# The Modern Law of Copyright and Designs

# The Modern Law of Copyright and Designs

Second edition

**Volume 2**

**Hugh Laddie**, MA (Cantab)
One of Her Majesty's Counsel
of the Middle Temple, Barrister

**Peter Prescott**, BSc, MSc,
One of Her Majesty's Counsel
of Lincoln's Inn, Barrister

**Mary Vitoria**,PhD, LLB,
of Lincoln's Inn, Barrister

**Butterworths**
London, Dublin, Edinburgh
1995

| United Kingdom | Butterworth & Co (Publishers) Ltd, Halsbury House, 35 Chancery Lane, London WC2A 1EL and 4 Hill Street, EDINBURGH EH2 3JZ |
| --- | --- |
| Australia | Butterworths, SYDNEY, MELBOURNE, BRISBANE, ADELAIDE, PERTH, CANBERRA and HOBART |
| Canada | Butterworth Canada Ltd, TORONTO and VANCOUVER |
| Ireland | Butterworth (Ireland) Ltd, DUBLIN |
| Malaysia | Malayan Law Journal Sdn Bhd, KUALA LUMPUR |
| New Zealand | Butterworth of New Zealand Ltd, WELLINGTON and AUCKLAND |
| Puerto Rico | Butterworth of Puerto Rico, Inc, SAN JUAN |
| Singapore | Butterworths Asia, SINGAPORE |
| South Africa | Butterworths Publishers (Pty) Ltd, DURBAN |
| USA | Butterworth Legal Publishers, CARLSBAD, California and SALEM, New Hampshire |

A CIP catalogue record for this book is available from the British Library.

ISBN for Volume 2: 0 406 04976 9
ISBN for the complete set: 0 406 61697 3


Typeset by Kerrypress Ltd, Luton, Beds
Printed in England by Clays Ltd, St Ives Plc

# Contents

# Appendix 1

# United Kingdom Statutes

## Part A    Copyright and Rights in Performances

### COPYRIGHT, DESIGNS AND PATENTS ACT 1988
### (c 48)

*General note*
As amended by the Companies Act 1989, Broadcasting Act 1990, Companies (No 2) (Northern Ireland) Order 1990 (SI 1990 No 1504), Courts and Legal Services Act 1990, National Health Service and Community Care Act 1990, High Court and County Courts Jurisdiction Order 1991 (SI 1991 No 724), Copyright (Computer Programs) Regulations 1992 (SI 1992 No 3233), Taxation of Chargeable Gains Act 1992, Tribunals and Inquiries Act 1992, Charities Act 1993, Judicial Pensions and Retirement Act 1993, Statute Law (Repeals) Act 1993, Trade Marks Act 1994, and Criminal Justice and Public Order Act 1994.

PART I
COPYRIGHT

**CHAPTER I**
**Subsistence, Ownership and Duration of Copyright**

**CHAPTER II**
**Rights of copyright owner**

**CHAPTER III**
**Acts permitted in relation to copyright works**

## CHAPTER VI
### Remedies for infringement

## CHAPTER VII
### Copyright licensing

**CHAPTER X**
**Miscellaneous and general**

**PART II**
**RIGHTS IN PERFORMANCES**

## PART III
## DESIGN RIGHT

## CHAPTER I
## Design right in original designs

## CHAPTER II
## Rights of design right owner and remedies

## CHAPTER III
## Exceptions to rights of design right owners

8

*An Act to restate the law of copyright, with amendments; to make fresh provision as to the rights of performers and others in performances; to confer a design right in original designs; to amend the Registered Designs Act 1949; to make provision with respect to patent agents and trade mark agents; to confer patents and designs jurisdiction on certain county courts; to amend the law of patents; to make provision with respect to devices designed to circumvent copy-protection of works in electronic form; to make fresh provision penalising the fraudulent reception of transmissions; to make the fraudulent application or use of a trade mark an offence; to make provision for the benefit of the Hospital for Sick Children, Great Ormond Street, London; to enable financial assistance to be given to certain international bodies; and for connected purposes*

[15th November 1988]

BE IT ENACTED by the Queen's most Excellent Majesty, by and with the advice and consent of the Lords Spiritual and Temporal, and Commons, in this present Parliament assembled, and by the authority of the same, as follows—

PART I
COPYRIGHT

CHAPTER I
SUBSISTENCE, OWNERSHIP AND DURATION OF COPYRIGHT

*Introductory*

**1. Copyright and copyright works**
(1) Copyright is a property right which subsists in accordance with this Part in the following descriptions of work—

    (a) original literary, dramatic, musical or artistic works,
    (b) sound recordings, films, broadcasts or cable programmes, and
    (c) the typographical arrangement of published editions.

    (2) In this Part 'copyright work' means a work of any of those descriptions in which copyright subsists.

    (3) Copyright does not subsist in a work unless the requirements of this Part with respect to qualification for copyright protection are met (see section 153 and the provisions referred to there).

## 2. Rights subsisting in copyright works

(1) The owner of the copyright in a work of any description has the exclusive right to do the acts specified in Chapter II as the acts restricted by the copyright in a work of that description.

(2) In relation to certain descriptions of copyright work the following rights conferred by Chapter IV (moral rights) subsist in favour of the author, director or commissioner of the work, whether or not he is the owner of the copyright—

    (a)  section 77 (right to be identified as author or director),

    (b)  section 80 (right to object to derogatory treatment of work), and

    (c)  section 85 (right to privacy of certain photographs and films).

*Descriptions of work and related provisions*

## 3. Literary, dramatic and musical works

(1) In this Part—

'literary work' means any work, other than a dramatic or musical work, which is written, spoken or sung, and accordingly includes—

    (a)  a table or compilation, *and*

    (b)  a computer program, **and**

    **(c)  preparatory design material for a computer program**;

'dramatic work' includes a work of dance or mime; and

'musical work' means a work consisting of music, exclusive of any words or action intended to be sung, spoken or performed with the music.

(2) Copyright does not subsist in a literary, dramatic or musical work unless and until it is recorded, in writing or otherwise; and references in this Part to the time at which such a work is made are to the time at which it is so recorded.

(3) It is immaterial for the purposes of subsection (2) whether the work is recorded by or with the permission of the author; and where it is not recorded by the author, nothing in that subsection affects the question whether copyright subsists in the record as distinct from the work recorded.

*General note*

Sub-s (1): word in italics repealed and words in bold type added by the Copyright (Computer Programs) Regulations 1992 SI 1992 No 3233, see Appendix 2, Part A.

## 4. Artistic works

(1) In this Part 'artistic work' means—

    (a)  a graphic work, photograph, sculpture or collage, irrespective of artistic quality,

    (b)  a work of architecture being a building or a model for a building, or

    (c)  a work of artistic craftsmanship.

(2) In this Part—

'building' includes any fixed structure, and a part of a building or fixed structure;

'graphic work' includes—

    (a)  any painting, drawing, diagram, map, chart or plan, and

    (b)  any engraving, etching, lithograph, woodcut or similar work;

'photograph' means a recording of light or other radiation on any medium on

which an image is produced or from which an image may by any means be produced, and which is not part of a film;
'sculpture' includes a cast or model made for purposes of sculpture.

## 5. Sound recordings and films
(1) In this Part—
'sound recording' means—

  (a) a recording of sounds, from which the sounds may be reproduced, or
  (b) a recording of the whole or any part of a literary, dramatic or musical work, from which sounds reproducing the work or part may be produced,

  regardless of the medium on which the recording is made or the method by which the sounds are reproduced or produced; and

'film' means a recording on any medium from which a moving image may by any means be produced.
(2) Copyright does not subsist in a sound recording or film which is, or to the extent that it is, a copy taken from a previous sound recording or film.

## 6. Broadcasts
(1) In this Part a 'broadcast' means a transmission by wireless telegraphy of visual images, sounds or other information which—

  (a) is capable of being lawfully received by members of the public, or
  (b) is transmitted for presentation to members of the public;

and references to broadcasting shall be construed accordingly.
(2) An encrypted transmission shall be regarded as capable of being lawfully received by members of the public only if decoding equipment has been made available to members of the public by or with the authority of the person making the transmission or the person providing the contents of the transmission.
(3) References in this Part to the person making a broadcast, broadcasting a work, or including a work in a broadcast are—

  (a) to the person transmitting the programme, if he has responsibility to any extent for its contents, and
  (b) to any person providing the programme who makes with the person transmitting it the arrangements necessary for its transmission;

and references in this Part to a programme, in the context of broadcasting, are to any item included in a broadcast.
(4) For the purposes of this Part the place from which a broadcast is made is, in the case of a satellite transmission, the place from which the signals carrying the broadcast are transmitted to the satellite.
(5) References in this Part to the reception of a broadcast include reception of a broadcast relayed by means of a telecommunications system.
(6) Copyright does not subsist in a broadcast which infringes, or to the extent that it infringes, the copyright in another broadcast or in a cable programme.

## 7. Cable programmes
(1) In this Part—
'cable programme' means any item included in a cable programme service; and
'cable programme service' means a service which consists wholly or mainly in sending visual images, sounds or other information by means of a

telecommunications system, otherwise than by wireless telegraphy, for reception—

    (a)  at two or more places (whether for simultaneous reception or at different times in response to requests by different users), or

    (b)  for presentation to members of the public,

and which is not, or so far as it is not, excepted by or under the following provisions of this section.

(2) The following are excepted from the definition of 'cable programme service'—

    (a)  a service or part of a service of which it is an essential feature that while visual images, sounds or other information are being conveyed by the person providing the service there will or may be sent from each place of reception, by means of the same system or (as the case may be) the same part of it, information (other than signals sent for the operation or control of the service) for reception by the person providing the service or other persons receiving it;

    (b)  a service run for the purposes of a business where—

        (i)  no person except the person carrying on the business is concerned in the control of the apparatus comprised in the system,

        (ii)  the visual images, sounds or other information are conveyed by the system solely for purposes internal to the running of the business and not by way of rendering a service or providing amenities for others, and

        (iii)  the system is not connected to any other telecommunications system;

    (c)  a service run by a single individual where—

        (i)  all the apparatus comprised in the system is under his control,

        (ii)  the visual images, sounds or other information conveyed by the system are conveyed solely for domestic purposes of his, and

        (iii)  the system is not connected to any other telecommunications system;

    (d)  services where—

        (i)  all the apparatus comprised in the system is situated in, or connects, premises which are in single occupation, and

        (ii)  the system is not connected to any other telecommunications system,

other than services operated as part of the amenities provided for residents or inmates of premises run as a business;

    (e)  services which are, or to the extent that they are, run for persons providing broadcasting or cable programme services or providing programmes for such services.

(3) The Secretary of State may by order amend subsection (2) so as to add or remove exceptions, subject to such transitional provision as appears to him to be appropriate.

(4) An order shall be made by statutory instrument; and no order shall be made

unless a draft of it has been laid before and approved by resolution of each House of Parliament.

(5) References in this Part to the inclusion of a cable programme or work in a cable programme service are to its transmission as part of the service; and references to the person including it are to the person providing the service.

(6) Copyright does not subsist in a cable programme—

   (a) if it is included in a cable programme service by reception and immediate re-transmission of a broadcast, or

   (b) if it infringes, or to the extent that it infringes, the copyright in another cable programme or in a broadcast.

## 8. Published editions

(1) In this Part 'published edition', in the context of copyright in the typographical arrangement of a published edition, means a published edition of the whole or any part of one or more literary, dramatic or musical works.

(2) Copyright does not subsist in the typographical arrangement of a published edition if, or to the extent that, it reproduces the typographical arrangement of a previous edition.

*Authorship and ownership of copyright*

## 9. Authorship of work

(1) In this Part 'author', in relation to a work, means the person who creates it.

(2) That person shall be taken to be—

   (a) in the case of a sound recording or film, the person by whom the arrangements necessary for the making of the recording or film are undertaken;

   (b) in the case of a broadcast, the person making the broadcast (see section 6(3)) or, in the case of a broadcast which relays another broadcast by reception and immediate re-transmission, the person making that other broadcast;

   (c) in the case of a cable programme, the person providing the cable programme service in which the programme is included;

   (d) in the case of the typographical arrangement of a published edition, the publisher.

(3) In the case of a literary, dramatic, musical or artistic work which is computer-generated, the author shall be taken to be the person by whom the arrangements necessary for the creation of the work are undertaken.

(4) For the purposes of this Part a work is of 'unknown authorship' if the identity of the author is unknown or, in the case of a work of joint authorship, if the identity of none of the authors is known.

(5) For the purposes of this Part the identity of an author shall be regarded as unknown if it is not possible for a person to ascertain his identity by reasonable inquiry; but if his identity is once known it shall not subsequently be regarded as unknown.

## 10. Works of joint authorship

(1) In this Part a 'work of joint authorship' means a work produced by the

collaboration of two or more authors in which the contribution of each author is not distinct from that of the other author or authors.

(2) A broadcast shall be treated as a work of joint authorship in any case where more than one person is to be taken as making the broadcast (see section 6(3)).

(3) References in this Part to the author of a work shall, except as otherwise provided, be construed in relation to a work of joint authorship as references to all the authors of the work.

### 11. First ownership of copyright

(1) The author of a work is the first owner of any copyright in it, subject to the following provisions.

(2) Where a literary, dramatic, musical or artistic work is made by an employee in the course of his employment, his employer is the first owner of any copyright in the work subject to any agreement to the contrary.

(3) This section does not apply to Crown copyright or Parliamentary copyright (see sections 163 and 165) or to copyright which subsists by virtue of section 168 (copyright of certain international organisations).

## *Duration of copyright*

### 12. Duration of copyright in literary, dramatic, musical or artistic works

(1) Copyright in a literary, dramatic, musical or artistic work expires at the end of the period of 50 years from the end of the calendar year in which the author dies, subject to the following provisions of this section.

(2) If the work is of unknown authorship, copyright expires at the end of the period of 50 years from the end of the calendar year in which it is first made available to the public; and subsection (1) does not apply if the identity of the author becomes known after the end of that period.

For this purpose making available to the public includes—

    (a) in the case of a literary, dramatic or musical work—

        (i) performance in public, or
        (ii) being broadcast or included in a cable programme service;

    (b) in the case of an artistic work—

        (i) exhibition in public,
        (ii) a film including the work being shown in public, or
        (iii) being included in a broadcast or cable programme service;

but in determining generally for the purposes of this subsection whether a work has been made available to the public no account shall be taken of any unauthorised act.

(3) If the work is computer-generated neither of the above provisions applies and copyright expires at the end of the period of 50 years from the end of the calendar year in which the work was made.

(4) In relation to a work of joint authorship—

    (a) the reference in subsection (1) to the death of the author shall be construed—

        (i) if the identity of all the authors is known, as a reference to the death of the last of them to die, and

      (ii)  if the identity of one or more of the authors is known and the identity of one or more others is not, as a reference to the death of the last of the authors whose identity is known; and

    (b)  the reference in subsection (2) to the identity of the author becoming known shall be construed as a reference to the identity of any of the authors becoming known.

(5) This section does not apply to Crown copyright or Parliamentary copyright (see sections 163 to 166) or to copyright which subsists by virtue of section 168 (copyright of certain international organisations).

### 13. Duration of copyright in sound recordings and films

(1) Copyright in a sound recording or film expires—

    (a)  at the end of the period of 50 years from the end of the calendar year in which it is made, or

    (b)  if it is released before the end of that period, 50 years from the end of the calendar year in which it is released.

(2) A sound recording or film is 'released' when—

    (a)  it is first published, broadcast or included in a cable programme service, or

    (b)  in the case of a film or film sound-track, the film is first shown in public;

but in determining whether a work has been released no account shall be taken of any unauthorised act.

### 14. Duration of copyright in broadcasts and cable programmes

(1) Copyright in a broadcast or cable programme expires at the end of the period of 50 years from the end of the calendar year in which the broadcast was made or the programme was included in a cable programme service.

(2) Copyright in a repeat broadcast or cable programme expires at the same time as the copyright in the original broadcast or cable programme; and accordingly no copyright arises in respect of a repeat broadcast or cable programme which is broadcast or included in a cable programme service after the expiry of the copyright in the original broadcast or cable programme.

(3) A repeat broadcast or cable programme means one which is a repeat either of a broadcast previously made or of a cable programme previously included in a cable programme service.

### 15. Duration of copyright in typographical arrangement of published editions

Copyright in the typographical arrangement of a published edition expires at the end of the period of 25 years from the end of the calendar year in which the edition was first published.

CHAPTER II
RIGHTS OF COPYRIGHT OWNER

*The acts restricted by copyright*

### 16. The acts restricted by copyright in a work

(1) The owner of the copyright in a work has, in accordance with the following provisions of this Chapter, the exclusive right to do the following acts in the United Kingdom—

(a)  to copy the work (see section 17);

(b)  to issue copies of the work to the public (see section 18);

(c)  to perform, show or play the work in public (see section 19);

(d)  to broadcast the work or include it in a cable programme service (see section 20);

(e)  to make an adaptation of the work or do any of the above in relation to an adaptation (see section 21);

and those acts are referred to in this Part as the 'acts restricted by the copyright'.

(2)  Copyright in a work is infringed by a person who without the licence of the copyright owner does, or authorises another to do, any of the acts restricted by the copyright.

(3)  References in this Part to the doing of an act restricted by the copyright in a work are to the doing of it—

(a)  in relation to the work as a whole or any substantial part of it, and

(b)  either directly or indirectly;

and it is immaterial whether any intervening acts themselves infringe copyright.

(4)  This Chapter has effect subject to—

(a)  the provisions of Chapter III (acts permitted in relation to copyright works), and

(b)  the provisions of Chapter VII (provisions with respect to copyright licensing).

## 17.  Infringement of copyright by copying

(1)  The copying of the work is an act restricted by the copyright in every description of copyright work; and references in this Part to copying and copies shall be construed as follows.

(2)  Copying in relation to a literary, dramatic, musical or artistic work means reproducing the work in any material form.
This includes storing the work in any medium by electronic means.

(3)  In relation to an artistic work copying includes the making of a copy in three dimensions of a two-dimensional work and the making of a copy in two dimensions of a three-dimensional work.

(4)  Copying in relation to a film, television broadcast or cable programme includes making a photograph of the whole or any substantial part of any image forming part of the film, broadcast or cable programme.

(5)  Copying in relation to the typographical arrangement of a published edition means making a facsimile copy of the arrangement.

(6)  Copying in relation to any description of work includes the making of copies which are transient or are incidental to some other use of the work.

## 18.  Infringement by issue of copies to the public

(1)  The issue to the public of copies of the work is an act restricted by the copyright in every description of copyright work.

(2)  References in this Part to the issue to the public of copies of a work are **except where the work is a computer program** to the act of putting into circulation copies not previously put into circulation, in the United Kingdom or elsewhere, and not to—

(a)  any subsequent distribution, sale, hiring or loan of those copies, or

(b)  any subsequent importation of those copies into the United Kingdom;

except that in relation to sound recordings, *films and computer programs* **and films** the restricted act of issuing copies to the public includes any rental of copies to the public.

**(3) References in this Part to the issue to the public of copies of a work where the work is a computer program are to the act of putting into circulation copies of that program not previously put into circulation in the United Kingdom or any other Member State, by or with the consent of the copyright owner, and not to—**

> **(a) any subsequent distribution, sale, hiring or loan of those copies, or**
> **(b) any subsequent importation of those copies into the United Kingdom,**

**except that the restricted act of issuing copies to the public includes any rental of copies to the public.**

*General note*
Sub-s (2): first words in bold type added, final words in bold type substituted, by the Copyright (Computer Programs) Regulations 1992, SI 1992 No 3233, see Appendix 2, Part A.
Sub-s (3): added by the Copyright (Computer Programs) Regulations 1992.

### 19. Infringement by performance, showing or playing of work in public

(1) The performance of the work in public is an act restricted by the copyright in a literary, dramatic or musical work.

(2) In this Part 'performance', in relation to a work—

> (a) includes delivery in the case of lectures, addresses, speeches and sermons, and
> (b) in general, includes any mode of visual or acoustic presentation, including presentation by means of a sound recording, film, broadcast or cable programme of the work.

(3) The playing or showing of the work in public is an act restricted by the copyright in a sound recording, film, broadcast or cable programme.

(4) Where copyright in a work is infringed by its being performed, played or shown in public by means of apparatus for receiving visual images or sounds conveyed by electronic means, the person by whom the visual images or sounds are sent, and in the case of a performance the performers, shall not be regarded as responsible for the infringement.

### 20. Infringement by broadcasting or inclusion in a cable programme service

The broadcasting of the work or its inclusion in a cable programme service is an act restricted by the copyright in—

> (a) a literary, dramatic, musical or artistic work,
> (b) a sound recording or film, or
> (c) a broadcast or cable programme.

### 21. Infringement by making adaptation or act done in relation to adaptation

(1) The making of an adaptation of the work is an act restricted by the copyright in a literary, dramatic or musical work.

For this purpose an adaptation is made when it is recorded, in writing or otherwise.

(2) The doing of any of the acts specified in sections 17 to 20, or subsection

(1) above, in relation to an adaptation of the work is also an act restricted by the copyright in a literary, dramatic or musical work.

For this purpose it is immaterial whether the adaptation has been recorded, in writing or otherwise, at the time the act is done.

(3) In this Part 'adaptation'—

(a) in relation to a literary **work, other than a computer program,** or dramatic work, means—

(i) a translation of the work;

(ii) a version of a dramatic work in which it is converted into a non-dramatic work or, as the case may be, of a non-dramatic work in which it is converted into a dramatic work;

(iii) a version of the work in which the story or action is conveyed wholly or mainly by means of pictures in a form suitable for reproduction in a book, or in a newspaper, magazine or similar periodical;

(a) **in relation to a computer program, means an arrangement or altered version of the program or a translation of it;**

(b) in relation to a musical work, means an arrangement or transcription of the work.

(4) In relation to a computer program a 'translation' includes a version of the program in which it is converted into or out of a computer language or code or into a different computer language or code, *otherwise than incidentally in the course of running the program.*

(5) No inference shall be drawn from this section as to what does or does not amount to copying a work.

*General note*

Sub-s (3): words in bold type added by the Copyright (Computer Programs) Regulations 1992, SI 1992 No 3233, see Appendix 2, Part A.

Sub-s (4): words in italics repealed by the Copyright (Computer Programs) Regulations 1992.

## *Secondary infringement of copyright*

### 22. Secondary infringement: importing infringing copy

The copyright in a work is infringed by a person who, without the licence of the copyright owner, imports into the United Kingdom, otherwise than for his private and domestic use, an article which is, and which he knows or has reason to believe is, an infringing copy of the work.

### 23. Secondary infringement: possessing or dealing with infringing copy

The copyright in a work is infringed by a person who, without the licence of the copyright owner—

(a) possesses in the course of a business,

(b) sells or lets for hire, or offers or exposes for sale or hire,

(c) in the course of a business exhibits in public or distributes, or

(d) distributes otherwise than in the course of a business to such an extent as to affect prejudicially the owner of the copyright,

an article which is, and which he knows or has reason to believe is, an infringing copy of the work.

## 24. Secondary infringement: providing means for making infringing copies

(1) Copyright in a work is infringed by a person who, without the licence of the copyright owner—

(a) makes,

(b) imports into the United Kingdom,

(c) possesses in the course of a business, or

(d) sells or lets for hire, or offers or exposes for sale or hire,

an article specifically designed or adapted for making copies of that work, knowing or having reason to believe that it is to be used to make infringing copies.

(2) Copyright in a work is infringed by a person who without the licence of the copyright owner transmits the work by means of a telecommunications system (otherwise than by broadcasting or inclusion in a cable programme service), knowing or having reason to believe that infringing copies of the work will be made by means of the reception of the transmission in the United Kingdom or elsewhere.

## 25. Secondary infringement: permitting use of premises for infringing performance

(1) Where the copyright in a literary, dramatic or musical work is infringed by a performance at a place of public entertainment, any person who gave permission for that place to be used for the performance is also liable for the infringement unless when he gave permission he believed on reasonable grounds that the performance would not infringe copyright.

(2) In this section 'place of public entertainment' includes premises which are occupied mainly for other purposes but are from time to time made available for hire for the purposes of public entertainment.

## 26. Secondary infringement: provision of apparatus for infringing performance, etc

(1) Where copyright in a work is infringed by a public performance of the work, or by the playing or showing of the work in public, by means of apparatus for—

(a) playing sound recordings,

(b) showing films, or

(c) receiving visual images or sounds conveyed by electronic means,

the following persons are also liable for the infringement.

(2) A person who supplied the apparatus, or any substantial part of it, is liable for the infringement if when he supplied the apparatus or part—

(a) he knew or had reason to believe that the apparatus was likely to be so used as to infringe copyright, or

(b) in the case of apparatus whose normal use involves a public performance, playing or showing, he did not believe on reasonable grounds that it would not be so used as to infringe copyright.

(3) An occupier of premises who gave permission for the apparatus to be brought onto the premises is liable for the infringement if when he gave permission he knew or had reason to believe that the apparatus was likely to be so used as to infringe copyright.

(4) A person who supplied a copy of a sound recording or film used to infringe copyright is liable for the infringement if when he supplied it he knew or had

reason to believe that what he supplied, or a copy made directly or indirectly from it, was likely to be so used as to infringe copyright.

## *Infringing copies*

### 27. Meaning of 'infringing copy'

(1) In this Part 'infringing copy', in relation to a copyright work, shall be construed in accordance with this section.

(2) An article is an infringing copy if its making constituted an infringement of the copyright in the work in question.

(3) **Subject to subsection (3A)** an article is also an infringing copy if—

    (a) it has been or is proposed to be imported into the United Kingdom, and

    (b) its making in the United Kingdom would have constituted an infringement of the copyright in the work in question, or a breach of an exclusive licence agreement relating to that work.

**(3A) A copy of a computer program which has previously been sold in any other member State, by or with the consent of the copyright owner, is not an infringing copy for the purposes of subsection (3).**

(4) Where in any proceedings the question arises whether an article is an infringing copy and it is shown—

    (a) that the article is a copy of the work, and

    (b) that copyright subsists in the work or has subsisted at any time,

it shall be presumed until the contrary is proved that the article was made at a time when copyright subsisted in the work.

(5) Nothing in subsection (3) shall be construed as applying to an article which may lawfully be imported into the United Kingdom by virtue of any enforceable Community right within the meaning of section 2(1) of the European Communities Act 1972.

(6) In this Part 'infringing copy' includes a copy falling to be treated as an infringing copy by virtue of any of the following provisions—

    section 32(5) (copies made for purposes of instruction or examination),

    section 35(3) (recordings made by educational establishments for educational purposes),

    section 36(5) (reprographic copying by educational establishments for purposes of instruction),

    section 37(3)(b) (copies made by librarian or archivist in reliance on false declaration),

    section 56(2) (further copies, adaptations, etc of work in electronic form retained on transfer of principal copy),

    section 63(2) (copies made for purpose of advertising artistic work for sale),

    section 68(4) (copies made for purpose of broadcast or cable programme), or

    any provision of an order under section 141 (statutory licence for certain reprographic copying by educational establishments).

*General note*
Sub-s (3): words in bold type added by the Copyright (Computer Programs) Regulations 1992, SI 1992 No 3233, see Appendix 2, Part A.
Sub-s (3A): added by the Copyright (Computer Programs) Regulations 1992.

## CHAPTER III
## ACTS PERMITTED IN RELATION TO COPYRIGHT WORKS

*Introductory*

**28. Introductory provisions**

(1) The provisions of this Chapter specify acts which may be done in relation to copyright works notwithstanding the subsistence of copyright; they relate only to the question of infringement of copyright and do not affect any other right or obligation restricting the doing of any of the specified acts.

(2) Where it is provided by this Chapter that an act does not infringe copyright, or may be done without infringing copyright, and no particular description of copyright work is mentioned, the act in question does not infringe the copyright in a work of any description.

(3) No inference shall be drawn from the description of any act which may by virtue of this Chapter be done without infringing copyright as to the scope of the acts restricted by the copyright in any description of work.

(4) The provisions of this Chapter are to be construed independently of each other, so that the fact that an act does not fall within one provision does not mean that it is not covered by another provision.

*General*

**29. Research and private study**

(1) Fair dealing with a literary, dramatic, musical or artistic work for the purposes of research or private study does not infringe any copyright in the work or, in the case of a published edition, in the typographical arrangement.

(2) Fair dealing with the typographical arrangement of a published edition for the purposes mentioned in subsection (1) does not infringe any copyright in the arrangement.

(3) Copying by a person other than the researcher or student himself is not fair dealing if—

(a) in the case of a librarian, or a person acting on behalf of a librarian, he does anything which regulations under section 40 would not permit to be done under section 38 or 39 (articles or parts of published works: restriction on multiple copies of same material), or

(b) in any other case, the person doing the copying knows or has reason to believe that it will result in copies of substantially the same material being provided to more than one person at substantially the same time and for substantially the same purpose.

**(4) It is not fair dealing—**

**(a) to convert a computer program expressed in a low level language into a version expressed in a higher level language, or**

**(b) incidentally in the course of so converting the program, to copy it,**

**(these acts being permitted if done in accordance with section 50B (decompilation)).**

*General note*
Sub-s (4): added by the Copyright (Computer Programs) Regulations 1992, SI 1992 No 3233, see Appendix 2, Part A.

**30. Criticism, review and news reporting**

(1) Fair dealing with a work for the purpose of criticism or review, of that or another work or of a performance of a work, does not infringe any copyright in the work provided that it is accompanied by a sufficient acknowledgement.

(2) Fair dealing with a work (other than a photograph) for the purpose of reporting current events does not infringe any copyright in the work provided that (subject to subsection (3)) it is accompanied by a sufficient acknowledgement.

(3) No acknowledgement is required in connection with the reporting of current events by means of a sound recording, film, broadcast or cable programme.

**31. Incidental inclusion of copyright material**

(1) Copyright in a work is not infringed by its incidental inclusion in an artistic work, sound recording, film, broadcast or cable programme.

(2) Nor is the copyright infringed by the issue to the public of copies, or the playing, showing, broadcasting or inclusion in a cable programme service, of anything whose making was, by virtue of subsection (1), not an infringement of the copyright.

(3) A musical work, words spoken or sung with music, or so much of a sound recording, broadcast or cable programme as includes a musical work or such words, shall not be regarded as incidentally included in another work if it is deliberately included.

*Education*

**32. Things done for purposes of instruction or examination**

(1) Copyright in a literary, dramatic, musical or artistic work is not infringed by its being copied in the course of instruction or of preparation for instruction, provided the copying—

    (a) is done by a person giving or receiving instruction, and

    (b) is not by means of a reprographic process.

(2) Copyright in a sound recording, film, broadcast or cable programme is not infringed by its being copied by making a film or film sound-track in the course of instruction, or of preparation for instruction, in the making of films or film sound-tracks, provided the copying is done by a person giving or receiving instruction.

(3) Copyright is not infringed by anything done for the purposes of an examination by way of setting the questions, communicating the questions to the candidates or answering the questions.

(4) Subsection (3) does not extend to the making of a reprographic copy of a musical work for use by an examination candidate in performing the work.

(5) Where a copy which would otherwise be an infringing copy is made in accordance with this section but is subsequently dealt with, it shall be treated as an infringing copy for the purpose of that dealing, and if that dealing infringes copyright for all subsequent purposes.

For this purpose 'dealt with' means sold or let for hire or offered or exposed for sale or hire.

**33. Anthologies for educational use**

(1) The inclusion of a short passage from a published literary or dramatic work in a collection which—

(a) is intended for use in educational establishments and is so described in its title, and in any advertisements issued by or on behalf of the publisher, and

(b) consists mainly of material in which no copyright subsists,

does not infringe the copyright in the work if the work itself is not intended for use in such establishments and the inclusion is accompanied by a sufficient acknowledgement.

(2) Subsection (1) does not authorise the inclusion of more than two excerpts from copyright works by the same author in collections published by the same publisher over any period of five years.

(3) In relation to any given passage the reference in subsection (2) to excerpts from works by the same author—

(a) shall be taken to include excerpts from works by him in collaboration with another, and

(b) if the passage in question is from such a work, shall be taken to include excerpts from works by any of the authors, whether alone or in collaboration with another.

(4) References in this section to the use of a work in an educational establishment are to any use for the educational purposes of such an establishment.

### 34. Performing, playing or showing work in course of activities of educational establishment

(1) The performance of a literary, dramatic or musical work before an audience consisting of teachers and pupils at an educational establishment and other persons directly connected with the activities of the establishment—

(a) by a teacher or pupil in the course of the activities of the establishment, or

(b) at the establishment by any person for the purposes of instruction,

is not a public performance for the purposes of infringement of copyright.

(2) The playing or showing of a sound recording, film, broadcast or cable programme before such an audience at an educational establishment for the purposes of instruction is not a playing or showing of the work in public for the purposes of infringement of copyright.

(3) A person is not for this purpose directly connected with the activities of the educational establishment simply because he is the parent of a pupil at the establishment.

### 35. Recording by educational establishments of broadcasts and cable programmes

(1) A recording of a broadcast or cable programme, or a copy of such a recording, may be made by or on behalf of an educational establishment for the educational purposes of that establishment without thereby infringing the copyright in the broadcast or cable programme, or in any work included in it.

(2) This section does not apply if or to the extent that there is a licensing scheme certified for the purposes of this section under section 143 providing for the grant of licences.

(3) Where a copy which would otherwise be an infringing copy is made in accordance with this section but is subsequently dealt with, it shall be treated as an infringing copy for the purposes of that dealing, and if that dealing infringes copyright for all subsequent purposes.

For this purpose 'dealt with' means sold or let for hire or offered or exposed for sale or hire.

## 36. Reprographic copying by educational establishments of passages from published works

(1) Reprographic copies of passages from published literary, dramatic or musical works may, to the extent permitted by this section, be made by or on behalf of an educational establishment for the purposes of instruction without infringing any copyright in the work, or in the typographical arrangement.

(2) Not more than one per cent of any work may be copied by or on behalf of an establishment by virtue of this section in any quarter, that is, in any period 1st January to 31st March, 1st April to 30th June, 1st July to 30th September or 1st October to 31st December.

(3) Copying is not authorised by this section if, or to the extent that, licences are available authorising the copying in question and the person making the copies knew or ought to have been aware of that fact.

(4) The terms of a licence granted to an educational establishment authorising the reprographic copying for the purposes of instruction of passages from published literary, dramatic or musical works are of no effect so far as they purport to restrict the proportion of a work which may be copied (whether on payment or free of charge) to less than that which would be permitted under this section.

(5) Where a copy which would otherwise be an infringing copy is made in accordance with this section but is subsequently dealt with, it shall be treated as an infringing copy for the purposes of that dealing, and if that dealing infringes copyright for all subsequent purposes.

For this purpose 'dealt with' means sold or let for hire or offered or exposed for sale or hire.

## *Libraries and archives*

## 37. Libraries and archives: introductory

(1) In sections 38 to 43 (copying by librarians and archivists)—

    (a) references in any provision to a prescribed library or archive are to a library or archive of a description prescribed for the purposes of that provision by regulations made by the Secretary of State; and

    (b) references in any provision to the prescribed conditions are to the conditions so prescribed.

(2) The regulations may provide that, where a librarian or archivist is required to be satisfied as to any matter before making or supplying a copy of a work—

  (a) he may rely on a signed declaration as to that matter by the person requesting the copy, unless he is aware that it is false in a material particular, and

  (b) in such cases as may be prescribed, he shall not make or supply a copy in the absence of a signed declaration in such form as may be prescribed.

(3) Where a person requesting a copy makes a declaration which is false in a material particular and is supplied with a copy which would have been an infringing copy if made by him—

  (a) he is liable for infringement of copyright as if he had made the copy himself, and

  (b) the copy shall be treated as an infringing copy.

(4) The regulations may make different provision for different descriptions of libraries or archives and for different purposes.

(5) Regulations shall be made by statutory instrument which shall be subject to annulment in pursuance of a resolution of either House of Parliament.

(6) References in this section, and in sections 38 to 43, to the librarian or archivist include a person acting on his behalf.

**38. Copying by librarians: articles in periodicals**
(1) The librarian of a prescribed library may, if the prescribed conditions are complied with, make and supply a copy of an article in a periodical without infringing any copyright in the text, in any illustrations accompanying the text or in the typographical arrangement.

(2) The prescribed conditions shall include the following—

  (a) that copies are supplied only to persons satisfying the librarian that they require them for purposes of research or private study, and will not use them for any other purpose;

  (b) that no person is furnished with more than one copy of the same article or with copies of more than one article contained in the same issue of a periodical; and

  (c) that persons to whom copies are supplied are required to pay for them a sum not less than the cost (including a contribution to the general expenses of the library) attributable to their production.

**39. Copying by librarians: parts of published works**
(1) The librarian of a prescribed library may, if the prescribed conditions are complied with, make and supply from a published edition a copy of part of a literary, dramatic or musical work (other than an article in a periodical) without infringing any copyright in the work, in any illustrations accompanying the work or in the typographical arrangement.

(2) The prescribed conditions shall include the following—

  (a) that copies are supplied only to persons satisfying the librarian that they require them for purposes of research or private study, and will not use them for any other purpose;

  (b) that no person is furnished with more than one copy of the same material or with a copy of more than a reasonable proportion of any work; and

(c) that person to whom copies are supplied are required to pay for them a sum not less than the cost (including a contribution to the general expenses of the library) attributable to their production.

## 40. Restriction on production of multiple copies of the same material
(1) Regulations for the purposes of sections 38 and 39 (copying by librarian of article or part of published work) shall contain provision to the effect that a copy shall be supplied only to a person satisfying the librarian that his requirement is not related to any similar requirement of another person.

(2) The regulations may provide—

(a) that requirements shall be regarded as similar if the requirements are for copies of substantially the same material at substantially the same time and for substantially the same purpose; and
(b) that requirements of persons shall be regarded as related if those persons receive instruction to which the material is relevant at the same time and place.

## 41. Copying by librarians: supply of copies to other libraries
(1) The librarian of a prescribed library may, if the prescribed conditions are complied with, make and supply to another prescribed library a copy of—

(a) an article in a periodical, or
(b) the whole or part of a published edition of a literary, dramatic or musical work,

without infringing any copyright in the text of the article or, as the case may be, in the work, in any illustrations accompanying it or in the typographical arrangement.

(2) Subsection (1)(b) does not apply if at the time the copy is made the librarian making it knows, or could by reasonable inquiry ascertain, the name and address of a person entitled to authorise the making of the copy.

## 42. Copying by librarians or archivists: replacement copies of works
(1) The librarian or archivist of a prescribed library or archive may, if the prescribed conditions are complied with, make a copy from any item in the permanent collection of the library or archive—

(a) in order to preserve or replace that item by placing the copy in its permanent collection in addition to or in place of it, or
(b) in order to replace in the permanent collection of another prescribed library or archive an item which has been lost, destroyed or damaged,

without infringing the copyright in any literary, dramatic or musical work, in any illustrations accompanying such a work or, in the case of a published edition, in the typographical arrangement.

(2) The prescribed conditions shall include provision for restricting the making of copies to cases where it is not reasonably practicable to purchase a copy of the item in question to fulfil that purpose.

## 43. Copying by librarians or archivists: certain unpublished works
(1) The librarian or archivist of a prescribed library or archive may, if the prescribed conditions are complied with, make and supply a copy of the whole or part of a literary, dramatic or musical work from a document in the library or

archive without infringing any copyright in the work or any illustrations accompanying it.

(2) This section does not apply if—

    (a) the work had been published before the document was deposited in the library or archive, or

    (b) the copyright owner has prohibited copying of the work,

and at the time the copy is made the librarian or archivist making it is, or ought to be, aware of that fact.

(3) The prescribed conditions shall include the following—

    (a) that copies are supplied only to persons satisfying the librarian or archivist that they require them for purposes of research or private study and will not use them for any other purpose;

    (b) that no person is furnished with more than one copy of the same material; and

    (c) that persons to whom copies are supplied are required to pay for them a sum not less than the cost (including a contribution to the general expenses of the library or archive) attributable to their production.

### 44. Copy of work required to be made as condition of export

If an article of cultural or historical importance or interest cannot lawfully be exported from the United Kingdom unless a copy of it is made and deposited in an appropriate library or archive, it is not an infringement of copyright to make that copy.

*Public administration*

### 45. Parliamentary and judicial proceedings

(1) Copyright is not infringed by anything done for the purposes of parliamentary or judicial proceedings.

(2) Copyright is not infringed by anything done for the purposes of reporting such proceedings; but this shall not be construed as authorising the copying of a work which is itself a published report of the proceedings.

### 46. Royal Commissions and statutory inquiries

(1) Copyright is not infringed by anything done for the purposes of the proceedings of a Royal Commission or statutory inquiry.

(2) Copyright is not infringed by anything done for the purpose of reporting any such proceedings held in public; but this shall not be construed as authorising the copying of a work which is itself a published report of the proceedings.

(3) Copyright in a work is not infringed by the issue to the public of copies of the report of a Royal Commission or statutory inquiry containing the work or material from it.

(4) In this section—

'Royal Commission' includes a Commission appointed for Northern Ireland by the Secretary of State in pursuance of the prerogative powers of Her Majesty delegated to him under section 7(2) of the Northern Ireland Constitution Act 1973; and

'statutory inquiry' means an inquiry held or investigation conducted in pursuance of a duty imposed or power conferred by or under an enactment.

## 47. Material open to public inspection or on official register

(1) Where material is open to public inspection pursuant to a statutory requirement, or is on a statutory register, any copyright in the material as a literary work is not infringed by the copying of so much of the material as contains factual information of any description, by or with the authority of the appropriate person, for a purpose which does not involve the issuing of copies to the public.

(2) Where material is open to public inspection pursuant to a statutory requirement, copyright is not infringed by the copying or issuing to the public of copies of the material, by or with the authority of the appropriate person, for the purpose of enabling the material to be inspected at a more convenient time or place or otherwise facilitating the exercise of any right for the purpose of which the requirement is imposed.

(3) Where material which is open to public inspection pursuant to a statutory requirement, or which is on a statutory register, contains information about matters of general scientific, technical, commercial or economic interest, copyright is not infringed by the copying or issuing to the public of copies of the material, by or with the authority of the appropriate person, for the purpose of disseminating that information.

(4) The Secretary of State may by order provide that subsection (1), (2) or (3) shall, in such cases as may be specified in the order, apply only to copies marked in such manner as may be so specified.

(5) The Secretary of State may by order provide that subsections (1) to (3) apply, to such extent and with such modifications as may be specified in the order—

(a) to material made open to public inspection by—

(i) an international organisation specified in the order, or

(ii) a person so specified who has functions in the United Kingdom under an international agreement to which the United Kingdom is party, or

(b) to a register maintained by an international organisation specified in the order,

as they apply in relation to material open to public inspection pursuant to a statutory requirement or to a statutory register.

(6) In this section—

'appropriate person' means the person required to make the material open to public inspection or, as the case may be, the person maintaining the register;

'statutory register' means a register maintained in pursuance of a statutory requirement; and

'statutory requirement' means a requirement imposed by provision made by or under an enactment.

(7) An order under this section shall be made by statutory instrument which shall be subject to annulment in pursuance of a resolution of either House of Parliament.

*General note*

See the Copyright (Material Open to Public Inspection) (International Organisations) Order 1989, SI 1989 No 1098 for modifications to sub-s (1) and (3) in respect of material published by (a) the European Patent Office under the European Patent Convention and (b) the World Intellectual Property Organisation under the Patent Co-operation Treaty.

29

### 48. Material communicated to the Crown in the course of public business

(1) This section applies where a literary, dramatic, musical or artistic work has in the course of public business been communicated to the Crown for any purpose, by or with the licence of the copyright owner and a document or other material thing recording or embodying the work is owned by or in the custody or control of the Crown.

(2) The Crown may, for the purpose for which the work was communicated to it, or any related purpose which could reasonably have been anticipated by the copyright owner, copy the work and issue copies of the work to the public without infringing any copyright in the work.

(3) The Crown may not copy a work, or issue copies of a work to the public, by virtue of this section if the work has previously been published otherwise than by virtue of this section.

(4) In subsection (1) 'public business' includes any activity carried on by the Crown.

(5) This section has effect subject to any agreement to the contrary between the Crown and the copyright owner.

**(6) In this section 'the Crown' includes a health service body, as defined in section 60(7) of the National Health Service and Community Care Act 1990, and a National Health Service trust established under Part I of that Act or the National Health Service (Scotland) Act 1978 [and also includes a health and social services body, as defined in Article 7(6) of the Health and Personal Social Services (Northern Ireland) Order 1991, and a Health and Social Services trust established under that Order]; and the reference in subsection (1) above to public business shall be construed accordingly.**

*General note*

Sub-s (6): added by the National Health Service and Community Care Act 1990, s 60, Sch 8, Part I, para 3. Words in square brackets added by the Health and Personal Social Services (Northern Ireland) Order 1991, SI 1991 No 194 (NI), art 7(2)(a), Sch 2, Part I.

### 49. Public records

Material which is comprised in public records within the meaning of the Public Records Act 1958, the Public Records (Scotland) Act 1937 or the Public Records Act (Northern Ireland) 1923 which are open to public inspection in pursuance of that Act, may be copied, and a copy may be supplied to any person, by or with the authority of any officer appointed under that Act, without infringement of copyright.

### 50. Acts done under statutory authority

(1) Where the doing of a particular act is specifically authorised by an Act of Parliament, whenever passed, then, unless the Act provides otherwise, the doing of that act does not infringe copyright.

(2) Subsection (1) applies in relation to an enactment contained in Northern Ireland legislation as it applies in relation to an Act of Parliament.

(3) Nothing in this section shall be construed as excluding any defence of statutory authority otherwise available under or by virtue of any enactment.

*Computer programs: lawful users*

### 50A. Back up copies

**(1) It is not an infringement of copyright for a lawful user of a copy of a**

computer program to make any back up copy of it which it is necessary for him to have for the purposes of his lawful use.

(2) For the purposes of this section and sections 50B and 50C a person is a lawful user of a computer program if (whether under a licence to do any acts restricted by the copyright in the program or otherwise), he has a right to use the program.

(3) Where an act is permitted under this section, it is irrelevant whether or not there exists any term or condition in an agreement which purports to prohibit or restrict the act (such terms being, by virtue of section 296A, void).

*General note*
Added by the Copyright (Computer Programs) Regulations 1992, SI 1992 No 3233, see Appendix 2, Part A.

## 50B. Decompilation

(1) It is not an infringement of copyright for a lawful user of a copy of a computer program expressed in a low level language—

   (a) to convert it into a version expressed in a higher level language, or
   (b) incidentally in the course of so converting the program, to copy it,

(that is, to 'decompile' it), provided that the conditions in subsection (2) are met.

(2) The conditions are that—

   (a) it is necessary to decompile the program to obtain the information necessary to create an independent program which can be operated with the program decompiled or with another program ('the permitted objective'); and
   (b) the information so obtained is not used for any purpose other than the permitted objective.

(3) In particular, the conditions in subsection (2) are not met if the lawful user—

   (a) has readily available to him the information necessary to achieve the permitted objective;
   (b) does not confine the decompiling to such acts as are necessary to achieve the permitted objective;
   (c) supplies the information obtained by the decompiling to any person to whom it is not necessary to supply it in order to achieve the permitted objective; or
   (d) uses the information to create a program which is substantially similar in its expression to the program decompiled or to do any act restricted by copyright.

(4) Where an act is permitted under this section, it is irrelevant whether or not there exists any term or condition in an agreement which purports to prohibit or restrict the act (such terms being, by virtue of section 296A, void).

*General note*
Added by the Copyright (Computer Programs) Regulations 1992, SI 1992 No 3233, see Appendix 2, Part A.

**50C. Other acts permitted to lawful users**

**(1) It is not an infringement of copyright for a lawful user of a copy of a computer program to copy or adapt it, provided that the copying or adapting—**

    **(a) is necessary for his lawful use; and**

    **(b) is not prohibited under any term or condition of an agreement regulating the circumstances in which his use is lawful.**

**(2) It may, in particular, be necessary for the lawful use of a computer program to copy it or adapt it for the purpose of correcting errors in it.**

**(3) This section does not apply to any copying or adapting permitted under section 50A or 50B.**

*General note*

Added by the Copyright (Computer Programs) Regulations 1992, SI 1992 No 3233, see Appendix 2, Part A.

## Designs

**51. Design documents and models**

(1) It is not an infringement of any copyright in a design document or model recording or embodying a design for anything other than an artistic work or a typeface to make an article to the design or to copy an article made to the design.

(2) Nor is it an infringement of the copyright to issue to the public, or include in a film, broadcast or cable programme service, anything the making of which was, by virtue of subsection (1), not an infringement of that copyright.

(3) In this section—

'design' means the design of any aspect of the shape or configuration (whether internal or external) of the whole or part of an article, other than surface decoration; and

'design document' means any record of a design, whether in the form of a drawing, a written description, a photograph, data stored in a computer or otherwise.

**52. Effect of exploitation of design derived from artistic work**

(1) This section applies where an artistic work has been exploited, by or with the licence of the copyright owner, by—

    (a) making by an industrial process articles falling to be treated for the purposes of this Part as copies of the work, and

    (b) marketing such articles, in the United Kingdom or elsewhere.

(2) After the end of the period of 25 years from the end of the calendar year in which such articles are first marketed, the work may be copied by making articles of any description, or doing anything for the purpose of making articles of any description, and anything may be done in relation to articles so made, without infringing copyright in the work.

(3) Where only part of an artistic work is exploited as mentioned in subsection (1), subsection (2) applies only in relation to that part.

(4) The Secretary of State may by order make provision—

    (a) as to the circumstances in which an article, or any description of an article, is to be regarded for the purposes of this section as made by an industrial process;

(b) excluding from the operation of this section such articles of a primarily literary or artistic character as he thinks fit.

(5) An order shall be made by statutory instrument which shall be subject to annulment in pursuance of a resolution of either House of Parliament.

(6) In this section—

(a) references to articles do not include films; and

(b) references to the marketing of an article are to its being sold or let for hire or offered or exposed for sale or hire.

## 53. Things done in reliance on registration of design

(1) The copyright in an artistic work is not infringed by anything done—

(a) in pursuance of an assignment or licence made or granted by a person registered under the Registered Designs Act 1949 as the proprietor of a corresponding design, and

(b) in good faith in reliance on the registration and without notice of any proceedings for the cancellation of the registration or for rectifying the relevant entry in the register of designs;

and this is so notwithstanding that the person registered as the proprietor was not the proprietor of the design for the purposes of the 1949 Act.

(2) In subsection (1) a 'corresponding design', in relation to an artistic work, means a design within the meaning of the 1949 Act which if applied to an article would produce something which would be treated for the purposes of this Part as a copy of the artistic work.

## *Typefaces*

## 54. Use of typeface in ordinary course of printing

(1) It is not an infringement of copyright in an artistic work consisting of the design of a typeface—

(a) to use the typeface in the ordinary course of typing, composing text, typesetting or printing,

(b) to possess an article for the purpose of such use, or

(c) to do anything in relation to material produced by such use;

and this is so notwithstanding that an article is used which is an infringing copy of the work.

(2) However, the following provisions of this Part apply in relation to persons making, importing or dealing with articles specifically designed or adapted for producing material in a particular typeface, or possessing such articles for the purpose of dealing with them, as if the production of material as mentioned in subsection (1) did infringe copyright in the artistic work consisting of the design of the typeface—

section 24 (secondary infringement: making, importing, possessing or dealing with an article for making infringing copy),

sections 99 and 100 (order for delivery up and right of seizure),

section 107(2) (offence of making or possessing such an article), and

section 108 (order for delivery up in criminal proceedings).

(3) The references in subsection (2) to 'dealing with' an article are to selling, letting for hire, or offering or exposing for sale or hire, exhibiting in public, or distributing.

### 55. Articles for producing material in particular typeface
(1) This section applies to the copyright in an artistic work consisting of the design of a typeface where articles specifically designed or adapted for producing material in that typeface have been marketed by or with the licence of the copyright owner.

(2) After the period of 25 years from the end of the calendar year in which the first such articles are marketed, the work may be copied by making further such articles, or doing anything for the purpose of making such articles, and anything may be done in relation to articles so made, without infringing copyright in the work.

(3) In subsection (1) 'marketed' means sold, let for hire or offered or exposed for sale or hire, in the United Kingdom or elsewhere.

*Works in electronic form*

### 56. Transfers of copies of works in electronic form
(1) This section applies where a copy of a work in electronic form has been purchased on terms which, expressly or impliedly or by virtue of any rule of law, allow the purchaser to copy the work, or to adapt it or make copies of an adaptation, in connection with his use of it.

(2) If there are no express terms—

    (a) prohibiting the transfer of the copy by the purchaser, imposing obligations which continue after a transfer, prohibiting the assignment of any licence or terminating any licence on a transfer, or

    (b) providing for the terms on which a transferee may do the things which the purchaser was permitted to do,

anything which the purchaser was allowed to do may also be done without infringement of copyright by a transferee; but any copy, adaptation or copy of an adaptation made by the purchaser which is not also transferred shall be treated as an infringing copy for all purposes after the transfer.

(3) The same applies where the original purchased copy is no longer usable and what is transferred is a further copy used in its place.

(4) The above provisions also apply on a subsequent transfer, with the substitution for references in subsection (2) to the purchaser of references to the subsequent transferor.

*Miscellaneous: literary, dramatic, musical and artistic works*

### 57. Anonymous or pseudonymous works: acts permitted on assumptions as to expiry of copyright or death of author
(1) Copyright in a literary, dramatic, musical or artistic work is not infringed by an act done at a time when, or in pursuance of arrangements made at a time when—

    (a) it is not possible by reasonable inquiry to ascertain the identity of the author, and

    (b) it is reasonable to assume—

- (i) that copyright has expired, or
- (ii) that the author died 50 years or more before the beginning of the calendar year in which the act is done or the arrangements are made.

(2) Subsection (1)(b)(ii) does not apply in relation to—

- (a) a work in which Crown copyright subsists, or
- (b) a work in which copyright originally vested in an international organisation by virtue of section 168 and in respect of which an Order under that section specifies a copyright period longer than 50 years.

(3) In relation to a work of joint authorship—

- (a) the reference in subsection (1) to its being possible to ascertain the identity of the author shall be construed as a reference to its being possible to ascertain the identity of any of the authors, and
- (b) the reference in subsection (1)(b)(ii) to the author having died shall be construed as a reference to all the authors having died.

## 58. Use of notes or recordings of spoken words in certain cases

(1) Where a record of spoken words is made, in writing or otherwise, for the purpose—

- (a) of reporting current events, or
- (b) of broadcasting or including in a cable programme service the whole or part of the work,

it is not an infringement of any copyright in the words as a literary work to use the record or material taken from it (or to copy the record, or any such material, and use the copy) for that purpose, provided the following conditions are met.

(2) The conditions are that—

- (a) the record is a direct record of the spoken words and is not taken from a previous record or from a broadcast or cable programme;
- (b) the making of the record was not prohibited by the speaker and, where copyright already subsisted in the work, did not infringe copyright;
- (c) the use made of the record or material taken from it is not of a kind prohibited by or on behalf of the speaker or copyright owner before the record was made; and
- (d) the use is by or with the authority of a person who is lawfully in possession of the record.

## 59. Public reading or recitation

(1) The reading or recitation in public by one person of a reasonable extract from a published literary or dramatic work does not infringe any copyright in the work if it is accompanied by a sufficient acknowledgement.

(2) Copyright in a work is not infringed by the making of a sound recording, or the broadcasting or inclusion in a cable programme service, of a reading or recitation which by virtue of subsection (1) does not infringe copyright in the work, provided that the recording, broadcast or cable programme consists mainly of material in relation to which it is not necessary to rely on that subsection.

### 60. Abstracts of scientific or technical articles

(1) Where an article on a scientific or technical subject is published in a periodical accompanied by an abstract indicating the contents of the article, it is not an infringement of copyright in the abstract, or in the article, to copy the abstract or issue copies of it to the public.

(2) This section does not apply if or to the extent that there is a licensing scheme certified for the purposes of this section under section 143 providing for the grant of licences.

### 61. Recordings of folksongs

(1) A sound recording of a performance of a song may be made for the purpose of including it in an archive maintained by a designated body without infringing any copyright in the words as a literary work or in the accompanying musical work, provided the conditions in subsection (2) below are met.

(2) The conditions are that—

  (a) the words are unpublished and of unknown authorship at the time the recording is made,
  (b) the making of the recording does not infringe any other copyright, and
  (c) its making is not prohibited by any performer.

(3) Copies of a sound recording made in reliance on subsection (1) and included in an archive maintained by a designated body may, if the prescribed conditions are met, be made and supplied by the archivist without infringing copyright in the recording or the works included in it.

(4) The prescribed conditions shall include the following—

  (a) that copies are only supplied to persons satisfying the archivist that they require them for purposes of research or private study and will not use them for any other purpose; and
  (b) that no person is furnished with more than one copy of the same recording.

(5) In this section—

  (a) 'designated' means designated for the purposes of this section by order of the Secretary of State, who shall not designate a body unless satisfied that it is not established or conducted for profit,
  (b) 'prescribed' means prescribed for the purposes of this section by order of the Secretary of State, and
  (c) references to the archivist include a person acting on his behalf.

(6) An order under this section shall be made by statutory instrument which shall be subject to annulment in pursuance of a resolution of either House of Parliament.

### 62. Representation of certain artistic works on public display

(1) This section applies to—

  (a) buildings, and
  (b) sculptures, models for buildings and works of artistic craftsmanship, if permanently situated in a public place or in premises open to the public.

(2) The copyright in such a work is not infringed by—

  (a) making a graphic work representing it,

(b) making a photograph or film of it, or

(c) broadcasting or including in a cable programme service a visual image of it.

(3) Nor is the copyright infringed by the issue to the public of copies, or the broadcasting or inclusion in a cable programme service, of anything whose making was, by virtue of this section, not an infringement of the copyright.

### 63. Advertisement of sale of artistic work

(1) It is not an infringement of copyright in an artistic work to copy it, or to issue copies to the public, for the purpose of advertising the sale of the work.

(2) Where a copy which would otherwise be an infringing copy is made in accordance with this section but is subsequently dealt with for any other purpose, it shall be treated as an infringing copy for the purposes of that dealing, and if that dealing infringes copyright for all subsequent purposes.

For this purpose 'dealt with' means sold or let for hire, offered or exposed for sale or hire, exhibited in public or distributed.

### 64. Making of subsequent works by same artist

Where the author of an artistic work is not the copyright owner, he does not infringe the copyright by copying the work in making another artistic work, provided he does not repeat or imitate the main design of the earlier work.

### 65. Reconstruction of buildings

Anything done for the purposes of reconstructing a building does not infringe any copyright—

(a) in the building, or

(b) in any drawings or plans in accordance with which the building was, by or with the licence of the copyright owner, constructed.

*Sound recordings, films and computer programs*

### 66. Rental of sound recordings, films and computer programs

(1) The Secretary of State may by order provide that in such cases as may be specified in the order the rental to the public of copies of sound recordings, films or computer programs shall be treated as licensed by the copyright owner subject only to the payment of such reasonable royalty or other payment as may be agreed or determined in default of agreement by the Copyright Tribunal.

(2) No such order shall apply if, or to the extent that, there is a licensing scheme certified for the purposes of this section under section 143 providing for the grant of licences.

(3) An order may make different provision for different cases and may specify cases by reference to any factor relating to the work, the copies rented, the renter or the circumstances of the rental.

(4) An order shall be made by statutory instrument; and no order shall be made unless a draft of it has been laid before and approved by a resolution of each House of Parliament.

(5) Copyright in a computer program is not infringed by the rental of copies to the public after the end of the period of 50 years from the end of the calendar year in which copies of it were first issued to the public in electronic form.

(6) Nothing in this section affects any liability under section 23 (secondary infringement) in respect of the rental of infringing copies.

### 67. Playing of sound recordings for purposes of club, society, etc

(1) It is not an infringement of the copyright in a sound recording to play it as part of the activities of, or for the benefit of, a club, society or other organisation if the following conditions are met.

(2) The conditions are—

    (a) that the organisation is not established or conducted for profit and its main objects are charitable or are otherwise concerned with the advancement of religion, education or social welfare, and

    (b) that the proceeds of any charge for admission to the place where the recording is to be heard are applied solely for the purposes of the organisation.

## Miscellaneous: broadcasts and cable programmes

### 68. Incidental recording for purposes of broadcast or cable programme

(1) This section applies where by virtue of a licence or assignment of copyright a person is authorised to broadcast or include in a cable programme service—

    (a) a literary, dramatic or musical work, or an adaptation of such a work,

    (b) an artistic work, or

    (c) a sound recording or film.

(2) He shall by virtue of this section be treated as licensed by the owner of the copyright in the work to do or authorise any of the following for the purposes of the broadcast or cable programme—

    (a) in the case of a literary, dramatic or musical work, or an adaptation of such a work, to make a sound recording or film of the work or adaptation;

    (b) in the case of an artistic work, to take a photograph or make a film of the work;

    (c) in the case of a sound recording or film, to make a copy of it.

(3) That licence is subject to the condition that the recording, film, photograph or copy in question—

    (a) shall not be used for any other purpose, and

    (b) shall be destroyed within 28 days of being first used for broadcasting the work or, as the case may be, including it in a cable programme service.

(4) A recording, film, photograph or copy made in accordance with this section shall be treated as an infringing copy—

    (a) for the purposes of any use in breach of the condition mentioned in subsection (3)(a), and

    (b) for all purposes after that condition or the condition mentioned in subsection (3)(b) is broken.

### 69. Recording for purposes of supervision and control of broadcasts and cable programmes

(1) Copyright is not infringed by the making or use by the British Broadcasting

Corporation, for the purpose of maintaining supervision and control over programmes broadcast by them, of recordings of those programmes.

*(2) Copyright is not infringed by—*

> *(a) the making or use of recordings by the Independent Broadcasting Authority for the purposes mentioned in section 4(7) of the Broadcasting Act 1981 (maintenance of supervision and control over programmes and advertisements); or*
>
> *(b) anything done under or in pursuance of provision included in a contract between a programme contractor and the Authority in accordance with section 21 of that Act.*

*(3) Copyright is not infringed by—*

> *(a) the making by or with the authority of the Cable Authority, or the use by that Authority, for the purpose of maintaining supervision and control over programmes included in services licensed under Part I of the Cable and Broadcasting Act 1984, of recordings of those programmes; or*
>
> *(b) anything done under or in pursuance of—*
>
> > *(i) a notice or direction given under section 16 of the Cable and Broadcasting Act 1984 (power of Cable Authority to require production of recordings); or*
> >
> > *(ii) a condition included in a licence by virtue of section 35 of that Act (duty of Authority to secure that recordings are available for certain purposes).*

**(2) Copyright is not infringed by anything done in pursuance of—**

> **(a) sections 11(1), 95(1), 145(4), (5) or (7), 155(3) or 167(1) of the Broadcasting Act 1990;**
>
> **(b) a condition which, by virtue of sections 11(2) or 95(2) of that Act, is included in a licence granted under Part I or III of that Act; or**
>
> **(c) a direction given under section 109(2) of that Act (power of Radio Authority to require production of recordings etc).**

**(3) Copyright is not infringed by—**

> **(a) the use by the Independent Television Commission or the Radio Authority, in connection with the performance of any of their functions under the Broadcasting Act 1990, of any recording, script or transcript which is provided to them under or by virtue of any provision of that Act; or**
>
> **(b) the use by the Broadcasting Complaints Commission or the Broadcasting Standards Council, in connection with any complaint made to them under that Act, of any recording or transcript requested or required to be provided to them, and so provided, under section 145(4) or (7) or section 155(3) of that Act.**

*General note*
Sub-ss (2), (3): substituted by the Broadcasting Act 1990, s 203(1), Sch 20, para 50.

## 70. Recording for purposes of time-shifting

The making for private and domestic use of a recording of a broadcast or cable programme solely for the purpose of enabling it to be viewed or listened to at a more convenient time does not infringe any copyright in the broadcast or cable programme or in any work included in it.

## 71. Photographs of television broadcasts or cable programmes
The making for private and domestic use of a photograph of the whole or any part of an image forming part of a television broadcast or cable programme, or a copy of such a photograph, does not infringe any copyright in the broadcast or cable programme or in any film included in it.

## 72. Free public showing or playing of broadcast or cable programme
(1) The showing or playing in public of a broadcast or cable programme to an audience who have not paid for admission to the place where the broadcast or programme is to be seen or heard does not infringe any copyright in—

    (a)  the broadcast or cable programme, or
    (b)  any sound recording or film included in it.

  (2) The audience shall be treated as having paid for admission to a place—

    (a)  if they have paid for admission to a place of which that place forms part; or
    (b)  if goods or services are supplied at that place (or a place of which it forms part)—

        (i)  at prices which are substantially attributable to the facilities afforded for seeing or hearing the broadcast or programme, or
        (ii)  at prices exceeding those usually charged there and which are partly attributable to those facilities.

  (3) The following shall not be regarded as having paid for admission to a place—

    (a)  persons admitted as residents or inmates of the place;
    (b)  persons admitted as members of a club or society where the payment is only for membership of the club or society and the provision of facilities for seeing or hearing broadcasts or programmes is only incidental to the main purposes of the club or society.

  (4) Where the making of the broadcast or inclusion of the programme in a cable programme service was an infringement of the copyright in a sound recording or film, the fact that it was heard or seen in public by the reception of the broadcast or programme shall be taken into account in assessing the damages for that infringement.

## 73. Reception and re-transmission of broadcast in cable programme service
(1) This section applies where a broadcast made from a place in the United Kingdom is, by reception and immediate re-transmission, included in a cable programme service.

  (2) The copyright in the broadcast is not infringed—

    (a)  *if the inclusion is in pursuance of a requirement imposed under section 13(1) of the Cable and Broadcasting Act 1984 (duty of Cable Authority to secure inclusion in cable service of certain programmes),* or
    (b)  if and to the extent that the broadcast is made for reception in the area in which the cable programme service is provided and is not a satellite transmission or an encrypted transmission.

(3) The copyright in any work included in the broadcast is not infringed—

(a) *if the inclusion is in pursuance of a requirement imposed under section 13(1) of the Cable and Broadcasting Act 1984 (duty of Cable Authority to secure inclusion in cable service of certain programmes), or*

(b) if and to the extent that the broadcast is made for reception in the area in which the cable programme service is provided;

but where the making of the broadcast was an infringement of the copyright in the work, the fact that the broadcast was re-transmitted as a programme in a cable programme service shall be taken into account in assessing the damages for that infringement.

*General note*
Sub-ss (2), (3): words in italics repealed by the Broadcasting Act 1990, s 203(3), Sch 21.

## 74. Provision of sub-titled copies of broadcast or cable programme

(1) A designated body may, for the purpose of providing people who are deaf or hard of hearing, or physically or mentally handicapped in other ways, with copies which are sub-titled or otherwise modified for their special needs, make copies of television broadcasts or cable programmes and issue copies to the public, without infringing any copyright in the broadcasts or cable programmes or works included in them.

(2) A 'designated body' means a body designated for the purposes of this section by order of the Secretary of State, who shall not designate a body unless he is satisfied that it is not established or conducted for profit.

(3) An order under this section shall be made by statutory instrument which shall be subject to annulment in pursuance of a resolution of either House of Parliament.

(4) This section does not apply if, or to the extent that, there is a licensing scheme certified for the purposes of this section under section 143 providing for the grant of licences.

## 75. Recording for archival purposes

(1) A recording of a broadcast or cable programme of a designated class, or a copy of such a recording, may be made for the purpose of being placed in an archive maintained by a designated body without thereby infringing any copyright in the broadcast or cable programme or in any work included in it.

(2) In subsection (1) 'designated' means designated for the purposes of this section by order of the Secretary of State, who shall not designate a body unless he is satisfied that it is not established or conducted for profit.

(3) An order under this section shall be made by statutory instrument which shall be subject to annulment in pursuance of a resolution of either House of Parliament.

*Adaptations*

## 76. Adaptations

An act which by virtue of this Chapter may be done without infringing copyright in a literary, dramatic or musical work does not, where that work is an adaptation, infringe any copyright in the work from which the adaptation was made.

CHAPTER IV
MORAL RIGHTS

*Right to be identified as author or director*

**77. Right to be identified as author or director**
(1) The author of a copyright literary, dramatic, musical or artistic work, and the director of a copyright film, has the right to be identified as the author or director of the work in the circumstances mentioned in this section; but the right is not infringed unless it has been asserted in accordance with section 78.

(2) The author of a literary work (other than words intended to be sung or spoken with music) or a dramatic work has the right to be identified whenever—

    (a) the work is published commercially, performed in public, broadcast or included in a cable programme service; or

    (b) copies of a film or sound recording including the work are issued to the public;

and that right includes the right to be identified whenever any of those events occur in relation to an adaptation of the work as the author of the work from which the adaptation was made.

(3) The author of a musical work, or a literary work consisting of words intended to be sung or spoken with music, has the right to be identified whenever—

    (a) the work is published commercially;

    (b) copies of a sound recording of the work are issued to the public; or

    (c) a film of which the sound-track includes the work is shown in public or copies of such a film are issued to the public;

and that right includes the right to be identified whenever any of those events occur in relation to an adaptation of the work as the author of the work from which the adaptation was made.

(4) The author of an artistic work has the right to be identified whenever—

    (a) the work is published commercially or exhibited in public, or a visual image of it is broadcast or included in a cable programme service;

    (b) a film including a visual image of the work is shown in public or copies of such a film are issued to the public; or

    (c) in the case of a work of architecture in the form of a building or a model for a building, a sculpture or a work of artistic craftsmanship, copies of a graphic work representing it, or of a photograph of it, are issued to the public.

(5) The author of a work of architecture in the form of a building also has the right to be identified on the building as constructed or, where more than one building is constructed to the design, on the first to be constructed.

(6) The director of a film has the right to be identified whenever the film is shown in public, broadcast or included in a cable programme service or copies of the film are issued to the public.

(7) The right of the author or director under this section is—

    (a) in the case of commercial publication or the issue to the public of copies of a film or sound recording, to be identified in or on each copy or, if that is not appropriate, in some other manner likely to bring his identity to the notice of a person acquiring a copy,

(b) in the case of identification on a building, to be identified by appropriate means visible to persons entering or approaching the building, and

(c) in any other case, to be identified in a manner likely to bring his identity to the attention of a person seeing or hearing the performance, exhibition, showing, broadcast or cable programme in question;

and the identification must in each case be clear and reasonably prominent.

(8) If the author or director in asserting his right to be identified specifies a pseudonym, initials or some other particular form of identification, that form shall be used; otherwise any reasonable form of identification may be used.

(9) This section has effect subject to section 79 (exceptions to right).

## 78. Requirement that right be asserted

(1) A person does not infringe the right conferred by section 77 (right to be identified as author or director) by doing any of the acts mentioned in that section unless the right has been asserted in accordance with the following provisions so as to bind him in relation to that act.

(2) The right may be asserted generally, or in relation to any specified act or description of acts—

(a) on an assignment of copyright in the work, by including in the instrument effecting the assignment a statement that the author or director asserts in relation to that work his right to be identified, or

(b) by instrument in writing signed by the author or director.

(3) The right may also be asserted in relation to the public exhibition of an artistic work—

(a) by securing that when the author or other first owner of copyright parts with possession of the original, or of a copy made by him or under his direction or control, the author is identified on the original or copy, or on a frame, mount or other thing to which it is attached, or

(b) by including in a licence by which the author or other first owner of copyright authorises the making of copies of the work a statement signed by or on behalf of the person granting the licence that the author asserts his right to be identified in the event of the public exhibition of a copy made in pursuance of the licence.

(4) The persons bound by an assertion of the right under subsection (2) or (3) are—

(a) in the case of an assertion under subsection (2)(*a*), the assignee and anyone claiming through him, whether or not he has notice of the assertion;

(b) in the case of an assertion under subsection (2)(*b*), anyone to whose notice the assertion is brought;

(c) in the case of an assertion under subsection (3)(*a*), anyone into whose hands that original or copy comes, whether or not the identification is still present or visible;

(d) in the case of an assertion under subsection (3)(*b*), the licensee and anyone into whose hands a copy made in pursuance of the licence comes, whether or not he has notice of the assertion.

(5) In an action for infringement of the right the court shall, in considering remedies, take into account any delay in asserting the right.

## 79. Exceptions to right

(1) The right conferred by section 77 (right to be identified as author or director) is subject to the following exceptions.

(2) The right does not apply in relation to the following descriptions of work—

    (a) a computer program;
    (b) the design of a typeface;
    (c) any computer-generated work.

(3) The right does not apply to anything done by or with the authority of the copyright owner where copyright in the work originally vested—

    (a) in the author's employer by virtue of section 11(2) (works produced in course of employment), or
    (b) in the director's employer by virtue of section 9(2)(a) (person to be treated as author of film).

(4) The right is not infringed by an act which by virtue of any of the following provisions would not infringe copyright in the work—

    (a) section 30 (fair dealing for certain purposes), so far as it relates to the reporting of current events by means of a sound recording, film, broadcast or cable programme;
    (b) section 31 (incidental inclusion of work in an artistic work, sound recording, film, broadcast or cable programme);
    (c) section 32(3) (examination questions);
    (d) section 45 (Parliamentary and judicial proceedings);
    (e) section 46(1) or (2) (Royal Commissions and statutory inquiries);
    (f) section 51 (use of design documents and models);
    (g) section 52 (effect of exploitation of design derived from artistic work);
    (h) section 57 (anonymous or pseudonymous works: acts permitted on assumptions as to expiry of copyright or death of author).

(5) The right does not apply in relation to any work made for the purpose of reporting current events.

(6) The right does not apply in relation to the publication in—

    (a) a newspaper, magazine or similar periodical, or
    (b) an encyclopaedia, dictionary, yearbook or other collective work of reference,

of a literary, dramatic, musical or artistic work made for the purposes of such publication or made available with the consent of the author for the purposes of such publication.

(7) The right does not apply in relation to—

    (a) a work in which Crown copyright or Parliamentary copyright subsists, or
    (b) a work in which copyright originally vested in an international organisation by virtue of section 168,

unless the author or director has previously been identified as such in or on published copies of the work.

*Right to object to derogatory treatment of work*

**80. Right to object to derogatory treatment of work**

(1) The author of a copyright literary, dramatic, musical or artistic work, and the director of a copyright film, has the right in the circumstances mentioned in this section not to have his work subjected to derogatory treatment.

(2) For the purposes of this section—

(a) 'treatment' of a work means any addition to, deletion from or alteration to or adaptation of the work, other than—

(i) a translation of a literary or dramatic work, or

(ii) an arrangement or transcription of a musical work involving no more than a change of key or register; and

(b) the treatment of a work is derogatory if it amounts to distortion or mutilation of the work or is otherwise prejudicial to the honour or reputation of the author or director;

and in the following provisions of this section references to a derogatory treatment of a work shall be construed accordingly.

(3) In the case of a literary, dramatic or musical work the right is infringed by a person who—

(a) publishes commercially, performs in public, broadcasts or includes in a cable programme service a derogatory treatment of the work; or

(b) issues to the public copies of a film or sound recording of, or including, a derogatory treatment of the work.

(4) In the case of an artistic work the right is infringed by a person who—

(a) publishes commercially or exhibits in public a derogatory treatment of the work, or broadcasts or includes in a cable programme service a visual image of a derogatory treatment of the work,

(b) shows in public a film including a visual image of a derogatory treatment of the work or issues to the public copies of such a film, or

(c) in the case of—

(i) a work of architecture in the form of a model for a building,

(ii) a sculpture, or

(iii) a work of artistic craftsmanship,

issues to the public copies of a graphic work representing, or of a photograph of, a derogatory treatment of the work.

(5) Subsection (4) does not apply to a work of architecture in the form of a building; but where the author of such a work is identified on the building and it is the subject of derogatory treatment he has the right to require the identification to be removed.

(6) In the case of a film, the right is infringed by a person who—

(a) shows in public, broadcasts or includes in a cable programme service a derogatory treatment of the film; or

(b) issues to the public copies of a derogatory treatment of the film,

or who, along with the film, plays in public, broadcasts or includes in a cable programme service, or issues to the public copies of, a derogatory treatment of the film sound-track.

(7) The right conferred by this section extends to the treatment of parts of a work resulting from a previous treatment by a person other than the author or director, if those parts are attributed to, or are likely to be regarded as the work of, the author or director.

(8) This section has effect subject to sections 81 and 82 (exceptions to and qualifications of right).

### 81. Exceptions to right

(1) The right conferred by section 80 (right to object to derogatory treatment of work) is subject to the following exceptions.

(2) The right does not apply to a computer program or to any computer-generated work.

(3) The right does not apply in relation to any work made for the purpose of reporting current events.

(4) The right does not apply in relation to the publication in—

(a) a newspaper, magazine or similar periodical, or
(b) an encyclopaedia, dictionary, yearbook or other collective work of reference,

of a literary, dramatic, musical or artistic work made for the purposes of such publication or made available with the consent of the author for the purposes of such publication.

Nor does the right apply in relation to any subsequent exploitation elsewhere of such a work without any modification of the published version.

(5) The right is not infringed by an act which by virtue of section 57 (anonymous or pseudonymous works: acts permitted on assumptions as to expiry of copyright or death of author) would not infringe copyright.

(6) The right is not infringed by anything done for the purpose of—

(a) avoiding the commission of an offence,
(b) complying with a duty imposed by or under an enactment, or
(c) in the case of the British Broadcasting Corporation, avoiding the inclusion in a programme broadcast by them of anything which offends against good taste or decency or which is likely to encourage or incite to crime or to lead to disorder or to be offensive to public feeling,

provided, where the author or director is identified at the time of the relevant act or has previously been identified in or on published copies of the work, that there is a sufficient disclaimer.

### 82. Qualification of right in certain cases

(1) This section applies to—

(a) works in which copyright originally vested in the author's employer by virtue of section 11(2) (works produced in course of employment) or in the director's employer by virtue of section 9(2)(a) (person to be treated as author of film),
(b) works in which Crown copyright or Parliamentary copyright subsists, and
(c) works in which copyright originally vested in an international organisation by virtue of section 168.

(2) The right conferred by section 80 (right to object to derogatory treatment

of work) does not apply to anything done in relation to such a work by or with the authority of the copyright owner unless the author or director—

    (a)  is identified at the time of the relevant act, or

    (b)  has previously been identified in or on published copies of the work;

and where in such a case the right does apply, it is not infringed if there is a sufficient disclaimer.

**83. Infringement of right by possessing or dealing with infringing article**
(1) The right conferred by section 80 (right to object to derogatory treatment of work) is also infringed by a person who—

    (a)  possesses in the course of a business, or

    (b)  sells or lets for hire, or offers or exposes for sale or hire, or

    (c)  in the course of a business exhibits in public or distributes, or

    (d)  distributes otherwise than in the course of a business so as to affect prejudicially the honour or reputation of the author or director,

an article which is, and which he knows or has reason to believe is, an infringing article.

    (2) An 'infringing article' means a work or a copy of a work which—

    (a)  has been subjected to derogatory treatment within the meaning of section 80, and

    (b)  has been or is likely to be the subject of any of the acts mentioned in that section in circumstances infringing that right.

*False attribution of work*

**84. False attribution of work**
(1) A person has the right in the circumstances mentioned in this section—

    (a)  not to have a literary, dramatic, musical or artistic work falsely attributed to him as author, and

    (b)  not to have a film falsely attributed to him as director;

and in this section an 'attribution', in relation to such a work, means a statement (express or implied) as to who is the author or director.

    (2) The right is infringed by a person who—

    (a)  issues to the public copies of a work of any of those descriptions in or on which there is a false attribution, or

    (b)  exhibits in public an artistic work, or a copy of an artistic work, in or on which there is a false attribution.

    (3) The right is also infringed by a person who—

    (a)  in the case of a literary, dramatic or musical work, performs the work in public, broadcasts it or includes it in a cable programme service as being the work of a person, or

    (b)  in the case of a film, shows it in public, broadcasts it or includes it in a cable programme service as being directed by a person,

knowing or having reason to believe that the attribution is false.

    (4) The right is also infringed by the issue to the public or public display of

material containing a false attribution in connection with any of the acts mentioned in subsection (2) or (3).

(5) The right is also infringed by a person who in the course of a business—

    (a) possesses or deals with a copy of a work of any of the descriptions mentioned in subsection (1) in or on which there is a false attribution, or

    (b) in the case of an artistic work, possesses or deals with the work itself when there is a false attribution in or on it,

knowing or having reason to believe that there is such an attribution and that it is false.

(6) In the case of an artistic work the right is also infringed by a person who in the course of a business—

    (a) deals with a work which has been altered after the author parted with possession of it as being the unaltered work of the author, or

    (b) deals with a copy of such a work as being a copy of the unaltered work of the author,

knowing or having reason to believe that that is not the case.

(7) References in this section to dealing are to selling or letting for hire, offering or exposing for sale or hire, exhibiting in public, or distributing.

(8) This section applies where, contrary to the fact—

    (a) a literary, dramatic or musical work is falsely represented as being an adaptation of the work of a person, or

    (b) a copy of an artistic work is falsely represented as being a copy made by the author of the artistic work,

as it applies where the work is falsely attributed to a person as author.

### Right to privacy of certain photographs and films

**85. Right to privacy of certain photographs and films**

(1) A person who for private and domestic purposes commissions the taking of a photograph or the making of a film has, where copyright subsists in the resulting work, the right not to have—

    (a) copies of the work issued to the public,

    (b) the work exhibited or shown in public, or

    (c) the work broadcast or included in a cable programme service;

and, except as mentioned in subsection (2), a person who does or authorises the doing of any of those acts infringes that right.

(2) The right is not infringed by an act which by virtue of any of the following provisions would not infringe copyright in the work—

    (a) section 31 (incidental inclusion of work in an artistic work, film, broadcast or cable programme);

    (b) section 45 (Parliamentary and judicial proceedings);

    (c) section 46 (Royal Commissions and statutory inquiries);

    (d) section 50 (acts done under statutory authority);

    (e) section 57 (anonymous or pseudonymous works: acts permitted on assumptions as to expiry of copyright or death of author).

*Supplementary*

### 86. Duration of rights

(1) The rights conferred by section 77 (right to be identified as author or director), section 80 (right to object to derogatory treatment of work) and section 85 (right to privacy of certain photographs and films) continue to subsist so long as copyright subsists in the work.

(2) The right conferred by section 84 (false attribution) continues to subsist until 20 years after a person's death.

### 87. Consent and waiver of rights

(1) It is not an infringement of any of the rights conferred by this Chapter to do any act to which the person entitled to the right has consented.

(2) Any of those rights may be waived by instrument in writing signed by the person giving up the right.

(3) A waiver—

    (a) may relate to a specific work, to works of a specified description or to works generally, and may relate to existing or future works, and

    (b) may be conditional or unconditional and may be expressed to be subject to revocation;

and if made in favour of the owner or prospective owner of the copyright in the work or works to which it relates, it shall be presumed to extend to his licensees and successors in title unless a contrary intention is expressed.

(4) Nothing in this Chapter shall be construed as excluding the operation of the general law of contract or estoppel in relation to an informal waiver or other transaction in relation to any of the rights mentioned in subsection (1).

### 88. Application of provisions to joint works

(1) The right conferred by section 77 (right to be identified as author or director) is, in the case of a work of joint authorship, a right of each joint author to be identified as a joint author and must be asserted in accordance with section 78 by each joint author in relation to himself.

(2) The right conferred by section 80 (right to object to derogatory treatment of work) is, in the case of a work of joint authorship, a right of each joint author and his right is satisfied if he consents to the treatment in question.

(3) A waiver under section 87 of those rights by one joint author does not affect the rights of the other joint authors.

(4) The right conferred by section 84 (false attribution) is infringed, in the circumstances mentioned in that section—

    (a) by any false statement as to the authorship of a work of joint authorship, and

    (b) by the false attribution of joint authorship in relation to a work of sole authorship;

and such a false attribution infringes the right of every person to whom authorship of any description is, whether rightly or wrongly, attributed.

(5) The above provisions also apply (with any necessary adaptations) in relation to a film which was, or is alleged to have been, jointly directed, as they apply to a work which is, or is alleged to be, a work of joint authorship.

A film is 'jointly directed' if it is made by the collaboration of two or more directors and the contribution of each director is not distinct from that of the other director or directors.

(6) The right conferred by section 85 (right to privacy of certain photographs and films) is, in the case of a work made in pursuance of a joint commission, a right of each person who commissioned the making of the work, so that—

(a) the right of each is satisfied if he consents to the act in question, and
(b) a waiver under section 87 by one of them does not affect the rights of the others.

### 89. Application of provisions to parts of works

(1) The rights conferred by section 77 (right to be identified as author or director) and section 85 (right to privacy of certain photographs and films) apply in relation to the whole or any substantial part of a work.

(2) The rights conferred by section 80 (right to object to derogatory treatment of work) and section 84 (false attribution) apply in relation to the whole or any part of a work.

CHAPTER V
DEALINGS WITH RIGHTS IN COPYRIGHT WORKS

*Copyright*

### 90. Assignment and licences

(1) Copyright is transmissible by assignment, by testamentary disposition or by operation of law, as personal or moveable property.

(2) An assignment or other transmission of copyright may be partial, that is, limited so as to apply—

(a) to one or more, but not all, of the things the copyright owner has the exclusive right to do;
(b) to part, but not the whole, of the period for which the copyright is to subsist.

(3) An assignment of copyright is not effective unless it is in writing signed by or on behalf of the assignor.

(4) A licence granted by a copyright owner is binding on every successor in title to his interest in the copyright, except a purchaser in good faith for valuable consideration and without notice (actual or constructive) of the licence or a person deriving title from such a purchaser; and references in this Part to doing anything with, or without, the licence of the copyright owner shall be construed accordingly.

### 91. Prospective ownership of copyright

(1) Where by an agreement made in relation to future copyright, and signed by or on behalf of the prospective owner of the copyright, the prospective owner purports to assign the future copyright (wholly or partially) to another person, then if, on the copyright coming into existence, the assignee or another person claiming under him would be entitled as against all other persons to require the copyright to be vested in him, the copyright shall vest in the assignee or his successor in title by virtue of this subsection.

(2) In this Part—

'future copyright' means copyright which will or may come into existence in respect of a future work or class of works or on the occurrence of a future event; and

'prospective owner' shall be construed accordingly, and includes a person who is prospectively entitled to copyright by virtue of such an agreement as is mentioned in subsection (1).

(3) A licence granted by a prospective owner of copyright is binding on every successor in title to his interest (or prospective interest) in the right, except a purchaser in good faith for valuable consideration and without notice (actual or constructive) of the licence or a person deriving title from such a purchaser; and references in this Part to doing anything with, or without, the licence of the copyright owner shall be construed accordingly.

## 92. Exclusive licences

(1) In this Part an 'exclusive licence' means a licence in writing signed by or on behalf of the copyright owner authorising the licensee to the exclusion of all other persons, including the person granting the licence, to exercise a right which would otherwise be exercisable exclusively by the copyright owner.

(2) The licensee under an exclusive licence has the same rights against a successor in title who is bound by the licence as he has against the person granting the licence.

## 93. Copyright to pass under will with unpublished work

Where under a bequest (whether specific or general) a person is entitled, beneficially or otherwise, to—

(a) an original document or other material thing recording or embodying a literary, dramatic, musical or artistic work which was not published before the death of the testator, or

(b) an original material thing containing a sound recording or film which was not published before the death of the testator,

the bequest shall, unless a contrary intention is indicated in the testator's will or a codicil to it, be construed as including the copyright in the work in so far as the testator was the owner of the copyright immediately before his death.

## *Moral rights*

## 94. Moral rights not assignable

The rights conferred by Chapter IV (moral rights) are not assignable.

## 95. Transmission of moral rights on death

(1) On the death of a person entitled to the right conferred by section 77 (right to identification of author or director), section 80 (right to object to derogatory treatment of work) or section 85 (right to privacy of certain photographs and films)—

(a) the right passes to such person as he may by testamentary disposition specifically direct,

(b) if there is no such direction but the copyright in the work in question forms part of his estate, the right passes to the person to whom the copyright passes, and

(c)  if or to the extent that the right does not pass under paragraph (a) or (b) it is exercisable by his personal representatives.

(2)  Where copyright forming part of a person's estate passes in part to one person and in part to another, as for example where a bequest is limited so as to apply—

(a)  to one or more, but not all, of the things the copyright owner has the exclusive right to do or authorise, or

(b)  to part, but not the whole, of the period for which the copyright is to subsist,

any right which passes with the copyright by virtue of subsection (1) is correspondingly divided.

(3)  Where by virtue of subsection (1)(a) or (b) a right becomes exercisable by more than one person—

(a)  it may, in the case of the right conferred by section 77 (right to identification of author or director), be asserted by any of them;

(b)  it is, in the case of the right conferred by section 80 (right to object to derogatory treatment of work) or section 85 (right to privacy of certain photographs and films), a right exercisable by each of them and is satisfied in relation to any of them if he consents to the treatment or act in question; and

(c)  any waiver of the right in accordance with section 87 by one of them does not affect the rights of the others.

(4)  A consent or waiver previously given or made binds any person to whom a right passes by virtue of subsection (1).

(5)  Any infringement after a person's death of the right conferred by section 84 (false attribution) is actionable by his personal representatives.

(6)  Any damages recovered by personal representatives by virtue of this section in respect of an infringement after a person's death shall devolve as part of his estate as if the right of action had subsisted and been vested in him immediately before his death.

CHAPTER VI
REMEDIES FOR INFRINGEMENT

*Rights and remedies of copyright owner*

**96. Infringement actionable by copyright owner**
(1)  An infringement of copyright is actionable by the copyright owner.

(2)  In an action for infringement of copyright all such relief by way of damages, injunctions, accounts or otherwise is available to the plaintiff as is available in respect of the infringement of any other property right.

(3)  This section has effect subject to the following provisions of this Chapter.

**97. Provisions as to damages in infringement action**
(1)  Where in an action for infringement of copyright it is shown that at the time of the infringement the defendant did not know, and had no reason to believe, that copyright subsisted in the work to which the action relates, the plaintiff is not entitled to damages against him, but without prejudice to any other remedy.

(2) The court may in an action for infringement of copyright having regard to all the circumstances, and in particular to—

    (a) the flagrancy of the infringement, and

    (b) any benefit accruing to the defendant by reason of the infringement,

award such additional damages as the justice of the case may require.

### 98. Undertaking to take licence of right in infringement proceedings

(1) If in proceedings for infringement of copyright in respect of which a licence is available as of right under section 144 (powers exercisable in consequence of report of Monopolies and Mergers Commission) the defendant undertakes to take a licence on such terms as may be agreed or, in default of agreement, settled by the Copyright Tribunal under that section—

    (a) no injunction shall be granted against him,

    (b) no order for delivery up shall be made under section 99, and

    (c) the amount recoverable against him by way of damages or on an account of profits shall not exceed double the amount which would have been payable by him as licensee if such a licence on those terms had been granted before the earliest infringement.

(2) An undertaking may be given at any time before final order in the proceedings, without any admission of liability.

(3) Nothing in this section affects the remedies available in respect of an infringement committed before licences of right were available.

### 99. Order for delivery up

(1) Where a person—

    (a) has an infringing copy of a work in his possession, custody or control in the course of a business, or

    (b) has in his possession, custody or control an article specifically designed or adapted for making copies of a particular copyright work, knowing or having reason to believe that it has been or is to be used to make infringing copies,

the owner of the copyright in the work may apply to the court for an order that the infringing copy or article be delivered up to him or to such other person as the court may direct.

(2) An application shall not be made after the end of the period specified in section 113 (period after which remedy of delivery up not available); and no order shall be made unless the court also makes, or it appears to the court that there are grounds for making, an order under section 114 (order as to disposal of infringing copy or other article).

(3) A person to whom an infringing copy or other article is delivered up in pursuance of an order under this section shall, if an order under section 114 is not made, retain it pending the making of an order, or the decision not to make an order, under that section.

(4) Nothing in this section affects any other power of the court.

### 100. Right to seize infringing copies and other articles

(1) An infringing copy of a work which is found exposed or otherwise immediately available for sale or hire, and in respect of which the copyright owner

would be entitled to apply for an order under section 99, may be seized and detained by him or a person authorised by him.

The right to seize and detain is exercisable subject to the following conditions and is subject to any decision of the court under section 114.

(2) Before anything is seized under this section notice of the time and place of the proposed seizure must be given to a local police station.

(3) A person may for the purpose of exercising the right conferred by this section enter premises to which the public have access but may not seize anything in the possession, custody or control of a person at a permanent or regular place of business of his, and may not use any force.

(4) At the time when anything is seized under this section there shall be left at the place where it was seized a notice in the prescribed form containing the prescribed particulars as to the person by whom or on whose authority the seizure is made and the grounds on which it is made.

(5) In this section—

'premises' includes land, buildings, moveable structures, vehicles, vessels, aircraft and hovercraft; and

'prescribed' means prescribed by order of the Secretary of State.

(6) An order of the Secretary of State under this section shall be made by statutory instrument which shall be subject to annulment in pursuance of a resolution of either House of Parliament.

## *Rights and remedies of exclusive licensee*

### 101. Rights and remedies of exclusive licensee

(1) An exclusive licensee has, except against the copyright owner, the same rights and remedies in respect of matters occurring after the grant of the licence as if the licence had been an assignment.

(2) His rights and remedies are concurrent with those of the copyright owner; and references in the relevant provisions of this Part to the copyright owner shall be construed accordingly.

(3) In an action brought by an exclusive licensee by virtue of this section a defendant may avail himself of any defence which would have been available to him if the action had been brought by the copyright owner.

### 102. Exercise of concurrent rights

(1) Where an action for infringement of copyright brought by the copyright owner or an exclusive licensee relates (wholly or partly) to an infringement in respect of which they have concurrent rights of action, the copyright owner or, as the case may be, the exclusive licensee may not, without the leave of the court, proceed with the action unless the other is either joined as a plaintiff or added as a defendant.

(2) A copyright owner or exclusive licensee who is added as a defendant in pursuance of subsection (1) is not liable for any costs in the action unless he takes part in the proceedings.

(3) The above provisions do not affect the granting of interlocutory relief on an application by a copyright owner or exclusive licensee alone.

(4) Where an action for infringement of copyright is brought which relates (wholly or partly) to an infringement in respect of which the copyright owner and an exclusive licensee have or had concurrent rights of action—

    (a)  the court shall in assessing damages take into account—

        (i)  the terms of the licence, and

        (ii)  any pecuniary remedy already awarded or available to either of them in respect of the infringement;

    (b)  no account of profits shall be directed if an award of damages has been made, or an account of profits has been directed, in favour of the other of them in respect of the infringement; and

    (c)  the court shall if an account of profits is directed apportion the profits between them as the court considers just, subject to any agreement between them;

and these provisions apply whether or not the copyright owner and the exclusive licensee are both parties to the action.

    (5)  The copyright owner shall notify any exclusive licensee having concurrent rights before applying for an order under section 99 (order for delivery up) or exercising the right conferred by section 100 (right of seizure); and the court may on the application of the licensee make such order under section 99 or, as the case may be, prohibiting or permitting the exercise by the copyright owner of the right conferred by section 100, as it thinks fit having regard to the terms of the licence.

*Remedies for infringement of moral rights*

### 103. Remedies for infringement of moral rights
(1)  An infringement of a right conferred by Chapter IV (moral rights) is actionable as a breach of statutory duty owed to the person entitled to the right.

    (2)  In proceedings for infringement of the right conferred by section 80 (right to object to derogatory treatment of work) the court may, if it thinks it is an adequate remedy in the circumstances, grant an injunction on terms prohibiting the doing of any act unless a disclaimer is made, in such terms and in such manner as may be approved by the court, dissociating the author or director from the treatment of the work.

*Presumptions*

### 104. Presumptions relevant to literary, dramatic, musical and artistic works
(1)  The following presumptions apply in proceedings brought by virtue of this Chapter with respect to a literary, dramatic, musical or artistic work.

    (2)  Where a name purporting to be that of the author appeared on copies of the work as published or on the work when it was made, the person whose name appeared shall be presumed, until the contrary is proved—

    (a)  to be the author of the work;

    (b)  to have made it in circumstances not falling within sections 11(2), 163, 165 or 168 (works produced in course of employment, Crown copyright, Parliamentary copyright or copyright of certain international organisations).

    (3)  In the case of a work alleged to be a work of joint authorship, subsection (2) applies in relation to each person alleged to be one of the authors.

    (4)  Where no name purporting to be that of the author appeared as mentioned in subsection (2) but—

(a) the work qualifies for copyright protection by virtue of section 155 (qualification by reference to country of first publication), and

(b) a name purporting to be that of the publisher appeared on copies of the work as first published,

the person whose name appeared shall be presumed, until the contrary is proved, to have been the owner of the copyright at the time of publication.

(5) If the author of the work is dead or the identity of the author cannot be ascertained by reasonable inquiry, it shall be presumed, in the absence of evidence to the contrary—

(a) that the work is an original work, and

(b) that the plaintiff's allegations as to what was the first publication of the work and as to the country of first publication are correct.

## 105. Presumptions relevant to sound recordings and films

(1) In proceedings brought by virtue of this Chapter with respect to a sound recording, where copies of the recording as issued to the public bear a label or other mark stating—

(a) that a named person was the owner of copyright in the recording at the date of issue of the copies, or

(b) that the recording was first published in a specified year or in a specified country,

the label or mark shall be admissible as evidence of the facts stated and shall be presumed to be correct until the contrary is proved.

(2) In proceedings brought by virtue of this Chapter with respect to a film, where copies of the film as issued to the public bear a statement—

(a) that a named person was the author or director of the film,

(b) that a named person was the owner of copyright in the film at the date of issue of the copies, or

(c) that the film was first published in a specified year or in a specified country,

the statement shall be admissible as evidence of the facts stated and shall be presumed to be correct until the contrary is proved.

(3) In proceedings brought by virtue of this Chapter with respect to a computer program, where copies of the program are issued to the public in electronic form bearing a statement—

(a) that a named person was the owner of copyright in the program at the date of issue of the copies, or

(b) that the program was first published in a specified country or that copies of it were first issued to the public in electronic form in a specified year,

the statement shall be admissible as evidence of the facts stated and shall be presumed to be correct until the contrary is proved.

(4) The above presumptions apply equally in proceedings relating to an infringement alleged to have occurred before the date on which the copies were issued to the public.

(5) In proceedings brought by virtue of this Chapter with respect to a film, where the film as shown in public, broadcast or included in a cable programme service bears a statement—

(a) that a named person was the author or director of the film, or

(b) that a named person was the owner of copyright in the film immediately after it was made,

the statement shall be admissible as evidence of the facts stated and shall be presumed to be correct until the contrary is proved.

This presumption applies equally in proceedings relating to an infringement alleged to have occurred before the date on which the film was shown in public, broadcast or included in a cable programme service.

### 106. Presumptions relevant to works subject to Crown copyright

In proceedings brought by virtue of this Chapter with respect to a literary, dramatic or musical work in which Crown copyright subsists, where there appears on printed copies of the work a statement of the year in which the work was first published commercially, that statement shall be admissible as evidence of the fact stated and shall be presumed to be correct in the absence of evidence to the contrary.

## *Offences*

### 107. Criminal liability for making or dealing with infringing articles, etc

(1) A person commits an offence who, without the licence of the copyright owner—

(a) makes for sale or hire, or

(b) imports into the United Kingdom otherwise than for his private and domestic use, or

(c) possesses in the course of a business with a view to committing any act infringing the copyright, or

(d) in the course of a business—

    (i) sells or lets for hire, or

    (ii) offers or exposes for sale or hire, or

    (iii) exhibits in public, or

    (iv) distributes, or

(e) distributes otherwise than in the course of a business to such an extent as to affect prejudicially the owner of the copyright,

an article which is, and which he knows or has reason to believe is, an infringing copy of a copyright work.

(2) A person commits an offence who—

(a) makes an article specifically designed or adapted for making copies of a particular copyright work, or

(b) has such an article in his possession,

knowing or having reason to believe that it is to be used to make infringing copies for sale or hire or for use in the course of a business.

(3) Where copyright is infringed (otherwise than by reception of a broadcast or cable programme)—

(a) by the public performance of a literary, dramatic or musical work, or

(b) by the playing or showing in public of a sound recording or film, any person who caused the work to be so performed, played or shown is guilty of an offence if he knew or had reason to believe that copyright would be infringed.

(4) A person guilty of an offence under subsection (1)(a), (b), (d)(iv) or (e) is liable—

(a) on summary conviction to imprisonment for a term not exceeding six months or a fine not exceeding the statutory maximum, or both;

(b) on conviction on indictment to a fine or imprisonment for a term not exceeding two years, or both.

(5) A person guilty of any other offence under this section is liable on summary conviction to imprisonment for a term not exceeding six months or a fine not exceeding level 5 on the standard scale, or both.

(6) Sections 104 to 106 (presumptions as to various matters connected with copyright) do not apply to proceedings for an offence under this section; but without prejudice to their application in proceedings for an order under section 108 below.

**"Enforcement by local weights and measures authority**
**107A—(1) It is the duty of every local weights and measures authority to enforce within their area the provisions of section 107.**

**(2) The following provisions of the Trade Descriptions Act 1968 apply in relation to the enforcement of that section by such an authority as in relation to the enforcement of that Act—**

**section 27 (power to make test purchases),**
**section 28 (power to enter premises and inspect and seize goods and documents),**
**section 29 (obstruction of authorised officers), and**
**section 33 (compensation for loss, &c. of goods seized).**

**(3) Subsection (1) above does not apply in relation to the enforcement of section 107 in Northern Ireland, but it is the duty of the Department of Economic Development to enforce that section in Northern Ireland.**

**For that purpose the provisions of the Trade Descriptions Act 1968 specified in subsection (2) apply as if for the references to a local weights and measures authority and any officer of such an authority there were substituted references to that Department and any of its officers.**

**(4) Any enactment which authorises the disclosure of information for the purpose of facilitating the enforcement of the Trade Descriptions Act 1968 shall apply as if section 107 were contained in that Act and as if the functions of any person in relation to the enforcement of that section were functions under that Act.**

**(5) Nothing in this section shall be construed as authorising a local weights and measures authority to bring proceedings in Scotland for an offence.".**

*General note*
This section added by the Criminal Justice and Public Order Act 1994, s 165(1), (2), as from a day to be appointed.

**108. Order for delivery up in criminal proceedings**
(1) The court before which proceedings are brought against a person for an offence under section 107 may, if satisfied that at the time of his arrest or charge—

(a) he had in his possession, custody or control in the course of a business an infringing copy of a copyright work, or

(b) he had in his possession, custody or control an article specifically designed or adapted for making copies of a particular copyright work, knowing or having reason to believe that it had been or was to be used to make infringing copies,

order that the infringing copy or article be delivered up to the copyright owner or to such other person as the court may direct.

(2) For this purpose a person shall be treated as charged with an offence—

(a) in England, Wales and Northern Ireland, when he is orally charged or is served with a summons or indictment;

(b) in Scotland, when he is cautioned, charged or served with a complaint or indictment.

(3) An order may be made by the court of its own motion or on the application of the prosecutor (or, in Scotland, the Lord Advocate or procurator-fiscal), and may be made whether or not the person is convicted of the offence, but shall not be made—

(a) after the end of the period specified in section 113 (period after which remedy of delivery up not available), or

(b) if it appears to the court unlikely that any order will be made under section 114 (order as to disposal of infringing copy or other article);

(4) An appeal lies from an order made under this section by a magistrates' court—

(a) in England and Wales, to the Crown Court, and

(b) in Northern Ireland, to the county court;

and in Scotland, where an order has been made under this section, the person from whose possession, custody or control the infringing copy or article has been removed may, without prejudice to any other form of appeal under any rule of law, appeal against that order in the same manner as against sentence.

(5) A person to whom an infringing copy or other article is delivered up in pursuance of an order under this section shall retain it pending the making of an order, or the decision not to make an order, under section 114.

(6) Nothing in this section affects the powers of the court under section 43 of the Powers of Criminal Courts Act 1973, sections 223 or 436 of the Criminal Procedure (Scotland) Act 1975 or Article 7 of the Criminal Justice (Northern Ireland) Order 1980 (general provisions as to forfeiture in criminal proceedings).

## 109. Search warrants

(1) Where a justice of the peace (in Scotland, a sheriff or justice of the peace) is satisfied by information on oath given by a constable (in Scotland, by evidence on oath) that there are reasonable grounds for believing—

(a) that an offence under section 107(1)(a), (b), (d)(iv) or (e) has been or is about to be committed in any premises, and

(b) that evidence that such an offence has been or is about to be committed is in those premises,

he may issue a warrant authorising a constable to enter and search the premises, using such reasonable force as is necessary.

(2) The power conferred by subsection (1) does not, in England and Wales, extend to authorising a search for material of the kinds mentioned in section 9(2) of the Police and Criminal Evidence Act 1984 (certain classes of personal or confidential material).

(3) A warrant under this section—

(a) may authorise persons to accompany any constable executing the warrant, and

(b) remains in force for 28 days from the date of its issue.

(4) In executing a warrant issued under this section a constable may seize an article if he reasonably believes that it is evidence that any offence under section 107(1) has been or is about to be committed.

(5) In this section 'premises' includes land, buildings, moveable structures, vehicles, vessels, aircraft and hovercraft.

## 110. Offence by body corporate: liability of officers

(1) Where an offence under section 107 committed by a body corporate is proved to have been committed with the consent or connivance of a director, manager, secretary or other similar officer of the body, or a person purporting to act in any such capacity, he as well as the body corporate is guilty of the offence and liable to be proceeded against and punished accordingly.

(2) In relation to a body corporate whose affairs are managed by its members 'director' means a member of the body corporate.

## *Provision for preventing importation of infringing copies*

## 111. Infringing copies may be treated as prohibited goods

(1) The owner of the copyright in a published literary, dramatic or musical work may give notice in writing to the Commissioners of Customs and Excise—

(a) that he is the owner of the copyright in the work, and

(b) that he requests the Commissioners, for a period specified in the notice, to treat as prohibited goods printed copies of the work which are infringing copies.

(2) The period specified in a notice under subsection (1) shall not exceed five years and shall not extend beyond the period for which copyright is to subsist.

(3) The owner of the copyright in a sound recording or film may give notice in writing to the Commissioners of Customs and Excise—

(a) that he is the owner of the copyright in the work,

(b) that infringing copies of the work are expected to arrive in the United Kingdom at a time and a place specified in the notice, and

(c) that he requests the Commissioners to treat the copies as prohibited goods.

(4) When a notice is in force under this section the importation of goods to which the notice relates, otherwise than by a person for his private and domestic use, is prohibited; but a person is not by reason of the prohibition liable to any penalty other than forfeiture of the goods.

## 112. Power of Commissioners of Customs and Excise to make regulations

(1) The Commissioners of Customs and Excise may make regulations prescribing

the form in which notice is to be given under section 111 and requiring a person giving notice—

(a) to furnish the Commissioners with such evidence as may be specified in the regulations, either on giving notice or when the goods are imported, or at both those times, and

(b) to comply with such other conditions as may be specified in the regulations.

(2) The regulations may, in particular, require a person giving such a notice—

(a) to pay such fees in respect of the notice as may be specified by the regulations;

(b) to give such security as may be so specified in respect of any liability or expense which the Commissioners may incur in consequence of the notice by reason of the detention of any article or anything done to an article detained;

(c) to indemnify the Commissioners against any such liability or expense, whether security has been given or not.

(3) The regulations may make different provision as respects different classes of case to which they apply and may include such incidental and supplementary provisions as the Commissioners consider expedient.

(4) Regulations under this section shall be made by statutory instrument which shall be subject to annulment in pursuance of a resolution of either House of Parliament.

(5) Section 17 of the Customs and Excise Management Act 1979 (general provisions as to Commissioners' receipts) applies to fees paid in pursuance of regulations under this section as to receipts under the enactments relating to customs and excise.

*Supplementary*

**113. Period after which remedy of delivery up not available**
(1) An application for an order under section 99 (order for delivery up in civil proceedings) may not be made after the end of the period of six years from the date on which the infringing copy or article in question was made, subject to the following provisions.

(2) If during the whole or any part of that period the copyright owner—

(a) is under a disability, or

(b) is prevented by fraud or concealment from discovering the facts entitling him to apply for an order,

an application may be made at any time before the end of the period of six years from the date on which he ceased to be under a disability or, as the case may be, could with reasonable diligence have discovered those facts.

(3) In subsection (2) 'disability'—

(a) in England and Wales, has the same meaning as in the Limitation Act 1980;

(b) in Scotland, means legal disability within the meaning of the Prescription and Limitation (Scotland) Act 1973;

(c) in Northern Ireland, has the same meaning as in the Statute of Limitations (Northern Ireland) 1958.

(4) An order under section 108 (order for delivery up in criminal proceedings) shall not, in any case, be made after the end of the period of six years from the date on which the infringing copy or article in question was made.

## 114. Order as to disposal of infringing copy or other article
(1) An application may be made to the court for an order that an infringing copy or other article delivered up in pursuance of an order under sections 99 or 108, or seized and detained in pursuance of the right conferred by section 100, shall be—

    (a) forfeited to the copyright owner, or

    (b) destroyed or otherwise dealt with as the court may think fit,

or for a decision that no such order should be made.

(2) In considering what order (if any) should be made, the court shall consider whether other remedies available in an action for infringement of copyright would be adequate to compensate the copyright owner and to protect his interests.

(3) Provision shall be made by rules of court as to the service of notice on persons having an interest in the copy or other articles, and any such person is entitled—

    (a) to appear in proceedings for an order under this section, whether or not he was served with notice, and

    (b) to appeal against any order made, whether or not he appeared;

and an order shall not take effect until the end of the period within which notice of an appeal may be given or, if before the end of that period notice of appeal is duly given, until the final determination or abandonment of the proceedings on the appeal.

(4) Where there is more than one person interested in a copy or other article, the court shall make such order as it thinks just and may (in particular) direct that the article be sold, or otherwise dealt with, and the proceeds divided.

(5) If the court decides that no order should be made under this section, the person in whose possession, custody or control the copy or other article was before being delivered up or seized is entitled to its return.

(6) References in this section to a person having an interest in a copy or other article include any person in whose favour an order could be made in respect of it under this section or under sections 204 or 231 of this Act or *section 58C of the Trade Marks Act 1938* **section 19 of the Trade Marks Act 1994** (which make similar provision in relation to infringement of rights in performances, design right and trade marks).

*General note*
Sub-s (6): words in italics repealed and words in bold type substituted by the Trade Marks Act 1994, s 106(1), Sch 4, para 8(2).

## 115. Jurisdiction of county court and sheriff court
(1) In England, Wales and Northern Ireland a county court may entertain proceedings under—

    section 99 (order for delivery up of infringing copy or other article),

    section 101(5) (order as to exercise of rights by copyright owner where exclusive licensee has concurrent rights), or

    section 114 (order as to disposal of infringing copy or other article),

**save that, in Northern Ireland, a county court may entertain such proceedings only** where the value of the infringing copies and other articles in question does not exceed the county court limit for actions in tort.

(2) In Scotland proceedings for an order under any of those provisions may be brought in the sheriff court.

(3) Nothing in this section shall be construed as affecting the jurisdiction of the High Court or, in Scotland, the Court of Session.

*General note*
Sub-s (1): words in bold type added by the High Court and County Courts Jurisdiction Order 1991, SI 1991 No 724. The reference in sub-s (1) to "section 101(5)" should read "section 102(5)"; this is a mistake on the Queen's printers copy of the Act.

CHAPTER VII
COPYRIGHT LICENSING

*Licensing schemes and licensing bodies*

**116. Licensing schemes and licensing bodies**
(1) In this Part a 'licensing scheme' means a scheme setting out—

(a) the classes of case in which the operator of the scheme, or the person on whose behalf he acts, is willing to grant copyright licences, and

(b) the terms on which licences would be granted in those classes of case;

and for this purpose a 'scheme' includes anything in the nature of a scheme, whether described as a scheme or as a tariff or by any other name.

(2) In this Chapter a 'licensing body' means a society or other organisation which has as its main object, or one of its main objects, the negotiation or granting, either as owner or prospective owner of copyright or as agent for him, of copyright licences, and whose objects include the granting of licences covering works of more than one author.

(3) In this section 'copyright licences' means licences to do, or authorise the doing of, any of the acts restricted by copyright.

(4) References in this Chapter to licences or licensing schemes covering works of more than one author do not include licences or schemes covering only—

(a) a single collective work or collective works of which the authors are the same, or

(b) works made by, or by employees of or commissioned by, a single individual, firm, company or group of companies.

For this purpose a group of companies means a holding company and its subsidiaries, within the meaning of section 736 of the Companies Act 1985.

*References and applications with respect to licensing schemes*

**117. Licensing schemes to which ss 118 to 123 apply**
Sections 118 to 123 (references and applications with respect to licensing schemes) apply to—

(a) licensing schemes operated by licensing bodies in relation to the copyright in literary, dramatic, musical or artistic works or films (or film sound-tracks when accompanying a film) which cover works of more than one author, so far as they relate to licences for—

    (i)  copying the work,

    (ii)  performing, playing or showing the work in public, or

    (iii)  broadcasting the work or including it in a cable programme service;

  (b)  all licensing schemes in relation to the copyright in sound recordings (other than film sound-tracks when accompanying a film), broadcasts or cable programmes, or the typographical arrangement of published editions; and

  (c)  all licensing schemes in relation to the copyright in sound recordings, films or computer programs so far as they relate to licences for the rental of copies to the public;

and in those sections 'licensing scheme' means a licensing scheme of any of those descriptions.

### 118. Reference of proposed licensing scheme to tribunal

(1) The terms of a licensing scheme proposed to be operated by a licensing body may be referred to the Copyright Tribunal by an organisation claiming to be representative of persons claiming that they require licences in cases of a description to which the scheme would apply, either generally or in relation to any description of case.

(2) The Tribunal shall first decide whether to entertain the reference, and may decline to do so on the ground that the reference is premature.

(3) If the Tribunal decides to entertain the reference it shall consider the matter referred and make such order, either confirming or varying the proposed scheme, either generally or so far as it relates to cases of the description to which the reference relates, as the Tribunal may determine to be reasonable in the circumstances.

(4) The order may be made so as to be in force indefinitely or for such period as the Tribunal may determine.

### 119. Reference of licensing scheme to tribunal

(1) If while a licensing scheme is in operation a dispute arises between the operator of the scheme and—

  (a)  a person claiming that he requires a licence in a case of a description to which the scheme applies, or

  (b)  an organisation claiming to be representative of such persons,

that person or organisation may refer the scheme to the Copyright Tribunal in so far as it relates to cases of that description.

(2) A scheme which has been referred to the Tribunal under this section shall remain in operation until proceedings on the reference are concluded.

(3) The Tribunal shall consider the matter in dispute and make such order, either confirming or varying the scheme so far as it relates to cases of the description to which the reference relates, as the Tribunal may determine to be reasonable in the circumstances.

(4) The order may be made so as to be in force indefinitely or for such period as the Tribunal may determine.

**120. Further reference of scheme to tribunal**

(1) Where the Copyright Tribunal has on a previous reference of a licensing scheme under sections 118 or 119, or under this section, made an order with respect to the scheme, then, while the order remains in force—

(a) the operator of the scheme,

(b) a person claiming that he requires a licence in a case of the description to which the order applies, or

(c) an organisation claiming to be representative of such persons

may refer the scheme again to the Tribunal so far as it relates to cases of that description.

(2) A licensing scheme shall not, except with the special leave of the Tribunal, be referred again to the Tribunal in respect of the same description of cases—

(a) within twelve months from the date of the order on the previous reference, or

(b) if the order was made so as to be in force for 15 months or less, until the last three months before the expiry of the order.

(3) A scheme which has been referred to the Tribunal under this section shall remain in operation until proceedings on the reference are concluded.

(4) The Tribunal shall consider the matter in dispute and make such order, either confirming, varying or further varying the scheme so far as it relates to cases of the description to which the reference relates, as the Tribunal may determine to be reasonable in the circumstances.

(5) The order may be made so as to be in force indefinitely or for such period as the Tribunal may determine.

**121. Application for grant of licence in connection with licensing scheme**

(1) A person who claims, in a case covered by a licensing scheme, that the operator of the scheme has refused to grant him or procure the grant to him of a licence in accordance with the scheme, or has failed to do so within a reasonable time after being asked, may apply to the Copyright Tribunal.

(2) A person who claims, in a case excluded from a licensing scheme, that the operator of the scheme either—

(a) has refused to grant him a licence or procure the grant to him of a licence, or has failed to do so within a reasonable time of being asked, and that in the circumstances it is unreasonable that a licence should not be granted, or

(b) proposes terms for a licence which are unreasonable,

may apply to the Copyright Tribunal.

(3) A case shall be regarded as excluded from a licensing scheme for the purposes of subsection (2) if—

(a) the scheme provides for the grant of licences subject to terms excepting matters from the licence and the case falls within such an exception, or

(b) the case is so similar to those in which licences are granted under the scheme that it is unreasonable that it should not be dealt with in the same way.

(4) If the Tribunal is satisfied that the claim is well-founded, it shall make an order declaring that, in respect of the matters specified in the order, the applicant

is entitled to a licence on such terms as the Tribunal may determine to be applicable in accordance with the scheme or, as the case may be, to be reasonable in the circumstances.

(5) The order may be made so as to be in force indefinitely or for such period as the Tribunal may determine.

**122. Application for review of order as to entitlement to licence**
(1) Where the Copyright Tribunal has made an order under section 121 that a person is entitled to a licence under a licensing scheme, the operator of the scheme, or the original applicant may apply to the Tribunal to review its order.

(2) An application shall not be made, except with the special leave of the Tribunal—

(a) within twelve months from the date of the order, or of the decision on a previous application under this section, or

(b) if the order was made so as to be in force for 15 months or less, or as a result of the decision on a previous application under this section is due to expire within 15 months of that decision, until the last three months before the expiry date.

(3) The Tribunal shall on an application for review confirm or vary its order as the Tribunal may determine to be reasonable having regard to the terms applicable in accordance with the licensing scheme or, as the case may be, the circumstances of the case.

**123. Effect of order of tribunal as to licensing scheme**
(1) A licensing scheme which has been confirmed or varied by the Copyright Tribunal—

(a) under section 118 (reference of terms of proposed scheme), or

(b) under sections 119 or 120 (reference of existing scheme to Tribunal),

shall be in force or, as the case may be, remain in operation, so far as it relates to the description of case in respect of which the order was made, so long as the order remains in force.

(2) While the order is in force a person who in a case of a class to which the order applies—

(a) pays to the operator of the scheme any charges payable under the scheme in respect of a licence covering the case in question or, if the amount cannot be ascertained, gives an undertaking to the operator to pay them when ascertained, and

(b) complies with the other terms applicable to such a licence under the scheme,

shall be in the same position as regards infringement of copyright as if he had at all material times been the holder of a licence granted by the owner of the copyright in question in accordance with the scheme.

(3) The Tribunal may direct that the order, so far as it varies the amount of charges payable, has effect from a date before that on which it is made, but not earlier than the date on which the reference was made or, if later, on which the scheme came into operation.

If such a direction is made—

(a) any necessary repayments or further payments shall be made in respect of charges already paid, and

(b) the reference in subsection (2)(a) to the charges payable under the scheme shall be construed as a reference to the charges so payable by virtue of the order.

No such direction may be made where subsection (4) below applies.

(4) An order of the Tribunal under sections 119 or 120 made with respect to a scheme which is certified for any purpose under section 143 has effect, so far as it varies the scheme by reducing the charges payable for licences, from the date on which the reference was made to the Tribunal.

(5) Where the Tribunal has made an order under section 121 (order as to entitlement to licence under licensing scheme) and the order remains in force, the person in whose favour the order is made shall if he—

(a) pays to the operator of the scheme any charges payable in accordance with the order or, if the amount cannot be ascertained, gives an undertaking to pay the charges when ascertained, and

(b) complies with the other terms specified in the order,

be in the same position as regards infringement of copyright as if he had at all material times been the holder of a licence granted by the owner of the copyright in question on the terms specified in the order.

*References and applications with respect to licensing by licensing bodies*

**124. Licences to which ss 125 to 128 apply**
Sections 125 to 128 (references and applications with respect to licensing by licensing bodies) apply to the following descriptions of licence granted by a licensing body otherwise than in pursuance of a licensing scheme—

(a) licences relating to the copyright in literary, dramatic, musical or artistic works or films (or film sound-tracks when accompanying a film) which cover works of more than one author, so far as they authorise—

    (i) copying the work,
    (ii) performing, playing or showing the work in public, or
    (iii) broadcasting the work or including it in a cable programme service;

(b) any licence relating to the copyright in a sound recording (other than a film sound-track when accompanying a film), broadcast or cable programme, or the typographical arrangement of a published edition; and

(c) all licences in relation to the copyright in sound recordings, films or computer programs so far as they relate to the rental of copies to the public;

and in those sections a 'licence' means a licence of any of those descriptions.

**125. Reference to tribunal of proposed licence**
(1) The terms on which a licensing body proposes to grant a licence may be referred to the Copyright Tribunal by the prospective licensee.

(2) The Tribunal shall first decide whether to entertain the reference, and may decline to do so on the ground that the reference is premature.

(3) If the Tribunal decides to entertain the reference it shall consider the terms

of the proposed licence and make such order, either confirming or varying the terms, as it may determine to be reasonable in the circumstances.

(4)  The order may be made so as to be in force indefinitely or for such period as the Tribunal may determine.

### 126.  Reference to tribunal of expiring licence

(1)  A licensee under a licence which is due to expire, by effluxion of time or as a result of notice given by the licensing body, may apply to the Copyright Tribunal on the ground that it is unreasonable in the circumstances that the licence should cease to be in force.

(2)  Such an application may not be made until the last three months before the licence is due to expire.

(3)  A licence in respect of which a reference has been made to the Tribunal shall remain in operation until proceedings on the reference are concluded.

(4)  If the Tribunal finds the application well-founded, it shall make an order declaring that the licensee shall continue to be entitled to the benefit of the licence on such terms as the Tribunal may determine to be reasonable in the circumstances.

(5)  An order of the Tribunal under this section may be made so as to be in force indefinitely or for such period as the Tribunal may determine.

### 127.  Application for review of order as to licence

(1)  Where the Copyright Tribunal has made an order under sections 125 or 126, the licensing body or the person entitled to the benefit of the order may apply to the Tribunal to review its order.

(2)  An application shall not be made, except with the special leave of the Tribunal—

  (a)  within twelve months from the date of the order or of the decision on a previous application under this section, or
  (b)  if the order was made so as to be in force for 15 months or less, or as a result of the decision on a previous application under this section is due to expire within 15 months of that decision, until the last three months before the expiry date.

(3)  The Tribunal shall on an application for review confirm or vary its order as the Tribunal may determine to be reasonable in the circumstances.

### 128.  Effect of order of Tribunal as to licence

(1)  Where the Copyright Tribunal has made an order under sections 125 or 126 and the order remains in force, the person entitled to the benefit of the order shall if he—

  (a)  pays to the licensing body any charges payable in accordance with the order or, if the amount cannot be ascertained, gives an undertaking to pay the charges when ascertained, and
  (b)  complies with the other terms specified in the order,

be in the same position as regards infringement of copyright as if he had at all material times been the holder of a licence granted by the owner of the copyright in question on the terms specified in the order.

(2)  The benefit of the order may be assigned—

  (a)  in the case of an order under section 125, if assignment is not prohibited under the terms of the Tribunal's order; and

(b) in the case of an order under section 126, if assignment was not prohibited under the terms of the original licence.

(3) The Tribunal may direct that an order under sections 125 or 126, or an order under section 127 varying such an order, so far as it varies the amount of charges payable, has effect from a date before that on which it is made, but not earlier than the date on which the reference or application was made or, if later, on which the licence was granted or, as the case may be, was due to expire.

If such a direction is made—

(a) any necessary repayments or further payments shall be made in respect of charges already paid, and
(b) the reference in subsection (1)(a) to the charges payable in accordance with the order shall be construed, where the order is varied by a later order, as a reference to the charges so payable by virtue of the later order.

*Factors to be taken into account in certain classes of case*

## 129. General considerations: unreasonable discrimination
In determining what is reasonable on a reference or application under this Chapter relating to a licensing scheme or licence, the Copyright Tribunal shall have regard to—

(a) the availability of other schemes, or the granting of other licences, to other persons in similar circumstances, and
(b) the terms of those schemes or licences,

and shall exercise its powers so as to secure that there is no unreasonable discrimination between licensees, or prospective licensees, under the scheme or licence to which the reference or application relates and licensees under other schemes operated by, or other licences granted by, the same person.

## 130. Licences for reprographic copying
Where a reference or application is made to the Copyright Tribunal under this Chapter relating to the licensing of reprographic copying of published literary, dramatic, musical or artistic works, or the typographical arrangement of published editions, the Tribunal shall have regard to—

(a) the extent to which published editions of the works in question are otherwise available,
(b) the proportion of the work to be copied, and
(c) the nature of the use to which the copies are likely to be put.

## 131. Licences for educational establishments in respect of works included in broadcasts or cable programmes
(1) This section applies to references or applications under this Chapter relating to licences for the recording by or on behalf of educational establishments of broadcasts or cable programmes which include copyright works, or the making of copies of such recordings, for educational purposes.

(2) The Copyright Tribunal shall, in considering what charges (if any) should be paid for a licence, have regard to the extent to which the owners of copyright

in the works included in the broadcast or cable programme have already received, or are entitled to receive, payment in respect of their inclusion.

### 132. Licences to reflect conditions imposed by promoters of events
(1) This section applies to references or applications under this Chapter in respect of licences relating to sound recordings, films, broadcasts or cable programmes which include, or are to include, any entertainment or other event.

(2) The Copyright Tribunal shall have regard to any conditions imposed by the promoters of the entertainment or other event; and, in particular, the Tribunal shall not hold a refusal or failure to grant a licence to be unreasonable if it could not have been granted consistently with those conditions.

(3) Nothing in this section shall require the Tribunal to have regard to any such conditions in so far as they—

    (a) purport to regulate the charges to be imposed in respect of the grant of licences, or

    (b) relate to payments to be made to the promoters of any event in consideration of the grant of facilities for making the recording, film, broadcast or cable programme.

### 133. Licences to reflect payments in respect of underlying rights
(1) In considering what charges should be paid for a licence—

    (a) on a reference or application under this Chapter relating to licences for the rental to the public of copies of sound recordings, films or computer programs, or

    (b) on an application under section 142 (settlement of royalty or other sum payable for deemed licence),

the Copyright Tribunal shall take into account any reasonable payments which the owner of the copyright in the sound recording, film or computer program is liable to make in consequence of the the the granting of the licence, or of the acts authorised by the licence, to owners of copyright in works included in that work.

(2) On any reference or application under this Chapter relating to licensing in respect of the copyright in sound recordings, films, broadcasts or cable programmes, the Copyright Tribunal shall take into account, in considering what charges should be paid for a licence, any reasonable payments which the copyright owner is liable to make in consequence of the granting of the licence, or of the acts authorised by the licence, in respect of any performance included in the recording, film, broadcast or cable programme.

### 134. Licences in respect of works included in re-transmissions
(1) This section applies to references or applications under this Chapter relating to licences to include in a broadcast or cable programme service—

    (a) literary, dramatic, musical or artistic works, or,

    (b) sound recordings or films,

where one broadcast or cable programme ('the first transmission') is, by reception and immediate re-transmission, to be further broadcast or included in a cable programme service ('the further transmission').

(2) So far as the further transmission is to the same area as the first transmission, the Copyright Tribunal shall, in considering what charges (if any) should be paid for licences for either transmission, have regard to the extent to which the

copyright owner has already received, or is entitled to receive, payment for the other transmission which adequately remunerates him in respect of transmissions to that area.

(3) So far as the further transmission is to an area outside that to which the first transmission was made, the Tribunal shall (except where subsection (4) applies) leave the further transmission out of account in considering what charges (if any) should be paid for licences for the first transmission.

(4) *If the Tribunal is satisfied that requirements imposed under section 13(1) of the Cable and Broadcasting Act 1984 (duty of Cable Authority to secure inclusion of certain broadcasts in cable programme services) will result in the further transmission being to areas part of which fall outside the area to which the first transmission is made, the Tribunal shall exercise its powers so as to secure that the charges payable for licences for the first transmission adequately reflect that fact.*

*General note*
Sub-s (4): repealed by the Broadcasting Act 1990, s 203(3), Sch 21.

## 135. Mention of specific matters not to exclude other relevant considerations

The mention in sections 129 to 134 of specific matters to which the Copyright Tribunal is to have regard in certain classes of case does not affect the Tribunal's general obligation in any case to have regard to all relevant considerations.

*Use as of right of sound recordings in broadcasts and cable programme services*

## 135A. Circumstances in which right available
(1) Section 135C applies to the inclusion in a broadcast or cable programme service of any sound recordings if—

(a) a licence to include those recordings in the broadcast or cable programme service could be granted by a licensing body or such a body could procure the grant of a licence to do so,

(b) the condition in subsection (2) or (3) applies, and

(c) the person including those recordings in the broadcast or cable programme service has complied with section 135B.

(2) Where the person including the recordings in the broadcast or cable programme service does not hold a licence to do so, the condition is that the licensing body refuses to grant, or procure the grant of, such a licence, being a licence—

(a) whose terms as to payment for including the recordings in the broadcast or cable programme service would be acceptable to him or comply with an order of the Copyright Tribunal under section 135D relating to such a licence or any scheme under which it would be granted, and

(b) allowing unlimited needletime or such needletime as he has demanded.

(3) Where he holds a licence to include the recordings in the broadcast or cable programme service, the condition is that the terms of the licence limit

needletime and the licensing body refuses to substitute or procure the substitution of terms allowing unlimited needletime or such needletime as he has demanded, or refuses to do so on terms that fall within subsection (2)(a).

(4) The references in subsection (2) to refusing to grant, or procure the grant of, a licence, and in subsection (3) to refusing to substitute or procure the substitution of terms, include failing to do so within a reasonable time of being asked.

(5) In the group of sections from this section to section 135G—

'needletime' means the time in any period (whether determined as a number of hours in the period or a proportion of the period, or otherwise) in which any proceedings may be included in a broadcast or cable programme service;
'sound recording' does not include a film sound-track when accompanying a film.

(6) In sections 135B to 135G, 'terms of payment' means terms as to payment for including sound recordings in a broadcast or cable programme service.

*General note*
Added by the Broadcasting Act 1990, s 175(1).

### 135B. Notice of intention to exercise right

(1) A person intending to avail himself of the right conferred by section 135C must—

(a) give notice to the licensing body of his intention to exercise the right, asking the body to propose terms of payment, and

(b) after receiving the proposal or the expiry of a reasonable period, give reasonable notice to the licensing body of the date on which he proposes to begin exercising that right, and the terms of payment in accordance with which he intends to do so.

(2) Where he has a licence to include the recordings in a broadcast or cable programme service, the date specified in a notice under subsection (1)(b) must not be sooner than the date of expiry of that licence except in a case falling within section 135A(3).

(3) Before the person intending to avail himself of the right begins to exercise it, he must—

(a) give reasonable notice to the Copyright Tribunal of his intention to exercise the right, and of the date on which he proposes to begin to do so, and

(b) apply to the Tribunal under section 135D to settle the terms of payment.

*General note*
Added by the Broadcasting Act 1990, s 175(1).

### 135C. Conditions for exercise of right

(1) A person who, on or after the date specified in a notice under section 135B(1)(b), includes in a broadcast or cable programme service any sound recordings in circumstances in which this section applies, and who—

(a) complies with any reasonable condition, notice of which has been given to him by the licensing body, as to inclusion in the broadcasting or cable programme service of those recordings,

(b) provides that body with such information about their inclusion in the broadcast or cable programme service as it may reasonably require, and

(c) makes the payments to the licensing body that are required by this section,

shall be in the same position as regards infringement of copyright as if he had at all material times been the holder of a licence granted by the owner of the copyright in question.

(2) Payments are to be made at not less than quarterly intervals in arrears.

(3) The amount of any payment is that determined in accordance with any order of the Copyright Tribunal under section 135D or, if no such order has been made—

(a) in accordance with any proposal for terms of payment made by the licensing body pursuant to a request under section 135B, or

(b) where no proposal has been so made or the amount determined in accordance with the proposal so made is unreasonably high, in accordance with the terms of payment notified to the licensing body under section 135B(1)(b).

(4) Where this section applies to the inclusion in a broadcast or cable programme service of any sound recordings, it does so in place of any licence.

*General note*
Added by the Broadcasting Act 1990, s 175(1).

## 135D. Applications to settle payments

(1) On an application to settle the terms of payment, the Copyright Tribunal shall consider the matter and make such order as it may determine to be reasonable in the circumstances.

(2) An order under subsection (1) has effect from the date the applicant begins to exercise the right conferred by section 135C and any necessary repayments, or further payments, shall be made in respect of amounts that have fallen due.

*General note*
Added by the Broadcasting Act 1990, s 175(1).

## 135E. References etc about conditions, information and other terms

(1) A person exercising the right conferred by section 135C, or who has given notice to the Copyright Tribunal of his intention to do so, may refer to the Tribunal—

(a) any question whether any condition as to the inclusion in a broadcast or cable programme service of sound recordings, notice of which has been given to him by the licensing body in question, is a reasonable condition, or

(b) any question whether any information is information which the licensing body can reasonably require him to provide.

(2) On a reference under this section, the Tribunal shall consider the matter and make such order as it may determine to be reasonable in the circumstances.

*General note*
Added by the Broadcasting Act 1990, s 175(1).

**135F. Application for review of order**
(1) A person exercising the right conferred by section 135C or the licensing body may apply to the Copyright Tribunal to review any order under section 135D or 135E.

(2) An application shall not be made, except with the special leave of the Tribunal—

    (a) within twelve months from the date of the order, or of the decision on a previous application under this section, or

    (b) if the order was made so as to be in force for fifteen months or less, or as a result of a decision on a previous application is due to expire within fifteen months of that decision, until the last three months before the expiry date.

(3) On the application the Tribunal shall consider the matter and make such order confirming or varying the original order as it may determine to be reasonable in the circumstances.

(4) An order under this section has effect from the date on which it is made or such later date as may be specified by the Tribunal.

*General note*
Added by the Broadcasting Act 1990, s 175(1).

**135G. Factors to be taken into account**
(1) In determining what is reasonable on an application or reference under section 135D or 135E, or on reviewing any order under section 135F, the Copyright Tribunal shall—

    (a) have regard to the terms of any orders which it has made in the case of persons in similar circumstances exercising the right conferred by section 135C, and

    (b) exercise its powers so as to secure that there is no unreasonable discrimination between persons exercising that right against the same licensing body.

(2) In settling the terms of payment under section 135D, the Tribunal shall not be guided by any order it has made under any enactment other than that section.

(3) Section 134 (factors to be taken into account: re-transmissions) applies on an application or reference under sections 135D to 135F as it applies on an application or reference relating to a licence.

*General note*
Added by the Broadcasting Act 1990, s 175(1).

*Implied indemnity in schemes or licences for reprographic copying*

**136. Implied indemnity in certain schemes and licences for reprographic copying**

(1) This section applies to—

    (a) schemes for licensing reprographic copying of published literary, dramatic, musical or artistic works, or the typographical arrangement of published editions, and

    (b) licences granted by licensing bodies for such copying,

where the scheme or licence does not specify the works to which it applies with such particularity as to enable licensees to determine whether a work falls within the scheme or licence by inspection of the scheme or licence and the work.

(2) There is implied—

    (a) in every scheme to which this section applies an undertaking by the operator of the scheme to indemnify a person granted a licence under the scheme, and

    (b) in every licence to which this section applies an undertaking by the licensing body to indemnify the licensee,

against any liability incurred by him by reason of his having infringed copyright by making or authorising the making of reprographic copies of a work in circumstances within the apparent scope of his licence.

(3) The circumstances of a case are within the apparent scope of a licence if—

    (a) it is not apparent from inspection of the licence and the work that it does not fall within the description of works to which the licence applies; and

    (b) the licence does not expressly provide that it does not extend to copyright of the description infringed.

(4) In this section 'liability' includes liability to pay costs; and this section applies in relation to costs reasonably incurred by a licensee in connection with actual or contemplated proceedings against him for infringement of copyright as it applies to sums which he is liable to pay in respect of such infringement.

(5) A scheme or licence to which this section applies may contain reasonable provision—

    (a) with respect to the manner in which, and time within which, claims under the undertaking implied by this section are to be made;

    (b) enabling the operator of the scheme or, as the case may be, the licensing body to take over the conduct of any proceedings affecting the amount of his liability to indemnify.

*Reprographic copying by educational establishments*

**137. Power to extend coverage of scheme or licence**

(1) This section applies to—

    (a) a licensing scheme to which sections 118 to 123 apply (see section 117) and which is operated by a licensing body, or

    (b) a licence to which sections 125 to 128 apply (see section 124),

so far as it provides for the grant of licences, or is a licence, authorising the making by or on behalf of educational establishments for the purposes of instruction of reprographic copies of published literary, dramatic, musical or artistic works, or of the typographical arrangement of published editions.

(2) If it appears to the Secretary of State with respect to a scheme or licence to which this section applies that—

    (a)  works of a description similar to those covered by the scheme or licence are unreasonably excluded from it, and

    (b)  making them subject to the scheme or licence would not conflict with the normal exploitation of the works or unreasonably prejudice the legitimate interests of the copyright owners,

he may by order provide that the scheme or licence shall extend to those works.

(3) Where he proposes to make such an order, the Secretary of State shall give notice of the proposal to—

    (a)  the copyright owners,

    (b)  the licensing body in question, and

    (c)  such persons or organisations representative of educational establishments, and such other persons or organisations, as the Secretary of State thinks fit.

(4) The notice shall inform those persons of their right to make written or oral representations to the Secretary of State about the proposal within six months from the date of the notice; and if any of them wishes to make oral representations, the Secretary of State shall appoint a person to hear the representations and report to him.

(5) In considering whether to make an order the Secretary of State shall take into account any representations made to him in accordance with subsection (4), and such other matters as appear to him to be relevant.

## 138. Variation or discharge of order extending scheme or licence

(1) The owner of the copyright in a work in respect of which an order is in force under section 137 may apply to the Secretary of State for the variation or discharge of the order, stating his reasons for making the application.

(2) The Secretary of State shall not entertain an application made within two years of the making of the original order, or of the making of an order on a previous application under this section, unless it appears to him that the circumstances are exceptional.

(3) On considering the reasons for the application the Secretary of State may confirm the order forthwith; if he does not do so, he shall give notice of the application to—

    (a)  the licensing body in question, and

    (b)  such persons or organisations representative of educational establishments, and such other persons or organisations, as he thinks fit.

(4) The notice shall inform those persons of their right to make written or oral representations to the Secretary of State about the application within the period of two months from the date of the notice; and if any of them wishes to make oral representations, the Secretary of State shall appoint a person to hear the representations and report to him.

(5) In considering the application the Secretary of State shall take into account the reasons for the application, any representations made to him in accordance with subsection (4), and such other matters as appear to him to be relevant.

(6) The Secretary of State may make such order as he thinks fit confirming or discharging the order (or, as the case may be, the order as previously varied), or varying (or further varying) it so as to exclude works from it.

### 139. Appeals against orders

(1) The owner of the copyright in a work which is the subject of an order under section 137 (order extending coverage of scheme or licence) may appeal to the Copyright Tribunal which may confirm or discharge the order, or vary it so as to exclude works from it, as it thinks fit having regard to the considerations mentioned in subsection (2) of that section.

(2) Where the Secretary of State has made an order under section 138 (order confirming, varying or discharging order extending coverage of scheme or licence)—

    (a)  the person who applied for the order, or

    (b)  any person or organisation representative of educational establishments who was given notice of the application for the order and made representations in accordance with subsection (4) of that section,

may appeal to the Tribunal which may confirm or discharge the order or make any other order which the Secretary of State might have made.

(3) An appeal under this section shall be brought within six weeks of the making of the order or such further period as the Tribunal may allow.

(4) An order under sections 137 or 138 shall not come into effect until the end of the period of six weeks from the making of the order or, if an appeal is brought before the end of that period, until the appeal proceedings are disposed of or withdrawn.

(5) If an appeal is brought after the end of that period, any decision of the Tribunal on the appeal does not affect the validity of anything done in reliance on the order appealed against before that decision takes effect.

### 140. Inquiry whether new scheme or general licence required

(1) The Secretary of State may appoint a person to inquire into the question whether new provision is required (whether by way of a licensing scheme or general licence) to authorise the making by or on behalf of educational establishments for the purposes of instruction of reprographic copies of—

    (a)  published literary, dramatic, musical or artistic works, or

    (b)  the typographical arrangement of published editions,

of a description which appears to the Secretary of State not to be covered by an existing licensing scheme or general licence and not to fall within the power conferred by section 137 (power to extend existing schemes and licences to similar works).

(2) The procedure to be followed in relation to an inquiry shall be such as may be prescribed by regulations made by the Secretary of State.

(3) The regulations shall, in particular, provide for notice to be given to—

    (a)  persons or organisations appearing to the Secretary of State to represent the owners of copyright in works of that description, and

    (b)  persons or organisations appearing to the Secretary of State to represent educational establishments,

and for the making of written or oral representations by such persons; but without prejudice to the giving of notice to, and the making of representations by, other persons and organisations.

(4) The person appointed to hold the inquiry shall not recommend the making of new provision unless he is satisfied—

    (a) that it would be of advantage to educational establishments to be authorised to make reprographic copies of the works in question, and

    (b) that making those works subject to a licensing scheme or general licence would not conflict with the normal exploitation of the works or unreasonably prejudice the legitimate interests of the copyright owners.

(5) If he does recommend the making of new provision he shall specify any terms, other than terms as to charges payable, on which authorisation under the new provision should be available.

(6) Regulations under this section shall be made by statutory instrument which shall be subject to annulment in pursuance of a resolution of either House of Parliament.

(7) In this section (and section 141) a 'general licence' means a licence granted by a licensing body which covers all works of the description to which it applies.

## 141. Statutory licence where recommendation not implemented

(1) The Secretary of State may, within one year of the making of a recommendation under section 140 by order provide that if, or to the extent that, provision has not been made in accordance with the recommendation, the making by or on behalf of an educational establishment, for the purposes of instruction, of reprographic copies of the works to which the recommendation relates shall be treated as licensed by the owners of the copyright in the works.

(2) For that purpose provision shall be regarded as having been made in accordance with the recommendation if—

    (a) a certified licensing scheme has been established under which a licence is available to the establishment in question, or

    (b) a general licence has been—

        (i) granted to or for the benefit of that establishment, or

        (ii) referred by or on behalf of that establishment to the Copyright Tribunal under section 125 (reference of terms of proposed licence), or

        (iii) offered to or for the benefit of that establishment and refused without such a reference,

and the terms of the scheme or licence accord with the recommendation.

(3) The order shall also provide that any existing licence authorising the making of such copies (not being a licence granted under a certified licensing scheme or a general licence) shall cease to have effect to the extent that it is more restricted or more onerous than the licence provided for by the order.

(4) The order shall provide for the licence to be free of royalty but, as respects other matters, subject to any terms specified in the recommendation and to such other terms as the Secretary of State may think fit.

(5) The order may provide that where a copy which would otherwise be an infringing copy is made in accordance with the licence provided by the order but is subsequently dealt with, it shall be treated as an infringing copy for the purposes of that dealing, and if that dealing infringes copyright for all subsequent purposes.

In this subsection 'dealt with' means sold or let for hire, offered or exposed for sale or hire, or exhibited in public.

(6) The order shall not come into force until at least six months after it is made.

(7) An order may be varied from time to time, but not so as to include works other than those to which the recommendation relates or remove any terms specified in the recommendation, and may be revoked.

(8) An order under this section shall be made by statutory instrument which shall be subject to annulment in pursuance of a resolution of either House of Parliament.

(9) In this section a 'certified licensing scheme' means a licensing scheme certified for the purposes of this section under section 143.

*Royalty or other sum payable for rental of certain works*

**142. Royalty or other sum payable for rental of sound recording, film or computer program**

(1) An application to settle the royalty or other sum payable in pursuance of section 66 (rental of sound recordings, films and computer programs) may be made to the Copyright Tribunal by the copyright owner or the person claiming to be treated as licensed by him.

(2) The Tribunal shall consider the matter and make such order as it may determine to be reasonable in the circumstances.

(3) Either party may subsequently apply to the Tribunal to vary the order, and the Tribunal shall consider the matter and make such order confirming or varying the original order as it may determine to be reasonable in the circumstances.

(4) An application under subsection (3) shall not, except with the special leave of the Tribunal, be made within twelve months from the date of the original order or of the order on a previous application under that subsection.

(5) An order under subsection (3) has effect from the date on which it is made or such later date as may be specified by the Tribunal.

*Certification of licensing schemes*

**143. Certification of licensing schemes**

(1) A person operating or proposing to operate a licensing scheme may apply to the Secretary of State to certify the scheme for the purposes of—

    (a) section 35 (educational recording of broadcasts or cable programmes),
    (b) section 60 (abstracts of scientific or technical articles),
    (c) section 66 (rental of sound recordings, films and computer programs),
    (d) section 74 (sub-titled copies of broadcasts or cable programmes for people who are deaf or hard of hearing), or
    (e) section 141 (reprographic copying of published works by educational establishments).

(2) The Secretary of State shall by order made by statutory instrument certify the scheme if he is satisfied that it—

    (a) enables the works to which it relates to be identified with sufficient certainty by persons likely to require licences, and
    (b) sets out clearly the charges (if any) payable and the other terms on which licences will be granted.

(3) The scheme shall be scheduled to the order and the certification shall come into operation for the purposes of sections 35, 60, 66, 74 or 141, as the case may be—

    (a) on such date, not less than eight weeks after the order is made, as may be specified in the order, or

    (b) if the scheme is the subject of a reference under section 118 (reference of proposed scheme), any later date on which the order of the Copyright Tribunal under that section comes into force or the reference is withdrawn.

(4) A variation of the scheme is not effective unless a corresponding amendment of the order is made; and the Secretary of State shall make such an amendment in the case of a variation ordered by the Copyright Tribunal on a reference under sections 118, 119 or 120, and may do so in any other case if he thinks fit.

(5) The order shall be revoked if the scheme ceases to be operated and may be revoked if it appears to the Secretary of State that it is no longer being operated according to its terms.

## *Powers exercisable in consequence of competition report*

### 144. Powers exercisable in consequence of report of Monopolies and Mergers Commission

(1) Where the matters specified in a report of the Monopolies and Mergers Commission as being those which in the Commission's opinion operate, may be expected to operate or have operated against the public interest include—

    (a) conditions in licences granted by the owner of copyright in a work restricting the use of the work by the licensee or the right of the copyright owner to grant other licences, or

    (b) a refusal of a copyright owner to grant licences on reasonable terms,

the powers conferred by Part I of Schedule 8 to the Fair Trading Act 1973 (powers exercisable for purpose of remedying or preventing adverse effects specified in report of Commission) include power to cancel or modify those conditions and, instead or in addition, to provide that licences in respect of the copyright shall be available as of right.

(2) The references in sections 56(2) and 73(2) of that Act, and sections 10(2)(b) and 12(5) of the Competition Act 1980, to the powers specified in that Part of that Schedule shall be construed accordingly.

(3) A Minister shall only exercise the powers available by virtue of this section if he is satisfied that to do so does not contravene any Convention relating to copyright to which the United Kingdom is a party.

(4) The terms of a licence available by virtue of this section shall, in default of agreement, be settled by the Copyright Tribunal on an application by the person requiring the licence; and terms so settled shall authorise the licensee to do everything in respect of which a licence is so available.

(5) Where the terms of a licence are settled by the Tribunal, the licence has effect from the date on which the application to the Tribunal was made.

CHAPTER VIII
THE COPYRIGHT TRIBUNAL

*The Tribunal*

## 145. The Copyright Tribunal

(1) The Tribunal established under section 23 of the Copyright Act 1956 is renamed the Copyright Tribunal.

(2) The Tribunal shall consist of a chairman and two deputy chairmen appointed by the Lord Chancellor, after consultation with the Lord Advocate, and not less than two or more than eight ordinary members appointed by the Secretary of State.

(3) A person is not eligible for appointment as chairman or deputy chairman *unless he is a barrister, advocate or solicitor of not less than seven years' standing or has held judicial office.*

**unless—**

(a) **he has a 7 year general qualification, within the meaning of section 71 of the Courts and Legal Services Act 1990;**

(b) **he is an advocate or solicitor in Scotland of at least 7 years' standing;**

(c) **he is a member of the Bar of Northern Ireland or solicitor of the Supreme Court of Northern Ireland of at least 7 years' standing; or**

(d) **he has held judicial office.**

*General note*
Sub-s (3): words in bold type substituted by the Courts and Legal Services Act 1990, s 71(2), Sch 10, para 73; original words italicised.

## 146. Membership of the Tribunal

(1) The members of the Copyright Tribunal shall hold and vacate office in accordance with their terms of appointment, subject to the following provisions.

(2) A member of the Tribunal may resign his office by notice in writing to the Secretary of State or, in the case of the chairman or a deputy chairman, to the Lord Chancellor.

(3) The Secretary of State or, in the case of the chairman or a deputy chairman, the Lord Chancellor may by notice in writing to the member concerned remove him from office if—

(a) he has become bankrupt or made an arrangement with his creditors or, in Scotland, his estate has been sequestrated or he has executed a trust deed for his creditors or entered into a composition contract, or

(b) he is incapacitated by physical or mental illness,

or if he is in the opinion of the Secretary of State or, as the case may be, the Lord Chancellor otherwise unable or unfit to perform his duties as member.

**(3A) A person who is the chairman or a deputy chairman of the Tribunal shall vacate his office on the day on which he attains the age of 70 years; but this subsection is subject to section 26(4) to (6) of the Judicial Pensions and Retirement Act 1993 (power to authorise continuance in office up to the age of 75 years).**

(4) If a member of the Tribunal is by reason of illness, absence or other reasonable cause for the time being unable to perform the duties of his office,

either generally or in relation to particular proceedings, a person may be appointed to discharge his duties for a period not exceeding six months at one time or, as the case may be, in relation to those proceedings.

(5) The appointment shall be made—

(a) in the case of the chairman or deputy chairman, by the Lord Chancellor, who shall appoint a person who would be eligible for appointment to that office, and

(b) in the case of an ordinary member, by the Secretary of State;

and a person so appointed shall have during the period of his appointment, or in relation to the proceedings in question, the same powers as the person in whose place he is appointed.

(6) The Lord Chancellor shall consult the Lord Advocate before exercising his powers under this section.

*General note*
Sub-s (3A): prospectively added with savings by the Judicial Pensions and Retirement Act 1993, s 26, Sch 6, para 49, as from a day to be appointed; for savings see s 27, Sch 7 thereof.

## 147. Financial provisions

(1) There shall be paid to the members of the Copyright Tribunal such remuneration (whether by way of salaries or fees), and such allowances, as the Secretary of State with the approval of the Treasury may determine.

(2) The Secretary of State may appoint such staff for the Tribunal as, with the approval of the Treasury as to numbers and remuneration, he may determine.

(3) The remuneration and allowances of members of the Tribunal, the remuneration of any staff and such other expenses of the Tribunal as the Secretary of State with the approval of the Treasury may determine shall be paid out of money provided by Parliament.

## 148. Constitution for purposes of proceedings

(1) For the purposes of any proceedings the Copyright Tribunal shall consist of—

(a) a chairman, who shall be either the chairman or a deputy chairman of the Tribunal, and

(b) two or more ordinary members.

(2) If the members of the Tribunal dealing with any matter are not unanimous, the decision shall be taken by majority vote; and if, in such a case, the votes are equal the chairman shall have a further, casting vote.

(3) Where part of any proceedings before the Tribunal has been heard and one or more members of the Tribunal are unable to continue, the Tribunal shall remain duly constituted for the purpose of those proceedings so long as the number of members is not reduced to less than three.

(4) If the chairman is unable to continue, the chairman of the Tribunal shall—

(a) appoint one of the remaining members to act as chairman, and

(b) appoint a suitably qualified person to attend the proceedings and advise the members on any questions of law arising.

(5) A person is 'suitably qualified' for the purposes of subsection (4)(b) if he is, or is eligible for appointment as, a deputy chairman of the Tribunal.

*Jurisdiction and procedure*

## 149. Jurisdiction of the Tribunal

The function of the Copyright Tribunal is to hear and determine proceedings under—

(a) sections 118, 119 or 120 (reference of licensing scheme);

(b) sections 121 or 122 (application with respect to entitlement to licence under licensing scheme);

(c) sections 125, 126 or 127 (reference or application with respect to licensing by licensing body);

**(cc) section 135D or 135E (application or reference with respect to use as of right of sound recordings in broadcasts or cable programme services);**

(d) section 139 (appeal against order as to coverage of licensing scheme or licence);

(e) section 142 (application to settle royalty or other sum payable for rental of sound recording, film or computer program);

(f) section 144(4) (application to settle terms of copyright licence available as of right);

(g) section 190 (application to give consent for purposes of Part II on behalf of performer);

(h) paragraph 5 of Schedule 6 (determination of royalty or other remuneration to be paid to trustees for the Hospital for Sick Children).

*General note*

Para (cc): added by the Broadcasting Act 1990, s 175(2). Proceedings under the Broadcasting Act 1990, Sch 17 are also subject to the jurisdiction of the Tribunal, see ibid, Sch 17, para 7(7).

## 150. General power to make rules

(1) The Lord Chancellor may, after consultation with the Lord Advocate, make rules for regulating proceedings before the Copyright Tribunal and, subject to the approval of the Treasury, as to the fees chargeable in respect of such proceedings.

(2) The rules may apply in relation to the Tribunal—

(a) as respects proceedings in England and Wales, any of the provisions of the Arbitration Act 1950;

(b) as respects proceedings in Northern Ireland, any of the provisions of the Arbitration Act (Northern Ireland) 1937

and any provisions so applied shall be set out in or scheduled to the rules.

(3) Provision shall be made by the rules—

(a) prohibiting the Tribunal from entertaining a reference under sections 118, 119, or 120 by a representative organisation unless the Tribunal is satisfied that the organisation is reasonably representative of the class of persons which it claims to represent;

(b) specifying the parties to any proceedings and enabling the Tribunal to make a party to the proceedings any person or organisation satisfying the Tribunal that they have a substantial interest in the matter; and

(c) requiring the Tribunal to give the parties to proceedings an opportunity to state their case, in writing or orally as the rules may provide.

(4) The rules may make provision for regulating or prescribing any matters

incidental to or consequential upon any appeal from the Tribunal under section 152 (appeal to the court on point of law).

(5) Rules under this section shall be made by statutory instrument which shall be subject to annulment in pursuance of a resolution of either House of Parliament.

### 151. Costs, proof of orders, etc

(1) The Copyright Tribunal may order that the costs of a party to proceedings before it shall be paid by such other party as the Tribunal may direct; and the Tribunal may tax or settle the amount of the costs, or direct in what manner they are to be taxed.

(2) A document purporting to be a copy of an order of the Tribunal and to be certified by the chairman to be a true copy shall, in any proceedings, be sufficient evidence of the order unless the contrary is proved.

(3) As respect proceedings in Scotland, the Tribunal has the like powers for securing the attendance of witnesses and the production of documents, and with regard to the examination of witnesses on oath, as an arbiter under a submission.

## *Appeals*

### 152. Appeal to the court on point of law

(1) An appeal lies on any point of law arising from a decision of the Copyright Tribunal to the High Court or, in the case of proceedings of the Tribunal in Scotland, to the Court of Session.

(2) Provision shall be made by rules under section 150 limiting the time within which an appeal may be brought.

(3) Provision may be made by rules under that section—

  (a)  for suspending, or authorising or requiring the Tribunal to suspend, the operation of orders of the Tribunal in cases where its decision is appealed against;
  (b)  for modifying in relation to an order of the Tribunal whose operation is suspended the operation of any provision of this Act as to the effect of the order;
  (c)  for the publication of notices or the taking of other steps for securing that persons affected by the suspension of an order of the Tribunal will be informed of its suspension.

CHAPTER IX
QUALIFICATION FOR AND EXTENT OF COPYRIGHT PROTECTION

## *Qualification for copyright protection*

### 153. Qualification for copyright protection

(1) Copyright does not subsist in a work unless the qualification requirements of this Chapter are satisfied as regards—

  (a)  the author (see section 154), or
  (b)  the country in which the work was first published (see section 155), or
  (c)  in the case of a broadcast or cable programme, the country from which the broadcast was made or the cable programme was sent (see section 156).

(2) Subsection (1) does not apply in relation to Crown copyright or Parliamentary copyright (see sections 163 to 166) or to copyright subsisting by virtue of section 168 (copyright of certain international organisations).

(3) If the qualification requirements of this Chapter, or sections 163, 165 or 168, are once satisfied in respect of a work, copyright does not cease to subsist by reason of any subsequent event.

### 154. Qualification by reference to author

(1) A work qualifies for copyright protection if the author was at the material time a qualifying person, that is—

(a) a British citizen, a British Dependent Territories citizen, a British National (Overseas), a British Overseas citizen, a British subject or a British protected person within the meaning of the British Nationality Act 1981, or

(b) an individual domiciled or resident in the United Kingdom or another country to which the relevant provisions of this Part extend, or

(c) a body incorporated under the law of a part of the United Kingdom or of another country to which the relevant provisions of this Part extend.

(2) Where, or so far as, provision is made by Order under section 159 (application of this Part to countries to which it does not extend), a work also qualifies for copyright protection if at the material time the author was a citizen or subject of, an individual domiciled or resident in, or a body incorporated under the law of, a country to which the Order relates.

(3) A work of joint authorship qualifies for copyright protection if at the material time any of the authors satisfies the requirements of subsection (1) or (2); but where a work qualifies for copyright protection only under this section, only those authors who satisfy those requirements shall be taken into account for the purposes of—

section 11(1) and (2) (first ownership of copyright; entitlement of author or author's employer),

section 12(1) and (2) (duration of copyright; dependent on life of author unless work of unknown authorship), and section 9(4) (meaning of 'unknown authorship') so far as it applies for the purposes of section 12(2), and

section 57 (anonymous or pseudonymous works: acts permitted on assumptions as to expiry of copyright or death of author).

(4) The material time in relation to a literary, dramatic, musical or artistic work is—

(a) in the case of an unpublished work, when the work was made or, if the making of the work extended over a period, a substantial part of that period;

(b) in the case of a published work, when the work was first published or, if the author had died before that time, immediately before his death.

(5) The material time in relation to other descriptions of work is as follows—

(a) in the case of a sound recording or film, when it was made;

(b) in the case of a broadcast, when the broadcast was made;

(c) in the case of a cable programme, when the programme was included in a cable programme service;

(d) in the case of the typographical arrangement of a published edition, when the edition was first published.

### 155. Qualification by reference to country of first publication

(1) A literary, dramatic, musical or artistic work, a sound recording or film, or the typographical arrangement of a published edition, qualifies for copyright protection if it is first published—

(a) in the United Kingdom, or
(b) in another country to which the relevant provisions of this Part extend.

(2) Where, or so far as, provision is made by Order under section 159 (application of this Part to countries to which it does not extend), such a work also qualifies for copyright protection if it is first published in a country to which the Order relates.

(3) For the purposes of this section, publication in one country shall not be regarded as other than the first publication by reason of simultaneous publication elsewhere; and for this purpose publication elsewhere within the previous 30 days shall be treated as simultaneous.

### 156. Qualification by reference to place of transmission

(1) A broadcast qualifies for copyright protection if it is made from, and a cable programme qualifies for copyright protection if it is sent from, a place in—

(a) the United Kingdom, or
(b) another country to which the relevant provisions of this Part extend.

(2) Where, or so far as, provision is made by Order under section 159 (application of this Part to countries to which it does not extend), a broadcast or cable programme also qualifies for copyright protection if it is made from or, as the case may be, sent from a place in a country to which the Order relates.

*Extent and application of this Part*

### 157. Countries to which this Part extends

(1) This Part extends to England and Wales, Scotland and Northern Ireland.

(2) Her Majesty may by Order in Council direct that this Part shall extend, subject to such exceptions and modifications as may be specified in the Order, to—

(a) any of the Channel Islands,
(b) the Isle of Man, or
(c) any colony.

(3) That power includes power to extend, subject to such exceptions and modifications as may be specified in the Order, any Order in Council made under the following provisions of this Chapter.

(4) The legislature of a country to which this Part has been extended may modify or add to the provisions of this Part, in their operation as part of the law of that country, as the legislature may consider necessary to adapt the provisions to the circumstances of that country—

(a) as regards procedure and remedies, or

(b) as regards works qualifying for copyright protection by virtue of a connection with that country.

(5) Nothing in this section shall be construed as restricting the extent of paragraph 36 of Schedule 1 (transitional provisions: dependent territories where the Copyright Act 1956 or the Copyright Act 1911 remains in force) in relation to the law of a dependent territory to which this Part does not extend.

## 158. Countries ceasing to be colonies

(1) The following provisions apply where a country to which this Part has been extended ceases to be a colony of the United Kingdom.

(2) As from the date on which it ceases to be a colony it shall cease to be regarded as a country to which this Part extends for the purposes of—

(a) section 160(2)(a) (denial of copyright protection to citizens of countries not giving adequate protection to British works), and
(b) sections 163 and 165 (Crown and Parliamentary copyright).

(3) But it shall continue to be treated as a country to which this Part extends for the purposes of sections 154 to 156 (qualification for copyright protection) until—

(a) an Order in Council is made in respect of that country under section 159 (application of this Part to countries to which it does not extend), or
(b) an Order in Council is made declaring that it shall cease to be so treated by reason of the fact that the provisions of this Part as part of the law of that country have been repealed or amended.

(4) A statutory instrument containing an Order in Council under subsection (3)(b) shall be subject to annulment in pursuance of a resolution of either House of Parliament.

## 159. Application of this Part to countries to which it does not extend

(1) Her Majesty may by Order in Council make provision for applying in relation to a country to which this Part does not extend any of the provisions of this Part specified in the Order, so as to secure that those provisions—

(a) apply in relation to persons who are citizens or subjects of that country or are domiciled or resident there, as they apply to persons who are British citizens or are domiciled or resident in the United Kingdom, or
(b) apply in relation to bodies incorporated under the law of that country as they apply in relation to bodies incorporated under the law of a part of the United Kingdom, or
(c) apply in relation to works first published in that country as they apply in relation to works first published in the United Kingdom, or
(d) apply in relation to broadcasts made from or cable programmes sent from that country as they apply in relation to broadcasts made from or cable programmes sent from the United Kingdom.

(2) An Order may make provision for all or any of the matters mentioned in subsection (1) and may—

(a) apply any provisions of this Part subject to such exceptions and modifications as are specified in the Order; and

(b) direct that any provisions of this Part apply either generally or in relation to such classes of works, or other classes of case, as are specified in the Order.

(3) Except in the case of a Convention country or another Member State of the European Economic Community, Her Majesty shall not make an Order in Council under this section in relation to a country unless satisfied that provision has been or will be made under the law of that country, in respect of the class of works to which the Order relates, giving adequate protection to the owners of copyright under this Part.

(4) In subsection (3) 'Convention country' means a country which is a party to a Convention relating to copyright to which the United Kingdom is also a party.

(5) A statutory instrument containing an Order in Council under this section shall be subject to annulment in pursuance of a resolution of either House of Parliament.

## 160. Denial of copyright protection to citizens of countries not giving adequate protection to British works

(1) If it appears to Her Majesty that the law of a country fails to give adequate protection to British works to which this section applies, or to one or more classes of such works, Her Majesty may make provision by Order in Council in accordance with this section restricting the rights conferred by this Part in relation to works of authors connected with that country.

(2) An Order in Council under this section shall designate the country concerned and provide that, for the purposes of specified in the Order, works first published after a date specified in the Order shall not be treated as qualifying for copyright protection by virtue of such publication if at that time the authors are—

(a) citizens or subjects of that country (not domiciled or resident in the United Kingdom or another country to which the relevant provisions of this Part extend), or

(b) bodies incorporated under the law of that country;

and the Order may make such provision for all the purposes of this Part or for such purposes as are specified in the Order, and either generally or in relation to such class of cases as are specified in the Order, having regard to the nature and extent of that failure referred to in subsection (1).

(3) This section applies to literary, dramatic, musical and artistic works, sound recordings and films; and 'British works' means works of which the author was a qualifying person at the material time within the meaning of section 154.

(4) A statutory instrument containing an Order in Council under this section shall be subject to annulment in pursuance of a resolution of either House of Parliament.

*Supplementary*

## 161. Territorial waters and the continental shelf

(1) For the purposes of this Part the territorial waters of the United Kingdom shall be treated as part of the United Kingdom.

(2) This Part applies to things done in the United Kingdom sector of the continental shelf on a structure or vessel which is present there for purposes

directly connected with the exploration of the sea bed or subsoil or the exploitation of their natural resources as it applies to things done in the United Kingdom.

(3) The United Kingdom sector of the continental shelf means the areas designated by order under section 1(7) of the Continental Shelf Act 1964.

**162. British ships, aircraft and hovercraft**
(1) This Part applies to things done on a British ship, aircraft or hovercraft as it applies to things done in the United Kingdom.

(2) In this section—

'British ship' means a ship which is a British ship for the purposes of the Merchant Shipping Acts (see section 2 of the Merchant Shipping Act 1988) otherwise than by virtue of registration in a country outside the United Kingdom; and

'British aircraft' and 'British hovercraft' mean an aircraft or hovercraft registered in the United Kingdom.

CHAPTER X
MISCELLANEOUS AND GENERAL

*Crown and Parliamentary copyright*

**163. Crown copyright**
(1) Where a work is made by Her Majesty or by an officer or servant of the Crown in the course of his duties—

(a) the work qualifies for copyright protection notwithstanding section 153(1) (ordinary requirement as to qualification for copyright protection), and
(b) Her Majesty is the first owner of any copyright in the work.

(2) Copyright in such a work is referred to in this Part as 'Crown copyright', notwithstanding that it may be, or have been, assigned to another person.

(3) Crown copyright in a literary, dramatic, musical or artistic work continues to subsist—

(a) until the end of the period of 125 years from the end of the calendar year in which the work was made, or
(b) if the work is published commercially before the end of the period of 75 years from the end of the calendar year in which it was made, until the end of the period of 50 years from the end of the calendar year in which it was first so published.

(4) In the case of a work of joint authorship where one or more but not all of the authors are persons falling within subsection (1), this section applies only in relation to those authors and the copyright subsisting by virtue of their contribution to the work.

(5) Except as mentioned above, and subject to any express exclusion elsewhere in this Part, the provisions of this Part apply in relation to Crown copyright as to other copyright.

(6) This section does not apply to work if, or to the extent that, Parliamentary copyright subsists in the work (see sections 165 and 166).

**164. Copyright in Acts and Measures**

(1) Her Majesty is entitled to copyright in every Act of Parliament or Measure of the General Synod of the Church of England.

(2) The copyright subsists from Royal Assent until the end of the period of 50 years from the end of the calendar year in which Royal Assent was given.

(3) References in this Part to Crown copyright (except in section 163) include copyright under this section; and, except as mentioned above, the provisions of this Part apply in relation to copyright under this section as to other Crown copyright.

(4) No other copyright, or right in the nature of copyright, subsists in an Act or Measure.

**165. Parliamentary copyright**

(1) Where a work is made by or under the direction or control of the House of Commons or the House of Lords—

    (a) the work qualifies for copyright protection notwithstanding section 153(1) (ordinary requirement as to qualification for copyright protection), and

    (b) the House by whom, or under whose direction or control, the work is made is the first owner of any copyright in the work, and if the work is made by or under the direction or control of both Houses, the two Houses are joint first owners of copyright.

(2) Copyright in such a work is referred to in this Part as 'Parliamentary copyright', notwithstanding that it may be, or have been, assigned to another person.

(3) Parliamentary copyright in a literary, dramatic, musical or artistic work continues to subsist until the end of the period of 50 years from the end of the calendar year in which the work was made.

(4) For the purposes of this section, works made by or under the direction or control of the House of Commons or the House of Lords include—

    (a) any work made by an officer or employee of that House in the course of his duties, and

    (b) any sound recording, film, live broadcast or live cable programme of the proceedings of that House;

but a work shall not be regarded as made by or under the direction or control of either House by reason only of its being commissioned by or on behalf of that House.

(5) In the case of a work of joint authorship where one or more but not all of the authors are acting on behalf of, or under the direction or control of, the House of Commons or the House of Lords, this section applies only in relation to those authors and the copyright subsisting by virtue of their contribution to the work.

(6) Except as mentioned above, and subject to any express exclusion elsewhere in this Part, the provisions of this Part apply in relation to Parliamentary copyright as to other copyright.

(7) The provisions of this section also apply, subject to any exceptions or modifications specified by Order in Council, to works made by or under the direction or control of any other legislative body of a country to which this Part extends; and references in this Part to 'Parliamentary copyright' shall be construed accordingly.

(8) A statutory instrument containing an Order in Council under subsection (7) shall be subject to annulment in pursuance of a resolution of either House of Parliament.

### 166. Copyright in Parliamentary Bills

(1) Copyright in every Bill introduced into Parliament belongs, in accordance with the following provisions, to one or both of the Houses of Parliament.

(2) Copyright in a public Bill belongs in the first instance to the House into which the Bill is introduced, and after the Bill has been carried to the second House to both Houses jointly, and subsists from the time when the text of the Bill is handed in to the House in which it is introduced.

(3) Copyright in a private Bill belongs to both Houses jointly and subsists from the time when a copy of the Bill is first deposited in either House.

(4) Copyright in a personal Bill belongs in the first instance to the House of Lords, and after the Bill has been carried to the House of Commons to both Houses jointly, and subsists from the time when it is given a First Reading in the House of Lords.

(5) Copyright under this section ceases—

    (a)  on Royal Assent, or

    (b)  if the Bill does not receive Royal Assent, on the withdrawal or rejection of the Bill or the end of the Session:

provided that copyright in a Bill continues to subsist notwithstanding its rejection in any Session by the House of Lords if, by virtue of the Parliament Acts 1911 and 1949, it remains possible for it to be presented for Royal Assent in that Session.

(6) References in this Part to Parliamentary copyright (except in section 165) include copyright under this section; and, except as mentioned above, the provisions of this Part apply in relation to copyright under this section as to other Parliamentary copyright.

(7) No other copyright, or right in the nature of copyright, subsists in a Bill after copyright has once subsisted under this section; but without prejudice to the subsequent operation of this section in relation to a Bill which, not having passed in one Session, is reintroduced in a subsequent Session.

### 167. Houses of Parliament: supplementary provisions with respect to copyright

(1) For the purposes of holding, dealing with and enforcing copyright, and in connection with all legal proceedings relating to copyright, each House of Parliament shall be treated as having the legal capacities of a body corporate, which shall not be affected by a prorogation or dissolution.

(2) The functions of the House of Commons as owner of copyright shall be exercised by the Speaker on behalf of the House; and if so authorised by the Speaker, or in case of a vacancy in the office of Speaker, those functions may be discharged by the Chairman of Ways and Means or a Deputy Chairman.

(3) For this purpose a person who on the dissolution of Parliament was Speaker of the House of Commons, Chairman of Ways and Means or a Deputy Chairman may continue to act until the corresponding appointment is made in the next Session of Parliament.

(4) The functions of the House of Lords as owner of copyright shall be exercised by the Clerk of the Parliaments on behalf of the House; and if so authorised by him, or in case of a vacancy in the office of Clerk of the Parliaments, those functions may be discharged by the Clerk Assistant or the Reading Clerk.

(5) Legal proceedings relating to copyright—

(a) shall be brought by or against the House of Commons in the name of 'The Speaker of the House of Commons'; and

(b) shall be brought by or against the House of Lords in the name of 'The Clerk of the Parliaments'.

## Other miscellaneous provisions

### 168. Copyright vesting in certain international organisations

(1) Where an original literary, dramatic, musical or artistic work—

(a) is made by an officer or employee of, or is published by, an international organisation to which this section applies, and

(b) does not qualify for copyright protection under section 154 (qualification by reference to author) or section 155 (qualification by reference to country of first publication),

copyright nevertheless subsists in the work by virtue of this section and the organisation is first owner of that copyright.

(2) The international organisations to which this section applies are those as to which Her Majesty has by Order in Council declared that it is expedient that this section should apply.

(3) Copyright of which an international organisation is first owner by virtue of this section continues to subsist until the end of the period of 50 years from the end of the calendar year in which the work was made or such longer period as may be specified by Her Majesty by Order in Council for the purpose of complying with the international obligations of the United Kingdom.

(4) An international organisation to which this section applies shall be deemed to have, and to have had at all material times, the legal capacities of a body corporate for the purpose of holding, dealing with and enforcing copyright and in connection with all legal proceedings relating to copyright.

(5) A statutory instrument containing an Order in Council under this section shall be subject to annulment in pursuance of a resolution of either House of Parliament.

### 169. Folklore, etc: anonymous unpublished works

(1) Where in the case of an unpublished literary, dramatic, musical or artistic work of unknown authorship there is evidence that the author (or, in the case of a joint work, any of the authors) was a qualifying individual by connection with a country outside the United Kingdom, it shall be presumed until the contrary is proved that he was such a qualifying individual and that copyright accordingly subsists in the work, subject to the provisions of this Part.

(2) If under the law of that country a body is appointed to protect and enforce copyright in such works, Her Majesty may by Order in Council designate that body for the purposes of this section.

(3) A body so designated shall be recognised in the United Kingdom as having authority to do in place of the copyright owner anything, other than assign copyright, which it is empowered to do under the law of that country; and it may, in particular, bring proceedings in its own name.

(4) A statutory instrument containing an Order in Council under this section

shall be subject to annulment in pursuance of a resolution of either House of Parliament.

(5) In subsection (1) a 'qualifying individual' means an individual who at the material time (within the meaning of section 154) was a person whose works qualified under that section for copyright protection.

(6) This section does not apply if there has been an assignment of copyright in the work by the author of which notice has been given to the designated body; and nothing in this section affects the validity of an assignment of copyright made, or licence granted, by the author or a person lawfully claiming under him.

## *Transitional provisions and savings*

### 170. Transitional provisions and savings
Schedule 1 contains transitional provisions and savings relating to works made, and acts or events occurring, before the commencement of this Part, and otherwise with respect to the operation of the provisions of this Part.

### 171. Rights and privileges under other enactments or the common law
(1) Nothing in this Part affects—

(a) any right or privilege of any person under any enactment (except where the enactment is expressly repealed, amended or modified by this Act);
(b) any right or privilege of the Crown subsisting otherwise than under an enactment;
(c) any right or privilege of either House of Parliament;
(d) the right of the Crown or any person deriving title from the Crown to sell, use or otherwise deal with articles forfeited under the laws relating to customs and excise;
(e) the operation of any rule of equity relating to breaches of trust or confidence.

(2) Subject to those savings, no copyright or right in the nature of copyright shall subsist otherwise than by virtue of this Part or some other enactment in that behalf.

(3) Nothing in this Part affects any rule of law preventing or restricting the enforcement of copyright, on grounds of public interest or otherwise.

(4) Nothing in this Part affects any right of action or other remedy, whether civil or criminal, available otherwise than under this Part in respect of acts infringing any of the rights conferred by Chapter IV (moral rights).

(5) The savings in subsection (1) have effect subject to section 164(4) and section 166(7) (copyright in Acts, Measures and Bills: exclusion of other rights in the nature of copyright).

## *Interpretation*

### 172. General provisions as to construction
(1) This Part restates and amends the law of copyright, that is, the provisions of the Copyright Act 1956, as amended.

(2) A provision of this Part which corresponds to a provision of the previous law shall not be construed as departing from the previous law merely because of a change of expression.

(3) Decisions under the previous law may be referred to for the purpose of

establishing whether a provision of this Part departs from the previous law, or otherwise for establishing the true construction of this Part.

## 173. Construction of references to copyright owner

(1) Where different persons are (whether in consequence of a partial assignment or otherwise) entitled to different aspects of copyright in a work, the copyright owner for any purpose of this Part is the person who is entitled to the aspect of copyright relevant for that purpose.

(2) Where copyright (or any aspect of copyright) is owned by more than one person jointly, references in this Part to the copyright owner are to all the owners, so that, in particular, any requirement of the licence of the copyright owner requires the licence of all of them.

## 174. Meaning of 'educational establishment' and related expressions

(1) The expression 'educational establishment' in a provision of this Part means—

(a) any school, and

(b) any other description of educational establishment specified for the purposes of this Part, or that provision, by order of the Secretary of State.

(2) The Secretary of State may by order provide that the provisions of this Part relating to educational establishments shall apply, with such modifications and adaptations as may be specified in the order, in relation to teachers who are employed by a local education authority to give instruction elsewhere to pupils who are unable to attend an educational establishment.

(3) In subsection (1)(a) 'school'—

(a) in relation to England and Wales, has the same meaning as in the Education Act 1944;

(b) in relation to Scotland, has the same meaning as in the Education (Scotland) Act 1962, except that it includes an approved school within the meaning of the Social Work (Scotland) Act 1968; and

(c) in relation to Northern Ireland, has the same meaning as in the Education and Libraries (Northern Ireland) Order 1986.

(4) An order under subsection (1)(b) may specify a description of educational establishment by reference to the instruments from time to time in force under any enactment specified in the order.

(5) In relation to an educational establishment the expressions 'teacher' and 'pupil' in this Part include, respectively, any person who gives and any person who receives instruction.

(6) References in this Part to anything being done 'on behalf of' an educational establishment are to its being done for the purposes of that establishment by any person.

(7) An order under this section shall be made by statutory instrument which shall be subject to annulment in pursuance of a resolution of either House of Parliament.

## 175. Meaning of publication and commercial publication

(1) In this Part 'publication', in relation to a work—

(a) means the issue of copies to the public, and

(b) includes, in the case of a literary, dramatic, musical or artistic work, making it available to the public by means of an electronic retrieval system;

and related expressions shall be construed accordingly.

(2) In this Part 'commercial publication', in relation to a literary, dramatic, musical or artistic work means—

    (a) issuing copies of the work to the public at a time when copies made in advance of the receipt of orders are generally available to the public, or

    (b) making the work available to the public by means of an electronic retrieval system;

and related expressions shall be construed accordingly.

(3) In the case of a work of architecture in the form of a building, or an artistic work incorporated in a building, construction of the building shall be treated as equivalent to publication of the work.

(4) The following do not constitute publication for the purposes of this Part and references to commercial publication shall be construed accordingly—

    (a) in the case of a literary, dramatic or musical work—

        (i) the performance of the work, or

        (ii) the broadcasting of the work or its inclusion in a cable programme service (otherwise than for the purposes of an electronic retrieval system);

    (b) in the case of an artistic work—

        (i) the exhibition of the work;

        (ii) the issue to the public of copies of a graphic work representing, or of photographs of, a work of architecture in the form of a building or a model for a building, a sculpture or a work of artistic craftsmanship,

        (iii) the issue to the public of copies of a film including the work, or

        (iv) the broadcasting of the work or its inclusion in a cable programme service (otherwise than for the purposes of an electronic retrieval system);

    (c) in the case of a sound recording or film—

        (i) the work being played or shown in public, or

        (ii) the broadcasting of the work or its inclusion in a cable programme service.

(5) References in this Part to publication or commercial publication do not include publication which is merely colourable and not intended to satisfy the reasonable requirements of the public.

(6) No account shall be taken for the purposes of this section of any unauthorised act.

### 176. Requirement of signature: application in relation to body corporate

(1) The requirement in the following provisions that an instrument be signed by or on behalf of a person is also satisfied in the case of a body corporate by the affixing of its seal—

    section 78(3)(b) (assertion by licensor of right to identification of author in case of public exhibition of copy made in pursuance of the licence),

section 90(3) (assignment of copyright),
section 91(1) (assignment of future copyright),
section 92(1) (grant of exclusive licence).

(2) The requirement in the following provisions that an instrument be signed by a person is satisfied in the case of a body corporate by signature on behalf of the body or by the affixing of its seal—

section 78(2)(b) (assertion by instrument in writing of right to have author identified),
section 87(2) (waiver of moral rights).

## 177. Adaptation of expressions for Scotland
In the application of this Part to Scotland—

'account of profits' means accounting and payment of profits;
'accounts' means count, reckoning and payment;
'assignment' means assignation;
'costs' means expenses;
'defendant' means defender;
'delivery up' means delivery;
'estoppel' means personal bar;
'injunction' means interdict;
'interlocutory relief' means interim remedy; and
'plaintiff' means pursuer.

## 178. Minor definitions
In this Part—

'article', in the context of an article in a periodical, includes an item of any description;
'business' includes a trade or profession;
'collective work' means—

(a) a work of joint authorship, or
(b) a work in which there are distinct contributions by different authors or in which works or parts of works of different authors are incorporated;

'computer-generated', in relation to a work, means that the work is generated by computer in circumstances such that there is no human author of the work;
'country' includes any territory;
'the Crown' includes the Crown in right of Her Majesty's Government in Northern Ireland or in any country outside the United Kingdom to which this Part extends;
'electronic' means actuated by electric, magnetic, electro-magnetic, electro-chemical or electro-mechanical energy, and 'in electronic form' means in a form usable only by electronic means;
'employed', 'employee', 'employer' and 'employment' refer to employment under a contract of service or of apprenticeship;
'facsimile copy' includes a copy which is reduced or enlarged in scale;
'international organisation' means an organisation the members of which include one or more states;

'judicial proceedings' includes proceedings before any court, tribunal or person having authority to decide any matter affecting a person's legal rights or liabilities;

'parliamentary proceedings' includes proceedings of the Northern Ireland Assembly or of the European Parliament;

'rental' means any arrangement under which a copy of a work is made available—

(a) for payment (in money or money's worth), or

(b) in the course of a business, as part of services or amenities for which payment is made

on terms that it will or may be returned;

'reprographic copy' and 'reprographic copying' refer to copying by means of a reprographic process;

'reprographic process' means a process—

(a) for making facsimile copies, or

(b) involving the use of an appliance for making multiple copies,

and includes, in relation to a work held in electronic form, any copying by electronic means, but does not include the making of a film or sound recording;

'sufficient acknowledgement' means an acknowledgement identifying the work in question by its title or other description, and identifying the author unless—

(a) in the case of a published work, it is published anonymously;

(b) in the case of an unpublished work, it is not possible for a person to ascertain the identity of the author by reasonable inquiry;

'sufficient disclaimer', in relation to an act capable of infringing the right conferred by section 80 (right to object to derogatory treatment of work), means a clear and reasonably prominent indication—

(a) given at the time of the act, and

(b) if the author or director is then identified, appearing along with the identification,

that the work has been subjected to treatment to which the author or director has not consented;

'telecommunications system' means a system for conveying visual images, sounds or other information by electronic means;

'typeface' includes an ornamental motif used in printing;

'unauthorised', as regards anything done in relation to a work, means done otherwise than—

(a) by or with the licence of the copyright owner, or

(b) if copyright does not subsist in the work, by or with the licence of the author or, in a case where section 11(2) would have applied, the author's employer or, in either case, persons lawfully claiming under him, or

(c) in pursuance of section 48 (copying, etc of certain material by the Crown);

'wireless telegraphy' means the sending of electro-magnetic energy over paths not provided by a material substance constructed or arranged for that purpose;

'writing' includes any form of notation or code, whether by hand or otherwise and regardless of the method by which, or medium in or on which, it is recorded, and 'written' shall be construed accordingly.

## 179. Index of defined expressions

The following Table shows provisions defining or otherwise explaining expressions used in this Part (other than provisions defining or explaining an expression used only in the same section)—

| | |
|---|---|
| account of profits and accounts (in Scotland) | section 177 |
| acts restricted by copyright | section 16(1) |
| adaptation | section 21(3) |
| archivist (in sections 37 to 43) | section 37(6) |
| article (in a periodical) | section 178 |
| artistic work | section 4(1) |
| assignment (in Scotland) | section 177 |
| author | sections 9 and 10(3) |
| broadcast (and related expressions) | section 6 |
| building | section 4(2) |
| business | section 178 |
| cable programme, cable programme service (and related expressions) | section 7 |
| collective work | section 178 |
| commencement (in Schedule 1) | paragraph 1(2) of that Schedule |
| commercial publication | section 175 |
| computer-generated | section 178 |
| copy and copying | section 17 |
| copyright (generally) | section 1 |
| copyright (in Schedule 1) | paragraph 2(2) of that Schedule |
| copyright owner | sections 101(2) and 173 |
| Copyright Tribunal | section 145 |
| copyright work | section 1(2) |
| costs (in Scotland) | section 177 |
| country | section 178 |
| the Crown | section 178 |
| Crown copyright | sections 163(2) and 164(3) |
| defendant (in Scotland) | section 177 |
| delivery up (in Scotland) | section 177 |
| dramatic work | section 3(1) |
| educational establishment | section 174(1) to (4) |
| electronic and electronic form | section 178 |
| employed, employee, employer and employment | section 178 |
| exclusive licence | section 92(1) |
| existing works (in Schedule 1) | paragraph 1(3) of that Schedule |
| facsimile copy | section 178 |
| film | section 5 |
| future copyright | section 91(2) |
| general licence (in sections 140 and 141) | section 140(7) |
| graphic work | section 4(2) |

| | |
|---|---|
| infringing copy | section 27 |
| injunction (in Scotland) | section 177 |
| interlocutory relief (in Scotland) | section 177 |
| international organisation | section 178 |
| issue of copies to the public | section 18(2) |
| joint authorship (work of) | sections 10(1) and (2) |
| judicial proceedings | section 178 |
| **lawful user (in sections 50A to 50C)** | **section 50A(2)** |
| librarian (in sections 37 to 43) | section 37(6) |
| licence (in sections 125 to 128) | section 124 |
| licence of copyright owner | sections 90(4), 91(3) and 173 |
| licensing body (in Chapter VII) | section 116(2) |
| licensing scheme (generally) | section 116(1) |
| licensing scheme (in sections 118 to 121) | section 117 |
| literary work | section 3(1) |
| made (in relation to a literary, dramatic or musical work) | section 3(2) |
| musical work | section 3(1) |
| **needletime** | **section 135A** |
| the new copyright provisions (in Schedule 1) | paragraph 1(1) of that Schedule |
| the 1911 Act (in Schedule 1) | paragraph 1(1) of that Schedule |
| the 1956 Act (in Schedule 1) | paragraph 1(1) of that Schedule |
| on behalf of (in relation to an educational establishment) | section 174(5) |
| Parliamentary copyright | sections 165(2) and (7) and 166(6) |
| parliamentary proceedings | section 178 |
| performance | section 19(2) |
| photograph | section 4(2) |
| plaintiff (in Scotland) | section 177 |
| prescribed conditions (in sections 38 to 43) | section 37(1)(b) |
| prescribed library or archive (in sections 38 to 43) | section 37(1)(a) |
| programme (in the context of broadcasting) | section 6(3) |
| prospective owner (of copyright) | section 91(2) |
| publication and related expressions | section 175 |
| published edition (in the context of copyright in the typographical arrangement | section 8 |
| pupil | section 174(5) |
| rental | section 178 |
| reprographic copies and reprographic copying | section 178 |
| reprographic process | section 178 |
| sculpture | section 4(2) |
| signed | section 176 |
| sound recording | sections 5 **and 135A** |
| sufficient acknowledgement | section 178 |
| sufficient disclaimer | section 178 |
| teacher | section 174(5) |
| telecommunications system | section 178 |
| **terms of payment** | **section 135A** |
| typeface | section 178 |

| | |
|---|---|
| unauthorised (as regards things done in relation to a work) | section 178 |
| unknown (in relation to the author of a work) | section 9(5) |
| unknown authorship (work of) | section 9(4) |
| wireless telegraphy | section 178 |
| work (in Schedule 1) | paragraph 2(1) of that Schedule |
| work of more than one author (in Chapter VII) | section 116(4) |
| writing and written | section 178 |

*General note*
Entry 'lawful user' added by the Copyright (Computer Programs) Regulations 1992 SI 1992 No 3233, reg 9; entries 'needletime' and 'terms of payment' added, and in entry 'sound recording' words in bold type added by the Broadcasting Act 1990, s 175(3).

## PART II
## RIGHTS IN PERFORMANCES

*Introductory*

**180. Rights conferred on performers and persons having recording rights**
(1) This Part confers rights—

(a) on a performer, by requiring his consent to the exploitation of his performances (see sections 181 to 184), and
(b) on a person having recording rights in relation to a performance, in relation to recordings made without his consent or that of the performer (see sections 185 to 188),

and creates offences in relation to dealing with or using illicit recordings and certain other related acts (see sections 198 and 201).
(2) In this Part—
'performance' means—

(a) a dramatic performance (which includes dance and mime),
(b) a musical performance,
(c) a reading or recitation of a literary work, or
(d) a performance of a variety act or any similar presentation,

which is, or so far as it is, a live performance given by one or more individuals; and
'recording', in relation to a performance, means a film or sound recording—

(a) made directly from the live performance,
(b) made from a broadcast of, or cable programme including, the performance, or
(c) made, directly or indirectly, from another recording of the performance.

(3) The rights conferred by this Part apply in relation to performances taking place before the commencement of this Part; but no act done before commencement, or in pursuance of arrangements made before commencement, shall be regarded as infringing those rights.
(4) The rights conferred by this Part are independent of—

    (a)  any copyright in, or moral rights relating to, any work performed or any film or sound recording of, or broadcast or cable programme including, the performance, and

    (b)  any other right or obligation arising otherwise than under this Part.

## *Performers' rights*

### 181. Qualifying performances

A performance is a qualifying performance for the purposes of the provisions of this Part relating to performers' rights if it is given by a qualifying individual (as defined in section 206) or takes place in a qualifying country (as so defined).

### 182. Consent required for recording or live transmission of performance

(1) A performer's rights are infringed by a person who, without his consent—

    (a)  makes, otherwise than for his private and domestic use, a recording of the whole or any substantial part of a qualifying performance, or

    (b)  broadcasts live, or includes live in a cable programme service, the whole or any substantial part of a qualifying performance.

(2) In an action for infringement of a performer's rights brought by virtue of this section damages shall not be awarded against a defendant who shows that at the time of the infringement he believed on reasonable grounds that consent had been given.

### 183. Infringement of performer's rights by use of recording made without consent

A performer's rights are infringed by a person who, without his consent—

    (a)  shows or plays in public the whole or any substantial part of a qualifying performance, or

    (b)  broadcasts or includes in a cable programme service the whole or any substantial part of a qualifying performance,

by means of a recording which was, and which that person knows or has reason to believe was, made without the performer's consent.

### 184. Infringement of performer's rights by importing, possessing or dealing with illicit recording

(1) A performer's rights are infringed by a person who, without his consent—

    (a)  imports into the United Kingdom otherwise than for his private and domestic use, or

    (b)  in the course of a business possesses, sells or lets for hire, offers or exposes for sale or hire, or distributes,

a recording of a qualifying performance which is, and which that person knows or has reason to believe is, an illicit recording.

(2) Where in an action for infringement of a performer's rights brought by virtue of this section a defendant shows that the illicit recording was innocently acquired by him or a predecessor in title of his, the only remedy available against him in respect of the infringement is damages not exceeding a reasonable payment in respect of the act complained of.

(3) In subsection (2) 'innocently acquired' means that the person acquiring the recording did not know and had no reason to believe that it was an illicit recording.

*Rights of person having recording rights*

**185. Exclusive recording contracts and persons having recording rights**

(1) In this Part an 'exclusive recording contract' means a contract between a performer and another person under which that person is entitled to the exclusion of all other persons (including the performer) to make recordings of one or more of his performances with a view to their commercial exploitation.

(2) References in this Part to a 'person having recording rights', in relation to a performance, are (subject to subsection (3)) to a person—

(a) who is party to and has the benefit of an exclusive recording contract to which the performance is subject, or

(b) to whom the benefit of such a contract has been assigned,

and who is a qualifying person.

(3) If a performance is subject to an exclusive recording contract but the person mentioned in subsection (2) is not a qualifying person, references in this Part to a 'person having recording rights' in relation to the performance are to any person—

(a) who is licensed by such a person to make recordings of the performance with a view to their commercial exploitation, or

(b) to whom the benefit of such a licence has been assigned,

and who is a qualifying person.

(4) In this section 'with a view to commercial exploitation' means with a view to the recordings being sold or let for hire, or shown or played in public.

**186. Consent required for recording of performance subject to exclusive contract**

(1) A person infringes the rights of a person having recording rights in relation to a performance who, without his consent or that of the performer, makes a recording of the whole or any substantial part of the performance, otherwise than for his private and domestic use.

(2) In an action for infringement of those rights brought by virtue of this section damages shall not be awarded against a defendant who shows that at the time of the infringement he believed on reasonable grounds that consent had been given.

**187. Infringement of recording rights by use of recording made without consent**

(1) A person infringes the rights of a person having recording rights in relation to a performance who, without his consent or, in the case of a qualifying performance, that of the performer—

(a) shows or plays in public the whole or any substantial part of the performance, or

(b) broadcasts or includes in a cable programme service the whole or any substantial part of the performance,

by means of a recording which was, and which that person knows or has reason to believe was, made without the appropriate consent.

(2) The reference in subsection (1) to 'the appropriate consent' is to the consent of—

(a) the performer, or

(b) the person who at the time the consent was given had recording rights in relation to the performance (or, if there was more than one such person, of all of them).

## 188. Infringement of recording rights by importing, possessing or dealing with illicit recording

(1) A person infringes the rights of a person having recording rights in relation to a performance who, without his consent or, in the case of a qualifying performance, that of the performer—

(a) imports into the United Kingdom otherwise than for his private and domestic use, or

(b) in the course of a business possesses, sells or lets for hire, offers or exposes for sale or hire, or distributes,

a recording of the performance which is, and which that person knows or has reason to believe is, an illicit recording.

(2) Where in an action for infringement of those rights brought by virtue of this section a defendant shows that the illicit recording was innocently acquired by him or a predecessor in title of his, the only remedy available against him in respect of the infringement is damages not exceeding a reasonable payment in respect of the act complained of.

(3) In subsection (2) 'innocently acquired' means that the person acquiring the recording did not know and had no reason to believe that it was an illicit recording.

## *Exceptions to rights conferred*

### 189. Acts permitted notwithstanding rights conferred by this Part

The provisions of Schedule 2 specify acts which may be done notwithstanding the rights conferred by this Part, being acts which correspond broadly to certain of those specified in Chapter III of Part I (acts permitted notwithstanding copyright).

### 190. Power of tribunal to give consent on behalf of performer in certain cases

(1) The Copyright Tribunal may, on the application of a person wishing to make a recording from a previous recording of a performance, give consent in a case where—

(a) the identity or whereabouts of a performer cannot be ascertained by reasonable inquiry, or

(b) a performer unreasonably withholds his consent.

(2) Consent given by the Tribunal has effect as consent of the performer for the purposes of—

(a) the provisions of this Part relating to performers' rights, and

(b) section 198(3)(a) (criminal liability: sufficient consent in relation to qualifying performances),

and may be given subject to any conditions specified in the Tribunal's order.

(3) The Tribunal shall not give consent under subsection (1)(a) except after the service or publication of such notices as may be required by rules made under section 150 (general procedural rules) or as the Tribunal may in any particular case direct.

(4) The Tribunal shall not give consent under subsection (1)(b) unless satisfied that the performer's reasons for withholding consent do not include the protection of any legitimate interest of his; but it shall be for the performer to show what his reasons are for withholding consent, and in default of evidence as to his reasons the Tribunal may draw such inferences as it thinks fit.

(5) In any case the Tribunal shall take into account the following factors—

    (a) whether the original recording was made with the performer's consent and is lawfully in the possession or control of the person proposing to make the further recording;

    (b) whether the making of the further recording is consistent with the obligations of the parties to the arrangements under which, or is otherwise consistent with the purposes for which, the original recording was made.

(6) Where the Tribunal gives consent under this section it shall, in default of agreement between the applicant and the performer, make such order as it thinks fit as to the payment to be made to the performer in consideration of consent being given.

*Duration and transmission of rights; consent*

### 191. Duration of rights
The rights conferred by this Part continue to subsist in relation to a performance until the end of the period of 50 years from the end of the calendar year in which the performance takes place.

### 192. Transmission of rights
(1) The rights conferred by this Part are not assignable or transmissible, except to the extent that performers' rights are transmissible in accordance with the following provisions.

(2) On the death of a person entitled to performer's rights—

    (a) the rights pass to such person as he may by testamentary disposition specifically direct, and

    (b) if or to the extent that there is no such direction, the rights are exercisable by his personal representatives;

and references in this Part to the performer, in the context of the person having performers' rights, shall be construed as references to the person for the time being entitled to exercise those rights.

(3) Where by virtue of subsection (2)(a) a right becomes exercisable by more than one person, it is exercisable by each of them independently of the other or others.

(4) The above provisions do not affect section 185(2)(b) or (3)(b), so far as those provisions confer rights under this Part on a person to whom the benefit of a contract or licence is assigned.

(5) Any damages recovered by personal representatives by virtue of this section in respect of an infringement after a person's death shall devolve as part of his estate as if the right of action had subsisted and been vested in him immediately before his death.

### 193. Consent
(1) Consent for the purposes of this Part may be given in relation to a specific

performance, a specified description of performances or performances generally, and may relate to past or future performances.

(2) A person having recording rights in a performance is bound by any consent given by a person through whom he derives his rights under the exclusive recording contract or licence in question, in the same way as if the consent had been given by him.

(3) Where a right conferred by this Part passes to another person, any consent binding on the person previously entitled binds the person to whom the right passes in the same way as if the consent had been given by him.

*Remedies for infringement*

### 194. Infringement actionable as breach of statutory duty
An infringement of any of the rights conferred by this Part is actionable by the person entitled to the right as a breach of statutory duty.

### 195. Order for delivery up
(1) Where a person has in his possession, custody or control in the course of a business an illicit recording of a performance, a person having performer's rights or recording rights in relation to the performance under this Part may apply to the court for an order that the recording be delivered up to him or to such other person as the court may direct.

(2) An application shall not be made after the end of the period specified in section 203; and no order shall be made unless the court also makes, or it appears to the court that there are grounds for making, an order under section 204 (order as to disposal of illicit recording).

(3) A person to whom a recording is delivered up in pursuance of an order under this section shall, if an order under section 204 is not made, retain it pending the making of an order, or the decision not to make an order, under that section.

(4) Nothing in this section affects any other power of the court.

### 196. Right to seize illicit recordings
(1) An illicit recording of a performance which is found exposed or otherwise immediately available for sale or hire, and in respect of which a person would be entitled to apply for an order under section 195, may be seized and detained by him or a person authorised by him.

The right to seize and detain is exercisable subject to the following conditions and is subject to any decision of the court under section 204 (order as to disposal of illicit recording).

(2) Before anything is seized under this section notice of the time and place of the proposed seizure must be given to a local police station.

(3) A person may for the purpose of exercising the right conferred by this section enter premises to which the public have access but may not seize anything in the possession, custody or control of a person at a permanent or regular place of business of his and may not use any force.

(4) At the time when anything is seized under this section there shall be left at the place where it was seized a notice in the prescribed form containing the prescribed particulars as to the person by whom or on whose authority the seizure is made and the grounds on which it is made.

(5) In this section—

'premises' includes land, buildings, fixed or moveable structures, vehicles, vessels, aircraft and hovercraft; and

'prescribed' means prescribed by order of the Secretary of State.

(6) An order of the Secretary of State under this section shall be made by statutory instrument which shall be subject to annulment in pursuance of a resolution of either House of Parliament.

**197. Meaning of 'illicit recording'**

(1) In this Part 'illicit recording', in relation to a performance, shall be construed in accordance with this section.

(2) For the purposes of a performer's rights, a recording of the whole or any substantial part of a performance of his is an illicit recording if it is made, otherwise than for private purposes, without his consent.

(3) For the purposes of the rights of a person having recording rights, a recording of the whole or any substantial part of a performance subject to the exclusive recording contract is an illicit recording if it is made, otherwise than for private purposes, without his consent or that of the performer.

(4) For the purposes of sections 198 and 199 (offences and orders for delivery up in criminal proceedings), a recording is an illicit recording if it is an illicit recording for the purposes mentioned in subsection (2) or subsection (3).

(5) In this Part 'illicit recording' includes a recording falling to be treated as an illicit recording by virtue of any of the following provisions of Schedule 2—

paragraph 4(3) (recordings made for purposes of instruction or examination),

paragraph 6(2) (recordings made by educational establishments for educational purposes),

paragraph 12(2) (recordings of performance in electronic form retained on transfer of principal recording), or

paragraph 16(3) (recordings made for purposes of broadcast or cable programme),

but otherwise does not include a recording made in accordance with any of the provisions of that Schedule.

(6) It is immaterial for the purposes of this section where the recording was made.

*Offences*

**198. Criminal liability for making, dealing with or using illicit recordings**

(1) A person commits an offence who without sufficient consent—

(a) makes for sale or hire, or

(b) imports into the United Kingdom otherwise than for his private and domestic use, or

(c) possesses in the course of a business with a view to committing any act infringing the rights conferred by this Part, or

(d) in the course of a business—

(i) sells or lets for hire, or

(ii) offers or exposes for sale or hire, or

(iii) distributes,

a recording which is, and which he knows or has reason to believe is, an illicit recording.

(2) A person commits an offence who causes a recording of a performance made without sufficient consent to be—

(a) shown or played in public, or
(b) broadcast or included in a cable programme service,

thereby infringing any of the rights conferred by this Part, if he knows or has reason to believe that those rights are thereby infringed.

(3) In subsections (1) and (2) 'sufficient consent' means—

(a) in the case of a qualifying performance, the consent of the performer, and
(b) in the case of a non-qualifying performance subject to an exclusive recording contract—

(i) for the purposes of subsection (1)(a) (making of recording), the consent of the performer or the person having recording rights, and
(ii) for the purposes of subsection (1)(b), (c) and (d) and subsection (2) (dealing with or using recording), the consent of the person having recording rights.

The references in this subsection to the person having recording rights are to the person having those rights at the time the consent is given or, if there is more than one such person, to all of them.

(4) No offence is committed under subsection (1) or (2) by the commission of an act which by virtue of any provision of Schedule 2 may be done without infringing the rights conferred by this Part.

(5) A person guilty of an offence under subsection (1)(a), (b) or (d)(iii) is liable—

(a) on summary conviction to imprisonment for a term not exceeding six months or a fine not exceeding the statutory maximum, or both;
(b) on conviction on indictment to a fine or imprisonment for a term not exceeding two years, or both.

(6) A person guilty of any other offence under this section is liable on summary conviction to a fine not exceeding level 5 on the standard scale or imprisonment for a term not exceeding six months, or both.

**Enforcement by local weights and measures authority**
**198A—(1) It is the duty of every local weights and measures authority to enforce within their area the provisions of section 198.**

**(2) The following provisions of the Trade Descriptions Act 1968 apply in relation to the enforcement of that section by such an authority as in relation to the enforcement of that Act—**

**section 27 (power to make test purchases),**
**section 28 (power to enter premises and inspect and seize goods and documents),**
**section 29 (obstruction of authorised officers), and**
**section 33 (compensation for loss, &c. of goods seized).**

**(3) Subsection (1) above does not apply in relation to the enforcement of section 198 in Northern Ireland, but it is the duty of the Department of Economic Development to enforce that section in Northern Ireland.**

For that purpose the provisions of the Trade Descriptions Act 1968 specified in subsection (2) apply as if for the references to a local weights and measures authority and any officer of such an authority there were substituted references to that Department and any of its officers.

(4) Any enactment which authorises the disclosure of information for the purpose of facilitating the enforcement of the Trade Descriptions Act 1968 shall apply as if section 198 were contained in that Act and as if the functions of any person in relation to the enforcement of that section were functions under that Act.

(5) Nothing in this section shall be construed as authorising a local weights and measures authority to bring proceedings in Scotland for an offence.

*General note*
This section added by the Criminal Justice and Public Order Act 1994, s 165(1), (3), as from a day to be appointed.

### 199. Order for delivery up in criminal proceedings

(1) The court before which proceedings are brought against a person for an offence under section 198 may, if satisfied that at the time of his arrest or charge he had in his possession, custody or control in the course of a business an illicit recording of a performance, order that it be delivered up to a person having performers' rights or recording rights in relation to the performance or to such other person as the court may direct.

(2) For this purpose a person shall be treated as charged with an offence—

(a) in England, Wales and Northern Ireland, when he is orally charged or is served with a summons or indictment;
(b) in Scotland, when he is cautioned, charged or served with a complaint or indictment.

(3) An order may be made by the court of its own motion or on the application of the prosecutor (or, in Scotland, the Lord Advocate or procurator-fiscal), and may be made whether or not the person is convicted of the offence, but shall not be made—

(a) after the end of the period specified in section 203 (period after which remedy of delivery up not available), or
(b) if it appears to the court unlikely that any order will be made under section 204 (order as to disposal of illicit recording).

(4) An appeal lies from an order made under this section by a magistrates' court—

(a) in England and Wales, to the Crown Court, and
(b) in Northern Ireland, to the county court;

and in Scotland, where an order has been made under this section, the person from whose possession, custody or control the illicit recording has been removed may, without prejudice to any other form of appeal under any rule of law, appeal against that order in the same manner as against sentence.

(5) A person to whom an illicit recording is delivered up in pursuance of an order under this section shall retain it pending the making of an order, or the decision not to make an order, under section 204.

(6) Nothing in this section affects the powers of the court under section 43 of the Powers of Criminal Courts Act 1973, sections 223 or 436 of the Criminal

Procedure (Scotland) Act 1975 or Article 7 of the Criminal Justice (Northern Ireland) Order 1980 (general provisions as to forfeiture in criminal proceedings).

**200. Search warrants**
(1) Where a justice of the peace (in Scotland, a sheriff or justice of the peace) is satisfied by information on oath given by a constable (in Scotland, by evidence on oath) that there are reasonable grounds for believing—

(a) that an offence under section 198(1)(a), (b) or (d)(iii) (offences of making, importing or distributing illicit recordings) has been or is about to be committed in any premises, and

(b) that evidence that such an offence has been or is about to be committed is in those premises,

he may issue a warrant authorising a constable to enter and search the premises, using such reasonable force as is necessary.

(2) The power conferred by subsection (1) does not, in England and Wales, extend to authorising a search for material of the kinds mentioned in section 9(2) of the Police and Criminal Evidence Act 1984 (certain classes of personal or confidential material).

(3) A warrant under subsection (1)—

(a) may authorise persons to accompany any constable executing the warrant, and

(b) remains in force for 28 days from the date of its issue.

(4) In this section 'premises' includes land, buildings, fixed or moveable structures, vehicles, vessels, aircraft and hovercraft.

**201. False representation of authority to give consent**
(1) It is an offence for a person to represent falsely that he is authorised by any person to give consent for the purposes of this Part in relation to a performance, unless he believes on reasonable grounds that he is so authorised.

(2) A person guilty of an offence under this section is liable on summary conviction to imprisonment for a term not exceeding six months or a fine not exceeding level 5 on the standard scale, or both.

**202. Offence by body corporate: liability of officers**
(1) Where an offence under this Part committed by a body corporate is proved to have been committed with the consent or connivance of a director, manager, secretary or other similar officer of the body, or a person purporting to act in any such capacity, he as well as the body corporate is guilty of the offence and liable to be proceeded against and punished accordingly.

(2) In relation to a body corporate whose affairs are managed by its members 'director' means a member of the body corporate.

*Supplementary provisions with respect to delivery up and seizure*

**203. Period after which remedy of delivery up not available**
(1) An application for an order under section 195 (order for delivery up in civil proceedings) may not be made after the end of the period of six years from the date on which the illicit recording in question was made, subject to the following provisions.

(2)  If during the whole or any part of that period a person entitled to apply for an order—

(a)  is under a disability, or

(b)  is prevented by fraud or concealment from discovering the facts entitling him to apply,

an application may be made by him at any time before the end of the period of six years from the date on which he ceased to be under a disability or, as the case may be, could with reasonable diligence have discovered those facts.

(3)  In subsection (2) 'disability'—

(a)  in England and Wales, has the same meaning as in the Limitation Act 1980;

(b)  in Scotland, means legal disability within the meaning of the Prescription and Limitations (Scotland) Act 1973;

(c)  in Northern Ireland, has the same meaning as in the Statute of Limitation (Northern Ireland) 1958.

(4)  An order under section 199 (order for delivery up in criminal proceedings) shall not, in any case, be made after the end of the period of six years from the date on which the illicit recording in question was made.

## 204.  Order as to disposal of illicit recording

(1)  An application may be made to the court for an order that an illicit recording of a performance delivered up in pursuance of an order under sections 195 or 199, or seized and detained in pursuance of the right conferred under section 196, shall be—

(a)  forfeited to such person having performer's rights or recording rights in relation to the performance as the court may direct, or

(b)  destroyed or otherwise dealt with as the court may think fit,

or for a decision that no such order should be made.

(2)  In considering what order (if any) should be made, the court shall consider whether other remedies available in an action for infringement of the rights conferred by this Part would be adequate to compensate the person or persons entitled to the rights and to protect their interests.

(3)  Provision shall be made by rules of court as to the service of notice on persons having an interest in the recording, and any such person is entitled—

(a)  to appear in proceedings for an order under this section, whether or not he was served with notice, and

(b)  to appeal against any order made, whether or not he appeared;

and an order shall not take effect until the end of the period within which notice of an appeal may be given or, if before the end of that period notice of appeal is duly given, until the final determination or abandonment of the proceedings on the appeal.

(4)  Where there is more than one person interested in a recording, the court shall make such order as it thinks just and may (in particular) direct that the recording be sold, or otherwise dealt with, and the proceeds divided.

(5)  If the court decides that no order should be made under this section, the person in whose possession, custody or control the recording was before being delivered up or seized is entitled to its return.

(6) References in this section to a person having an interest in a recording include any person in whose favour an order could be made in respect of the recording under this section or under sections 114 or 231 of this Act or *section 58C of the Trade Marks Act 1938* **section 19 of the Trade Marks Act 1994** (which make similar provision in relation to infringement of copyright, design right and trade marks).

*General note*
Sub-s (6): words in italics repealed and words in bold type substituted by the Trade Marks Act 1994, s 106(1), Sch 4, para 8(2).

### 205 Jurisdiction of county court and sheriff court

(1) In England, Wales and Northern Ireland a county court may entertain proceedings under—

section 195 (order for delivery up of illicit recording), or
section 204 (order as to disposal of illicit recording),

**save that, in Northern Ireland, a county court may entertain such proceedings only** where the value of the illicit recordings in question does not exceed the county court limit for actions in tort.

(2) In Scotland proceedings for an order under either of those provisions may be brought in the sheriff court.

(3) Nothing in this section shall be construed as affecting the jurisdiction of the High Court or, in Scotland, the Court of Session.

*General note*
Sub-s (1): words in bold type added by the High Court and County Courts Jurisdiction Order 1991, SI 1991 No 724.

*Qualification for protection and extent*

### 206. Qualifying countries, individuals and persons

(1) In this Part—

'qualifying country' means—

    (a) the United Kingdom,
    (b) another Member State of the European Economic Community, or
    (c) to the extent that an Order under section 208 so provides, a country designated under that section as enjoying reciprocal protection;

'qualifying individual' means a citizen or subject of, or an individual resident in, a qualifying country; and
'qualifying person' means a qualifying individual or a body corporate or other body having legal personality which—

    (a) is formed under the law of a part of the United Kingdom or another qualifying country, and
    (b) has in any qualifying country a place of business at which substantial business activity is carried on.

(2) The reference in the definition of 'qualifying individual' to a person's being a citizen or subject of a qualifying country shall be construed—

(a) in relation to the United Kingdom, as a reference to his being a British citizen, and

(b) in relation to a colony of the United Kingdom, as a reference to his being a British Dependent Territories' citizen by connection with that colony.

(3) In determining for the purpose of the definition of 'qualifying person' whether substantial business activity is carried on at a place of business in any country, no account shall be taken of dealings in goods which are at all material times outside that country.

## 207. Countries to which this Part extends

This Part extends to England and Wales, Scotland and Northern Ireland.

## 208. Countries enjoying reciprocal protection

(1) Her Majesty may by Order in Council designate as enjoying reciprocal protection under this Part—

(a) a Convention country, or

(b) a country as to which Her Majesty is satisfied that provision has been or will be made under its law giving adequate protection for British performances.

(2) A 'Convention country' means a country which is a party to a Convention relating to performers' rights to which the United Kingdom is also a party.

(3) A 'British performance' means a performance—

(a) given by an individual who is a British citizen or resident in the United Kingdom, or

(b) taking place in the United Kingdom.

(4) If the law of that country provides adequate protection only for certain descriptions of performance, an Order under subsection (1)(b) designating that country shall contain provision limiting to a corresponding extent the protection afforded by this Part in relation to performances connected with that country.

(5) The power conferred by subsection (1)(b) is exercisable in relation to any of the Channel Islands, the Isle of Man or any colony of the United Kingdom, as in relation to a foreign country.

(6) A statutory instrument containing an Order in Council under this section shall be subject to annulment in pursuance of a resolution of either House of Parliament.

## 209. Territorial waters and the continental shelf

(1) For the purposes of this Part the territorial waters of the United Kingdom shall be treated as part of the United Kingdom.

(2) This Part applies to things done in the United Kingdom sector of the continental shelf on a structure or vessel which is present there for purposes directly connected with the exploration of the sea bed or subsoil or the exploitation of their natural resources as it applies to things done in the United Kingdom.

(3) The United Kingdom sector of the continental shelf means the areas designated by order under section 1(7) of the Continental Shelf Act 1964.

**210. British ships, aircraft and hovercraft**
(1) This Part applies to things done on a British ship, aircraft or hovercraft as it applies to things done in the United Kingdom.
  (2) In this section—
    'British ship' means a ship which is a British ship for the purposes of the Merchant Shipping Acts (see section 2 of the Merchant Shipping Act 1988) otherwise than by virtue of registration in a country outside the United Kingdom; and
    'British aircraft' and 'British hovercraft' mean an aircraft or hovercraft registered in the United Kingdom.

*Interpretation*

**211. Expressions having same meaning as in copyright provisions**
(1) The following expressions have the same meaning in this Part as in Part I (copyright)—

broadcast,
business,
cable programme,
cable programme service,
country,
defendant (in Scotland),
delivery up (in Scotland),
film,
literary work,
published, and
sound recording.

  (2) The provisions of section 6(3) to (5), sections 7(5) and 19(4) (supplementary provisions relating to broadcasting and cable programme services) apply for the purposes of this Part, and in relation to an infringement of the rights conferred by this Part, as they apply for the purposes of Part I and in relation to an infringement of copyright.

**212. Index of defined expressions**
The following Table shows provisions defining or otherwise explaining expressions used in this Part (other than provisions defining or explaining an expression used only in the same section)—

| | |
|---|---|
| broadcast (and related expressions) | section 211 (and section 6) |
| business | section 211(account of 1) |
| | (and section 178) |
| cable programme, cable programme service | |
| (and related expressions) | section 211 (and section 7) |
| country | section 211(1) (and section 178) |
| defendant (in Scotland) | section 211(1) (and section 177) |
| delivery up (in Scotland) | section 211(1) (and section 177) |
| exclusive recording contract | section 185(1) |
| film | section 211(1) (and section 5) |
| illicit recording | section 197 |
| literary work | section 211(1) (and section 3(1)) |

| performance | section 180(2) |
| published | section 211(1) (and section 175) |
| qualifying country | section 206(1) |
| qualifying individual | section 206(1) and (2) |
| qualifying performance | section 181 |
| qualifying person | section 206(1) and (3) |
| recording (of a performance) | section 180(2) |
| recording rights (person having) | section 185(2) and (3) |
| sound recording | section 211(1) (and section 5). |

## PART III
## DESIGN RIGHT

## CHAPTER I
## DESIGN RIGHT IN ORIGINAL DESIGNS

*General note*
See the Design Right (Semiconductor Topographies) Regulations 1989, SI 1989 No 1100 (see Appendix 2, Part D) for modifications to Part III of the Act in relation to semiconductor topographies.

## *Introductory*

**213. Design right**
(1) Design right is a property right which subsists in accordance with this Part in an original design.

(2) In this Part 'design' means the design of any aspect of the shape or configuration (whether internal or external) of the whole or any substantial part of an article.

(3) Design right does not subsist in—

(a) a method or principle of construction,
(b) features of shape or configuration of an article which—

    (i) enable the article to be connected to, or placed in, around or against, another article so that either article may perform its function, or
    (ii) are dependent upon the appearance of another article of which the article is intended by the designer to form an integral part, or

(c) surface decoration.

(4) A design is not 'original' for the purposes of this Part if it is commonplace in the design field in question at the time of its creation.

(5) Design right subsists in a design only if the design qualifies for design right protection by reference to—

(a) the designer or the person by whom the design was commissioned or the designer employed (see sections 218 and 219), or
(b) the person by whom and country in which articles made to the design were first marketed (see section 220),

or in accordance with any Order under section 221 (power to make further provision with respect to qualification).

(6) Design right does not subsist unless and until the design has been recorded in a design document or an article has been made to the design.

(7) Design right does not subsist in a design which was so recorded, or to which an article was made, before the commencement of this Part.

*General note*
Sub-s (5): see also Design Right (Semiconductor Topographies) Regulations 1989, SI 1989 No 1100, reg 4(1).

### 214. The designer
(1) In this Part the 'designer', in relation to a design, means the person who creates it.

(2) In the case of a computer-generated design the person by whom the arrangements necessary for the creation of the design are undertaken shall be taken to be the designer.

### 215. Ownership of design right
(1) The designer is the first owner of any design right in a design which is not created in pursuance of a commission or in the course of employment.

(2) Where a design is created in pursuance of a commission, the person commissioning the design is the first owner of any design right in it.

(3) Where, in a case not falling within subsection (2) a design is created by an employee in the course of his employment, his employer is the first owner of any design right in the design.

(4) If a design qualifies for design right protection by virtue of section 220 (qualification by reference to first marketing of articles made to the design), the above rules do not apply and the person by whom the articles in question are marketed is the first owner of the design right.

*General note*
Section 215 substituted by the Design Right (Semiconductor Topographies) Regulations 1989, SI 1989 No 1100, reg 5 in relation to semiconductor topographies.

### 216. Duration of design right
(1) Design right expires—

    (a) fifteen years from the end of the calendar year in which the design was first recorded in a design document or an article was first made to the design, whichever first occurred, or

    (b) if articles made to the design are made available for sale or hire within five years from the end of that calendar year, ten years from the end of the calendar year in which that first occurred.

(2) The reference in subsection (1) to articles being made available for sale or hire is to their being made so available anywhere in the world by or with the licence of the design right owner.

*General note*
Section 216 substituted by the Design Right (Semiconductor Topographies) Regulations 1989, SI 1989 No 1100, regs 6, 7 in relation to semiconductor topographies.

## *Qualification for design right protection*

### 217. Qualifying individuals and qualifying persons
(1) In this Part—

'qualifying individual' means a citizen or subject of, or an individual habitually resident in, a qualifying country; and

'qualifying person' means a qualifying individual or a body corporate or other body having legal personality which—

(a) is formed under the law of a part of the United Kingdom or another qualifying country, and

(b) has in any qualifying country a place of business at which substantial business activity is carried on.

(2) References in this Part to a qualifying person include the Crown and the government of any other qualifying country.

(3) In this section 'qualifying country' means—

(a) the United Kingdom,

(b) a country to which this Part extends by virtue of an Order under section 255,

(c) another Member State of the European Economic Community, or

(d) to the extent that an Order under section 256 so provides, a country designated under that section as enjoying reciprocal protection.

(4) The reference in the definition of 'qualifying individual' to a person's being a citizen or subject of a qualifying country shall be construed—

(a) in relation to the United Kingdom, as a reference to his being a British citizen, and

(b) in relation to a colony of the United Kingdom, as a reference to his being a British Dependent Territories' citizen by connection with that colony.

(5) In determining for the purpose of the definition of 'qualifying person' whether substantial business activity is carried on at a place of business in any country, no account shall be taken of dealings in goods which are at all material times outside that country.

*General note*
See also the Design Right (Semiconductor Topographies) Regulations 1989, SI 1989 No 1100, reg 4(2) which substitutes s 217 in relation to semiconductor topographies.

## 218. Qualification by reference to designer

(1) This section applies to a design which is not created in pursuance of a commission or in the course of employment.

(2) A design to which this section applies qualifies for design right protection if the designer is a qualifying individual or, in the case of a computer-generated design, a qualifying person.

(3) A joint design to which this section applies qualifies for design right protection if any of the designers is a qualifying individual or, as the case may be, a qualifying person.

(4) Where a joint design qualifies for design right protection under this section, only those designers who are qualifying individuals or qualifying persons are entitled to design right under section 215(1) (first ownership of design right: entitlement of designer).

*General note*
See the Design Right (Semiconductor Topographies) Regulations 1989, SI 1989 No 1100, reg 4(3) for modifications in relation to semiconductor topographies.

## 219. Qualification by reference to commissioner or employer

(1) A design qualifies for design right protection if it is created in pursuance of a commission from, or in the course of employment with, a qualifying person.

(2) In the case of a joint commission or joint employment a design qualifies for design right protection if any of the commissioners or employers is a qualifying person.

(3) Where a design which is jointly commissioned or created in the course of joint employment qualifies for design right protection under this section, only those commissioners or employers who are qualifying persons are entitled to design right under section 215(2) or (3) (first ownership of design right: entitlement of commissioner or employer).

*General note*
See the Design Right (Semiconductor Topographies) Regulations 1989, SI 1989 No 1100, reg 4(3) for modifications in relation to semiconductor topographies.

## 220. Qualification by reference to first marketing

(1) A design which does not qualify for design right protection under sections 218 or 219 (qualification by reference to designer, commissioner or employer) qualifies for design right protection if the first marketing of articles made to the design—

    (a) is by a qualifying person who is exclusively authorised to put such articles on the market in the United Kingdom, and

    (b) takes place in the United Kingdom, another country to which this Part extends by virtue of an Order under section 255, or another member State of the European Economic Community.

(2) If the first marketing of articles made to the design is done jointly by two or more persons, the design qualifies for design right protection if any of those persons meets the requirements specified in subsection (1)(a).

(3) In such a case only the persons who meet those requirements are entitled to design right under section 215(4) (first ownership of design right: entitlement of first marketer of articles made to the design).

(4) In subsection (1)(a) 'exclusively authorised' refers—

    (a) to authorisation by the person who would have been first owner of design right as designer, commissioner of the design or employer of the designer if he had been a qualifying person, or by a person lawfully claiming under such a person, and

    (b) to exclusivity capable of being enforced by legal proceedings in the United Kingdom.

*General note*
Section 220(1) substituted and (4) modified by the Design Right (Semiconductor Topographies) Regulations 1989, SI 1989 No 1100, reg 4(4) in relation to semiconductor topographies.

## 221. Power to make further provision as to qualification

(1) Her Majesty may, with a view to fulfilling an international obligation of the United Kingdom, by Order in Council provide that a design qualifies for design right protection if such requirements as are specified in the Order are met.

(2) An Order may make different provision for different descriptions of design or article; and may make such consequential modifications of the operation of

section 215 (ownership of design right) and sections 218 to 220 (other means of qualification) as appear to Her Majesty to be appropriate.

(3) A statutory instrument containing an Order in Council under this section shall be subject to annulment in pursuance of a resolution of either House of Parliament.

## *Dealings with design right*

### 222. Assignment and licences

(1) Design right is transmissible by assignment, by testamentary disposition or by operation of law, as personal or moveable property.

(2) An assignment or other transmission of design right may be partial, that is, limited so as to apply—

(a) to one or more, but not all, of the things the design right owner has the exclusive right to do;

(b) to part, but not the whole, of the period for which the right is to subsist.

(3) An assignment of design right is not effective unless it is in writing signed by or on behalf of the assignor.

(4) A licence granted by the owner of design right is binding on every successor in title to his interest in the right, except a purchaser in good faith for valuable consideration and without notice (actual or constructive) of the licence or a person deriving title from such a purchaser; and references in this Part to doing anything with, or without, the licence of the design right owner shall be construed accordingly.

### 223. Prospective ownership of design right

(1) Where by an agreement made in relation to future design right, and signed by or on behalf of the prospective owner of the design right, the prospective owner purports to assign the future design right (wholly or partially) to another person, then if, on the right coming into existence, the assignee or another person claiming under him would be entitled as against all other persons to require the right to be vested in him, the right shall vest in him by virtue of this section.

(2) In this section—

'future design right' means design right which will or may come into existence in respect of a future design or class of designs or on the occurrence of a future event; and

'prospective owner' shall be construed accordingly, and includes a person who is prospectively entitled to design right by virtue of such an agreement as is mentioned in subsection (1).

(3) A licence granted by a prospective owner of design right is binding on every successor in title to his interest (or prospective interest) in the right, except a purchaser in good faith for valuable consideration and without notice (actual or constructive) of the licence or a person deriving title from such a purchaser; and references in this Part to doing anything with, or without, the licence of the design right owner shall be construed accordingly.

### 224. Assignment of right in registered design presumed to carry with it design right

Where a design consisting of a design in which design right subsists is registered under the Registered Designs Act 1949 and the proprietor of the registered design is also the design right owner, an assignment of the right in the registered design shall be taken to be also an assignment of the design right, unless a contrary intention appears.

### 225. Exclusive licences

(1) In this Part an 'exclusive licence' means a licence in writing signed by or on behalf of the design right owner authorising the licensee to the exclusion of all other persons, including the person granting the licence, to exercise a right which would otherwise be exercisable exclusively by the design right owner.

(2) The licensee under an exclusive licence has the same rights against any successor in title who is bound by the licence as he has against the person granting the licence.

## CHAPTER II
## RIGHTS OF DESIGN RIGHT OWNER AND REMEDIES

*Infringement of design right*

### 226. Primary infringement of design right

(1) The owner of design right in a design has the exclusive right to reproduce the design for commercial purposes—

(a) by making articles to that design, or
(b) by making a design document recording the design for the purpose of enabling such articles to be made.

(2) Reproduction of a design by making articles to the design means copying the design so as to produce articles exactly or substantially to that design, and references in this Part to making articles to a design shall be construed accordingly.

(3) Design right is infringed by a person who without the licence of the design right owner does, or authorises another to do, anything which by virtue of this section is the exclusive right of the design right owner.

(4) For the purposes of this section reproduction may be direct or indirect, and it is immaterial whether any intervening acts themselves infringe the design right.

(5) This section has effect subject to the provisions of Chapter III (exceptions to rights of design right owner).

*General note*
Section 226(1) substituted and s 226(1A) added by the Design Right (Semiconductor Topographies) Regulations 1989, SI 1989 No 1100, reg 8(1) in relation to semiconductor topographies. See also ibid reg 8(4).

### 227. Secondary infringement: importing or dealing with infringing article

(1) Design right is infringed by a person who, without the licence of the design right owner—

(a) imports into the United Kingdom for commercial purposes, or
(b) has in his possession for commercial purposes, or
(c) sells, lets for hire, or offers or exposes for sale or hire, in the course of a business,

an article which is, and which he knows or has reason to believe is, an infringing article.

(2) This section has effect subject to the provisions of Chapter III (exceptions to rights of design right owner).

*General note*
Section 227 modified by the Design Right (Semiconductor Topographies) Regulations 1989, SI 1989 No 1100, reg 8(2) in relation to semiconductor topographies.

## 228. Meaning of 'infringing article'

(1) In this Part 'infringing article', in relation to a design, shall be construed in accordance with this section.

(2) An article is an infringing article if its making to that design was an infringement of design right in the design.

(3) An article is also an infringing article if—

(a) it has been or is proposed to be imported into the United Kingdom, and
(b) its making to that design in the United Kingdom would have been an infringement of design right in the design or a breach of an exclusive licence agreement relating to the design.

(4) Where it is shown that an article is made to a design in which design right subsists or has subsisted at any time, it shall be presumed until the contrary is proved that the article was made at a time when design right subsisted.

(5) Nothing in subsection (3) shall be construed as applying to an article which may lawfully be imported into the United Kingdom by virtue of any enforceable Community right within the meaning of section 2(1) of the European Communities Act 1972.

(6) The expression 'infringing article' does not include a design document, notwithstanding that its making was or would have been an infringement of design right.

*General note*
Section 228(6) does not apply to semiconductor topographies: Design Right (Semiconductor Topographies) Regulations 1989, SI 1989 No 1100, reg 8(3).

## *Remedies for infringement*

## 229. Rights and remedies of design right owner

(1) An infringement of design right is actionable by the design right owner.

(2) In an action for infringement of design right all such relief by way of damages, injunctions, accounts or otherwise is available to the plaintiff as is available in respect of the infringement of any other property right.

(3) The court may in an action for infringement of design right, having regard to all the circumstances and in particular to—

(a) the flagrancy of the infringement, and
(b) any benefit accruing to the defendant by reason of the infringement,

award such additional damages as the justice of the case may require.

(4) This section has effect subject to section 233 (innocent infringement).

## 230. Order for delivery up

(1) Where a person—

(a) has in his possession, custody or control for commercial purposes an infringing article, or

(b)  has in his possession, custody or control anything specifically designed or adapted for making articles to a particular design, knowing or having reason to believe that it has been or is to be used to make an infringing article,

the owner of the design right in the design in question may apply to the court for an order that the infringing article or other thing be delivered up to him or to such other person as the court may direct.

(2)  An application shall not be made after the end of the period specified in the following provisions of this section; and no order shall be made unless the court also makes, or it appears to the court that there are grounds for making, an order under section 231 (order as to disposal of infringing article, etc).

(3)  An application for an order under this section may not be made after the end of the period of six years from the date on which the article or thing in question was made, subject to subsection (4).

(4)  If during the whole or any part of that period the design right owner—

(a)  is under a disability, or
(b)  is prevented by fraud or concealment from discovering the facts entitling him to apply for an order,

an application may be made at any time before the end of the period of six years from the date on which he ceased to be under a disability or, as the case may be, could with reasonable diligence have discovered those facts.

(5)  In subsection (4) 'disability'—

(a)  in England and Wales, has the same meaning as in the Limitation Act 1980;
(b)  in Scotland, means legal disability within the meaning of the Prescription and Limitation (Scotland) Act 1973;
(c)  in Northern Ireland, has the same meaning as in the Statute of Limitations (Northern Ireland) 1958.

(6)  A person to whom an infringing article or other thing is delivered up in pursuance of an order under this section shall, if an order under section 231 is not made, retain it pending the making of an order, or the decision not to make an order, under that section.

(7)  Nothing in this section affects any other power of the court.

## 231.  Order as to disposal of infringing articles, etc

(1)  An application may be made to the court for an order that an infringing article or other thing delivered up in pursuance of an order under section 230 shall be—

(a)  forfeited to the design right owner, or
(b)  destroyed or otherwise dealt with as the court may think fit,

or for a decision that no such order should be made.

(2)  In considering what order (if any) should be made, the court shall consider whether other remedies available in an action for infringement of design right would be adequate to compensate the design right owner and to protect his interests.

(3)  Provision shall be made by rules of court as to the service of notice on persons having an interest in the article or other thing, and any such person is entitled—

(a) to appear in proceedings for an order under this section, whether or not he was served with notice, and

(b) to appeal against any order made, whether or not he appeared;

and an order shall not take effect until the end of the period within which notice of an appeal may be given or, if before the end of that period notice of appeal is duly given, until the final determination or abandonment of the proceedings on the appeal.

(4) Where there is more than one person interested in an article or other thing, the court shall make such order as it thinks just and may (in particular) direct that the thing be sold, or otherwise dealt with, and the proceeds divided.

(5) If the court decides that no order should be made under this section, the person in whose possession, custody or control the article or other thing was before being delivered up or seized is entitled to its return.

(6) References in this section to a person having an interest in an article or other thing include any person in whose favour an order could be made in respect of it under this section or under sections 114 or 204 of this Act or *section 58C of the Trade Marks Act 1938* **section 19 of the Trade Marks Act 1994** (which make similar provision in relation to infringement of copyright, rights in performances and trade marks).

*General note*
Sub-s (6): words in italics repealed and words in bold type substituted by the Trade Marks Act 1994, s 106(1), Sch 4, para 8(2).

## 232. Jurisdiction of county court and sheriff court

(1) In England, Wales and Northern Ireland a county court may entertain proceedings under—

section 230 (order for delivery up of infringing article, etc),

section 231 (order as to disposal of infringing article, etc), or

section 235(5) (application by exclusive licensee having concurrent rights),

**save that, in Northern Ireland, a county court may entertain such proceedings only** where the value of the infringing articles and other things in question does not exceed the county court limit for actions in tort.

(2) In Scotland proceedings for an order under any of those provisions may be brought in the sheriff court.

(3) Nothing in this section shall be construed as affecting the jurisdiction of the High Court or, in Scotland, the Court of Session.

*General note*
Sub-s (1): words in bold type added by the High Court and County Courts Jurisdiction Order 1991, SI 1991 No 724.

## 233. Innocent infringement

(1) Where in an action for infringement of design right brought by virtue of section 226 (primary infringement) it is shown that at the time of the infringement the defendant did not know, and had no reason to believe, that design right subsisted in the design to which the action relates, the plaintiff is not entitled to damages against him, but without prejudice to any other remedy.

(2) Where in an action for infringement of design right brought by virtue of section 227 (secondary infringement) a defendant shows that the infringing article was innocently acquired by him or a predecessor in title of his, the only remedy

available against him in respect of the infringement is damages not exceeding a reasonable royalty in respect of the act complained of.

(3) In subsection (2) 'innocently acquired' means that the person acquiring the article did not know and had no reason to believe that it was an infringing article.

## 234. Rights and remedies of exclusive licensee

(1) An exclusive licensee has, except against the design right owner, the same rights and remedies in respect of matters occurring after the grant of the licence as if the licence had been an assignment.

(2) His rights and remedies are concurrent with those of the design right owner; and references in the relevant provisions of this Part to the design right owner shall be construed accordingly.

(3) In an action brought by an exclusive licensee by virtue of this section a defendant may avail himself of any defence which would have been available to him if the action had been brought by the design right owner.

## 235. Exercise of concurrent rights

(1) Where an action for infringement of design right brought by the design right owner or an exclusive licensee relates (wholly or partly) to an infringement in respect of which they have concurrent rights of action, the design right owner or, as the case may be, the exclusive licensee may not, without the leave of the court, proceed with the action unless the other is either joined as a plaintiff or added as a defendant.

(2) A design right owner or exclusive licensee who is added as a defendant in pursuance of subsection (1) is not liable for any costs in the action unless he takes part in the proceedings.

(3) The above provisions do not affect the granting of interlocutory relief on the application of the design right owner or an exclusive licensee.

(4) Where an action for infringement of design right is brought which relates (wholly or partly) to an infringement in respect of which the design right owner and an exclusive licensee have concurrent rights of action—

(a) the court shall, in assessing damages, take into account—

(i) the terms of the licence, and
(ii) any pecuniary remedy already awarded or available to either of them in respect of the infringement;

(b) no account of profits shall be directed if an award of damages has been made, or an account of profits has been directed, in favour of the other of them in respect of the infringement; and

(c) the court shall if an account of profits is directed apportion the profits between them as the court considers just, subject to any agreement between them;

and these provisions apply whether or not the design right owner and the exclusive licensee are both parties to the action.

(5) The design right owner shall notify any exclusive licensee having concurrent rights before applying for an order under section 230 (order for delivery up of infringing article, etc); and the court may on the application of the licensee make such order under that section as it thinks fit having regard to the terms of the licence.

## CHAPTER III
## EXCEPTIONS TO RIGHTS OF DESIGN RIGHT OWNERS

### *Infringement of copyright*

### 236. Infringement of copyright

Where copyright subsists in a work which consists of or includes a design in which design right subsists, it is not an infringement of design right in the design to do anything which is an infringement of the copyright in that work.

*General note*
See also the Design Right (Semiconductor Topographies) Regulations 1989, SI 1989 No 1100, regs 8(4), (5) in relation to semiconductor topographies.

### *Availability of licences of right*

### 237. Licences available in last five years of design right

(1) Any person is entitled as of right to a licence to do in the last five years of the design right term anything which would otherwise infringe the design right.

(2) The terms of the licence shall, in default of agreement, be settled by the comptroller.

(3) The Secretary of State may if it appears to him necessary in order to—

(a) comply with an international obligation of the United Kingdom, or
(b) secure or maintain reciprocal protection for British designs in other countries,

by order exclude from the operation of subsection (1) designs of a description specified in the order or designs applied to articles of a description so specified.

(4) An order shall be made by statutory instrument; and no order shall be made unless a draft of it has been laid before and approved by a resolution of each House of Parliament.

*General note*
Section 237 does not apply to semiconductor topographies: Design Right (Semiconductor Topographies) Regulations 1989, SI 1989 No 1100, reg 9.

### 238. Powers exercisable for protection of the public interest

(1) Where the matters specified in a report of the Monopolies and Mergers Commission as being those which in the Commission's opinion operate, may be expected to operate or have operated against the public interest include—

(a) conditions in licences granted by a design right owner restricting the use of the design by the licensee or the right of the design right owner to grant other licences, or
(b) a refusal of a design right owner to grant licences on reasonable terms,

the powers conferred by Part I of Schedule 8 to the Fair Trading Act 1973 (powers exercisable for purpose of remedying or preventing adverse effects specified in report of Commission) include power to cancel or modify those conditions and, instead or in addition, to provide that licences in respect of the design right shall be available as of right.

(2) The references in sections 56(2) and 73(2) of that Act, and sections 10(2)(b)

and 12(5) of the Competition Act 1980, to the powers specified in that Part of that Schedule shall be construed accordingly.

(3) The terms of a licence available by virtue of this section shall, in default of agreement, be settled by the comptroller.

### 239. Undertaking to take licence of right in infringement proceedings

(1) If in proceedings for infringement of design right in a design in respect of which a licence is available as of right under sections 237 or 238 the defendant undertakes to take a licence on such terms as may be agreed or, in default of agreement, settled by the comptroller under that section—

(a) no injunction shall be granted against him,

(b) no order for delivery up shall be made under section 230, and

(c) the amount recoverable against him by way of damages or on an account of profits shall not exceed double the amount which would have been payable by him as licensee if such a licence on those terms had been granted before the earliest infringement.

(2) An undertaking may be given at any time before final order in the proceedings, without any admission of liability.

(3) Nothing in this section affects the remedies available in respect of an infringement committed before licences of right were available.

## Crown use of designs

### 240. Crown use of designs

(1) A government department, or a person authorised in writing by a government department, may without the licence of the design right owner—

(a) do anything for the purpose of supplying articles for the services of the Crown, or

(b) dispose of articles no longer required for the services of the Crown;

and nothing done by virtue of this section infringes the design right.

(2) References in this Part to 'the services of the Crown' are to—

(a) the defence of the realm,

(b) foreign defence purposes, and

(c) health service purposes.

(3) The reference to the supply of articles for 'foreign defence purposes' is to their supply—

(a) for the defence of a country outside the realm in pursuance of an agreement or arrangement to which the government of that country and Her Majesty's Government in the United Kingdom are parties; or

(b) for use by armed forces operating in pursuance of a resolution of the United Nations or one of its organs.

(4) The reference to the supply of articles for 'health service purposes' are to their supply for the purpose of providing—

(a) pharmaceutical services,

(b) general medical services, or

(c) general dental services,

that is, services of those kinds under Part II of the National Health Service Act 1977, Part II of the National Health Service (Scotland) Act 1978 or the corresponding provisions of the law in force in Northern Ireland.

(5) In this Part—

'Crown use', in relation to a design, means the doing of anything by virtue of this section which would otherwise be an infringement of design right in the design; and

'the government department concerned', in relation to such use, means the government department by whom or on whose authority the act was done.

(6) The authority of a government department in respect of Crown use of a design may be given to a person either before or after the use and whether or not he is authorised, directly or indirectly, by the design right owner to do anything in relation to the design.

(7) A person acquiring anything sold in the exercise of powers conferred by this section, and any person claiming under him, may deal with it in the same manner as if the design right were held on behalf of the Crown.

## 241. Settlement of terms for Crown use

(1) Where Crown use is made of a design, the government department concerned shall—

(a) notify the design right owner as soon as practicable, and

(b) give him such information as to the extent of the use as he may from time to time require,

unless it appears to the department that it would be contrary to the public interest to do so or the identity of the design right owner cannot be ascertained on reasonable inquiry.

(2) Crown use of a design shall be on such terms as, either before or after the use, are agreed between the government department concerned and the design right owner with the approval of the Treasury or, in default of agreement, are determined by the court.

In the application of this subsection to Northern Ireland the reference to the Treasury shall, where the government department referred to in that subsection is a Northern Ireland department, be construed as a reference to the Department of Finance and Personnel.

(3) Where the identity of the design right owner cannot be ascertained on reasonable inquiry, the government department concerned may apply to the court who may order that no royalty or other sum shall be payable in respect of Crown use of the design until the owner agrees terms with the department or refers the matter to the court for determination.

## 242. Rights of third parties in case of Crown use

(1) The provisions of any licence, assignment or agreement made between the design right owner (or anyone deriving title from him or from whom he derives title) and any person other than a government department are of no effect in relation to Crown use of a design, or any act incidental to Crown use, so far as they—

(a) restrict or regulate anything done in relation to the design, or the use of any model, document or other information relating to it, or

(b) provide for the making of payments in respect of, or calculated by reference to such use;

and the copying or issuing to the public of copies of any such model or document in connection with the thing done, or any such use, shall be deemed not to be an infringement of any copyright in the model or document.

(2) Subsection (1) shall not be construed as authorising the disclosure of any such model, document or information in contravention of the licence, assignment or agreement.

(3) Where an exclusive licence is in force in respect of the design—

(a) if the licence was granted for royalties—

(i) any agreement between the design right owner and a government department under section 241 (settlement of terms for Crown use) requires the consent of the licensee, and

(ii) the licensee is entitled to recover from the design right owner such part of the payment for Crown use as may be agreed between them or, in default of agreement, determined by the court;

(b) if the licence was granted otherwise than for royalties—

(i) section 241 applies in relation to anything done which but for section 240 (Crown use) and subsection (1) above would be an infringement of the rights of the licensee with the substitution for references to the design right owner of references to the licensee, and

(ii) section 241 does not apply in relation to anything done by the licensee by virtue of an authority given under section 240.

(4) Where the design right has been assigned to the design right owner in consideration of royalties—

(a) section 241 applies in relation to Crown use of the design as if the references to the design right owner included the assignor, and any payment for Crown use shall be divided between them in such proportion as may be agreed or, in default of agreement, determined by the court; and

(b) section 241 applies in relation to any act incidental to Crown use as it applies in relation to Crown use of the design.

(5) Where any model, document or other information relating to a design is used in connection with Crown use of the design, or any act incidental to Crown use, section 241 applies to the use of the model, document or other information with the substitution for the references to the design right owner of references to the person entitled to the benefit of any provision of an agreement rendered inoperative by subsection (1) above.

(6) In this section—

'act incidental to Crown use' means anything done for the services of the Crown to the order of a government department by the design right owner in respect of a design;

'payment for Crown use' means such amount as is payable by the government department concerned by virtue of section 241; and

'royalties' includes any benefit determined by reference to the use of the design.

**243. Crown use: compensation for loss of profit**
(1) Where Crown use is made of a design, the government department concerned shall pay—

(a) to the design right owner, or
(b) if there is an exclusive licence in force in respect of the design, to the exclusive licensee,

compensation for any loss resulting from his not being awarded a contract to supply the articles made to the design.

(2) Compensation is payable only to the extent that such a contract could have been fulfilled from his existing manufacturing capacity; but is payable notwithstanding the existence of circumstances rendering him ineligible for the award of such a contract.

(3) In determining the loss, regard shall be had to the profit which would have been made on such a contract and to the extent to which any manufacturing capacity was underused.

(4) No compensation is payable in respect of any failure to secure contracts for the supply of articles made to the design otherwise than for the services of the Crown.

(5) The amount payable shall, if not agreed between the design right owner or licensee and the government department concerned with the approval of the Treasury, be determined by the court on a reference under section 252; and it is in addition to any amount payable under sections 241 or 242.

(6) In the application of this section to Northern Ireland, the reference in subsection (5) to the Treasury shall, where the government department concerned is a Northern Ireland department, be construed as a reference to the Department of Finance and Personnel.

**244. Special provision for Crown use during emergency**
(1) During a period of emergency the powers exercisable in relation to a design by virtue of section 240 (Crown use) include power to do any act which would otherwise be an infringement of design right for any purpose which appears to the government department concerned necessary or expedient—

(a) for the efficient prosecution of any war in which Her Majesty may be engaged;
(b) for the maintenance of supplies and services essential to the life of the community;
(c) for securing a sufficiency of supplies and services essential to the well-being of the community;
(d) for promoting the productivity of industry, commerce and agriculture;
(e) for fostering and directing exports and reducing imports, or imports of any classes, from all or any countries and for redressing the balance of trade;
(f) generally for ensuring that the whole resources of the community are available for use, and are used, in a manner best calculated to serve the interests of the community; or
(g) for assisting the relief of suffering and the restoration and distribution of essential supplies and services in any country outside the United Kingdom which is in grave distress as the result of war.

(2) References in this Part to the services of the Crown include, as respects a

period of emergency, those purposes; and references to 'Crown use' include any act which would apart from this section be an infringement of design right.

(3) In this section 'period of emergency' means a period beginning with such date as may be declared by Order in Council to be the beginning, and ending with such date as may be so declared to be the end, of a period of emergency for the purposes of this section.

(4) No Order in Council under this section shall be submitted to Her Majesty unless a draft of it has been laid before and approved by a resolution of each House of Parliament.

## *General*

### 245. Power to provide for further exceptions

(1) The Secretary of State may if it appears to him necessary in order to—

(a) comply with an international obligation of the United Kingdom, or
(b) secure or maintain reciprocal protection for British designs in other countries,

by order provide that acts of a description specified in the order do not infringe design right.

(2) An order may make different provision for different descriptions of design or article.

(3) An order shall be made by statutory instrument and no order shall be made unless a draft of it has been laid before and approved by a resolution of each House of Parliament.

## CHAPTER IV
## JURISDICTION OF THE COMPTROLLER AND THE COURT

## *Jurisdiction of the comptroller*

### 246. Jurisdiction to decide matters relating to design right

(1) A party to a dispute as to any of the following matters may refer the dispute to the comptroller for his decision—

(a) the subsistence of design right,
(b) the term of design right, or
(c) the identity of the person in whom design right first vested;

and the comptroller's decision on the reference is binding on the parties to the dispute.

(2) No other court or tribunal shall decide any such matter except—

(a) on a reference or appeal from the comptroller,
(b) in infringement or other proceedings in which the issue arises incidentally, or
(c) in proceedings brought with the agreement of the parties or the leave of the comptroller.

(3) The comptroller has jurisdiction to decide any incidental question of fact or law arising in the course of a reference under this section.

**247. Application to settle terms of licence of right**

(1) A person requiring a licence which is available as of right by virtue of—

    (a)  section 237 (licences available in last five years of design right), or

    (b)  an order under section 238 (licences made available in the public interest),

may apply to the comptroller to settle the terms of the licence.

(2)  No application for the settlement of the terms of a licence available by virtue of section 237 may be made earlier than one year before the earliest date on which the licence may take effect under that section.

(3)  The terms of a licence settled by the comptroller shall authorise the licensee to do—

    (a)  in the case of licence available by virtue of section 237, everything which would be an infringement of the design right in the absence of a licence;

    (b)  in the case of a licence available by virtue of section 238, everything in respect of which a licence is so available.

(4)  In settling the terms of a licence the comptroller shall have regard to such factors as may be prescribed by the Secretary of State by order made by statutory instrument.

(5)  No such order shall be made unless a draft of it has been laid before and approved by a resolution of each House of Parliament.

(6)  Where the terms of a licence are settled by the comptroller, the licence has effect—

    (a)  in the case of an application in respect of a licence available by virtue of section 237 made before the earliest date on which the licence may take effect under that section, from that date;

    (b)  in any other case, from the date on which the application to the comptroller was made.

**248. Settlement of terms where design right owner unknown**

(1)  This section applies where a person making an application under section 247 (settlement of terms of licence of right) is unable on reasonable inquiry to discover the identity of the design right owner.

(2)  The comptroller may in settling the terms of the licence order that the licence shall be free of any obligation as to royalties or other payments.

(3)  If such an order is made the design right owner may apply to the comptroller to vary the terms of the licence with effect from the date on which his application is made.

(4)  If the terms of a licence are settled by the comptroller and it is subsequently established that a licence was not available as of right, the licensee shall not be liable in damages for, or for an account of profits in respect of, anything done before he was aware of any claim by the design right owner that a licence was not available.

**249. Appeals as to terms of licence of right**

(1)  An appeal lies from any decision of the comptroller under sections 247 or 248 (settlement of terms of licence of right) to the Appeal Tribunal constituted under section 28 of the Registered Designs Act 1949.

(2)  Section 28 of that Act applies to appeals from the comptroller under this

section as it applies to appeals from the registrar under that Act; but rules made under that section may make different provision for appeals under this section.

## 250. Rules

(1) The Secretary of State may make rules for regulating the procedure to be followed in connection with any proceeding before the comptroller under this Part.

(2) Rules may, in particular, make provision—

(a) prescribing forms;

(b) requiring fees to be paid;

(c) authorising the rectification of irregularities of procedure;

(d) regulating the mode of giving evidence and empowering the comptroller to compel the attendance of witnesses and the discovery of and production of documents;

(e) providing for the appointment of advisers to assist the comptroller in proceedings before him;

(f) prescribing time limits for doing anything required to be done (and providing for the alteration of any such limit); and

(g) empowering the comptroller to award costs and to direct how, to what party and from what parties, costs are to be paid.

(3) Rules prescribing fees require the consent of the Treasury.

(4) The remuneration of an adviser appointed to assist the comptroller shall be determined by the Secretary of State with the consent of the Treasury and shall be defrayed out of money provided by Parliament.

(5) Rules shall be made by statutory instrument which shall be subject to annulment in pursuance of a resolution of either House of Parliament.

## *Jurisdiction of the court*

## 251. References and appeals on design right matters

(1) In any proceedings before him under section 246 (reference of matter relating to design right), the comptroller may at any time order the whole proceedings or any question or issue (whether of fact or law) to be referred, on such terms as he may direct, to the High Court or, in Scotland, the Court of Session.

(2) The comptroller shall make such an order if the parties to the proceedings agree that he should do so.

(3) On a reference under this section the court may exercise any power available to the comptroller by virtue of this Part as respects the matter referred to it and, following its determination, may refer any matter back to the comptroller.

(4) An appeal lies from any decision of the comptroller in proceedings before him under section 246 (decisions on matters relating to design right) to the High Court or, in Scotland, the Court of Session.

## 252. Reference of disputes relating to Crown use

(1) A dispute as to any matter which falls to be determined by the court in default of agreement under—

(a) section 241 (settlement of terms for Crown use),

(b) section 242 (rights of third parties in case of Crown use), or

(c) section 243 (Crown use: compensation for loss of profit),

may be referred to the court by any party to the dispute.

(2) In determining a dispute between a government department and any person as to the terms for Crown use of a design the court shall have regard to—

  (a) any sums which that person or a person from whom he derives title has received or is entitled to receive, directly or indirectly, from any government department in respect of the design; and

  (b) whether that person or a person from whom he derives title has in the court's opinion without reasonable cause failed to comply with a request of the department for the use of the design on reasonable terms.

(3) One of two or more joint owners of design right may, without the concurrence of the others, refer a dispute to the court under this section, but shall not do so unless the others are made parties; and none of those others is liable for any costs unless he takes part in the proceedings.

(4) Where the consent of an exclusive licensee is required by section 242(3)(a)(i) to the settlement by agreement of the terms for Crown use of a design, a determination by the court of the amount of any payment to be made for such use is of no effect unless the licensee has been notified of the reference and given an opportunity to be heard.

(5) On the reference of a dispute as to the amount recoverable as mentioned in section 242(3)(a)(ii) (right of exclusive licensee to recover part of amount payable to design right owner) the court shall determine what is just having regard to any expenditure incurred by the licensee—

  (a) in developing the design, or

  (b) in making payments to the design right owner in consideration of the licence (other than royalties or other payments determined by reference to the use of the design).

(6) In this section 'the court' means—

  (a) in England and Wales, the High Court or any patents county court having jurisdiction by virtue of an order under section 287 of this Act,

  (b) in Scotland, the Court of Session, and

  (c) in Northern Ireland, the High Court.

## CHAPTER V
## MISCELLANEOUS AND GENERAL

*Miscellaneous*

### 253. Remedy for groundless threats of infringement proceedings

(1) Where a person threatens another person with proceedings for infringement of design right, a person aggrieved by the threats may bring an action against him claiming—

  (a) a declaration to the effect that the threats are unjustifiable;

  (b) an injunction against the continuance of the threats;

  (c) damages in respect of any loss which he has sustained by the threats.

(2) If the plaintiff proves that the threats were made and that he is a person aggrieved by them, he is entitled to the relief claimed unless the defendant shows

that the acts in respect of which proceedings were threatened did constitute, or if done would have constituted, an infringement of the design right concerned.

(3) Proceedings may not be brought under this section in respect of a threat to bring proceedings for an infringement alleged to consist of making or importing anything.

(4) Mere notification that a design is protected by design right does not constitute a threat of proceedings for the purposes of this section.

**254. Licensee under licence of right not to claim connection with design right owner**

(1) A person who has a licence in respect of a design by virtue of section 237 or 238 (licences of right) shall not, without the consent of the design right owner—

(a) apply to goods which he is marketing, or proposes to market, in reliance on that licence a trade description indicating that he is the licensee of the design right owner, or

(b) use any such trade description in an advertisement in relation to such goods.

(2) A contravention of subsection (1) is actionable by the design right owner.

(3) In this section 'trade description', the reference to applying a trade description to goods and 'advertisement' have the same meaning as in the Trade Descriptions Act 1968.

*Extent of operation of this Part*

**255. Countries to which this Part extends**

(1) This Part extends to England and Wales, Scotland and Northern Ireland.

(2) Her Majesty may by Order in Council direct that this Part shall extend, subject to such exceptions and modifications as may be specified in the Order, to—

(a) any of the Channel Islands,

(b) the Isle of Man, or

(c) any colony.

(3) That power includes power to extend, subject to such exceptions and modifications as may be specified in the Order, any Order in Council made under section 221 (further provision as to qualification for design right protection) or section 256 (countries enjoying reciprocal protection).

(4) The legislature of a country to which this Part has been extended may modify or add to the provisions of this Part, in their operation as part of the law of that country, as the legislature may consider necessary to adapt the provisions to the circumstances of that country; but not so as to deny design right protection in a case where it would otherwise exist.

(5) Where a country to which this Part extends ceases to be a colony of the United Kingdom, it shall continue to be treated as such a country for the purposes of this Part until—

(a) an Order in Council is made under section 256 designating it as a country enjoying reciprocal protection, or

(b) an Order in Council is made declaring that it shall cease to be so treated by reason of the fact that the provisions of this Part as part of the law of that country have been amended or repealed.

(6) A statutory instrument containing an Order in Council under subsection (5)(b) shall be subject to annulment in pursuance of a resolution of either House of Parliament.

### 256. Countries enjoying reciprocal protection

(1) Her Majesty may, if it appears to Her that the law of a country provides adequate protection for British designs, by Order in Council designate that country as one enjoying reciprocal protection under this Part.

(2) If the law of a country provides adequate protection only for certain classes of British design, or only for designs applied to certain classes of article, any Order designating that country shall contain provision limiting, to a corresponding extent, the protection afforded by this Part in relation to designs connected with that country.

(3) An Order under this section shall be subject to annulment in pursuance of a resolution of either House of Parliament.

### 257. Territorial waters and the continental shelf

(1) For the purposes of this Part the territorial waters of the United Kingdom shall be treated as part of the United Kingdom.

(2) This Part applies to things done in the United Kingdom sector of the continental shelf on a structure or vessel which is present there for purposes directly connected with the exploration of the sea bed or subsoil or the exploitation of their natural resources as it applies to things done in the United Kingdom.

(3) The United Kingdom sector of the continental shelf means the areas designated by order under section 1(7) of the Continental Shelf Act 1964.

*Interpretation*

### 258. Construction of references to design right owner

(1) Where different persons are (whether in consequence of a partial assignment or otherwise) entitled to different aspects of design right in a work, the design right owner for any purpose of this Part is the person who is entitled to the right in the respect relevant for that purpose.

(2) Where design right (or any aspect of design right) is owned by more than one person jointly, references in this Part to the design right owner are to all the owners, so that, in particular, any requirement of the licence of the design right owner requires the licence of all of them.

### 259. Joint designs

(1) In this Part a 'joint design' means a design produced by the collaboration of two or more designers in which the contribution of each is not distinct from that of the other or others.

(2) References in this Part to the designer of a design shall, except as otherwise provided, be construed in relation to a joint design as references to all the designers of the design.

### 260. Application of provisions to articles in kit form

(1) The provisions of this Part apply in relation to a kit, that is, a complete or substantially complete set of components intended to be assembled into an article, as they apply in relation to the assembled article.

(2) Subsection (1) does not affect the question whether design right subsists in

any aspect of the design of the components of a kit as opposed to the design of the assembled article.

## 261. Requirement of signature: application in relation to body corporate

The requirement in the following provisions that an instrument be signed by or on behalf of a person is also satisfied in the case of a body corporate by the affixing of its seal—

section 222(3) (assignment of design right),
section 223(1) (assignment of future design right),
section 225(1) (grant of exclusive licence).

## 262. Adaptation of expressions in relation to Scotland

In the application of this Part to Scotland—

'account of profits' means accounting and payment of profits;
'accounts' means count, reckoning and payment;
'assignment' means assignation;
'costs' means expenses;
'defendant' means defender;
'delivery up' means delivery;
'injunction' means interdict;
'interlocutory relief' means interim remedy; and
'plaintiff' means pursuer.

## 263. Minor definitions

(1) In this Part—

'British design' means a design which qualifies for design right protection by reason of a connection with the United Kingdom of the designer or the person by whom the design is commissioned or the designer is employed;
'business' includes a trade or profession;
'commission' means a commission for money or money's worth;
'the comptroller' means the Comptroller-General of Patents, Designs and Trade Marks;
'computer-generated', in relation to a design, means that the design is generated by computer in circumstances such that there is no human designer;
'country' includes any territory;
'the Crown' includes the Crown in right of Her Majesty's Government in Northern Ireland;
'design document' means any record of a design, whether in the form of a drawing, a written description, a photograph, data stored in a computer or otherwise;
'employee', 'employment' and 'employer' refer to employment under a contract of service or of apprenticeship;
'government department' includes a Northern Ireland department.

(2) References in this Part to 'marketing', in relation to an article, are to its being sold or let for hire, or offered or exposed for sale or hire, in the course of a business, and related expressions shall be construed accordingly; but no account shall be taken for the purposes of this Part of marketing which is merely colourable and not intended to satisfy the reasonable requirements of the public.

(3) References in this Part to an act being done in relation to an article for 'commercial purposes' are to its being done with a view to the article in question being sold or hired in the course of a business.

*General note*
Section 263(2) modified by the Design Right (Semiconductor Topographies) Regulations 1989, SI 1989 No 1100, reg 6(2) in relation to semiconductor topographies.

## 264. Index of defined expressions
The following Table shows provisions defining or otherwise explaining expressions used in this Part (other than provisions defining or explaining an expression used only in the same section)—

| | |
|---|---|
| account of profits and accounts (in Scotland) | section 262 |
| assignment (in Scotland) | section 262 |
| British designs | section 263(1) |
| business | section 263(1) |
| commercial purposes | section 263(3) |
| commission | section 263(1) |
| the comptroller | section 263(1) |
| computer-generated | section 263(1) |
| costs (in Scotland) | section 262 |
| country | section 263(1) |
| the Crown | section 263(1) |
| Crown use | sections 240(5) and 244(2) |
| defendant (in Scotland) | section 262 |
| delivery up (in Scotland) | section 262 |
| design | section 213(2) |
| design document | section 263(1) |
| designer | sections 214 and 259(2) |
| design right | section 213(1) |
| design right owner | sections 234(2) and 258 |
| employee, employment and employer | section 263(1) |
| exclusive licence | section 225(1) |
| government department | section 263(1) |
| government department concerned (in relation to Crown use) | section 240(5) |
| infringing article | section 228 |
| injunction (in Scotland) | section 262 |
| interlocutory relief (in Scotland) | section 262 |
| joint design | section 259(1) |
| licence (of the design right owner) | sections 222(4), 223(3) and 258 |
| making articles to a design | section 226(2) |
| marketing (and related expressions) | section 263(3) |
| original | section 213(4) |
| plaintiff (in Scotland) | section 262 |
| qualifying individual | section 217(1) |
| qualifying person | section 217(1) and (2) |
| signed | section 261 |

PART IV
REGISTERED DESIGNS

*Amendments of the Registered Designs Act 1949*

## 265. Registrable designs

(1) < . . . >

(2) The above amendment does not apply in relation to applications for registration made before the commencement of this Part; but the provisions of section 266 apply with respect to the right in certain designs registered in pursuance of such an application.

*General note*
Sub-s (1): substitutes the Registered Designs Act 1949, s 1, which Act is printed, as amended, in Part C of Appendix 1 to this work.

## 266. Provisions with respect to certain designs registered in pursuance of application made before commencement

(1) Where a design is registered under the Registered Designs Act 1949 in pursuance of an application made after 12th January 1988 and before the commencement of this Part which could not have been registered under section 1 of that Act as substituted by section 265 above—

  (a) the right in the registered design expires ten years after the commencement of this Part, if it does not expire earlier in accordance with the 1949 Act, and

  (b) any person is, after the commencement of this Part, entitled as of right to a licence to do anything which would otherwise infringe the right in the registered design.

(2) The terms of a licence available by virtue of this section shall, in default of agreement, be settled by the registrar on an application by the person requiring the licence; and the terms so settled shall authorise the licensee to do everything which would be an infringement of the right in the registered design in the absence of a licence.

(3) In settling the terms of a licence the registrar shall have regard to such factors as may be prescribed by the Secretary of State by order made by statutory instrument.

No such order shall be made unless a draft of it has been laid before and approved by a resolution of each House of Parliament.

(4) Where the terms of a licence are settled by the registrar, the licence has effect from the date on which the application to the registrar was made.

(5) Section 11B of the 1949 Act (undertaking to take licence of right in infringement proceedings), as inserted by section 270 below, applies where a licence is available as of right under this section, as it applies where a licence is available as of right under section 11A of that Act.

(6) Where a licence is available as of right under this section, a person to whom a licence was granted before the commencement of this Part may apply to the registrar for an order adjusting the terms of that licence.

(7) An appeal lies from any decision of the registrar under this section.

(8) This section shall be construed as one with the Registered Designs Act 1949.

## 267. Authorship and first ownership of designs
(1)-(3) < . . . >

(4) The amendments made by this section do not apply in relation to an application for registration made before the commencement of this Part.

*General note*
Sub-ss (1)-(3): amend the Registered Designs Act 1949, s 2, which Act is printed, as amended, in Part C of Appendix 1 to this work.

## 268. Right given by registration of design
(1) < . . . >

(2) The above amendment does not apply in relation to a design registered in pursuance of an application made before the commencement of this Part.

*General note*
Sub-s (1): substitutes the Registered Designs Act 1949, s 7, which Act is printed, as amended, in Part C of Appendix 1 to this work.

## 269. Duration of right in registered design
(1) < . . . >

(2) The above amendment does not apply in relation to the right in a design registered in pursuance of an application made before the commencement of this Part.

*General note*
Sub-s (1): substitutes the Registered Designs Act 1949, ss 8, 8A, 8B, for existing s 8, which Act is printed, as amended, in Part C of Appendix 1 to this work.

## 270. Powers exercisable for protection of the public interest
< . . . >

*General note*
This section adds the Registered Designs Act 1949, ss 11A, 11B, which Act is printed, as amended, in Part C of Appendix 1 to this work.

## 271. Crown use: compensation for loss of profit
(1), (2) < . . . >

(3) The above amendments apply in relation to any Crown use of a registered design after the commencement of this section, even if the terms for such use were settled before commencement.

*General note*
Sub-ss (1), (2): amend the Registered Designs Act 1949, Schedule 1, which Act is printed, as amended, in Part C of Appendix 1 to this work.

## 272. Minor and consequential amendments
The Registered Designs Act 1949 is further amended in accordance with Schedule 3 which contains minor amendments and amendments consequential upon the provisions of this Act.

## *Supplementary*

## 273. Text of Registered Designs Act 1949 as amended
Schedule 4 contains the text of the Registered Designs Act 1949 as amended.

PART V
PATENT AGENTS AND TRADE MARK AGENTS

*Patent agents*

**274. Persons permitted to carry on business of a patent agent**

(1) Any individual, partnership or body corporate may, subject to the following provisions of this Part, carry on the business of acting as agent for others for the purpose of—

(a) applying for or obtaining patents, in the United Kingdom or elsewhere, or

(b) conducting proceedings before the comptroller relating to applications for, or otherwise in connection with, patents.

(2) This does not affect any restriction under the European Patent Convention as to who may act on behalf of another for any purpose relating to European patents.

**275. The register of patent agents**

(1) The Secretary of State may make rules requiring the keeping of a register of persons who act as agent for others for the purposes of applying for or obtaining patents; and in this Part a 'registered patent agent' means a person whose name is entered in the register kept under this section.

(2) The rules may contain such provision as the Secretary of State thinks fit regulating the registration of persons, and may in particular—

(a) require the payment of such fees as may be prescribed, and

(b) authorise in prescribed cases the erasure from the register of the name of any person registered in it, or the suspension of a person's registration.

(3) The rules may delegate the keeping of the register to another person, and may confer on that person—

(a) power to make regulations—

(i) with respect to the payment of fees, in the cases and subject to the limits prescribed by rules, and

(ii) with respect to any other matter which could be regulated by rules, and

(b) such other functions, including disciplinary functions, as may be prescribed by rules.

(4) Rules under this section shall be made by statutory instrument which shall be subject to annulment in pursuance of a resolution of either House of Parliament.

**276. Persons entitled to describe themselves as patent agents**

(1) An individual who is not a registered patent agent shall not—

(a) carry on a business (otherwise than in partnership) under any name or other description which contains the words 'patent agent' or 'patent attorney'; or

(b) in the course of a business otherwise describe himself, or permit himself to be described, as a 'patent agent' or 'patent attorney'.

(2) A partnership shall not—

(a) carry on a business under any name or other description which contains the words 'patent agent' or 'patent attorney'; or

(b) in the course of a business otherwise describe itself, or permit itself to be described as, a firm of 'patent agents' or 'patent attorneys',

unless all the partners are registered patent agents or the partnership satisfies such conditions as may be prescribed for the purposes of this section.

(3) A body corporate shall not—

(a) carry on a business (otherwise than in partnership) under any name or other description which contains the words 'patent agent' or 'patent attorney'; or

(b) in the course of a business otherwise describe itself, or permit itself to be described as, a 'patent agent' or 'patent attorney',

unless all the directors of the body corporate are registered patent agents or the body satisfies such conditions as may be prescribed for the purposes of this section.

(4) Subsection (3) does not apply to a company which began to carry on business as a patent agent before 17th November 1917 if the name of a director or the manager of the company who is a registered patent agent is mentioned as being so registered in all professional advertisements, circulars or letters issued by or with the company's consent on which its name appears.

(5) Where this section would be contravened by the use of the words 'patent agent' or 'patent attorney' in reference to an individual, partnership or body corporate, it is equally contravened by the use of other expressions in reference to that person, or his business or place of business, which are likely to be understood as indicating that he is entitled to be described as a 'patent agent' or 'patent attorney'.

(6) A person who contravenes this section commits an offence and is liable on summary conviction to a fine not exceeding level 5 on the standard scale; and proceedings for such an offence may be begun at any time within a year from the date of the offence.

(7) This section has effect subject to—

(a) section 277 (persons entitled to describe themselves as European patent attorneys, etc), and

(b) section 278(1) (use of term 'patent attorney' in reference to solicitors).

**277. Persons entitled to describe themselves as European patent attorneys, etc**

(1) The term 'European patent attorney' or 'European patent agent' may be used in the following cases without any contravention of section 276.

(2) An individual who is on the European list may—

(a) carry on business under a name or other description which contains the words 'European patent attorney' or 'European patent agent', or

(b) otherwise describe himself, or permit himself to be described, as a 'European patent attorney' or 'European patent agent'.

(3) A partnership of which not less than the prescribed number or proportion of partners is on the European list may—

(a) carry on a business under a name or other description which contains the words 'European patent attorneys' or 'European patent agents', or

(b) otherwise describe itself, or permit itself to be described, as a firm which carries on the business of a 'European patent attorney' or 'European patent agent'.

(4) A body corporate of which not less than the prescribed number or proportion of directors is on the European list may—

(a) carry on a business under a name or other description which contains the words 'European patent attorney' or 'European patent agent', or

(b) otherwise describe itself, or permit itself to be described as, a company which carries on the business of a 'European patent attorney' or 'European patent agent'.

(5) Where the term 'European patent attorney' or 'European patent agent' may, in accordance with this section, be used in reference to an individual, partnership or body corporate, it is equally permissible to use other expressions in reference to that person, or to his business or place of business, which are likely to be understood as indicating that he is entitled to be described as a 'European patent attorney' or 'European patent agent.'

### 278. Use of the term 'patent attorney': supplementary provisions

(1) The term 'patent attorney' may be used in reference to a solicitor, and a firm of solicitors may be described as a firm of 'patent attorneys', without any contravention of section 276.

(2) No offence is committed under the enactments restricting the use of certain expressions in reference to persons not qualified to act as solicitors—

(a) by the use of the term 'patent attorney' in reference to a registered patent agent, or

(b) by the use of the term 'European patent attorney' in reference to a person on the European list.

(3) The enactments referred to in subsection (2) are section 21 of the Solicitors Act 1974, section 31 of the Solicitors (Scotland) Act 1980 and Article 22 of the Solicitors (Northern Ireland) Order 1976.

### 279. Power to prescribe conditions, etc for mixed partnerships and bodies corporate

(1) The Secretary of State may make rules—

(a) prescribing the conditions to be satisfied for the purposes of section 276 (persons entitled to describe themselves as patent agents) in relation to a partnership where not all the partners are qualified persons or a body corporate where not all the directors are qualified persons, and

(b) imposing requirements to be complied with by such partnerships and bodies corporate.

(2) The rules may, in particular—

(a) prescribe conditions as to the number or proportion of partners or directors who must be qualified persons;

(b) impose requirements as to—

(i) the identification of qualified and unqualified persons in

141

professional advertisements, circulars or letters issued by or with the consent of the partnership or body corporate and which relate to it or to its business; and

(ii) the manner in which a partnership or body corporate is to organise its affairs so as to secure that qualified persons exercise a sufficient degree of control over the activities of unqualified persons.

(3) Contravention of a requirement imposed by the rules is an offence for which a person is liable on summary conviction to a fine not exceeding level 5 on the standard scale.

(4) The Secretary of State may make rules prescribing for the purposes of section 277 the number or proportion of partners of a partnership or directors of a body corporate who must be qualified persons in order for the partnership or body to take advantage of that section.

(5) In this section 'qualified person'—

(a) in subsections (1) and (2), means a person who is a registered patent agent, and

(b) in subsection (4), means a person who is on the European list.

(6) Rules under this section shall be made by statutory instrument which shall be subject to annulment in pursuance of a resolution of either House of Parliament.

## 280. Privilege for communications with patent agents
(1) This section applies to communications as to any matter relating to the protection of any invention, design, technical information, *trade mark or service mark* **or trade mark,** or as to any matter involving passing off.

(2) Any such communication—

(a) between a person and his patent agent, or

(b) for the purpose of obtaining, or in response to a request for, information which a person is seeking for the purpose of instructing his patent agent,

is privileged from disclosure in legal proceedings in England, Wales or Northern Ireland in the same way as a communication between a person and his solicitor or, as the case may be, a communication for the purpose of obtaining, or in response to a request for, information which a person seeks for the purpose of instructing his solicitor.

(3) In subsection (2) 'patent agent' means—

(a) a registered patent agent or a person who is on the European list,

(b) a partnership entitled to describe itself as a firm of patent agents or as a firm carrying on the business of a European patent attorney, or

(c) a body corporate entitled to describe itself as a patent agent or as a company carrying on the business of a European patent attorney.

(4) It is hereby declared that in Scotland the rules of law which confer privilege from disclosure in legal proceedings in respect of communications extend to such communications as are mentioned in this section.

*General note*
Sub-s (1): words in italics repealed and words in bold type substituted by the Trade Marks Act 1994, s 106(1), Sch 4, para 8(3).

### 281. Power of comptroller to refuse to deal with certain agents

(1) This section applies to business under the Patents Act 1949, the Registered Designs Act 1949 or the Patents Act 1977.

(2) The Secretary of State may make rules authorising the comptroller to refuse to recognise as agent in respect of any business to which this section applies—

(a) a person who has been convicted of an offence under section 88 of the Patents Act 1949, section 114 of the Patents Act 1977 or section 276 of this Act;

(b) an individual whose name has been erased from and not restored to, or who is suspended from, the register of patent agents on the ground of misconduct;

(c) a person who is found by the Secretary of State to have been guilty of such conduct as would, in the case of an individual registered in the register of patent agents, render him liable to have his name erased from the register on the ground of misconduct;

(d) a partnership or body corporate of which one of the partners or directors is a person whom the comptroller could refuse to recognise under paragraph (a), (b) or (c) above.

(3) The rules may contain such incidental and supplementary provisions as appear to the Secretary of State to be appropriate and may, in particular, prescribe circumstances in which a person is or is not to be taken to have been guilty of misconduct.

(4) Rules made under this section shall be made by statutory instrument which shall be subject to annulment in pursuance of a resolution of either House of Parliament.

(5) The comptroller shall refuse to recognise as agent in respect of any business to which this section applies a person who neither resides nor has a place of business in the United Kingdom, the Isle of Man or another Member State of the European Economic Community.

## Trade mark agents

*282. The register of trade mark agents*

*(1) The Secretary of State may make rules requiring the keeping of a register of persons who act as agent for others for the purpose of applying for or obtaining the registration of trade marks; and in this Part a 'registered trade mark agent' means a person whose name is entered in the register kept under this section.*

*(2) The rules may contain such provision as the Secretary of State thinks fit regulating the registration of persons, and may in particular—*

*(a) require the payment of such fees as may be prescribed, and*

*(b) authorise in prescribed cases the erasure from the register of the name of any person registered in it, or the suspension of a person's registration.*

*(3) The rules may delegate the keeping of the register to another person, and may confer on that person—*

*(a) power to make regulations—*

*(i) with respect to the payment of fees, in the cases and subject to the limits prescribed by rules, and*

   *(ii) with respect to any other matter which could be regulated by rules, and*

 *(b) such other functions, including disciplinary functions, as may be prescribed by rules.*

*(4) Rules under this section shall be made by statutory instrument which shall be subject to annulment in pursuance of a resolution of either House of Parliament.*

*General note*
This section is repealed by the Trade Marks Act 1994, s 106(2), Sch 5.

**283. *Unregistered persons not to be described as registered trade mark agents***
*(1) An individual who is not a registered trade mark agent shall not—*

 *(a) carry on a business (otherwise than in partnership) under any name or other description which contains the words 'registered trade mark agent'; or*
 *(b) in the course of a business otherwise describe or hold himself out, or permit himself to be described or held out, as a registered trade mark agent.*

*(2) A partnership shall not—*

 *(a) carry on a business under any name or other description which contains the words 'registered trade mark agent'; or*
 *(b) in the course of a business otherwise describe or hold itself out, or permit itself to be described or held out, as a firm of registered trade mark agents,*

*unless all the partners are registered trade mark agents or the partnership satisfies such conditions as may be prescribed for the purposes of this section.*
*(3) A body corporate shall not—*

 *(a) carry on a business (otherwise than in partnership) under any name or other description which contains the words 'registered trade mark agent'; or*
 *(b) in the course of a business otherwise describe or hold itself out, or permit itself to be described or held out, as a registered trade mark agent,*

*unless all the directors of the body corporate are registered trade mark agents or the body satisfies such conditions as may be prescribed for the purposes of this section.*
*(4) The Secretary of State may make rules prescribing the conditions to be satisfied for the purposes of this section in relation to a partnership where not all the partners are registered trade mark agents or a body corporate where not all the directors are registered trade mark agents; and the rules may, in particular, prescribe conditions as to the number or proportion of partners or directors who must be registered trade mark agents.*
*(5) Rules under this section shall be made by statutory instrument which shall be subject to annulment in pursuance of a resolution of either House of Parliament.*
*(6) A person who contravenes this section commits an offence and is liable on summary conviction to a fine not exceeding level 5 on the standard scale; and proceedings for such an offence may be begun at any time within a year from the date of the offence.*

*General note*
This section is repealed by the Trade Marks Act 1994, s 106(2), Sch 5.

*284. Privilege for communications with registered trade mark agents*
*(1) This section applies to communications as to any matter relating to the protection of any design, trade mark or service mark, or as to any matter involving passing off.*

*(2) Any such communication—*

(a) *between a person and his trade mark agent, or*

(b) *for the purpose of obtaining, or in response to a request for, information which a person is seeking for the purpose of instructing his trade mark agent,*

*is privileged from disclosure in legal proceedings in England, Wales or Northern Ireland in the same way as a communication between a person and his solicitor or, as the case may be, a communication for the purpose of obtaining, or in response to a request for, information which a person seeks for the purpose of instructing his solicitor.*

*(3) In subsection (1) 'trade mark agent' means—*

(a) *a registered trade mark agent, or*

(b) *a partnership entitled to describe itself as a firm of registered trade mark agents, or*

(c) *a body corporate entitled to describe itself as a registered trade mark agent.*

*(4) It is hereby declared that in Scotland the rules of law which confer privilege from disclosure in legal proceedings in respect of communications extend to such communications as are mentioned in subsection (1).*

*General note*
This section is repealed by the Trade Marks Act 1994, s 106(2), Sch 5.

## *Supplementary*

### 285. Offences committed by partnerships and bodies corporate

(1) Proceedings for an offence under this Part alleged to have been committed by a partnership shall be brought in the name of the partnership and not in that of the partners; but without prejudice to any liability of theirs under subsection (4) below.

(2) The following provisions apply for the purposes of such proceedings as in relation to a body corporate—

(a) any rules of court relating to the service of documents;

(b) in England, Wales or Northern Ireland, Schedule 3 to the Magistrates' Courts Act 1980 or Schedule 4 to the Magistrates' Courts (Northern Ireland) Order 1981 (procedure on charge of offence).

(3) A fine imposed on a partnership on its conviction in such proceedings shall be paid out of the partnership assets.

(4) Where a partnership is guilty of an offence under this Part, every partner, other than a partner who is proved to have been ignorant of or to have attempted to prevent the commission of the offence, is also guilty of the offence and liable to be proceeded against and punished accordingly.

(5) Where an offence under this Part committed by a body corporate is proved

to have been committed with the consent or connivance of a director, manager, secretary or other similar officer of the body, or a person purporting to act in any such capacity, he as well as the body corporate is guilty of the offence and liable to be proceeded against and punished accordingly.

### 286. Interpretation
In this Part—

'the comptroller' means the Comptroller-General of Patents, Designs and Trade Marks;

'director', in relation to a body corporate whose affairs are managed by its members, means any member of the body corporate;

'the European list' means the list of professional representatives maintained by the European Patent Office in pursuance of the European Patent Convention;

'registered patent agent' has the meaning given by section 275(1);

*'registered trade mark agent' has the meaning given by section 282(1).*

*General note*
Definition 'registered trade mark agent' repealed by the Trade Marks Act 1994, s 106(2), Sch 5.

## PART VI
## PATENTS

*Patents county courts*

### 287. Patents county courts: special jurisdiction
(1) The Lord Chancellor may by order made by statutory instrument designate any county court as a patents county court and confer on it jurisdiction (its 'special jurisdiction') to hear and determine such descriptions of proceedings—

(a) relating to patents or designs, or

(b) ancillary to, or arising out of the same subject matter as, proceedings relating to patents or designs,

as may be specified in the order.

(2) The special jurisdiction of a patents county court is exercisable throughout England and Wales, but rules of court may provide for a matter pending in one such court to be heard and determined in another or partly in that and partly in another.

(3) A patents county court may entertain proceedings within its special jurisdiction notwithstanding that no pecuniary remedy is sought.

(4) An order under this section providing for the discontinuance of any of the special jurisdiction of a patents county court may make provision as to proceedings pending in the court when the order comes into operation.

(5) Nothing in this section shall be construed as affecting the ordinary jurisdiction of a county court.

### 288. Financial limits in relation to proceedings within special jurisdiction of patents county court
(1) Her Majesty may by Order in Council provide for limits of amount or value

in relation to any description of proceedings within the special jurisdiction of a patents county court.

(2) If a limit is imposed on the amount of a claim of any description and the plaintiff has a cause of action for more than that amount, he may abandon the excess; in which case a patents county court shall have jurisdiction to hear and determine the action, but the plaintiff may not recover more than that amount.

(3) Where the court has jurisdiction to hear and determine an action by virtue of subsection (2), the judgment of the court in the action is in full discharge of all demands in respect of the cause of action, and entry of the judgment shall be made accordingly.

(4) If the parties agree, by a memorandum signed by them or by their respective solicitors or other agents, that a patents county court shall have jurisdiction in any proceedings, that court shall have jurisdiction to hear and determine the proceedings notwithstanding any limit imposed under this section.

(5) No recommendation shall be made to Her Majesty to make an Order under this section unless a draft of the Order has been laid before and approved by a resolution of each House of Parliament.

## 289. Transfer of proceedings between High Court and patents county court

(1) No order shall be made under section 41 of the County Courts Act 1984 (power of High Court to order proceedings to be transferred from the county court) in respect of proceedings within the special jurisdiction of a patents county court.

(2) In considering in relation to proceedings within the special jurisdiction of a patents county court whether an order should be made under sections 40 or 42 of the County Courts Act 1984 (transfer of proceedings from or to the High Court), the court shall have regard to the financial position of the parties and may order the transfer of the proceedings to a patents county court or, as the case may be, refrain from ordering their transfer to the High Court notwithstanding that the proceedings are likely to raise an important question of fact or law.

## 290. Limitation of costs where pecuniary claim could have been brought in patents county court

(1) Where an action is commenced in the High Court which could have been commenced in a patents county court and in which a claim for a pecuniary remedy is made, then, subject to the provisions of this section, if the plaintiff recovers less than the prescribed amount, he is not entitled to recover any more costs than those to which he would have been entitled if the action had been brought in the county court.

(2) For this purpose a plaintiff shall be treated as recovering the full amount recoverable in respect of his claim without regard to any deduction made in respect of matters not falling to be taken into account in determining whether the action could have been commenced in a patents county court.

(3) This section does not affect any question as to costs if it appears to the High Court that there was reasonable ground for supposing the amount recoverable in respect of the plaintiff's claim to be in excess of the prescribed amount.

(4) The High Court, if satisfied that there was sufficient reason for bringing the action in the High Court, may make an order allowing the costs or any part of the costs on the High Court scale or on such one of the county court scales as it may direct.

(5) This section does not apply to proceedings brought by the Crown.

(6) In this section 'the prescribed amount' means such amount as may be prescribed by Her Majesty for the purposes of this section by Order in Council.

(7) No recommendation shall be made to Her Majesty to make an Order under this section unless a draft of the Order has been laid before and approved by a resolution of each House of Parliament.

*General note*
Prospectively repealed by the Courts and Legal Services Act 1990, s 125(7), Sch 20, as from a day to be appointed.

### 291. Proceedings in patents county court

(1) Where a county court is designated a patents county court, the Lord Chancellor shall nominate a person entitled to sit as a judge of that court as the patents judge.

(2) County court rules shall make provision for securing that, so far as is practicable and appropriate—

(a) proceedings within the special jurisdiction of a patents county court are dealt with by the patents judge, and

(b) the judge, rather than a registrar or other officer of the court, deals with interlocutory matters in the proceedings.

(3) County court rules shall make provision empowering a patents county court in proceedings within its special jurisdiction, on or without the application of any party—

(a) to appoint scientific advisers or assessors to assist the court, or

(b) to order the Patent Office to inquire into and report on any question of fact or opinion.

(4) Where the court exercises either of those powers on the application of a party, the remuneration or fees payable to the Patent Office shall be at such rate as may be determined in accordance with county court rules and shall be costs of the proceedings unless otherwise ordered by the judge.

(5) Where the court exercises either of those powers of its own motion, the remuneration or fees payable to the Patent Office shall be at such rate as may be determined by the Lord Chancellor with the approval of the Treasury and shall be paid out of money provided by Parliament.

### 292. Rights and duties of registered patent agents in relation to proceedings in patents county court

(1) A registered patent agent may do, in or in connection with proceedings in a patents county court which are within the special jurisdiction of that court, anything which a solicitor of the Supreme Court might do, other than prepare a deed.

(2) The Lord Chancellor may by regulations provide that the right conferred by subsection (1) shall be subject to such conditions and restrictions as appear to the Lord Chancellor to be necessary or expedient; and different provision may be made for different descriptions of proceedings.

(3) A patents county court has the same power to enforce an undertaking given by a registered patent agent acting in pursuance of this section as it has, by virtue of section 142 of the County Courts Act 1984, in relation to a solicitor.

(4) Nothing in section 143 of the County Courts Act 1984 (prohibition on persons other than solicitors receiving remuneration) applies to a registered patent agent acting in pursuance of this section.

(5) The provisions of county court rules prescribing scales of costs to be paid to solicitors apply in relation to registered patent agents acting in pursuance of this section.

(6) Regulations under this section shall be made by statutory instrument which shall be subject to annulment in pursuance of a resolution of either House of Parliament.

## *Licences of right in respect of certain patents*

### 293. Restriction of acts authorised by certain licences

*General note*
This section restricted to patents and the text is not printed here.

### 294. When application may be made for settlement of terms of licence

*General note*
This section restricted to patents and the text is not printed here.

## *Patents: miscellaneous amendments*

### 295. Patents: miscellaneous amendments

*General note*
This section restricted to patents and the text is not printed here.

## PART VII
## MISCELLANEOUS AND GENERAL

## *Devices designed to circumvent copy-protection*

### 296. Devices designed to circumvent copy-protection

(1) This section applies where copies of a copyright work are issued to the public, by or with the licence of the copyright owner, in an electronic form which is copy-protected.

(2) The person issuing the copies to the public has the same rights against a person who, knowing or having reason to believe that it will be used to make infringing copies—

    (a) makes, imports, sells or lets for hire, offers or exposes for sale or hire, or advertises for sale or hire, any device or means specifically designed or adapted to circumvent the form of copy-protection employed, or

    (b) publishes information intended to enable or assist persons to circumvent that form of copy-protection,

as a copyright owner has in respect of an infringement of copyright.

**(2A) Where the copies being issued to the public as mentioned in subsection (1) are copies of a computer program, subsection (2) applies as if for the words 'or advertises for sale or hire' there were substituted 'advertises for sale or hire or possesses in the course of a business'.**

(3) Further, he has the same rights under sections 99 or 100 (delivery up or seizure of certain articles) in relation to any such device or means which a person

has in his possession, custody or control with the intention that it should be used to make infringing copies of copyright works, as a copyright owner has in relation to an infringing copy.

(4) References in this section to copy-protection include any device or means intended to prevent or restrict copying of a work or to impair the quality of copies made.

(5) Expressions used in this section which are defined for the purposes of Part I of this Act (copyright) have the same meaning as in that Part.

(6) The following provisions apply in relation to proceedings under this section as in relation to proceedings under Part I (copyright)—

(a) sections 104 to 106 of this Act (presumptions as to certain matters relating to copyright), and

(b) section 72 of the Supreme Court Act 1981, section 15 of the Law Reform (Miscellaneous Provisions) (Scotland) Act 1985 and section 94A of the Judicature (Northern Ireland) Act 1978 (withdrawal of privilege against self-incrimination in certain proceedings relating to intellectual property);

and section 114 of this Act applies, with the necessary modifications, in relation to the disposal of anything delivered up or seized by virtue of subsection (3) above.

*General note*
Sub-s (2A): added by the Copyright (Computer Programs) Regulations 1992, SI 1992 No 3233, see Appendix 2, Part A.

## Computer programs

**296A. Avoidance of certain terms**
**(1) Where a person has the use of a computer program under an agreement, any term or condition in the agreement shall be void in so far as it purports to prohibit or restrict—**

(a) **the making of any back up copy of the program which it is necessary for him to have for the purposes of the agreed use;**

(b) **where the conditions in section 50B(2) are met, the decompiling of the program; or**

(c) **the use of any device or means to observe, study or test the functioning of the program in order to understand the ideas and principles which underlie any element of the program.**

**(2) In this section, decompile, in relation to a computer program, has the same meaning as in section 50B.**

*General note*
Added by the Copyright (Computer Programs) Regulations 1992, SI 1992 No 3233, see Appendix 2, Part A.

## Fraudulent reception of transmissions

**297. Offence of fraudulently receiving programmes**
(1) A person who dishonestly receives a programme included in a broadcasting or cable programme service provided from a place in the United Kingdom with intent to avoid payment of any charge applicable to the reception of the programme commits an offence and is liable on summary conviction to a fine not exceeding level 5 on the standard scale.

(2) Where an offence under this section committed by a body corporate is proved to have been committed with the consent or connivance of a director, manager, secretary or other similar officer of the body, or a person purporting to act in any such capacity, he as well as the body corporate is guilty of the offence and liable to be proceeded against and punished accordingly.

In relation to a body corporate whose affairs are managed by its members 'director' means a member of the body corporate.

### 297A. Unauthorised decoders

**(1) A person who makes, imports, sells or lets for hire any unauthorised decoder shall be guilty of an offence and liable on summary conviction to a fine not exceeding level 5 on the standard scale.**

**(2) It is a defence to any prosecution for an offence under this section for the defendant to prove that he did not know, and had no reasonable ground for knowing, that the decoder was an unauthorised decoder.**

**(3) In this section—**

> **'apparatus' includes any device, component or electronic data;**
>
> **'decoder' means any apparatus which is designed or adapted to enable (whether on its own or with any other apparatus) an encrypted transmission to be decoded;**
>
> **'transmission' means any programme included in a broadcasting or cable programme service which is provided from a place in the United Kingdom; and**
>
> **'unauthorised', in relation to a decoder, means a decoder which will enable encrypted transmissions to be viewed in decoded form without payment of the fee (however imposed) which the person making the transmission, or on whose behalf it is made, charges for viewing those transmissions, or viewing any service of which they form part.**

*General note*
Added by the Broadcasting Act 1990, s 179(1).

### 298. Rights and remedies in respect of apparatus, etc for unauthorised reception of transmissions

(1) A person who—

(a) makes charges for the reception of programmes included in a broadcasting or cable programme service provided from a place in the United Kingdom, or

(b) sends encrypted transmissions of any other description from a place in the United Kingdom,

is entitled to the following rights and remedies.

(2) He has the same rights and remedies against a person who—

(a) makes, imports or sells or lets for hire any apparatus or device designed or adapted to enable or assist persons to receive the programmes or other transmissions when they are not entitled to do so, or

(b) publishes any information which is calculated to enable or assist persons to receive the programmes or other transmissions when they are not entitled to do so,

as a copyright owner has in respect of an infringement of copyright.

(3) Further, he has the same rights under sections 99 or 100 (delivery up or seizure of certain articles) in relation to any such apparatus or device as a copyright owner has in relation to an infringing copy.

(4) Section 72 of the Supreme Court Act 1981, section 15 of the Law Reform (Miscellaneous Provisions) (Scotland) Act 1985 and section 94A of the Judicature (Northern Ireland) Act 1978 (withdrawal of privilege against self-incrimination in certain proceedings relating to intellectual property) apply to proceedings under this section as to proceedings under Part I of this Act (copyright).

(5) In section 97(1) (innocent infringement of copyright) as it applies to proceedings for infringement of the rights conferred by this section, the reference to the defendant not knowing or having reason to believe that copyright subsisted in the work shall be construed as a reference to his not knowing or having reason to believe that his acts infringed the rights conferred by this section.

(6) Section 114 of this Act applies, with the necessary modifications, in relation to the disposal of anything delivered up or seized by virtue of subsection (3) above.

## 299. Supplementary provisions as to fraudulent reception

(1) Her Majesty may by Order in Council—

    (a) provide that section 297 applies in relation to programmes included in services provided from a country or territory outside the United Kingdom, and

    (b) provide that section 298 applies in relation to such programmes and to encrypted transmissions sent from such a country or territory.

*(2) No such Order shall be made unless it appears to Her Majesty that provision has been or will be made under the laws of that country or territory giving adequate protection to persons making charges for programmes included in broadcasting or cable programme services provided from the United Kingdom or, as the case may be, for encrypted transmissions sent from the United Kingdom.*

(3) A statutory instrument containing an Order in Council under subsection (1) shall be subject to annulment in pursuance of a resolution of either House of Parliament.

(4) Where sections 297 and 298 apply in relation to a broadcasting service or cable programme service, they also apply to any service run for the person providing that service, or a person providing programmes for that service, which consists wholly or mainly in the sending by means of a telecommunications system of sounds or visual images, or both.

(5) In sections 297**, 297A** and 298, and this section, 'programme', 'broadcasting' and 'cable programme service', and related expressions, have the same meaning as in Part I (copyright).

*General note*
Sub-s (2): repealed by the Broadcasting Act 1990, ss 179(2), 203(3), Sch 21.
Sub-s (5): figure in bold type added by the Broadcasting Act 1990, s 179(2).

*Fraudulent application or use of trade mark*

## 300. Fraudulent application or use of trade mark an offence

*General note*
This section which inserted ss 58A to 58D into the Trade Marks Act 1938 has now been repealed by the Trade Marks Act 1994, s 106(2), Sch 5.

*Provisions for the benefit of the Hospital for Sick Children*

**301. Provisions for the benefit of the Hospital for Sick Children**
The provisions of Schedule 6 have effect for conferring on trustees for the benefit of the Hospital for Sick Children, Great Ormond Street, London, a right to a royalty in respect of the public performance, commercial publication, broadcasting or inclusion in a cable programme service of the play 'Peter Pan' by Sir James Matthew Barrie, or of any adaptation of that work, notwithstanding that copyright in the work expired on 31st December 1987.

**302. Financial assistance for certain international bodies**
(1) The Secretary of State may give financial assistance, in the form of grants, loans or guarantees to—

  (a) any international organisation having functions relating to trade marks or other intellectual property, or

  (b) any Community institution or other body established under any of the Community Treaties having any such functions,

with a view to the establishment or maintenance by that organisation, institution or body of premises in the United Kingdom.

(2) Any expenditure of the Secretary of State under this section shall be defrayed out of money provided by Parliament; and any sums received by the Secretary of State in consequence of this section shall be paid into the Consolidated Fund.

*General*

**303. Consequential amendments and repeals**
(1) The enactments specified in Schedule 7 are amended in accordance with that Schedule, the amendments being consequential on the provisions of this Act.

  (2) The enactments specified in Schedule 8 are repealed to the extent specified.

**304. Extent**
(1) Provision as to the extent of Part I (copyright), Part II (rights in performances) and Part III (design right) is to be found in sections 157, 207 and 255 respectively; the extent of the other provisions of this Act is as follows.

(2) Parts IV to VII extend to England and Wales, Scotland and Northern Ireland, except that—

  (a) sections 287 to 292 (patents county courts) extend to England and Wales only,

  (b) the proper law of the trust created by Schedule 6 (provisions for the benefit of the Hospital for Sick Children) is the law of England and Wales, and

  (c) the amendments and repeals in Schedules 7 and 8 have the same extent as the enactments amended or repealed.

(3) The following provisions extend to the Isle of Man subject to any modifications contained in an Order made by Her Majesty in Council—

  (a) sections 293 and 294 (patents: licences of right), and

  (b) paragraphs 24 and 29 of Schedule 5 (patents: effect of filing international application for patent and power to extend time limits).

(4) Her Majesty may by Order in Council direct that the following provisions extend to the Isle of Man, with such exceptions and modifications as may be specified in the Order—

(a) Part IV (registered designs),

(b) Part V (patent agents),

(c) the provisions of Schedule 5 (patents: miscellaneous amendments) not mentioned in subsection (3) above,

(d) sections 297 to 299 (fraudulent reception of transmissions), and

(e) section 300 (fraudulent application or use of trade mark).

(5) Her Majesty may by Order in Council direct that sections 297 to 299 (fraudulent reception of transmissions) extend to any of the Channel Islands, with such exceptions and modifications as may be specified in the Order.

(6) Any power conferred by this Act to make provision by Order in Council for or in connection with the extent of provisions of this Act to a country outside the United Kingdom includes power to extend to that country, subject to any modifications specified in the Order, any provision of this Act which amends or repeals an enactment extending to that country.

## 305. Commencement

(1) The following provisions of this Act come into force on Royal Assent—

paragraphs 24 and 29 of Schedule 5 (patents: effect of filing international application for patent and power to extend time limits);

section 301 and Schedule 6 (provisions for the benefit of the Hospital for Sick Children).

(2) Sections 293 and 294 (licences of right) come into force at the end of the period of two months beginning with the passing of this Act.

(3) The other provisions of this Act come into force on such day as the Secretary of State may appoint by order made by statutory instrument, and different days may be appointed for different provisions and different purposes.

## 306. Short title

This Act may be cited as the Copyright, Designs and Patents Act 1988.

SCHEDULE 1

COPYRIGHT: TRANSITIONAL PROVISIONS AND SAVINGS

Section 170

*Introductory*

1.—(1) In this Schedule—

'the 1911 Act' means the Copyright Act 1911,

'the 1956 Act' means the Copyright Act 1956, and

'the new copyright provisions' means the provisions of this Act relating to copyright, that is, Part I (including this Schedule) and Schedules 3, 7 and 8 so far as they make amendments or repeals consequential on the provisions of Part I.

(2) References in this Schedule to 'commencement', without more, are to the date on which the new copyright provisions come into force.

(3) References in this Schedule to 'existing works' are to works made before commencement; and for this purpose a work of which the making extended over a period shall be taken to have been made when its making was completed.

**2.**—(1) In relation to the 1956 Act, references in this Schedule to a work include any work or other subject-matter within the meaning of that Act.

(2) In relation to the 1911 Act—

(a) references in this Schedule to copyright include the right conferred by section 24 of that Act in substitution for a right subsisting immediately before the commencement of that Act;

(b) references in this Schedule to copyright in a sound recording are to the copyright under that Act in records embodying the recording; and

(c) references in this Schedule to copyright in a film are to any copyright under that Act in the film (so far as it constituted a dramatic work for the purposes of that Act) or in photographs forming part of the film.

*General principles: continuity of the law*

**3.**—The new copyright provisions apply in relation to things existing at commencement as they apply in relation to things coming into existence after commencement, subject to any express provision to the contrary.

**4.**—(1) The provisions of this paragraph have effect for securing the continuity of the law so far as the new copyright provisions re-enact (with or without modification) earlier provisions.

(2) A reference in an enactment, instrument or other document to copyright, or to a work or other subject-matter in which copyright subsists, which apart from this Act would be construed as referring to copyright under the 1956 Act shall be construed, so far as may be required for continuing its effect, as being, or as the case may require, including, a reference to copyright under this Act or to works in which copyright subsists under this Act.

(3) Anything done (including subordinate legislation made), or having effect as done, under or for the purposes of a provision repealed by this Act has effect as if done under or for the purposes of the corresponding provision of the new copyright provisions.

(4) References (expressed or implied) in this Act or any other enactment, instrument or document to any of the new copyright provisions shall, so far as the context permits, be construed as including, in relation to times, circumstances and purposes before commencement, a reference to corresponding earlier provisions.

(5) A reference (express or implied) in an enactment, instrument or other document to a provision repealed by this Act shall be construed, so far as may be required for continuing its effect, as a reference to the corresponding provision of this Act.

(6) The provisions of this paragraph have effect subject to any specific transitional provision or saving and to any express amendment made by this Act.

*Subsistence of copyright*

**5.**—(1) Copyright subsists in an existing work after commencement only if copyright subsisted in it immediately before commencement.

(2) Sub-paragraph (1) does not prevent an existing work qualifying for copyright protection after commencement—

(a) under section 155 (qualification by virtue of first publication), or

(b) by virtue of an Order under section 159 (application of Part I to countries to which it does not extend).

**6.**—(1) Copyright shall not subsist by virtue of this Act in an artistic work made before 1st June 1957 which at the time when the work was made constituted a design capable of registration under the Registered Designs Act 1949 or under the enactments repealed by that Act, and was used, or intended to be used, as a model or pattern to be multiplied by an industrial process.

(2) For this purpose a design shall be deemed to be used as a model or pattern to be multiplied by any industrial process—

(a) when the design is reproduced or is intended to be reproduced on more than 50 single articles, unless all the articles in which the design is reproduced or is intended to be reproduced together form only a single set of articles as defined in section 44(1) of the Registered Designs Act 1949, or

(b) when the design is to be applied to—

      (i)   printed paper hangings,
     (ii)   carpets, floor cloths or oil cloths, manufactured or sold in lengths or pieces,
   (iii)   textile piece goods, or textile goods manufactured or sold in lengths or pieces, or
   (iv)   lace, not made by hand.

**7.**—(1) No copyright subsists in a film, as such, made before 1st June 1957.

(2) Where a film made before that date was an original dramatic work within the meaning of the 1911 Act, the new copyright provisions have effect in relation to the film as if it was an original dramatic work within the meaning of Part I.

(3) The new copyright provisions have effect in relation to photographs forming part of a film made before 1st June 1957 as they have effect in relation to photographs not forming part of a film.

**8.**—(1) A film sound-track to which section 13(9) of the 1956 Act applied before commencement (film to be taken to include sounds in associated sound-track) shall be treated for the purposes of the new copyright provisions not as part of the film, but as a sound recording.

(2) However—

(a)   copyright subsists in the sound recording only if copyright subsisted in the film immediately before commencement, and it continues to subsist until copyright in the film expires;

(b)   the author and first owner of copyright in the film shall be treated as having been author and first owner of the copyright in the sound recording; and

(c)   anything done before commencement under or in relation to the copyright in the film continues to have effect in relation to the sound recording as in relation to the film.

**9.**—No copyright subsists in—

(a)   a broadcast made before 1st June 1957, or

(b)   a cable programme included in a cable programme service before 1st January 1985;

and any such broadcast or cable programme shall be disregarded for the purposes of section 14(2) (duration of copyright in repeats).

*Authorship of work*

**10.**—The question who was the author of an existing work shall be determined in accordance with the new copyright provisions for the purposes of the rights conferred by Chapter IV of Part I (moral rights), and for all other purposes shall be determined in accordance with the law in force at the time the work was made.

*First ownership of copyright*

**11.**—(1) The question who was first owner of copyright in an existing work shall be determined in accordance with the law in force at the time the work was made.

(2) Where before commencement a person commissioned the making of a work in circumstances falling within—

(a)   section 4(3) of the 1956 Act or paragraph (a) of the proviso to section 5(1) of the 1911 Act (photographs, portraits and engravings), or

(b)   the proviso to section 12(4) of the 1956 Act (sound recordings),

those provisions apply to determine first ownership of copyright in any work made in pursuance of the commission after commencement.

*Duration of copyright in existing works*

**12.**—(1) The following provisions have effect with respect to the duration of copyright in existing works.

The question which provision applies to a work shall be determined by reference to the facts immediately before commencement; and expressions used in this paragraph which were defined for the purposes of the 1956 Act have the same meaning as in that Act.

(2) Copyright in the following descriptions of work continues to subsist until the date on which it would have expired under the 1956 Act—

   (a)   literary, dramatic or musical works in relation to which the period of 50 years mentioned in the proviso to section 2(3) of the 1956 Act (duration of copyright in works made available to the public after the death of the author) has begun to run;

   (b)   engravings in relation to which the period of 50 years mentioned in the proviso to section 3(4) of the 1956 Act (duration of copyright in works published after the death of the author) has begun to run;

   (c)   published photographs and photographs taken before 1st June 1957;

   (d)   published sound recordings and sound recordings made before 1st June 1957;

   (e)   published films and films falling within section 13(3)(a) of the 1956 Act (films registered under former enactments relating to registration of films).

(3) Copyright in anonymous or pseudonymous literary, dramatic, musical or artistic works (other than photographs) continues to subsist—

   (a)   if the work is published, until the date on which it would have expired in accordance with the 1956 Act, and

   (b)   if the work is unpublished, until the end of the period of 50 years from the end of the calendar year in which the new copyright provisions come into force or, if during that period the work is first made available to the public within the meaning of section 12(2) (duration of copyright in works of unknown authorship), the date on which copyright expires in accordance with that provision;

unless, in any case, the identity of the author becomes known before that date, in which case section 12(1) applies (general rule: life of the author plus 50 years).

(4) Copyright in the following descriptions of work continues to subsist until the end of the period of 50 years from the end of the calendar year in which the new copyright provisions come into force—

   (a)   literary, dramatic and musical works of which the author has died and in relation to which none of the acts mentioned in paragraphs (a) to (e) of the proviso to section 2(3) of the 1956 Act has been done;

   (b)   unpublished engravings of which the author has died;

   (c)   unpublished photographs taken on or after 1st June 1957.

(5) Copyright in the following descriptions of work continues to subsist until the end of the period of 50 years from the end of the calendar year in which the new copyright provisions come into force—

   (a)   unpublished sound recordings made on or after 1st June 1957;

   (b)   films not falling within sub-paragraph (2)(e) above,

unless the recording or film is published before the end of that period in which case copyright in it shall continue until the end of the period of 50 years from the end of the calendar year in which the recording or film is published.

(6) Copyright in any other description of existing work continues to subsist until the date on which copyright in that description of work expires in accordance with sections 12 to 15 of this Act.

(7) The above provisions do not apply to works subject to Crown or Parliamentary copyright (see paragraphs 41 to 43 below).

*Perpetual copyright under the Copyright Act 1775*

**13.**—(1) The rights conferred on universities and colleges by the Copyright Act 1775 shall continue to subsist until the end of the period of 50 years from the end of the calendar year in which the new copyright provisions come into force and shall then expire.

(2) The provisions of the following Chapters of Part I—

Chapter III (acts permitted in relation to copyright works),

Chapter VI (remedies for infringement),

Chapter VII (provisions with respect to copyright licensing), and

Chapter VIII (the Copyright Tribunal)

apply in relation to those rights as they apply in relation to copyright under this Act.

*Acts infringing copyright*

**14.**—(1) The provisions of Chapters II and III of Part I as to the acts constituting an infringement of copyright apply only in relation to acts done after commencement; the provisions of the 1956 Act continue to apply in relation to acts done before commencement.

(2) So much of section 18(2) as extends the restricted act of issuing copies to the public to include the rental to the public of copies of sound recordings, films or computer programs does not apply in relation to a copy of a sound recording, film or computer program acquired by any person before commencement for the purpose of renting it to the public.

(3) For the purposes of section 27 (meaning of 'infringing copy') the question whether the making of an article constituted an infringement of copyright, or would have done if the article had been made in the United Kingdom, shall be determined—

    (a)   in relation to an article made on or after 1st June 1957 and before commencement, by reference to the 1956 Act, and

    (b)   in relation to an article made before 1st June 1957, by reference to the 1911 Act.

(4) For the purposes of the application of sections 31(2), 51(2) and 62(3) (subsequent exploitation of things whose making was, by virtue of an earlier provision of the section, not an infringement of copyright) to things made before commencement, it shall be assumed that the new copyright provisions were in force at all material times.

(5) Section 55 (articles for producing material in a particular typeface) applies where articles have been marketed as mentioned in subsection (1) before commencement with the substitution for the period mentioned in subsection (3) of the period of 25 years from the end of the calendar year in which the new copyright provisions come into force.

(6) Section 56 (transfer of copies, adaptations, etc of work in electronic form) does not apply in relation to a copy purchased before commencement.

(7) In section 65 (reconstruction of buildings) the reference to the owner of the copyright in the drawings or plans is, in relation to buildings constructed before commencement, to the person who at the time of the construction was the owner of the copyright in the drawings or plans under the 1956 Act, the 1911 Act or any enactment repealed by the 1911 Act.

**15.**—(1) Section 57 (anonymous or pseudonymous works: acts permitted on assumptions as to expiry of copyright or death of author) has effect in relation to existing works subject to the following provisions.

(2) Subsection (1)(b)(i) (assumption as to expiry of copyright) does not apply in relation to—

    (a)   photographs, or

    (b)   the rights mentioned in paragraph 13 above (rights conferred by the Copyright Act 1775).

(3) Subsection (1)(b)(ii) (assumption as to death of author) applies only—

    (a)   where paragraph 12(3)(b) above applies (unpublished anonymous or pseudonymous works), after the end of the period of 50 years from the end of the calendar year in which the new copyright provisions come into force, or

    (b)   where paragraph 12(6) above applies (cases in which the duration of copyright is the same under the new copyright provisions as under the previous law).

**16.**—The following provisions of section 7 of the 1956 Act continue to apply in relation to existing works—

    (a)   subsection (6) (copying of unpublished works from manuscript or copy in library, museum or other institution);

    (b)   subsection (7) (publication of work containing material to which subsection (6) applies), except paragraph (a) (duty to give notice of intended publication);

    (c)   subsection (8) (subsequent broadcasting, performance, etc of material published in accordance with subsection (7));

and subsection (9)(d) (illustrations) continues to apply for the purposes of those provisions.

**17.**—Where in the case of a dramatic or musical work made before 1st July 1912, the right conferred by the 1911 Act did not include the sole right to perform the work in public, the acts restricted by the copyright shall be treated as not including—

    (a)   performing the work in public,

(b)  broadcasting the work or including it in a cable programme service, or

(c)  doing any of the above in relation to an adaptation of the work;

and where the right conferred by the 1911 Act consisted only of the sole right to perform the work in public, the acts restricted by the copyright shall be treated as consisting only of those acts.

**18**—Where a work made before 1st July 1912 consists of an essay, article or portion forming part of and first published in a review, magazine or other periodical or work of a like nature, the copyright is subject to any right of publishing the essay, article, or portion in a separate form to which the author was entitled at the commencement of the 1911 Act, or would if that Act had not been passed, have become entitled under section 18 of the Copyright Act 1842.

*Designs*

**19.**—(1) Section 51 (exclusion of copyright protection in relation to works recorded or embodied in design document or models) does not apply for ten years after commencement in relation to a design recorded or embodied in a design document or model before commencement.

(2) During those ten years the following provisions of Part III (design right) apply to any relevant copyright as in relation to design right—

(a)  sections 237 to 239 (availability of licences of right), and

(b)  sections 247 and 248 (application to comptroller to settle terms of licence of right).

(3) In section 237 as it applies by virtue of this paragraph, for the reference in subsection (1) to the last five years of the design right term there shall be substituted a reference to the last five years of the period of ten years referred to in sub-paragraph (1) above, or to so much of those last five years during which copyright subsists.

(4) In section 239 as it applies by virtue of this paragraph, for the reference in subsection (1)(b) to section 230 there shall be substituted a reference to section 99.

(5) Where a licence of right is available by virtue of this paragraph, a person to whom a licence was granted before commencement may apply to the comptroller for an order adjusting the terms of that licence.

(6) The provisions of sections 249 and 250 (appeals and rules) apply in relation to proceedings brought under or by virtue of this paragraph as to proceedings under Part III.

(7) A licence granted by virtue of this paragraph shall relate only to acts which would be permitted by section 51 if the design document or model had been made after commencement.

(8) Section 100 (right to seize infringing copies, etc) does not apply during the period of ten years referred to in sub-paragraph (1) in relation to anything to which it would not apply if the design in question had been first recorded or embodied in a design document or model after commencement.

(9) Nothing in this paragraph affects the operation of any rule of law preventing or restricting the enforcement of copyright in relation to a design.

*General note*

Sch 19 modified in relation to semiconductor topographies by the Design Right (Semiconductor Topographies) Regulations 1989, SI 1989 No 1100, reg 10.

**20.**—(1) Where section 10 of the 1956 Act (effect of industrial application of design corresponding to artistic work) applied in relation to an artistic work at any time before commencement, section 52(2) of this Act applies with the substitution for the period of 25 years mentioned there of the relevant period of 15 years as defined in section 10(3) of the 1956 Act.

(2) Except as provided in sub-paragraph (1), section 52 applies only where articles are marketed as mentioned in subsection (1)(b) after commencement.

*Abolition of statutory recording licence*

**21.**—Section 8 of the 1956 Act (statutory licence to copy records sold by retail) continues to apply where notice under subsection (1)(b) of that section was given before the repeal of that section by this Act, but only in respect of the making of records—

(a)  within one year of the repeal coming into force, and

(b)  up to the number stated in the notice as intended to be sold.

*Appendix 1*

*Moral rights*

**22.**—(1) No act done before commencement is actionable by virtue of any provision of Chapter IV of Part I (moral rights).

(2) Section 43 of the 1956 Act (false attribution of authorship) continues to apply in relation to acts done before commencement.

**23.**—(1) The following provisions have effect with respect to the rights conferred by—

    (a)   section 77 (right to be identified as author or director), and

    (b)   section 80 (right to object to derogatory treatment of work).

(2) The rights do not apply—

    (a)   in relation to a literary, dramatic, musical and artistic work of which the author died before commencement; or

    (b)   in relation to a film made before commencement.

(3) The rights in relation to an existing literary, dramatic, musical or artistic work do not apply—

    (a)   where copyright first vested in the author, to anything which by virtue of an assignment of copyright made or licence granted before commencement may be done without infringing copyright;

    (b)   where copyright first vested in a person other than the author, to anything done by or with the licence of the copyright owner.

(4) The rights do not apply to anything done in relation to a record made in pursuance of section 8 of the 1956 Act (statutory recording licence).

**24.**—The right conferred by section 85 (right to privacy of certain photographs and films) does not apply to photographs taken or films made before commencement.

*Assignments and licences*

**25.**—(1) Any document made or event occurring before commencement which had any operation—

    (a)   affecting the ownership of the copyright in an existing work, or

    (b)   creating, transferring or terminating an interest, right or licence in respect of the copyright in an existing work,

has the corresponding operation in relation to copyright in the work under this Act.

(2) Expressions used in such a document shall be construed in accordance with their effect immediately before commencement.

**26.**—(1) Section 91(1) of this Act (assignment of future copyright: statutory vesting of legal interest on copyright coming into existence) does not apply in relation to an agreement made before 1st June 1957.

(2) The repeal by this Act of section 37(2) of the 1956 Act (assignment of future copyright: devolution of right where assignee dies before copyright comes into existence) does not affect the operation of that provision in relation to an agreement made before commencement.

**27.**—(1) Where the author of a literary, dramatic, musical or artistic work was the first owner of the copyright in it, no assignment of the copyright and no grant of any interest in it, made by him (otherwise than by will) after the passing of the 1911 Act and before 1st June 1957, shall be operative to vest in the assignee or grantee any rights with respect to the copyright in the work beyond the expiration of 25 years from the death of the author.

(2) The reversionary interest in the copyright expectant on the termination of that period may after commencement be assigned by the author during his life but in the absence of any assignment shall, on his death, devolve on his legal personal representatives as part of his estate.

(3) Nothing in this paragraph affects—

    (a)   an assignment of the reversionary interest by a person to whom it has been assigned,

    (b)   an assignment of the reversionary interest after the death of the author by his personal representatives or any person becoming entitled to it, or

    (c)   any assignment of the copyright after the reversionary interest has fallen in.

(4) Nothing in this paragraph applies to the assignment of the copyright in a collective work or a licence to publish a work or part of a work as part of a collective work.

(5) In sub-paragraph (4) 'collective work' means—

    (a)   any encyclopaedia, dictionary, yearbook, or similar work;

    (b)   a newspaper, review, magazine, or similar periodical; and

    (c)   any work written in distinct parts by different authors, or in which works or parts of works of different authors are incorporated.

**28.**—(1) This paragraph applies where copyright subsists in a literary, dramatic, musical or artistic work made before 1st July 1912 in relation to which the author, before the commencement of the 1911 Act, made such an assignment or grant as was mentioned in paragraph (a) of the proviso to section 24(1) of that Act (assignment or grant of copyright or performing right for full term of the right under the previous law).

(2) If before commencement any event has occurred or notice has been given which by virtue of paragraph 38 of Schedule 7 to the 1956 Act had any operation in relation to copyright in the work under that Act, the event or notice has the corresponding operation in relation to copyright under this Act.

(3) Any right which immediately before commencement would by virtue of paragraph 38(3) of that Schedule have been exercisable in relation to the work, or copyright in it, is exercisable in relation to the work or copyright in it under this Act.

(4) If in accordance with paragraph 38(4) of that Schedule copyright would, on a date after the commencement of the 1956 Act, have reverted to the author or his personal representatives and that date falls after the commencement of the new copyright provisions—

    (a)   the copyright in the work shall revert to the author or his personal representatives, as the case may be, and

    (b)   any interest of any other person in the copyright which subsists on that date by virtue of any document made before the commencement of the 1911 Act shall thereupon determine.

**29.**—Section 92(2) of this Act (rights of exclusive licensee against successors in title of person granting licence) does not apply in relation to an exclusive licence granted before commencement.

*Bequests*

**30.**—(1) Section 93 of this Act (copyright to pass under will with original document or other material thing embodying unpublished work)—

    (a)   does not apply where the testator died before 1st June 1957, and

    (b)   where the testator died on or after that date and before commencement, applies only in relation to an original document embodying a work.

(2) In the case of an author who died before 1st June 1957, the ownership after his death of a manuscript of his, where such ownership has been acquired under a testamentary disposition made by him and the manuscript is of a work which has not been published or performed in public, is prima facie proof of the copyright being with the owner of the manuscript.

*Remedies for infringement*

**31.**—(1) Sections 96 and 97 of this Act (remedies for infringement) apply only in relation to an infringement of copyright committed after commencement; section 17 of the 1956 Act continues to apply in relation to infringements committed before commencement.

(2) Sections 99 and 100 of this Act (delivery up or seizure of infringing copies, etc) apply to infringing copies and other articles made before or after commencement; section 18 of the 1956 Act, and section 7 of the 1911 Act, (conversion damages, etc), do not apply after commencement except for the purposes of proceedings begun before commencement.

(3) Sections 101 to 102 of this Act (rights and remedies of exclusive licensee) apply where sections 96 to 100 of this Act apply; section 19 of the 1956 Act continues to apply where sections 17 or 18 of that Act applies.

(4) Sections 104 to 106 of this Act (presumptions) apply only in proceedings brought by virtue of this Act; section 20 of the 1956 Act continues to apply in proceedings brought by virtue of that Act.

**32.**—Sections 101 and 102 of this Act (rights and remedies of exclusive licensee) do not apply to a licence granted before 1st June 1957.

**33.**—(1) The provisions of section 107 of this Act (criminal liability for making or dealing with infringing articles, etc) apply only in relation to acts done after commencement; section 21 of the 1956 Act (penalties and summary proceedings in respect of dealings which infringe copyright) continues to apply in relation to acts done before commencement.

(2) Section 109 of this Act (search warrants) applies in relation to offences committed before commencement in relation to which sections 21A or 21B of the 1956 Act applied; sections 21A and 21B continue to apply in relation to warrants issued before commencement.

*Copyright Tribunal: proceedings pending on commencement*

**34.**—(1) The Lord Chancellor may, after consultation with the Lord Advocate, by rules make such provision as he considers necessary or expedient with respect to proceedings pending under Part IV of the 1956 Act immediately before commencement.

(2) Rules under this paragraph shall be made by statutory instrument which shall be subject to annulment in pursuance of a resolution of either House of Parliament.

*Qualification for copyright protection*

**35.**—Every work in which copyright subsisted under the 1956 Act immediately before commencement shall be deemed to satisfy the requirements of Part I of this Act as to qualification for copyright protection.

*Dependent territories*

**36.**—(1) The 1911 Act shall remain in force as part of the law of any dependent territory in which it was in force immediately before commencement until—

    (a)   the new copyright provisions come into force in that territory by virtue of an Order under section 157 of this Act (power to extend new copyright provisions), or

    (b)   in the case of any of the Channel Islands, the Act is repealed by Order under sub-paragraph (3) below.

(2) An Order in Council in force immediately before commencement which extends to any dependent territory any provisions of the 1956 Act shall remain in force as part of the law of that territory until—

    (a)   the new copyright provisions come into force in that territory by virtue of an Order under section 157 of this Act (power to extend new copyright provisions), or

    (b)   in the case of the Isle of Man, the Order is revoked by Order under sub-paragraph (3) below;

and while it remains in force such an Order may be varied under the provisions of the 1956 Act under which it was made.

(3) If it appears to Her Majesty that provision with respect to copyright has been made in the law of any of the Channel Islands or the Isle of Man otherwise than by extending the provisions of Part I of this Act, Her Majesty may by Order in Council repeal the 1911 Act as it has effect as part of the law of that territory or, as the case may be, revoke the Order extending the 1956 Act there.

(4) A dependent territory in which the 1911 or 1956 Act remains in force shall be treated, in the law of the countries to which Part I extends, as a country to which that Part extends; and those countries shall be treated in the law of such a territory as countries to which the 1911 Act or, as the case may be, the 1956 Act extends.

(5) If a country in which the 1911 or 1956 Act is in force ceases to be a colony of the United Kingdom, section 158 of this Act (consequences of country ceasing to be colony) applies with the substitution for the reference in subsection (3)(b) to the provisions of Part I of this Act of a reference to the provisions of the 1911 or 1956 Act, as the case may be.

(6) In this paragraph 'dependent territory' means any of the Channel Islands, the Isle of Man or any colony.

**37.**—(1) This paragraph applies to a country which immediately before commencement was not a dependent territory within the meaning of paragraph 36 above but—

(a)   was a country to which the 1956 Act extended, or

(b)   was treated as such a country by virtue of paragraph 39(2) of Schedule 7 to that Act (countries to which the 1911 Act extended or was treated as extending);

and Her Majesty may by Order in Council conclusively declare for the purposes of this paragraph whether a country was such a country or was so treated.

(2)   A country to which this paragraph applies shall be treated as a country to which Part I extends for the purposes of sections 154 to 156 (qualification for copyright protection) until—

(a)   an Order in Council is made in respect of that country under section 159 (application of Part I to countries to which it does not extend), or

(b)   an Order in Council is made declaring that it shall cease to be so treated by reason of the fact that the provisions of the 1956 Act or, as the case may be, the 1911 Act, which extended there as part of the law of that country have been repealed or amended.

(3)   A statutory instrument containing an Order in Council under this paragraph shall be subject to annulment in pursuance of a resolution of either House of Parliament.


*Territorial waters and the continental shelf*

**38.**—Section 161 of this Act (application of Part I to things done in territorial waters or the United Kingdom sector of the continental shelf) does not apply in relation to anything done before commencement.


*British ships, aircraft and hovercraft*

**39.**—Section 162 (British ships, aircraft and hovercraft) does not apply in relation to anything done before commencement.


*Crown copyright*

**40.**—(1) Section 163 of this Act (general provisions as to Crown copyright) applies to an existing work if—

(a)   section 39 of the 1956 Act applies to the work immediately before commencement, and

(b)   the work is not one to which sections 164, 165 or 166 applies (copyright in Acts, Measures and Bills and Parliamentary copyright: see paragraphs 42 and 43 below).

(2)   Section 163(1)(b) (first ownership of copyright) has effect subject to any agreement entered into before commencement under section 39(6) of the 1956 Act.

**41.**—(1) The following provisions have effect with respect to the duration of copyright in existing works to which section 163 (Crown copyright) applies.

The question which provision applies to a work shall be determined by reference to the facts immediately before commencement; and expressions used in this paragraph which were defined for the purposes of the 1956 Act have the same meaning as in that Act.

(2)   Copyright in the following descriptions of work continues to subsist until the date on which it would have expired in accordance with the 1956 Act—

(a)   published literary, dramatic or musical works;

(b)   artistic works other than engravings or photographs;

(c)   published engravings;

(d)   published photographs and photographs taken before 1st June 1957;

(e)   published sound recordings and sound recordings made before 1st June 1957;

(f)   published films and films falling within section 13(3)(a) of the 1956 Act (films registered under former enactments relating to registration of films).

(3)   Copyright in unpublished literary, dramatic or musical works continues to subsist until—

(a)   the date on which copyright expires in accordance with section 163(3), or

(b)   the end of the period of 50 years from the end of the calendar year in which the new copyright provisions come into force,

whichever is the later.

(4) Copyright in the following descriptions of work continues to subsist until the end of the period of 50 years from the end of the calendar year in which the new copyright provisions come into force—

    (a)   unpublished engravings;

    (b)   unpublished photographs taken on or after 1st June 1957.

(5) Copyright in a film or sound recording not falling within sub-paragraph (2) above continues to subsist until the end of the period of 50 years from the end of the calendar year in which the new copyright provisions come into force, unless the film or recording is published before the end of that period, in which case copyright expires 50 years from the end of the calendar year in which it is published.

**42.**—(1) Section 164 (copyright in Acts and Measures) applies to existing Acts of Parliament and Measures of the General Synod of the Church of England.

(2) References in that section to Measures of the General Synod of the Church of England include Church Assembly Measures.

*Parliamentary copyright*

**43.**—(1) Section 165 of this Act (general provisions as to Parliamentary copyright) applies to existing unpublished literary, dramatic, musical or artistic works, but does not otherwise apply to existing works.

(2) Section 166 (copyright in Parliamentary Bills) does not apply—

    (a)   to a public Bill which was introduced into Parliament and published before commencement,

    (b)   to a private Bill of which a copy was deposited in either House before commencement, or

    (c)   to a personal Bill which was given a First Reading in the House of Lords before commencement.

*Copyright vesting in certain international organisations*

**44.**—(1) Any work in which immediately before commencement copyright subsisted by virtue of section 33 of the 1956 Act shall be deemed to satisfy the requirements of section 168(1); but otherwise section 168 does not apply to works made or, as the case may be, published before commencement.

(2) Copyright in any such work which is unpublished continues to subsist until the date on which it would have expired in accordance with the 1956 Act, or the end of the period of 50 years from the end of the calendar year in which the new copyright provisions come into force, whichever is the earlier.

*Meaning of 'publication'*

**45.**—Section 175(3) (construction of building treated as equivalent to publication) applies only where the construction of the building began after commencement.

*Meaning of 'unauthorised'*

**46.**—For the purposes of the application of the definition in section 178 (minor definitions) of the expression 'unauthorised' in relation to things done before commencement—

    (a)   paragraph (a) applies in relation to things done before 1st June 1957 as if the reference to the licence of the copyright owner were a reference to his consent or acquiescence;

    (b)   paragraph (b) applies with the substitution for the words from 'or, in a case' to the end of the words 'or any person lawfully claiming under him'; and

    (c)   paragraph (c) shall be disregarded.

SCHEDULE 2
RIGHTS IN PERFORMANCES: PERMITTED ACTS

Section 189

*Introductory*

**1.**—(1)  The provisions of this Schedule specify acts which may be done in relation to a performance or recording notwithstanding the rights conferred by Part II; they relate only to the question of infringement of those rights and do not affect any other right or obligation restricting the doing of any of the specified acts.

(2)  No inference shall be drawn from the description of any act which may by virtue of this Schedule be done without infringing the rights conferred by Part II as to the scope of those rights.

(3)  The provisions of this Schedule are to be construed independently of each other, so that the fact that an act does not fall within one provision does not mean that it is not covered by another provision.

*Criticism, reviews and news reporting*

**2.**—(1)  Fair dealing with a performance or recording—

(a)  for the purpose of criticism or review, of that or another performance or recording, or of a work, or

(b)  for the purpose of reporting current events,

does not infringe any of the rights conferred by Part II.

(2)  Expressions used in this paragraph have the same meaning as in section 30.

*Incidental inclusion of performance or recording*

**3.**—(1)  The rights conferred by Part II are not infringed by the incidental inclusion of a performance or recording in a sound recording, film, broadcast or cable programme.

(2)  Nor are those rights infringed by anything done in relation to copies of, or the playing, showing, broadcasting or inclusion in a cable programme service of, anything whose making was, by virtue of sub-paragraph (1), not an infringement of those rights.

(3)  A performance or recording so far as it consists of music, or words spoken or sung with music, shall not be regarded as incidentally included in a sound recording, broadcast or cable programme if it is deliberately included.

(4)  Expressions used in this paragraph have the same meaning as in section 31.

*Things done for purposes of instruction or examination*

**4.**—(1)  The rights conferred by Part II are not infringed by the copying of a recording of a performance in the course of instruction, or of preparation for instruction, in the making of films or film sound-tracks, provided the copying is done by a person giving or receiving instruction.

(2)  The rights conferred by Part II are not infringed—

(a)  by the copying of a recording of a performance for the purposes of setting or answering the questions in an examination, or

(b)  by anything done for the purposes of an examination by way of communicating the questions to the candidates.

(3)  Where a recording which would otherwise be an illicit recording is made in accordance with this paragraph but is subsequently dealt with, it shall be treated as an illicit recording for the purposes of that dealing, and if that dealing infringes any right conferred by Part II for all subsequent purposes.

For this purpose 'dealt with' means sold or let for hire, or offered or exposed for sale or hire.

(4)  Expressions used in this paragraph have the same meaning as in section 32.

*Playing or showing sound recording, film, broadcast or cable programme at educational establishment*

**5.**—(1)  The playing or showing of a sound recording, film, broadcast or cable programme at an educational establishment for the purposes of instruction before an audience consisting of teachers and pupils at the establishment and other persons directly connected with the activities of the establishment is not a playing or showing of a performance in public for the purposes of infringement of the rights conferred by Part II.

(2) A person is not for this purpose directly connected with the activities of the educational establishment simply because he is the parent of a pupil at the establishment.

(3) Expressions used in this paragraph have the same meaning as in section 34 and any provision made under section 174(2) with respect to the application of that section also applies for the purposes of this paragraph.

*Recording of broadcasts and cable programmes by educational establishments*

**6.**—(1) A recording of a broadcast or cable programme, or a copy of such a recording, may be made by or on behalf of an educational establishment for the educational purposes of that establishment without thereby infringing any of the rights conferred by Part II in relation to any performance or recording included in it.

(2) Where a recording which would otherwise be an illicit recording is made in accordance with this paragraph but is subsequently dealt with, it shall be treated as an illicit recording for the purposes of that dealing, and if that dealing infringes any right conferred by Part II for all subsequent purposes.

For this purpose 'dealt with' means sold or let for hire, or offered or exposed for sale or hire.

(3) Expressions used in this paragraph have the same meaning as in section 35 and any provision made under section 174(2) with respect to the application of that section also applies for the purposes of this paragraph.

*Copy of work required to be made as condition of export*

**7.**—(1) If an article of cultural or historical importance or interest cannot lawfully be exported from the United Kingdom unless a copy of it is made and deposited in an appropriate library or archive, it is not an infringement of any right conferred by Part II to make that copy.

(2) Expressions used in this paragraph have the same meaning as in section 44.

*Parliamentary and judicial proceedings*

**8.**—(1) The rights conferred by Part II are not infringed by anything done for the purposes of parliamentary or judicial proceedings or for the purpose of reporting such proceedings.

(2) Expressions used in this paragraph have the same meaning as in section 45.

*Royal Commissions and statutory inquiries*

**9.**—(1) The rights conferred by Part II are not infringed by anything done for the purposes of the proceedings of a Royal Commission or statutory inquiry or for the purpose of reporting any such proceedings held in public.

(2) Expressions used in this paragraph have the same meaning as in section 46.

*Public records*

**10.**—(1) Material which is comprised in public records within the meaning of the Public Records Act 1958, the Public Records (Scotland) Act 1937 or the Public Records (Northern Ireland) Act 1923 which are open to public inspection in pursuance of that Act, may be copied, and a copy may be supplied to any person, by or with the authority of any officer appointed under that Act, without infringing any right conferred by Part II.

(2) Expressions used in this paragraph have the same meaning as in section 49.

*Acts done under statutory authority*

**11.**—(1) Where the doing of a particular act is specifically authorised by an Act of Parliament, whenever passed, then, unless the Act provides otherwise, the doing of that act does not infringe the rights conferred by Part II.

(2) Sub-paragraph (1) applies in relation to an enactment contained in Northern Ireland legislation as it applies to an Act of Parliament.

(3) Nothing in this paragraph shall be construed as excluding any defence of statutory authority otherwise available under or by virtue of any enactment.

(4) Expressions used in this paragraph have the same meaning as in section 50.

*Transfer of copies of works in electronic form*

**12.**—(1) This paragraph applies where a recording of a performance in electronic form has been purchased on terms which, expressly or impliedly or by virtue of any rule of law, allow the purchaser to make further recordings in connection with his use of the recording.

(2) If there are no express terms—

(a) prohibiting the transfer of the recording by the purchaser, imposing obligations which continue after a transfer, prohibiting the assignment of any consent or terminating any consent on a transfer, or

(b) providing for the terms on which a transferee may do the things which the purchaser was permitted to do,

anything which the purchaser was allowed to do may also be done by a transferee without infringement of the rights conferred by this Part, but any recording made by the purchaser which is not also transferred shall be treated as an illicit recording for all purposes after the transfer.

(3) The same applies where the original purchased recording is no longer usable and what is transferred is a further copy used in its place.

(4) The above provisions also apply on a subsequent transfer, with the substitution for references in sub-paragraph (2) to the purchaser of references to the subsequent transferor.

(5) This paragraph does not apply in relation to a recording purchased before the commencement of Part II.

(6) Expressions used in this paragraph have the same meaning as in section 56.

*Use of recordings of spoken works in certain cases*

**13.**—(1) Where a recording of the reading or recitation of a literary work is made for the purpose—

(a) of reporting current events, or

(b) of broadcasting or including in a cable programme service the whole or part of the reading or recitation,

it is not an infringement of the rights conferred by Part II to use the recording (or to copy the recording and use the copy) for that purpose, provided the following conditions are met.

(2) The conditions are that—

(a) the recording is a direct recording of the reading or recitation and is not taken from a previous recording or from a broadcast or cable programme;

(b) the making of the recording was not prohibited by or on behalf of the person giving the reading or recitation;

(c) the use made of the recording is not of a kind prohibited by or on behalf of that person before the recording was made; and

(d) the use is by or with the authority of a person who is lawfully in possession of the recording.

(3) Expressions used in this paragraph have the same meaning as in section 58.

*Recordings of folksongs*

**14.**—(1) A recording of a performance of a song may be made for the purpose of including it in an archive maintained by a designated body without infringing any of the rights conferred by Part II, provided the conditions in sub-paragraph (2) below are met.

(2) The conditions are that—

(a) the words are unpublished and of unknown authorship at the time the recording is made,

(b) the making of the recording does not infringe any copyright, and

(c) its making is not prohibited by any performer.

(3) Copies of a recording made in reliance on sub-paragraph (1) and included in an archive maintained by a designated body may, if the prescribed conditions are met, be made and supplied by the archivist without infringing any of the rights conferred by Part II.

(4) In this paragraph—

'designated body' means a body designated for the purposes of section 61, and
'the prescribed conditions' means the conditions prescribed for the purposes of subsection (3) of
that section;

and other expressions used in this paragraph have the same meaning as in that section.

*Playing of sound recordings for purposes of club, society, etc*

**15.**—(1) It is not an infringement of any right conferred by Part II to play a sound recording as part of the activities of, or for the benefit of, a club, society or other organisation if the following conditions are met.

(2) The conditions are—

    (a)  that the organisation is not established or conducted for profit and its main objects are charitable or are otherwise concerned with the advancement of religion, education or social welfare, and

    (b)  that the proceeds of any charge for admission to the place where the recording is to be heard are applied solely for the purposes of the organisation.

(3) Expressions used in this paragraph have the same meaning as in section 67.

*Incidental recording for purposes of broadcast or cable programme*

**16.**—(1) A person who proposes to broadcast a recording of a performance, or include a recording of a performance in a cable programme service, in circumstances not infringing the rights conferred by Part II shall be treated as having consent for the purposes of that Part for the making of a further recording for the purposes of the broadcast or cable programme.

(2) That consent is subject to the condition that the further recording—

    (a)  shall not be used for any other purpose, and

    (b)  shall be destroyed within 28 days of being first used for broadcasting the performance or including it in a cable programme service.

(3) A recording made in accordance with this paragraph shall be treated as an illicit recording—

    (a)  for the purposes of any use in breach of the condition mentioned in sub-paragraph (2)(a), and

    (b)  for all purposes after that condition or the condition mentioned in sub-paragraph (2)(b) is broken.

(4) Expressions used in this paragraph have the same meaning as in section 68.

*Recordings for purposes of supervision and control of broadcasts and cable programmes*

**17.**—(1) The rights conferred by Part II are not infringed by the making or use by the British Broadcasting Corporation, for the purpose of maintaining supervision and control over programmes broadcast by them, of recordings of those programmes.

*(2) The rights conferred by Part II are not infringed by—*

    *(a)  the making or use of recordings by the Independent Broadcasting Authority for the purposes mentioned in section 4(7) of the Broadcasting Act 1981 (maintenance of supervision and control over programmes and advertisements); or*

    *(b)  anything done under or in pursuance of provision included in a contract between a programme contractor and the Authority in accordance with section 21 of that Act.*

*(3) The rights conferred by Part II are not infringed by—*

    *(a)  the making by or with the authority of the Cable Authority, or the use by that Authority, for the purpose of maintaining supervision and control over programmes included in services licensed under Part I of the Cable and Broadcasting Act 1984, of recordings of those programmes; or*

    *(b)  anything done under or in pursuance of—*

(i)  a notice or direction given under section 16 of the Cable and Broadcasting Act 1984 (power of Cable Authority to require production of recordings); or

(ii)  a condition included in a licence by virtue of section 35 of that Act (duty of Authority to secure that recordings are available for certain purposes).

(4)  Expressions used in this paragraph have the same meaning as in section 69.

(2)  **The rights conferred by Part II are not infringed by anything done in pursuance of—**

(a)  **sections 11(1), 95(1), 145(4), (5) or (7), 155(3) or 167(1) of the Broadcasting Act 1990;**

(b)  **a condition which, by virtue of sections 11(2) or 95(2) of that Act, is included in a licence granted under Part I or III of that Act; or**

(c)  **a direction given under section 109(2) of that Act (power of Radio Authority to require production of recordings etc).**

(3)  **The rights conferred by Part II are not infringed by—**

(a)  **the use by the Independent Television Commission or the Radio Authority, in connection with the performance of any of their functions under the Broadcasting Act 1990, of any recording, script or transcript which is provided to them under or by virtue of any provision of that Act; or**

(b)  **the use by the Broadcasting Complaints Commission or the Broadcasting Standards Council, in connection with any complaint made to them under that Act, of any recording or transcript requested or required to be provided to them, and so provided, under section 145(4) or (7) or section 155(3) of that Act.**

*General note*
Paras 17(2), (3), substituted for sub-paras (2)–(4) as originally enacted by the Broadcasting Act 1990, Sch 20, para 50(2).

*Free public showing or playing of broadcast or cable programme*

**18.**—(1)  The showing or playing in public of a broadcast or cable programme to an audience who have not paid for admission to the place where the broadcast or programme is to be seen or heard does not infringe any right conferred by Part II in relation to a performance or recording included in—

(a)  the broadcast or cable programme, or

(b)  any sound recording or film which is played or shown in public by reception of the broadcast or cable programme.

(2)  The audience shall be treated as having paid for admission to a place—

(a)  if they have paid for admission to a place of which that place forms part; or

(b)  if goods or services are supplied at that place (or a place of which it forms part)—

(i)  at prices which are substantially attributable to the facilities afforded for seeing or hearing the broadcast or programme, or

(ii)  at prices exceeding those usually charged there and which are partly attributable to those facilities.

(3)  The following shall not be regarded as having paid for admission to a place—

(a)  persons admitted as residents or inmates of the place;

(b)  persons admitted as members of a club or society where the payment is only for membership of the club or society and the provision of facilities for seeing or hearing broadcasts or programmes is only incidental to the main purposes of the club or society.

(4)  Where the making of the broadcast or inclusion of the programme in a cable programme service was an infringement of the rights conferred by Part II in relation to a performance or recording, the fact that it was heard or seen in public by the reception of the broadcast or programme shall be taken into account in assessing the damages for that infringement.

(5)  Expressions used in this paragraph have the same meaning as in section 72.

*Reception and re-transmission of broadcast in cable programme service*

**19.**—(1)  This paragraph applies where a broadcast made from a place in the United Kingdom is, by reception and immediate re-transmission, included in a cable programme service.

(2) The rights conferred by Part II in relation to a performance or recording included in the broadcast are not infringed—

    (a)   *if the inclusion of the broadcast in the cable programme service is in pursuance of a requirement imposed under section 13(1) of the Cable and Broadcasting Act 1984 (duty of Cable Authority to secure inclusion in cable services of certain programmes), or*

    (b)   if and to the extent that the broadcast is made for reception in the area in which the cable programme service is provided;

but where the making of the broadcast was an infringement of those rights, the fact that the broadcast was re-transmitted as a programme in a cable programme service shall be taken into account in assessing the damages for that infringement.

(3) Expressions used in this paragraph have the same meaning as in section 73.

*General note*
Para 19(2)(a) deleted by the Broadcasting Act 1990, s 203(3) and Sch 21.

*Provision of sub-titled copies of broadcast or cable programme*

**20.**—(1) A designated body may, for the purpose of providing people who are deaf or hard of hearing, or physically or mentally handicapped in other ways, with copies which are sub-titled or otherwise modified for their special needs, make recordings of television broadcasts or cable programmes without infringing any right conferred by Part II in relation to a performance or recording included in the broadcast or cable programme.

(2) In this paragraph 'designated body' means a body designated for the purposes of section 74 and other expressions used in this paragraph have the same meaning as in that section.

*Recording of broadcast or cable programme for archival purposes*

**21.**—(1) A recording of a broadcast or cable programme of a designated class, or a copy of such a recording, may be made for the purpose of being placed in an archive maintained by a designated body without thereby infringing any right conferred by Part II in relation to a performance or recording included in the broadcast or cable programme.

(2) In this paragraph 'designated class' and 'designated body' means a class or body designated for the purposes of section 75 and other expressions used in this paragraph have the same meaning as in that section.

SCHEDULE 3

REGISTERED DESIGNS: MINOR AND CONSEQUENTIAL AMENDMENTS OF 1949 ACT

Section 272

*General note*
This Schedule amends certain sections of the Registered Designs Act 1949, which is printed, as amended, in Part C of Appendix 1 to this work.

SCHEDULE 4

THE REGISTERED DESIGNS ACT 1949 AS AMENDED

Section 273

*General note*
This Schedule sets out the text of the Registered Designs Act 1949 as amended by this Act, which is printed in Part C of Appendix 1 to this work.

SCHEDULE 5

PATENTS: MISCELLANEOUS AMENDMENTS

Section 295
**11. Cancellation of registration**
(1) The registrar may, upon a request made in the prescribed manner by the registered proprietor, cancel the registration of a design.

*General note*
Sch 5 relates solely to patents and, apart from para 11(1), is not printed here.


SCHEDULE 6

PROVISIONS FOR THE BENEFIT OF THE HOSPITAL FOR SICK CHILDREN

Section 301

**1. Interpretation**
(1) In this Schedule—
'the Hospital' means The Hospital for Sick Children, Great Ormond Street, London,
'the trustees' means the special trustees appointed for the Hospital under the National Health Service Act 1977; and
'the work' means the play 'Peter Pan' by Sir James Matthew Barrie.
(2) Expressions used in this Schedule which are defined for the purposes of Part I of this Act (copyright) have the same meaning as in that Part.

**2. Entitlement to royalty**
(1) The trustees are entitled, subject to the following provisions of this Schedule, to a royalty in respect of any public performance, commercial publication, broadcasting or inclusion in a cable programme service of the whole or any substantial part of the work or an adaptation of it.
(2) Where the trustees are or would be entitled to a royalty, another form of remuneration may be agreed.

**3. Exceptions**
No royalty is payable in respect of—
    (a)    anything which immediately before copyright in the work expired on 31st December 1987 could lawfully have been done without the licence, or further licence, of the trustees as copyright owners; or
    (b)    anything which if copyright still subsisted in the work could, by virtue of any provision of Chapter III of Part I of this Act (acts permitted notwithstanding copyright), be done without infringing copyright.

**4. Saving**
No royalty is payable in respect of anything done in pursuance of arrangements made before the passing of this Act.

**5. Procedure for determining amount payable**
(1) In default of agreement application may be made to the Copyright Tribunal which shall consider the matter and make such order regarding the royalty or other remuneration to be paid as it may determine to be reasonable in the circumstances.
(2) Application may subsequently be made to the Tribunal to vary its order, and the Tribunal shall consider the matter and make such order confirming or varying the original order as it may determine to be reasonable in the circumstances.
(3) An application for variation shall not, except with the special leave of the Tribunal, be made within twelve months from the date of the original order or of the order on a previous application for variation.
(4) A variation order has effect from the date on which it is made or such later date as may be specified by the Tribunal.

**6. Sums received to be held on trust**
The sums received by the trustees by virtue of this Schedule, after deduction of any relevant expenses, shall be held by them on trust for the purposes of the Hospital.

**7. Right only for the benefit of the Hospital**
    (1) The right of the trustees under this Schedule may not be assigned and shall cease if the trustees purport to assign or charge it.
    (2) The right may not be the subject of an order under section 92 of the National Health Service Act 1977 (transfers of trust property by order of the Secretary of State) and shall cease if the Hospital ceases to have a separate identity or ceases to have purposes which include the care of sick children.
    (3) Any power of Her Majesty, the court (within the meaning of *the Charities Act 1960* **the Charities Act 1993**) or any other person to alter the trusts of a charity is not exercisable in relation to the trust created by this Schedule.

*General note*
Para 7: in sub-para (3) words in bold type substituted for the words in italics by the Charities Act 1993, s 98(1), Sch 6, para 30.


SCHEDULE 7

CONSEQUENTIAL AMENDMENTS: GENERAL


*British Mercantile Marine Uniform Act 1919 (c 62)*

1—For section 2 of the British Mercantile Marine Uniform Act 1919 (copyright in distinctive marks of uniform) substitute—

'**2   Right in registered design of distinctive marks of uniform**

*The right of the Secretary of State in any design forming part of the British mercantile marine uniform which is registered under the Registered Designs Act 1949 is not limited to the period prescribed by section 8 of that Act but shall continue to subsist so long as the design remains on the register.'*


*Chartered Associations (Protection of Names and Uniforms) Act 1926 (c 26)*

**2.**—In section 1(5) of the Chartered Associations (Protection of Names and Uniforms) Act 1926 for 'the copyright in respect thereof' substitute 'the right in the registered design'.


*Patents, Designs, Copyright and Trade Marks (Emergency) Act 1939 (c 107)*

**3.**—(1) The Patents, Designs, Copyright and Trade Marks (Emergency) Act 1939 is amended as follows.
    (2) in section 1 (effect of licence where owner is enemy or enemy subject)—

    (a)  in subsection (1) after 'a copyright' and 'the copyright' insert 'or design right';
    (b)  in subsection (2) after 'the copyright' insert 'or design right' and for 'or copyright' substitute ', copyright or design right'.

    (3) In section 2 (power of comptroller to grant licences)—

    (a)  in subsection (1) after 'a copyright', 'the copyright' (twice) and 'the said copyright' insert 'or design right' and for 'or copyright' (twice) substitute ', copyright or design right';
    (b)  in subsections (2) and (3) for ', or copyright' substitute ', copyright or design right';
    (c)  in subsection (4) and in subsection (5) (twice), after 'the copyright' insert 'or design right';
    (d)  in subsection (8)(c) for 'or work in which copyright subsists' substitute 'work in which copyright subsists or design in which design right subsists'.

    (4) In section 5 (effect of war on international arrangements)—

    (a)  in subsection (1) for 'section twenty-nine of the Copyright Act 1911' substitute 'section 159 or 256 of the Copyright, Designs and Patents Act 1988 (countries enjoying reciprocal copyright or design right protection)';

(b) in subsection (2) after 'copyright' (four times) insert 'or design right' and for 'the Copyright Act 1911' (twice) substitute 'Part I or III of the Copyright, Designs and Patents Act 1988'.

(5) In section 10(1) (interpretation) omit the definition of 'copyright', and for the definitions of 'design', 'invention', 'patent' and 'patentee' substitute—

"'design' has in reference to a registered design the same meaning as in the Registered Designs Act 1949, and in reference to design right the same meaning as in Part III of the Copyright, Designs and Patents Act 1988;
'invention' and 'patent' have the same meaning as in the Patents Act 1977.'

*Crown Proceedings Act 1947 (c 44)*

**4.**—(1) In the Crown Proceedings Act 1947 for section 3 (provisions as to industrial property) substitute—

### '3   Infringement of intellectual property rights

(1) Civil proceedings lie against the Crown for an infringement committed by a servant or agent of the Crown, with the authority of the Crown, of—

(a) a patent,
(b) a registered trade mark or registered service mark,
(c) the right in a registered design,
(d) design right, or
(e) copyright;

but save as provided by this subsection no proceedings lie against the Crown by virtue of this Act in respect of an infringement of any of those rights.

(2) Nothing in this section, or any other provision of this Act, shall be construed as affecting—

(a) the rights of a government department under section 55 of the Patents Act 1977, Schedule 1 to the Registered Designs Act 1949 or section 240 of the Copyright, Designs and Patents Act 1988 (Crown use of patents and designs), or
(b) the rights of the Secretary of State under section 22 of the Patents Act 1977 or section 5 of the Registered Designs Act 1949 (security of information prejudicial to defence or public safety).'

(3) In the application of sub-paragraph (1) to Northern Ireland—

(a) the reference to the Crown Proceedings Act 1947 is to that Act as it applies to the Crown in right of Her Majesty's Government in Northern Ireland, as well as to the Crown in right of Her Majesty's Government in the United Kingdom, and
(b) in the substituted section 3 as it applies in relation to the Crown in right of Her Majesty's Government in Northern Ireland, subsection (2)(b) shall be omitted.

*Patents Act 1949 (c 87)*

**5.**—In section 47 of the Patents Act 1949 (rights of third parties in respect of Crown use of patent), in the closing words of subsection (1) (which relate to the use of models or documents), after 'copyright' insert 'or design right'.

*Public Libraries (Scotland) Act 1955 (c 27)*

**6.**—In section 4 of the Public Libraries (Scotland) Act 1955 (extension of lending power of public libraries), make the existing provision subsection (1) and after it add—

'(2) The provisions of Part I of the Copyright, Designs and Patents Act 1988 (copyright) relating to the rental of copies of sound recordings, films and computer programs apply to any lending by a statutory library authority of copies of such works, whether or not a charge is made for that facility.'

*Appendix 1*

*London County Council (General Powers) Act 1958*

**7.**—In section 36 of the London County Council (General Powers) Act 1958 (power as to libraries: provision and repair of things other than books) for subsection (5) substitute—

'(5) Nothing in this section shall be construed as authorising an infringement of copyright.'

*Public Libraries and Museums Act 1964 (c 75)*

**8.**—In section 8 of the Public Libraries and Museums Act 1964 (restrictions on charges for library facilities), after subsection (5) add—

'(6) The provisions of Part I of the Copyright, Designs and Patents Act 1988 (copyright) relating to the rental of copies of sound recordings, films and computer programs apply to any lending by a library authority of copies of such works, whether or not a charge is made for that facility.'

*Marine etc, Broadcasting (Offences) Act 1967 (c 41)*

**9.**—In section 5 of the Marine etc, Broadcasting (Offences) Act 1967 (provision of material for broadcasting by pirate radio stations)—

(a) in subsection (3)(a) for the words from 'cinematograph film' to 'in the record' substitute 'film or sound recording with intent that a broadcast of it'; and

(b) in subsection (6) for the words from 'and references' to the end substitute 'and 'film', 'sound recording', 'literary, dramatic or musical work' and 'artistic work' have the same meaning as in Part I of the Copyright, Designs and Patents Act 1988 (copyright)'.

*Medicines Act 1968 (c 67)*

**10.**—(1) Section 92 of the Medicines Act 1968 (scope of provisions restricting promotion of sales of medicinal products) is amended as follows.

(2) In subsection (1) (meaning of 'advertisement') for the words from 'or by the exhibition' to 'service' substitute 'or by means of a photograph, film, sound recording, broadcast or cable programme.'

(3) In subsection (2) (exception for the spoken word)—

(a) in paragraph (a) omit the words from 'or embodied' to 'film'; and

(b) in paragraph (b) for the words from 'by way of' to the end substitute 'or included in a cable programme service'.

(4) For subsection (6) substitute—

'(6) In this section 'film', 'sound recording', 'broadcast', 'cable programme', 'cable programme service', and related expressions, have the same meaning as in Part I of the Copyright, Designs and Patents Act 1988 (copyright).'

*Post Office Act 1969 (c 48)*

**11.**—In Schedule 10 to the Post Office Act 1969 (special transitional provisions relating to use of patents and registered designs), in the closing words of paragraphs 8(1) and 18(1) (which relate to the use of models and documents), after 'copyright' insert 'or design right'.

*Merchant Shipping Act 1970 (c 36)*

**12.**—In section 87 of the Merchant Shipping Act 1970 (merchant navy uniform), for subsection (4) substitute—

'(4) Where any design forming part of the merchant navy uniform has been registered under the Registered Designs Act 1949 and the Secretary of State is the proprietor of the design, his right in the design is not limited to the period prescribed by section 8 of that Act but shall continue to subsist so long as the design remains registered.'

*Taxes Management Act 1970 (c 9)*

**13.**—In section 16 of the Taxes Management Act 1970 (returns to be made in respect of certain payments)—

    (a)   in subsection (1)(c), and
    (b)   in subsection (2)(b),

for 'or public lending right' substitute ', public lending right, right in a registered design or design right'.

*Tribunals and Inquiries Act 1971 (c 62)*

***14.****—In Part I of Schedule 1 to the Tribunals and Inquiries Act 1971 (tribunals under direct supervision of Council on Tribunals) renumber the entry inserted by the Data Protection Act 1984 as '5B' and before it insert—*

                          *'Copyright     5A. The Copyright Tribunal.'*

*General note*
This paragraph is repealed by the Tribunals and Inquiries Act 1992, s 18(2), Sch 4, Pt I.

*Fair Trading Act 1973 (c 41)*

**15.**—In Schedule 4 to the Fair Trading Act 1973 (excluded services), for paragraph 10 (services of patent agents) substitute—

    **'10.** The services of registered patent agents (within the meaning of Part V of the Copyright, Designs and Patents Act 1988) in their capacity as such.';

and in paragraph 10A (services of European patent attorneys) for 'section 84(7) of the Patents Act 1977' substitute 'Part V of the Copyright, Designs and Patents Act 1988''.

*House of Commons Disqualification Act 1975 (c 24)*

**16.**—In Part II of Schedule 1 to the House of Commons Disqualification Act 1975 (bodies of which all members are disqualified), at the appropriate place insert 'The Copyright Tribunal'.

*Northern Ireland Assembly Disqualification Act 1975 (c 25)*

**17.**—In Part II of Schedule 1 to the Northern Ireland Assembly Disqualification Act 1975 (bodies of which all members are disqualified), at the appropriate place insert 'The Copyright Tribunal'.

*Restrictive Trade Practices Act 1976 (c 34)*

**18.**—(1) The Restrictive Trade Practices Act 1976 is amended as follows.
    (2) In Schedule 1 (excluded services) for paragraph 10 (services of patent agents) substitute—

    **'10.** The services of registered patent agents (within the meaning of Part V of the Copyright, Designs and Patents Act 1988) in their capacity as such.';

and in paragraph 10A (services of European patent attorneys) for 'section 84(7) of the Patents Act 1977' substitute 'Part V of the Copyright, Designs and Patents Act 1988'.
    (3) In Schedule 3 (excepted agreements), after paragraph 5A insert—

*'Design right*

**5B.**—(1) This Act does not apply to—

    (a)   a licence granted by the owner or a licensee of any design right,
    (b)   an assignment of design right, or
    (c)   an agreement for such a licence or assignment,

if the licence, assignment or agreement is one under which no such restrictions as are described in section 6(1) above are accepted, or no such information provisions as are described in section 7(1) above are made, except in respect of articles made to the design; but subject to the following provisions.

(2) Sub-paragraph (1) does not exclude a licence, assignment or agreement which is a design pooling agreement or is granted or made (directly or indirectly) in pursuance of a design pooling agreement.

(3) In this paragraph a 'design pooling agreement' means an agreement—

(a) to which the parties are or include at least three persons (the 'principal parties') each of whom has an interest in one or more design rights, and

(b) by which each principal party agrees, in respect of design right in which he has, or may during the currency of the agreement acquire, an interest to grant an interest (directly or indirectly) to one or more of the other principal parties, or to one or more of those parties and to other persons.

(4) In this paragraph—

'assignment', in Scotland, means assignation; and
'interest' means an interest as owner or licensee of design right.

(5) This paragraph applies to an interest held by or granted to more than one person jointly as if they were one person.

(6) References in this paragraph to the granting of an interest to a person indirectly are to its being granted to a third person for the purpose of enabling him to make a grant to the person in question.'

*Resale Prices Act 1976 (c 53)*

**19.**—In section 10(4) of the Resale Prices Act 1976 (patented articles: articles to be treated in same way), in paragraph (a) after 'protected' insert 'by design right or'.

*Patents Act 1977 (c 37)*

**20.**—In section 57 of the Patents Act 1977 (rights of third parties in respect of Crown use of patent), in the closing words of subsection (1) (which relate to the use of models or documents), after 'copyright' insert 'or design right'.

**21.**—In section 105 of the Patents Act 1977 (privilege in Scotland for communications relating to patent proceedings), omit 'within the meaning of section 104 above', make the existing text subsection (1) and after it insert—

'(2) In this section—

'patent proceedings' means proceedings under this Act or any of the relevant conventions, before the court, the comptroller or the relevant convention court, whether contested or uncontested and including an application for a patent; and

'the relevant conventions' means the European Patent Convention, the Community Patent Convention and the Patent Co-operation Treaty.'

**22.**—In section 123(7) of the Patents Act 1977 (publication of case reports by the comptroller—
(a) for 'and registered designs' substitute 'registered designs or design right',
(b) for 'and copyright' substitute ', copyright and design right'.

**23.**—In section 130(1) of the Patents Act 1977 (interpretation), in the definition of 'court', for paragraph (a) substitute—

'(a) as respects England and Wales, the High Court or any patents county court having jurisdiction by virtue of an order under section 287 of the Copyright, Designs and Patents Act 1988;'.

*Unfair Contract Terms Act 1977 (c 50)*

**24.**—In paragraph 1 of Schedule 1 to the Unfair Contract Terms Act 1977 (scope of main provisions: excluded contracts), in paragraph (c) (contracts relating to grant or transfer of interest in intellectual property) after 'copyright' insert 'or design right'.

*Judicature (Northern Ireland) Act 1978 (c 23)*

**25.**—In section 94A of the Judicature (Northern Ireland) Act 1978 (withdrawal of privilege against self-incrimination in certain proceedings relating to intellectual property), in subsection (5) (meaning of 'intellectual property') after 'copyright' insert 'or design right'.

*Capital Gains Tax Act 1979 (c 14)*

**26.**—*In section 18(4) of the Capital Gains Tax Act 1979 (situation of certain assets for purposes of Act), for paragraph (h) (intellectual property) substitute—*

> *'(ha) patents, trade marks, service marks and registered designs are situated where they are registered, and if registered in more than one register, where each register is situated, and rights or licences to use a patent, trade mark, service mark or registered design are situated in the United Kingdom if they or any right derived from them are exercisable in the United Kingdom,*
>
> *(hb) copyright, design right and franchises, and rights or licences to use any copyright work or design in which design right subsists, are situated in the United Kingdom if they or any right derived from them are exercisable in the United Kingdom,'.*

*General note*
This paragraph is repealed by the Taxation of Chargeable Gains Act 1992, s 290(3), Sch 12.

*British Telecommunications Act 1981 (c 38)*

**27.**—In Schedule 5 to the British Telecommunications Act 1981 (special transitional provisions relating to use of patents and registered designs), in the closing words of paragraphs 9(1) and 19(1) (which relate to the use of models and documents), after 'copyright' insert 'or design right'.

*Supreme Court Act 1981 (c 54)*

**28.**—(1) The Supreme Court Act 1981 is amended as follows.

(2) In section 72 (withdrawal of privilege against self-incrimination in certain proceedings relating to intellectual property), in subsection (5) (meaning of 'intellectual property') after 'copyright' insert, 'design right'.

(3) In Schedule 1 (distribution of business in the High Court), in paragraph 1(i) (business assigned to the Chancery Division: causes and matters relating to certain intellectual property) for 'or copyright' substitute ', copyright or design right'.

*Broadcasting Act 1981 (c 68)*

**29.**—*(1) The Broadcasting Act 1981 is amended as follows.*

*(2) In section 4 (general duties of IBA as regards programmes) for subsection (7) substitute—*

> '(7) For the purpose of maintaining supervision and control over the programmes (including advertisements) broadcast by them the Authority may make and use recordings of those programmes or any part of them.'

*(3) In section 20(9), omit paragraph (a).*

*General note*
This paragraph is repealed by the Broadcasting Act 1990, s 203(3), Sch 21.

*Appendix 1*

*Cable and Broadcasting Act 1984 (c 46)*

**30.**—*(1) The Cable and Broadcasting Act 1984 is amended as follows.*
*(2) In section 8, omit subsection (8).*
*(3) In section 49 (power of Secretary of State to give directions in the public interest), for subsection (7) substitute—*

'*(7) For the purposes of this section the place from which a broadcast is made is, in the case of a satellite transmission, the place from which the signals carrying the broadcast are transmitted to the satellite.*'
*(4) In section 56(2) (interpretation) omit the definition of 'the 1956 Act'.*

*General note*
This paragraph is repealed by the Broadcasting Act 1990, s 203(3), Sch 21.

*Companies Act 1985 (c 6)*

**31.**—*(1) Part XII of the Companies Act 1985 (registration of charges) is amended as follows.*
*(2) In section 396 (registration of charges in England and Wales: charges which must be registered), in subsection (1)(j) for the words from 'on a patent' to the end substitute 'or on any intellectual property', and after subsection (3) insert—*
'*(3A) The following are 'intellectual property' for the purposes of this section—*

*(a)   any patent, trade mark, service mark, registered design, copyright or design right;*
*(b)   any licence under or in respect of any such right.*'.

*(3)   In section 410 (registration of charges in Scotland: charges which must be registered), in subsection (4)(c) (incorporeal moveable property) after subparagraph (vi) insert—*

'*(vii) a registered design or a licence in respect of such a design,*
*(viii) a design right or a licence under a design right,*'.

*General note*
This paragraph is prospectively repealed by the Companies Act 1989, s 212, Sch 24.

*Law Reform (Miscellaneous Provisions) (Scotland) Act 1985 (c 73)*

**32.**—In section 15 of the Law Reform (Miscellaneous Provisions) (Scotland) Act 1985 (withdrawal of privilege against self-incrimination in certain proceedings relating to intellectual property), in subsection (5) (meaning of 'intellectual property') after 'copyright' insert 'or design right'.

*Atomic Energy Authority Act 1986 (c 3)*

**33.**—In section 8(2) of the Atomic Energy Authority Act 1986 (powers of Authority as to exploitation of research: meaning of 'intellectual property'), after 'copyrights' insert ', design rights'.

*Education and Libraries (Northern Ireland) Order 1986 (SI 1986/594 (NI 3))*

**34.**—In Article 77 of the Education and Libraries (Northern Ireland) Order 1986 (charges for library services), after paragraph (2) add—

'(3)  The provisions of Part I of the Copyright, Designs and Patents Act 1988 (copyright) relating to the rental of copies of sound recordings, films and computer programs apply to any lending by a board of copies of such works, whether or not a charge is made for that facility.'

*Companies (Northern Ireland) Order 1986 (SI 1986/1032 (NI 6))*

**35.**—*In Article 403 of the Companies (Northern Ireland) Order 1986 (registration of charges: charges which must be registered), in paragraph (1)(j) for the words from 'on a patent' to the end substitute 'or on any intellectual property', and after paragraph (3) insert—*
'*(3A) The following are 'intellectual property' for the purposes of this Article—*

(a)   any patent, trade mark, service mark, registered design, copyright or design right;
(b)   any licence under or in respect of any such right.'.

*General note*
This paragraph is prospectively repealed by the the Companies (No 2) (Northern Ireland) Order 1990, SI 1990 No 1504.


*Income and Corporation Taxes Act 1988 (c 1)*

**36.**—(1) The Income and Corporation Taxes Act 1988 is amended as follows.
(2) In section 83 (fees and expenses deductible in computing profits and gains of trade) for 'the extension of the period of copyright in a design' substitute 'an extension of the period for which the right in a registered design subsists'.
(3) In section 103 (charge on receipts after discontinuance of trade, profession or vocation), in subsection (3) (sums to which the section does not apply), after paragraph (b) insert—

'(bb)  a lump sum paid to the personal representatives of the designer of a design in which design right subsists as consideration for the assignment by them, wholly or partially, of that right,'

(4) In section 387 (carry forward as losses of certain payments made under deduction of tax), in subsection (3) (payments to which the section does not apply), in paragraph (e) (copyright royalties) after 'applies' insert 'or royalties in respect of a right in a design to which section 537B applies'.
(5) In section 536 (taxation of copyright royalties where owner abroad), for the definition of 'copyright' in subsection (2) substitute—

'copyright' does not include copyright in—

(i)   a cinematograph film or video recording, or
(ii)  the sound-track of such a film or recording, so far as it is not separately exploited; and'.

(6)   In Chapter I of Part XIII (miscellaneous special provisions: intellectual property), after section 537 insert—

'*Designs*

**537A.  Relief for payments in respect of designs**
(1)   Where the designer of a design in which design right subsists assigns that right, or the author of a registered design assigns the right in the design, wholly or partially, or grants an interest in it by licence, and—

(a)   the consideration for the assignment or grant consists, in whole or in part, of a payment to which this section applies, the whole amount of which would otherwise be included in computing the amount of his profits or gains for a single year of assessment, and
(b)   he was engaged in the creation of the design for a period of more than 12 months,

he may, on making a claim, require that effect shall be given to the following provisions in connection with that payment.
(2)   If the period for which he was engaged in the creation of the design does not exceed 24 months, then, for all income tax purposes, one-half only of the amount of the payment shall be treated as having become receivable on the date on which it actually became receivable and the remaining half shall be treated as having become receivable 12 months before that date.
(3)   If the period for which he was engaged in the creation of the design exceeds 24 months, then, for all income tax purposes, one-third only of the amount of the payment shall be treated as having become receivable on the date on which it actually became receivable, and one-third shall be treated as having become receivable 12 months, and one-third 24 months, before that date.
(4)   This section applies to—

(a)   a lump sum payment, including an advance on account of royalties which is not returnable, and
(b)   any other payment of or on account of royalties or sums payable periodically which does not only become receivable more than two years after articles made to the design or, as the case may be, articles to which the design is applied are first made available for sale or hire.

(5) A claim under this section with respect to any payment to which it applies by virtue only of subsection (4)(b) above shall have effect as a claim with respect to all such payments in respect of rights in the design in question which are receivable by the claimant, whether before or after the claim; and such a claim may be made at any time not later than 5th April next following the expiration of eight years after articles made to the design or, as the case may be, articles to which the design is applied were first made available for sale or hire.

(6) In this section—

    (a) 'designer' includes a joint designer, and

    (b) any reference to articles being made available for sale or hire is to their being so made available anywhere in the world by or with the licence of the design right owner or, as the case may be, the proprietor of the registered design.

**537B**

(1) Where the usual place of abode of the owner of a right in a design is not within the United Kingdom, section 349(1) shall apply to any payment of or on account of any royalties or sums paid periodically for or in respect of that right as it applies to annual payments not payable out of profits or gains brought into charge to income tax.

(2) In subsection (1) above—

    (a) 'right in a design' means design right or the right in a registered design,

    (b) the reference to the owner of a right includes a person who, notwithstanding that he has assigned the right to some other person, is entitled to receive periodical payments in respect of the right, and

    (c) the reference to royalties or other sums paid periodically for or in respect of a right does not include royalties or sums paid in respect of articles which are shown on a claim to have been exported from the United Kingdom for distribution outside the United Kingdom.

(3) Where a payment to which subsection (1) above applies is made through an agent resident in the United Kingdom and that agent is entitled as against the owner of the right to deduct any sum by way of commission in respect of services rendered, the amount of the payment shall for the purposes of section 349(1) be taken to be diminished by the sum which the agent is entitled to deduct.

(4) Where the person by or through whom the payment is made does not know that any such commission is payable or does not know the amount of any such commission, any income tax deducted by or assessed and charged on him shall be computed in the first instance on, and the account to be delivered of the payment shall be an account of, the total amount of the payment without regard being had to any diminution thereof, and in that case, on proof of the facts on a claim, there shall be made to the agent on behalf of the owner of the right such repayment of income tax as is proper in respect of the sum deducted by way of commission.

(5) The time of the making of a payment to which subsection (1) above applies shall, for all tax purposes, be taken to be the time when it is made by the person by whom it is first made and not the time when, it is made by or through any other person.

(6) Any agreement for the making of any payment to which subsection (1) above applies in full and without deduction of income tax shall be void.'

(7) In section 821 (payment made under deduction of tax before passing of Act imposing income tax for that year), in subsection (3) (payments subject to adjustment) after paragraph (a) insert

    '(aa) any payment for or in respect of a right in a design to which section 537B applies; and'

(8) In Schedule 19 (apportionment of income of close companies), in paragraph 10(4) (cessation or liquidation: debts taken into account although creditor is participator or associate), in paragraph (c) (payments for use of certain property) for the words from 'tangible property' to 'extend') substitute—

    '—

    (i) tangible property,

    (ii) copyright in a literary, dramatic, musical or artistic work within the meaning of Part I of the Copyright, Designs and Patents Act 1988 (or any similar right under the law of a country to which that Part does not extend), or

    (iii) design right,'.

(9) in Schedule 25 (taxation of UK-controlled foreign companies: exempt activities), in paragraph 9(1)(a) (investment business: holding of property) for 'patents or copyrights' substitute 'or intellectual property' and after that sub-paragraph insert—

'(1A) In sub-paragraph (1)(a) above 'intellectual property' means patents, registered designs, copyright and design right (or similar rights under the law of a country outside the United Kingdom).'

## SCHEDULE 8

REPEALS

Section 303(2)

| Chapter | Short title | Extent of repeal |
|---|---|---|
| 1939 c 107. | Patents, Designs, Copyright and Trade Marks (Emergency) Act 1939. | In section 10(1), the definition of 'copyright'. |
| 1945 c 16. | Limitation (Enemies and War Prisoners) Act 1945. | In section 2(1) and 4(a), the reference to section 10 of the Copyright Act 1911. |
| 1949 c 88. | Registered Designs Act 1949. | In section 3(2), the words 'or original'. Section 5(5). In section 11(2), the words 'or original'. In section 14(3), the words 'or the Isle of Man'. Section 32. Section 33(2). Section 37(1). Section 38. In section 44(1),. the definitions of 'copyright' and 'Journal'. In section 45, paragraphs (1) and (2). In section 46, paragraphs (1) and (2). Section 48(1). In Schedule 1, in paragraph 3(1), the words 'in such manner as may be prescribed by rules of court'. Schedule 2. |
| 1956 c 74. | Copyright Act 1956. | The whole Act. |
| 1957 c 6. | Ghana Independence Act 1957. | In Schedule 2, paragraph 12. |
| 1957 c 60. | Federation of Malaya Independence Act 1957. | In Schedule 1, paragraphs 14 and 15. |
| 1958 c 44. | Dramatic and Musical Performers' Protection Act 1958. | The whole Act. |
| 1958 c 51. | Public Records Act 1958. | Section 11. Schedule 3. |
| 1960 c 52. | Cyprus Independence Act 1960. | In the Schedule, paragraph 13. |
| 1960 c 55. | Nigeria Independence Act 1960. | In Schedule 2, paragraphs 12 and 13. |
| 1961 c 1. | Tanganyika Independence Act 1961. | In Schedule 2, paragraphs 13 and 14. |
| 1961 c 16. | Sierra Leone Independence Act 1961. | In Schedule 3, paragraphs 13 and 14. |
| 1961 c 25. | Patents and Designs (Renewals, Extensions and Fees) Act 1961. | The whole Act. |
| 1962 c 40. | Jamaica Independence Act 1962. | In Schedule 2, paragraph 13. |
| 1962 c 54. | Trinidad and Tobago Independence Act 1962. | In Schedule 2, paragraph 13. |
| 1963 c 53. | Performers' Protection Act 1963. | The whole Act. |
| 1964 c 46. | Malawi Independence Act 1964. | In Schedule 2, paragraph 13. |
| 1964 c 65. | Zambia Independence Act 1964. | In Schedule 1, paragraph 9. |
| *1964 c86* | *Malta Independence Act 1964* | *In Schedule 1, paragraph 11.* |
| 1964 c 93. | Gambia Independence Act 1964. | In Schedule 2, paragraph 12. |
| 1966 c 24. | Lesotho Independence Act 1966. | In the Schedule, paragraph 9. |
| 1966 c 37. | Barbados Independence Act 1966. | In Schedule 2, paragraph 12. |

| | | |
|---|---|---|
| 1967 c 80. | Criminal Justice Act 1967. | In Parts I and IV of Schedule 3, the entries relating to the Registered Designs Act 1949. |
| 1968 c 56. | Swaziland Independence Act 1968. | In the Schedule, paragraph 9. |
| 1968 c 67. | Medicines Act 1968. | In section 92(2)(a), the words from 'or embodied' to 'film'. Section 98. |
| 1968 c 68. | Design Copyright Act 1968. | The whole Act. |
| 1971 c 4. | Copyright (Amendment) Act 1971. | The whole Act. |
| 1971 c 23. | Courts Act 1971. | In Schedule 9, the entry relating to the Copyright Act 1956. |
| 1971 c 62. | Tribunals and Inquiries Act 1971. | In Schedule 1, paragraph 24. |
| 1972 c 32. | Performers' Protection Act 1972. | The whole Act. |
| 1975 c 24. | House of Commons Disqualification Act 1975 | In Part II of Schedule 1, the entry relating to the Performing Right Tribunal. |
| 1975 c 25. | Northern Ireland Assembly Disqualification Act 1975 | *.In Part II of Schedule 1, the entry relating to the Performing Right Tribunal.* |
| 1977 c 37. | Patents Act 1977. | Section 14(4) and (8). |
| | | In section 28(3), paragraph (b) and the word 'and' preceding it. |
| | | Section 28(5) to (9). |
| | | Section 49(3). |
| | | Section 72(3). |
| | | Sections 84 and 85. |
| | | Section 88. |
| | | Section 104. |
| | | In section 105, the words 'within the meaning of section 104 above'. |
| | | Sections 114 and 115. |
| | | Section 123(2)(k) |
| | | In section 130(1), the definition of 'patent agent'. |
| | | In section 130(7), the words '88(6) and (7),'. |
| | | In Schedule 5, paragraphs 1 and 2, in paragraph 3 the words 'and 44(1)' and 'in each case', and paragraphs 7 and 8. |
| 1979 c 2. | Customs and Excise Management Act 1979. | In Schedule 4, the entry relating to the Copyright Act 1956. |
| 1980 c 21. | Competition Act 1980. | Section 14. |
| 1981 c 68. | Broadcasting Act 1981. | Section 20(9)(a). |
| 1982 c 35. | Copyright Act 1956 (Amendment) Act 1982. | The whole Act. |
| 1983 c 42. | Copyright (Amendment) Act 1983. | The whole Act. |
| 1984 c 46. | Cable and Broadcasting Act 1984. | Section 8(8). |
| | | Section 16(4) and (5). |
| | | Sections 22 to 24. |
| | | Section 35(2) and (3). |
| | | Sections 53 and 54. |
| | | In section 56(2), the definition of 'the 1956 Act'. |
| | | In Schedule 5, paragraphs 6, 7, 13 and 23. |
| 1985 c 21. | Films Act 1985. | Section 7(2). |
| 1985 c 41. | Copyright (Computer Software) Amendment Act 1985. | The whole Act. |
| 1985 c 61. | Administration of Justice Act 1985. | Section 60. |
| 1986 c 39. | Patents, Designs and Marks Act 1986. | In Schedule 2, paragraph 1(2)(a), in paragraph 1(2)(k) the words 'subsection (1)(j) of section 396 and' and in paragraph 1(2)(l) the words 'subsection (2)(i) of section 93'. |
| 1988 c 1. | Income and Corporation Taxes Act 1988. | In Schedule 29, paragraph 5. |

*General note*
Entry in italics repealed by the Statute Law (Repeals) Act 1993.

# COPYRIGHT ACT 1911
## (1 & 2 Geo 5 c 46)

*General note*
This Act was repealed by the Copyright Act 1956.

## Arrangement of sections

*An Act to amend and consolidate the law relating to copyright*

[16 December 1911]

PART I
IMPERIAL COPYRIGHT

## *Rights*

### 1. Copyright

(1) Subject to the provisions of this Act, copyright shall subsist throughout the parts of His Majesty's dominions to which this Act extends for the term hereinafter mentioned in every original literary, dramatic, musical and artistic work, if—

(a) in the case of a published work, the work was first published within such parts of His Majesty's dominions as aforesaid; and

(b) in the case of an unpublished work, the author was at the date of the making of the work a British subject or resident within such parts of His Majesty's dominions as aforesaid;

but in no other works, except so far as the protection conferred by this Act is extended by Orders in Council thereunder relating to self-governing dominions to which this Act does not extend and to foreign countries.

(2) For the purposes of this Act, 'copyright' means the sole right to produce or reproduce the work or any substantial part thereof in any material form whatsoever, to perform, or in the case of a lecture to deliver, the work or any substantial part thereof in public; if the work is unpublished to publish the work or any substantial part thereof; and shall include the sole right,—

(a) to produce, reproduce, perform, or publish any translation of the work;

(b) in the case of a dramatic work, to convert it into a novel or other non-dramatic work;

(c) in the case of a novel or other non-dramatic work, or of an artistic work, to convert it into a dramatic work, by way of performance in public or otherwise;

(d) in the case of a literary, dramatic, or musical work, to make any record, perforated roll, cinematograph film, or other contrivance by means of which the work may be mechanically performed or delivered,

and to authorise any such acts as aforesaid.

(3) For the purposes of this Act, publication, in relation to any work, means the issue of copies of the work to the public, and does not include the performance in public of a dramatic or musical work, the delivery in public of a lecture, the exhibition in public of an artistic work, or the construction of an architectural work of art, but, for the purposes of this provision, the issue of photographs and engravings of works of sculpture and architectural works of art shall not be deemed to be publication of such works.

### 2. Infringement of copyright

(1) Copyright in a work shall be deemed to be infringed by any person who, without the consent of the owner of the copyright, does anything the sole right to do which is by this Act conferred on the owner of the copyright: Provided that the following acts shall not constitute an infringement of copyright—

(i) any fair dealing with any work for the purposes of private study, research, criticism, review, or newspaper summary;

(ii) where the author of an artistic work is not the owner of the copyright therein, the use by the author of any mould, cast, sketch, plan, model, or study made by him for the purpose of the work, provided that he does not thereby repeat or imitate the main design of that work;

(iii) the making or publishing of paintings, drawings, engravings, or photographs of a work of sculpture or artistic craftsmanship, if permanently situate in a public place or building, or the making or publishing of paintings, drawings, engravings, or photographs (which are not in the nature of architectural drawings or plans) of any architectural work of art;

(iv) the publication in a collection, mainly composed of non-copyright matter, bona fide intended for the use of schools, and so described in the title and in any advertisements issued by the publisher, of short passages from published literary works not themselves published for the use of schools in which copyright subsists: Provided that not more than two of such passages from works by the same author are published by the same publisher within five years, and that the source from which such passages are taken is acknowledged;

(v) the publication in a newspaper of a report of a lecture delivered in public, unless the report is prohibited by conspicuous written or printed notice affixed before and maintained during the lecture at or about the main entrance of the building in which the lecture is given, and, except whilst the building is being used for public worship, in a position near the lecturer; but nothing in this paragraph shall affect the provisions in paragraph (i) as to newspaper summaries;

(vi) the reading or recitation in public by one person of any reasonable extract from any published works.

(2) Copyright in a work shall also be deemed to be infringed by any person who—

(a) sells or lets for hire, or by way of trade exposes or offers for sale or hire; or

(b) distributes either for the purposes of trade or to such an extent as to affect prejudicially the owner of the copyright; or

(c) by way of trade exhibits in public; or

(d) imports for sale or hire into any part of His Majesty's dominions to which this Act extends, any work which to his knowledge infringes copyright or would infringe copyright if it had been made within the part of His Majesty's dominions in or into which the sale or hiring, exposure, offering for sale or hire, distribution, exhibition, or importation took place.

(3) Copyright in a work shall also be deemed to be infringed by any person who for his private profit permits a theatre or other place of entertainment to be used for the performance in public of the work without the consent of the owner of the copyright, unless he was not aware, and had no reasonable ground for suspecting, that the performance would be an infringement of copyright.

## 3. Term of copyright

The term for which copyright shall subsist shall, except as otherwise expressly provided by this Act, be the life of the author and a period of fifty years after his death:

Provided that at any time after the expiration of twenty-five years, or in the case of a work in which copyright subsists at the passing of this Act thirty years, from the death of the author of a published work, copyright in the work shall not be deemed to be infringed by the reproduction of the work for sale if the person reproducing the work proves that he has given the prescribed notice in writing of his intention to reproduce the work, and that he has paid in the prescribed manner to, or for the benefit of, the owner of the copyright royalties in respect of all copies of the work sold by him calculated at the rate of ten per cent on the price at which he publishes the work; and, for the purposes of this proviso, the Board of Trade may make regulations prescribing the mode in which notices are to be given, and the particulars to be given in such notices, and the mode, time, and frequency of the payment of royalties, including (if they think fit) regulations requiring payment in advance or otherwise securing the payment of royalties.

### 4. Compulsory licences

If at any time after the death of the author of a literary, dramatic, or musical work which has been published or performed in public a complaint is made to the Judicial Committee of the Privy Council that the owner of the copyright in the work has refused to republish or to allow the republication of the work or has refused to allow the performance in public of the work, and that by reason of such refusal the work is withheld from the public, the owner of the copyright may be ordered to grant a licence to reproduce the work or perform the work in public, as the case may be, on such terms and subject to such conditions as the Judicial Committee may think fit.

### 5. Ownership of copyright, etc

(1) Subject to the provisions of this Act, the author of a work shall be the first owner of the copyright therein:
Provided that—

  (a) where, in the case of an engraving, photograph, or portrait, the plate or other original was ordered by some other person and was made for valuable consideration in pursuance of that order, then, in the absence of any agreement to the contrary, the person by whom such plate or other original was ordered shall be the first owner of the copyright; and

  (b) where the author was in the employment of some other person under a contract of service or apprenticeship and the work was made in the course of his employment by that person, the person by whom the author was employed shall, in the absence of any agreement to the contrary, be the first owner of the copyright, but where the work is an article or other contribution to a newspaper, magazine, or similar periodical, there shall, in the absence of any agreement to the contrary, be deemed to be reserved to the author a right to restrain the publication of the work, otherwise than as part of a newspaper, magazine, or similar periodical.

(2) The owner of the copyright in any work may assign the right, either wholly or partially, and either generally or subject to limitations to the United Kingdom or any self-governing dominion or other part of His Majesty's dominions to which this Act extends, and either for the whole term of the copyright or for any part thereof, and may grant any interest in the right by licence, but no such assignment or grant shall be valid unless it is in writing signed by the owner of the right in respect of which the assignment or grant is made, or by his duly authorised agent:
Provided that, where the author of a work is the first owner of the copyright therein, no assignment of the copyright, and no grant of any interest therein, made

by him (otherwise than by will) after the passing of this Act, shall be operative to vest in the assignee or grantee any rights with respect to the copyright in the work beyond the expiration of twenty-five years from the death of the author, and the reversionary interest in the copyright expectant on the termination of that period shall, on the death of the author, notwithstanding any agreement to the contrary, devolve on his legal personal representatives as part of his estate, and any agreement entered into by him as to the disposition of such reversionary interest shall be null and void, but nothing in this proviso shall be construed as applying to the assignment of the copyright in a collective work or a licence to publish a work or part of a work as part of a collective work.

(3) Where, under any partial assignment of copyright, the assignee becomes entitled to any right comprised in copyright, the assignee as respects the right so assigned, and the assignor as respects the rights not assigned, shall be treated for the purposes of this Act as the owner of the copyright, and the provisions of this Act shall have effect accordingly.

## Civil remedies

### 6. Civil remedies for infringement of copyright
(1) Where copyright in any work has been infringed, the owner of the copyright shall, except as otherwise provided by this Act, be entitled to all such remedies by way of injunction or interdict, damages, accounts, and otherwise, as are or may be conferred by law for the infringement of a right.

(2) The costs of all parties in any proceedings in respect of the infringement of copyright shall be in the absolute discretion of the court.

(3) In any action for infringement of copyright in any work, the work shall be presumed to be a work in which copyright subsists and the plaintiff shall be presumed to be the owner of the copyright, unless the defendant puts in issue the existence of the copyright, or, as the case may be, the title of the plaintiff, and where any such question is in issue, then—

    (a) if a name purporting to be that of the author of the work is printed or otherwise indicated thereon in the usual manner, the person whose name is so printed or indicated shall, unless the contrary is proved, be presumed to be the author of the work;

    (b) if no name is so printed or indicated, or if the name so printed or indicated is not the author's true name or the name by which he is commonly known, and a name purporting to be that of the publisher or proprietor of the work is printed or otherwise indicated thereon in the usual manner the person whose name is so printed or indicated shall, unless the contrary is proved, be presumed to be the owner of the copyright in the work for the purposes of proceedings in respect of the infringement of copyright therein.

### 7. Rights of owner against persons possessing or dealing with infringing copies, etc
All infringing copies of any work in which copyright subsists, or of any substantial part thereof, and all plates used or intended to be used for the production of such infringing copies, shall be deemed to be the property of the owner of the copyright, who accordingly may take proceedings for the recovery of the possession thereof or in respect of the conversion thereof.

## 8. Exemption of innocent infringer from liability to pay damages, etc

Where proceedings are taken in respect of the infringement of the copyright in any work and the defendant in his defence alleges that he was not aware of the existence of the copyright in the work, the plaintiff shall not be entitled to any remedy other than an injunction or interdict in respect of the infringement if the defendant proves that at the date of the infringement he was not aware and had no reasonable grounds for suspecting that copyright subsisted in the work.

## 9. Restriction on remedies in the case of architecture

(1) Where the construction of a building or other structure which infringes or which, if completed, would infringe the copyright in some other work has been commenced, the owner of the copyright shall not be entitled to obtain an injunction or interdict to restrain the construction of such building or structure or to order its demolition.

(2) Such of the other provisions of this Act as provide that an infringing copy of a work shall be deemed to be the property of the owner of the copyright, or as impose summary penalties, shall not apply in any case to which this section applies.

## 10. Limitation of actions

An action in respect of infringement of copyright shall not be commenced after the expiration of three years next after the infringement.

*Summary remedies*

## 11. Penalties for dealing with infringing copies, etc

(1) If any person knowingly—

(a) makes for sale or hire any infringing copy of a work in which copyright subsists; or

(b) sells or lets for hire, or by way of trade exposes or offers for sale or hire any infringing copy of any such work; or

(c) distributes infringing copies of any such work either for the purposes of trade or to such an extent as to affect prejudicially the owner of the copyright; or

(d) by way of trade exhibits in public any infringing copy of any such work; or

(e) imports for sale or hire into the United Kingdom any infringing copy of any such work:

he shall be guilty of an offence under this Act and be liable on summary conviction to a fine not exceeding forty shillings for every copy dealt with in contravention of this section, but not exceeding fifty pounds in respect of the same transaction; or, in the case of a second or subsequent offence, either to such fine or to imprisonment with or without hard labour for a term not exceeding two months.

(2) If any person knowingly makes or has in his possession any plate for the purpose of making infringing copies of any work in which copyright subsists, or knowingly and for his private profit causes any such work to be performed in public without the consent of the owner of the copyright, he shall be guilty of an offence under this Act, and be liable on summary conviction to a fine not exceeding fifty pounds, or, in the case of a second or subsequent offence, either to such fine

or to imprisonment with or without hard labour for a term not exceeding two months.

(3) The court before which any such proceedings are taken may, whether the alleged offender is convicted or not, order that all copies of the work or all plates in the possession of the alleged offender, which appear to it to be infringing copies or plates for the purpose of making infringing copies, be destroyed or delivered up to the owner of the copyright or otherwise dealt with as the court may think fit.

(4) Nothing in this section shall, as respects musical works, affect the provisions of the Musical (Summary Proceedings) Copyright Act 1902, or the Musical Copyright Act 1906.

## 12. Appeals to quarter sessions

Any person aggrieved by a summary conviction of an offence under the foregoing provisions of this Act may in England and Ireland appeal to a court of quarter sessions and in Scotland under and in terms of the Summary Jurisdiction (Scotland) Acts.

## 13. Extent of provisions as to summary remedies

The provisions of this Act with respect to summary remedies shall extend only to the United Kingdom.

## 14. Importation of copies

(1) Copies made out of the United Kingdom of any work in which copyright subsists which if made in the United Kingdom would infringe copyright, and as to which the owner of the copyright gives notice in writing by himself or his agent to the Commissioners of Customs and Excise, that he is desirous that such copies should not be imported into the United Kingdom, shall not be so imported, and shall, subject to the provisions of this section, be deemed to be included in the table of prohibitions and restrictions contained in section forty-two of the Customs Consolidation Act 1876, and that section shall apply accordingly.

(2) Before detaining any such copies or taking any further proceedings with a view to the forfeiture thereof under the law relating to the Customs, the Commissioners of Customs and Excise may require the regulations under this section, whether as to information, conditions, or other matters, to be complied with, and may satisfy themselves in accordance with those regulations that the copies are such as are prohibited by this section to be imported.

(3) The Commissioners of Customs and Excise may make regulations, either general or special, respecting the detention and forfeiture of copies the importation of which is prohibited by this section, and the conditions, if any, to be fulfilled before such detention and forfeiture, and may, by such regulations, determine the information, notices, and security to be given, and the evidence requisite for any of the purposes of this section, and the mode of verification of such evidence.

(4) The regulations may apply to copies of all works the importation of copies of which is prohibited by this section, or different regulations may be made respecting different classes of such works.

(5) The regulations may provide for the informant reimbursing the Commissioners of Customs and Excise all expenses and damages incurred in respect of any detention made on his information, and of any proceedings consequent on such detention; and may provide for notices under any enactment repealed by this Act being treated as notices given under this section.

(6) The foregoing provisions of this section shall have effect as if they were

part of the Customs Consolidation Act 1876: Provided that, notwithstanding anything in that Act, the Isle of Man shall not be treated as part of the United Kingdom for the purposes of this section.

(7) This section shall, with the necessary modifications, apply to the importation into a British possession to which this Act extends of copies of works made out of that possession.

## *Delivery of books to libraries*

### 15. Delivery of copies to British Museum and other libraries

(1) The publisher of every book published in the United Kingdom shall, within one month after the publication, deliver, at his own expense, a copy of the book to the trustees of the British Museum, who shall give a written receipt for it....

(2) He shall also, if written demand is made before the expiration of twelve months after publication, deliver within one month after receipt of that written demand or, if the demand was made before publication, within one month after publication, to some depot in London named in the demand a copy of the book for, or in accordance with the directions of, the authority having the control of each of the following libraries, namely: the Bodleian Library, Oxford, the University Library, Cambridge, [the National Library of Scotland], and the Library of Trinity College, Dublin, and subject to the provisions of this section the National Library of Wales. In the case of an encyclopaedia, newspaper, review, magazine, or work published in a series of numbers or parts, the written demand may include all numbers or parts of the work which may be subsequently published.

(3) The copy delivered to the trustees of the British Museum shall be a copy of the whole book with all maps and illustrations belonging thereto, finished and coloured in the same manner as the best copies of the book are published, and shall be bound, sewed, or stitched together, and on the best paper on which the book is printed.

(4) The copy delivered for the other authorities mentioned in this section shall be on the paper on which the largest number of copies of the book is printed for sale, and shall be in the like condition as the books prepared for sale.

(5) The books of which copies are to be delivered to the National Library of Wales shall not include books of such classes as may be specified in regulations to be made by the Board of Trade.

(6) If a publisher fails to comply with this section, he shall be liable on summary conviction to a fine not exceeding five pounds and the value of the book, and the fine shall be paid to the trustees or authority to whom the book ought to have been delivered.

(7) For the purposes of this section, the expression 'book' includes every part or division of a book, pamphlet, sheet of letterpress, sheet of music, map, plan, chart or table separately published, but shall not include any second or subsequent edition of a book unless such edition contains additions or alterations either in the letterpress or in the maps, prints, or other engravings belonging thereto.

## *Special provisions as to certain works*

### 16. Works of joint authors

(1) In the case of a work of joint authorship, copyright shall subsist during the life of the author who first dies and for a term of fifty years after his death, or during

the life of the author who dies last, whichever period is the longer, and references in this Act to the period after the expiration of any specified number of years from the death of the author shall be construed as references to the period after the expiration of the like number of years from the death of the author who dies first or after the death of the author who dies last, whichever period may be the shorter, and in the provisions of this Act with respect to the grant of compulsory licences a reference to the date of the death of the author who dies last shall be substituted for the reference to the date of the death of the author.

(2) Where, in the case of a work of joint authorship, some one or more of the joint authors do not satisfy the conditions conferring copyright laid down by this Act, the work shall be treated for the purposes of this Act as if the other author or authors had been the sole author or authors thereof:

Provided that the term of the copyright shall be the same as it would have been if all the authors had satisfied such conditions as aforesaid.

(3) For the purposes of this Act, 'a work of joint authorship' means a work produced by the collaboration of two or more authors in which the contribution of one author is not distinct from the contribution of the other author or authors.

(4) Where a married woman and her husband are joint authors of a work the interest of such married woman therein shall be her separate property.

*General note*
Amended by the Law Reform (Married Women and Tortfeasors) Act 1935 (c 30), s 5(2) and Sch 2.

## 17. Posthumous works

(1) In the case of a literary, dramatic, or musical work, or an engraving, in which copyright subsists at the date of the death of the author or, in the case of a work of joint authorship, at or immediately before the date of the death of the author who dies last, but which has not been published, nor, in the case of a dramatic or musical work, been performed in public, nor, in the case of a lecture, been delivered in public, before that date, copyright shall subsist till publication, or performance or delivery in public, whichever may first happen, and for a term of fifty years thereafter, and the proviso to section three of this Act shall, in the case of such a work, apply as if the author had died at the date of such publication or performance or delivery in public as aforesaid.

(2) The ownership of an author's manuscript after his death, where such ownership has been acquired under a testamentary disposition made by the author and the manuscript is of a work which has not been published nor performed in public nor delivered in public, shall be prima facie proof of the copyright being with the owner of the manuscript.

## 18. Provisions as to Government publications

Without prejudice to any rights or privileges of the Crown, where any work has, whether before or after the commencement of this Act, been prepared or published by or under the direction or control of His Majesty or any Government department, the copyright in the work shall, subject to any agreement with the author, belong to His Majesty, and in such case shall continue for a period of fifty years from the date of the first publication of the work.

## 19. Provisions as to mechanical instruments

(1) Copyright shall subsist in records, perforated rolls, and other contrivances by means of which sounds may be mechanically reproduced, in like manner as if such

contrivances were musical works, but the term of copyright shall be fifty years from the making of the original plate from which the contrivance was directly or indirectly derived, and the person who was the owner of such original plate at the time when such plate was made shall be deemed to be the author of the work, and, where such owner is a body corporate, the body corporate shall be deemed for the purposes of this Act to reside within the parts of His Majesty's dominions to which this Act extends if it has established a place of business within such parts.

(2) It shall not be deemed to be an infringement of copyright in any musical work for any person to make within the parts of His Majesty's dominions to which this Act extends records, perforated rolls, or other contrivances by means of which the work may be mechanically performed, if such person proves—

(a) that such contrivances have previously been made by, or with the consent or acquiescence of, the owner of the copyright in the work; and

(b) that he has given the prescribed notice of his intention to make the contrivances, and has paid in the prescribed manner to, or for the benefit of, the owner of the copyright in the work royalties in respect of all such contrivances sold by him, calculated at the rate hereinafter mentioned:

Provided that—

(i) nothing in this provision shall authorise any alterations in, or omissions from, the work reproduced, unless contrivances reproducing the work subject to similar alterations and omissions have been previously made by, or with the consent or acquiescence of, the owner of the copyright, or unless such alterations or omissions are reasonably necessary for the adaptation of the work to the contrivances in question; and

(ii) for the purposes of this provision, a musical work shall be deemed to include any words so closely associated therewith as to form part of the same work, but shall not be deemed to include a contrivance by means of which sounds may be mechanically reproduced.

(3) The rate at which such royalties as aforesaid are to be calculated shall—

(a) in the case of contrivances sold within two years after the commencement of this Act by the person making the same, be two and one-half per cent; and

(b) in the case of contrivances sold as aforesaid after the expiration of that period, five per cent

on the ordinary retail selling price of the contrivance calculated in the prescribed manner, so however that the royalties payable in respect of a contrivance shall, in no case, be less than a halfpenny for each separate musical work in which copyright subsists reproduced thereon, and, where the royalty calculated as aforesaid includes a fraction of a farthing, such fraction shall be reckoned as a farthing:

Provided that, if, at any time after the expiration of seven years from the commencement of this Act, it appears to the Board of Trade that such rate as aforesaid is no longer equitable, the Board of Trade may, after holding a public inquiry, make an order either decreasing or increasing that rate to such extent as under the circumstances may seem just, but any order so made shall be provisional only and shall not have any effect unless and until confirmed by Parliament; but, where an order revising the rate has been so made and confirmed, no further revision shall be made before the expiration of fourteen years from the date of the last revision.

(4) If any such contrivance is made reproducing two or more different works in which copyright subsists and the owners of the copyright therein are different persons, the sums payable by way of royalties under this section shall be apportioned amongst the several owners of the copyright in such proportions as, failing agreement, may be determined by arbitration.

(5) When any such contrivances by means of which a musical work may be mechanically performed have been made, then, for the purposes of this section, the owner of the copyright in the work shall, in relation to any person who makes the prescribed inquiries, be deemed to have given his consent to the making of such contrivances if he fails to reply to such inquiries within the prescribed time.

(6) For the purposes of this section, the Board of Trade may make regulations prescribing anything which under this section is to be prescribed, and prescribing the mode in which notices are to be given and the particulars to be given in such notices, and the mode, time, and frequency of the payment of royalties, and any such regulations may, if the Board think fit, include regulations requiring payment in advance or otherwise securing the payment of royalties.

(7) In the case of musical works published before the commencement of this Act, the foregoing provisions shall have effect, subject to the following modifications and additions:—

(a) the conditions as to the previous making by, or with the consent or acquiescence of, the owner of the copyright in the work, and the restrictions as to alterations in or omissions from the work, shall not apply;

(b) the rate of two and one-half per cent shall be substituted for the rate of five per cent as the rate at which royalties are to be calculated, but no royalties shall be payable in respect of contrivances sold before the first day of July, nineteen-hundred and thirteen, if contrivances reproducing the same work had been lawfully made, or placed on sale, within the parts of His Majesty's dominions to which this Act extends before the first day of July, nineteen hundred and ten;

(c) notwithstanding any assignment made before the passing of this Act of the copyright in a musical work, any rights conferred by this Act in respect of the making, or authorising the making, of contrivances by means of which the work may be mechanically performed shall belong to the author or his legal personal representatives and not to the assignee, and the royalties aforesaid shall be payable to, and for the benefit of, the author of the work or his legal personal representatives;

(d) the saving contained in this Act of the rights and interests arising from, or in connection with, action taken before the commencement of this Act shall not be construed as authorising any person who has made contrivances by means of which the work may be mechanically performed to sell any such contrivances, whether made before or after the passing of this Act, except on the terms and subject to the conditions laid down in this section;

(e) where the work is a work on which copyright is conferred by an Order in Council relating to a foreign country, the copyright so conferred shall not, except to such extent as may be provided by the Order, include any rights with respect to the making of records, perforated rolls, or other contrivances by means of which the work may be mechanically performed.

(8) Notwithstanding anything in this Act, where a record, perforated roll, or other contrivance by means of which sounds may be mechanically reproduced has been made before the commencement of this Act, copyright shall, as from the commencement of this Act, subsist therein in like manner and for the like term as if this Act had been in force at the date of the making of the original plate from which the contrivance was directly or indirectly derived:

Provided that—

(i) the person who, at the commencement of this Act, is the owner of such original plate shall be the first owner of such copyright; and

(ii) nothing in this provision shall be construed as conferring copyright in any such contrivance if the making thereof would have infringed copyright in some other such contrivance, if this provision had been in force at the time of the making of the first-mentioned contrivance.

## 20. Provision as to political speeches

Notwithstanding anything in this Act, it shall not be an infringement of copyright in an address of a political nature delivered at a public meeting to publish a report thereof in a newspaper.

## 21. Provisions as to photographs

The term for which copyright shall subsist in photographs shall be fifty years from the making of the original negative from which the photograph was directly or indirectly derived, and the person who was owner of such negative at the time when such negative was made shall be deemed to be the author of the work, and, where such owner is a body corporate, the body corporate shall be deemed for the purposes of this Act to reside within the parts of His Majesty's dominions to which this Act extends if it has established a place of business within such parts.

## 22. Provisions as to designs registrable under 7 Edw 7 c 29

(1) This Act shall not apply to designs capable of being registered under the Patents and Designs Act 1907, except designs which, though capable of being so registered, are not used or intended to be used as models or patterns to be multiplied by any industrial process.

(2) General rules under section eighty-six of the Patents and Designs Act 1907, may be made for determining the conditions under which a design shall be deemed to be used for such purposes as aforesaid.

## 23. Works of foreign authors first published in parts of His Majesty's dominions to which Act extends

If it appears to His Majesty that a foreign country does not give, or has not undertaken to give, adequate protection to the works of British authors, it shall be lawful for His Majesty by Order in Council to direct that such of the provisions of this Act as confer copyright on works first published within the parts of His Majesty's dominions to which this Act extends, shall not apply to works published after the date specified in the Order, the authors whereof are subjects or citizens of such foreign country, and are not resident in His Majesty's dominions, and thereupon those provisions shall not apply to such works.

## 24. Existing works

(1) Where any person is immediately before the commencement of this Act entitled to any such right in any work as is specified in the first column of the First

Schedule to this Act, or to any interest in such a right, he shall, as from that date, be entitled to the substituted right set forth in the second column of that schedule, or to the same interest in such a substituted right, and to no other right or interest, and such substituted right shall subsist for the term for which it would have subsisted if this Act had been in force at the date when the work was made and the work had been one entitled to copyright thereunder:

Provided that—

(a) if the author of any work in which any such right as is specified in the first column of the First Schedule to this Act subsists at the commencement of this Act has, before that date, assigned the right or granted any interest therein for the whole term of the right, then at the date when, but for the passing of this Act, the right would have expired the substituted right conferred by this section shall, in the absence of express agreement, pass to the author of the work, and any interest therein created before the commencement of this Act and then subsisting shall determine; but the person who immediately before the date at which the right would so have expired was the owner of the right or interest shall be entitled at his option either—

(i) on giving such notice as hereinafter mentioned, to an assignment of the right or the grant of a similar interest therein for the remainder of the term of the right for such consideration as, failing agreement, may be determined by arbitration; or

(ii) without any such assignment or grant, to continue to reproduce or perform the work in like manner as theretofore subject to the payment, if demanded by the author within three years after the date at which the right would have so expired, of such royalties to the author as, failing agreement, may be determined by arbitration, or, where the work is incorporated in a collective work and the owner of the right or interest is the proprietor of that collective work, without any such payment.

The notice above referred to must be given not more than one year nor less than six months before the date at which the right would have so expired, and must be sent by registered post to the author, or, if he cannot with reasonable diligence be found, advertised in the London Gazette and in two London newspapers;

(b) where any person has, before the twenty-sixth day of July nineteen hundred and ten, taken any action whereby he has incurred any expenditure or liability in connection with the reproduction or performance of any work in a manner which at the time was lawful, or for the purpose of or with a view to the reproduction or performance of a work at a time when such reproduction or performance would, but for the passing of this Act, have been lawful, nothing in this section shall diminish or prejudice any rights or interest arising from or in connection with such action which are subsisting and valuable at the said date, unless the person who by virtue of this section becomes entitled to restrain such reproduction or performance agrees to pay such compensation as, failing agreement, may be determined by arbitration.

(2) For the purposes of this section, the expression 'author' includes the legal personal representatives of a deceased author.

(3) Subject to the provisions of section nineteen subsections (7) and (8) and of section thirty-three of this Act, copyright shall not subsist in any work made before the commencement of this Act, otherwise than under, and in accordance with, the provisions of this section.

## Application to British possessions

### 25. Application of Act to British dominions

(1) This Act, except such of the provisions thereof as are expressly restricted to the United Kingdom, shall extend throughout His Majesty's dominions: Provided that it shall not extend to a self-governing dominion, unless declared by the Legislature of that dominion to be in force therein either without any modifications or additions, or with such modifications and additions relating exclusively to procedure and remedies, or necessary to adapt this Act to the circumstances of the dominion, as may be enacted by such Legislature.

(2) If the Secretary of State certifies by notice published in the London Gazette that any self-governing dominion has passed legislation under which works, the authors whereof were at the date of the making of the works British subjects resident elsewhere than in the dominion or (not being British subjects) were resident in the parts of His Majesty's dominions to which this Act extends, enjoy within the dominion rights substantially identical with those conferred by this Act, then, whilst such legislation continues in force, the dominion shall, for the purposes of the rights conferred by this Act, be treated as if it were a dominion to which this Act extends; and it shall be lawful for the Secretary of State to give such a certificate as aforesaid, notwithstanding that the remedies for enforcing the rights, or the restrictions on the importation of copies of works, manufactured in a foreign country, under the law of the dominion, differ from those under this Act.

### 26. Legislative powers of self-governing dominions

(1) The Legislature of any self-governing dominion may, at any time, repeal all or any of the enactments relating to copyright passed by Parliament (including this Act) so far as they are operative within that dominion: Provided that no such repeal shall prejudicially affect any legal rights existing at the time of the repeal, and that, on this Act or any part thereof being so repealed by the Legislature of a self-governing dominion, that dominion shall cease to be a dominion to which this Act extends.

(2) In any self-governing dominion to which this Act does not extend, the enactments repealed by this Act shall, so far as they are operative in that dominion, continue in force until repealed by the Legislature of that dominion.

(3) Where His Majesty in Council is satisfied that the law of a self-governing dominion to which this Act does not extend provides adequate protection within the dominion for the works (whether published or unpublished) of authors who at the time of the making of the work were British subjects resident elsewhere than in that dominion, His Majesty in Council may, for the purpose of giving reciprocal protection, direct that this Act, except such parts (if any) thereof as may be specified in the Order, and subject to any conditions contained therein, shall, within the parts of His Majesty's dominions to which this Act extends, apply to works the authors whereof were, at the time of the making of the work, resident within the first-mentioned dominion, and to works first published in that dominion; but, save as provided by such an Order, works the authors whereof were resident in a dominion to which this Act does not extend shall not, whether they

are British subjects or not, be entitled to any protection under this Act except such protection as is by this Act conferred on works first published within the parts of His Majesty's dominions to which this Act extends:

Provided that no such Order shall confer any rights within a self-governing dominion, but the Governor in Council of any self-governing dominion to which this Act extends, may, by Order, confer within that dominion the like rights as His Majesty in Council is, under the foregoing provisions of this subsection, authorised to confer within other parts of His Majesty's dominions.

For the purposes of this subsection, the expression 'a dominion to which this Act extends' includes a dominion which is for the purposes of this Act to be treated as if it were a dominion to which this Act extends.

## 27. Power of Legislatures of British possessions to pass supplemental legislation

The Legislature of any British possession to which this Act extends may modify or add to any of the provisions of this Act in its application to the possession, but, except so far as such modifications and additions relate to procedure and remedies, they shall apply only to work the authors whereof were, at the time of the making of the work, resident in the possession, and to works first published in the possession.

## 28. Application to protectorates

His Majesty may, by Order in Council, extend this Act to any territories under his protection and to Cyprus, and, on the making of any such Order, this Act shall, subject to the provisions of the Order, have effect as if the territories to which it applies or Cyprus were part of His Majesty's dominions to which this Act extends.

PART II
INTERNATIONAL COPYRIGHT

## 29. Power to extend Act to foreign works

(1) His Majesty may, by order in Council, direct that this Act (except such parts, if any, thereof as may be specified in the Order) shall apply—

(a) to works first published in a foreign country to which the Order relates, in like manner as if they were first published within the parts of His Majesty's dominions to which this Act extends;

(b) to literary, dramatic, musical, and artistic works, or any class thereof, the authors whereof were at the time of the making of the work subjects or citizens of a foreign country to which the Order relates, in like manner as if the authors were British subjects;

(c) in respect of residence in a foreign country to which the Order relates, in like manner as if such residence were residence in the parts of His Majesty's dominions to which this Act extends;

and thereupon, subject to the provisions of this Part of this Act and of the Order, this Act shall apply accordingly:

Provided that—

(i) before making an Order in Council under this section in respect of any foreign country (other than a country with which His Majesty has entered into a convention relating to copyright) His Majesty shall be satisfied that that foreign country has made, or has undertaken to make, such provisions, if any, as it appears to His Majesty expedient to require for the protection of works entitled to copyright under the provisions of Part I of this Act;

(ii) the Order in Council may provide that the term of copyright within such parts of His Majesty's dominions as aforesaid shall not exceed that conferred by the law of the country to which the Order relates;

(iii) the provisions of this Act as to the delivery of copies of books shall not apply to works first published in such country, except so far as is provided by the Order;

(iv) the Order in Council may provide that the enjoyment of the rights conferred by this Act shall be subject to the accomplishment of such conditions and formalities (if any) as may be prescribed by the Order;

(v) in applying the provision of this Act as to ownership of copyright, the Order in Council may make such modifications as appear necessary having regard to the law of the foreign country;

(vi) in applying the provisions of this Act as to existing works, the Order in Council may make such modifications as appear necessary, and may provide that nothing in those provisions as so applied shall be construed as reviving any right of preventing the production or importation of any translation in any case where the right has ceased by virtue of section five of the International Copyright Act 1886.

(2) An Order in Council under this section may extend to all the several countries named or described therein.

### 30. Application of Part II to British possessions

(1) An Order in Council under this Part of this Act shall apply to all His Majesty's dominions to which this Act extends except self-governing dominions and any other possession specified in the Order with respect to which it appears to His Majesty expedient that the Order should not apply.

(2) The Governor in Council of any self-governing dominion to which this Act extends may, as respects that dominion, make the like orders as under this Part of this Act His Majesty in Council is authorised to make with respect to His Majesty's dominions other than self-governing dominions, and the provisions of this Part of this Act shall, with the necessary modifications, apply accordingly.

(3) Where it appears to His Majesty expedient to except from the provisions of any order any part of his dominions not being a self-governing dominion, it shall be lawful for His Majesty by the same or any other Order in Council to declare that such order and this Part of this Act shall not, and the same shall not, apply to such part, except so far as is necessary for preventing any prejudice to any rights acquired previously to the date of such Order.

PART III
SUPPLEMENTAL PROVISIONS

### 31. Abrogation of common law rights

No person shall be entitled to copyright or any similar right in any literary, dramatic, musical, or artistic work, whether published or unpublished, otherwise than under and in accordance with the provisions of this Act, or of any other statutory enactment for the time being in force, but nothing in this section shall be construed as abrogating any right or jurisdiction to restrain a breach of trust or confidence.

**32. Provisions as to Orders in Council**
(1) His Majesty in Council may make Orders for altering, revoking, or varying any Order in Council made under this Act, or under any enactments repealed by this Act, but any Order made under this section shall not affect prejudicially any rights or interests acquired or accrued at the date when the Order comes into operation, and shall provide for the protection of such rights and interests.

(2) Every Order in Council made under this Act shall be published in the London Gazette and shall be laid before both Houses of Parliament as soon as may be after it is made, and shall have effect as if enacted in this Act.

**33. Saving of university copyright**
Nothing in this Act shall deprive any of the universities and colleges mentioned in the Copyright Act 1775, of any copyright they already possess under that Act, but the remedies and penalties for infringement of any such copyright shall be under this Act and not under that Act.

**34. Saving of compensation to certain libraries**
There shall continue to be charged on, and paid out of, the Consolidated Fund of the United Kingdom such annual compensation as was immediately before the commencement of this Act payable in pursuance of any Act as compensation to a library for the loss of the right to receive gratuitous copies of books:

Provided that this compensation shall not be paid to a library in any year, unless the Treasury are satisfied that the compensation for the previous year has been applied in the purchase of books for the use of and to be preserved in the library.

**35. Interpretation**
(1) In this Act, unless the context otherwise requires—

'Literary work' includes maps, charts, plans, tables, and compilations;
'Dramatic work' includes any piece for recitation, choreographic work or entertainment in dumb show, the scenic arrangement or acting form of which is fixed in writing or otherwise, and any cinematograph production where the arrangement or acting form or the combination of incidents represented give the work an original character;
'Artistic work' includes works of painting, drawing, sculpture and artistic craftsmanship, and architectural works of art and engravings and photographs;
'Work of sculpture' includes casts and models;
'Architectural work of art' means any building or structure having an artistic character or design, in respect of such character or design, or any model for such building or structure, provided that the protection afforded by this Act shall be confined to the artistic character and design, and shall not extend to processes or methods of construction;
'Engravings' include etchings, lithographs, wood-cuts, prints, and other similar works, not being photographs;
'Photograph' includes photo-lithograph and any work produced by any process analogous to photography;
'Cinematograph' includes any work produced by any process analogous to cinematography;
'Collective work' means—

    (a) an encyclopaedia, dictionary, year book, or similar work;

(b) a newspaper, review, magazine, or similar periodical; and

(c) any work written in distinct parts by different authors, or in which works or parts of works of different authors are incorporated;

'Infringing,' when applied to a copy of a work in which copyright subsists, means any copy, including any colourable imitation, made, or imported in contravention of the provisions of this Act;

'Performance' means any acoustic representation of a work and any visual representation of any dramatic action in a work, including such a representation made by means of any mechanical instrument;

'Delivery,' in relation to a lecture, includes delivery by means of any mechanical instrument;

'Plate' includes any stereotype or other plate, stone, block, mould, matrix, transfer, or negative used or intended to be used for printing or reproducing copies of any work, and any matrix or other appliance by which records, perforated rolls or other contrivances for the acoustic representation of the work are or are intended to be made;

'Lecture' includes address, speech, and sermon;

'Self-governing dominion' means the Dominion of Canada, the Commonwealth of Australia, the Dominion of New Zealand, the Union of South Africa, and Newfoundland.

(2) For the purposes of this Act (other than those relating to infringements of copyright), a work shall not be deemed to be published or performed in public, and a lecture shall not be deemed to be delivered in public, if published, performed in public, or delivered in public, without the consent or acquiescence of the author, his executors, administrators or assigns.

(3) For the purposes of this Act, a work shall be deemed to be first published within the parts of His Majesty's dominions to which this Act extends, notwithstanding that it has been published simultaneously in some other place, unless the publication in such parts of His Majesty's dominions as aforesaid is colourable only and is not intended to satisfy the reasonable requirements of the public, and a work shall be deemed to be published simultaneously in two places if the time between the publication in one such place and the publication in the other place does not exceed fourteen days, or such longer period as may, for the time being, be fixed by Order in Council.

(4) Where, in the case of an unpublished work, the making of a work has extended over a considerable period, the conditions of this Act conferring copyright shall be deemed to have been complied with, if the author was, during any substantial part of that period, a British subject or a resident within the parts of His Majesty's dominions to which this Act extends.

(5) For the purposes of the provisions of this Act as to residence, an author of a work shall be deemed to be a resident in the parts of His Majesty's dominions to which this Act extends if he is domiciled within any such part.

## 36. Repeal

Subject to the provisions of this Act, the enactments mentioned in the Second Schedule to this Act are hereby repealed to the extent specified in the third column of that Schedule: Provided that this repeal shall not take effect in any part of His Majesty's dominions until this Act comes into operation in that part.

### 37. Short title and commencement

(1) This Act may be cited as the Copyright Act 1911.

(2) This Act shall come into operation—

(a) in the United Kingdom, on the first day of July nineteen hundred and twelve or such earlier date as may be fixed by Order in Council;

(b) in a self-governing dominion to which this Act extends, at such date as may be fixed by the Legislature of that dominion;

(c) in the Channel Islands, at such date as may be fixed by the States of those islands respectively;

(d) in any other British possession to which this Act extends, on the proclamation thereof within the possession by the Governor.

SCHEDULES

Section 24                    FIRST SCHEDULE

EXISTING RIGHTS

| Existing Right | Substituted Right |
|---|---|
| *(a) In the case of works other than dramatic and musical works* | |
| Copyright     . .      . .     . .     . . | Copyright as defined by this Act.* |
| *(b) In the case of musical and dramatic works* | |
| Both copyright and performing right . . | Copyright as defined by this Act.* |

| Existing Right | Substituted Right |
|---|---|
| Copyright, but not performing right   . . | Copyright as defined by this Act, except the sole right to perform the work or any substantial part thereof in public. |
| Performing right, but not copyright   . . | The sole right to perform the work in public, but none of the other rights comprised in copyright as defined by this Act. |

For the purposes of this Schedule the following expressions, where used in the first column thereof, have the following meanings:—

'Copyright,' in the case of a work which according to the law in force immediately before the commencement of this Act has not been published before that date and statutory copyright wherein depends on publication, includes the right at common law (if any) to restrain publication or other dealing with the work;

'Performing right,' in the case of a work which has not been performed in public before the commencement of this Act, includes the right at common law (if any) to restrain the performance thereof in public.

---

\* In the case of an essay, article, or portion forming part of and first published ina review, magazine, or other periodical or work of a like nature, the right shall be subject to any right of publishing the essay, article, or portion in a separate form to which the author is entitled at the commencement of this Act, or would, if this Act had not been passed, have become entitled under s 18, Copyright Act 1842 (repealed).

Section 36            *SECOND SCHEDULE*

*ENACTMENTS REPEALED*

| Session and Chapter | Short Title | Extent of Repeal |
|---|---|---|
| *8 Geo 2 c 13* | *The Engraving Copyright Act 1734* | *The whole Act.* |
| *7 Geo 3 c 38* | *The Engraving Copyright Act 1767* | *The whole Act.* |
| *15 Geo 3 c 53* | *The Copyright Act 1775* | *The whole Act.* |
| *17 Geo 3 c 57* | *The Prints Copyright Act 1777* | *The whole Act.* |
| *54 Geo 3 c 56* | *The Sculpture Copyright Act 1814* | *The whole Act.* |
| *3 & 4 Will 4 c 15* | *The Dramatic Copyright Act 1833* | *The whole Act.* |
| *5 & 6 Will 4 c 65* | *The Lectures Copyright Act 1835* | *The whole Act.* |
| *6 & 7 Will 4 c 59* | *The Prints and Engravings Copyright (Ireland) Act 1836* | *The whole Act.* |
| *6 & 7 Will 4 c 110* | *The Copyright Act 1836* | *The whole Act.* |
| *5 & 6 Vict c 45* | *The Copyright Act 1842* | *The whole Act.* |
| *7 & 8 Vict c 12* | *The International Copyright Act 1844* | *The whole Act.* |
| *10 & 11 Vict c 95* | *The Colonial Copyright Act 1847* | *The whole Act.* |
| *15 & 16 Vict c 12* | *The International Copyright Act 1852* | *The whole Act.* |
| *25 & 26 Vict c 68* | *The Fine Arts Copyright Act 1862* | *Sections one to six. In section eight the words 'and pursuant to any Act for the protection of copyright engravings,' and 'and in any such Act as aforesaid.' Sections nine to twelve.* |
| *38 & 39 Vict c 12* | *The International Copyright Act 1875* | *The whole Act.* |
| *39 & 40 Vic c 36* | *The Customs Consolidation Act 1876* | *Section forty-two, from 'Books wherein' to 'such copyright will expire.' Sections forty-four, forty-five, and one hundred and fifty-two.* |
| *45 & 46 Vict c 40* | *The Copyright (Musical Compositions) Act 1882* | *The whole Act.* |
| *49 & 50 Vict c 33* | *The International Copyright Act 1886* | *The whole Act.* |
| *51 & 52 Vict c 17* | *The Copyright (Musical Compositions) Act 1888* | *The whole Act.* |
| *52 & 53 Vict c 42* | *The Revenue Act 1889* | *Section one, from 'Books first published' to 'as provided in that section.'* |
| *6 Edw 7 c 36* | *The Musical Copyright Act 1906* | *In section three the words 'and which has been registered in accordance with the provisions of the Copyright Act 1842, or of the International Copyright Act 1844, which registration may be effected notwithstanding anything in the International Copyright Act 1886.'* |

*General note*
This Schedule repealed by the Statute Law Repeals Act 1977 (c 42).

WIRELESS TELEGRAPHY ACT 1949
(12, 13 & 14 Geo 6 c 54)

### 19. Interpretation

(1) In this Act, except where the context otherwise requires, the expression 'wireless telegraphy' means the emitting or receiving, over paths which are not provided by any material substance constructed or arranged for that purpose, of electro-magnetic energy of a frequency not exceeding three million megacycles a second, being energy which either—

(a) serves for the conveying of messages, sound or visual images (whether the messages, sound or images are actually received by any person or not), or for the actuation or control of machinery or apparatus; or

(b) is used in connection with the determination of position, bearing, or distance, or for the gaining of information as to the presence, absence, position or motion of any object or of any objects of any class,

and references to stations for wireless telegraphy and apparatus for wireless telegraphy or wireless telegraphy apparatus shall be construed as references to stations and apparatus for the emitting or receiving as aforesaid of such electro-magnetic energy as aforesaid:

*Provided that where—*

(i) *a station or apparatus for wireless telegraphy cannot lawfully be used without a wireless telegraphy licence or could not lawfully be used without such a licence but for regulations under section one of this Act; and*

(ii) *any such electro-magnetic energy as aforesaid which is received by that station or apparatus serves for the conveying of messages, sound or visual images; and*

(iii) *any apparatus is electrically coupled with that station or apparatus for the purpose of enabling any person to receive any of the said messages, sound or visual images,*

*the apparatus so coupled shall itself be deemed for the purposes of this Act to be apparatus for wireless telegraphy.*

. . .

(3) Any reference in this Act to the emission of electro-magnetic energy, or to emission (as opposed to reception), shall be construed as including a reference to the deliberate reflection of electro-magnetic energy by means of any apparatus designed or specially adapted for that purpose, whether the reflection is continuous or intermittent.

. . .

(6) Any reference in this Act to the sending or the conveying of messages includes a reference to the making of any signal or the sending or conveying of any warning or information, and any reference to the reception of messages shall be construed accordingly.

*General note*
Words in italics repealed by the Cable and Broadcasting Act 1984.

# COPYRIGHT ACT 1956 (AS AMENDED)
(4 & 5 Eliz 2 c 74)

*General note*

This Act was amended by the House of Commons Disqualification Act 1957, the Dramatic and Musical Performers' Protection Act 1958, the Films Act 1960, the Northern Ireland Act 1968, the Design Copyright Act 1968, the Industrial Expansion Act 1968, the Copyright (Amendment) Act 1971, the Statute Law (Repeals) Act 1974, the Customs and Excise Management Act 1979, the Limitation Act 1980, the British Nationality (Modification of Enactments) Order 1982, SI 1982/1832, the Copyright Act 1956 (Amendment) Act 1982, the Criminal Justice Act 1982, the Copyright (Amendment) Act 1983, the Cable and Broadcasting Act 1984, the Films Act 1985 and the Statute Law (Repeals) Act 1986.

## Arrangement of sections

*An Act to make new provision in respect of copyright and related matters, in substitution for the provisions of the Copyright Act 1991, and other enactments relating thereto; to amend the Registered Designs Act 1949, with respect to designs related to artistic works in which copyright subsists, and to amend the Dramatic and Musical Performers' Protection Act 1925; and for purposes connected with the matters aforesaid.* [5 November 1956]

PART I
COPYRIGHT IN ORIGINAL WORKS

## 1. Nature of copyright under this Act

(1) In this Act 'copyright' in relation to a work (except where the context otherwise requires) means the exclusive right, by virtue and subject to the provisions of this Act, to do, and to authorise other persons to do, certain acts in relation to that work in the United Kingdom or in any other country to which the relevant provision of this Act extends.

The said acts, in relation to a work of any description, are those acts which, in the relevant provision of this Act, are designated as the acts restricted by the copyright in a work of that description.

(2) In accordance with the preceding subsection, but subject to the following provisions of this Act, the copyright in a work is infringed by any person who, not being the owner of the copyright, and without the licence of the owner thereof, does, or authorises another person to do, any of the said acts in relation to the work in the United Kingdom or in any other country to which the relevant provision of this Act extends.

(3) In the preceding subsections references to the relevant provision of this Act, in relation to a work of any description, are references to the provision of this Act whereby it is provided that (subject to compliance with the conditions specified therein) copyright shall subsist in works of that description.

(4) The preceding provisions of this section shall apply, in relation to any subject-matter (other than a work) of a description to which any provision of Part II of this Act relates, as they apply in relation to a work.

(5) For the purposes of any provision of this Act which specifies the conditions under which copyright may subsist in any description of work or other subject-matter, 'qualified person'—

(a) in the case of an individual, means a person who is a British subject or British protected person or a citizen of the Republic of Ireland or (not being a British subject or British protected person or a citizen of the Republic of Ireland) is domiciled or resident in the United Kingdom or in another country to which that provision extends, and

(b) in the case of a body corporate, means a body incorporated under the laws of any part of the United Kingdom or of another country to which that provision extends.

In this subsection 'British protected person' has the same meaning as in the *British Nationality Act 1948 and* **the British Nationality Act 1981.**

*General note*
As amended by the British Nationality (Modification of Enactments) Order 1982, SI 1982/1832.

## 2. Copyright in literary, dramatic and musical works

(1) Copyright shall subsist, subject to the provisions of this Act, in every original literary, dramatic or musical work which is unpublished, and of which the author was a qualified person at the time when the work was made, or, if the making of the work extended over a period, was a qualified person for a substantial part of that period.

(2) Where an original literary, dramatic or musical work has been published, then, subject to the provisions of this Act, copyright shall subsist in the work (or, if copyright in the work subsisted immediately before its first publication, shall continue to subsist) if, but only if,—

(a) the first publication of the work took place in the United Kingdom, or in another country to which this section extends, or

(b) the author of the work was a qualified person at the time when the work was first published, or

(c) the author had died before that time, but was a qualified person immediately before his death.

(3) Subject to the last preceding subsection, copyright subsisting in a work by virtue of this section shall continue to subsist until the end of the period of fifty years from the end of the calendar year in which the author died, and shall then expire:

Provided that if before the death of the author none of the following acts had been done, that is to say,—

(a) the publication of the work,

(b) the performance of the work in public,

(c) the offer for sale to the public of records of the work, *and*

(d) the broadcasting of the work,

(e) **the inclusion of the work in a cable programme,**

the copyright shall continue to subsist until the end of the period of fifty years from the end of the calendar year which includes the earliest occasion on which one of those acts is done.

(4) In the last preceding subsection references to the doing of any act in relation to a work include references to the doing of that act in relation to an adaptation of the work.

(5) The acts restricted by the copyright in a literary, dramatic or musical work are—

(a) reproducing the work in any material form;

(b) publishing the work;

(c) performing the work in public;

(d) broadcasting the work;

(e) *causing the work to be transmitted to subscribers to a diffusion service;* **including the work in a cable programme;**

(f) making any adaptation of the work;

(g) doing, in relation to an adaptation of the work, any of the acts specified in relation to the work in paragraphs (a) to (e) of this subsection.

(6) In this Act 'adaptation'—

(a) in relation to a literary or dramatic work, means any of the following, that is to say,—

(i) In the case of a non-dramatic work, a version of the work (whether in its original language or a different language) in which it is converted into a dramatic work;

(ii) in the case of a dramatic work, a version of the work (whether in its original language or a different language) in which it is converted into a non-dramatic work;

(iii) a translation of the work;

(iv) a version of the work in which the story or action is conveyed wholly or mainly by means of pictures in a form suitable for reproduction in a book, or in a newspaper, magazine or similar periodical; and

(b) in relation to a musical work, means an arrangement or transcription of the work,

so however that the mention of any matter in this definition shall not affect the generality of paragraph (a) of the last preceding subsection.

*General note*
As amended by the Cable and Broadcasting Act 1984.

## 3. Copyright in artistic works

(1) In this Act 'artistic work' means a work of any of the following descriptions, that is to say,—

    (a)  the following, irrespective of artistic quality, namely paintings, sculptures, drawings, engravings and photographs;

    (b)  works of architecture, being either buildings or models for buildings;

    (c)  works of artistic craftsmanship, not falling within either of the preceding paragraphs.

(2) Copyright shall subsist, subject to the provisions of this Act, in every original artistic work which is unpublished, and of which the author was a qualified person at the time when the work was made, or, if the making of the work extended over a period, was a qualified person for a substantial part of that period.

(3) Where an original artistic work has been published, then, subject to the provisions of this Act, copyright shall subsist in the work (or, if copyright in the work subsisted immediately before its first publication, shall continue to subsist) if, but only if,—

    (a)  the first publication of the work took place in the United Kingdom, or in another country to which this section extends, or

    (b)  the author of the work was a qualified person at the time when the work was first published, or

    (c)  the author had died before that time, but was a qualified person immediately before his death.

(4) Subject to the last preceding subsection, copyright subsisting in a work by virtue of this section shall continue to subsist until the end of the period of fifty years from the end of the calendar year in which the author died, and shall then expire:

Provided that—

    (a)  in the case of an engraving, if before the death of the author the engraving had not been published, the copyright shall continue to subsist until the end of the period of fifty years from the end of the calendar year in which it is first published;

    (b)  the copyright in a photograph shall continue to subsist until the end of the period of fifty years from the end of the calendar year in which the photograph is first published, and shall then expire.

(5) The acts restricted by the copyright in an artistic work are—

    (a)  reproducing the work in any material form;

    (b)  publishing the work;

    (c)  including the work in a television broadcast;

    (d)  *causing a television programme which includes the work to be transmitted to subscribers to a diffusion service.*

    **(d)  including the work in a cable programme**.

*General note*
As amended by the Cable and Broadcasting Act 1984. Italicised words repealed; words in bold type added.

**4. Ownership of copyright in literary, dramatic, musical and artistic works**
(1) Subject to the provisions of this section, the author of a work shall be entitled to any copyright subsisting in the work by virtue of this Part of this Act.

(2) Where a literary, dramatic or artistic work is made by the author in the course of his employment by the proprietor of a newspaper, magazine or similar periodical under a contract of service or apprenticeship, and is so made for the purpose of publication in a newspaper, magazine or similar periodical, the said proprietor shall be entitled to the copyright in the work in so far as the copyright relates to publication of the work in any newspaper, magazine or similar periodical, or to reproduction of the work for the purpose of its being so published; but in all other respects the author shall be entitled to any copyright subsisting in the work by virtue of this Part of this Act.

(3) Subject to the last preceding subsection, where a person commissions the taking of a photograph, or the painting or drawing of a portrait, or the making of an engraving, and pays or agrees to pay for it in money or money's worth, and the work is made in pursuance of that commission, the person who so commissioned the work shall be entitled to any copyright subsisting therein by virtue of this Part of this Act.

(4) Where, in the case not falling within either of the two last preceding subsections, a work is made in the course of the author's employment by another person under a contract of service or apprenticeship, that other person shall be entitled to any copyright subsisting in the work by virtue of this Part of this Act.

(5) Each of the three last preceding subsections shall have effect subject, in any particular case, to any agreement excluding the operation thereof in that case.

(6) The preceding provisions of this section shall all have effect subject to the provisions of Part VI of this Act.

**5. Infringements by importation, sale and other dealings**
(1) Without prejudice to the general provisions of section one of this Act as to infringements of copyright, the provisions of this section shall have effect in relation to copyright subsisting by virtue of this Part of this Act.

(2) The copyright in a literary, dramatic, musical or artistic work is infringed by any person who, without the licence of the owner of the copyright, imports an article (otherwise than for his private and domestic use) into the United Kingdom, or into any other country to which this section extends, if to his knowledge the making of that article constituted an infringement of that copyright, or would have constituted such an infringement if the article had been made in the place into which it is so imported.

(3) The copyright in a literary, dramatic, musical or artistic work is infringed by any person who, in the United Kingdom, or in any other country to which this section extends, and without the licence of the owner of the copyright,—

(a) sells, lets for hire, or by way of trade offers or exposes for sale or hire any article, or
(b) by way of trade exhibits any article in public,

if to his knowledge the making of the article constituted an infringement of that copyright, or (in the case of an imported article) would have constituted an infringement of that copyright if the article had been made in the place into which it was imported.

(4) The last preceding subsection shall apply in relation to the distribution of any articles either—

    (a)  for purposes of trade, or

    (b)  for other purposes, but to such an extent as to affect prejudicially the owner of the copyright in question,

as it applies in relation to the sale of an article.

(5) The copyright in a literary, dramatic or musical work is also infringed by any person who permits a place of public entertainment to be used for a performance in public of the work, where the performance constitutes an infringement of the copyright in the work:

Provided that this subsection shall not apply in a case where the person permitting the place to be so used—

    (a)  was not aware, and had no reasonable grounds for suspecting, that the performance would be an infringement of the copyright, or

    (b)  gave the permission gratuitously, or for a consideration which was only nominal or (if more than nominal) did not exceed a reasonable estimate of the expenses to be incurred by him in consequence of the use of the place for the performance.

(6) In this section 'place of public entertainment' includes any premises which are occupied mainly for other purposes, but are from time to time made available for hire to such persons as may desire to hire them for purposes of public entertainment.

### 6. General exceptions from protection of literary, dramatic and musical works

(1) No fair dealing with a literary, dramatic or musical work for purposes of research or private study shall constitute an infringement of the copyright in the work.

(2) No fair dealing with a literary, dramatic or musical work shall constitute an infringement of the copyright in the work if it is for purposes of criticism or review, whether of that work or of another work, and is accompanied by a sufficient acknowledgment.

(3) No fair dealing with a literary, dramatic or musical work shall constitute an infringement of the copyright in the work if it is for the purpose of reporting current events—

    (a)  in a newspaper, magazine or similar periodical, or

    (b)  by means of broadcasting, or in a cinematograph film,

and, in a case falling within paragraph (a) of this subsection, is accompanied by a sufficient acknowledgment.

(4) The copyright in a literary, dramatic or musical work is not infringed by reproducing it for the purposes of a judicial proceeding, or for the purposes of a report of a judicial proceeding.

(5) The reading or recitation in public by one person of any reasonable extract from a published literary or dramatic work, if accompanied by a sufficient acknowledgment, shall not constitute an infringement of the copyright in the work:

Provided that this subsection shall not apply to anything done for the purposes of broadcasting.

(6) The copyright in a published literary or dramatic work is not infringed by the inclusion of a short passage therefrom in a collection intended for the use of schools, if—

(a) the collection is described in its title, and in any advertisements thereof issued by or on behalf of the publisher, as being so intended, and

(b) the work in question was not published for the use of schools, and

(c) the collection consists mainly of material in which no copyright subsists, and

(d) the inclusion of the passage is accompanied by a sufficient acknowledgment.

Provided that this subsection shall not apply in relation to the copyright in a work if, in addition to the passage in question, two or more other excerpts from works by the author thereof (being works in which copyright subsists at the time when the collection is published) are contained in that collection, or are contained in that collection taken together with every similar collection (if any) published by the same publisher within the period of five years immediately preceding the publication of that collection.

(7) Where by virtue of an assignment or licence a person is authorised to broadcast a literary, dramatic or musical work from a place in the United Kingdom, or in another country to which section two of this Act extends, but (apart from this subsection) would not be entitled to make reproductions of it in the form of a record or of a cinematograph film, the copyright in the work is not infringed by his making such a reproduction of the work solely for the purpose of broadcasting the work:

Provided that this subsection shall not apply if—

(a) the reproduction is used for making any further reproduction therefrom, or for any other purpose except that of broadcasting in accordance with the assignment or licence, or

(b) the reproduction is not destroyed before the end of the period of twenty-eight days beginning with the day on which it is first used for broadcasting the work in pursuance of the assignment or licence, or such extended period (if any) as may be agreed between the person who made the reproduction and the person who (in relation to the making of reproductions of the description in question) is the owner of the copyright.

(8) The preceding provisions of this section shall apply to the doing of any act in relation to an adaptation of a work as they apply in relation to the doing of that act in relation to the work itself.

(9) The provisions of this section shall apply where a work, or adaptation of a work, *is caused to be transmitted to subscribers to a diffusion service as* **included in a cable programme** they apply where a work or adaptation is broadcast.

(10) In this Act 'sufficient acknowledgment' means an acknowledgment identifying the work in question by its title or other description and, unless the work is anonymous or the author has previously agreed or required that no acknowledgment of his name should be made, also identifying the author.

*General note*
As amended by the Cable and Broadcasting Act 1984. Italicised words repealed; words in bold type added.

## 7. Special exceptions as respects libraries and archives

(1) The copyright in an article contained in a periodical publication is not infringed by the making or supplying of a copy of the article, if the copy is made or supplied by or on behalf of the librarian of a library of a class prescribed by

regulations made under this subsection by the Board of Trade, and the conditions prescribed by those regulations are complied with.

(2) In making any regulations for the purposes of the preceding subsection the Board of Trade shall make such provision as the Board may consider appropriate for securing—

    (a) that the libraries to which the regulations apply are not established or conducted for profit;

    (b) that the copies in question are supplied only to persons satisfying the librarian, or a person acting on his behalf, that they require them for purposes of research or private study and will not use them for any other purpose;

    (c) that no person is furnished under the regulations with two or more copies of the same article;

    (d) that no copy extends to more than one article contained in any one publication; and

    (e) that persons to whom copies are supplied under the regulations are required to pay for them a sum not less than the cost (including a contribution to the general expenses of the library) attributable to their production,

and may impose such other requirements (if any) as may appear to the Board to be expedient.

(3) The copyright in a published literary, dramatic or musical work, other than an article contained in a periodical publication, is not infringed by the making or supplying of a copy of part of the work, if the copy is made or supplied by or on behalf of the librarian of a library of a class prescribed by regulations made under this subsection by the Board of Trade, and the conditions prescribed by those regulations are complied with:

Provided that this subsection shall not apply if, at the time when the copy is made, the librarian knows the name and address of a person entitled to authorise the making of the copy, or could by reasonable inquiry ascertain the name and address of such a person.

(4) The provisions of subsection (2) of this section shall apply for the purposes of the last preceding subsection:

Provided that paragraph (d) of the said subsection (2) shall not apply for those purposes, but any regulations made under the last preceding subsection shall include such provision as the Board of Trade may consider appropriate for securing that no copy to which the regulations apply extends to more than a reasonable proportion of the work in question.

(5) The copyright in a published literary, dramatic or musical work is not infringed by the making or supplying of a copy of the work, or of part of it, by or on behalf of the librarian of a library of a class prescribed by regulations made under this subsection by the Board of Trade, if—

    (a) the copy is supplied to the librarian of any library of a class so prescribed;

    (b) at the time when the copy is made, the librarian by or on whose behalf it is supplied does not know the name and address of any person entitled to authorise the making of the copy, and could not by reasonable inquiry ascertain the name and address of such a person; and

    (c) any other conditions prescribed by the regulations are complied with:

Provided that the condition specified in paragraph (b) of this subsection shall not apply in the case of an article contained in a periodical publication.

(6) Where, at a time more than fifty years from the end of the calendar year in which the author of a literary, dramatic or musical work died, and more than one hundred years after the time, or the end of the period, at or during which the work was made,—

(a) copyright subsists in the work, but
(b) the work has not been published, and
(c) the manuscript or a copy of the work is kept in a library, museum or other institution where (subject to any provisions regulating the institution in question) it is open to public inspection,

the copyright in the work is not infringed by a person who reproduces the work for purposes of research or private study, or with a view to publication.

(7) Where a published literary, dramatic or musical work (in this subsection referred to as 'the new work') incorporates the whole or part of a work (in this subsection referred to as 'the old work') in the case of which the circumstances specified in the last preceding subsection existed immediately before the new work was published, and—

(a) before the new work was published, such notice of the intended publication as may be prescribed by regulations made under this subsection by the Board of Trade had been given, and
(b) immediately before the new work was published, the identity of the owner of the copyright in the old work was not known to the publisher of the new work,

then for the purposes of this Act—

(i) that publication of the new work, and
(ii) any subsequent publication of the new work, either in the same or in an altered form,

shall, in so far as it constitutes a publication of the old work, not be treated as an infringement of the copyright in the old work or as an unauthorised publication of the old work:

Provided that this subsection shall not apply to a subsequent publication incorporating a part of the old work which was not included in the new work as originally published, unless (apart from this subsection) the circumstances specified in the last preceding subsection, and in paragraphs (a) and (b) of this subsection, existed immediately before that subsequent publication.

(8) In so far as the publication of a work, or of part of a work, is, by virtue of the last preceding subsection, not to be treated as an infringement of the copyright in the work, a person who subsequently broadcasts the work, or that part thereof, as the case may be, or *causes it to be transmitted to subscribers to a diffusion service*, **includes it in a cable programme** or performs it in public, or makes a record of it, does not thereby infringe copyright in the work.

(9) In relation to an article or other work which is accompanied by one or more artistic works provided for explaining or illustrating it (in this subsection referred to as 'illustrations'), the preceding provisions of this section shall apply as if—

(a) wherever they provide that the copyright in the article or work is not infringed, the reference to that copyright included a reference to any copyright in any of the illustrations;

(b)  in subsections (1) and (2), references to a copy of the article included references to a copy of the article together with a copy of the illustrations or any of them;

(c)  in subsections (3) to (5), references to a copy of the work included references to a copy of the work together with a copy of the illustrations or any of them, and references to a copy of part of the work included references to a copy of that part of the work together with a copy of any of the illustrations which were provided for explaining or illustrating that part; and

(d)  in subsections (6) and (7), references to the doing of any act in relation to the work included references to the doing of that act in relation to the work together with any of the illustrations.

(10)  In this section 'article' includes an item of any description.

*General note*
As amended by the Cable and Broadcasting Act 1984. Italicised words repealed; words in bold type added.

## 8. Special exception in respect of records of musical works

(1)  The copyright in a musical work is not infringed by a person (in this section referred to as 'the manufacturer') who makes a record of the work or of an adaptation thereof in the United Kingdom, if—

(a)  records of the work, or, as the case may be, of a similar adaptation of the work, have previously been made in, or imported into, the United Kingdom for the purposes of retail sale, and were so made or imported by, or with the licence of, the owner of the copyright in the work;

(b)  before making the record, the manufacturer gave to the owner of the copyright the prescribed notice of his intention to make it;

(c)  the manufacturer intends to sell the record by retail, or to supply it for the purpose of its being sold by retail by another person, or intends to use it for making other records which are to be sold or supplied; and

(d)  in the case of a record which is sold by retail, the manufacturer pays to the owner of the copyright, in the prescribed manner and at the prescribed time, a royalty of an amount ascertained in accordance with the following provisions of this section.

(2)  Subject to the following provisions of this section, the royalty mentioned in paragraph (d) of the preceding subsection shall be of an amount equal to six and one-quarter per cent of the ordinary retail selling price of the record, calculated in the prescribed manner:

Provided that, if the amount so calculated includes a fraction of a farthing, that fraction shall be reckoned as one farthing, and if, apart from this proviso, the amount of the royalty would be less than three farthings, the amount thereof shall be three farthings.

(3)  If, at any time after the end of the period of one year beginning with the coming into operation of this section, it appears to the Board of Trade that the ordinary rate of royalty, or the minimum amount thereof, in accordance with the provisions of the last preceding subsection, or in accordance with those provisions as last varied by an order under this subsection, has ceased to be equitable, either generally or in relation to any class of records, the Board may hold a public inquiry in the prescribed manner; and if, in consequence of such an inquiry, the Board are

satisfied of the need to do so, the Board may make an order prescribing such different rate or amount, either generally or in relation to any one or more classes of records, as the Board may consider just:

Provided that—

(a) no order shall be made under this subsection unless a draft of the order has been laid before Parliament and approved by a resolution of each House of Parliament; and

(b) where an order comprising a class of records (that is to say, either a general order or an order relating specifically to that class, or to that class together with one or more other classes of records) has been made under this subsection, no further order comprising that class of records shall be made thereunder less than five years after the date on which the previous order comprising that class (or, if more than one, the last previous order comprising that class) was made thereunder.

(4) In the case of a record which comprises (with or without other material, and either in their original form or in the form of adaptations) two or more musical works in which copyright subsists—

(a) the minimum royalty shall be three-farthings in respect of each of those works, or, if a higher or lower amount is prescribed by an order under the last preceding subsection as the minimum royalty, shall be that amount in respect of each of those works; and

(b) if the owners of the copyright in the works are different persons, the royalty shall be apportioned among them in such manner as they may agree or as, in default of agreement, may be determined by arbitration.

(5) Where a record comprises (with or without other material) a performance of a musical work, or of an adaptation of a musical work, in which words are sung, or are spoken incidentally to or in association with the music, and either no copyright subsists in that work or, if such copyright subsists, the conditions specified in subsection (1) of this section are fulfilled in relation to that copyright, then if—

(a) the words consist or form part of a literary or dramatic work in which copyright subsists, and

(b) such previous records as are referred to in paragraph (a) of subsection (1) of this section were made or imported by, or with the licence of, the owner of the copyright in that literary or dramatic work, and

(c) the conditions specified in paragraphs (b) and (d) of subsection (1) of this section are fulfilled in relation to the owner of that copyright,

the making of the record shall not constitute an infringement of the copyright in the literary or dramatic work:

Provided that this subsection shall not be construed as requiring more than one royalty to be paid in respect of a record; and if copyright subsists both in the musical work and in the literary or dramatic work, and their owners are different persons, the royalty shall be apportioned among them (or among them and any other person entitled to a share thereof in accordance with the last preceding subsection) as they may agree or as, in default of agreement, may be determined by arbitration.

(6) For the purposes of this section an adaptation of a work shall be taken to be similar to an adaptation thereof contained in previous records if the two

adaptations do not substantially differ in their treatment of the work, either in respect of style or (apart from any difference in numbers) in respect of the performers required for performing them.

(7) Where, for the purposes of paragraph (a) of subsection (1) of this section, the manufacturer requires to know whether such previous records as are mentioned in that paragraph were made or imported as therein mentioned, the manufacturer may make the prescribed inquiries; and if the owner of the copyright fails to reply to those inquiries within the prescribed period, the previous records shall be taken to have been made or imported, as the case may be, with the licence of the owner of the copyright.

(8) The preceding provisions of this section shall apply in relation to records of a part of a work or adaptation as they apply in relation to records of the whole of it:

Provided that subsection (1) of this section—

(a) shall not apply to a record of the whole of a work or adaptation unless the previous records referred to in paragraph (a) of that subsection were records of the whole of the work or of a similar adaptation, and

(b) shall not apply to a record of part of a work or adaptation unless those previous records were records of, or comprising, that part of the work or of a similar adaptation.

(9) In relation to musical works published before the first day of July, nineteen hundred and twelve, the preceding provisions of this section shall apply as if paragraph (a) of subsection (1), paragraph (b) of subsection (5), subsections (6) and (7), and the proviso to the last preceding subsection, were omitted:

Provided that this subsection shall not extend the operation of subsection (5) of this section to a record in respect of which the condition specified in paragraph (b) of that subsection is not fulfilled, unless the words comprised in the record (as well as the musical work) were published before the first day of July, nineteen hundred and twelve, and were so published as words to be sung to, or spoken incidentally to or in association with, the music.

(10) Nothing in this section shall be construed as authorising the importation of records which could not lawfully be imported apart from this section; and accordingly, for the purposes of any provision of this Act relating to imported articles, where the question arises whether the making of a record made outside the United Kingdom would have constituted an infringement of copyright if the record had been made in the United Kingdom, that question shall be determined as if subsection (1) of this section had not been enacted.

(11) In this section 'prescribed' means prescribed by regulations made under this section by the Board of Trade; and any such regulations made for the purposes of paragraph (d) of subsection (1) of this section may provide that the taking of such steps as may be specified in the regulations (being such steps as the Board consider most convenient for ensuring the receipt of the royalties by the owner of the copyright) shall be treated as constituting payment of the royalties in accordance with that paragraph.

## 9. General exceptions from protection of artistic works

(1) No fair dealing with an artistic work for purposes of research or private study shall constitute an infringement of the copyright in the work.

(2) No fair dealing with an artistic work shall constitute an infringement of the

copyright in the work if it is for purposes of criticism or review, whether of that work or of another work, and is accompanied by a sufficient acknowledgment.

(3) The copyright in a work to which this subsection applies which is permanently situated in a public place, or in premises open to the public, is not infringed by the making of a painting, drawing, engraving or photograph of the work, or the inclusion of the work in a cinematograph film or in a television broadcast.

This subsection applies to sculptures, and to such works of artistic craftsmanship as are mentioned in paragraph (c) of subsection (1) of section three of this Act.

(4) The copyright in a work of architecture is not infringed by the making of a painting, drawing, engraving or photograph of the work, or the inclusion of the work in a cinematograph film or in a television broadcast.

(5) Without prejudice to the two last preceding subsections, the copyright in an artistic work is not infringed by the inclusion of the work in a cinematograph film or in a television broadcast, if its inclusion therein is only by way of background or is otherwise only incidental to the principal matters represented in the film or broadcast.

(6) The copyright in an artistic work is not infringed by the publication of a painting, drawing, engraving, photograph or cinematograph film, if by virtue of any of the three last preceding subsections the making of that painting, drawing, engraving, photograph or film did not constitute an infringement of the copyright.

(7) The copyright in an artistic work is not infringed by reproducing it for the purposes of a judicial proceeding or for the purposes of a report of a judicial proceeding.

(8) The making of an object of any description which is in three dimensions shall not be taken to infringe the copyright in an artistic work in two dimensions, if the object would not appear, to persons who are not experts in relation to objects of that description, to be a reproduction of the artistic work.

(9) The copyright in an artistic work is not infringed by the making of a subsequent artistic work by the same author, notwithstanding that part of the earlier work—

(a) is reproduced in the subsequent work, and
(b) is so reproduced by the use of a mould, cast, sketch, plan, model or study made for the purposes of the earlier work,

if in making the subsequent work the author does not repeat or imitate the main design of the earlier work.

(10) Where copyright subsists in a building as a work of architecture, the copyright is not infringed by any reconstruction of that building; and where a building has been constructed in accordance with architectural drawings or plans in which copyright subsists, and has been so constructed by, or with the licence of, the owner of that copyright, any subsequent reconstruction of the building by reference to those drawings or plans shall not constitute an infringement of that copyright.

(11) The provisions of this section shall apply in relation to *a television programme which is caused to be transmitted to subscribers to a diffusion service* **cable programme** as they apply in relation to a television broadcast.

*General note*
As amended by the Cable and Broadcasting Act 1984. Italicised words repealed; words in bold type added.

## 10. Special exception in respect of industrial designs

(1) *Where copyright subsists in an artistic work, and a corresponding design is registered under the Registered Designs Act 1949 (in this section referred to as 'the Act of 1949'), it shall not be an infringement of the copyright in the work—*

> (*a*) *to do anything, during the subsistence of the copyright in the registered design under the Act of 1949, which is within the scope of the copyright in the design, or*
>
> (*b*) *to do anything, after the copyright in the registered design has come to an end, which, if it had been done while the copyright in the design subsisted, would have been within the scope of that copyright as extended to all associated designs and articles:*

*Provided that this subsection shall have effect subject to the provisions of the first Schedule to this Act in cases falling within that Schedule.*

(2) Where copyright subsists in an artistic work, and—

> (a) a corresponding design is applied industrially by or with the licence of the owner of the copyright in the work, and
>
> (b) articles to which the design has been so applied are sold, let for hire, or offered for sale or hire [whether in the United Kingdom or elsewhere], and
>
> (c) *at the time when those articles are sold, let for hire, or offered for sale or hire, they are not articles in respect of which the design has been registered under the Act of 1949,*

the following provisions of this section shall apply.

(3) *Subject to the next following subsection,—*

> (*a*) *during the relevant period of fifteen years, it shall not be an infringement of the copyright in the work to do anything which, at the time when it is done, would have been within the scope of the copyright in the design if the design had, immediately before that time, been registered in respect of all relevant articles; and*
>
> (*b*) *after the end of the relevant period of fifteen years, it shall not be an infringement of the copyright in the work to do anything which, at the time when it is done, would, if the design had been registered immediately before that time, have been within the scope of the copyright in the design as extended to all associated designs and articles.*

*In this subsection 'the relevant period of fifteen years' means the period of fifteen years beginning with the date on which articles, such as are mentioned in paragraph (b) of the last preceding subsection, were first sold, let for hire, or offered for sale or hire in the circumstances mentioned in paragraph (c) of that subsection; and 'all relevant articles', in relation to any time within that period, means all articles falling within the said paragraph (b) which had before that time been sold, let for hire, or offered for sale or hire in those circumstances.*

(3) **Subject to the next following subsection, after the end of the relevant period of 15 years it shall not be an infringement of the copyright in the work to do anything which at the time when it was done would, if a corresponding design had been registered under the Registered Designs Act 1949 (in this section referred to as 'the Act of 1949') immediately before that time, have been within the scope of the copyright in the design as extended to all associated designs and articles.**

**In this subsection 'the relevant period of 15 years' means the period of 15 years beginning with the date on which articles, such as are mentioned in paragraph (b) of the last preceding subsection, were first sold, let for hire or offered for sale or hire, whether in the United Kingdom or elsewhere.**

(4) For the purposes of subsections (2) and (3) of this section, no account shall be taken of any articles in respect of which, at the time when they were sold, let for hire, or offered for sale or hire, the design in question was excluded from registration under the Act of 1949 by rules made under subsection (4) of section one of that Act (which relates to the exclusion of designs for articles which are primarily literary or artistic in character); and for the purposes of any proceedings under this Act a design shall be conclusively presumed to have been so excluded if—

(a) before the commencement of those proceedings, an application for the registration of the design under the Act of 1949 in respect of those articles had been refused;

(b) the reason or one of the reasons stated for the refusal was that the design was excluded from such registration by rules made under the said subsection (4); and

(c) no appeal against that refusal had been allowed before the date of the commencement of the proceedings or was pending on that date.

(5) The power of the Board of Trade to make rules under section thirty-six of the Act of 1949 shall include power to make rules for the purpose of this section for determining the circumstances in which a design is to be taken to be applied industrially.

(6) In this section, references to the scope of the copyright in a registered design are references to the aggregate of the things, which, by virtue of section seven of the Act of 1949, the registered proprietor of the design has the exclusive right to do, and references to the scope of the copyright in a registered design as extended to all associated designs and articles are references to the aggregate of the things which, by virtue of that section, the registered proprietor would have had the exclusive right to do if—

(a) when that design was registered, there had at the same time been registered every possible design consisting of that design with modifications or variations not sufficient to alter the character or substantially to affect the identity thereof, and the said proprietor had been registered as the proprietor of every such design, and

(b) the design in question, and every other design such as is mentioned in the preceding paragraph, had been registered in respect of all the articles to which it was capable of being applied.

(7) In this section 'corresponding design', in relation to an artistic work, means a design which, when applied to an article, results in a reproduction of that work.

*General note*
As amended by the Design Copyright Act 1968. Italicised words repealed; words in bold added.

## 11. Provisions as to anonymous and pseudonymous works, and works of joint authorship
(1) The preceding provisions of this Part of this Act shall have effect subject to the modifications specified in the Second Schedule to this Act in the case of works published anonymously or pseudonymously.

(2) The provisions of the Third Schedule to this Act shall have effect with respect to works of joint authorship.

(3) In this Act 'work of joint authorship' means a work produced by the collaboration of two or more authors in which the contribution of each author is not separate from the contribution of the other author or authors.

PART II
COPYRIGHT IN SOUND RECORDINGS, CINEMATOGRAPH FILMS, BROADCASTS, ETC.

### 12. Copyright in sound recordings

(1) Copyright shall subsist, subject to the provisions of this Act, in every sound recording of which the maker was a qualified person at the time when the recording was made.

(2) Without prejudice to the preceding subsection, copyright shall subsist, subject to the provisions of this Act, in every sound recording which has been published, if the first publication of the recording took place in the United Kingdom or in another country to which this section extends.

(3) Copyright subsisting in a sound recording by virtue of this section shall continue to subsist until the end of the period of fifty years from the end of the calendar year in which the recording is first published, and shall then expire.

(4) Subject to the provisions of this Act, the maker of a sound recording shall be entitled to any copyright subsisting in the recording by virtue of this section:

Provided that where a person commissions the making of a sound recording, and pays or agrees to pay for it in money or money's worth, and the recording is made in pursuance of that commission, that person, in the absence of any agreement to the contrary, shall, subject to the provisions of Part VI of this Act, be entitled to any copyright subsisting in the recording by virtue of this section.

(5) The acts restricted by the copyright in a sound recording are the following, whether a record embodying the recording is utilised directly or indirectly in doing them, that is to say,—

    (a)  making a record embodying the recording;
    (b)  causing the recording to be heard in public;
    (c)  broadcasting the recording **or including it in a cable programme**.

(6) The copyright in a sound recording is not infringed by a person who does any of those acts in the United Kingdom in relation to a sound recording, or part of a sound recording, if—

    (a)  records embodying that recording, or that part of the recording, as the case may be, have previously been issued to the public in the United Kingdom, and
    (b)  at the time when those records were so issued, neither the records nor the containers in which they were so issued, bore a label or other mark indicating the year in which the recording was first published:

Provided that this subsection shall not apply if it is shown that the records in question were not issued by or with the licence of the owner of the copyright, or that the owner of the copyright had taken all reasonable steps for securing that records embodying the recording or part thereof would not be issued to the public in the United Kingdom without such a label or mark either on the records themselves or on their containers.

(7) Where a sound recording is caused to be heard in public—

(a) at any premises where persons reside or sleep, as part of the amenities provided exclusively or mainly for residents or inmates therein, or

(b) as part of the activities of, or for the benefit of, a club, society or other organisation which is not established or conducted for profit and whose main objects are charitable or are otherwise concerned with the advancement of religion, education or social welfare,

the act of causing it to be so heard shall not constitute an infringement of the copyright in the recording:

Provided that this subsection shall not apply—

(i) in the case of such premises as are mentioned in paragraph (a) of this subsection, if a special charge is made for admission to the part of the premises where the recording is to be heard; or

(ii) in the case of such an organisation as is mentioned in paragraph (b) of this subsection, if a charge is made for admission to the place where the recording is to be heard, and any of the proceeds of the charge are applied otherwise than for the purposes of the organisation.

(8) For the purposes of this Act a sound recording shall be taken to be made at the time when the first record embodying the recording is produced, and the maker of a sound recording is the person who owns that record at the time when the recording is made.

(9) In this Act 'sound recording' means the aggregate of the sounds embodied in, and capable of being reproduced by means of, a record of any description, other than a sound-track associated with a cinematograph film; and 'publication', in relation to a sound recording, means the issue to the public of records embodying the recording or any part thereof.

*General note*
Words in bold type added by the Cable and Broadcasting Act 1984.

### 13. Copyright in cinematograph films

(1) Copyright shall subsist, subject to the provisions of this Act, in every cinematograph film of which the maker was a qualified person for the whole or a substantial part of the period during which the film was made.

(2) Without prejudice to the preceding subsection, copyright shall subsist, subject to the provisions of this Act, in every cinematograph film which has been published, if the first publication of the film took place in the United Kingdom or in another country to which this section extends.

(3) Copyright subsisting in a cinematograph film by virtue of this section—

(a) *in the case of a film which is registrable under (Part III of the Cinematograph Films Act 1938) Part II of the Films Act 1960; shall continue to subsist until the film is registered thereunder, and thereafter until the end of the period of fifty years from the end of the calendar year in which it is so registered*; **in the case of any film which was registered under a former enactment relating to the registration of films, shall continue until the end of the period of fifty years from the end of the calender year in which it was so registered**;

(b) in the case of *a film which is not so registrable* **any other film**, shall continue until the film is published, and thereafter until the end of the period of fifty years from the end of the calendar year which includes the date of its first publication, or, if copyright in the film subsists by virtue only of the last preceding subsection, shall continue as from the date of first publication until the end of the period of fifty years from the end of the calendar year which includes that date,

and shall then expire:

*Provided that if the Parliament of Northern Ireland passes legislation for purposes similar to those of (Part III of the said Act of 1938) [Part II of the Films Act 1960], then, in the case of a cinematograph film which is registered under that legislation, at a time when it has not been registered (the said Part III) [the said Part II], the copyright shall continue to subsist until the end of the period of fifty years from the end of the calendar year which includes the date on which the film is registered under that legislation, and shall then expire.* **In this subsection 'former enactment relating to the registration of films' means Part II of the Films Act 1960 or Part III of the Cinematograph Films Act 1938.**

(4) Subject to the provisions of Part VI of this Act, the maker of a cinematograph film shall be entitled to any copyright subsisting in the film by virtue of this section.

(5) The acts restricted by the copyright in a cinematograph film are—

(a) making a copy of the film;
(b) causing the film, in so far as it consists of visual images, to be seen in public, or, in so far as it consists of sounds, to be heard in public;
(c) broadcasting the film;
(d) *causing the film to be transmitted to subscribers to a diffusion service* **including the film in a cable programme**.

(6) The copyright in a cinematograph film is not infringed by making a copy of it for the purposes of a judicial proceeding, or by causing it to be seen or heard in public for the purposes of such a proceeding.

(7) Where by virtue of this section copyright has subsisted in a cinematograph film, a person who, after that copyright has expired, causes the film to be seen, or to be seen and heard, in public does not thereby infringe any copyright subsisting by virtue of Part I of this Act in any literary, dramatic, musical or artistic work.

(8) In the case of *any such film as is mentioned in (paragraph (a) of section thirty-five of the Cinematograph Films Act 1938) [paragraph (a) of subsection (1) of section thirty-eight of the Films Act 1960] (which relates to newsreels),* **any film consisting wholly or mainly of photographs which, at the time when they were taken, were means of communicating news,** the copyright in the film is not infringed by causing it to be seen or heard in public after the end of the period of fifty years from the end of the calendar year in which the principal events depicted in the film occurred.

(9) For the purposes of this Act a cinematograph film shall be taken to include the sounds embodied in any sound-track associated with the film, and references to a copy of a cinematograph film shall be construed accordingly:

Provided that where those sounds are also embodied in a record, other than such a sound-track or a record derived (directly or indirectly) from such a sound-track, the copyright in the film is not infringed by any use made of that record.

(10) In this Act—

'cinematograph film' means any sequence of visual images recorded on material of any description (whether translucent or not) so as to be capable, by the use of that material—

(a) of being shown as a moving picture, or

(b) of being recorded on other material (whether translucent or not), by the use of which it can be so shown;

'the maker', in relation to a cinematograph film, means the person by whom the arrangements necessary for the making of the film are undertaken;

'publication', in relation to a cinematograph film, means the sale, letting on hire, or offer for sale or hire, of copies of the film to the public;

'copy', in relation to a cinematograph film, means any print, negative, tape or other article on which the film or part of it is recorded,

and references in this Act to a sound-track associated with a cinematograph film are references to any record of sounds which is incorporated in any print, negative, tape or other article on which the film or part of it, in so far as it consists of visual images, is recorded, or which is issued by the maker of the film for use in conjunction with such an article.

*((11) References in this section to Part III of the Cinematograph Films Act 1938, shall be construed as including references to any enactments for the time being in force amending or substituted for the provisions of the said Part III.)*

[(11) References in this section to Part II of the Films Act 1960, shall be construed as including references to any enactments for the time being in force amending or substituted for the provisions of the said Part II and, in relation to any time before the commencement of that Act, as references to the enactments replaced by those provisions.]

*General note*

Sub-s (3)(a), the words in bold in sub-s (3)(b), the words in square brackets at the end of that subsection and those in sub-s (8) were substituted, and the proviso to sub-s (3) and sub-s (11) were repealed, by the Films Act 1985. Added words are in bold type; repealed words are italicised. Sub-s (3)(a), the proviso to that subsection, sub-s (8) and sub-s (11), as repealed, were originally amended by the Films Act 1960. Added words are in square brackets; repealed words are in round brackets. Sub-s (5)(d) was substituted by the Cable and Broadcasting Act 1984. Italicised words repealed; words in bold type added.

## 14. Copyright in television broadcasts and sound broadcasts

(1) Copyright shall subsist, subject to the provisions of this Act,—

(a) in every television broadcast made by the British Broadcasting Corporation (in this Act referred to as 'the Corporation') or by the Independent Television Authority (in this Act referred to as 'the Authority') from a place in the United Kingdom or in any other country to which this section extends, and

(b) in every sound broadcast made by the Corporation or the Authority from such a place.

(2) Subject to the provisions of this Act, the Corporation or the Authority, as the case may be, shall be entitled to any copyright subsisting in a television broadcast or sound broadcast made by them; and any such copyright shall continue to subsist until the end of the period of fifty years from the end of the calendar year in which the broadcast is made, and shall then expire.

(3) In so far as a television broadcast or sound broadcast is a repetition (whether the first or any subsequent repetition) of a television broadcast or sound broadcast

previously made as mentioned in subsection (1) of this section (whether by the Corporation or by the Authority), and is made by broadcasting material recorded on film, records or otherwise—

    (a) copyright shall not subsist therein by virtue of this section if it is made after the end of the period of fifty years from the end of the calendar year in which the previous broadcast was made; and

    (b) if it is made before the end of that period, any copyright subsisting therein by virtue of this section shall expire at the end of that period.

(4) The acts restricted by the copyright in a television broadcast or sound broadcast are—

    (a) in the case of a television broadcast in so far as it consists of visual images, making, otherwise than for private purposes, a cinematograph film of it or a copy of such a film;

    (b) in the case of a sound broadcast, or of a television broadcast in so far as it consists of sounds, making, otherwise than for private purposes, a sound recording of it or a record embodying such a recording;

    (c) in the case of a television broadcast, causing it, in so far as it consists of visual images, to be seen in public, or, in so far as it consists of sounds, to be heard in public, if it is seen or heard by a paying audience;

    (d) in the case either of a television broadcast or of a sound broadcast, re-broadcasting it **or including it in a cable programme**.

(5) The restrictions imposed by virtue of the last preceding subsection in relation to a television broadcast or sound broadcast made by the Corporation or by the Authority shall apply whether the act in question is done by the reception of the broadcast or by making use of any record, print, negative, tape or other article on which the broadcast has been recorded.

(6) In relation to copyright in television broadcasts, in so far as they consist of visual images, the restrictions imposed by virtue of subsection (4) of this section shall apply to any sequence of images sufficient to be seen as a moving picture; and accordingly, for the purpose of establishing an infringement of such copyright, it shall not be necessary to prove that the act in question extended to more than such a sequence of images.

(7) For the purposes of subsection (4) of this section a cinematograph film or a copy thereof, or a sound recording or a record embodying a recording, shall be taken to be made otherwise than for private purposes if it is made for the purposes of the doing by any person of any of the following acts, that is to say—

    (a) the sale or letting for hire of any copy of the film, or, as the case may be, of any record embodying the recording;

    (b) broadcasting the film or recording;

    (c) causing the film or recording to be seen or heard in public.

(8) For the purposes of paragraph (c) of subsection (4) of this section, a television broadcast shall be taken to be seen or heard by a paying audience if it is seen or heard by persons who either—

    (a) have been admitted for payment to the place where the broadcast is to be seen or heard, or have been admitted for payment to a place of which that place forms part, or

    (b) have been admitted to the place where the broadcast is to be seen or heard in circumstances where goods or services are supplied there at prices which exceed the prices usually charged at that place and are partly attributable to the facilities afforded for seeing or hearing the broadcast:

Provided that for the purposes of paragraph (a) of this subsection no account shall be taken—

(i) of persons admitted to the place in question as residents or inmates therein, or

(ii) of persons admitted to that place as members of a club or society, where the payment is only for membership of the club or society and the provision of facilities for seeing or hearing television broadcasts is only incidental to the main purposes of the club or society.

**(8A) The Copyright in a television broadcast or sound broadcast is not infringed by any person who, by the reception and immediate re-transmission of the broadcast, includes a programme in a cable programme service—**

**(a) if the programme is so included in pursuance of a requirement imposed under subsection (1) of section 13 of the Cable and Broadcasting Act 1984; or**

**(b) where the broadcast is made otherwise than in a DBS service (as defined in subsection (6) of that section) or an additional teletext service (as so defined), if and to the extent that it is made for reception in the area in which the cable programme service is provided.**

(9) The copyright in a television broadcast or sound broadcast is not infringed by anything done in relation to the broadcast for the purposes of a judicial proceeding.

(10) In this Act 'television broadcast' means visual images broadcast by way of television, together with any sounds broadcast for reception along with those images, and 'sound broadcast' means sounds broadcast otherwise than as part of a television broadcast; and for the purposes of this Act a television broadcast or sound broadcast shall be taken to be made by the body by whom, at the time when, and from the place from which, *the visual* images or sounds in question, or both, as the case may be, are broadcast.

**(a) the visual images or sounds in question, or both, as the case may be, are broadcast; or**

**(b) in the case of a television broadcast or sound broadcast made by the technique known as direct broadcasting by satellite, the visual images or sounds in question, or both, as the case may be, are transmitted to the satellite transponder.**

**(11) The foregoing provisions of this section shall have effect as if references in those provisions and in section 12(9) of this Act to sounds included references to signals serving for the impartation of matter otherwise than in the form of sounds or visual images.**

*General note*
Amended by the Cable and Broadcasting Act 1984. Italicised words repealed; words in bold added.

## 14A Copyright in cable programmes

**(1) Copyright shall subsist, subject to the provisions of this Act, in every cable programme which is included in a cable programme service provided**

by a qualified person in the United Kingdom or in any other country to which this section extends.

(2) Copyright shall not subsist in a cable programme by virtue of this section of the programme is included in the cable programme service by the reception and immediate re-transmission of a television broadcast or a sound broadcast.

(3) Subject to the provisions of this Act, a person providing a cable programme service shall be entitled to any copyright subsisting in a cable programme included in that service and any such copyright shall continue to subsist until the end of the period of fifty years from the end of the calendar year in which the cable programme is so included, and shall then expire.

(4) In so far as a cable programme is a repetition (whether the first or any subsequent repetition) of a cable programme previously included as mentioned in subsection (1) of this section—

(a) copyright shall not subsist therein by virtue of this section if it is so included after the end of the period of fifty years from the end of the calendar year in which it was previously so included; and

(b) if it is so included before the end of that period any copyright subsisting therein by virtue of this section shall expire at the end of that period.

(5) The acts restricted by the copyright in a cable programme are—

(a) in so far as it consists of visual images, making, otherwise than for private purposes, a cinematograph film of it or a copy of such a film;

(b) in so far as it consists of sounds, making, otherwise than for private purposes, a sound recording of it or a record embodying such a recording;

(c) causing it, in so far as it consists of visual images, to be seen in public, or, in so far as it consists of sounds, to be heard in public, if it is seen or heard by a paying audience;

(d) broadcasting it or including it in a cable programme service.

(6) The restrictions imposed by virtue of the last preceding subsection in relation to a cable programme shall apply whether the act in question is done by the reception of the programme or by making use of any record, print, negative, tape or other article on which the programme has been recorded.

(7) In relation to copyright in cable programmes, in so far as they consist of visual images, the restrictions imposed by virtue of subsection (5) of this section shall apply to any sequence of images sufficient to be seen as a moving picture; and accordingly, for the purpose of establishing an infringement of such copyright, it shall not be necessary to prove that the act in question extended to more than such a sequence of images.

(8) For the purposes of subsection (5) of this section a cinematograph film or a copy thereof, or a sound recording or a record embodying a recording, shall be taken to be made otherwise than for private purposes if it is made for the purposes of the doing by any person of any of the following acts, that is to say,—

(a) the sale or letting for hire of any copy of the film, or, as the case may be, of any record embodying the recording;

(b) broadcasting the film or recording or including it in a cable programme service;

(c) causing the film or recording to be seen or heard in public.

(9) For the purposes of paragraph (c) of subsection (5) of this section, a cable programme shall be taken to be seen or heard by a paying audience if it is seen or heard by persons who either—

(a) have been admitted for payment to the place where the programme is to be seen or heard, or have been admitted for payment to a place of which that place forms part, or

(b) have been admitted to the place where the programme is to be seen or heard in circumstances where goods or services are supplied there at prices which exceed the prices usually charged at that place and are partly attributable to the facilities afforded for seeing or hearing the programme:

Provided that for the purposes of paragraph (a) of this subsection no account shall be taken—

(i) of persons admitted to the place in question as residents or inmates therein, or

(ii) of persons admitted to that place as members of a club or society, where payment is only for membership of the club or society and the provision of facilities for seeing or hearing cable programmes is only incidental to the main purposes of the club or society.

(10) The copyright in a cable programme is not infringed by anything done in relation to the programme for the purposes of a judicial proceeding.

(11) In this Act—

'cable programme' means a programme which is included, after the commencement of section 22 of the Cable and Broadcasting Act 1984, in a cable programme service;

'cable programme service' means a cable programme service within the meaning of the said Act of 1984 or a service provided outside the United Kingdom which would be such a service if subsection (7) of section 2 of that Act and references in subsection (1) of that section to the United Kingdom were omitted;

'programme', in relation to a cable programme service, includes any item included in that service.

(12) The foregoing provisions of this section shall have effect as if references in those provisions and in section 12(9) of this Act to sounds included references to signals for the impartation of matter otherwise than in the form of sounds or visual images.

*General note*
Inserted by the Cable and Broadcasting Act 1984.

## 15. Copyright in published editions of works

(1) Copyright shall subsist, subject to the provisions of this Act, in every published edition of any one or more literary, dramatic or musical works in the case of which either—

(a) the first publication of the edition took place in the United Kingdom, or in another country to which this section extends, or

(b) the publisher of the edition was a qualified person at the date of the first publication thereof:

Provided that this subsection does not apply to an edition which reproduces the typographical arrangement of a previous edition of the same work or works.

(2) Subject to the provisions of this Act, the publisher of an edition shall be entitled to any copyright subsisting in the edition by virtue of this section; and any such copyright shall continue to subsist until the end of the period of twenty-five years from the end of the calendar year in which the edition was first published, and shall then expire.

(3) The act restricted by the copyright subsisting by virtue of this section in a published edition is the making, by any photographic or similar process, of a reproduction of the typographical arrangement of the edition.

(4) The copyright under this section in a published edition is not infringed by the making by or on behalf of a librarian of a reproduction of the typographical arrangement of the edition, if he is the librarian of a library of a class prescribed by regulations made under this subsection by the Board of Trade, and the conditions prescribed by those regulations are complied with.

## 16. Supplementary provisions for purposes of Part II

(1) The provisions of this section shall have effect with respect to copyright subsisting by virtue of this Part of this Act in sound recordings, cinematograph films, television broadcasts *and sound broadcasts*, **sound broadcasts and cable programmes** and in published editions of literary, dramatic and musical works; and in those provisions references to the relevant provision of this Part of this Act, in relation to copyright in a subject-matter of any of those descriptions, are references to the provision of this Part of this Act whereby it is provided that (subject to compliance with the conditions specified therein) copyright shall subsist in that description of subject-matter.

(2) Any copyright subsisting by virtue of this Part of this Act is infringed by any person who, without the licence of the owner of the copyright, imports an article (otherwise than for his private and domestic use) into the United Kingdom, or into any other country to which the relevant provision of this Part of this Act extends, if to his knowledge the making of that article constituted an infringement of that copyright, or would have constituted such an infringement if the article had been made in the place into which it is so imported.

(3) Any such copyright is also infringed by any person who, in the United Kingdom, or in any other country to which the relevant provision of this Part of this Act extends, and without the licence of the owner of the copyright,—

(a) sells, lets for hire, or by way of trade offers or exposes for sale or hire any article, or
(b) by way of trade exhibits any article in public,

if to his knowledge the making of the article constituted an infringement of that copyright, or (in the case of an imported article) would have constituted an infringement of that copyright if the article had been made in the place into which it was imported.

(4) The last preceding subsection shall apply in relation to the distribution of any articles either—

(a) for purposes of trade, or

(b) for other purposes, but to such an extent as to affect prejudicially the owner of the copyright in question,

as it applies in relation to the sale of an article.

(5) The three last preceding subsections shall have effect without prejudice to the general provisions of section one of this Act as to infringements of copyright.

(6) Where by virtue of this Part of this Act copyright subsists in a sound recording, cinematograph film, broadcast, **cable programme** or other subject-matter, nothing in this Part of this Act shall be construed as affecting the operation of Part I of this Act in relation to any literary, dramatic, musical or artistic work from which that subject-matter is wholly or partly derived; and copyright subsisting by virtue of this Part of this Act shall be additional to, and independent of, any copyright subsisting by virtue of Part I of this Act:

Provided that this subsection shall have effect subject to the provisions of subsection (7) of section thirteen of this Act.

(7) The subsistence of copyright under any of the preceding sections of this Part of this Act shall not affect the operation of any other of those sections under which copyright can subsist.

*General note*
As amended by the Cable and Broadcasting Act 1984. Italicised words repealed; words in bold type added.

PART III
REMEDIES FOR INFRINGEMENTS OF COPYRIGHT

## 17.—Action by owner of copyright for infringement

(1) Subject to the provisions of this Act, infringements of copyright shall be actionable at the suit of the owner of the copyright; and in any action for such an infringement all such relief, by way of damages, injunction, accounts or otherwise, shall be available to the plaintiff as is available in any corresponding proceedings in respect of infringements of other proprietary rights.

(2) Where in an action for infringement of copyright it is proved or admitted—

(a) that an infringement was committed, but

(b) that at the time of the infringement the defendant was not aware, and had no reasonable grounds for suspecting, that copyright subsisted in the work or other subject-matter to which the action relates,

the plaintiff shall not be entitled under this section to any damages against the defendant in respect of the infringement, but shall be entitled to an account of profits in respect of the infringement whether any other relief is granted under this section or not.

(3) Where in an action under this section an infringement of copyright is proved or admitted, and the court, having regard (in addition to all other material considerations) to—

(a) the flagrancy of the infringement, and

(b) any benefit shown to have accrued to the defendant by reason of the infringement,

is satisfied that effective relief would not otherwise be available to the plaintiff, the court, in assessing damages for the infringement, shall have power to award such additional damages by virtue of this subsection as the court may consider appropriate in the circumstances.

(4) In an action for infringement of copyright in respect of the construction of a building, no injunction or other order shall be made—

    (*a*) after the construction of the building has been begun, so as to prevent it from being completed, or

    (*b*) so as to require the building, in so far as it has been constructed, to be demolished.

(5) In this Part of this Act 'action' includes a counterclaim, and references to the plaintiff and to the defendant in an action shall be construed accordingly.

(6) In the application of this Part of this Act to Scotland, 'injunction' means an interdict and 'interlocutory injunction' means an interim interdict, 'accounts' means count, reckoning and payment, 'an account of profits' means an accounting and payment of profits, 'plaintiff' means pursuer, 'defendant' means defender and 'costs' means expenses.

### 18. Rights of owner of copyright in respect of infringing copies etc

(1) Subject to the provisions of this Act, the owner of any copyright shall be entitled to all such rights and remedies, in respect of the conversion or detention by any person of any infringing copy, or of any plate used or intended to be used for making infringing copies, as he would be entitled to if he were the owner of every such copy or plate and had been the owner thereof since the time when it was made:

Provided that if, by virtue of subsection (2) of section three of the Limitation Act 1939 (which relates to successive conversions or detentions), or of any corresponding provision which may be enacted by the Parliament of Northern Ireland, the title of the owner of the copyright to such a copy or plate would (if he had then been the owner of the copy or plate) have been extinguished at the end of the period mentioned in that subsection or corresponding provision, he shall not be entitled to any rights or remedies under this subsection in respect of anything done in relation to that copy or plate after the end of that period.

(2) A plaintiff shall not be entitled by virtue of this section to any damages or to any other pecuniary remedy (except costs) if it is proved or admitted that, at the time of the conversion or detention in question,—

    (a) the defendant was not aware, and had no reasonable grounds for suspecting, that copyright subsisted in the work or other subject-matter to which the action relates, or

    (b) where the articles converted or detained were infringing copies, the defendant believed, and had reasonable grounds for believing, that they were not infringing copies, or

    (c) where the article converted or detained was a plate used or intended to be used for making any articles, the defendant believed, and had reasonable grounds for believing, that the articles so made or intended to be made were not, or (as the case may be) would not be, infringing copies.

(3) In this Part of this Act 'infringing copy'—

    (a) in relation to a literary, dramatic, musical or artistic work, or to such a published edition as is mentioned in section fifteen of this Act, means a reproduction otherwise than in the form of a cinematograph film,

(b) in relation to a sound recording, means a record embodying that recording,

(c) in relation to a cinematograph film, means a copy of the film, and

(d) in relation to a television broadcast or *a sound broadcast*, **a sound broadcast or a cable programme**, means a copy of a cinematograph film of it or a record embodying a sound recording of it,

being (in any such case) an article the making of which constituted an infringement of the copyright in the work, edition, recording, film *or broadcast*, **broadcast or programme**, or, in the case of an imported article, would have constituted an infringement of that copyright if the article had been made in the place into which it was imported; and 'plate' includes any stereotype, stone, block, mould, matrix, transfer, negative or other appliance.

(4) In the application of this section to Scotland, for any reference to the conversion or detention by any person of an infringing copy there shall be substituted a reference to an intromission by any person with an infringing copy, and for any reference to articles converted or detained there shall be substituted a reference to articles intromitted with.

*General note*
As amended by the Cable and Broadcasting Act 1984. Repealed by Limitation Act 1939 and replaced by Limitation Act 1980.

## 19. Proceedings in case of copyright subject to exclusive licence

(1) The provisions of this section shall have effect as to proceedings in the case of any copyright in respect of which an exclusive licence has been granted and is in force at the time of the events to which the proceedings relate.

(2) Subject to the following provisions of this section—

(a) the exclusive licensee shall (except against the owner of the copyright) have the same rights of action, and be entitled to the same remedies, under section seventeen of this Act as if the licence had been an assignment, and those rights and remedies shall be concurrent with the rights and remedies of the owner of the copyright under that section;

(b) the exclusive licensee shall (except against the owner of the copyright) have the same rights of action, and be entitled to the same remedies, by virtue of the last preceding section as if the licence had been an assignment; and

(c) the owner of the copyright shall not have any rights of action, or be entitled to any remedies, by virtue of the last preceding section which he would not have had or been entitled to if the licence had been an assignment.

(3) Where an action is brought either by the owner of the copyright or by the exclusive licensee, and the action, in so far as it is brought under section seventeen of this Act, relates (wholly or partly) to an infringement in respect of which they have concurrent rights of action under that section, the owner or licensee, as the case may be, shall not be entitled, except with the leave of the court, to proceed with the action, in so far as it is brought under that section and relates to that infringement, unless the other party is either joined as a plaintiff in the action or added as a defendant:

Provided that this subsection shall not affect the granting of an interlocutory injunction on the application of either of them.

(4) In any action brought by the exclusive licensee by virtue of this section, any defence which would have been available to a defendant in the action, if this section had not been enacted and the action had been brought by the owner of the copyright, shall be available to that defendant as against the exclusive licensee.

(5) Where an action is brought in the circumstances mentioned in subsection (3) of this section, and the owner of the copyright and the exclusive licensee are not both plaintiffs in the action, the court, in assessing damages in respect of any such infringement as is mentioned in that subsection,—

(a) if the plaintiff is the exclusive licensee, shall take into account any liabilities (in respect of royalties or otherwise) to which the licence is subject, and

(b) whether the plaintiff is the owner of the copyright or the exclusive licensee, shall take into account any pecuniary remedy already awarded to the other party under section seventeen of this Act in respect of that infringement, or, as the case may require, any right of action exercisable by the other party under that section in respect thereof.

(6) Where an action, in so far as it is brought under section seventeen of this Act, relates (wholly or partly) to an infringement in respect of which the owner of the copyright and the exclusive licensee have concurrent rights of action under that section, and in that action (whether they are both parties to it or not) an account of profits is directed to be taken in respect of that infringement, then, subject to any agreement of which the court is aware, whereby the application of those profits is determined as between the owner of the copyright and the exclusive licensee, the court shall apportion the profits between them as the court may consider just, and shall give such directions as the court may consider appropriate for giving effect to that apportionment.

(7) In an action brought either by the owner of the copyright or by the exclusive licensee,—

(a) no judgment or order for the payment of damages in respect of an infringement of copyright shall be given or made under section seventeen of this Act, if a final judgment or order has been given or made awarding an account of profits to the other party under that section in respect of the same infringement; and

(b) no judgment or order for an account of profits in respect of an infringement of copyright shall be given or made under that section, if a final judgment or order has been given or made awarding either damages or an account of profits to the other party under that section in respect of the same infringement.

(8) Where, in an action brought in the circumstances mentioned in subsection (3) of this section, whether by the owner of the copyright or by the exclusive licensee, the other party is not joined as a plaintiff (either at the commencement of the action or subsequently), but is added as a defendant, he shall not be liable for any costs in the action unless he enters an appearance and takes part in the proceedings.

(9) In this section 'exclusive licence' means a licence in writing, signed by or on behalf of an owner or prospective owner of copyright, authorising the licensee, to the exclusion of all other persons, including the grantor of the licence, to exercise a right which by virtue of this Act would (apart from the licence) be exercisable exclusively by the owner of the copyright, and 'exclusive licensee' shall be

construed accordingly; 'the other party', in relation to the owner of the copyright, means the exclusive licensee, and, in relation to the exclusive licensee, means the owner of the copyright; and 'if the licence had been an assignment' means if, instead of the licence, there had been granted (subject to terms and conditions corresponding as nearly as may be with those subject to which the licence was granted) an assignment of the copyright in respect of its application to the doing, at the places and times authorised by the licence, of the acts so authorised.

**20. Proof of facts in copyright actions**
(1) In any action brought by virtue of this Part of this Act—

    (a) copyright shall be presumed to subsist in the work or other subject matter to which the action relates, if the defendant does not put in issue the question whether copyright subsists therein, and

    (b) where the subsistence of the copyright is proved or admitted, or is presumed in pursuance of the preceding paragraph, the plaintiff shall be presumed to be the owner of the copyright, if he claims to be the owner of the copyright and the defendant does not put in issue the question of his ownership thereof.

(2) Subject to the preceding subsection, where, in the case of a literary, dramatic, musical or artistic work, a name purporting to be that of the author appeared on copies of the work as published, or, in the case of an artistic work, appeared on the work when it was made, the person whose name so appeared (if it was his true name or a name by which he was commonly known) shall, in any action brought by virtue of this Part of this Act, be presumed, unless the contrary is proved,—

    (a) to be the author of the work, and

    (b) to have made the work in circumstances not falling within subsection (2), subsection (3) or subsection (4) of section four of this Act.

(3) In the case of a work alleged to be a work of joint authorship, the last preceding subsection shall apply in relation to each person alleged to be one of the authors of the work, as if references in that subsection to the author were references to one of the authors.

(4) Where, in an action brought by virtue of this Part of this Act with respect to a literary, dramatic, musical or artistic work, subsection (2) of this section does not apply, but it is established—

    (a) that the work was first published in the United Kingdom, or in another country to which section two, or, as the case may be, section three, of this Act extends, and was so published within the period of fifty years ending with the beginning of the calendar year in which the action was brought, and

    (b) that a name purporting to be that of the publisher appeared on copies of the work as first published,

then, unless the contrary is shown, copyright shall be presumed to subsist in the work and the person whose name so appeared shall be presumed to have been the owner of that copyright at the time of the publication.

For the purposes of this subsection a fact shall be taken to be established if it is proved or admitted, or if it is presumed in pursuance of the following provisions of this section.

(5) Where in an action brought by virtue of this Part of this Act with respect to a literary, dramatic, musical or artistic work it is proved or admitted that the author of the work is dead,—

(a) the work shall be presumed to be an original work unless the contrary is proved, and

(b) if it is alleged by the plaintiff that a publication specified in the allegation was the first publication of the work, and that it took place in a country and on a date so specified, that publication shall be presumed, unless the contrary is proved, to have been the first publication of the work, and to have taken place in that country and on that date.

(6) Paragraphs (a) and (b) of the last preceding subsection shall apply where a work has been published, and—

(a) the publication was anonymous, or was under a name alleged by the plaintiff to have been a pseudonym, and

(b) it is not shown that the work has ever been published under the true name of the author, or under a name by which he was commonly known, or that it is possible for a person without previous knowledge of the facts to ascertain the identity of the author by reasonable inquiry,

as those paragraphs apply in a case where it is proved that the author is dead.

(7) In any action brought by virtue of this Part of this Act with respect to copyright in a sound recording, if records embodying that recording or part thereof have been issued to the public, and at the time when those records were so issued they bore a label or other mark comprising any one or more of the following statements, that is to say—

(a) that a person named on the label or mark was the maker of the sound recording;

(b) that the recording was first published in a year specified on the label or mark;

(c) that the recording was first published in a country specified on the label or mark,

that label or mark shall be sufficient evidence of the facts so stated except in so far as the contrary is proved.

## 21. Penalties and summary proceedings in respect of dealings which infringe copyright

(1) Any person who, at a time when copyright subsists in a work,—

(a) makes for sale or hire, or

(b) sells or lets for hire, or by way of trade offers or exposes for sale or hire, or

(c) by way of trade exhibits in public, or

(d) imports into the United Kingdom, otherwise than for his private and domestic use,

any article which he knows to be an infringing copy of the work, shall be guilty of an offence under this subsection.

(2) Any person who, at a time when copyright subsists in a work, distributes, either—

(a) for purposes of trade, or

(b) for other purposes, but to such an extent as to affect prejudicially the owner of the copyright,

articles which he knows to be infringing copies of the work, shall be guilty of an offence under this subsection.

(3) Any person who, at a time when copyright subsists in a work, makes or has in his possession a plate, knowing that it is to be used for making infringing copies of the work, shall be guilty of an offence under this subsection.

(4) The preceding subsections shall apply in relation to copyright subsisting in any subject-matter by virtue of Part II of this Act, as they apply in relation to copyright subsisting by virtue of Part I of this Act.

**(4A) Any person who, at a time when copyright subsists in a sound recording or in a cinematograph film, by way of trade has in his possession any article which he knows to be an infringing copy of the sound recording or cinematograph film, as the case may be, shall be guilty of an offence under this subsection.**

(5) Any person who causes a literary, dramatic or musical work to be performed in public, knowing that copyright subsists in the work and that the performance constitutes an infringement of the copyright, shall be guilty of an offence under this subsection.

(6) The preceding provisions of this section apply only in respect of acts done in the United Kingdom.

(7) A person guilty of an offence under subsection (1) *or subsection (2) of this section* **or subsection (2) of this section, other than an offence, for which a penalty is provided by subsection (7A) or (7B) of this section** shall on summary conviction—

(a) *if it is his first conviction of an offence under this section, be liable to a fine not exceeding forty shillings for each article to which the offence relates*;

(b) *in any other case, be liable to such a fine, or to imprisonment for a term not exceeding two months:* **be liable to a fine not exceeding level 1 on the standard scale or to imprisonment for a term not exceeding two months for each article to which the offence relates:**

Provided that a fine imposed by virtue of this subsection shall not exceed *fifty pounds* **level 3 on the standard scale** in respect of articles comprised in the same transaction.

**(7A) A person guilty of an offence under subsection (1)(b) or (c) or (4A) of this section relating to an infringing copy of a sound recording or cinematograph film shall be liable on summary conviction to a fine not exceeding level 5 on the standard scale or imprisonment for a term not exceeding two months or to both.**

**(7B) A person guilty of an offence under subsection (1)(a) or (d) or (2) of this section relating to an infringing copy of a sound recording or cinematograph film shall be liable—**

(a) **on summary conviction, to a fine not exceeding the statutory maximum;**

(b) **on conviction on indictment, to a fine or to imprisonment for a term not exceeding two years or to both.**

**(7C) In subsection (7A) of this section 'the standard scale' has the meaning given by section 75 of the Criminal Justice Act 1982 . . .**

**(7D)** In subsection **(7B)** of this section 'statutory maximum' has the meaning given by section 74 of the Criminal Justice Act 1982 . . .

(8) A person guilty of an offence under subsection (3) or subsection (5) of this section shall on summary conviction—

(a) *if it is his first conviction of an offence under this section, be liable to a fine not exceeding fifty pounds;*

(b) *in any other case, be liable to such a fine, or to imprisonment for a term not exceeding two months.* **be liable to a fine not exceeding level 3 on the standard scale or to imprisonment for a term not exceeding two months**.

(9) The court before which a person is charged with an offence under this section may, whether he is convicted of the offence or not, order that any article in his possession which appears to the court to be an infringing copy, or to be a plate used or intended to be used for making infringing copies, shall be destroyed or delivered up to the owner of the copyright in question or otherwise dealt with as the court may think fit.

(10) An appeal shall lie to *a court of quarter sessions* **the Crown Court** from any order made under the last preceding subsection by a court of summary jurisdiction; and where such an order is made by the sheriff there shall be a like right of appeal against the order as if it were a conviction.

*General note*

Sub-s (4A) was inserted by the Copyright Act 1956 (Amendment) Act 1982. Words in bold type added; italicised words repealed.

The first set of words in bold type in Sub-s (7) were added, and Sub-ss (7A)–(7D) were inserted, by the Copyright (Amendment) Act 1983. Words in bold type added; italicised words repealed.

The second set of words in bold type in sub-s (7) were added by the Criminal Justice Act 1982; italicised words were repealed.

## 21A. Search warrants

**(1) Where, on information on oath given by a constable, a justice of the peace is satisfied that there are reasonable grounds for believing—**

(a) **that an offence under subsection (1)(a) or (d) or (2) of section 21 of this Act relating to an infringing copy of a sound recording or a cinematograph film has been or is about to be committed in any premises, and**

(b) **that evidence that the offence has been or is about to be committed is in those premises,**

**he may issue a warrant authorising a constable to enter and search the premises, using such reasonable force as is necessary.**

**(2) A warrant under this section may authorise persons to accompany any constable who is executing it and must be executed within twenty-eight days from the date of its issue.**

**(3) In executing a warrant issued under this section a constable may seize any article if he reasonably believes that it is evidence that an offence under subsection (1) (2) or (4A) of section 21 of this Act relating to an infringing copy of a sound recording or a cinematograph film has been or is about to be committed.**

**(4) In this section 'premises' includes land, buildings, moveable structures, vehicles, vessels aircraft and hovercraft.**

**(5)** This section shall have effect in Northern Ireland as if in subsection (1)—

    (a) for the reference to an information there were substituted a reference to a complaint, and

    (b) for the reference to a justice of the peace there were substituted a reference to a resident magistrate.

**(6)** This section shall not extend to Scotland.

*General note*
Inserted by the Copyright (Amendment) Act 1983.

**21B Persons accompanying constable under search warrant or order of Court in Scotland**
**(1)** Where in Scotland an application is made for a warrant or order of court to authorise a constable to enter and search any premises where there are reasonable grounds for believing that an offence under subsection (1)(*a*) or (*d*) or (2) of section 21 of this Act relating to an infringing copy of a sound recording or a cinematograph film has been or is about to be committed, the court may in any such warrant or order of court authorise any person named in the warrant or order to accompany any constable who is executing the warrant or order.

**(2)** In this section 'premises' includes land, buildings, moveable structures, vehicles, vessels, aircraft and hovercraft.

**(3)** This section applies to Scotland only.

*General note*
Inserted by the Copyright (Amendment) Act 1983.

**22. Provision for restricting importation of printed copies**
(1) The owner of the copyright in any published literary, dramatic or musical work may give notice in writing to the Commissioners of Customs and Excise (in this section referred to as 'the Commissioners')—

    (a) that he is the owner of the copyright in the work, and

    (b) that he requests the Commissioners, during a period specified in the notice, to treat as prohibited goods copies of the work to which this section applies:

Provided that the period specified in a notice under this subsection shall not exceed five years and shall not extend beyond the end of the period for which the copyright is to subsist.

(2) This section applies, in the case of a work, to any printed copy made outside the United Kingdom which, if it had been made in the United Kingdom, would be an infringing copy of the work.

(3) Where a notice has been given under this section in respect of a work, and has not been withdrawn, the importation into the United Kingdom, at a time before the end of the period specified in the notice, of any copy of the work to which this section applies shall, subject to the following provisions of this section, be prohibited:

Provided that this subsection shall not apply to the importation of any article by a person for his private and domestic use.

(4) The Commissioners may make regulations prescribing the form in which notices are to be given under this section, and requiring a person giving such a notice, either at the time of giving the notice or at the time when the goods in question are imported, or at both those times, to furnish the Commissioners with such evidence, and to comply with such other conditions (if any), as may be specified in the regulations; and any such regulations may include such incidental and supplementary provisions as the Commissioners consider expedient for the purposes of this section.

(5) Without prejudice to the generality of the last preceding subsection, regulations made under that subsection may include provision for requiring a person who has given a notice under subsection (1) of this section, or a notice purporting to be a notice under that subsection,—

(a) to pay such fees in respect of the notice as may be prescribed by the regulations;

(b) to give to the Commissioners such security as may be so prescribed, in respect of any liability or expense which they may incur in consequence of the detention, at any time within the period specified in the notice, of any copy of the work to which the notice relates, or in consequence of anything done in relation to a copy so detained;

(c) whether any such security is given or not, to keep the Commissioners indemnified against any such liability or expense as is mentioned in the last preceding paragraph.

(6) For the purposes of *section eleven of the Customs and Excise Act 1952* **section 17 of the Customs and Excise Management Act 1979** (which relates to the disposal of duties), any fees paid in pursuance of regulations made under this section shall be treated as money collected on account of customs.

(7) Notwithstanding anything in *the Customs and Excise Act 1952* **the Customs and Excise Management Act 1979**, a person shall not be liable to any penalty under that Act (other than forfeiture of the goods) by reason that any goods are treated as prohibited goods by virtue of this section.

*General note*
As amended by the Customs and Excise Management Act 1979. Italicised words repealed, words in bold type added.

PART IV
PERFORMING RIGHT TRIBUNAL

## 23. Establishment of tribunal

(1) There shall be established a tribunal, to be called the Performing Right Tribunal (in this Act referred to as 'the tribunal'), for the purpose of exercising the jurisdiction conferred by the provisions of this Part of this Act.

(2) The tribunal shall consist of a chairman appointed by the Lord Chancellor, who shall be a barrister, advocate or solicitor of not less than seven years' standing or a person who has held judicial office, and of not less than two nor more than four other members appointed by the Board of Trade.

*(3) A person shall be disqualified from being appointed, or being, a member of the tribunal so long as he is a member of the Commons House of Parliament, or of the Senate or House of Commons of Northern Ireland.*

(4) The provisions of the Fourth Schedule to this Act shall have effect with respect to the tribunal.

(5) There shall be paid to the members of the tribunal such remuneration (whether by way of salaries or fees), and such allowances, as the Board of Trade, with the approval of the Treasury, may determine in the case of those members respectively.

(6) The Board of Trade may appoint such officers and servants of the tribunal as the Board, with the approval of the Treasury as to numbers and remuneration, may determine.

(7) The remuneration and allowances of members of the tribunal, the remuneration of any officers and servants appointed under the last preceding subsection, and such other expenses of the tribunal as the Board of Trade with the approval of the Treasury may determine, shall be paid out of moneys provided by Parliament.

*General note*
Subsection (3) repealed by the House of Commons Disqualification Act 1957, s 14 (1) and Sch 4, Part I. See the House of Commons Disqualification Act 1975.

## 24. General provisions as to jurisdiction of tribunal
(1) Subject to the provisions of this Part of this Act, the function of the tribunal shall be to determine disputes arising between licensing bodies and persons requiring licences, or organisations claiming to be representative of such persons, either—

    (a)  on the reference of a licence scheme to the tribunal, or

    (b)  on the application of a person requiring a licence either in accordance with a licence scheme or in a case not covered by a licence scheme.

(2) In this Part of this Act 'licence' means a licence granted by or on behalf of the owner, or prospective owner, of the copyright in a literary, dramatic or musical work, or in a sound recording or a television broadcast, being—

    (a)  in the case of a literary, dramatic or musical work, a licence to perform in public, or to broadcast, the work or an adaptation thereof, or to *cause the work or an adaptation thereof to be transmitted to subscribers to a diffusion service* **including the work or an adaption thereof in a cable programme**;

    (b)  in the case of a sound recording, a licence to cause it to be heard in public, *or to broadcast it* **to broadcast it or to include it in a cable programme**;

    (c)  in the case of a television broadcast, a licence to cause it, in so far as it consists of visual images, to be seen in public and, in so far as it consists of sound, to be heard in public.

(3) In this Part of this Act 'licensing body'—

    (a)  in relation to such licences as are mentioned in paragraph (a) of the last preceding subsection, means a society or other organisation which has as its main object, or one of its main objects, the negotiation or granting of such licences, either as owner or prospective owner of copyright or as agent for the owners or prospective owners thereof;

    (b)  in relation to such licences as are mentioned in paragraph (b) of the last preceding subsection, means any owner or prospective owner of copyright in sound recordings, or any person or body of persons acting as agent for any owners or prospective owners of copyright in sound recordings in relation to the negotiation or granting of such licences; and

(c) in relation to such licences as are mentioned in paragraph (c) of the last preceding subsection, means the Corporation or the Authority or any organisation appointed by them, or either of them, in accordance with the provisions of the Fifth Schedule to this Act:

Provided that paragraph (a) of this subsection shall not apply to an organisation by reason that its objects include the negotiation or granting of individual licences, each relating to a single work or the works of a single author, if they do not include the negotiation or granting of general licences, each extending to the works of several authors.

(4) In this Part of this Act 'licence scheme', in relation to licences of any description, means a scheme made by one or more licensing bodies, setting out the classes of cases in which they, or the persons on whose behalf they act, are willing to grant licences of that description, and the charges (if any), and terms and conditions, subject to which licences would be granted in those classes of cases; and in this subsection 'scheme' includes anything in the nature of a scheme, whether described therein as a scheme or as a tariff or by any other name.

(5) References in this Part of this Act to terms and conditions are references to any terms and conditions other than those relating to the amount of a charge for a licence; and references to giving an opportunity to a person of presenting his case are references to giving him an opportunity, at his option, of submitting representations in writing, or of being heard, or of submitting representations in writing and being heard.

*General note*
As amended by the Cable and Broadcasting Act 1984. Italicised words repealed; words in bold type added.

## 25. Reference of licence schemes to tribunal

(1) Where, at any time while a licence scheme is in operation, a dispute arises with respect to the scheme between the licensing body operating the scheme and—

(a) an organisation claiming to be representative of persons requiring licences in cases of a class to which the scheme applies, or
(b) any person claiming that he requires a licence in a case of a class to which the scheme applies,

the organisation or person in question may refer the scheme to the tribunal in so far as it relates to cases of that class.

(2) The parties to a reference under this section shall be—

(a) the organisation or person at whose instance the reference is made;
(b) the licensing body operating the scheme to which the reference relates; and
(c) such other organisations or persons (if any) as apply to the tribunal to be made parties to the reference and, in accordance with the next following subsection, are made parties thereto.

(3) Where an organisation (whether claiming to be representative of persons requiring licences or not) or a person (whether requiring a licence or not) applies to the tribunal to be made a party to a reference, and the tribunal is satisfied that the organisation or person has a substantial interest in the matter in dispute, the tribunal may, if it thinks fit, make that organisation or person a party to the reference.

(4) The tribunal shall not entertain a reference under this section by an organisation unless the tribunal is satisfied that the organisation is reasonably representative of the class of persons which it claims to represent.

(5) Subject to the last preceding subsection, the tribunal, on any reference under this section, shall consider the matter in dispute, and, after giving to the parties to the reference an opportunity of presenting their cases respectively, shall make such order, either confirming or varying the scheme, in so far as it relates to cases of the class to which the reference relates, as the tribunal may determine to be reasonable in the circumstances.

(6) An order of the tribunal under this section may, notwithstanding anything contained in the licence scheme to which it relates, be made so as to be in force either indefinitely or for such period as the tribunal may determine.

(7) Where a licence scheme has been referred to the tribunal under this section, then, notwithstanding anything contained in the scheme,—

(a) the scheme shall remain in operation until the tribunal has made an order in pursuance of the reference, and

(b) after such an order has been made, the scheme shall remain in operation, in so far as it relates to the class of cases in respect of which the order was made, so long as the order remains in force:

Provided that this subsection shall not apply in relation to a reference as respects any period after the reference has been withdrawn, or has been discharged by virtue of subsection (4) of this section.

## 26. Further reference of scheme to tribunal

(1) Where the tribunal has made an order under the last preceding section with respect to a licence scheme, then, subject to the next following subsection, at any time while the order remains in force,—

(a) the licensing body operating the scheme, or

(b) any organisation claiming to be representative of persons requiring licences in cases of the class to which the order applies, or

(c) any person claiming that he requires a licence in a case of that class, may refer the scheme again to the tribunal in so far as it relates to cases of that class.

(2) A licence scheme shall not, except with the special leave of the tribunal, be referred again to the tribunal under the preceding subsection at a time earlier than—

(a) the end of the period of twelve months beginning with the date on which the order in question was made, in the case of an order made so as to be in force indefinitely or for a period exceeding fifteen months, or

(b) the beginning of the period of three months ending with the date of expiry of the order, in the case of an order made so as to be in force for fifteen months or less.

(3) The parties to a reference under this section shall be—

(a) the licensing body, organisation or person at whose instance the reference is made;

(b) the licensing body operating the scheme to which the reference relates, if the reference is not made at their instance; and

(c) such other organisations or persons (if any) as apply to the tribunal to be made parties to the reference and, in accordance with the provisions applicable in that behalf by virtue of subsection (5) of this section are made parties thereto.

(4) Subject to the next following subsection, the tribunal, on any reference under this section, shall consider the matter in dispute, and, after giving to the parties to the reference an opportunity of presenting their cases respectively, shall make such order in relation to the scheme as previously confirmed or varied, in so far as it relates to cases of the class in question, either by way of confirming, varying or further varying the scheme, as the tribunal may determine to be reasonable in the circumstances.

(5) Subsections (3), (4), (6) and (7) of the last preceding section shall apply for the purposes of this section.

(7) Nothing in this section shall be construed as preventing a licence scheme, in respect of which an order has been made under the last preceding section, from being again referred to the tribunal under that section, either—

    (a) at any time, in so far as the scheme relates to cases of a class to which the order does not apply, or

    (b) after the expiration of the order, in so far as the scheme relates to cases of the class to which the order applied while it was in force.

## 27. Applications to tribunal

(1) For the purposes of this Part of this Act a case shall be taken to be covered by a licence scheme if, in accordance with a licence scheme for the time being in operation, licences would be granted in cases of the class to which that case belongs:

Provided that where, in accordance with the provisions of a licence scheme,—

    (a) the licences which would be so granted would be subject to terms and conditions whereby particular matters would be excepted from the licences, and

    (b) the case in question relates to one or more matters falling within such an exception,

that case shall be taken not to be covered by the scheme.

(2) Any person who claims, in a case covered by a licence scheme, that the licensing body operating the scheme have refused or failed to grant him a licence in accordance with the provisions of the scheme, or to procure the grant to him of such a licence, may apply to the tribunal under this section.

(3) Any person who claims that he requires a licence in a case not covered by a licence scheme, and either—

    (a) that a licensing body have refused or failed to grant the licence, or to procure the grant thereof, and that in the circumstances it is unreasonable that the licence should not be granted, or

    (b) that any charges, terms or conditions subject to which a licensing body propose that the licence should be granted are unreasonable, may apply to the tribunal under this section.

(4) Where an organisation (whether claiming to be representative of persons requiring licences or not) or a person (whether requiring a licence or not) applies to the tribunal to be made a party to an application under the preceding provisions of this section, and the tribunal is satisfied that the organisation or person has a

substantial interest in the matter in dispute, the tribunal may, if it thinks fit, make that organisation or person a party to the application.

(5) On any application under subsection (2) or subsection (3) of this section the tribunal shall give to the applicant and to the licensing body in question and to every other party (if any) to the application an opportunity of presenting their cases respectively; and if the tribunal is satisfied that the claim of the applicant is well-founded, the tribunal shall make an order declaring that, in respect of the matters specified in the order, the applicant is entitled to a licence on such terms and conditions, and subject to the payment of such charges (if any), as—

(a) in the case of an application under subsection (2) of this section, the tribunal may determine to be applicable in accordance with the licence scheme, or

(b) in the case of an application under subsection (3) of this section, the tribunal may determine to be reasonable in the circumstances.

(6) Any reference in this section to a failure to grant or procure the grant of a licence shall be construed as a reference to a failure to grant it, or to procure the grant thereof, within a reasonable time after being requested to do so.

### 27A. Applications for review by tribunal or orders

(1) Where the tribunal has made an order under subsection (5) of the last preceding section, then subject to the next following subsection, at any time while the order remains in force,—

(a) the licensing body in question, or

(b) the original applicant,

may apply to the tribunal to review its original order.

(2) An application shall not be made pursuant to subsection (1) of this section, except with the special leave of the tribunal, at a time earlier than—

(a) the end of a period of twelve months beginning with the date on which the original order was made, in the case of an order made so as to be in force indefinitely or for a period exceeding fifteen months, or

(b) the beginning of the period of three months ending with the date of expiry of the order in the case of an order made so as to be in force for fifteen months or less.

(3) The parties to an application under this section shall be—

(a) the parties to the original application proceedings; and

(b) any organisation or person who is made party thereto pursuant to subsection (5) of this section.

(4) The tribunal, on any application under this section, after giving all the parties an opportunity of presenting their cases shall make such order in relation to the application either by way of confirming or varying the order in question as—

(a) in the case of an order made pursuant to an application under subsection (2) of the last preceding section, the tribunal may determine to be applicable in accordance with the licence scheme, or

(b) in the case of an order made pursuant to an application under subsection (3) of the last preceding section, the tribunal may determine to be reasonable in the circumstances.

**(5)** Subsection (4) of section 27 (applications by organisations and persons to be made party to proceedings) shall apply in relation to proceedings under this section as it applies in relation to proceedings under that section.

**(6)** The preceding provisions of this section shall have effect in relation to orders made under this section as they have in relation to orders made under the last preceding section.

*General note*
Added by the Copyright (Amendment) Act 1971.

### 27B Exercise of jurisdiction of tribunal in relation to inclusion of broadcasts in cable programmes

**(1)** On a reference to the tribunal under this Part of this Act relating to licences to broadcast works or sound recordings for reception in any area, the tribunal shall exercise its powers under this Part of this Act so as to secure that the charges payable for the licences adequately reflect the extent to which the works or recordings will be included, in pursuance of requirements imposed under section 13(1) of the Cable and Broadcasting Act 1984, in cable programme services provided in areas parts of which fall outside that area.

**(2)** The preceding subsection shall have effect, with the necessary modifications, in relation to applications under this Part of this Act as it has effect in relation to references thereunder.

*General note*
Added by the Cable and Broadcasting Act 1984.

### 28. Exercise of jurisdiction of tribunal in relation to diffusion of foreign broadcasts

(1) Where, on a reference to the tribunal under this Part of this Act relating to licences to *cause works to be transmitted to subscribers to a diffusion service* **include works or sound recordings in a cable programme service provided** in the United Kingdom, the tribunal is satisfied—

(a) that the licences are required wholly or partly for the purpose of *distributing* **including in such service** programmes broadcast, from a place outside the United Kingdom, by an organisation other than the Corporation and the authority, and

(b) that, under the arrangements in accordance with which the programmes are broadcast by that organisation, charges are payable by or on behalf of the organisation to another body, as being the body entitled under the relevant copyright law to authorise the broadcasting of those works **or recordings** from that place,

the tribunal shall, subject to the next following subsection, exercise its powers under this Part of this Act as the tribunal may consider appropriate for securing that the persons requiring the licences are exempted from the payment of any charges for them in so far as the licences are required for the purpose of *distributing those programmes* **including those programmes in a cable programme service**.

(2) If on such a reference as is mentioned in the last preceding subsection the tribunal is satisfied as to the matters mentioned in paragraphs (a) and (b) of that subsection, but it is shown to the satisfaction of the tribunal that the charges payable by or on behalf of the organisation, as mentioned in paragraph (b) of that subsection,—

(a) make no allowance for the fact that, in consequence of the broadcasting of the works **or recordings** in question by that organisation, the persons requiring the licences may be enabled to *cause those works to be transmitted to subscribers* **include those works or recoverings in cable programme services provided** to diffusion services in the United Kingdom, or

(b) do not adequately reflect the extent to which it is likely that those persons will *cause those works to be so transmitted* **so include those works or recordings** in consequence of their being so broadcast,

the last preceding subsection shall not apply, but the tribunal shall exercise its powers under this Part of this Act so as to secure that the charges payable for the licences, in so far as the licences are required for the purpose mentioned in the last preceding subsection, are on a scale not exceeding that appearing to the tribunal to be requisite for making good the deficiency (as mentioned in paragraph (a) or paragraph (b) of this subsection, as the case may be) in the charges payable by or on behalf of the organisation broadcasting the works **or recordings**.

(3) The preceding provisions of this section shall have effect, with the necessary modifications, in relation to applications under this Part of this Act as they have effect in relation to references thereunder.

(4) In this section 'the relevant copyright law', in relation to works **or sound recordings** broadcast from a place outside the United Kingdom, means so much of the laws of the country in which that place is situated as confers rights similar to copyright under this Act or as otherwise relates to such rights; and any reference to works includes a reference to adaptations thereof.

*General Note*
As amended by the Cable and Broadcasting Act 1984; italicised words replaced; words in bold type added.

### 29. Effect of orders of tribunal, and supplementary provisions relating thereto

(1) Where an order made on a reference under this Part of this Act with respect to a licence scheme is for the time being in force, any person who, in a case covered by the scheme as confirmed or varied by the order, does anything which—

(a) apart from this subsection would be an infringement of copyright, but

(b) would not be such an infringement if he were the holder of a licence granted in accordance with the scheme, as confirmed or varied by the order, in so far as the scheme relates to cases comprised in the order,

shall, if he has complied with the requirements specified in the next following subsection, be in the like position, in any proceedings for infringement of that copyright, as if he had at the material time been the holder of such a licence.

(2) The said requirements are—

(a) that, at all material times, the said person has complied with the terms and conditions which, in accordance with the licence scheme as confirmed or varied by the order, would be applicable to a licence covering the case in question, and

(b) if, in accordance with the scheme as so confirmed or varied, any charges are payable in respect of such a licence, that at the material time he had paid those charges to the licensing body operating the scheme, or, if at that time the amount payable could not be ascertained, he had given an undertaking to the licensing body to pay the charges when ascertained.

(3) Where the tribunal has made an order under section twenty-seven **or section twenty-seven A** of this Act declaring that a person is entitled to a licence in respect of any matters specified in the order, then if—

(a) that person has complied with the terms and conditions specified in the order, and

(b) in a case where the order requires the payment of charges, he has paid those charges to the licensing body in accordance with the order, or, if the order so provides, has given to the licensing body an undertaking to pay the charges when ascertained,

he shall be in the like position, in any proceedings for infringement of copyright relating to any of those matters, as if he had at all material times been the holder of a licence granted by the owner of the copyright in question on the terms and conditions specified in the order.

(4) In the exercise of its jurisdiction in respect of licences relating to television broadcasts, the tribunal shall have regard (among other matters) to any conditions imposed by the promoters of any entertainment or other event which is to be comprised in the broadcasts; and, in particular, the tribunal shall not hold a refusal or failure to grant a licence to be unreasonable if it could not have been granted consistently with those conditions:

Provided that nothing in this subsection shall require the tribunal to have regard to any such conditions in so far as they purport to regulate the charges to be imposed in respect of the grant of licences, or in so far as they relate to payments to be made to the promoters of any event in consideration of the grant of facilities for broadcasting.

(5) Where, on a reference to the tribunal under this Part of this Act,—

(a) the reference relates to licences in respect of copyright in sound recordings or in television broadcasts, and

(b) the tribunal is satisfied that any of the licences in question are required for the purposes of organisations such as are mentioned in paragraph (b) of subsection (7) of section twelve of this Act,

the tribunal may, if it thinks fit, exercise its powers under this Part of this Act so as to reduce, in the case of those organisations, to such extent as the tribunal thinks fit, the charges which it determines generally to be reasonable in relation to cases of the class to which the reference relates, or, if it thinks fit, so as to exempt those organisations from the payment of any such charges.

(6) The last preceding subsection shall have effect, with the necessary modifications, in relation to applications under this Part of this Act as it has effect in relation to references thereunder.

(7) In relation to copyright in a literary, dramatic or musical work, any reference in this section to proceedings for infringement of copyright includes a reference to proceedings brought by virtue of subsection (5) of section twenty-one of this Act.

*General note*
Amended by the Copyright (Amendment) Act 1971. Words in bold added.

**30. Reference of questions of law to the court**

(1) Any question of law arising in the course of proceedings before the tribunal may, at the request of any party to the proceedings, be referred by the tribunal to the court for decision, whether before or after the tribunal has given its decision in the proceedings:

Provided that a question shall not be referred to the court by virtue of this subsection in pursuance of a request made after the date on which the tribunal gave its decision, unless the request is made before the end of such period as may be prescribed by rules made under the Fourth Schedule to this Act.

(2) If the tribunal, after giving its decision in any proceedings, refuses any such request to refer a question to the court, the party by whom the request was made may, within such period as may be prescribed by rules of court, apply to the court for an order directing the tribunal to refer the question to the court.

(3) On any reference to the court under this section with respect to any proceedings before the tribunal, and on any application under the last preceding subsection with respect to any such proceedings, every party to the proceedings before the tribunal shall be entitled to appear and to be heard.

(4) Where, after the tribunal has given its decision in any proceedings, the tribunal refers to the court under this section a question of law which arose in the course of the proceedings, and the court decides that the question was erroneously determined by the tribunal,—

(a) the tribunal, if it considers it requisite to do so for the purpose of giving effect to the decision of the court, shall give to the parties to the proceedings a further opportunity of presenting their cases respectively;

(b) in any event, the tribunal shall consider the matter in dispute in conformity with the decision of the court;

(c) if on such reconsideration it appears to the tribunal to be appropriate to do so, the tribunal shall make such order revoking or modifying any order previously made by it in the proceedings, or, in the case of proceedings under section twenty-seven of this Act where the tribunal refused to make an order, shall make such order under that section, as on such reconsideration the tribunal determines to be appropriate.

(5) Any reference of a question by the tribunal to the court under this section shall be by way of stating a case for the opinion of the court; and the decision of the court on any such reference shall be final.

(6) In this section 'the court'—

(a) in relation to any proceedings of the tribunal in England or Wales, or in Northern Ireland, means the High Court; and

(b) in relation to any proceedings of the tribunal in Scotland, means the Court of Session.

*General note*
This section has effect, in its application to Northern Ireland, with the omission from sub-s(2) of the words 'within such period as may be prescribed by rules of court'; see the Northern Ireland Act 1962, s 7(9), (10) and Sch 1, Part I.

PART V
EXTENSION OR RESTRICTION OF OPERATION OF ACT

## 31. Extension of Act to Isle of Man, Channel Islands, colonies and dependencies

(1) Her Majesty may by Order in Council direct that any of the provisions of this Act specified in the Order (including any enactments for the time being in force amending or substituted for those provisions) shall extend, subject to such exceptions and modifications (if any) as may be specified in the Order, to—

(a) the Isle of Man;
(b) any of the Channel Islands;
(c) any colony;
(d) any country outside Her Majesty's dominions in which for the time being Her Majesty has jurisdiction;
(e) any country consisting partly of one or more colonies and partly of one or more such countries as are mentioned in the last preceding paragraph.

(2) The powers conferred by the preceding subsection shall be exercisable in relation to any Order in Council made under the following provisions of this Part of this Act, as those powers are exercisable by virtue of that subsection in relation to the provisions of this Act.

(3) The legislature of any country to which any provisions of this Act have been extended may modify or add to those provisions, in their operation as part of the law of that country, in such manner as that legislature may consider necessary to adapt the provisions to the circumstances of that country:

Provided that no such modifications or additions, except in so far as they relate to procedure and remedies, shall be made so as to apply to any work or other subject-matter in which copyright can subsist unless—

(a) in the case of a literary, dramatic, musical or artistic work, the author of the work, or, in the case of a sound recording or a cinematograph film, the maker of the recording or film, was domiciled or resident in that country at the time when, or during the period while, the work, recording or film was made, or
(b) in the case of a published edition of a literary, dramatic or musical work, the publisher of the edition was domiciled or resident in that country at the date of its first publication, or
(c) in the case of a literary, dramatic, musical or artistic work, or of a sound recording or a cinematograph film or a published edition, it was first published in that country, or
(d) in the case of a television broadcast or sound broadcast, it was made from a place in that country, or.
(e) **in the case of a cable programme, it was sent from a place in that country**

(4) For the purposes of any proceedings under this Act in the United Kingdom, where the proceedings relate to an act done in a country to which any provisions of this Act extend subject to exceptions, modifications or additions,—

(a) the procedure applicable to the proceedings, including the time within which they may be brought, and the remedies available therein, shall be in accordance with this Act in its operation as part of the law of the United Kingdom; but

(b) if the act in question does not constitute an infringement of copyright under this Act in its operation as part of the law of the country where the act was done, it shall (notwithstanding anything in this Act) be treated as not constituting an infringement of copyright under this Act in its operation as part of the law of the United Kingdom.

*General note*
Sub-section (3)(e) added by the Cable and Broadcasting Act 1984.

## 32. Application of Act to countries to which it does not extend

(1) Her Majesty may by Order in Council make provision for applying any of the provisions of this Act specified in the Order, in the case of a country to which those provisions do not extend, in any one or more of the following ways, that is to say, so as to secure that those provisions—

(a) apply in relation to literary, dramatic, musical or artistic works, sound recordings, cinematograph films or editions first published in that country as they apply in relation to literary, dramatic, musical or artistic works, sound recordings, cinematograph films or editions first published in the United Kingdom;

(b) apply in relation to persons who, at a material time, are citizens or subjects of that country as they apply in relation to persons who, at such a time, are British subjects;

(c) apply in relation to persons who, at a material time, are domiciled or resident in that country as they apply in relation to persons who, at such a time, are domiciled or resident in the United Kingdom;

(d) apply in relation to bodies incorporated under the laws of that country as they apply in relation to bodies incorporated under the laws of any part of the United Kingdom;

(e) apply in relation to television broadcasts and sound broadcasts made from places in that country, by one or more organisations constituted in, or under the laws of, that country, as they apply in relation to television broadcasts and sound broadcasts made from places in the United Kingdom by the Corporation or the Authority;

(f) **apply in relation to cable programmes sent from places in that country as they apply in relation to cable programmes sent from places in the United Kingdom**.

(2) An Order in Council under this section—

(a) may apply the provisions in question as mentioned in the preceding subsection, but subject to exceptions or modifications specified in the Order;

(b) may direct that the provisions in question shall so apply either generally or in relation to such classes of works, or other classes of cases, as may be specified in the Order.

(3) Her Majesty shall not make an Order in Council under this section applying any of the provisions of this Act in the case of a country, other than a country which is a party to a Convention relating to copyright to which the United Kingdom is also a party, unless Her Majesty is satisfied that, in respect of the class of works or other subject-matter to which those provisions relate, provision has

been or will be made under the laws of that country whereby adequate protection will be given to owners of copyright under this Act.

*General note*
Words in bold type added by the Cable and Broadcasting Act 1984.

### 33. Provisions as to international organisations

(1) Where it appears to Her Majesty that one or more sovereign Powers, or the government or governments thereof, are members of an organisation, and that it is expedient that the provisions of this section should apply to that organisation, Her Majesty may by Order in Council declare that the organisation is one to which this section applies.

(2) Where an original literary, dramatic, musical or artistic work is made by or under the direction or control of an organisation to which this section applies in such circumstances that—

    (a)  copyright would not subsist in the work apart from this subsection, but,

    (b)  if the author of the work had been a British subject at the time when it was made, copyright would have subsisted in the work immediately after it was made and would thereupon have vested in the organisation,

copyright shall subsist in the work as if the author had been a British subject when it was made, that copyright shall continue to subsist so long as the work remains unpublished, and the organisation shall, subject to the provisions of this Act, be entitled to that copyright.

(3) Where an original literary, dramatic, musical or artistic work is first published by or under the direction or control of an organisation to which this section applies, in such circumstances that, apart from this subsection, copyright does not subsist in the work immediately after the first publication thereof, and either—

    (a)  the work is so published in pursuance of an agreement with the author which does not reserve to the author the copyright (if any) in the work, or

    (b)  the work was made in such circumstances that, if it had been first published in the United Kingdom, the organisation would have been entitled to the copyright in the work,

copyright shall subsist in the work (or, if copyright in the work subsisted immediately before its first publication, shall continue to subsist) as if it had been first published in the United Kingdom, that copyright shall subsist until the end of the period of fifty years from the end of the calendar year in which the work was first published, and the organisation shall, subject to the provisions of Part VI of this Act, be entitled to that copyright.

(4) The provisions of Part I of this Act, with the exception of provisions thereof relating to the subsistence, duration or ownership of copyright, shall apply in relation to copyright subsisting by virtue of this section as they apply in relation to copyright subsisting by virtue of the said Part I.

(5) An organisation to which this section applies which otherwise has not, or at some material time otherwise had not, the legal capacities of a body corporate shall have, and shall be deemed at all material times to have had, the legal capacities of a body corporate for the purpose of holding, dealing with and

enforcing copyright and in connection with all legal proceedings relating to copyright.

### 34. Extended application of provisions relating to broadcasts

Her Majesty may by Order in Council provide that, subject to such exceptions and modifications (if any) as may be specified in the Order, such provisions of this Act relating to television broadcasts or to sound broadcasts as may be so specified shall apply in relation to the operation of wireless telegraphy apparatus by way of the emission (as opposed to reception) of electro-magnetic energy—

- (a) by such persons or classes of persons, other than the Corporation and the Authority, as may be specified in the Order, and
- (b) for such purposes (whether involving broadcasting or not) as may be so specified,

as they apply in relation to television broadcasts, or, as the case may be, to sound broadcasts, made by the Corporation and the Authority.

### 35. Denial of copyright to citizens of countries not giving adequate protection to British works

(1) If it appears to Her Majesty that the laws of a country fail to give adequate protection to British works to which this section applies, or fail to give such protection in the case of one or more classes of such works (whether the lack of protection relates to the nature of the work or the country of its author or both), Her Majesty may make an Order in Council designating that country and making such provision in relation thereto as is mentioned in the following provisions of this section.

(2) An Order in Council under this section shall provide that, either generally or in such classes of cases as are specified in the Order, copyright under this Act shall not subsist in works to which this section applies which were first published after a date specified in the Order, if at the time of their first publication the authors thereof were—

- (a) citizens or subjects of the country designated by the Order, not being at that time persons domiciled or resident in the United Kingdom or in another country to which the relevant provision of this Act extends, or
- (b) bodies incorporated under the laws of the country designated by the Order.

(3) In making an Order in Council under this section Her Majesty shall have regard to the nature and extent of the lack of protection for British works in consequence of which the Order is made.

(4) This section applies to the following works, that is to say, literary, dramatic, musical and artistic works, sound recordings and cinematograph films.

(5) In this section—

'British work' means a work of which the author, at the time when the work was made, was a qualified person for the purposes of the relevant provision of this Act;
'author', in relation to a sound recording or a cinematograph film, means the maker of the recording or film;
'the relevant provision of this Act', in relation to literary, dramatic and musical works means section two, in relation to artistic works means section three,

in relation to sound recordings means section twelve, and in relation to cinematograph films means section thirteen, of this Act.

PART VI
MISCELLANEOUS AND SUPPLEMENTARY PROVISIONS

## 36. Assignments and licences in respect of copyright

(1) Subject to the provisions of this section, copyright shall be transmissible by assignment, by testamentary disposition, or by operation of law, as personal or moveable property.

(2) An assignment of copyright may be limited in any of the following ways, or in any combination of two or more of those ways, that is to say,—

(a) so as to apply to one or more, but not all, of the classes of acts which by virtue of this Act the owner of the copyright has the exclusive right to do (including any one or more classes of acts not separately designated in this Act as being restricted by the copyright, but falling within any of the classes of acts so designated);

(b) so as to apply to any one or more, but not all, of the countries in relation to which the owner of the copyright has by virtue of this Act that exclusive right;

(c) so as to apply to part, but not the whole, of the period for which the copyright is to subsist;

and references in this Act to a partial assignment are references to an assignment so limited.

(3) No assignment of copyright (whether total or partial) shall have effect unless it is in writing signed by or on behalf of the assignor.

(4) A licence granted in respect of any copyright by the person who, in relation to the matters to which the licence relates, is the owner of the copyright shall be binding upon every successor in title to his interest in the copyright, except a purchaser in good faith for valuable consideration and without notice (actual or constructive) of the licence or a person deriving title from such a purchaser; and references in this Act, in relation to any copyright, to the doing of anything with, or (as the case may be) without, the licence of the owner of the copyright shall be construed accordingly.

## 37. Prospective ownership of copyright

(1) Where by an agreement made in relation to any future copyright, and signed by or on behalf of the prospective owner of the copyright, the prospective owner purports to assign the future copyright (wholly or partially) to another person (in this subsection referred to as 'the assignee'), then if, on the coming into existence of the copyright, the assignee or a person claiming under him would, apart from this subsection, be entitled as against all other persons to require the copyright to be vested in him (wholly or partially, as the case may be), the copyright shall, on its coming into existence, vest in the assignee or his successor in title accordingly by virtue of this subsection and without further assurance.

(2) Where, at the time when any copyright comes into existence, the person who, if he were then living, would be entitled to the copyright is dead, the copyright shall devolve as if it had subsisted immediately before his death and he had then been the owner of the copyright.

(3) Subsection (4) of the last preceding section shall apply in relation to a

licence granted by a prospective owner of any copyright as it applies in relation to a licence granted by the owner of a subsisting copyright, as if any reference in that subsection to the owner's interest in the copyright included a reference to his prospective interest therein.

(4) The provisions of the Fifth Schedule to this Act shall have effect with respect to assignments and licences in respect of copyright (including future copyright) in television broadcasts.

(5) In this Act 'future copyright' means copyright which will or may come into existence in respect of any future work or class of works or other subject-matter, or on the coming into operation of any provisions of this Act, or in any other future event, and 'prospective owner' shall be construed accordingly and, in relation to any such copyright, includes a person prospectively entitled thereto by virtue of such an agreement as is mentioned in subsection (1) of this section.

## 38. Copyright to pass under will with unpublished work
Where under a bequest (whether specific or general) a person is entitled, beneficially or otherwise, to the manuscript of a literary, dramatic or musical work, or to an artistic work, and the work was not published before the death of the testator, the bequest shall, unless a contrary intention is indicated in the testator's will or a codicil thereto, be construed as including the copyright in the work in so far as the testator was the owner of the copyright immediately before his death.

## 39. Provisions as to Crown and Government departments
(1) In the case of every original literary, dramatic, musical or artistic work made by or under the direction or control of Her Majesty or a Government department,—

(a) if apart from this section copyright would not subsist in the work, copyright shall subsist therein by virtue of this subsection, and
(b) in any case, Her Majesty shall, subject to the provisions of this Part of this Act, be entitled to the copyright in the work.

(2) Her Majesty shall, subject to the provisions of this Part of this Act, be entitled—

(a) to the copyright in every original literary, dramatic or musical work first published in the United Kingdom, or in another country to which section two of this Act extends, if first published by or under the direction or control of Her Majesty or a Government department;
(b) to the copyright in every original artistic work first published in the United Kingdom, or in another country to which section three of this Act extends, if first published by or under such direction or control.

(3) Copyright in a literary, dramatic or musical work, to which Her Majesty is entitled in accordance with either of the preceding subsections,—

(a) where the work is unpublished, shall continue to subsist so long as the work remains unpublished, and
(b) where the work is published, shall subsist (or, if copyright in the work subsisted immediately before its first publication, shall continue to subsist) until the end of the period of fifty years from the end of the calendar year in which the work was first published, and shall then expire.

(4) Copyright in an artistic work to which Her Majesty is entitled in accordance with the preceding provisions of this section shall continue to subsist until the end

of the period of fifty years from the end of the calendar year in which the work was made, and shall then expire:

Provided that where the work in question is an engraving or a photograph, the copyright shall continue to subsist until the end of the period of fifty years from the end of the calendar year in which the engraving or photograph is first published.

(5) In the case of every sound recording or cinematograph film made by or under the direction or control of Her Majesty or a Government department,—

    (a) if apart from this section copyright would not subsist in the recording or film, copyright shall subsist therein by virtue of this subsection, and

    (b) in any case, Her Majesty shall, subject to the provisions of this Part of this Act, be entitled to the copyright in the recording or film, and it shall subsist for the same period as if it were copyright subsisting by virtue of, and owned in accordance with, section twelve or, as the case may be, section thirteen of this Act.

(6) The preceding provisions of this section shall have effect subject to any agreement made by or on behalf of Her Majesty or a Government department with the author of the work, or the maker of the sound recording or cinematograph film, as the case may be, whereby it is agreed that the copyright in the work, recording or film shall vest in the author or maker, or in another person designated in the agreement in that behalf.

(7) In relation to copyright subsisting by virtue of this section—

    (a) in the case of a literary, dramatic, musical or artistic work, the provisions of Part I of this Act, with the exception of provisions thereof relating to the subsistence, duration or ownership of copyright, and

    (b) in the case of a sound recording or cinematograph film, the provisions of Part II of this Act, with the exception of provisions thereof relating to the subsistence or ownership of copyright,

shall apply as those provisions apply in relation to copyright subsisting by virtue of Part I, or as the case may be, Part II of this Act.

(8) For the avoidance of doubt, it is hereby declared that the provisions of section three of the Crown Proceedings Act 1947 (which relates to infringements of industrial property by servants or agents of the Crown) apply to copyright under this Act.

(9) In this section 'Government department' means any department of Her Majesty's Government in the United Kingdom or of the Government of Northern Ireland, or any department or agency of the Government of any other country to which this section extends.

## 40. Broadcasts of sound recordings and cinematograph films, and diffusion of broadcast programmes

(1) Where a sound broadcast or television broadcast is made by the Corporation or the Authority, and a person, by the reception of that broadcast, causes a sound recording to be heard in public, he does not thereby infringe the copyright (if any) in that recording under section twelve of this Act.

(2) Where a television broadcast or sound broadcast is made by the Corporation or the Authority, and the broadcast is an authorised broadcast, any person who, by the reception of the broadcast, causes a cinematograph film to be seen or heard in public, shall be in the like position, in any proceedings for infringement of the copyright (if any) in the film under section thirteen of this Act, as if he had been

the holder of a licence granted by the owner of that copyright to cause the film to be seen or heard in public by the reception of the broadcast.

*(3) Where a television broadcast or sound broadcast is made by the Corporation or the Authority, and the broadcast is an authorised broadcast, any person who, by the reception of the broadcast, causes a programme to be transmitted to subscribers to a diffusion service, being a programme comprising a literary, dramatic or musical work, or an adaptation of such a work, or an artistic work, or a cinematograph film, shall be in the like position, in any proceedings for infringement of the copyright (if any) in the work or film, as if he had been the holder of a licence granted by the owner of that copyright to include the work, adaptation or film in any programme caused to be transmitted by him to subscribers to that service by the reception of the broadcast.*

**(3) Where a television broadcast or sound broadcast is made by the Corporation or the Authority, and the broadcast is an authorised broadcast, then, subject to subsection (3A) below, any person who, by the reception and immediate re-transmission of the broadcast, includes a programme in a cable programme service, being a programme comprising a literary, dramatic or musical work, or an adaptation of such a work, or an artistic work, or a sound recording or cinematograph film, shall be in the like position, in any proceedings for infringement of the copyright (if any) in the work, recording or film, as if he had been the holder of a licence granted by the owner of that copyright to include the work, adaptation, recording or film in any programme so included in that service.**

**(3A) Subsection (3) above applies only—**

(a) **if the programme is included in the service in pursuance of a requirement imposed under section 13(1) of the Cable and Broadcasting Act 1984; or**

(b) **if and to the extent that the broadcast is made for reception in the area in which the service is provided.**

(4) If, in the circumstances mentioned in either of the two last preceding subsections, the person causing the cinematograph film to be seen or heard, or *the programme to be transmitted* **including the programme in a cable programme service**, as the case may be, infringed the copyright in question, by reason that the broadcast was not an authorised broadcast,—

(a) no proceedings shall be brought against that person under this Act in respect of his infringement of that copyright, but

(b) it shall be taken into account in assessing damages in any proceedings against the Corporation or the Authority, as the case may be, in respect of that copyright, in so far as that copyright was infringed by them in making the broadcast.

(5) For the purposes of this section, a broadcast shall be taken, in relation to a work **or sound recording** or cinematograph film, to be an authorised broadcast if, but only if, it is made by, or with the licence of, the owner of the copyright in the work **or recording** or film.

*General note*
As amended by the Cable and Broadcasting Act 1984. Italicised words repealed; words in bold type added.

**40A Inclusion of sound recordings and cinematograph films in cable programmes**
**(1) Where a cable programme is sent and a person, by the reception of that programme, causes a sound recording to be heard in public, he does not thereby infringe the copyright (if any) in that recording under section 12 of this Act.**

**(2) Where a cable programme is sent and the programme is an authorised programme, any person who, by the reception of the programme, causes a cinematograph film to be seen or heard in public shall be in the like position, in any proceedings for infringement of copyright (if any) in the film under section 13 of this Act, as if he had been the holder of a licence granted by the owner of that copyright to cause the film to be seen or heard in public by the reception of the programme.**

**(3) If, in the circumstances mentioned in the last preceding subsection, a person causing a cinematograph film to be seen or heard infringes the copyright in the film by reason that the cable programme was not an authorised programme—**

    (a)  **no proceedings shall be brought against that person under this Act in respect of his infringement of that copyright, but**

    (b)  **it shall be taken into account in assessing damages in any proceedings against the person sending the programme, in so far as that copyright was infringed by him in sending the programme.**

**(4) For the purposes of this section, a cable programme shall be taken, in relation to a cinematograph film, to be an authorised programme if, but only if, it is sent by, or with the licence of, the owner of the copyright in the film.**

*General note*
Inserted by the Cable and Broadcasting Act 1984.

**41. Use of copyright material for education**
(1) Where copyright subsists in a literary, dramatic, musical or artistic work, the copyright shall not be taken to be infringed by reason only that the work is reproduced, or an adaptation of the work is made or reproduced,—

    (a)  in the course of instruction, whether at a school or elsewhere, where the reproduction or adaptation is made by a teacher or pupil otherwise than by the use of a duplicating process, or

    (b)  as part of the questions to be answered in an examination, or in an answer to such a question.

(2) Nothing in the preceding subsection shall apply to the publication of a work or of an adaptation of a work; and, for the purposes of section 5 of this Act, the fact that to a person's knowledge the making of an article would have constituted an infringement of copyright but for the preceding subsection shall have the like effect as if, to his knowledge, the making of it had constituted such an infringement.

(3) For the avoidance of doubt it is hereby declared that, where a literary, dramatic or musical work—

    (a)  is performed in class, or otherwise in the presence of an audience, and

    (b)  is so performed in the course of the activities of a school, by a person who is a teacher in, or a pupil in attendance at, the school, the performance shall not be taken for the purposes of this Act to be a performance in public if the audience is limited to persons who are teachers in, or pupils in attendance at, the school, or are otherwise directly connected with the activities of the school.

(4) For the purposes of the last preceding subsection a person shall not be taken to be directly connected with the activities of a school by reason only that he is a parent or guardian of a pupil in attendance at the school.

(5) The two last preceding subsections shall apply in relation to sound recordings, cinematograph films, **television broadcasts and cable programmes** as they apply in relation to literary, dramatic and musical works, as if any reference to performance were a reference to the act of causing the sounds or visual images in question to be heard or seen.

(6) Nothing in this section shall be construed—

(a) as extending the operation of any provision of this Act as to the acts restricted by copyright of any description, or

(b) as derogating from the operation of any exemption conferred by any provision of this Act other than this section.

(7) In this section 'school'—

(a) in relation to England and Wales, has the same meaning as in the Education Act 1944;

(b) in relation to Scotland, has the same meaning as in the Education (Scotland) Act 1946, except that it includes an approved school within the meaning of the Children and Young Persons (Scotland) Act 1937; and

(c) in relation to Northern Ireland, has the same meaning as in the Education Act (Northern Ireland) 1947;

and 'duplicating process' means any process involving the use of an appliance for producing multiple copies.

*General note*
As amended by the Cable and Broadcasting Act 1984. Italicised words repealed; words in bold type added.

## 42. Special provisions as to public records
(1) Where any work in which copyright subsists, or a reproduction of any such work, is comprised in—

(a) any records belonging to Her Majesty which are under the charge and superintendence of the Master of the Rolls by virtue of an Order in Council under section two of the Public Record Office Act 1838, and are open to public inspection in accordance with rules made under that Act, or

(b) any public records to which the Public Records Act (Northern Ireland) 1923, applies, being records which are open to public inspection in accordance with rules made under that Act,

the copyright in the work is not infringed by the making, or the supplying to any person, of any reproduction of the work by or under the direction of any officer appointed under the said Act of 1838 or the said Act of 1923, as the case may be.

(2) In the preceding subsection 'records'—

(a) in paragraph (a) of that subsection has the same meaning as in the Public Record Office Act 1838;

(b) in paragraph (b) of that subsection has the same meaning as in the Public Records Act (Northern Ireland) 1923.

(3) Any reference in this section to the Public Records Act (Northern Ireland) 1923, shall be construed as including a reference to that Act as for the time being amended or re-enacted (with or without modifications) by any enactment of the Parliament of Northern Ireland.

## 43. False attribution of authorship

(1) The restrictions imposed by this section shall have effect in relation to literary, dramatic, musical or artistic works; and any reference in this section to a work shall be construed as a reference to such a work.

(2) A person (in this subsection referred to as 'the offender') contravenes those restrictions as respects another person if, without the licence of that other person, he does any of the following acts in the United Kingdom, that is to say, he—

(a) inserts or affixes that other person's name in or on a work of which that person is not the author, or in or on a reproduction of such a work, in such a way as to imply that the other person is the author of the work, or

(b) publishes, or sells or lets for hire, or by way of trade offers or exposes for sale or hire, or by way of trade exhibits in public, a work in or on which the other person's name has been so inserted or affixed, if to the offender's knowledge that person is not the author of the work, or

(c) does any of the acts mentioned in the last preceding paragraph in relation to, or distributes, reproductions of a work, being reproductions in or on which the other person's name has been so inserted or affixed, if to the offender's knowledge that person is not the author of the work, or

(d) performs in public, *or broadcasts* **broadcasts or includes in a cable programme**, a work of which the other person is not the author, as being a work of which he is the author, if to the offender's knowledge that person is not the author of the work.

(3) The last preceding subsection shall apply where, contrary to the fact, a work is represented as being an adaptation of the work of another person as it applies where a work is so represented as being the work of another person.

(4) In the case of an artistic work which has been altered after the author parted with the possession of it, the said restrictions are contravened, in relation to the author, by a person who in the United Kingdom, without the licence of the author,—

(a) publishes, sells or lets for hire, or by way of trade offers or exposes for sale or hire the work as so altered, as being the unaltered work of the author, or

(b) publishes, sells or lets for hire, or by way of trade offers or exposes for sale or hire a reproduction of the work as so altered, as being a reproduction of the unaltered work of the author,

if to his knowledge it is not the unaltered work, or, as the case may be, a reproduction of the unaltered work, of the author.

(5) The three last preceding subsections shall apply with respect to anything done in relation to another person after that person's death, as if any reference to

that person's licence were a reference to a licence given by him or by his personal representatives:

Provided that nothing in those subsections shall apply to anything done in relation to a person more than twenty years after that person's death.

(6) In the case of an artistic work in which copyright subsists, the said restrictions are also contravened, in relation to the author of the work, by a person who in the United Kingdom—

(a) publishes, or sells or lets for hire, or by way of trade offers or exposes for sale or hire, or by way of trade exhibits in public, a reproduction of the work, as being a reproduction made by the author of the work, or

(b) distributes reproductions of the work as being reproductions made by the author of the work,

if (in any such case) the reproduction or reproductions was or were to his knowledge not made by the author.

(7) The preceding provisions of this section shall apply (with the necessary modifications) with respect to acts done in relation to two or more persons in connection with the same work.

(8) The restrictions imposed by this section shall not be enforceable by any criminal proceedings; but any contravention of those restrictions, in relation to a person, shall be actionable at his suit, or, if he is dead, at the suit of his personal representative, as a breach of statutory duty.

(9) Any damages recovered under this section by personal representatives, in respect of a contravention committed in relation to a person after his death, shall devolve as part of his estate, as if the right of action had subsisted and had been vested in him immediately before his death.

(10) Nothing in this section shall derogate from any right of action or other remedy (whether civil or criminal) in proceedings instituted otherwise than by virtue of this section:

Provided that this subsection shall not be construed as requiring any damages recovered by virtue of this section to be disregarded in assessing damages in any proceedings instituted otherwise than by virtue of this section and arising out of the same transaction.

(11) In this section 'name' includes initials or a monogram.

*General note*
As amended by the cable and Broadcasting Act 1984. Italicized words repealed; words in bold type added.

## 44. Amendments of Registered Designs Act 1949

(1) In section six of the Registered Designs Act 1949 (under which the disclosure of a design in certain circumstances is not to be a reason for refusing registration), the following subsections shall be inserted after subsection (3)—

'(4) Where copyright under the Copyright Act 1956, subsists in an artistic work, and an application is made by, or with the consent of, the owner of that copyright for the registration of a corresponding design, that design shall not be treated for the purposes of this Act as being other than new or original by reason only of any use previously made of the artistic work, unless—

*(a)* the previous use consisted of or included the sale, letting for hire, or offer for sale or hire of articles to which the design in question (or a design differing from it only as mentioned in subsection (2) of section one of

this Act) had been applied industrially, other than articles of a description specified in rules made under subsection (4) of section one of this Act, and

(b) that previous use was made by, or with the consent of, the owner of the copyright in the artistic work.

(5) Any rules made by virtue of subsection (5) of section ten of the Copyright Act 1956 (which relates to rules for determining the circumstances in which a design is to be taken to be applied industrially) shall apply for the purposes of the last foregoing subsection.'

(2) The following subsection shall be added at the end of section eight of the said Act of 1949 (which relates to the period of copyright in registered designs)—

'(3) Where in the case of a registered design it is shown—

(a) that the design, at the time when it was registered, was a corresponding design in relation to an artistic work in which copyright subsisted under the Copyright Act 1956;

(b) that, by reason of a previous use of that artistic work, the design would not have been registrable under this Act but for subsection (4) of section six of this Act; and

(c) that the copyright in that work under the Copyright Act 1956, expired before the date of expiry of the copyright in the design,

the copyright in the design shall, notwithstanding anything in this section, be deemed to have expired at the same time as the copyright in the artistic work, and shall not be renewable after that time.'

(3) In section eleven of the said Act of 1949 (which relates to cancellation of the registration of designs), the following subsection shall be inserted after subsection (2)—

'(2A) At any time after a design has been registered, any person interested may apply to the registrar for the cancellation of the registration of the design on the grounds—

(a) that the design, at the time when it was registered, was a corresponding design in relation to an artistic work in which copyright subsisted under the Copyright Act 1956;

(b) that, by reason of a previous use of that artistic work, the design would not have been registrable under this Act but for subsection (4) of section six of this Act; and

(c) that the copyright in that work under the Copyright Act 1956, has expired;

and the registrar may make such order on the application as he thinks fit.'

(4) In subsection (3) of the said section eleven, for the words 'the last foregoing subsection' there shall be substituted the words 'either of the two last foregoing subsections'.

(5) In subsection (1) of section forty-four of the said Act of 1949 (which relates to the interpretation of that Act)—

(a) after the definition of 'article' there shall be inserted the words 'artistic work' has the same meaning as in the Copyright Act 1956'; and

(b) after the definition of 'copyright' there shall be inserted the words 'corresponding design' has the same meaning as in section ten of the Copyright Act 1956'.

*General note*
The Registered Designs Act 1949 has been further amended by the Copyright, Designs and Patents Act 1988. For the amended text, see Appendix 1.

## PART C

### 45. Amendment of Dramatic and Musical Performers' Protection Act 1925
*In the Dramatic and Musical Performers' Protection Act 1925,—*

(a) *after section one there shall be inserted the two sections set out in Part of the Sixth Schedule to this Act; and*

(b) *after section three there shall be inserted the two sections set out in Part II of that Schedule;*

*and the provisions of that Act specified in Part III of that Schedule shall have effect subject to the amendments set out in relation thereto in the second column of the said Part III (being minor amendments of that Act and amendments consequential upon the insertion therein of the sections referred to in paragraphs (a) and (b) of this section).*

*General note*
Repealed by the Dramatic and Musical Performer's Protection Act 1958, s. 9(3).

### 46. Savings
(1) Any rights conferred on universities and colleges by the Copyright Act 1775, which continued to subsist in accordance with section thirty-three of the Copyright Act 1911; notwithstanding the repeal of the said Act of 1775, shall continue to subsist in accordance with the said Act of 1775 notwithstanding any repeal effected by this Act:

Provided that no proceedings shall be brought under the Copyright Act 1775, but the provisions of Part III of this Act shall apply for the enforcement of those rights as if they were copyright subsisting by virtue of this Act.

(2) Nothing in this Act shall affect any right or privilege of the Crown subsisting otherwise than by virtue of an enactment; and nothing in this Act shall affect any right or privilege of the Crown or of any other person under any enactment (including any enactment of the Parliament of Northern Ireland), except in so far as that enactment is expressly repealed, amended or modified by this Act.

(3) Nothing in this Act shall affect the right of the Crown or of any person deriving title from the Crown to sell, use or otherwise deal with articles forfeited under the laws relating to customs or excise, including any article so forfeited by virtue of this Act or of any enactment repealed by this Act.

(4) Nothing in this Act shall affect the operation of any rule of equity relating to breaches of trust or confidence.

(5) Subject to the preceding provisions of this section, no copyright, or right in the nature of copyright, shall subsist otherwise than by virtue of this Act or of some other enactment in that behalf.

### 47. General provisions as to Orders in Council, regulations, rules and orders, and as to the Board of Trade
(1) Any power to make regulations, rules or orders under this Act shall be exercisable by statutory instrument.

(2) Any statutory instrument containing—

    (a) any Order in Council or regulations made under this Act, or

    (b) any rules made by the Lord Chancellor under the Fourth Schedule to this Act,

shall be subject to annulment in pursuance of a resolution of either House of Parliament.

(3) Any Order in Council, or other order, made under any of the preceding provisions of this Act may be varied or revoked by a subsequent Order in Council or order made thereunder.

(4) Where a power to make regulations or rules is conferred by any provision of this Act, regulations or rules under that power may be made either as respects all, or as respects any one or more, of the matters to which the provision relates; and different provision may be made by any such regulations or rules as respects different classes of cases to which the regulations or rules apply.

(5) *Anything required or authorised by or under this Act to be done by, to or before the Board of Trade may be done by, to or before the President of the Board of Trade, any Minister of State with duties concerning the affairs of the Board, any secretary, under-secretary or assistant secretary of the board, or any person authorised in that behalf by the President.*

(6) In this section 'order' does not include an order of a court or of the tribunal.

*General note*
Subsection (5) repealed by the Industrial Expansion Act 1968, s 18(2) and Sch 4; see now s 14 of that Act.

## 48. Interpretation

(1) In this Act, except in so far as the context otherwise requires, the following expressions have the meanings hereby assigned to them respectively, that is to say:—

    'adaptation', in relation to a literary, dramatic or musical work, has the meaning assigned to it by section two of this Act;

    'artistic work' has the meaning assigned to it by section three of this Act;

    'building' includes any structure; **'cable programme', 'cable programme service' and 'programme' have the meanings assigned to them by section 14A of this Act**;

    'cinematograph film' has the meaning assigned to it by section thirteen of this Act;

    'construction' includes erection, and references to reconstruction shall be construed accordingly;

    'the Corporation' and 'the Authority' have the meanings assigned to them by section fourteen of this Act;

    'country' includes any territory;

    'dramatic work' includes a choreographic work or entertainment in dumb show if reduced to writing in the form in which the work or entertainment is to be presented, but does not include a cinematograph film, as distinct from a scenario or script for a cinematograph film;

    'drawing' includes any diagram, map, chart or plan;

    'engraving' includes any etching, lithograph, woodcut, print or similar work, not being a photograph;

'future copyright' and 'prospective owner' have the meanings assigned to them by section thirty-seven of this Act;

'judicial proceeding' means a proceeding before any court, tribunal or person having by law power to hear, receive and examine evidence on oath;

'literary work' includes any written table or compilation;

'manuscript', in relation to a work, means the original document embodying the work, whether written by hand or not;

'performance' includes delivery, in relation to lectures, addresses, speeches and sermons, and in general, subject to the provisions of subsection (5) of this section, includes any mode of visual or acoustic presentation, including any such presentation by the operation of wireless telegraphy apparatus, or by the exhibition of a cinematograph film, or by the use of a record, or by any other means, and references to performing a work or an adaptation of a work shall be construed accordingly;

'photograph' means any product of photography or of any process akin to photography, other than a part of a cinematograph film, and 'author', in relation to a photograph, means the person who, at the time when the photograph is taken, is the owner of the material on which it is taken;

'qualified person' has the meaning assigned to it by section one of this Act;

'record' means any disc, tape, perforated roll or other device in which sounds are embodied so as to be capable (with or without the aid of some other instrument) of being automatically reproduced therefrom, and references to a record of a work or other subject-matter are references to a record (as herein defined) by means of which it can be performed;

'reproduction', in the case of a literary, dramatic or musical work, includes a reproduction in the form of a record or of a cinematograph film, and, in the case of an artistic work, includes a version produced by converting the work into a three-dimensional form, or, if it is in three dimensions, by converting it into a two-dimensional form, and references to reproducing a work shall be construed accordingly;

'sculpture' includes any cast or model made for purposes of sculpture;

'sound recording' has the meaning assigned to it by section twelve of this Act;

'sufficient acknowledgment' has the meaning assigned to it by section six of this Act;

'television broadcast' and 'sound broadcast' have the meanings assigned to them by section fourteen of this Act;

'wireless telegraphy apparatus' has the same meaning as in the Wireless Telegraphy Act 1949;

'work of joint authorship' has the meaning assigned to it by section eleven of this Act;

'writing' includes any form of notation, whether by hand or by printing, typewriting or any similar process.

(2) References in this Act to broadcasting are references to broadcasting by wireless telegraphy (within the meaning of the Wireless Telegraphy Act 1949), whether by way of sound broadcasting or of television.

*(3) References in this Act to the transmission of a work or other subject-matter to subscribers to a diffusion service are references to the transmission thereof in the course of a service of distributing broadcast programmes, or other programmes (whether provided by the person operating the service or other persons), over wires, or other paths provided by a material substance, to the*

*premises of subscribers to the service; and for the purposes of this Act, where a work or other subject-matter is so transmitted,—*

> (a) *the person operating the service (that is to say, the person who, in the agreements with subscribers to the service, undertakes to provide them with the service, whether he is the person who transmits the programmes or not) shall be taken to be the person causing the work or other subject-matter to be so transmitted, and*
>
> (b) *no person, other than the person operating the service, shall be taken to be causing it to be so transmitted, notwithstanding that he provides any facilities for the transmission of the programmes:*

*Provided that, for the purposes of this subsection, and of references to which this subsection applies, no account shall be taken of a service of distributing broadcasts or other programmes, where the service is only incidental to a business of keeping or letting premises where persons reside or sleep, and is operated as part of the amenities provided exclusively or mainly for residents or inmates therein.*

**(3) References in this Act to the inclusion of a programme in a cable programme service are references to its inclusion in such a service by the person providing that service.**

**(3A) For the purposes of this Act no account shall be taken of a cable programme service if, and to the extent that, it is provided for—**

> **(a) a person providing another such service;**
>
> **(b) the Corporation; or**
>
> **(c) the Authority;**

**and for the purposes of this subsection a cable programme service provided for the Welsh Fourth Channel Authority, the subsidiary mentioned in section 12(2) of the Broadcasting Act 1981 or a programme contractor within the meaning of that Act shall be treated as provided for the Authority.**

**(3B) For the purposes of this Act no account shall be taken of cable programme service which is only incidental to a business of keeping or letting premises where persons reside or sleep, and is operated as part of the amenities provided exclusively or mainly for residents or inmates therein.**

(4) References in this Act to the doing of any act by the reception of a television broadcast or sound broadcast made by the Corporation or the Authority are references to the doing of that act by means of receiving the broadcast either—

> (a) from the transmission whereby the broadcast is made by the Corporation or the Authority, as the case may be, or
>
> (b) from a transmission made by the Corporation or the Authority, as the case may be, otherwise than by way of broadcasting, but simultaneously with the transmission mentioned in the preceding paragraph,

whether (in either case) the reception of the broadcast is directly from the transmission in question or from a re-transmission thereof made by any person from any place, whether in the United Kingdom or elsewhere; and in this subsection 're-transmission' means any re-transmission, whether over paths provided by a material substance or not, including any re-transmission made by making use of any record, print, negative, tape or other article on which the broadcast in question has been recorded.

(5) For the purposes of this Act, broadcasting, or *the causing of a work or other*

*subject-matter to be transmitted to subscribers to a diffusion service* **including a work or other subject matter in a cable programme**, shall not be taken to constitute performance, or to constitute causing visual images or sounds to be seen or heard; and where visual images or sounds are displayed or emitted by any receiving apparatus, to which they are conveyed by the transmission of electro-magnetic signals (whether over paths provided by a material substance or not),—

    (a)  the operation of any apparatus whereby the signals are transmitted, directly or indirectly, to the receiving apparatus shall not be taken to constitute performance or to constitute causing the visual images or sounds to be seen or heard; but

    (b)  in so far as the display or emission of the images or sounds constitutes a performance, or causes them to be seen or heard, the performance, or the causing of the images or sounds to be seen or heard, as the case may be, shall be taken to be effected by the operation of the receiving apparatus.

(6) Without prejudice to the last preceding subsection, where a work or an adaptation of a work is performed, or visual images or sounds are caused to be seen or heard, by the operation of any apparatus to which this subsection applies, being apparatus provided by or with the consent of the occupier of the premises where the apparatus is situated, the occupier of those premises shall, for the purposes of this Act, be taken to be the person giving the performance, or causing the images or sounds to be seen or heard, whether he is the person operating the apparatus or not.

This subsection applies to any such receiving apparatus as is mentioned in the last preceding subsection, and to any apparatus for reproducing sounds by the use of a record.

(7) Except in so far as the context otherwise requires, any reference in this Act to an enactment shall be construed as a reference to that enactment as amended or extended by or under any other enactment.

*General note*
Amended by the Cable and Broadcasting Act 1984. Italicized words repealed; words in bold type added.

### 49. Supplementary provisions as to interpretation

(1) Except in so far as the context otherwise requires, any reference in this Act to the doing of an act in relation to a work or other subject-matter shall be taken to include a reference to the doing of that act in relation to a substantial part thereof, and any reference to a reproduction, adaptation or copy of a work, or a record embodying a sound recording, shall be taken to include a reference to a reproduction, adaptation or copy of a substantial part of the work, or a record embodying a substantial part of the sound recording, as the case may be:

Provided that, for the purposes of the following provisions of this Act, namely subsections (1) and (2) of section two, subsections (2) and (3) of section three, subsections (2) and (3) of section thirty-three, section thirty-eight, and subsections (2) to (4) of section thirty-nine, this subsection shall not affect the construction of any reference to the publication, or absence of publication, of a work.

(2) With regard to publication, the provisions of this subsection shall have effect for the purposes of this Act, that is to say,—

    (a)  the performance, or the issue of records, of a literary, dramatic or musical work, the exhibition of an artistic work, the construction of a work of

architecture, and the issue of photographs or engravings of a work of architecture or of a sculpture, do not constitute publication of the work;
(b) except in so far as it may constitute an infringement of copyright, or a
contravention of any restriction imposed by section forty-three of this
Act, a publication which is merely colourable, and not intended to satisfy
the reasonable requirements of the public, shall be disregarded;
(c) subject to the preceding paragraphs, a literary, dramatic or musical work,
or an edition of such a work, or an artistic work, shall be taken to have
been published if, but only if, reproductions of the work or edition have
been issued to the public;
(d) a publication in the United Kingdom, or in any other country, shall not
be treated as being other than the first publication by reason only of an
earlier publication elsewhere, if the two publications took place within a
period of not more than thirty days;

and in determining, for the purposes of paragraph (c) of this subsection, whether
reproductions of a work or edition have been issued to the public, the preceding
subsection shall not apply.

(3) In determining for the purposes of any provision of this Act—

(a) whether a work or other subject-matter has been published, or
(b) whether a publication of a work or other subject-matter was the first
publication thereof, or
(c) whether a work or other subject-matter was published or otherwise dealt
with in the lifetime of a person,

no account shall be taken of any unauthorised publication or of the doing of any
other unauthorised act; and (subject to subsection (7) of section seven of this Act)
a publication or other act shall for the purposes of this subsection be taken to have
been unauthorised—

(i) if copyright subsisted in the work or other subject-matter and the act in
question was done otherwise than by, or with the licence of, the owner
of the copyright, or
(ii) if copyright did not subsist in the work, or other subject-matter, and the
act in question was done otherwise than by, or with the licence of, the
author (or, in the case of a sound recording or a cinematograph film, or
an edition of a literary, dramatic or musical work, the maker or publisher,
as the case may be) or persons lawfully claiming under him:

Provided that nothing in this subsection shall affect any provisions of this Act
as to the acts restricted by any copyright or as to acts constituting infringements
of copyrights, or any provisions of section forty-three of this Act.

(4) References in this Act to the time at which, or the period during which, a
literary, dramatic or musical work was made are references to the time or period
at or during which it was first reduced to writing or some other material form.

(5) In the case of any copyright to which (whether in consequence of a partial
assignment or otherwise) different persons are entitled in respect of the application
of the copyright—

(a) to the doing of different acts or classes of acts, or
(b) to the doing of one or more acts or classes of acts in different countries
or at different times,

the owner of the copyright, for any purpose of this Act, shall be taken to be the person who is entitled to the copyright in respect of its application to the doing of the particular act or class of acts, or, as the case may be, to the doing thereof in the particular country or at the particular time, which is relevant to the purpose in question; and, in relation to any future copyright to which different persons are prospectively entitled, references in this Act to the prospective owner of the copyright shall be construed accordingly.

(6) Without prejudice to the generality of the last preceding subsection, where under any provision of this Act a question arises whether an article of any description has been imported or sold, or otherwise dealt with, without the licence of the owner of any copyright, the owner of the copyright, for the purpose of determining that question shall be taken to be the person entitled to the copyright in respect of its application to the making of articles of that description in the country into which the article was imported, or, as the case may be, in which it was sold or otherwise dealt with.

(7) Where the doing of anything is authorised by the grantee of a licence, or a person deriving title from the grantee, and it is within the terms (including any implied terms) of the licence for him to authorise it, it shall for the purposes of this Act be taken to be done with the licence of the grantor and of every other person (if any) upon whom the licence is binding.

(8) References in this Act to deriving title are references to deriving title either directly or indirectly.

(9) Where, in the case of copyright of any description,—

   (a) provisions contained in this Act specify certain acts as being restricted by the copyright, or as constituting infringements thereof, and
   (b) other provisions of this Act specify certain acts as not constituting infringements of the copyright,

the omission or exclusion of any matter from the latter provisions shall not be taken to extend the operation of the former provisions.

(10) Any reference in this Act to countries to which a provision of this Act extends includes a country to which that provision extends subject to exceptions, modifications or additions.

## 50. Transitional provisions, and repeals

(1) The transitional provisions contained in the Seventh Schedule to this Act shall have effect for the purposes of this Act; and the provisions of the Eighth Schedule to this Act shall have effect in accordance with those transitional provisions.

*(2) Subject to the said transitional provisions, the enactments specified in the Ninth Schedule to this Act are hereby repealed to the extent specified in the third column of that Schedule.*

*General note*
Sub-section (2) repealed by the Statute Law (Repeals) Act 1974.

## 51. Short title, commencement and extent

(1) This Act may be cited as the Copyright Act 1956.

(2) This Act shall come into operation on such day as the Board of Trade may by order appoint; and different days may be appointed for the purposes of different provisions of this Act, and, for the purposes of any provision of this Act whereby enactments are repealed, different days may be appointed for the operation of the

repeal in relation to different enactments, including different enactments contained in the same Act.

(3) It is hereby declared that this Act extends to Northern Ireland.

SCHEDULES

Section 10                      FIRST SCHEDULE

FALSE REGISTRATION OF INDUSTRIAL DESIGNS

1. The provisions of this Schedule shall have effect where—

    (a)    copyright subsists in an artistic work, and proceedings are brought under this Act relating to that work;

    (b)    a corresponding design has been registered under the Act of 1949, and the copyright in the design subsisting by virtue of that registration has not expired by effluxion of time before the commencement of those proceedings; and

    (c)    it is proved or admitted in the proceedings that the person registered as the proprietor of the design was not the proprietor thereof for the purposes of the Act of 1949, and was so registered without the knowledge of the owner of the copyright in the artistic work.

2. For the purposes of those proceedings (but subject to the next following paragraph) the registration shall be treated as never having been effected, and accordingly, in relation to that registration, *subsection (1) of section ten of this Act shall not apply*, and nothing in section seven of the Act of 1949 shall be construed as affording any defence in those proceedings.

3. Notwithstanding anything in the last preceding paragraph, if in the proceedings it is proved or admitted that any act to which the proceedings relate—

    (a)    was done in pursuance of an assignment or licence made or granted by the person registered as proprietor of the design, and

    (b)    was so done in good faith in reliance upon the registration, and without notice of any proceedings for the cancellation of the registration or for rectifying the entry in the register of designs relating thereto,

*subsection (1) of section ten of this Act shall apply in relation to that act for the purposes of the first-mentioned proceedings* **this shall be a good defence to such proceedings**s.

4. In this Schedule 'the Act of 1949' means the Registered Designs Act 1949, and 'corresponding design' has the meaning assigned to it by subsection (6) of section ten of this Act.

*General note*
Amended by the Design Copyright Act 1968. Italicised words repealed; words in bold added.

Section 11                    SECOND SCHEDULE

DURATION OF COPYRIGHT IN ANONYMOUS AND PSEUDONYMOUS WORKS

1. Where the first publication of a literary, dramatic, or musical work, or of an artistic work other than a photograph, is anonymous or pseudonymous, then subject to the following provisions of this Schedule—

    (a)    subsection (3) of section two of this Act, or, as the case may be, subsection (4) of section three of this Act, shall not apply, and

    (b)    any copyright subsisting in the work by virtue of either of those sections shall continue to subsist until the end of the period of fifty years from the end of the calendar year in which the work was first published, and shall then expire.

2. The preceding paragraph shall not apply in the case of a work if, at any time before the end of the period mentioned in that paragraph, it is possible for a person without previous knowledge of the facts to ascertain the identity of the author by reasonable inquiry.

3. For the purposes of this Act a publication of a work under two or more names shall not be taken to be pseudonymous unless all those names are pseudonyms.

THIRD SCHEDULE

WORKS OF JOINT AUTHORSHIP

1. In relation to a work of joint authorship, the references to the author in subsections (1) and (2) of

section two of this Act, in subsections (2) and (3) of section three of this Act, and in paragraph 2 of the Second Schedule to this Act, shall be construed as references to any one or more of the authors.

2. In relation to a work of joint authorship, other than a work to which the next following paragraph applies, references to the author in subsection (3) of section two, in subsection (4) of section three, and in subsection (6) of section seven, of this Act, shall be construed as references to the author who died last.

3.—(1) This paragraph applies to any work of joint authorship which was first published under two or more names, of which one or more (but not all) were pseudonyms.

(2) This paragraph also applies to any work of joint authorship which was first published under two or more names all of which were pseudonyms, if, at any time within the period of fifty years from the end of the calendar year in which the work was first published, it is possible for a person without previous knowledge of the facts to ascertain the identity of any one or more (but not all) of the authors by reasonable inquiry.

(3) In relation to a work to which this paragraph applies, references to the author in subsection (3) of section two of this Act, and in subsection (4) of section three of this Act, shall be construed as references to the author whose identity was disclosed, or, if the identity of two or more of the authors was disclosed, as references to that one of those authors who died last.

(4) For the purposes of this paragraph the identity of an author shall be taken to have been disclosed if either—

(a) in his case, the name under which the work was published was not a pseudonym, or

(b) it is possible to ascertain his identity as mentioned in subparagraph (2) of this paragraph.

4.—(1) In relation to a work of joint authorship of which one or more of the authors are persons to whom this paragraph applies, subsection (1) of section four of this Act shall have effect as if the author or authors, other than persons to whom this paragraph applies, had been the sole author, or (as the case may be) sole joint authors, of the work.

(2) This paragraph applies, in the case of a work, to any person such that, if he had been the sole author of the work, copyright would not have subsisted in the work by virtue of Part I of this Act.

5. In the proviso to subsection (6) of section six of this Act, the reference to other excerpts from works by the author of the passage in question—

(a) shall be taken to include a reference to excerpts from works by the author of that passage in collaboration with any other person, or

(b) if the passage in question is from a work of joint authorship, shall be taken to include a reference to excerpts from works by any one or more of the authors of that passage, or by any one or more of those authors in collaboration with any other person.

6. Subject to the preceding provisions of this Schedule, any reference in this Act to the author of a work shall (unless it is otherwise expressly provided) be construed, in relation to a work of joint authorship, as a reference to all the authors of the work.


Sections 23, 30, 47                    FOURTH SCHEDULE

PROVISIONS AS TO PERFORMING RIGHT TRIBUNAL

1.—(1) Subject to the provisions of this paragraph, the members of the tribunal shall hold office for such period as may be determined at the time of their respective appointments; and a person who ceases to hold office as a member of the tribunal shall be eligible for reappointment.

(2) Any member of the tribunal may at any time by notice in writing to the Board of Trade, or, in the case of the chairman of the tribunal, to the Lord Chancellor, resign his appointment.

(3) The Board of Trade, or, in the case of the chairman of the tribunal, the Lord Chancellor, may declare the office of any member of the tribunal vacant on the ground of his unfitness to continue in office or incapacity to perform the duties thereof.

2. If any member of the tribunal is, by reason of illness, absence or other reasonable cause, for the time being unable to perform the duties of his office, either generally or in relation to any particular proceedings, the Board of Trade, or, in the case of the chairman of the tribunal, the Lord Chancellor, may appoint some other duly qualified person to discharge the duties of that member for any period, not exceeding six months at one time, or, as the case may be, in relation to those proceedings; and a person so appointed shall, during that period or in relation to those proceedings, have the same powers as the person in whose place he is appointed.

3. If at any time there are more than two members of the tribunal, in addition to the chairman, then, for the purposes of any proceedings, the tribunal may consist of the chairman together with any two or more of those members.

4. If the members of the tribunal dealing with any reference or application are unable to agree as to the order to be made by the tribunal, a decision shall be taken by the votes of the majority; and, in the event of an equality of votes, the chairman shall be entitled to a second or casting vote.

5. The tribunal may order that the costs or expenses of any proceedings before it incurred by any party shall be paid by any other party, and may tax or settle the amount of any costs or expenses to be paid under any such order or direct in what manner they are to be taxed.

6.—(1) The Lord Chancellor may make rules as to the procedure in connection with the making of references and applications to the tribunal, and for regulating proceedings before the tribunal and, subject to the approval of the Treasury, as to the fees chargeable in respect of those proceedings.

(2) Any such rules may apply in relation to the tribunal—

    (a)    as respects proceedings in England and Wales, any of the provisions of the Arbitration Act 1950, and

    (b)    as respects proceedings in Northern Ireland, any of the provisions of the Arbitration Act (Northern Ireland) 1937.

(3) Any such rules may include provision—

    (a)    for prescribing the period within which, after the tribunal has given its decision in any proceedings, a request may be made to the tribunal to refer a question of law to the court;

    (b)    for requiring notice of any intended application to the court under subsection (2) of section thirty of this Act to be given to the tribunal and to the other parties to the proceedings, and for limiting the time within which any such notice is to be given;

    (c)    for suspending, or authorising or requiring the tribunal to suspend, the operation of orders of the tribunal, in cases where, after giving its decision, the tribunal refers a question of law to the court;

    (d)    for modifying, in relation to orders of the tribunal whose operation is suspended, the operation of any provisions of Part IV of this Act as to the effect of orders made thereunder;

    (e)    for the publication of notices, or the taking of any other steps, for securing that persons affected by the suspension of an order of the tribunal will be informed of its suspension;

    (f)    for regulating or prescribing any other matters incidental to or consequential upon any request, application, order or decision under section thirty of this Act.

(4) Provision shall be made by rules of court for limiting the time for instituting proceedings under subsection (2) of section thirty of this Act, and for authorising or requiring the court, where it makes an order directing the tribunal to refer a question of law to the court, to provide in the order for suspending the operation of any order made by the tribunal in the proceedings in which the question of law arose.

(5) In this paragraph 'the court' has the same meaning as in section thirty of this Act.

7. As respects proceedings in Scotland, the tribunal shall have the like powers for securing the attendance of witnesses and the production of documents, and with regard to the examination of witnesses on oath, as if the tribunal were an arbiter under a submission.

8. Without prejudice to any method available by law for the proof of orders of the tribunal, a document purporting to be a copy of any such order, and to be certified by the chairman of the tribunal to be a true copy thereof, shall, in any legal proceedings, be sufficient evidence of the order unless the contrary is proved.

Sections 24, 37                    FIFTH SCHEDULE

APPOINTMENT OF TELEVISION COPYRIGHT ORGANISATIONS BY BRITISH BROADCASTING CORPORATION AND INDEPENDENT TELEVISION AUTHORITY

1. In this Schedule—

    (a)    references to a right to which the Schedule applies are references to the copyright (including any future copyright) in any televison broadcast, in so far as the copyright relates, or when it comes into existence will relate, to the acts specified in paragraph (c) of subsection (4) of section fourteen of this Act;

    (b)    references to the purposes of this Schedule are references to the purposes of negotiating or granting licences in respect of rights to which this Schedule applies.

2. The Corporation and the Authority may jointly appoint an organisation for the purposes of this Schedule; and if they do so, no other organisation shall be appointed by them or either of them for those purposes until the appointment of that organisation has been duly terminated.

3. Subject to the last preceding paragraph, the Corporation or the Authority, or each of them, may appoint an organisation for the purposes of this Schedule; and if an organisation is so appointed by the Corporation or by the Authority, no other organisation shall be appointed for the purposes of this Schedule by the Corporation or the Authority, as the case may be, until the appointment of that organisation has been duly terminated.

4. A right to which this Schedule applies shall not be assignable by the Corporation or by the Authority except to an organisation duly appointed for the purposes of this Schedule; and where such a right has been assigned to such an organisation, it shall not be assignable by the organisation except to the Corporation or the Authority, as the case may be, or to another organisation subsequently appointed for the purposes of this Schedule.

5.—(1) Neither the Corporation nor the Authority shall authorise any organisation or person, other than any person in their employment under a contract of service, to negotiate or act for them with respect to the granting of licences in respect of rights to which this Schedule applies, except an organisation duly appointed for the purposes of this Schedule.

(2) An organisation appointed for the purposes of this Schedule shall not authorise any other organisation or person, other than any person in their employment under a contract of service, to negotiate or act for them, or for the Corporation or the Authority, with respect to the granting of licences in respect of rights to which this Schedule applies.

6. The appointment, or the termination of the appointment, of an organisation for the purposes of this Schedule shall not have effect unless, not less than fourteen days before the appointment or termination is to take effect, a notice is published in the London Gazette, the Edinburgh Gazette and the Belfast Gazette, specifying the name and address of the organisation, and the date on which the appointment or termination is to take effect, and stating whether the appointment, or termination of appointment, is made by the Corporation or the Authority or by both of them.

7. Where notice of the appointment of an organisation for the purposes of this Schedule has been given under the last preceding paragraph, the organisation shall be taken for the purposes of this Act to be authorised to act in accordance with the appointment until their appointment is duly terminated in pursuance of a notice published in accordance with that paragraph.


*Section 45*                                **SIXTH SCHEDULE**

*AMENDMENT OF DRAMATIC AND MUSICAL PERFORMERS' PROTECTION ACT 1925 PART I NEW SECTIONS 1A AND 1B*

*1A. Subject to the provisions of this Act, if any person knowingly—*

    (a)  *makes a cinematograph film, directly or indirectly, from or by means of the performance of any dramatic or musical work without the consent in writing of the performers, or*

    (b)  *sells or lets for hire, or distributes for the purposes of trade, or by way of trade exposes or offers for sale or hire, a cinematograph film made in contravention of this Act, or*

    (c)  *uses for the purposes of exhibition to the public a cinematograph film made in contravenion of this Act,*

*he shall be guilty of an offence under this Act, and shall be liable on summary conviction to a fine not exceeding fifty pounds:*

    *Provided that, where a person is charged with an offence under paragraph (a) of this section, it shall be a defence to prove that the cinematograph film was made for his private and domestic use only.*


*Penalties for broadcasting without consent of performers*

*1B. Subject to the provisions of this Act, any person who, otherwise than by the use of a record or a cinematograph film, knowingly broadcasts a performance of any dramatic or musical work, or any part of such a performance, without the consent in writing of the performers shall be guilty of an offence under this Act, and shall be liable on summary conviction to a fine not exceeding fifty pounds.*


*PART II NEW SECTIONS 3A AND 3B*
*Special defences*
*3A. Notwithstanding anything in the preceding provisions of this Act, it shall be a defence to any proceedings under this Act to prove—*

    (a)  *that the record, cinematograph film or broadcast to which the proceedings relate was made only for the purpose of reporting current events, or*

    (b)  *that the inclusion of the performance in question in the record, cinematograph film or broadcast to which the proceedings relate was only by way of background or was otherwise only incidental to the principal matters comprised or represented in the record, film or broadcast.*

*Consent on behalf of performers*
*3B. Where in any proceedings under this Act it is proved—*

    (a)  *that the record, cinematograph film or broadcast to which the proceedings relate was made with the consent in writing of a person who, at the time of giving the consent, represented that he was authorised by the performers to give it on their behalf, and,*

    (b)  *that the person making the record, film or broadcast had no reasonable grounds for believing that the person giving the consent was not so authorised,*

*the provisions of this Act shall apply as if it had been proved that the performers had themselves consented in writing to the making of the record, film or broadcast.*

*PART III   MINOR AND CONSEQUENTIAL AMENDMENTS*

| Provision amended | Amendment |
|---|---|
| Section one  .   .   .   . | *At the beginning of the section there shall be inserted the words 'Subject to the provisions of this Act'; and at the end of the section, for the words 'not made for purposes of trade' there shall be substituted the words 'made for his private and domestic use only'.* |
| Section three  .   . | *For the words 'records or' there shall be substituted the words 'records, cinematograph films'.* |
| Section four  .  .    .   . | *At the end of the definition of the expression 'record' there shall be inserted the words 'including the sound-track of a cinematograph film'; and at the end of the section there shall be inserted the following definitions—* |
| | *'The expression 'cinematograph film' means any print, negative, tape or other article on which a performance of a dramatic or musical work or part thereof is recorded for the purposes of visual reproduction, and any reference to the making of a cinematograph film is a reference to the carrying out of any process whereby such a performance or part thereof is so recorded;* |
| | *The expression 'broadcast' means broadcast by wireless telegraphy (within the meaning of the Wireless Telegraphy Act 1949) whether by way of sound broadcasting or of television'.* |

*General note*
Repealed by the Dramatic and Musical Performers' Protection Act 1958.

Section 50                               SEVENTH SCHEDULE

TRANSITIONAL PROVISIONS
PART I. PROVISIONS RELATING TO PART I OF THE ACT
*Conditions for subsistence of copyright*
1. In the application of sections two and three to works first published before the commencement of those sections, subsection (2) of section two, and subsection (3) of section three, shall apply as if paragraphs (b) and (c) of those subsections were omitted.

*Duration of copyright*
2. In relation to any photograph taken before the commencement of section three, subsection (4) of that section shall not apply, but, subject to subsection (3) of that section, copyright subsisting in the photograph by virtue of that section shall continue to subsist until the end of the period of fifty years from the end of the calendar year in which the photograph was taken, and shall then expire.

*Ownership of copyright*
3.—(1) Subsections (2) to (4) of section four shall not apply—

    (a)   to any work made as mentioned in subsection (2) or subsection (4) of that section, if the work was so made before the commencement of that section,

(b) to any work made as mentioned in subsection (3) of that section, if the work was or is so made in pursuance of a contract made before the commencement of that section.

(2) In relation to any work to which the preceding sub-paragraph applies, subsection (1) of section four shall have effect subject to the proviso set out in paragraph 1 of the Eighth Schedule to this Act (being the proviso to subsection (1) of section five of the Act of 1911).

*Infringements of copyright*

4. For the purposes of section five, the fact that, to a person's knowledge, the making of an article constituted an infringement of copyright under the Act of 1911, or would have constituted such an infringement if the article had been made in the place into which it is imported, shall have the like effect as if, to that person's knowledge, the making of the article had constituted an infringement of copyright under this Act.

5. Subsection (7) of section six does not apply to assignments made or licences granted before the commencement of that section.

6.—(1) References in section eight to records previously made by, or with the licence of, the owner of the copyright in a work include references to records previously made by, or with the consent of, the owner of the copyright in that work under the Act of 1911.

(2) The repeal by this Act of any provisions of section nineteen of the Act of 1911, or of the provisions of the Copyright Order Confirmation (Mechanical Instruments: Royalties) Act 1928, shall not affect the operation of those provisions, or of any regulations or order made thereunder, in relation to a record made before the repeal.

7.—(1) In relation to a painting, drawing, engraving, photograph or cinematograph film made before the commencement of section nine, subsection (6) of that section shall apply if, by virtue of subsection (3) or subsection (4) of that section, the making of the painting, drawing, engraving, photograph or film would not have constituted an infringement of copyright under this Act if this Act had been in operation at the time when it was made.

(2) In subsection (10) of section nine, the reference to construction by, or with the licence of, the owner of the copyright in any architectural drawings or plans includes a reference to construction by, or with the licence of, the person who, at the time of the construction, was the owner of the copyright in the drawings or plans under the Act of 1911, or under any enactment repealed by that Act.

8.—(1) Section ten and the First Schedule to this Act do not apply to artistic work made before the commencement of that section.

(2) Copyright shall not subsist by virtue of this Act in any artistic work made before the commencement of section ten which, at the time when the work was made, constituted a design capable of registration under the Registered Designs Act 1949, or under the enactments repealed by that Act, and was used, or intended to be used, as a model or pattern to be multiplied by any industrial process.

(3) The provisions set out in paragraph 2 of the Eighth Schedule to this Act (being the relevant provisions of the Copyright (Industrial Designs) Rules 1949) shall apply for the purposes of the last preceding sub-paragraph.

9.—(1) Where, before the repeal by this Act of section three of the Act of 1911, a person has, in the case of a work, given the notice requisite under the proviso set out in paragraph 3 of the Eighth Schedule to this Act (being the proviso to the said section three), then, as respects reproductions by that person of that work after the repeal of that section by this Act, that proviso shall have effect as if it had been re-enacted in this Act as a proviso to subsection (2) of section one:

Provided that the said proviso shall so have effect subject to the provisions set out in paragraphs 4 and 5 of the Eighth Schedule to this Act (being so much of subsection (1) of sections sixteen and seventeen respectively of the Act of 1911 as is applicable to the said proviso), as if those provisions had also been re-enacted in this Act.

(2) For the purposes of the operation of the said proviso in accordance with the preceding sub-paragraph, any regulations made by the Board of Trade thereunder before the repeal of section three of the Act of 1911 shall have effect as if they had been made under this Act, and the power of the Board of Trade to make further regulations thereunder shall apply as if the proviso had been re-enacted as mentioned in the preceding sub-paragraph.

*Works of joint authorship*

10.—(1) Notwithstanding anything in section eleven, or in the Third Schedule to this Act, copyright shall not subsist by virtue of Part I of this Act in any work of joint authorship first published before the commencement of section eleven, if the period of copyright had expired before the commencement of that section.

(2) In this paragraph 'the period of copyright' means whichever is the longer of the following periods, that is to say,—

    (a)   the life of the author who died first and a term of fifty years after his death, and

    (b)   the life of the author who died last.

## PART II. PROVISIONS RELATING TO PART II OF THE ACT

*Sound recordings*

11. In the case of a sound recording made before the commencement of section twelve, subsection (3) of that section shall apply with the substitution, for the period mentioned in that subsection, of the period of fifty years from the end of the calendar year in which the recording was made.

12. Subsection (6) of section twelve shall not apply to a sound recording made before the commencement of that section.

13. Notwithstanding anything in section twelve, copyright shall not subsist by virtue of that section in a sound recording made before the first day of July, nineteen hundred and twelve, unless, immediately before the commencement of that section, a corresponding copyright subsisted, in relation to that recording, by virtue of subsection (8) of section nineteen of the Act of 1911 (which relates to records made before the commencement of that Act).

*Cinematograph films*

14. Section thirteen shall not apply to cinematograph films made before the commencement of that section.

15. Where a cinematograph film made before the commencement of section thirteen was an original dramatic work within the definition of 'dramatic work' set out in paragraph 9 of the Eighth Schedule to this Act (being the definition thereof in the Act of 1911), the provisions of this Act, including the provisions of this Schedule other than this paragraph, shall have effect in relation to the film as if it had been an original dramatic work within the meaning of this Act; and the person who was the author of the work for the purposes of the Act of 1911 shall be taken to be the author thereof for the purposes of the said provisions as applied by this paragraph.

16. The provisions of this Act shall have effect in relation to photographs forming part of a cinematograph film made before the commencement of section thirteen as those provisions have effect in relation to photographs not forming part of a cinematograph film.

*Television broadcasts and sound broadcasts*

17. Copyright shall not subsist by virtue of section fourteen in any television broadcast or sound broadcast made before the commencement of that section.

18. For the purposes of subsection (3) of section fourteen, a previous television broadcast or sound broadcast shall be disregarded if it was made before the commencement of that section.

*Supplementary*

19. For the purposes of subsections (2) to (4) of section sixteen, the fact that, to a person's knowledge, the making of an article constituted an infringement of copyright under the Act of 1911, or would have constituted such an infringement if the article had been made in the place into which it is imported, shall have the like effect as if, to that person's knowledge, the making of the article had constituted an infringement of copyright under this Act.

## PART III. PROVISIONS RELATING TO PART III OF THE ACT

20. Nothing in section seventeen shall apply to any infringement of copyright under the Act of 1911, or shall affect any proceedings under that Act, whether begun before or after the commencement of that section.

21. Section eighteen shall not apply with respect to any article made, or, as the case may be, imported, before the commencement of that section; but, notwithstanding the repeal by this Act of section seven of the Act of 1911 (which contains provisions corresponding to subsection (1) of section eighteen), proceedings may (subject to the provisions of that Act) be brought or continued by virtue of the said section seven in respect of any article made or imported before the repeal, although the proceedings relate to the conversion or detention thereof after the repeal took effect.

22. Section nineteen shall not apply to any licence granted before the commencement of that section, and shall not affect any proceedings under the Act of 1991, whether begun before or after the commencement of that section.

23. For the purposes of section twenty-one the definition of 'infringing copy' in section eighteen shall apply as if any reference to copyright in that definition included a reference to copyright under the Act of 1911.

24. Where before the commencement of section twenty-two a notice had been given in respect of a work under section fourteen of the Act of 1911 (which contains provisions corresponding to section twenty-two), and that notice had not been withdrawn and had not otherwise ceased to have effect before

the commencement of section twenty-two, the notice shall have effect after the commencement of that section as if it had been duly given thereunder:

Provided that a notice shall not continue to have effect by virtue of this paragraph after the end of the period of six months beginning with the commencement of section twenty-two.

## PART IV. PROVISIONS RELATING TO PART IV OF THE ACT

25. The provisions of Part IV of this Act shall apply in relation to licence schemes made before the commencement of that Part as they apply in relation to licence schemes made thereafter, as if references in Part IV of this Act to copyright included references to copyright under the Act of 1911.

26. In section twenty-seven, references to a refusal or failure to grant or procure the grant of a licence, or to a proposal that a licence should be granted, do not include a refusal or failure which occurred, or a proposal made, before the commencement of that section.

## PART V. PROVISIONS RELATING TO PART V OF THE ACT

27. In section thirty-three, subsection (2) shall not apply to works made before the commencement of that section, and subsection (3) shall not apply to works first published before the commencement of that section.

## PART VI. PROVISIONS RELATING TO PART VI OF THE ACT

*Assignments, licences and bequests*

28.—(1) Where by virtue of any provision of this Act copyright subsists in a work, any document or event which—

(a) was made or occurred before the commencement of that provision, and

(b) had any operation affecting the title to copyright in the work under the Act of 1911, or would have had such an operation if the Act of 1911 had continued in force,

shall have the corresponding operation in relation to the copyright in the work under this Act;

Provided that, if the operation of any such document was or would have been limited to a period specified in the document, it shall not have any operation in relation to the copyright under this Act, except in so far as that period extends beyond the commencement of the provision of this Act by virtue of which copyright subsists in the work.

(2) For the purposes of the operation of a document in accordance with the preceding subparagraph,—

(a) expressions used in the document shall be construed in accordance with their effect immediately before the commencement of the provision in question, notwithstanding that a different meaning is assigned to them for the purposes of this Act; and

(b) subsection (1) of section thirty-seven shall not apply.

(3) Without prejudice to the generality of sub-paragraph (1) of this paragraph, the proviso set out in paragraph 6 of the Eighth Schedule to this Act (being the proviso to subsection (2) of section five of the Act of 1911) shall apply to assignments and licences having effect in relation to copyright under this Act in accordance with that sub-paragraph, as if that proviso had been re-enacted in this Act.

(4) In relation to copyright under this Act in a sound recording or in a cinematograph film, the preceding provisions of this paragraph shall apply subject to the following modifications, that is to say,—

(a) in the case of a sound recording, references to the copyright under the Act of 1911 shall be construed as references to the copyright under that Act in records embodying the recording, and

(b) in the case of a cinematograph film, references to the copyright under the Act of 1911 shall be construed as references to any copyright under that Act in the film (in so far as it constituted a dramatic work for the purposes of the Act of 1911) or in photographs forming part of the film.

(5) In this paragraph 'operation affecting the title', in relation to copyright under the Act of 1911, means any operation affecting the ownership of that copyright, or creating, transferring or terminating an interest, right or licence in respect of that copyright.

29.—(1) Section thirty-eight shall not apply to a bequest contained in the will, or a codicil to the will, of a testator who died before the commencement of that section.

(2) In the case of an author who died before the commencement of section thirty-eight, the provision set out in paragraph 7 of the Eighth Schedule to this Act (being subsection (2) of section seventeen of the Act of 1911) shall have effect as if it had been re-enacted in this Act.

*Appendix 1*

*Crown and Government departments*

30. Subsection (4) of section thirty-nine shall apply in relation to photographs taken before the commencement of that section as if the proviso to that subsection were omitted.

31.—(1) In the application of subsection (5) of section thirty-nine to a sound recording made before the commencement of that section, paragraph (b) of that subsection shall apply as if for the period mentioned in that paragraph there were substituted the period of fifty years from the end of the calendar year in which the recording was made.

(2) With respect to cinematograph films made before the commencement of section thirty-nine—

(a) subsection (5) of that section shall not apply, but

(b) in the case of a cinematograph film made as mentioned in that subsection, but before the commencement of section thirty-nine, if it was an original dramatic work as mentioned in paragraph 15 of this Schedule, the provisions of subsections (1) to (3) of section thirty-nine shall apply in accordance with that paragraph, and

(c) in relation to photographs forming part of such a cinematograph film the provisions of subsections (1), (2) and (4) of section thirty-nine (as modified by the last preceding paragraph) shall apply as they apply in relation to photographs not forming part of a cinematograph film.

*False attribution of authorship*

32.—(1) Paragraphs (b) and (c) of subsection (2) of section forty-three shall apply to any such act as is therein mentioned, if done after the commencement of that section, notwithstanding that the name in question was inserted or affixed before the commencement of that section.

(2) Subject to the preceding sub-paragraph, no act done before the commencement of section forty-three shall be actionable by virtue of that section.

(3) In this paragraph 'name' has the same meaning as in section forty-three.

*Other provisions*

33.—(1) In the application of subsection (2) of section forty-nine to a publication effected before the commencement of that section, the reference in paragraph (d) to thirty days shall be treated as a reference to fourteen days.

(2) For the purposes of the application of subsection (3) of section forty-nine to an act done before the commencement of a provision of this Act to which that subsection applies, references to copyright include references to copyright under the Act of 1911, and, in relation to copyright under that Act, references to the licence of the owner are references to the consent or acquiescence of the owner.

PART VII. WORKS MADE BEFORE 1ST JULY 1912

34.—(1) This Part of this Schedule applies to works made before the first day of July, nineteen hundred and twelve.

(2) In this Part of this Schedule, 'right conferred by the Act of 1911', in relation to a work, means such a substituted right as, by virtue of section twenty-four of the Act of 1911, was conferred in place of a right subsisting immediately before the commencement of that Act.

35. Notwithstanding anything in Part I of this Schedule, neither subsection (1) or subsection (2) of section two, nor subsection (2) or subsection (3) of section three, shall apply to a work to which this Part of this Schedule applies, unless a right conferred by the Act of 1911 subsisted in the work immediately before the commencement of section two or section three, as the case may be.

36.—(1) Where, in the case of a dramatic or musical work to which this Part of this Schedule applies, the right conferred by the Act of 1911 did not include the sole right to perform the work in public, then, in so far as copyright subsists in the work by virtue of this Act, the acts restricted by the copyright shall be treated as not including those specified in sub-paragraph (3) of this paragraph.

(2) Where, in the case of a dramatic or musical work to which this Part of this Schedule applies, the right conferred by the Act of 1911 consisted only of the sole right to perform the work in public, then, in so far as copyright subsists in the work by virtue of this Act, the acts restricted by the copyright shall be treated as consisting only of those specified in sub-paragraph (3) of this paragraph.

(3) The said acts are—

(a) performing the work or an adaptation thereof in public;

(b) broadcasting the work or an adaptation thereof;

(c) *causing the work or an adaptation thereof to be transmitted to subscribers to a diffusion service* **including the work or an adaption thereof in a cable programme**.

37. Where a work to which this Part of this Schedule applies consists of an essay, article or portion forming part of and first published in a review, magazine or other periodical or work of a like nature, and immediately before the commencement of section two a right of publishing the work in a separate

form subsisted by virtue of the provision set out in paragraph 8 of the Eighth Schedule to this Act (being the note appended to the First Schedule to the Act of 1911), that provision shall have effect, in relation to that work, as if it had been re-enacted in this Act with the substitution, for the word 'right' where it first occurs, of the word 'copyright'.

38.—(1) Without prejudice to the generality of sub-paragraph (1) of paragraph 28 of this Schedule, the provisions of this paragraph shall have effect where—

(a) the author of a work to which this Part of this Schedule applies had, before the commencement of the Act of 1911, made such an assignment or grant as is mentioned in paragraph (a) of the proviso to subsection (1) of section twenty-four of that Act (which relates to transactions whereby the author had assigned, or granted an interest in, the copyright or performing right in a work for the full term of that right under the law in force before the Act of 1911), and

(b) copyright subsists in the work by virtue of any provision of this Act.

(2) If, before the commencement of that provision of this Act, any event occurred, or notice was given, which in accordance with paragraph (a) of the said proviso had any operation affecting the ownership of the right conferred by the Act of 1911 in relation to the work, or creating, transferring or terminating an interest, right or licence in respect of that right, that event or notice shall have the corresponding operation in relation to the copyright in the work under this Act.

(3) Any right which, at a time after the commencement of that provision of this Act would, by virtue of paragraph (a) of the said proviso, have been exercisable in relation to the work, or to the right conferred by the Act of 1911, if this Act had not been passed, shall be exercisable in relation to the work or to the copyright therein under this Act, as the case may be.

(4) If, in accordance with paragraph (a) of the said proviso, the right conferred by the Act of 1911 would have reverted to the author or his personal representatives on the date referred to in that paragraph, and the said date falls after the commencement of the provision of this Act whereby copyright subsists in the work, then on that date—

(a) the copyright in the work under this Act shall revert to the author or his personal representatives, as the case may be, and

(b) any interest of any other person in that copyright which subsists on that date by virtue of any document made before the commencement of the Act of 1911 shall thereupon determine.

*General note*

As amended by the Cable and Broadcasting Act 1984. Italicized words repealed; words in bold type added.

## PART VIII. GENERAL AND SUPPLEMENTARY PROVISIONS

39.—(1) The provisions of this paragraph shall have effect for the construction of any reference in any provision of this Act—

(a) to countries to which that provision extends, or

(b) to qualified persons.

(2) Where, at any time after the commencement of any provisions of this Act, a provision which contains such a reference—

(a) has not yet been extended by virtue of section thirty-one to a country to which the Act of 1911 extended (or which, by virtue of that Act, was to be treated as a country to which it extended), and

(b) has not been applied in the case of that country by virtue of section thirty-two, then, with respect to any time before the provision is so extended or applied, the reference shall be construed as if the provision did extend to that country.

(3) For the purpose of determining whether copyright subsists in any work or other subject-matter at a time when a provision containing such a reference has been extended to a country other than the United Kingdom, the reference shall be construed, in relation to past events, as if that provision had always been in operation and had always extended to that country.

(4) In relation to photographs taken before the commencement of section three and to sound recordings made before the commencement of section twelve, the definition of 'qualified person' in subsection (5) of section one shall apply as if, in paragraph (b) of that subsection, for the words 'body

incorporated under the laws of' there were substituted the words 'body corporate which has established a place of business in'.

*40.—(1) The provisions of the two next following sub-paragraphs shall apply where—*

    *(a)   immediately before the date on which any provisions of the Act of 1911 (in this paragraph referred to as 'the repealed provisions') are repealed in the law of the United Kingdom by this Act, the repealed provisions have effect as applied by an Order in Council made in respect of a foreign country under section twenty-nine of the Act of 1911; and*

    *(b)   no Order in Council under section thirty-two of this Act, applying any provisions of this Act in the case of that country, is made so as to come into force on or before that date.*

*(2) The repealed provisions, as applied by the Order in Council under section twenty-nine of the Act of 1911 (or by that Order as varied by any subsequent Order thereunder), shall continue to have effect, notwithstanding the repeal, until the occurrence of whichever of the following events first occurs, that is to say—*

    *(a)   the revocation of the Order in Council under section twenty-nine of the Act of 1911;*

    *(b)   the coming into operation of an Order in Council under section thirty-two of this Act applying any of the provisions of this Act in the case of the foreign country in question;*

    *(c)   the expiration of the period of two years beginning with the date mentioned in the preceding sub-paragraph.*

*(3) For the purposes of continuing, varying or terminating the operation of the repealed provisions in accordance with the last preceding sub-paragraph, and for the purposes of any proceedings arising out of the operation of those provisions in accordance with that sub-paragraph, all the provisions of the Act of 1911 (including the power to revoke or vary Orders in Council under section twenty-nine of that Act) shall be treated as continuing in force as if none of those provisions had been repealed by this Act.*

*(4) In relation to a country in respect of which an Order in Council has been made under subsection (3) of section twenty-six of the Act of 1911 (which relates to countries therein referred to as self-governing dominions to which that Act does not extend), the preceding provisions of this paragraph shall apply as they apply in relation to a foreign country, with the substitution, for references to section twenty-nine of the Act of 1911, of references to the said subsection (3).*

*General note*
Paragraph 40 repealed by Statute Law (Repeals) Act 1986.

41.  In so far as the Act of 1911 or any Order in Council made thereunder forms part of the law of any country other than the United Kingdom, at a time after that Act has been wholly or partly repealed in the law of the United Kingdom, it shall, so long as it forms part of the law of that country, be construed and have effect as if that Act had not been so repealed.

42.  The mention of any particular matter in the preceding provisions of this Schedule with regard to the repeal of any of the provisions of the Act of 1911 shall not affect the general application to this Act of section thirty-eight of the Interpretation Act 1889 (which relates to the effect of repeals), either in relation to the Act of 1911 or to any other enactment repealed by this Act.

43.  For the purposes of the application, by virtue of any of the preceding paragraphs of this Schedule, of any of the provisions set out in the Eighth Schedule to this Act,—

    (a)   the expressions of which definitions are set out in paragraph 9 of that Schedule (being the definitions of those expressions in the Act of 1911) shall, notwithstanding anything in this Act, be construed in accordance with those definitions; and

    (b)   where, for those purposes, any of those provisions is to be treated as if re-enacted in this Act, it shall be treated as if it had been so re-enacted with the substitution, for the words 'this Act', wherever the reference is to the passing or the commencement of the Act of 1911, of the words 'the Copyright Act 1911'.

44.  Without prejudice to the operation of any of the preceding provisions of this Schedule—

    (a)   any enactment or other document referring to an enactment repealed by this Act shall be construed as referring (or as including a reference) to the corresponding enactment of this Act;

    (b)   any enactment or other document referring to copyright, or to works in which copyright subsists, if apart from this Act it would be construed as referring to copyright under the Act of 1911, or to works in which copyright subsists under that Act, shall be construed as referring (or as including a reference) to copyright under this Act, or, as the case may be, to works or any other subject-matter in which copyright subsists under this Act;

(c) any reference in an enactment or other document to the grant of an interest in copyright by licence shall be construed, in relation to copyright under this Act, as a reference to the grant of a licence in respect of that copyright.

45.—(1) Except in so far as it is otherwise expressly provided in this Schedule, the provisions of this Act apply in relation to things existing at the commencement of those provisions as they apply in relation to things coming into existence thereafter.

(2) For the purposes of any reference in this Schedule to works, sound recordings or cinematograph films made before the commencement of the provision of this Act, a work, recording or film, the making of which extended over a period, shall not be taken to have been so made unless the making of it was completed before the commencement of that provision.

46.—(1) Any reference in this Schedule to a numbered section shall, unless the reference is to a section of a specified Act, be construed as a reference to the section bearing that number in this Act.

(2) Any reference in this Schedule to the commencement of a provision of this Act is a reference to the date on which that provision comes into operation as part of the law of the United Kingdom.

47.—(1) In this Schedule 'photograph' has the meaning assigned to it in the definition set out in paragraph 9 of the Eighth Schedule to this Act, and not the meaning assigned to it by section forty-eight.

(2) In this Schedule 'the Act of 1911' means the Copyright Act 1911.

Section 50                 EIGHTH SCHEDULE

PROVISIONS OF COPYRIGHT ACT 1911 AND RULES REFERRED TO IN SEVENTH SCHEDULE

1. *proviso to s. 5(1) of the Copyright Act 1911 (referred to in paragraph 3 of Seventh Schedule)*—
Provided that—

(a) where, in the case of an engraving, photograph, or portrait, the plate or other original was ordered by some other person and was made for valuable consideration in pursuance of that order, then, in the absence of any agreement to the contrary, the person by whom such plate or other original was ordered shall be the first owner of the copyright; and

(b) where the author was in the employment of some other person under a contract of service or apprenticeship and the work was made in the course of his employment by that person, the person by whom the author was employed shall, in the absence of any agreement to the contrary, be the first owner of the copyright, but where the work is an article or other contribution to a newspaper, magazine, or similar periodical, there shall, in the absence of any agreement to the contrary, be deemed to be reserved to the author a right to restrain the publication of the work, otherwise than as part of a newspaper, magazine, or similar periodical.

2. *Rule 2 of the Copyright (Industrial Designs) Rules 1949 (referred to in paragraph 8 of Seventh Schedule)*—
A design shall be deemed to be used as a model or pattern to be multiplied by any industrial process—

(a) when the design is reproduced or is intended to be reproduced on more than 50 single articles, unless all the articles in which the design is reproduced or is intended to be reproduced together form only a single set of articles as defined in subsection (1) of section 44 of the Registered Designs Act 1949, or

(b) when the design is to be applied to—

    (i) printed paper hangings,

    (ii) carpets, floor cloths or oil cloths, manufactured or sold in lengths or pieces,

    (iii) textile piece goods, or textile goods manufactured or sold in lengths or pieces, or

    (iv) lace, not made by hand.

3. *Proviso to s 3 of the Copyright Act 1911 (referred to in paragraph 9 of Seventh Schedule)*—
Provided that at any time after the expiration of twenty-five years, or in the case of a work in which copyright subsists at the passing of this Act thirty years, from the death of the author of a published work, copyright in the work shall not be deemed to be infringed by the reproduction of the work for sale if the person reproducing the work proves that he has given the prescribed notice in writing of his intention to reproduce the work, and that he has paid in the prescribed manner to, or for the benefit of, the owner of the copyright royalties in respect of all copies of the work sold by him calculated at the

rate of ten per cent on the price at which he publishes the work; and, for the purposes of this proviso, the Board of Trade may make regulations prescribing the mode in which notices are to be given, and the particulars to be given in such notices, and the mode, time, and frequency of the payment of royalties, including (if they think fit) regulations requiring payment in advance or otherwise securing the payment of royalties.

4. *S 16 (1) of the Copyright Act 1991 (referred to in paragraph 9 of Seventh Schedule)*—

In the case of a work of joint authorship . . . references in this Act to the period after the expiration of any specified number of years from the death of the author shall be construed as references to the period after the expiration of the like number of years from the death of the author who dies first or after the death of the author who dies last, whichever period may be the shorter . . .

5. *S 17 (1) of Copyright Act 1911 (referred to in paragraph 9 of Seventh Schedule)*—

In the case of a literary, dramatic or musical work, or an engraving, in which copyright subsists at the date of the death of the author or, in the case of a work of joint authorship, at or immediately before the date of the death of the author who dies last, but which has not been published, nor, in the case of a dramatic or musical work, been performed in public, nor, in the case of a lecture, been delivered in public before that date, . . . the proviso to section three of this Act shall . . . apply as if the author had died at the date of such publication or performance or delivery in public as aforesaid.

6. *Proviso to s 5 (2) of the Copyright Act 1911 (referred to in paragraph 28 of Seventh Schedule)*—

Provided that, where the author of a work is the first owner of the copyright therein, no assignment of the copyright, and no grant of any interest therein, made by him (otherwise than by will) after the passing of this Act, shall be operative to vest in the assignee or grantee any rights with respect to the copyright in the work beyond the expiration of twenty-five years from the death of the author, and the reversionary interest in the copyright expectant on the termination of that period shall, on the death of the author, notwithstanding any agreement to the contrary, devolve on his legal personal representatives as part of his estate, and any agreement entered into by him as to the disposition of such reversionary interest shall be null and void, but nothing in this proviso shall be construed as applying to the assignment of the copyright in a collective work or a licence to publish a work or part of a work as part of a collective work.

7. *S 17 (2) of the Copyright Act 1911 (referred to in paragraph 29 of Seventh Schedule)*—

The ownership of an author's manuscript after his death, where such ownership has been acquired under a testamentary disposition made by the author and the manuscript is of a work which has not been published nor performed in public nor delivered in public, shall be prima facie proof of the copyright being with the owner of the manuscript.

8. *Note to First Schedule to the Copyright Act 1911 (referred to in paragraph 37 of Seventh Schedule)*—

In the case of an essay, article, or portion forming part of and first published in a review, magazine, or other periodical or work of a like nature, the right shall be subject to any right of publishing the essay, article, or portion in a separate form to which the author is entitled at the commencement of this Act, or would, if this Act had not been passed, have become entitled under section eighteen of the Copyright Act 1842.

9. *Definitions in s. 35 (1) of the Copyright Act 1911 (referred to in paragraphs 15, 43 and 47 of Seventh Schedule)*:—

> 'literary work' includes maps, charts, plans, tables, and compilations;
> 'dramatic work' includes any piece for recitation, choreographic work or entertainment in dumb show the scenic arrangement or acting form of which is fixed in writing or otherwise, and any cinematograph production where the arrangement or acting form or the combination of incidents represented give the work an original character;
> 'performance' means any acoustic representation of a work and any visual representation of any dramatic action in a work, including such a representation made by means of any mechanical instrument;
> 'photograph' includes photo-lithograph and any work produced by any process analogous to photography;
> 'collective work' means—
>
> (a)  any encyclopaedia, dictionary, year book, or similar work;
> (b)  a newspaper, review, magazine, or similar periodical; and
> (c)   any work written in distinct parts by different authors, or in which works or parts of works of different authors are incorporated;
>
> 'delivery' in relation to a lecture, includes delivery by means of any mechanical instrument;
> 'lecture' includes address, speech and sermon.

*Note*—In this Schedule 'this Act' means the Copyright Act 1911.

Section 50                                    NINTH SCHEDULE

ENACTMENTS REPEALED

| Session and Chapter | Short Title | Extent of Repeal |
|---|---|---|
| 25 & 26 Vict c 68 | The Fine Arts Copyright Act 1862 | The whole Act. |
| 2 Edw 7 c 15 | The Musical (Summary Proceedings) Copyright Act 1902 | The whole Act. |
| 6 Edw 7 c 36 | The Musical Copyright Act 1906 | The whole Act. |
| 1 & 2 Geo 5 c 46 | The Copyright Act 1911 | The whole Act, except sections fifteen, thirty-four and thirty seven thereof. |
| 18 & 19 Geo 5 c lii | The Copyright Order Confirmation (Mechanical Instruments: Royalties) Act 1928 | Thr whole Act. |
| 11 & 12 Geo 6 c 7 | The Ceylon Independence Act 1947 | Paragraph 10 of the Second Schedule. |

*General note*
Repealed by the Statute Law (Repeals) Act 1974.


COPYRIGHT (COMPUTER SOFTWARE) AMENDMENT ACT 1985
(1985 c 41)
*An Act to amend the Copyright Act 1956 in its application to computer programs and computer storage*                                    [16 July 1985]

*General note*
Repealed by the Copyright, Designs and Patents Act 1988, Sch 8, subject to savings in relation to the continued operation of parts of the Copyright Act 1956.

## 1. Copyright in computer programs
(1) The Copyright Act 1956 shall apply in relation to a computer program (including one made before the commencement of this Act) as it applies in relation to a literary work and shall so apply whether or not copyright would subsist in that program apart from this Act.

(2) For the purposes of the application of the said Act of 1956 in relation to a computer program, a version of the program in which it is converted into or out of a computer language or code, or into a different computer language or code, is an adaptation of the program.

## 2. Computer storage
References in the Copyright Act 1956 to the reduction of any work to a material form, or to the reproduction of any work in a material form, or to the reproduction of any work in a material form, shall include references to the storage of that work in a computer.

## 3. Offences and search warrants
Where an infringing copy of a computer program consists of a disc, tape or chip or of any other device which embodies signals serving for the impartation of the program or part of it, sections 21 to 21B of the Copyright Act 1956 (offences and

search warrants) shall apply in relation to that copy as they apply in relation to an infringing copy of a sound recording or cinematograph film.

### 4. Short title, interpretation, commencement and extent
(1)  This Act may be cited as the Copyright (Computer Software) Amendment Act 1985.

(2)  This Act shall be construed as one with the Copyright Act 1956 and Part V of that Act (extension and restriction of operation of Act) shall apply in relation to the provisions of this Act as it applies in relation to the provisions of that Act.

(3)  This Act shall come into force at the end of the period of two months beginning with the day on which it is passed.

(4)  Nothing in this Act shall affect—

    (a)  the determination of any question as to whether anything done before the commencement of this Act was an infringement of copyright or an offence under section 21 of the said Act of 1956; or

    (b)  the penalty which may be imposed for any offence under that section committed before the commencement of this Act.

(5)  This Act extends to Northern Ireland.

# DRAMATIC AND MUSICAL PERFORMERS' PROTECTION ACT 1958
(6 & 7 Eliz 2 c 44)

*General note*
This Act was repealed by the Copyright, Designs and Patents Act 1988. Printed as amended by the Performers Protection Act 1963, the Performers Protection Act 1972, Magistrates' Court Act 1980, Criminal Justice Act 1982, Cable and Broadcasting Act 1984.

## Arrangement of sections

*An Act to consolidate the Dramatic and Musical Performers' Protection Act 1925, and the provisions of the Copyright Act 1956, amending it.*

[23 July 1958]

## 1. Penalisation of making, &c, records without consent of performers
Subject to the provisions of this Act, if a person knowingly—

    (a) makes a record, directly or indirectly from or by means of the performance of a dramatic or musical work without the consent in writing of the performers, or

    (b) sells or lets for hire, or distributes for the purposes of trade, or by way of trade exposes or offers for sale or hire, a record made in contravention of this Act, or

    (c) uses for the purposes of a public performance a record so made,

he shall be guilty of an offence under this Act, and shall be liable, on summary conviction, to a fine not exceeding *forty shillings for each record in respect of which an offence is proved,* **the prescribed sum** *but not exceeding fifty pounds in respect of any one transaction;* **or, on conviction on indictment, to imprisonment for a term, not exceeding two years, or to a fine, or to both:**

Provided that, where a person is charged with an offence under paragraph (a) of this section, it shall be a defence to prove that the record was made for his private and domestic use only.

*General note*
First italicised words repealed, and first words in bold type, added, by the Magistrates' Court Act 1980; second italicised words repealed, and second words in bold added, by the Performers' Protection Act 1972.

## 2. Penalisation of making, &c, cinematograph films without consent of performers
Subject to the provisions of this Act, if a person knowingly—

    (a) makes a cinematograph film, directly or indirectly, from or by means of the performance of a dramatic or musical work without the consent in writing of the performers, or

    (b)  sells or lets for hire, or distributes for the purposes of trade, or by way of trade exposes or offers for sale or hire, a cinematograph film made in contravention of this Act, or

    (c)  uses for the purposes of exhibition to the public a cinematograph film so made;

he shall be guilty of an offence under this Act, and shall be liable, on summary conviction, to a fine not exceeding *fifty pounds* **level 5 on the standard scale**:

Provided that, where a person is charged with an offence under paragraph (a) of this section, it shall be a defence to prove that the cinematograph film was made for his private and domestic use only.

*General note*
As amended by the Criminal Justice Act 1982. Italicised words repealed; words in bold type added.

### 3. Penalisation of broadcasting without consent of performers

Subject to the provisions of this Act, a person who, otherwise than by the use of a record or cinematograph film, knowingly broadcasts a performance of a dramatic or musical work, or any part of such a performance, without the consent in writing of the performers, shall be guilty of an offence under this Act, and shall be liable, on summary conviction, to a fine not exceeding *fifty pounds* **level 5 on the standard scale**.

*General note*
As amended by the Criminal Justice Act 1982. Italicised words repealed; words in bold type added.

### 4. Penalisation of making or having plates, &c, for making records in contravention of Act

If a person makes, or has in his possession, a plate or similar contrivance for the purpose of making records in contravention of this Act, he shall be guilty of an offence under this Act, and shall be liable, on summary conviction, to a fine not exceeding *fifty pounds* **level 5 on the standard scale** for each plate or similar contrivance in respect of which an offence is proved.

*General note*
As amended by the Criminal Justice Act 1982. Italicised words repealed; words in bold type added.

### 5. Power of court to order destruction of records, &c, contravening Act

The court before which any proceedings are taken under this Act may, on conviction of the offender, order that all records, cinematograph films, plates or similar contrivances in the possession of the offender which appear to the court to have been made in contravention of this Act, or to be adapted for the making of records in contravention of this Act, and in respect of which the offender has been convicted, be destroyed, or otherwise dealt with as the court may think fit.

*General note*
As amended by the Criminal Justice Act 1982. Italicised words repealed; words in bold type added.

### 6. Special defences

Notwithstanding anything in the preceding provisions of this Act, it shall be a defence to any proceedings under this Act to prove—

    (a)  that the record, cinematograph film *or broadcast* **broadcast or [cable**

**programme]** to which the proceedings relate was made **or included** only for the purpose of reporting current events, or

(b) that the inclusion of the performance in question in the record, cinematograph film *or broadcast* **broadcast or [cable programme]** to which the proceedings relate was only by way of background or was otherwise only incidental to the principal matters comprised or represented in the record, film *or broadcast* **broadcast or [cable programme]**.

*General note*
The words in italics were repealed and the words 'broadcast or' were added by the Performers' Protection Act 1963. The words 'cable programme' and 'or included' were added by the Cable and Broadcasting Act 1984.

## 7. Consent on behalf of performers

Where in any proceedings under this Act it is proved—

(a) that the record, cinematograph film *or broadcast* **broadcast or [cable programme]** to which the proceedings relate was made **or included** with the consent in writing of a person who, at the time of giving the consent, represented that he was authorised by the performers to give it on their behalf, and

(b) that the person making **or including** the record, film *or broadcast* **broadcast or [cable programme]** had no reasonable grounds for believing that the person giving the consent was not so authorised,

the provisions of this Act shall apply as if it had been proved that the performers had themselves consented in writing to the making **or including** of the record, film *or broadcast* **broadcast or [cable programme]**.

*General note*
The words in italics were repealed and the words 'broadcast or' were added by the Performers' Protection Act 1963. The words 'cable programme' and 'or included' were added by the Cable and Broadcasting Act 1984.

## 8. Interpretation

(1) In this Act, unless the context otherwise requires, the following expressions have the meanings hereby respectively assigned to them, that is to say,—

'broadcast' means broadcast by wireless telegraphy (within the meaning of the Wireless Telegraphy Act 1949), whether by way of sound broadcasting or of television;

'cable programme' means a programme included in a cable programme service, and references to the inclusion of a cable programme shall be construed accordingly:

'cinematograph film' means any print, negative, tape or other article on which a performance of a dramatic or musical work or part thereof is recorded for the purposes of visual reproduction;

'performance of a dramatic or musical work' includes any performance, mechanical or otherwise, of any such work, being a performance rendered or intended to be rendered audible by mechanical or electrical means;

'performers', in the case of a mechanical performance, means the persons whose performance is mechanically reproduced;

'programme' in relation to a cable programme service, includes any item included in that service;

'record' means any record or similar contrivance for reproducing sound, including the sound-track of a cinematograph film.

(2) Any reference in this Act to the making of a cinematograph film is a reference to the carrying out of any process whereby a performance of a dramatic or musical work or part thereof is recorded for the purposes of visual reproduction.

(3) Section 48(3) of the Copyright Act 1956 (which explains the meaning of references in that Act to the inclusion of a programme in a cable programme service) shall apply for the purposes of this Act as it applies for the purposes of that Act.

*General note*
Words added by the Cable and Broadcasting Act 1984.

## 9. Short title, extent, repeal and commencement

(1) This Act may be cited as the Dramatic and Musical Performers' Protection Act 1958.

(2) It is hereby declared that this Act extends to Northern Ireland.

(3) The Dramatic and Musical Performers' Protection Act 1925, and section forty-five of, and the Sixth Schedule to, the Copyright Act 1956, are hereby repealed.

(4) This Act shall come into operation at the expiration of a period of one month beginning with the date of its passing.

## PERFORMERS' PROTECTION ACT 1963
(1963 c 53)

*General note*
This Act was repealed by the Copyright, Designs and Patents Act 1988. Printed as amended by the Performers Protection Act 1972, the Criminal Justice Act 1982 and the Cable and Broadcasting Act 1984.

## Arrangement of sections

*An Act to amend the law relating to the protection of performers so as to enable effect to be given to a Convention entered into at Rome on 26 October 1961*
[31 July 1963]

Whereas, with a view to the ratification by Her Majesty of the International Convention for the Protection of Performers, Producers of Phonograms and Broadcasting Organisations entered into at Rome on 26 October 1961, it is expedient to amend and supplement the Dramatic and Musical Performers' Protection Act 1958 (in this Act referred to as 'the principal Act'):

## 1. Performances to which principal Act applies

(1) The principal Act shall have effect as if for references therein to the performance of a dramatic or musical work there were substituted references to the performance of any actors, singers, musicians, dancers or other persons who act, sing, deliver, declaim, play in or otherwise perform literary, dramatic, musical or artistic works, and the definition contained in section 8(1) of that Act of the expression 'performance of a dramatic or musical work' (by which that expression is made to include a performance rendered or intended to be rendered audible by mechanical or electrical means) shall be construed accordingly.

(2) For the avoidance of doubt it is hereby declared that the principal Act applies as respects anything done in relation to a performance notwithstanding that the performance took place out of the United Kingdom, but this shall not cause anything done out of the United Kingdom to be treated as an offence.

## 2. Sales etc of records made abroad

For the purposes of paragraphs (b) and (c) of section 1 of the principal Act (by which sales of, and other dealings with, records made in contravention of the Act are rendered punishable), a record made in a country outside the United Kingdom directly or indirectly from or by means of a performance to which the principal Act applies shall, where the civil or criminal law of that country contains a provision for the protection of performers under which the consent of any person to the making of the record was required, be deemed to have been made in contravention of the principal Act if, whether knowingly or not, it was made without the consent so required and without the consent in writing of the performers.

## 3. Relaying of performances

(1) A person who, otherwise than by the use of a record or cinematograph film or the reception **and immediate re-transmission** of a broadcast, knowingly *causes a performance to which the principal Act applies, or any part of such a performance, to be transmitted without the consent in writing of the performers—*

    (a) *to subscribers to a diffusion service; or*

    (b) *over wires or other paths provided by a material substance so as to be seen or heard in public,* **includes a performance to which the principal Act applies, or any part of such performance, in a cable programme without the consent in writing of the performers,**

shall be guilty of an offence, and shall be liable, on summary conviction, to a fine not exceeding *fifty pounds* **level 5 on the standard scale**.

(2) *Section 48 (3) of the Copyright Act 1956 (which explains the meaning of references in that Act to the transmission of a work or other subject-matter to subscribers to a diffusion service) shall apply for the purposes of the preceding subsection as it applies for the purposes of that Act.*

(3) Section 6 of the principal Act (which provides for special defences) shall have effect as if the preceding subsections were inserted immediately before that section, and that section and section 7 of the principal Act (which provides for the giving of consent on behalf of performers) shall have effect as if for the words 'or broadcast' in each place where they occur there were substituted the words 'broadcast or transmission'.

*General note*
The words 'fifty pounds' in italics were repealed and the words 'level 5 an the standard scale' in bold

type were added, by the Criminal Justice Act 1982. The remaining repeals (in italics) and additions (in bold type) were made by the Cable and Broadcasting Act 1984.

## 4. Giving of consent without authority
(1) Where—

    (a) a record, cinematograph film, *broadcast or transmission is made* **or broadcast is made or a cable programme is included** with the consent in writing of a person who, at the time of giving the consent, represented that he was authorised by the performers to give it on their behalf when to his knowledge he was not so authorised, and

    (b) if proceedings were brought against the person to whom the consent was given, the consent would by virtue of section 7 of the principal Act afford a defence to those proceedings,

the person giving the consent shall be guilty of an offence, and shall be liable on summary conviction, to a fine not exceeding *fifty pounds* **level 5 on the standard scale**.

(2) The said section 7 shall not apply to proceedings under this section.

*General note*
The first words in italics were repealed and the first words in bold type, were added by the Cable and Broadcasting Act 1984. The second words in italics were repealed and the second words in bold type were added by the Criminal Justice Act 1982.

*General note*
Inserted by the Performers' Protection Act 1972.

## 4A  Offences by bodies corporate
**Where an offence under the principal Act or this Act committed by a body corporate is proved to have been committed with the consent or connivance of, or to be attributable to any neglect on the part of, any director, manager, secretary or other similar officer of the body corporate or any person who was purporting to act in any such capacity, he, as well as the body corporate, shall be guilty of that offence and shall be liable to be proceeded against and punished accordingly.**

*General note*
Inserted by the Performers' Protection Act 1972.

## 5. Citation, construction, commencement and extent
(1) This Act may be cited as the Performers' Protection Act 1963, and the principal Act and this Act may be cited together as the Performers' Protection Acts 1958 and 1963.

(2) This Act shall be construed as one with the principal Act.

(3) This Act shall come into operation at the expiration of the period of one month beginning with the date of its passing, and shall apply only in relation to performances taking place after its commencement.

(4) It is hereby declared that this Act extends to Northern Ireland.

PERFORMERS' PROTECTION ACT 1972
(1972 c 32)

*General note*
This Act was repealed by the Copyright, Designs and Patents Act 1988.

**Arrangement of sections**

*An Act to amend the Performers' Protection Acts 1958 and 1963.*
[29 June 1972]

**1. Increase of fines under Performers' Protection Acts 1958 and 1963**
The enactments specified in column 1 of the Schedule to this Act (being enactments creating the offences under the Performers' Protection Acts 1958 and 1963 broadly described in column 2 of that Schedule) shall each have effect as if the maximum fine which may be imposed on summary conviction of any offence specified in that enactment were a fine not exceeding the amount specified in column 4 of that Schedule instead of a fine not exceeding the amount specified in column 3 of that Schedule.

**2. Amendment of section 1 of Dramatic and Musical Performers' Protection Act 1958**
Section 1 of the Dramatic and Musical Performers' Protection Act 1958 (by which the making of records without the consent of the performers and sales of, and other dealings with, such records are rendered punishable) shall have effect as if after the word 'transaction' there were inserted the words 'or, on conviction on indictment, to imprisonment for a term not exceeding two years, or to a fine, or to both'.

**3. Amendment of Performers' Protection Act 1963**
In the Performers' Protection Act 1963 there shall be inserted after section 4 the following section:—

    **'4A. Offences by bodies corporate**
    Where an offence under the principal Act or this Act committed by a body corporate is proved to have been committed with the consent or connivance of, or to be attributable to any neglect on the part of, any director, manager, secretary or other similar officer of the body corporate or any person who was purporting to act in any such capacity, he, as well as the body corporate, shall be guilty of that offence and shall be liable to be proceeded against and punished accordingly.'

**4. Citation, construction, commencement and extent**
(1) This Act may be cited as the Performers' Protection Act 1972, and the

Performers' Protection Acts 1958 and 1963 and this Act may be cited together as the Performers' Protection Acts 1958 to 1972.

(2) This Act shall come into operation at the expiration of the period of one month beginning with the date of its passing, but nothing in this Act shall affect the punishment for an offence committed before the commencement of this Act.

(3) It is hereby declared that this Act extends to Northern Ireland.

## SCHEDULE

Section 1

INCREASE OF FINES

| (1)<br>Enactment | (2)<br>Description<br>of Offence | (3)<br>Old<br>Maximum Fine | (4)<br>New<br>Maximum Fine |
|---|---|---|---|
| The Dramatic and Musical Performers' Protection Act 1958— | | | |
| Section 1 | Making, etc, records without consent of performers. | £2 for each record in respect of which an offence is proved subject to a limit of £50 in respect of any one transaction. | £20 for each record in respect of which an offence is proved subject to a limit of £400 in respect of any one transaction. |
| Section 2 | Making, etc, cinematograph films without consent of performers. | £50 | £400 |
| Section 3 | Broadcasting without consent of performers. | £50 | £400 |
| Section 4 | Making or having plates, etc, for making records in contravention of Act | £50 | £400 |
| The Performers' Protection Act 1963— | | | |
| Section 3(1) | Relaying performances without consent of performers. | £50 | £400 |
| Section 4(1) | Giving consent without authority. | £50 | £400 |

## BROADCASTING ACT 1990
(1990 c 42)

PART IX
COPYRIGHT AND RELATED MATTERS

### 176. Duty to provide advance information about programmes
(1) A person providing a programme service to which this section applies must make available in accordance with this section information relating to the programmes to be included in the service to any person (referred to in this section and Schedule 17 to this Act as 'the publisher') wishing to publish in the United Kingdom any such information.

(2) The duty imposed by subsection (1) is to make available information as to the titles of the programmes which are to be, or may be, included in the service on any date,and the time of their inclusion, to any publisher who has asked the person providing the programme service to make such information available to him and reasonably requires it.

(3) Information to be made available to a publisher under this section is to be made available as soon after it has been prepared as is reasonably practicable but, in any event—

(a) not later than when it is made available to any other publisher, and
(b) in the case of information in respect of all the programmes to be included in the service in any period of seven days, not later than the beginning of the preceding period of fourteen days, or such other number of days as may be prescribed by the Secretary of State by order.

(4) An order under subsection (3) shall be subject to annulment in pursuance of a resolution of either House of Parliament.

(5) The duty imposed by subsection (1) is not satisfied by providing the information on terms, other than terms as to copyright, prohibiting or restricting publication in the United Kingdom by the publisher.

(6) Schedule 17 applies to any information or future information which the person providing a programme service to which this section applies is or may be required to make available under this section.

(7) For the purposes of this section and that Schedule, the following table shows the programme services to which the section and Schedule apply and the persons who provide them or are to be treated as providing them.

| **Programme service** | **Provider of service** |
| --- | --- |
| *Services other than services under the Act* | |
| Television and national radio services provided by the BBC for reception in the United Kingdom | The BBC |
| *Services under the Act* | |
| Television programme services subject to regulation by the Independent Television Commission | The person licensed to provide the service |
| The television broadcasting service provided by the Welsh Authority | The Authority |
| Any national service (see section 84(2)(a)(i)) subject to regulation by the Radio Authority | The person licensed to provide the service |
| *Services provided during interim period only* | |
| Television broadcasting services provided by the Independent Television Commission in accordance with Schedule 11, other than Channel 4 | The programme contractor |
| Channel 4, as so provided | The body corporate referred to in section 12(2) of the Broadcasting Act 1981 |

(8) This section does not require any information to be given about any advertisement.

## SCHEDULE 17

**Information About Programmes: Copyright**
Section 176

## PART I
## COPYRIGHT LICENSING

**1.**—(1) This paragraph applies where the person providing a programme service has assigned to another the copyright in works containing information to which this Schedule applies.

(2) The person providing the programme service, not the assignee, is to be treated as the owner of the copyright for the purposes of licensing any act restricted by the copyright done on or after the day on which this paragraph comes into force.

(3) Where the assignment by the person providing the programme service occurred before 29th September 1989 then, in relation to any act restricted by the copyright so assigned—

> (a) sub-paragraph (2) does not have effect, and
> (b) references below in this Schedule to the person providing the programme service are to the assignee.

## PART II
## USE OF INFORMATION AS OF RIGHT

*Circumstances in which right available*

**2.**—(1) Paragraph 4 applies to any act restricted by the copyright in works containing information to which this Schedule applies done by the publisher if—

> (a) a licence to do the act could be granted by the person providing the programme service but no such licence is held by the publisher,
> (b) the person providing the programme service refuses to grant to the publisher a licence to do the act, being a licence of such duration, and of which the terms as to payment for doing the act are such, as would be acceptable to the publisher, and
> (c) the publisher has complied with paragraph 3.

(2) The reference in sub-paragraph (1) to refusing to grant a licence includes failing to do so within a reasonable time of being asked.

(3) References below in this Schedule to the terms of payment are to the terms as to payment for doing any act restricted by the copyright in works containing information to which this Schedule applies.

*Notice of intention to exercise right*

**3.**—(1) A publisher intending to avail himself of the right conferred by paragraph 4 must—

> (a) give notice of his intention to the person providing the programme service, asking that person to propose terms of payment, and
> (b) after receiving the proposal or the expiry of a reasonable time, give reasonable notice to the person providing the programme service of the date on which he proposes to begin exercising the right and the terms of payment in accordance with which he intends to do so.

(2) Before exercising the right the publisher must—

> (a) give reasonable notice to the Copyright Tribunal of his intention to exercise the right and of the date on which he proposes to begin to do so, and
> (b) apply to the Tribunal under paragraph 5 to settle the terms of payment.

*Conditions for exercise of right*

**4.**—(1) Where the publisher, on or after the date specified in a notice under paragraph 3(1)(b), does any act in circumstances in which this paragraph applies, he shall, if he makes the payments required by this paragraph, be in the same position as regards infringement of copyright as if he had at all material times been the holder of a licence to do so granted by the person providing the programme service.

(2) Payments are to be made at not less than quarterly intervals in arrears.

(3) The amount of any payment is that determined in accordance with any order of the Copyright Tribunal under paragraph 5 or, if no such order has been made—

(a) in accordance with any proposal for terms of payment made by the person providing the programme service pursuant to a request under paragraph 3(1)(a), or

(b) where no proposal has been so made or the amount determined in accordance with the proposal so made appears to the publisher to be unreasonably high, in accordance with the terms of payment notified under paragraph 3(1)(b).

### Applications to settle payments

**5.**—(1) On an application to settle the terms of payment, the Copyright Tribunal shall consider the matter and make such order as it may determine to be reasonable in the circumstances.

(2) An order under sub-paragraph (1) has effect from the date the applicant begins to exercise the right conferred by paragraph 4 and any necessary repayments, or further payments, shall be made in respect of amounts that have fallen due.

### Application for review of order

**6.**—(1) A person exercising the right conferring by paragraph 4, or the person providing the programme service, may apply to the Tribunal to review any order under paragraph 5.

(2) An application under sub-paragraph (1) shall not be made, except with the special leave of the Tribunal—

(a) within twelve months from the date of the order, or of the decision on a previous application under this paragraph, or

(b) if the order was made so as to be in force for fifteen months or less, or as a result of a decision on a previous application is due to expire within fifteen months of that decision, until the last three months before the expiry date.

(3) On the application the Tribunal shall consider the matter and make such order confirming or varying the original order as it may determine to be reasonable in the circumstances.

(4) An order under this paragraph has effect from the date on which it is made or such later date as may be specified by the Tribunal.

## PART III
## SUPPLEMENTARY

**7.**—(1) This Schedule and the Copyright, Designs and Patents Act 1988 shall have effect as if the Schedule were included in Chapter III of Part I of that Act, and that Act shall have effect as if proceedings under this Schedule were listed in section 149 of that Act (jurisdiction of the Copyright Tribunal).

(2) References in this Schedule to anything done by the publisher include anything done on his behalf.

(3) References in this Schedule to works include future works, and references to the copyright in works include future copyright.

# Part B   Public Lending Right

## PUBLIC LENDING RIGHT ACT 1979
(c 10)

*General note*
Printed as amended by the Criminal Justice Act 1982.

### Arrangement of sections

*An Act to provide public lending right for authors, and for connected purposes.*
[22 March 1979]

### 1. Establishment of public lending right

(1) In accordance with a scheme to be prepared and brought into force by the Secretary of State, there shall be conferred on authors a right, known as 'public lending right', to receive from time to time out of a Central Fund payments in respect of such of their books as are lent out to the public by local library authorities in the United Kingdom.

(2) The classes, descriptions and categories of books in respect of which public lending right subsists, and the scales of payments to be made from the Central Fund in respect of it, shall be determined by or in accordance with the scheme; and in preparing the scheme the Secretary of State shall consult with representatives of authors and library authorities and of others who appear to be likely to be affected by it.

(3) The Secretary of State shall appoint an officer to be known as the Registrar of Public Lending Right; and the Schedule to this Act has effect with respect to the Registrar.

(4) The Registrar shall be charged with the duty of establishing and maintaining in accordance with the scheme a register showing the books in respect of which public lending right subsists and the persons entitled to the right in respect of any registered book.

(5) The Registrar shall, in the case of any registered book determine in accordance with the scheme the sums (if any) due by way of public lending right; and any sum so determined to be due shall be recoverable from the Registrar as a debt due to the person for the time being entitled to that right in respect of the book.

(6) Subject to any provision made by the scheme, the duration of public lending right in respect of a book shall be from the date of the book's first publication (or, if later, the beginning of the year in which application is made for it to be registered) until 50 years have elapsed since the end of the year in which the author died.

(7) Provision shall be made by the scheme for the right—

(a) to be established by registration;

   (b) to be transmissible by assignment or assignation, by testamentary disposition or by operation of law, as personal or moveable property;

   (c) to be claimed by or on behalf of the person for the time being entitled;

   (d) to be renounced (either in whole or in part, and either temporarily or for all time) on notice being given to the Registrar to that effect.

## 2. The Central Fund

(1) The Central Fund shall be constituted by the Secretary of State and placed under the control and management of the Registrar.

(2) There shall be paid into the Fund from time to time such sums, out of money provided by Parliament, as the Secretary of State with Treasury approval determines to be required for the purpose of satisfying the liabilities of the Fund; but in respect of the liabilities of any one financial year of the Fund the total of those sums shall not exceed £2 million less the total of any sums paid in that year, out of money so provided, under paragraph 2 of the Schedule to this Act (pay, pension, etc of Registrar).

(3) With the consent of the Treasury, the Secretary of State may from time to time by order in a statutory instrument increase the limit on the sums to be paid under subsection (2) above in respect of financial years beginning after that in which the order is made; but no such order shall be made unless a draft of it has been laid before the House of Commons and approved by a resolution of that House.

(4) There shall be paid out of the Central Fund—

   (a) such sums as may in accordance with the scheme be due from time to time in respect of public lending right; and

   (b) the administrative expenses of the Registrar and any other expenses and outgoings mentioned in this Act which are expressed to be payable from the Fund.

(5) Money received by the Registrar in respect of property disposed of, or otherwise in the course of his functions, or under this Act, shall be paid into the Central Fund, except in such cases as the Secretary of State otherwise directs with the approval of the Treasury; and in any such case the money shall be paid into the Consolidated Fund.

(6) The Registrar shall keep proper accounts and other records and shall prepare in respect of each financial year of the Fund statements of account in such form as the Secretary of State may direct with Treasury approval; and those statements shall, on or before 31st August next following the end of that year, be transmitted to the Comptroller and Auditor General, who shall examine and certify the statements and lay copies thereof, together with his report thereon, before each House of Parliament.

## 3. The scheme and its administration

(1) As soon as may be after this Act comes into force, the Secretary of State shall prepare the draft of a scheme for its purposes and lay a copy of the draft before each House of Parliament.

(2) If the draft scheme is approved by a resolution of each House, the Secretary of State shall bring the scheme into force (in the form of the draft) by means of an order in a statutory instrument, to be laid before Parliament after it is made; and the order may provide for different provisions of the scheme to come into force on different dates.

(3) The scheme shall be so framed as to make entitlement to public lending right dependent on, and its extent ascertainable by reference to, the number of occasions on which books are lent out from particular libraries, to be specified by the scheme or identified in accordance with provision made by it.

(4) For this purpose, 'library'—

(a) means any one of a local library authority's collections of books held by them for the purpose of being borrowed by the public; and

(b) includes any such collection which is taken about from place to place.

(5) The scheme may provide for requiring local library authorities—

(a) to give information as and when, and in the form in which, the Registrar may call for it or the Secretary of State may direct, as to loans made by them to the public of books in respect of which public lending rights subsists, or of other books; and

(b) to arrange for books to be numbered, or otherwise marked or coded, with a view to facilitating the maintenance of the register and the ascertainment and administration of public lending right.

(6) The Registrar shall, by means of payments out of the Central Fund, reimburse to local library authorities any expenditure incurred by them in giving effect to the scheme, the amount of that expenditure being ascertained in accordance with such calculations as the scheme may prescribe.

(7) Subject to the provisions of this Act (and in particular to the foregoing provisions of this section), the scheme may be varied from time to time by the Secretary of State, after such consultation as is mentioned in section 1 (2) above, and the variation brought into force by an order in a statutory instrument, subject to annulment in pursuance of a resolution of either House of Parliament; and the variation may comprise such incidental and transitional provisions as the Secretary of State thinks appropriate for the purposes of continuing the scheme as varied.

(8) The Secretary of State shall in each year prepare and lay before each House of Parliament a report on the working of the scheme.

## 4. The register

(1) The register shall be kept in such form, and contain such particulars of books and their authors, as may be prescribed.

(2) No application for an entry in the register is to be entertained in the case of any book unless it falls within a class, description or category of books prescribed as one in respect of which public lending right subsists.

(3) The scheme shall provide for the register to be conclusive both as to whether public lending right subsists in respect of a particular book and also as to the persons (if any) who are for the time being entitled to the right.

(4) Provision shall be included in the scheme for entries in the register to be made and amended, on application made in the prescribed manner and supported by prescribed particulars (verified as prescribed) so as to indicate, in the case of any book who (if anyone) is for the time being entitled to public lending right in respect of it.

(5) The Registrar may direct the removal from the register of every entry relating to a book in whose case no sum has become due by way of public lending right for a period of at least 10 years, but without prejudice to a subsequent application for the entries to be restored to the register.

(6) The Registrar may require the payment of fees, according to prescribed

scales and rates, for supplying copies of entries in the register; and a copy of an entry, certified under the hand of the Registrar or an officer of his with authority in that behalf (which authority it shall be unnecessary to prove) shall in all legal proceedings be admissible in evidence as of equal validity with the original.

(7) It shall be an offence for any person, in connection with the entry of any matter whatsoever in the register, to make any statement which he knows to be false in a material particular or recklessly to make any statement which is false in a material particular; and a person who commits an offence under this section shall be liable on summary conviction to a fine of not more than *£1,000* **level 5 on the standard scale**.

(8) Where an offence under subsection (7) above which has been committed by a body corporate is proved to have been committed with the consent or connivance of, or to be attributable to any neglect on the part of, a director, manager, secretary or other similar officer of the body corporate, or any person who was purporting to act in any such capacity, he (as well as the body corporate) shall be guilty of that offence and be liable to be proceeded against accordingly.

Where the affairs of a body corporate are managed by its members, this subsection applies in relation to the acts and defaults of a member in connection with his functions of management as if he were a director of the body corporate.

*General note*
As amended by the Criminal Justice Act 1982. Italicised words repealed: words in bold type added.

## 5. Citation, etc

(1) This Act may be cited as the Public Lending Right Act 1979.

(2) In this Act any reference to 'the scheme' is to the scheme prepared and brought into force by the Secretary of State in accordance with sections 1 and 3 of this Act (including the scheme as varied from time to time under section 3 (7)); and—

'local library authority' means—

(a) a library authority under the Public Libraries and Museums Act 1964;
(b) a statutory library authority within the Public Libraries (Scotland) Act 1955; and
(c) an Education and Library Board within the Education and Libraries (Northern Ireland) Order 1972;

'prescribed' means prescribed by the scheme;
'the register' means the register required by section 1 (4) to be established and maintained by the Registrar; and
'the Registrar' means the Registrar of Public Lending Right.

(3) This Act comes into force on a day to be appointed by an order made by the Secretary of State in a statutory instrument to be laid before Parliament after it has been made.

(4) This Act extends to Northern Ireland.

Section 1 (3)                                    SCHEDULE

THE REGISTRAR OF PUBLIC LENDING RIGHT
1. The Registrar shall hold and vacate office as such in accordance with the terms of his appointment; but he may at any time resign his office by notice in writing addressed to the Secretary of State; and the Secretary of State may at any time remove a person from the office of Registrar on the ground of incapacity or misbehaviour.

2. —(1) There shall be paid to the Registrar out of money provided by Parliament such remuneration and allowances as the Secretary of State may determine with the approval of the Minister for the Civil Service.

(2) In the case of any such holder of the office of Registrar as may be determined by the Secretary of State with that approval, there shall be paid out of money so provided such pension, allowance or gratuity to or in respect of him, or such contributions or payments towards provision of such a pension, allowance or gratuity, as may be so determined.

3. If, when a person ceases to hold office as Registrar, it appears to the Secretary of State that there are special circumstances which make it right that he should receive compensation, there may (with the approval of the Minister for the Civil Service) be paid to him out of the Central Fund a sum by way of compensation of such amount as may be so determined.

4. In the House of Commons Disqualification Act 1975, in Part III of Schedule 1 (other disqualifying offices), the following shall be inserted at the appropriate place in alphabetical order—

'Registrar of Public Lending Right';

and the like insertion shall be made in Part III of Schedule 1 to the Northern Ireland Assembly Disqualification Act 1975.

5.—(1) The Registrar of Public Lending Right shall be by that name a corporation sole, with a corporate seal.

(2) He is not to be regarded as the servant or agent of the Crown.

6. The Documentary Evidence Act 1868 shall have effect as if the Registrar were included in the first column of the Schedule to that Act, as if the Registrar and any person authorised to act on his behalf were mentioned in the second column of that Schedule, and as if the regulations referred to in that Act included any documents issued by the Registrar or by any such person.

7—(1) The Registrar may appoint such assistant registrars and staff as he thinks fit, subject to the approval of the Secretary of State as to their numbers; and their terms and conditions of service, and the remuneration and allowances payable to them, shall be such as the Registrar may determine.

(2) The Registrar may direct, in the case of persons appointed by him under this paragraph—

   (a)   that there be paid to and in respect of them such pensions, allowances and gratuities as he may determine;
   (b)   that payments be made towards the provision for them of such pensions, allowances and gratuities as he may determine; and
   (c)   that schemes be provided and maintained (whether contributory or not) for the payment to and in respect of them of such pensions, allowances and gratuities as he may determine.

(3) Any money required for the payment of remuneration and allowances under this paragraph, and of pensions, allowances and gratuities, and otherwise for the purposes of sub-paragraph (2) above, shall be paid from the Central Fund.

(4) The approval of the Secretary of State and the Minister for the Civil Service shall be required for any directions or determination by the Registrar under this paragraph.

**8.** Anything authorised or required under this Act (except paragraph 7 of this Schedule), or by or under the scheme, to be done by the Registrar may be done by an assistant registrar or member of the Registrar's staff who is authorised generally or specially in that behalf in writing by the Registrar.

# Part C  Registered Designs

REGISTERED DESIGNS ACT 1949
(12, 13 & 14 Geo 6 c 88)

*(Printed as amended by the Copyright Act 1956, the Defence Contracts Act 1958, the Patents and Designs (Renewals, Extensions and Fees) Act 1961, the Northern Ireland Act 1962, the Industrial Expansion Act 1968, the Administration of Justice Act 1969, the Administration of Justice Act 1970, the Patents Act 1977, the Patents, Designs and Marks Act 1986, the Statute Law (Repeals) Act 1986, the Semiconductor Products (Protection of Topography) Regulations 1987, the Copyright, Designs and Patents Act 1988)*

*Registrable designs and proceedings for registration*

**1. Designs registrable under Act**
*(1) Subject to the following provisions of this section, a design may, upon application made by the person claiming to be the proprietor, be registered under this Act in respect of any article or set of articles specified in the application.*

*(2) Subject to the provisions of this Act, a design shall not be registered thereunder unless it is new or original and in particular shall not be so registered in respect of any article if it is the same as a design which before the date of the application for registration has been registered or published in the United Kingdom in respect of the same or any other article or differs from such a design only in immaterial details or in features which are variants commonly used in the trade.*

*(3) In this Act the expression 'design' means features of shape, configuration, pattern or ornament applied to an article by any industrial process or means, being features which in the finished article appeal to and judged solely by the eye, but does not include a method or principle of construction or features of shape or configuration which are dictated solely by the function which the article to be made in that shape or configuration has to perform.*

*(4) Rules made by the Board of Trade under this Act may provide for excluding from registration thereunder designs for such articles, being articles which are primarily literary or artistic in character, as the Board think fit.*

**(1) In this Act 'design' means features of shape, configuration, pattern or ornament applied to an article by any industrial process, being features which in the finished article appeal to and are judged by the eye, but does not include—**

(a)  **a method or principle of construction, or**
(b)  **features of shape or configuration of an article which—**

  (i)  **are dictated solely by the function which the article has to perform, or**
  (ii)  **are dependent upon the appearance of another article of which the article is intended by the author of the design to form an integral part.**

**(2) A design which is new may, upon application by the person claiming**

to be the proprietor, be registered under this Act in respect of any article, or set of articles, specified in the application.

(3) A design shall not be registered in respect of an article if the appearance of the article is not material, that is, if aesthetic considerations are not normally taken into account to a material extent by persons acquiring or using articles of that description, and would not be so taken into account if the design were to be applied to the article.

(4) A design shall not be regarded as new for the purposes of this Act if it is the same as a design—

(a) registered in respect of the same or any other article in pursuance of a prior application, or

(b) published in the United Kingdom in respect of the same or any other article before the date of the application,

or if it differs from such a design only in immaterial details or in features which are variants commonly used in the trade.

This subsection has effect subject to the provisions of sections 4, 6 and 16 of this Act.

(5) The Secretary of State may by rules provide for excluding from registration under this Act designs for such articles of a primarily literary or artistic character as the Secretary of State thinks fit.

*General note*

As amended by the Copyright, Designs and Patents Act 1988. Italicised words apply to designs registered in pursuance of applications made before 1 August 1979; words in bold type added and apply to designs registered pursuant to applications made after 1 August 1989: see Copyright, Designs and Patents Act 1988, s 265(2) and 266.

## 2. Proprietorship of designs

*(1) Subject to the provisions of this section, the author of a design shall be treated for the purposes of this Act as the proprietor of the design:*

*Provided that where the design is executed by the author for another person for good consideration, that other person shall be treated for the purposes of this Act as the proprietor.*

(1) The author of a design shall be treated for the purposes of this Act as the original proprietor of the design, subject to the following provisions.

(1A) Where a design is created in pursuance of a commission for money or money's worth, the person commissioning the design shall be treated as the original proprietor of the design.

(1B) Where, in a case not falling within subsection (1A), a design is created by an employee in the course of his employment, his employer shall be treated as the original proprietor of the design.

(2) Where a design, or the right to apply a design to any article, becomes vested, whether by assignment, transmission or operation of law, in any person other than the original proprietor, either alone or jointly with the original proprietor, that other person, or as the case may be the original proprietor and that other person, shall be treated for the purposes of this Act as the proprietor of the design or as the proprietor of the design in relation to that article.

(3) In this Act the 'author' of a design means the person who creates it.

(4) In the case of a design generated by computer in circumstances such that there is no human author, the person by whom the arrangements

**necessary for the creation of the design are made shall be taken to be the author.**

*General note*

As amended by the Copyright, Designs and Patents Act 1988. Italicised words apply to designs registered in pursuance of applications made before 1 August 1979; words in bold type added and apply to designs, registered pursuant to applications made after 1 August 1989: see Copyright, Designs and Patents Act 1988, s 267.

### 3. Proceedings for registration

(1) An application for the registration of a design shall be made in the prescribed form and shall be filed at the Patent Office in the prescribed manner.

*(2) For the purpose of deciding whether a design is new or original, the registrar may make such searches, if any, as he thinks fit.*

*(3) The registrar may refuse any application for the registration of a design or may register the design in pursuance of the application subject to such modifications, if any, as he thinks fit.*

*(4) An application which, owing to any default or neglect on the part of the applicant, has not been completed so as to enable registration to be effected within such time as may be prescribed shall be deemed to be abandoned.*

*(5) Except as otherwise expressly provided by this Act, a design when registered shall be registered as of the date on which the application for registration was made, or such other date (whether earlier or later than that date) as the registrar may in any particular case direct:*

*Provided that no proceedings shall be taken in respect of any infringement committed before the date on which the certificate of registration of the design under this Act is issued.*

*(6) An appeal shall lie from any decision of the registrar under subsection (3) of this section.*

**(2) An application for the registration of a design in which design right subsists shall not be entertained unless made by the person claiming to be the design right owner.**

**(3) For the purpose of deciding whether a design is new, the registrar may make such searches, if any, as he thinks fit.**

**(4) The registrar may, in such cases as may be prescribed, direct that for the purpose of deciding whether a design is new an application shall be treated as made on a date earlier or later than that on which it was in fact made.**

**(5) The registrar may refuse an application for the registration of a design or may register the design in pursuance of the application subject to such modifications, if any, as he thinks fit; and a design when registered shall be registered as of the date on which the application was made or is treated as having been made.**

**(6) An application which, owing to any default or neglect on the part of the applicant, has not been completed so as to enable registration to be effected within such time as may be prescribed shall be deemed to be abandoned.**

**(7) An appeal lies from any decision of the registrar under this section.**

*General note*

As amended by the Copyright, Designs and Patents Act 1988, Sch 3, para 1. Italicised words repealed; words in bold type added.

### 4. Registration of same design in respect of other articles, etc

(1) Where the registered proprietor of a design registered in respect of any article makes an application—

(a) for registration in respect of one or more other articles, of the registered design, or

(b) for registration in respect of the same or one or more other articles, of a design consisting of the registered design with modifications or variations not sufficient to alter the character or substantially to affect the identity thereof,

the application shall not be refused and the registration made on that application shall not be invalidated by reason only of the previous registration or publication of the registered design:

*Provided that the period of copyright in a design registered by virtue of this section shall not extend beyond the expiration of the original and any extended period of copyright in the original registered design.* **Provided that the right in a design registered by virtue of this section shall not extend beyond the end of the period, and any extended period, for which the right subsists in the original registered design.**

(2) Where any person makes an application for the registration of a design in respect of any article and either—

(a) that design has been previously registered by another person in respect of some other article; or

(b) the design to which the application relates consists of a design previously registered by another person in respect of the same or some other article with modifications or variations not sufficient to alter the character or substantially to affect the identity thereof,

then, if at any time while the application is pending the applicant becomes the registered proprietor of the design previously registered, the foregoing provisions of this section shall apply as if at the time of making the application the applicant had been the registered proprietor of that design.

*General note*
As amended by the Copyright, Designs and Patents Act 1988, Sch 3, para 2. Italicised words repealed; words in bold type added.

## 5. Provisions for secrecy of certain designs

(1) Where, either before or after the commencement of this Act, an application for the registration of a design has been made, and it appears to the registrar that the design is one of a class notified to him by a competent authority as relevant for defence purposes, he may give directions for prohibiting or restricting the publication of information with respect to the design, or the communication of such information to any person or class of persons specified in the directions

*(2) Rules shall be made by the Board of Trade under this Act for securing that the representation or specimen of a design in the case of which directions are given under this section shall not be open to inspection at the Patent Office during the continuance in force of the directions.*

**(2) The Secretary of State shall by rules make provision for securing that where such directions are given—**

**(a) the representation or specimen of the design, and**

**(b) any evidence filed in support of the applicant's contention that the appearance of an article is material (for the purposes of section 1(3) of this Act),**

**shall not be open to public inspection at the Patent Office during the continuance in force of the directions.**

(3) Where the registrar gives any such directions as aforesaid, he shall give notice of the application and of the directions to a competent authority, and thereupon the following provisions shall have effect, that is to say—

(a) the competent authority shall, upon receipt of such notice, consider whether the publication of the design would be prejudicial to the defence of the realm and unless a notice under paragraph (c) of this subsection has previously been given by that authority to the registrar, shall reconsider that question before the expiration of nine months from the date of filing of the application for registration of the design and at least once in every subsequent year;

(b) for the purpose aforesaid, the competent authority may, at any time after the design has been registered or, with the consent of the applicant, at any time before the design has been registered, inspect the representation or specimen of the design filed in pursuance of the application;

(c) if upon consideration of the design at any time it appears to the competent authority that the publication of the design would not, or would no longer, be prejudicial to the defence of the realm, that authority shall give notice to the registrar to that effect;

(d) on the receipt of any such notice the registrar shall revoke the directions and may, subject to such conditions, if any, as he thinks fit, extend the time for doing anything required or authorised to be done by or under this Act in connection with the application or registration, whether or not that time has previously expired.

(4) No person resident in the United Kingdom shall, except under the authority of a written permit granted by or on behalf of the registrar, make or cause to be made any application outside the United Kingdom for the registration or a design of any class prescribed for the purposes of this subsection unless—

(a) an application for registration of the same design has been made in the United Kingdom not less than six weeks before the application outside the United Kingdom; and

(b) either no directions have been given under subsection (1) of this section in relation to the application in the United Kingdom or all such directions have been revoked:

Provided that this subsection shall not apply in relation to a design for which an application for protection has first been filed in a country outside the United Kingdom by a person resident outside the United Kingdom.

*(5) In this section the expression 'competent authority' means a Secretary of State, the Admiralty or the Minister of Supply.*

*General note*
As amended by the Copyright, Designs and Patents Act 1988, Sch 3, para 3. Italicised words repealed, words in bold added.

## 6. Provisions as to confidential disclosure, etc

(1) An application for the registration of a design shall not be refused, and the registration of a design shall not be invalidated, by reason only of—

(a) the disclosure of the design by the proprietor to any other person in such circumstances as would make it contrary to good faith for that other person to use or publish the design;

(b) the disclosure of the design in breach of good faith by any person other than the proprietor of the design; or

(c) in the case of a new or original textile design intended for registration, the acceptance of a first and confidential order for goods bearing the design.

(2) An application for the registration of a design shall not be refused and the registration of a design shall not be invalidated by reason only—

(a) that a representation of the design, or any article to which the design has been applied has been displayed, with the consent of the proprietor of the design, at an exhibition certified by the Board of Trade for the purposes of this subsection;

(b) that after any such display as aforesaid, and during the period of the exhibition, a representation of the design or any such article as aforesaid has been displayed by any person without the consent of the proprietor; or

(c) that a representation of the design has been published in consequence of any such display as is mentioned in paragraph (a) of this subsection,

if the application for registration of the design is made not later than six months after the opening of the exhibition.

(3) An application for the registration of a design shall not be refused and the registration of a design shall not be invalidated, by reason only of the communication of the design by the proprietor thereof to a Government department or to any person authorised by a Government department to consider the merits of the design, or of anything done in consequence of such a communication.

*(4) Where copyright under the Copyright Act 1956, subsists in an artistic work, and an application is made by, or with the consent of, the owner of that copyright for the registration of a corresponding design, that design shall not be treated for the purposes of this Act as being other than new or original by reason only of any use previously made of the artistic work, unless—*

*(a) the previous use consisted of or included the sale, letting for hire, or offer for sale or hire of articles to which the design in question (or a design differing from it only as mentioned in subsection (2) of section one of the Act) had been applied industrially, other than articles of a description specified in rules made under subsection (4) of section one of this Act, and*

*(b) that previous use was made by, or with the consent of, the owner of the copyright in the artistic work.*

*(5) Any rules made by virtue of subsection (5) of section ten of the Copyright Act 1956 (which relates to rules for determining the circumstances in which a design is to be taken to be applied industrially) shall apply for the purposes of the last foregoing subsection.*

**(4) Where an application is made by or with the consent of the owner of the copyright in an artistic work for the registration of a corresponding design, the design shall not be treated for the purposes of this Act as being other than new by reason only of any use previously made of the artistic work, subject to subsection (5).**

**(5) Subsection (4) does not apply if the previous use consisted of or**

included the sale, letting for hire or offer or exposure for sale or hire of articles to which had been applied industrially—

(a)  the design in question, or

(b)  a design differing from it only in immaterial details or in features which are variants commonly used in the trade,

and that previous use was made by or with the consent of the copyright owner.

(6)  The Secretary of State may make provision by rules as to the circumstances in which a design is to be regarded for the purposes of this section as 'applied industrially' to articles, or any description of articles.

*General note*
Italicised sub-ss (4), (5) originally added by the Copyright Act 1956, s 44. Subsequently substituted by new sub-ss (4)–(6) by the Copyright, Designs and Patents Act 1988, Sch 3, para 4.

## *Effect of registration, etc.*

### 7.  Right given by registration

*(1)  The registration of a design under this Act shall give to the registered proprietor the copyright in the registered design, that is to say, the exclusive right in the United Kingdom and the Isle of Man to make or import for sale or for use for the purposes of any trade or business, or to sell, hire or offer for sale or hire, any article in respect of which the design is registered, being an article to which the registered design or a design not substantially different from the registered design has been applied, and to make anything for enabling any such article to be made as aforesaid, whether in the United Kingdom or the Isle of Man or elsewhere.*

(2)  Subject to the provision of this Act and of subsection (3) of section three of the Crown Proceedings Act 1947, the registration of a design shall have the same effect against the Crown as it has against a subject.

### 7.  Right given by registration

(1)  The registration of a design under this Act gives the registered proprietor the exclusive right—

(a)  to make or import—
(i)  for sale or hire, or
(ii)  for use for the purposes of a trade or business, or
(b)  to sell, hire or offer or expose for sale or hire,

an article in respect of which the design is registered and to which that design or a design not substantially different from it has been applied.

(2)  The right in the registered design is infringed by a person who without the licence of the registered proprietor does anything which by virtue of subsection (1) is the exclusive right of the proprietor.

(3)  The right in the registered design is also infringed by a person who without the licence of the registered proprietor makes anything for enabling any such article to be made, in the United Kingdom or elsewhere, as mentioned in subsection (1).

(4)  The right in the registered design is also infringed by a person who without the licence of the registered proprietor—

(a)  does anything in relation to a kit that would be an infringement if done in relation to the assembled article (see subsection (1)), or

(b)  makes anything for enabling a kit to be made or assembled, in the

**United Kingdom or elsewhere, if the assembled article would be such an article as is mentioned in subsection (1);**

**and for this purpose a 'kit' means a complete or substantially complete set of components intended to be assembled into an article.**

**(5) No proceedings shall be taken in respect of an infringement committed before the date on which the certificate of registration of the design under this Act is granted.**

**(6) The right in a registered design is not infringed by the reproduction of a feature of the design which, by virtue of section 1 (1)(b), is left out of account in determining whether the design is registrable.**

*General note*
As amended by the Copyright, Designs and Patents Act 1988. Italicised words apply to designs registered in pursuance of applications made before 1 August 1979; words in bold type added and apply to designs, registered pursuant to applications made after 1 August 1989: see Copyright, Designs and Patents Act 1988, s 268.

## 8. Period of copyright

*(1) Copyright in a registered design shall, subject to the provisions of this Act, subsist for a period of five years from the date of registration.*

*(2) The registrar shall extend the period of copyright for a second period of five years from the expiration of the original period and for a third period of five years from the expiration of the second period if an application for extension of the period of copyright for the second or third period is made in the prescribed form before the expiration of the original period or the second period, as the case may be, and if the prescribed fee is paid before the expiration of the relevant period or within such further period (not exceeding (three) [six] months) as may be specified in a request made to the registrar and accompanied by the prescribed additional fee.*

*[(3) Where in the case of a registered design it is shown—*

    *(a) that the design, at the time when it was registered was a corresponding design in relation to an artistic work in which copyright subsisted under the Copyright Act 1956;*

    *(b) that, by reason of a previous use of that artistic work, the design would not have been registrable under this Act but for subsection (4) of section six of this Act; and*

    *(c) that the copyrigh in that work under the Copyright Act 1956, expired before the date of expiry of the copyright in the design,*

*the copyright in the design shall, notwithstanding anything in this section, be deemed to have expired at the same time as the copyright in the artistic work, and shall not be renewable after that time.]*

## 8. Duration of right in registered design

**(1) The right in a registered design subsists in the first instance for a period of five years from the date of the registration of the design.**

**(2) The period for which the right subsists may be extended for a second, third, fourth and fifth period of five years, by applying to the registrar for an extension and paying the prescribed renewal fee.**

**(3) If the first, second, third or fourth period expires without such application and payment being made, the right shall cease to have effect; and**

the registrar shall, in accordance with rules made by the Secretary of State, notify the proprietor of that fact.

(4) **If during the period of six months immediately following the end of that period an application for extension is made and the prescribed renewal fee and any prescribed additional fee is paid, the right shall be treated as if it had never expired, with the result that—**

(a) **anything done under or in relation to the right during that further period shall be treated as valid,**

(b) **an act which would have constituted an infringement of the right if it had not expired shall be treated as an infringement, and**

(c) **an act which would have constituted use of the design for the services of the Crown if the right had not expired shall be treated as such use.**

(5) **Where it is shown that a registered design—**

(a) **was at the time it was registered a corresponding design in relation to an artistic work in which copyright subsists, and**

(b) **by reason of a previous use of that work would not have been registrable but for section 6(4) of this Act (registration despite certain prior applications of design),**

**the right in the registered design expires when the copyright in that work expires, if that is earlier than the time at which it would otherwise expire, and it may not thereafter be renewed.**

(6) **The above provisions have effect subject to the proviso to section 4(1) (registration of same design in respect of other articles, & c).**

*General note*
As amended by the Copyright, Designs and Patents Act 1988. Italicised words apply to designs registered in pursuance of applications made before 1 August 1979; words in bold type added. Sub-s (2) originally amended by the Patents and Designs (Renewals, Extensions and Fees Act 1961; words in round brackets repealed, words in square brackets added. Sub-s (3) was originally added by the Copyright Act 1956.

## 8A. Restoration of lapsed right in design

(1) Where the right in a registered design has expired by reason of a failure to extend, in accordance with section 8(2) or (4), the period for which the right subsists, an application for the restoration of the right in the design may be made to the registrar within the prescribed period.

(2) The application may be made by the person who was the registered proprietor of the design or by any other person who would have been entitled to the right in the design if it had not expired; and where the design was held by two or more persons jointly, the application may, with the leave of the registrar, be made by one or more of them without joining the others.

(3) Notice of the application shall be published by the registrar in the prescribed manner.

(4) If the registrar is satisfied that the proprietor took reasonable care to see that the period for which the right subsisted was extended in accordance with section 8(2) or (4), he shall, on payment of any unpaid renewal fee and any prescribed additional fee, order the restoration of the right in the design.

(5) The order may be made subject to such conditions as the registrar thinks fit, and if the proprietor of the design does not comply with any condition the

registrar may revoke the order and give such consequential directions as he thinks fit.

(6) Rules altering the period prescribed for the purposes of subsection (1) may contain such transitional provisions and savings as appear to the Secretary of State to be necessary or expedient.

*General note*
Added by the Copyright, Designs and Patents Act 1988, s269 in respect of designs registered pursuant to applications made after 1 August 1989; see s269 (2) thereof.

## 8B. Effect of order for restoration of right

(1) The effect of an order under section 8A for the restoration of the right in a registered design is as follows.

(2) Anything done under or in relation to the right during the period between expiry and restoration shall be treated as valid.

(3) Anything done during that period which would have constituted an infringement if the right had not expired shall be treated as an infringement—

   (a) if done at a time when it was possible for an application for extension to be made under section 8(4); or
   (b) if it was a continuation or repetition of an earlier infringing act.

(4) If, after it was no longer possible for such an application for extension to be made and before publication of notice of the application for restoration, a person—

   (a) began in good faith to do an act which would have constituted an infringement of the right in the design if it had not expired, or
   (b) made in good faith effective and serious preparations to do such an act,

he has the right to continue to do the act or, as the case may be, to do the act, notwithstanding the restoration of the right in the design; but this does not extend to granting a licence to another person to do the act.

(5) If the act was done, or the preparations were made, in the course of a business, the person entitled to the right conferred by subsection (4) may—

   (a) authorise the doing of that act by any partners of his for the time being in that business, and
   (b) assign that right, or transmit it on death (or in the case of a body corporate on its dissolution), to any person who acquires that part of the business in the course of which the act was done or the preparations were made.

(6) Where an article is disposed of to another in exercise of the rights conferred by subsection (4) or subsection (5), that other and any person through him may deal with the article in the same way as if it had been disposed of by the registered proprietor of the design.

(7) The above provisions apply in relation to the use of a registered design for the services of the Crown as they apply in relation to infringement of the right in the design.

*General note*
Added by the Copyright, Designs and Patents Act 1988, s269 in respect of designs registered pursuant to applications made after 1 August 1989; see s 269 (2) thereof.

### 9. Exemption of innocent infringer from liability for damages

(1) In proceedings for the infringement of copyright in a registered design damages shall not be awarded against a defendant who proves that at the date of the infringement he was not aware, and had no reasonable ground for supposing, that the design was registered; and a person shall not be deemed to have been aware or to have had reasonable grounds for supposing as aforesaid by reason only of the marking of an article with the word registered or any abbreviation thereof, or any word or words expressing or implying that the design applied to the article has been registered, unless the number of the design accompanied the word or words or the abbreviation in question.

(2) Nothing in this section shall affect the power of the court to grant an injunction in any proceedings for infringement of copyright in a registered design.

### 10. Compulsory licence in respect of registered design

(1) At any time after a design has been registered any person interested may apply to the registrar for the grant of a compulsory licence in respect of the design on the ground that the design is not applied in the United Kingdom by any industrial process or means to the article in respect of which it is registered to such an extent as is reasonable in the circumstances of the case; and the registrar may make such order on the application as he thinks fit.

(2) An order for the grant of a licence shall, without prejudice to any other method of enforcement, have effect as if it were a deed executed by the registered proprietor and all other necessary parties, granting a licence in accordance with the order.

(3) No order shall be made under this section which would be at variance with any treaty, convention, arrangement or engagement applying to the United Kingdom and any convention country.

(4) An appeal shall lie from any order of the registrar under this section.

### 11. Cancellation of registration

(1) The Registrar may, upon a request made in the prescribed manner by the registered proprietor, cancel the registration of a design.

(2) At any time after a design has been registered any person interested may apply to the Registrar for the cancellation of the registration of the design on the ground that the design was not, at the date of the registration thereof, new or original, or on any other ground on which the Registrar could have refused to register the design; and the Registrar may make such order on the application as he thinks fit.

*(2A) At any time after a design has been registered, any person interested may apply to the Registrar for the cancellation of the registration of the design on the grounds—*

    *(a) that the design, at the time when it was registered, was a corresponding design in relation to an artistic work in which copyright subsisted under the Copyright Act 1956;*

    *(b) that, by reason of a previous use of that artistic work, the design would not have been registrable under this Act but for subsection (4) of section 6 of this Act; and*

    *(c) that the copyright in that work under the Copyright Act 1956, has expired;*

*and the Registrar may make such order on the application as he thinks fit.*

*(3) An appeal shall lie from any order of the Registrar under (the last foregoing subsection) either of the two last foregoing subsections].*

**(3) At any time after a design has been registered, any person interested may apply to the registrar for the cancellation of the registration on the ground that—**

    **(a) the design was at the time it was registered a corresponding design in relation to an artistic work in which copyright subsisted, and**

    **(b) the right in the registered design has expired in accordance with section 8(4) of this Act (expiry of right in registered design on expiry of copyright in artistic work);**

**and the registrar may make such order on the application as he thinks fit.**

**(4) A cancellation under this section takes effect—**

    **(a) in the case of cancellation under subsection (1), from the date of the registrar's decision,**

    **(b) in the case of cancellation under subsection (2), from the date of registration,**

    **(c) in the case of cancellation under subsection (3), from the date on which the right in the registered design expired,**

**or, in any case, from such other date as the registrar may direct.**

**(5) An appeal lies from any order of the registrar under this section.**

*General note*
Sub-ss (3)–(5) were substituted for original sub-ss (2A), (3) by the Copyright, Designs and Patents Act 1988, Sch 3, para 6. Italicised words repealed; words in bold type added. Sub-s (2A) was originally added, and the words in the original sub-s (3) were substituted, by the Copyright Act 1956. Words in round brackets repealed; words in square brackets added.

**11A.  Powers exercisable for protection of the public interest**
**(1) Where a report of the Monopolies and Mergers Commission has been laid before Parliament containing conclusions to the effect—**

    **(a) on a monopoly reference, that a monopoly situation exists and facts found by the Commission operate or may be expected to operate against the public interest,**

    **(b) on a merger reference, that a merger situation qualifying for investigation has been created and the creation of the situation, or particular elements in or consequences of it specified in the report, operate or may be expected to operate against the public interest,**

    **(c) on a competition reference, that a person was engaged in an anti-competitive practice which operated or may be expected to operate against the public interest, or**

    **(d) on a reference under section 11 of the Competition Act 1980 (reference of public bodies and certain other persons), that a person is pursuing a course of conduct which operates against the public interest,**

**the appropriate Minister or Ministers may apply to the registrar to take action under this section.**

**(2) Before making an application the appropriate Minister or Ministers shall publish, in such a manner as he or they think appropriate, a notice describing the nature of the proposed application and shall consider any**

representations which may be made within thirty days of such publication by persons whose interests appear to him or them to be affected.

(3) If on an application under this section it appears to the registrar that the matters specified in the Commission's report as being those which in the Commission's opinion operate or operated or may be expected to operate against the public interest include—

    (a)  conditions in licences granted in respect of a registered design by its proprietor restricting the use of the design by the licensee or the right of the proprietor to grant other licences, or

    (b)  a refusal by the proprietor of a registered design to grant licences on reasonable terms,

he may by order cancel or modify any such condition or may, instead or in addition, make an entry in the register to the effect that licences in respect of the design are to be available as of right.

(4) The terms of a licence available by virtue of this section shall, in default of agreement, be settled by the registrar on an application by the person requiring the licence; and terms so settled shall authorise the licensee to do everything which would be an infringement of the right in the registered design in the absence of a licence.

(5) Where the terms of a licence are settled by the registrar the licence has effect from the date on which the application to him was made.

(6) An appeal lies from any order of the registrar under this section.

(7) In this section 'the appropriate Minister or Ministers' means the Minister or Ministers to whom the report of the Monopolies and Mergers Commission was made.

*General note*
Added by the Copyright, Designs and Patents Act 1988, s270, in respect of designs registered pursuant to applications made after 1 August 1989.

## 11B. Undertaking to take licence of right in infringement proceedings

(1) If in proceedings for infringement of the right in a registered design in respect of which a licence is available as of right under section 11A of this Act the defendant undertakes to take a licence on such terms as may be agreed or, in default of agreement, settled by the registrar under that section—

    (a)  no injunction shall be granted against him, and

    (b)  the amount recoverable against him by way of damages or on an account of profits shall not exceed double the amount which would have been payable by him as licensee if such a licence on those terms had been granted before the earliest infringement.

(2) An undertaking may be given at any time before final order in the proceedings, without any admission of liability.

(3) Nothing in this section affects the remedies available in respect of an infringement committed before licences of right were available.

*General note*
Added by the Copyright, Designs and Patents Act 1988, s270, in respect of designs registered pursuant to application made after 1 August 1989.

### 12. Use for services of the Crown

The provisions of the First Schedule to this Act shall have effect with respect to the use of registered designs for the services of the Crown and the rights of third parties in respect of such use.

## *International Arrangements*

### 13. Orders in Council as to convention countries

(1) His Majesty may, with a view to the fulfilment of a treaty, convention, arrangement or engagement, by Order in Council declare that any country specified in the order is a convention country for the purposes of this Act:

Provided that a declaration may be made as aforesaid for the purposes of either of all or of some only of the provisions of this Act, and a country in the case of which a declaration made for the purposes of some only of the provisions of this Act is in force shall be deemed to be a convention country for the purposes of those provisions only.

(2) His Majesty may by Order in Council direct that any of the Channel Islands, any colony, any British protectorate or protected state or any territory administered by His Majesty's Government in the United Kingdom under the trusteeship system of the United Nations shall be deemed to be a convention country for the purposes of all or any of the provisions of this Act; and an Order made under this subsection may direct that any such provisions shall have effect, in relation to the territory in question, subject to such conditions or limitations, if any, as may be specified in the Order.

(3) For the purposes of subsection (1) of this section, every colony, protectorate, territory subject to the authority or under the suzerainty of another country, and territory administered by another country in accordance with a mandate from the League of Nations or under the trusteeship system of the United Nations, shall be deemed to be a country in the case of which a declaration may be made under that subsection.

*General note*
As amended by the Statute Law (Repeals) Act 1986; italicised words repealed.

### 14. Registration of design where application for protection in convention country has been made

(1) An application for registration of a design in respect of which protection has been applied for in a convention country may be made in accordance with the provisions of this Act by the person by whom the application for protection was made or his personal representative or assignee:

Provided that no applications shall be made by virtue of this section after the expiration of six months from the date of the application for protection in a convention country or, where more than one such application for protection has been made, from the date of the first application.

*(2) A design registered on an application made by virtue of this section shall be registered as of the date of the application for protection in the convention country or, where more than one such application for protection has been made, the date of the first such application:*

*Provided that no proceedings shall be taken in respect of any infringement committed before the date on which the certificate of registration of the design under this Act is issued.*

*(3) An application for the registration of a design made by virtue of this section shall not be refused, and the registration of a design on such an application shall not be invalidated, by reason only of the registration or publication of the design in the United Kingdom or the Isle of Man during the period specified in the proviso to subsection (1) of this section as that within which the application for registration may be made.*

**(2) Where an application for registration of a design is made by virtue of this section, the application shall be treated, for the purpose of determining whether that or any other design is new, as made on the date of the application for protection in the convention country or, if more than one such application was made, on the date of the first such application.**

**(3) Subsection (2) shall not be construed as excluding the power to give directions under section 3(4) of this Act in relation to an application made by virtue of this section.**

(4) Where a person has applied for protection for a design by an application which—

(a) in accordance with the terms of a treaty subsisting between two or more convention countries, is equivalent to an application duly made in any one of those convention countries; or

(b) in accordance with the law of any convention country, is equivalent to an application duly made in that convention country, he shall be deemed for the purposes of this section to have applied in that convention country.

*General note*
As amended by the Copyright, Designs and Patents Act 1988, Sch 3, para 7.

### 15. Extension of time for applications under s14 in certain cases

(1) If the Secretary of State is satisfied that provision substantially equivalent to the provision to be made by or under this section has been or will be made under the law of any convention country, he may make rules empowering the registrar to extend the time for making application under subsection (1) of section 14 of this Act for registration of a design in respect of which protection has been applied for in that country in any case where the period specified in the proviso to that subsection expires during a period prescribed by the rules.

(2) Rules made under this section—

(a) may, where any agreement or arrangement has been made between His Majesty's Government in the United Kingdom and the government of the convention country for the supply or mutual exchange of information or articles, provide, either generally or in any class of case specified in the rules, that an extension of time shall not be granted under this section unless the design has been communicated in accordance with the agreement or arrangement;

(b) may, either generally or in any class of case specified in the rules, fix the maximum extension which may be granted under this section;

(c) may prescribe or allow any special procedure in connection with applications made by virtue of this section;

(d) may empower the registrar to extend, in relation to an application made by virtue of this section, the time limited by or under the foregoing provisions of this Act for doing any act, subject to such conditions, if any, as may be imposed by or under the rules;

(e) may provide for securing that the rights conferred by registration on an application made by virtue of this section shall be subject to such restrictions or conditions as may be specified by or under the rules in particular to restrictions and conditions for the protection of persons (including persons acting on behalf of His Majesty) who, otherwise than as the result of a communication made in accordance with such an agreement or arrangement as is mentioned in paragraph (a) of this subsection, and before the date of the application in question or such later date as may be allowed by the rules, may have imported or made articles to which the design is applied or may have made an application for registration of the design.

## 16. Protection of designs communicated under international agreements

(1) Subject to the provisions of this section, the Board of Trade may make rules for securing that, where a design has been communicated in accordance with an agreement or arrangement made between His Majesty's Government in the United Kingdom and the government of any other country for the supply or mutual exchange of information or articles—

(a) an application for the registration of the design made by the person from whom the design was communicated or his personal representative or assignee shall not be prejudiced, and the registration of the design in pursuance of such an application shall not be invalidated, by reason only that the design has been communicated as aforesaid or that in consequence thereof—

   (i) the design has been published or applied, or

   (ii) an application for registration of the design has been made by any other person, or the design has been registered on such an application;

(b) any application for the registration of a design made in consequence of such a communication as aforesaid may be refused and any registration of a design made on such an application may be cancelled.

(2) Rules made under subsection (1) of this section may provide that the publication or application of a design, or the making of any application for registration thereof shall, in such circumstances and subject to such conditions or exceptions as may be prescribed by the rules, be presumed to have been in consequence of such a communication as is mentioned in that subsection.

(3) The powers of the Secretary of State under this section, so far as they are exercisable for the benefit of persons from whom designs have been communicated to His Majesty's Government in the United Kingdom by the government of any other country, shall only be exercised if and to the extent that the Secretary of State is satisfied that substantially equivalent provision has been or will be made under the law of that country for the benefit of persons from whom designs have been communicated by His Majesty's Government in the United Kingdom to the government of that country.

(4) References in the last foregoing subsection to the communication of a design to or by His Majesty's Government or the government of any other country shall be construed as including references to the communication of the design by or to any person authorised in that behalf by the government in question.

*Register of designs, etc*

**17. Register of designs**

*(1) There shall be kept at the Patent Office under the control of the registrar a register of designs, in which there shall be entered the names and addresses of proprietors of registered designs, notices of assignments and of transmissions of registered designs, and such other matters as may be prescribed or as the registrar may think fit.*

*(2) Subject to the provisions of this Act and to rules made by the Board of Trade thereunder, the register of designs shall, at all convenient times, be open to inspection by the public; and certified copies sealed with the seal of the Patent Office of any entry in the register shall be given to any person requiring them on payment of the prescribed fee.*

*(3) The register of designs shall be prima facie evidence of any matters required or authorised by this Act to be entered therein.*

*(4) No notice of any trust, whether expressed, implied or constructive, shall be entered in the register of designs, and the registrar shall not be affected by any such notice.*

(1) The registrar shall maintain the register of designs, in which shall be entered—

(a) the names and addresses of proprietors of registered designs;

(b) notices of assignments and of transmissions of registered designs; and

(c) such other matters as may be prescribed or as the registrar may think fit.

(2) No notice of any trust, whether express, implied or constructive, shall be entered in the register of designs, and the registrar shall not be affected by any such notice.

(3) The register need not be kept in documentary form.

(4) Subject to the provisions of this Act and to rules made by the Secretary of State under it, the public shall have a right to inspect the register at the Patent Office at all convenient times.

(5) Any person who applies for a certified copy of an entry in the register or a certified extract from the register shall be entitled to obtain such a copy or extract on payment of a fee prescribed in relation to certified copies and extracts; and rules made by the Secretary of State under this Act may provide that any person who applies for an uncertified copy or extract shall be entitled to such a copy or extract on payment of a fee prescribed in relation to uncertified copies and extracts.

(6) Applications under subsection (5) above or rules made by virtue of that subsection shall be made in such manner as may be prescribed.

(7) In relation to any portion of the register kept otherwise than in documentary form—

(a) the right of inspection conferred by subsection (4) above is a right to inspect the material on the register; and

(b) the right to a copy or extract conferred by subsection (5) above or rules is a right to a copy or extract in a form in which it can be taken away and in which it is visible and legible.

(8) Subject to subsection (11) below, the register shall be prima facie

evidence of anything required or authorised [by this Act] to be entered in it and in Scotland shall be sufficient evidence of any such thing.

**(9)** A certificate purporting to be signed by the registrar and certifying that any entry which he is authorised by or under this Act to make has or has not been made, or that any other thing which he is so authorised to do has or has not been done, shall be prima facie evidence, and in Scotland shall be sufficient evidence, of the matters so certified.

**(10)** Each of the following—

(a) a copy of an entry in the register or an extract from the register which is supplied under subsection (5) above;

(b) a copy of any representation, specimen or document kept in the Patent Office or an extract from any such document,

which purports to be a certified copy or certified extract shall, subject to subsection (11) below, be admitted in evidence without further proof and without production of any original and in Scotland such evidence shall be sufficient evidence.

**(11)** In the application of this section to England and Wales nothing in it shall be taken as detracting from section 69 or 70 of the Police and Criminal Evidence Act 1984 or any provision made by virtue of either of them.

**(12)** In this section 'certified copy' and 'certified extract' mean a copy and extract certified by the registrar and sealed with the seal of the Patent Office.

*General note*
As amended by the Patents, Designs and Marks Act 1986, Sch 1, para 3. Italicised words repealed; words in bold type added.

## 18. Certificate of registration

(1) The registrar shall grant a certificate of registration in the prescribed form to the registered proprietor of a design when the design is registered.

(2) The register may, in a case where he is satisfied that the certificate of registration has been lost or destroyed, or in any other case in which he thinks it expedient, furnish one or more copies of the certificate.

## 19. Registration of assignments, etc

(1) Where any person becomes entitled by assignment, transmission or operation of law to registered design or to a share in a registered design, or becomes entitled as mortgagee, licensee or otherwise to any other interest in a registered design, he shall apply to the registrar in the prescribed manner for the registration of his title as proprietor or co-proprietor or, as the case may be, of notice of his interest, in the register of designs.

(2) Without prejudice to the provisions of the foregoing subsection, an application for the registration of the title of any person becoming entitled by assignment to a registered design or a share in a registered design, or becoming entitled by virtue of a mortgage, licence or other instrument to any other interest in a registered design, may be made in the prescribed manner by the assignor, mortgagor, licensor or other party to that instrument, as the case may be.

(3) Where application is made under this section for the registration of the title of any person, the registrar shall, upon proof of title to his satisfaction—

(a) where that person is entitled to a registered design or a share in a registered design, register him in the register of designs as proprietor or co-proprietor of the design, and enter in that register particulars of the instrument or event by which he derives title; or

(b) where that person is entitled to any other interest in the registered design, enter in that register notice of his interest, with particulars of the instrument (if any) creating it.

**(3A) Where a design right subsists in a registered design, the registrar shall not register an interest under subsection (3) unless he is satisfied that the person entitled to that interest is also entitled to a corresponding interest in the design right.**

**(3B) Where a design right subsists in a registered design and the proprietor of the registered design is also the design right owner, an assignment of the design right shall be taken to be also an assignment of the right in the registered design, unless a contrary intention appears.**

(4) Subject to any rights vested in any other person of which notice is entered in the register of designs, the person or persons registered as proprietor of a registered design shall have power to assign, grant licences under, or otherwise deal with the design, and to give effectual receipts for any consideration for any such assignment, licence or dealing:

Provided that any equities in respect of the design may be enforced in like manner as in respect of any other personal property.

(5) Except for the purposes of an application to rectify the register under the following provisions of this Act, a document in respect of which no entry has been made in the register of designs under subsection (3) of this section shall not be admitted in any court as evidence of the title of any person to a registered design or share of or interest in a registered design unless the court otherwise directs.

*General note*
Words in bold type added by the Copyright, Designs and Patents Act 1988, Sch 3, para 10.

## 20. Rectification of register

(1) The court may, on the application of any person aggrieved, order the register of designs to be rectified by the making of any entry therein or the variation or deletion of any entry therein.

(2) In proceedings under this section the court may determine any question which it may be necessary or expedient to decide in connection with the rectification of the register.

(3) Notice of any application to the court under this section shall be given in the prescribed manner to the registrar, who shall be entitled to appear and be heard on the application, and shall appear if so directed by the court.

(4) Any order made by the court under this section shall direct that notice of the order shall be served on the registrar in the prescribed manner; and the registrar shall, on receipt of the notice, rectify the register accordingly.

**(5) A recification of the register under this section has effect as follows—**

**(a) an entry made has effect from the date on which it should have been made,**

**(b) an entry varied has effect as if it had originally been made in its varied form, and**

**(c) an entry deleted shall be deemed never to have had effect, unless, in any case, the court directs otherwise.**

*General note*
Sub-s (5) added by the Copyright, Designs and Patents Act 1988 Sch 3, para 11.

## 21. Power to correct clerical errors

(1) The registrar may, in accordance with the provisions of this section, correct any error in an application for the registration or in the representation of a design, or any error in the register of designs.

(2) A correction may be made in pursuance of this section either upon a request in writing made by any person interested and accompanied by the prescribed fee, or without such a request.

(3) Where the registrar proposes to make any such correction as aforesaid otherwise than in pursuance of a request made under this section, he shall give notice of the proposal to the registered proprietor or the applicant for registration of the design, as the case may be, and to any other person who appears to him to be concerned, and shall give them an opportunity to be heard before making the correction.

## 22. Inspection of registered designs

*(1) Subject to the following provisions of this section and to any rules made by the Board of Trade in pursuance of subsection (2) of section five of this Act, the representation or specimen of a design registered under this Act shall be open to inspection at the Patent Office on and after the day on which the certificate of registration is issued.*

**(1) Where a design has been registered under this Act, there shall be open to inspection at the Patent Office on and after the day on which the certificate of registration is issued—**

> **(a) the representation or specimen of the design, and**
> **(b) any evidence filed in support of the applicant's contention that the appearance of an article is material (for the purposes of section 1(3) of this Act).**

**This subsection has effect subject to the following provisions of this section and to any rules made under section 5(2) of this Act.**

(2) In the case of a design registered in respect of an article of any class prescribed for the purposes of this subsection, no representation or specimen of the design filed in pursuance of the application shall, until the expiration of such period after the day on which the certificate of registration is issued as may be prescribed in relation to articles of that class, be open to inspection at the Patent Office except by the registered proprietor, a person authorised in writing by the registered proprietor, or a person authorised by the registrar or by the court:

Provided that where the registrar proposes to refuse an application for the registration of any other design on the ground that it is the same as the first-mentioned design or differs from that design only in immaterial details or in features which are variants commonly used in the trade, the applicant shall be entitled to inspect the representation or specimen of the first-mentioned design filed in pursuance of the application for registration of that design.

(3) In the case of a design registered in respect of an article of any class prescribed for the purposes of the last foregoing subsection, the representation or specimen of the design shall not, during the period prescribed as aforesaid, be inspected by any person by virtue of this section except in the presence of the registrar or of an officer acting under him; and except in the case of an inspection

authorised by the proviso to that subsection, the person making the inspection shall not be entitled to take a copy of the representation or specimen of the design or any part thereof.

(4) Where an application for the registration of a design has been abandoned or refused, neither the application for registration nor any representation or specimen of the design filed in pursuance thereof shall at any time be open to inspection at the Patent Office or be published by the registrar.

*General note*
As amended by the Copyright, Designs and Patents Act, Sch 3, para 12. Italicised words repealed; words in bold type added.

## 23. Information as to existence of copyright

*On the request of any person furnishing such information as may enable the registrar to identify the design, and on payment of the prescribed fee the registrar shall inform him whether the design is registered, and if so, in respect of what articles, and whether any extension of the period of copyright has been granted and shall state the date of registration and the name and address of the registered proprietor.*

**On the request of a person furnishing such information as may enable the registrar to identify the design, and on payment of the prescribed fee, the registrar shall inform him—**

**(a) whether the design is registered and, if so, in respect of what articles, and**

**(b) whether any extension of the period of the right in the registered design has been granted,**

**and shall state the date of registration and the name and address of the registered proprietor.**

*General note*
As amended by the Copyright, Designs and Patents Act 1988, Sch 3, para 13. Italicised words repealed; words in bold type added.

## 24. Evidence of entries, documents, etc

*(1) A certificate purporting to be signed by the registrar and certifying that any entry which he is authorised by or under this Act to make has or has not been made, or that any other thing which he is so authorised to do has or has not been done shall be prima facie evidence of the matters so certified.*

*(2) A copy of any entry in the register of designs or of any representation, specimen or document kept in the Patent Office or an extract from the register or any such document, purporting to be certified by the registrar and to be sealed with the seal of the Patent Office, shall be admitted in evidence without further proof and without production of the original.*

*General note*
Repealed by the Patents, Designs and Marks Act 1986, Sch 3, Pt I.

## *Legal proceedings and Appeals*

## 25. Certificate of contested validity of registration

(1) If in any proceedings before the court the validity of the registration of a design is contested, and it is found by the court that the design is validly registered, the

court may certify that the validity of the registration of the design was contested in those proceedings.

(2) Where any such certificate has been granted, then if in any subsequent proceedings before the court for infringement of the copyright in the registered design or for cancellation of the registration of the design, a final order or judgment is made or given in favour of the registered proprietor, he shall, unless the court otherwise directs, be entitled to his costs as between solicitor and client:

Provided that this subsection shall not apply to the costs of any appeal in any such proceedings as aforesaid.

### 26. Remedy for groundless threats of infringement proceedings

(1) Where any person (whether entitled to or interested in a registered design or an application for registration of a design or not) by circulars, advertisements or otherwise threatens any other person with proceedings for infringement of the *copyright in a registered design* **right in a registered design**, any person aggrieved thereby may bring an action against him for any such relief as is mentioned in the next following subsection.

(2) Unless in any action brought by virtue of this section the defendant proves that the acts in respect of which proceedings were threatened constitute or, if done, would constitute, an infringement of the *copyright in a registered design* **right in a registered design** the registration of which is not shown by the plaintiff to be invalid, the plaintiff shall be entitled to the following relief, that is to say—

   (a) declaration to the effect that the threats are unjustifiable;
   (b) an injunction against the continuance of the threats; and
   (c) such damages, if any, as he has sustained thereby.

**(2A) Proceedings may not be brought under this section in respect of a threat to bring proceedings for an infringement alleged to consist of the making or importing of anything.**

(3) For the avoidance of doubt it is hereby declared that a mere notification that a design is registered does not constitute a threat of proceedings within the meaning of this section.

*General note*
As amended by the Copyright, Designs and Patents Act 1988, Sch 3, para 15. Italicised words repealed; words in bold bype added.

### 27. The Court

*Subject to the provisions of this Act relating to Scotland, Northern Ireland and the Isle of Man, any reference or application to the court under this Act, shall, subject to rules of court, be dealt with by such judge of the High Court as the Lord Chancellor may select for the purpose.*

   **(1) In this Act 'the court' means—**

   **(a) in England and Wales the High Court or any patents county court having jurisdiction by virtue of an order under section 287 of the Copyright, Designs and Patents Act 1988,**
   **(b) in Scotland, the Court of Session, and**
   **(c) in Northern Ireland, the High Court.**

   **(2) Provision may be made by rules of court with respect to proceedings in the High Court in England and Wales for references and applications**

**under this Act to be dealt with by such judge of that court as the Lord Chancellor may select for the purpose.**

*General note*
As amended by the Copyright, Designs, and Patents Act 1988, Sch 3, para 16. Italicised words repealed; words in bold type added.

### 28. The Appeal Tribunal
(1) Any appeal from the registrar under this Act shall lie to the Appeal Tribunal.

*(2) The Appeal Tribunal shall consist of one or more judges of the High Court nominated for the purpose by the Lord Chancellor.*

*(2A) At any time when it consists of two or more judges, the jurisdiction of the Appeal Tribunal*

> *(a) where in the case of any particular appeal the senior of those judges so directs, shall be exercised in relation to that appeal by both of the judges, or (if there are more than two) by two of them, sitting together, and*
> *(b) in relation to any appeal in respect of which no such direction is given, may be exercised by any one of the judges;*

*and, in the exercise of that jurisdiction, different appeals may be heard at the same time by different judges.*

(2) **The Appeal Tribunal shall consist of**

> (a) **one or more judges of the High Court nominated by the Lord Chancellor, and**
> (b) **one judge of the Court of Session nominated by the Lord President of that Court.**

(2A) **At any time when it consists of two or more judges, the jurisdiction of the Appeal Tribunal—**

> (a) **where in the case of any particular appeal the senior of those judges so directs, shall be exercised in relation to that, appeal by both of the judges, or (if there are more than two) by two of them, sitting together, and**
> (b) **in relation to any appeal in respect of which no such direction is given, may be exercised by any one of the judges;**

**and, in the exercise of that jurisdiction, different appeals may be heard at the same time by different judges.**

(3) The expenses of the Appeal Tribunal shall be defrayed and the fees to be taken therein may be fixed as if the Tribunal were a court of the High Court.

(4) The Appeal Tribunal may examine witnesses on oath and administer oaths for that purpose.

*(5) Upon any appeal under this Act the Appeal Tribunal may by order award to any party such costs as the Tribunal may consider reasonable and direct how and by what parties the costs are to be paid; and any such order may be made a rule of court.*

(5) **Upon any appeal under this Act the Appeal Tribunal may by order award to any party such costs or expenses as the Tribunal may consider reasonable and direct how and by what parties the costs or expenses are to be paid; and any such order may be enforced—**

(a) **in England and Wales or Northern Ireland, in the same way as an order of the High Court;**

(b) **in Scotland, in the same way as a decree for expenses granted by the Court of Session.**

*(6) The Appeal Tribunal shall with regard to the right of audience, observe the same practice as before the first day of November, nineteen hundred and thirty-two, was observed in the hearing of appeals by the law officer.*

(7) Upon any appeal under this Act the Appeal Tribunal may exercise any power which could have been exercised by the registrar in the proceeding from which the appeal is brought.

(8) Subject to the foregoing provisions of this section the Appeal Tribunal may make rules for regulating all matters relating to proceedings before it under this Act including right of audience.

**(8A) At any time when the Appeal Tribunal consists of two or more judges, the power to make rules under subsection (8) of this section shall be exercisable by the senior of those judges:**

**Provided that another of those judges may exercise that power if it appears to him that it is necessary for rules to be made and that the judge (or, if more than one, each of the judges) senior to him is for the time being prevented by illness, absence or otherwise from making them.**

(9) An appeal to the Appeal Tribunal under this Act shall not be deemed to be a proceeding in the High Court.

*(10) For the purposes of this section the seniority of judges shall be reckoned by reference to the dates on which they were appointed judges of the High Court respectively.*

**(10) In this section 'the High Court' means the High Court in England and Wales; and for the purposes of this section the seniority of judges shall be reckoned by reference to the dates on which they were appointed judges of that court or the Court of Session.**

*General note*

Sub-ss (2), (2A), (5), (10) were substituted by the Copyright, Designs and Patents Act 1988, Sch 3, para 17. Sub-ss (2), (2A), (10) were originally added, and sub-s (8A) was inserted by the Administration of Justice Act 1969, s24. Sub-s (6) was repealed, and the words in bold type in sub-s (8) were added, by the Administration of Justice Act 1970, ss10(5), 54(3), Sch 11.

*Powers and Duties of Registrar*

**29. Exercise of discretionary powers of registrar**

Without prejudice to any provisions of this Act requiring the registrar to hear any party to proceedings thereunder, or to give to any such party an opportunity to be heard, the registrar shall give to any applicant for registration of a design an opportunity to be heard before exercising adversely to the applicant any discretion vested in the registrar by or under this Act.

*General note*

As amended by the Copyright, Designs and Patents Act 1988, Sch 3, para 18. Italicised words repealed; words in square brackets added.

## 30. Costs and security for costs

*(1) The registrar may, in any proceedings before him under this Act, by order award to any party such costs as he may consider reasonable, and direct how and by what parties they are to be paid; and any such order may be made a rule of court.*

*(2) If any party by whom application is made to the registrar for the cancellation of the registration of a design or for the grant of a licence in respect of a registered design, or by whom notice of appeal is given from any decision of the registrar under this Act, neither resides nor carries on business in the United Kingdom or the Isle of Man, the registrar, or, in the case of appeal, and in default of such security being given may treat the application or appeal as abandoned.*

**(1) Rules made by the Secretary of State under this Act may make provision empowering the registrar, in any proceedings before him under this Act—**

  **(a) to award any party such costs as he may consider reasonable, and**
  **(b) to direct how and by what parties they are to be paid.**

**(2) Any such order of the registrar may be enforced—**

  **(a) in England and Wales or Northern Ireland, in the same way as an order of the High Court;**
  **(b) in Scotland, in the same way as a decree for expenses granted by the Court of Session.**

**(3) Rules made by the Secretary of State under this Act may make provision empowering the registrar to require a person, in such cases as may be prescribed, to give security for the costs of—**

  **(a) an application for cancellation of the registration of a design,**
  **(b) an application for the grant of a licence in respect of a registered design, or**
  **(c) an appeal from any decision of the registrar under this Act,**

**and enabling the application or appeal to be treated as abandoned in default of such security being given.**

*General note*
As amended by the Copyright, Designs and Patents Act 1988, Sch 3, para 19. Italicised words repealed; words in square brackets added.

## 31. Evidence before registrar

*(1) Subject to rules made by the Board of Trade under this Act the evidence to be given in any proceedings before the registrar under this Act may be given by affidavit or statutory declaration; but the registrar may if he thinks fit in any particular case take oral evidence in lieu of or in addition to such evidence as aforesaid, and may allow any witness to be cross-examined on his affidavit or declaration.*

*(2) Subject to any such rules as aforesaid, the registrar shall in respect of the examination of witnesses on oath and the discovery and production of documents have all the powers of an official referee of the Supreme Court, and the rules applicable to the attendance of witnesses in proceedings before such a referee shall apply to the attendance of witnesses in proceedings before the registrar.*

**Rules made by the Secretary of State under this Act may make provision—**

> **(a)** **as to the giving of evidence in proceedings before the registrar under this Act by affidavit or statutory declaration;**
> **(b)** **conferring on the registrar the powers of an official referee of the Supreme Court as regards the examination of witnesses on oath and the discovery and production of documents; and**
> **(c)** **applying in relation to the attendance of witnesses in proceedings before the registrar the rules applicable to the attendance of witnesses in proceedings before such a referee.**

*General note*
As amended by the Copyright, Designs and Patents Act 1988, Sch 3, para 20. Italicised words repealed; words in bold type added.

## 32. Power of registrar to refuse to deal with certain agents
*(1) Rules made by the Board of Trade under this Act may authorise the registrar to refuse to recognise as agent in respect of any business under this Act—*

> *(a) any individual whose name has been erased from, and not restored to, the register of patent agents kept in purusance of rules made under the* **Patents Act 1977;**
> *(b) any individual who is for the time being suspended in accordance with those rules from acting as a patent agent;*
> *(c) any person who has been convicted of an offence under section eighty-eight of the Patents Act 1949* **or section 114 of the Patents Act 1977;**
> *(d) any person who is found by the Board of Trade (after being given an opportunity to be heard) to have been convicted of any offence or to have been guilty of any such misconduct as, in the case of an individual registered in the register of patent agents aforesaid, would render him liable to have his name erased therefrom;*
> *(e) any person, not being registered as a patent agent, who in the opinion of the registrar is engaged wholly or mainly in acting as agent in applying for patents in the United Kingdom or elsewhere in the name or for the benefit of a person by whom he is employed;*
> *(f) any company or firm, if any person whom the registrar could refuse to recognise as agent in respect of any business under this Act is acting as a director or manager of the company or is a partner in the firm.*

*(2) The registrar shall refuse to recognise as agent in respect of any business under this Act any person who neither resides nor has a place of business in the United Kingdom or the Isle of Man.*

*General note*
Repealed by the Copyright, Designs and Patents Act 1988, Sch 3, para 21. Words in bold originally added by the Patents Act 1977, Sch 5, para 2.

*Offences*

## 33. Offences under s 5
(1) If any person fails to comply with any direction given under section five of this Act or makes or causes to be made an application for the registration of a design in contravention of that section, he shall be guilty of an offence and liable—

*(a)* *on summary conviction, to imprisonment for a term not exceeding three months or to a fine not exceeding* **the prescribed sum***, or to both such imprisonment and such fine, or*

*(b)* *on conviction on indictment, to imprisonment for a term not exceeding two years or to a fine . . . or to both such imprisonment and such fine.*

**(a)** **on conviction on indictment to imprisonment for a term not exceeding two years or a fine, or both;**

**(b)** **on summary conviction to imprisonment for a term not exceeding six months or a fine not exceeding the statutory maximum,or both.**

*(2) Where an offence under section five of this Act is committed by a body corporate, every person who at the time of commission of the offence is a director, general manager, secretary or other similar officer of the body corporate, or is purporting to act in any such capacity, shall be deemed to be guilty of that offence unless he proves that the offence was committed without his consent or connivance and that he exercised all such diligence to prevent the commission of the offence as he ought to have exercised having regard to the nature of his functions in that capactiy and to all the circumstances.*

*General note*
Sub-ss (1)(a), (b) sustituted, and sub-s (2) repealed, by the Copyright, Designs and Patents Act 1988, Sch 3, para 22, in relation to offences committed on or after 1 August 1989. Italicised words repealed; words in bold type added.

## 34. Falsification of register, etc

If any person makes or causes to be made a false entry in the register of designs, or a writing falsely purporting to be a copy of an entry in that register, or produces or tenders or causes to be produced or tendered in evidence any such writing, knowing the entry or writing to be false, he shall be guilty *of a misdemeanour* of an offence and liable—

**(a)** **on conviction on indictment to imprisonment for a term not exceeding two years or a fine, or both;**

**(b)** **on summary conviction to imprisonment for a term not exceeding six months or a fine not exceeding the statutory maximum, or both.**

*General note*
As amended by the Copyright, Designs and Patents Act 1988, Sch 3, para 23, in relation to offences committed on or after 1 August 1989. Italicised words repealed; words in bold type added.

## 35. Fine for falsely representing a design as registered

(1) If any person falsely represents that a design applied to any article sold by him is registered in respect of that article, he shall be liable on summary conviction to a fine **not exceeding level 3 on the standard scale**; and for the purposes of this provision a person who sells an article having stamped, engraved or impressed thereon or otherwise applied thereto the word 'registered', or any other word expressing or implying that the design applied to the article is registered, shall be deemed to represent that the design applied to the article is registered in respect of the article.

(2) If any person, after *the copyright in a registered design* **the right in a registered design** has expired, marks any article to which the design has been

applied with the word 'registered', or any word or words implying that there is a *subsisting copyright in the origin* **subsisting right in the design under this Act**, or causes any such article to be so marked, he shall be liable on summary conviction to a fine **not exceeding level 1 on the standard scale**.

*General note*
As amended by the Copyright, Designs and Patents Act 1988, Sch 3, para 24. The amendments to sub-s (2) do not apply to offences committed before 1 August 1989. Italicised words repealed; words in bold type added.

### 35.A  Offence by body corporate: liability of officers
(1) Where an offence under this Act committed by a body corporate is proved to have been committed with the consent or connivance of a director, manager, secretary or other similar officer of the body, or a person purporting to act in any such capacity, he as well as the body corporate is guilty of the offence and liable to be proceeded against and punished accordingly.

(2) In relation to a body corporate whose affairs are managed by its members 'directors' means a member of the body corporate.

*General note*
Inserted by the Copyright, Designs and Patents Act 1988, Sch 3, para 25, in relation to offences committed on or after 1 August 1989.

### 36.  General power of *Board of Trade* Secretary of State to make rules, etc
*(1) Subject to the provisions of this Act, the Board of Trade may make such rules as they think expedient for regulating the business of the Patent Office in relation to designs and for regulating all matters by this Act placed under the direction or control of the registrar or the Board, and in particular, but without prejudice to the generality of the foregoing provision—*

> *(a) for prescribing the form of applications for registration of designs and of any representations or specimens of designs or other documents which may be filed at the Patent Office, and for requiring copies to be furnished of any such representations, specimens or documents;*
> *(b) for regulating the procedure to be followed in connection with any application or request to the registrar or in connection with any proceeding before the registrar and for authorising the rectification of irregularities of procedure;*
> *(c) for regulating the keeping of the register of designs;*
> *(d) for authorising the publication and sale of copies or represetations of designs and other documents in the Patent Office;*
> *(e) for prescribing anything authorised or required by this Act to be prescribed by rules made by the Board.*

**(1) Subject to the provisions of this Act, the Secretary of State may make such rules as he thinks expedient for regulating the business of the Patent Office in relation to designs and for regulating all matters by this Act placed under the direction or control of the registrar or the Secretary of State.**

**(1A) Rules may, in particular, make provision—**

> **(a) prescribing the form of applications for registration of designs and of any representations or specimens of designs or other documents which may be filed at the Patent Office, and requiring copies to be furnished of any such representations, specimens or documents;**

(b) **regulationg the procedure to be followed in connection with any application or request to the registrar or in connection with any proceeding before him, and authorising the rectification or irregularities of procedure;**

(c) **providing for the appointment of advisers to assist the registrar in proceedings before him;**

(d) **regulating the keeping of the register of designs;**

(e) **authorising the publication and sale of copies of representations of designs and other documents in the Patent Office;**

(f) **prescribing anything authorised or required by this Act to be prescribed by rules.**

(1B) **The remuneration of an adviser appointed to assist the registrar shall be determined by the Secretary of State with the consent of the Treasury and shall be defrayed out of money provided by Parliament.**

(2) Rules made under this section may provide for the establishment of branch offices for designs and may authorise any document or thing required by or under this Act to be filed or done at the Patent Office, to be filed or done at the branch office at Manchester or any other branch office established in pursuance of the rules.

*General note*
As amended by the Copyright, Designs and Patents Act 1988, Sch 3, para 26. Italicised words repealed; words in bold type added.

### 37. Provisions as to rules and Orders

*(1) Any rules made by the Board of Trade under this Act shall be advertised twice in the Journal.*

(2) Any rules made by the *Board of Trade* **Secretary of State** in pursuance of section fifteen or section sixteen of this Act, and any order made, direction given, or other action taken under the rules by the registrar, may be made, given or taken so as to have effect as respects things done or omitted to be done on or after such date, whether before or after the coming into operation of the rules or of this Act, as may be specified in the rules.

(3) Any power to make rules conferred by this Act on the *Board of Trade* **Secretary of State** or on the Appeal Tribunal shall be exercisable by statutory instrument; and the Statutory Instruments Act 1946 shall apply to a statutory instrument containing rules made by the Appeal Tribunal in like manner as if the rules had been made by a Minister of the Crown.

(4) Any statutory instrument containing rules made by the Board of Trade under this Act shall be subject to annulment in pursuance of a resolution of either House of Parliament.

(5) An Order in Council made under this Act may be revoked or varied by a subsequent Order in Council.

*General note*
As amended by the Copyright, Designs and Patents Act 1988, Sch 3, para 27. Italicised words repealed; words in bold type added.

### *38. Proceedings of Board of Trade*

*(1) Anything required or authorised by this Act to be done by, to or before the Board of Trade may be done by, to or before the President of the Board of Trade,*

*any secretary, under-secretary or assistant secretary of the Board, or any person authorised in that behalf by the President.*

*(2) All documents purporting to be orders made by the Board of Trade and to be sealed with the seal of the Board, or to be signed by a secretary, under-secretary or assistant secretary of the Board, or by any person authorised in that behalf by the President of the Board, shall be received in evidence and shall be deemed to be such orders without further proof, unless the contrary is shown.*

*(3) A certificate, signed by the President of the Board of Trade, that any order made or act done is the order or act of the Board, shall be conclusive evidence of the fact so certified.*

*General note*
Sub-s (1) was repealed by the Industrial Expansion Act 1968, s 18(2), Sch 4. Whole section repealed by the Copyright, Designs and Patents Act 1988, Sch 3, para 28.

*Supplemental*

## 39. Hours of business and excluded days
(1) Rules made by the *Board of Trade* **Secretary of State** under this Act may specify the hour at which the Patent Office shall be deemed to be closed on any day for the purposes of the transaction by the public of business under this Act or of any class of such business, and may specify days as excluded days for any such purposes.

(2) Any business done under this Act on any day after the hour specified as aforesaid in relation to business of that class, or on a day which is an excluded day in relation to business of that class, shall be deemed to have been done on the next following day not being an excluded day, that time shall be extended to the next following day not being an excluded day.

*General note*
As amended by the Copyright, Designs and Patents Act 1988, Sch 3, para 29. Italicised words repealed; words in bold type added.

## 40. Fees
There shall be paid in respect of the registration of designs and applications therefore, and in respect of other matters relating to designs arising under this Act, such fees as may be prescribed by rules made by the *Board of Trade* **Secretary of State** with the consent of the Treasury.

*General note*
As amended by the Copyright, Designs and Patents Act 1988, Sch 3, para 30. Italicised words repealed; words in bold type added.

## 41. Service of notices, etc, by post
Any notice required or authorised to be given by or under this Act, and any application or other document so authorised or required to be made or filed, may be given, made or filed by post.

## 42. Annual report of registrar
The Comptroller-General of Patents, Designs and Trade Marks shall, in his annual report with respect to the execution of the **Patents Act 1977** include a report with respect to the execution of this Act as if it formed part of or was included in that Act.

*General note*
Words in bold type substituted by the Patents Act 1977, Sch 5, para 3.

### 43. Savings
(1) Nothing in this Act shall be construed as authorising or requiring the registrar to register a design the use of which would, in his opinion, be contrary to law or morality.

(2) Nothing in this Act shall affect the right of the Crown or of any person deriving title directly or indirectly from the Crown to sell or use articles forfeited under the laws relating to customs or excise.

### 44. Interpretation
(1) In this Act, except where the context otherwise requires, the following expressions have the meanings hereby respectively assigned by them, that is to say—

> *'Appeal Tribunal' means the judge nominated under section twenty-eight of this Act;*
> **'Appeal Tribunal' means the Appeal Tribunal constituted and acting in accordance with section 28 of this Act as amended by the Administration of Justice Act 1969;**
> 'article' means any article of manufacture and includes any part of an article if that part is made and sold separately;
> 'artistic work' has the same meaning as in the *Copyright Act 1956* **Part I of the Copyright, Designs and Patents Act 1988**;
> 'assignee' includes the personal representative of a deceased assignee, and references to the assignee of any person include references to the assignee of the personal representative or assignee of that person;
> 'author' in relation to a design, has the meaning given by section 2(3) and (4);
> *'copyright' has the meaning assigned to it by subsection (1) of section seven of this Act;*
> *['corresponding design' has the same meaning as in section ten of the Copyright Act 1956;] in relation to an artistic work, means a design which if applied to an article would produce something which would be treated for the purposes of Part I of the Copyright, Designs and Patents Act 1988 as a copy of that work,*
> *'court' means the High Court;*
> **'the court' shall be construed in accordance with section 27 of this Act,**
> 'design' has the meaning assigned to it by *subsection (3) of* **section one of this Act;**
> **'employee', 'employment' and 'employer' refer to employment under a contract of service or of apprenticeship;**
> *'Journal' means the journal published by the comptroller under the Patents Act 1949;*
> 'prescribed' means prescribed by rules made by *the Board of Trade* **the Secretary of State under this Act;**
> 'proprietor' has the meaning assigned to it by section two of this Act;
> 'registered proprietor' means the person or persons for the time being entered in the register of designs as proprietor of the design;
> 'registrar' means the Comptroller-General of Patents Designs and Trade Marks;
> 'set of articles' means a number of articles of the same general character

ordinarily on sale or intended to be used together, to each of which the same design, or the same design with modifications or variations not sufficient to alter the character or substantially to affect the identity thereof, is applied.

(2) Any reference in this Act to an article in respect of which a design is registered shall, in the case of a design registered in respect of a set of articles, be construed as a reference to any article of that set.

(3) Any question arising under this Act whether a number of articles constitute a set of articles shall be determined by the registrar; and notwithstanding anything in this Act any determination of the registrar under this subsection shall be final.

(4) For the purposes of subsection (1) of section fourteen and of section sixteen of this Act, the expression 'personal representative', in relation to a deceased person, includes the legal representative of the deceased appointed in any country outside the United Kingdom.

*General note*
The definition 'Appeal Tribunal' was substituted by the Administration of Justice Act 1969. The definitions 'artistic work' and 'corresponding design' were inserted by the Copyright Act 1956, and the words in square brackets within those definitions were substituted by the Copyright, Designs and Patents Act 1988.

The definitions 'author' and 'employee', 'employment' and 'employer' were inserted, the definition 'the court' and the words in square brackets in the definitions 'design' and 'prescribed' were substituted, and the definitions 'copyright' and 'Journal' were repeated by the Copyright, Designs and Patents Act 1988. Italicised words repealed; words in bold type added.

### 45. Application to Scotland
In the application of this Act to Scotland—

*(1) The provisions of this Act conferring a special jurisdiction on the court as defined by this Act shall not, except so far as the jurisdiction extends, affect the jurisdiction of any court in Scotland in any proceedings relating to designs; and with reference to any such proceedings, the term 'the Court' shall mean the Court of Session:*

*(2) If any rectification of a register under this Act is required in pursuance of any proceeding in a court, a copy of the order, decree, or other authority for the recitification, shall be served on the registrar, and he shall rectify the register accordingly:*

(3) The expression 'injunction' means 'interdict'; the expression 'arbitrator' means 'arbiter'; the expression 'plaintiff' means 'pursuer'; the expression 'defendant' means 'defender'.

*General note*
Sub-ss (1), (2) were repealed by the Copyright, Designs and Patents Act 1988, Sch 3, para 32.

### 46. Application to Northern Ireland
In the application of this Act to Northern Ireland—

*(1) The provisions of this Act conferring a special jurisdiction on the court, as defined by this Act, shall not, except so far as the jurisdiction extends, affect the jurisdiction of any court in Northern Ireland in any proceedings relating to designs; and with reference to any such proceedings the term 'the Court' means the High Court in Northern Ireland;*

*(2) If any rectification of a register under this Act is required in pursuance of any proceeding in a court, a copy of the order, decree or other authority for the*

*rectification shall be served on the registrar, and he shall rectify the register accordingly;*

*(3) References to enactments of the Parliament of the United Kingdom shall be construed as references to those enactments as they apply in Northern Ireland.*

**(3) References to enactments include enactments comprised in Northern Ireland legislation;**

**(3A) References to the Crown include the Crown in right of Her Majesty's Government in Northern Ireland.**

*(4) References to a Government department shall be construed as including references to a department of the Government of Northern Ireland:*

**(4) References to a Government department shall be construed as including references to a Northern Ireland department and in relation to a Northern Ireland department references to the Treasury shall be construed as references to the Department of Finance and Personnel.**

*(5) The expression 'summary conviction' shall be construed as meaning conviction subject to, and in accordance with, the Petty Sessions (Ireland) Act 1851, and any Act (including any Act of the Parliament of Northern Ireland) amending that Act.*

*General note*
Paras (1), (2) were repealed, paras (3), (4) were substituted and para (3A) was inserted, by the Copyright, Designs and Patents Act 1988, Sch 3, para 33.
Para (5) was repealed by the Northern Ireland Act 1962, Sch 4, Pt IV. Italicised words repealed: words in bold type added.

## 47. Isle of Man
*This Act shall extend to the Isle of Man subject to the following modifications—*

*(1) Nothing in this Act shall affect the jurisdiction of the courts in the Isle of Man in proceedings for infringement or in any action or proceeding respecting a design competent to those courts;*

*(2) The punishment for a misdemeanour under this Act in the Isle of Man shall be imprisonment for any term not exceeding two years, with or without hard labour, and with or without a fine not exceeding one hundred pounds, at the discretion of the court;*

*(3) Any offence under this Act committed in the Isle of Man which would in England be punishable on summary conviction may be prosecuted, and any fine in respect thereof, recovered, at the instance of any person aggrieved, in the manner in which offences punishable on summary conviction may for the time being be prosecuted.*

**This Act extends to the Isle of Man, subject to any modifications contained in an Order made by Her Majesty in Council, and accordingly, subject to any such Order, references in this Act to the United Kingdom shall be construed as including the Isle of Man.**

*General note*
As amended by the Copyright, Designs and Patents Act 1988, Sch 3, para 34. Italicised words repealed; words in bold type added.

## 47A. Territorial waters and the continental shelf
**(1) For the purposes of this Act the territorial waters of the United Kingdom shall be treated as part of the United Kingdom.**

**(2) This Act applies to things done in the United Kingdom sector of the continental shelf on a structure or vessel which is present there for purposes directly connected with the exploration of the sea bed or subsoil or the exploitation of their natural resources as it applies to things done in the United Kingdom.**

**(3) The United Kingdom sector of the continental shelf means the areas designated by order under section 1(7) of the Continental Shelf Act 1974.**

*General note*
Inserted by the Copyright, Designs and Patents Act 1988, Sch 3, para 35.

### 48. Repeals, savings, and transitional provisions

*(1) Subject to the provisions of this section the enactments specified in the Second Schedule to this Act are hereby repealed to the extent specified in the third column of that Schedule.*

(2) Subject to the provisions of this section, any Order in Council, rule, order, requirement, certificate, notice, decision, direction, authorisation, consent, application, request or thing made, issued, given or done under any enactment repealed by this Act shall, if in force at the commencement of this Act, and so far as it could have been made, issued, given or done under this Act, continue in force and have effect as if made, issued, given or done under the corresponding enactment of this Act.

(3) Any register kept under the Patents and Designs Act 1907, shall be deemed to form part of the corresponding register under this Act.

(4) Any design registered before the commencement of this Act shall be deemed to be registered under this Act in respect of articles of the class in which it is registered.

(5) Where, in relation to any design the time for giving notice to the registrar under section fifty-nine of the Patents and Designs Act 1907, expired before the commencement of this Act and the notice was not given, subsection (2) of section six of this Act shall not apply in relation to that design or any registration of that design.

(6) Any document referring to any enactment repealed by this Act shall be construed as referring to the corresponding enactment of this Act.

(7) Nothing in the foregoing provisions of this section shall be taken as prejudicing the operation of section thirty-eight of the Interpretation Act 1889, (which relates to the effect of repeals).

*General note*
Italicised words repealed by the Copyright, Designs and Patents Act 1988, Sch 3, para 36.

### 49. Short title and commencement

(1) This Act may be cited as the Registered Designs Act 1949.

(2) This Act shall come into operation on the first day of January, nineteen hundred and fifty, immediately after the coming into operation of the Patents and Designs Act 1949.

SCHEDULES

## FIRST SCHEDULE

Section 12

PROVISIONS AS TO THE USE OF REGISTERED DESIGNS FOR THE SERVICES OF THE CROWN AND AS TO THE
RIGHTS OF THIRD PARTIES IN RESPECT OF SUCH USE

### 1. Use of registered designs for services of the Crown

(1) Notwithstanding anything in this Act, any Government department, and any person authorised in writing by a Government department, may use any registered design for the services of the Crown in accordance with the following provisions of this paragraph.

(2) If and so far as the design has before the date of registration thereof been duly recorded by or applied by or on behalf of a Government department otherwise than in consequence of the communication of the design directly or indirectly by the registered proprietor or any person from whom he derives title, any use of the design by virtue of this paragraph may be made free of any royalty or other payment to the registered proprietor.

(3) If and so far as the design has not been so recorded or applied as aforesaid, any use of the design made by virtue of this paragraph at any time after the date of registration thereof, or in consequence of any such communication as aforesaid, shall be made upon such terms as may be agreed upon, either before or after the use, between the Government department and the registered proprietor with the approval of the Treasury, or as may in default of agreement be determined by the court on a reference under paragraph 3 of this Schedule.

(4) The authority of a Government department in respect of a design may be given under this paragraph either before or after the design is registered and either before or after the acts in respect of which the authority is given are done, and may be given to any person whether or not he is authorised directly or indirectly by the registered proprietor to use the design.

(5) Where any use of a design is made by or with the authority of a Government department under this paragraph, then, unless it appears to the department that it would be contrary to the public interest so to do, the department shall notify the registered proprietor as soon as practicable after the use is begun, and furnish him with such information as to the extent of the use as he may from time to time require.

**(6) For the purposes of this and the next following paragraph 'the services of the Crown' shall be deemed to include—**

   **(a)   the supply to the government of any country outside the United Kingdom, in pursuance of an agreement or arrangement between Her Majesty's Government in the United Kingdom and the government of that country, of articles required—**
      **(i)   for the defence of that country; or**
      **(ii)  for the defence of any other country whose government is party to any agreement or arrangement with Her Majesty's said Government in respect of defence matters;**
   **(b)   the supply to the United Nations, or to the government of any country belonging to that organisation, in pursuance of an agreement or arrangement between Her Majesty's Government and that organisation or government, of articles required for any armed forces operating in pursuance of a resolution of that organisation or any organ of that organisation;**

**and the power of a Government department or a person authorised by a Government department under this paragraph to use a design shall include power to sell to any such government or to the said organisation any articles the supply of which is authorised by this sub-paragraph, and to sell to any person any articles made in the exercise of the powers conferred by this paragraph which are no longer required for the purposes for which they were made.**

(7) The purchaser of any articles sold in the exercise of powers conferred by this paragraph, and any person claiming through him, shall have power to deal with them in the same manner as if the rights in the registered design were held on behalf on His Majesty.

*General note*
Sub-s(6) substituted by the Defence Contracts Act 1958, s 1.

### 2. Rights of third parties in respect of Crown use

(1) In relation to any use of a registered design, or a design in respect of which an application for registration is pending, made for the services of the Crown—

    (a)   by a Government department or a person authorised by a Government department under the last foregoing paragraph; or

    (b)   by the registered proprietor or applicant for registration to the order of a Government department.

the provisions of any licence, assignment or agreement made, whether before or after the commencement of this Act, between the registered proprietor or applicant for the registration or any person who derives title from him or from whom he derives title and any person other than a Government department shall be of no effect so far as those provisions restrict or regulate the use of the design, or any model, document or information relating thereto, or provide for the making of payments in respect of any such use, or calculated by reference thereto; and the reproduction or publication of any model or document in connection with the said use shall not be deemed to be an infringement of any copyright **or design right** subsisting in the model or document **or of any topography right**.

(2) Where an exclusive licence granted otherwise than for royalties or other benefits determined by reference to the use of the design is in force under the registered design then—

    (a)   in relation to any use of the design which, but for the provisions of this and the last foregoing paragraph, would constitute an infringement of the rights of the licensee, sub-paragraph (3) of the last foregoing paragraph shall have effect as if for the reference to the registered proprietor there were substituted a reference to the licensee; and

    (b)   in relation to any use of the design by the licensee by virtue of an authority given under the last foregoing paragraph, that paragraph shall have effect as if the said sub-paragraph (3) were omitted.

(3) Subject to the provisions of the last foregoing sub-paragraph, where the registered design or the right to apply for or obtain registration of the design has been assigned to the registered proprietor in consideration of royalties or other benefits determined by reference to the use of the design, then—

    (a)   in relation to any use of the design by virtue of paragraph 1 of this Schedule, sub-paragraph (3) of that paragraph shall have effect as if the reference to the registered proprietor included a reference to the assignor, and any sum payable by virtue of that sub-paragraph shall be divided between the registered proprietor and the assignor in such proportion as may be agreed upon between them or as may in default of agreement be determined by the court on a reference under the next following paragraph; and

    (b)   in relation to any use of the design made for the services of the Crown by the registered proprietor to the order of a Government department sub-paragraph (3) of paragraph 1 of this Schedule shall have effect as if that use were made by virtue of an authority given under that paragraph.

(4) Where, under sub-paragraph (3) of paragraph 1 of this Schedule, payments are required to be made by a Government department to a registered proprietor in respect of any use of a design, any person being the holder of an exclusive licence under the registered design (not being such a licence as is mentioned in sub-paragraph (2) of this paragraph) authorising him to make use of the design shall be entitled to recover from the registered proprietor, or as may in default of agreement be determined by the court under the next following paragraph to be just having regard to any expenditure incurred by that person—

    (a)   in developing the said design; or

    (b)   in making payments to the registered proprietor, other than royalties or other payments determined by reference to the use of the design, in consideration of the licence;

and, if, at any time before the amount of any such payment has been agreed upon between the Government department and the registered proprietor, that person gives notice in writing of his interest to the department, any agreement as to the amount of that payment shall be of no effect unless it is made with his consent.

(5) In this paragraph 'exclusive licence' means a licence from a registered proprietor which confers on the licensee, or on the licensee and persons authorised by him, to the exclusion of all other persons (including the registered proprietor) any right in respect of the registered design.

*General note*
Words 'or design right' added by the Copyright, Designs and Patents Act 1988, Sch 3, para 27. Words 'or of any topography right' added by the Semiconductor Products (Protection of Topography) Regulations 1987, SI 1987/1497, Sch 2, para 2.

**2A. Compensation for loss of profit**
(1) Where Crown use is made of a registered design, the government department concerned shall pay—

(a) to the registered proprietor, or
(b) if there is an exclusive licence in force in respect of the design, to the exclusive licensee,

compensation for any loss resulting from his not being awarded a contract to supply the articles to which the design is applied.

(2) Compensation is payable only to the extent that such a contract could have been fulfilled from his existing manufacturing capacity; but is payable notwithstanding the existence of circumstances rendering him ineligible for the award of such a contract.

(3) In determining the loss, regard shall be had to the profit which would have been made on such a contract and to the extent to which any manufacturing capacity was underused.

(4) No compensation is payable in respect of any failure to secure contracts for the supply of articles to which the design is applied otherwise than for the services of the Crown.

(5) The amount payable under this paragraph shall, if not agreed between the registered proprietor or licensee and the government department concerned with the approval of the Treasury, be determined by the court on a reference under paragraph 3; and it is in addition to any amount payable under paragraph 1 or 2 of this Schedule.

(6) In this paragraph—
'Crown use'; in relation to a design, means the doing of anything by virtue of paragraph 1 which would otherwise be an infringement of the right in the design; and
'the government department concerned', in relation to such use, means the government department by whom or on whose authority the act was done.

*General note*
Inserted by the Copyright, Designs and Patents Act 1988, s 271, in relation to any Crown use of a registered design after 1 August 1989.

**3. Reference of disputes as to Crown use**
*(1) Any dispute as to the exercise by a Government department or a person authorised by a Government department of the powers conferred by paragraph 1 of this Schedule, or as to terms for the use of a design for the services of the Crown thereunder, or as to the right of any person to receive any part of a payment made in pursuance of sub-paragraph (3) of that paragraph, may be referred to the court by either party to the dispute in such manner as may be prescribed by rules of court.*

**(1) Any dispute as to—**

**(a) the exercise by a Government department, or a person authorised by a Government department, of the powers conferred by paragraph 1 of this Schedule,**
**(b) terms for the use of a design for the services of the Crown under that paragraph,**
**(c) the right of any person to receive any part of a payment made under paragraph 1(3), or**
**(d) the right of any person to receive a payment under paragraph 2A, may be referred to the court by either party to the dispute.**

(2) In any proceedings under this paragraph to which a Government department are a party, the department may—

(a) if the registered proprietor is a party to the proceedings, apply for cancellation of the registration of the design upon any ground upon which the registration of a design may be cancelled on an application to the court under section twenty of this Act;
(b) in any case, put in issue the validity of the registration of the design without applying for its cancellation.

(3) If in such proceedings as aforesaid any question arises whether a design has been recorded or applied as mentioned in paragraph 1 of this Schedule, and the disclosure of any document recording the design, or of any evidence of the application thereof, would in the opinion of the department be prejudicial to the public interest, the disclosure may be made confidentially to counsel for the other party or to an independent expert mutually agreed upon.

(4) In determining under this paragraph any dispute between a Government department and any person as to terms for the  use of a design for the services of the Crown, the court shall have regard to any benefit or compensation which that person from whom he derives title may have received, or may be entitled to receive, directly or indirectly from any Government department in respect of the design in question.

(5) In any proceedings under this paragraph the court may at any time order the whole proceedings or any question or issue of fact arising therein to be referred to a special or official referee or an arbitrator on such terms as the court may direct; and references to the court in the foregoing provisions of this paragraph shall be construed accordingly.

*General note*

Sub-s(1) substituted by the Copyright, Designs and Patents Act 1988, s 271, in relation to any Crown use of a registered design after 1 August 1989. Italicised words repealed; words in bold type added.

### 4. Special provisions as to Crown use during emergency

(1) During any period of emergency within the meaning of this paragraph, the powers exercisable in relation to a design by a Government department, or a person authorised by a Government department under paragraph 1 of this Schedule shall include power to use the design for any purpose which appears to the department necessary or expedient—

    (a)   for the efficient prosecution of any war in which His Majesty may be engaged;

    (b)   for the maintenance of supplies and services essential to the life of the community;

    (c)   for securing a sufficiency of supplies and services essential to the well-being of the community;

    (d)   for promoting the productivity of industry, commerce and agriculture;

    (e)   for fostering and directing exports and reducing imports, or imports of any classes, from all or any countries and for redressing the balance of trade;

    (f)   generally for ensuring that the whole resources of the community are available for use, and are used, in a manner best calculated to serve the interests of the community; or

    (g)   for assisting the relief of suffering and the restoration and distribution of essential supplies and services in any part of His Majesty's dominions or any foreign countries that are in grave distress as the result of war;

and any reference in this Schedule to the services of the Crown shall be construed as including a reference to the purposes aforesaid.

*(2) In this paragraph the expression 'period of emergency' means the period ending with the tenth day of December, nineteen hundred and fifty, or such later date as may be prescribed by Order in Council, and any other period beginning on such date as may be declared by Order in Council to be the commencement, and ending on such date as may be so declared to be the termination, of a period of emergency for the purposes of this paragraph.*

*(3) A draft of any Order in Council under this paragraph shall be laid before Parliament; and the draft shall not be submitted to His Majesty except in pursuance of an Address presented by each House of Parliament praying that the Order be made.*

**(2) In this paragraph the expression 'period of emergency' means a period beginning on such date as may be declared by Order in Council to be the commencement, and ending on such date as may be so declared to be the termination, of a period of emergency for the purposes of this paragraph.**

**(3) No Order in Council under this paragraph shall be submitted to Her Majesty unless a draft of it has been laid before and approved by a resolution of each House of Parliament.**

*General note*

Sub-ss(2), (3) were substituted by the Copyright, Designs and Patents Act 1988, Sch 3, para 37. Italicised words repealed; words in bold type added.

SECOND SCHEDULE

*General note*

This Schedule set out enactments repealed by this Act and was itself repealed by the Copyright, Designs and Patents Act 1988, Sch 3, para 28.

# Part D   Miscellaneous

INTERPREATION ACT 1978
(1978 c 30)

## 6.  Gender and number

In any Act, unless the contrary intention appears,—

- (a)  words importing the masculine gender include the feminine;
- (b)  words importing the feminine gender include the masculine;
- (c)  words in the singular include the plural and words in the plural include the singular.

## 15.  Repeal of repeal

Where an Act repeals a repealing enactment, the repeal does not revive any enactment previously repealed unless words are added reviving it.

## 16.  General savings

(1)  Without prejudice to section 15, where an Act repeals an enactment, the repeal does not, unless the contrary intention appears,—

- (a)  revive anything not in force or existing at the time at which the repeal takes effect;
- (b)  affect the previous operation of the enactment repealed or anything duly done or suffered under that enactment;
- (c)  affect any right, privilege, obligation or liability acquired accrued or incurred under that enactment;
- (d)  affect any penalty, forfeiture or punishment incurred in respect of an offence committed against that enactment;
- (e)  affect any investigation, legal proceeding or remedy in respect of any such right, privilege, obligation, liability, penalty, forfeiture or punishment;

and any such investigation, legal proceeding or remedy may be instituted, continued or enforced, and any such penalty, forfeiture or punishment may be imposed as if the repealing Act had not been passed.

(2)  This section applies to the expiry of a temporary enactment as if it were repealed by an Act.

# Appendix 2

## Secondary legislation

### Part A    Copyright and Rights in Performances

BRITISH MUSEUM (DELIVERY OF BOOKS) REGULATION
(SR & O 1915 No 773)
*Dated 9 August 1915*

The Board of Trade on the application of the Trustees of the British Museum, and by virtue of the powers given them by section 1 of the Copyright (British Museum) Act 1915, hereby make the following Regulation, to come into operation as from the date hereof:

There shall be excepted from the provisions of section 15(1) of the Copyright Act 1911, whereby the publisher of any book published in the United Kingdom is required within one month after the publication to deliver, at his own expense, a copy of the book to the Trustees of the British Museum, the following publications, viz:

| | |
|---|---|
| Trade Advertisements, | Trade Labels, |
| Trade Cards, | Trade Leaflets, |
| Trade Catalogues, | Trade Plans, |
| Trade Circulars, | Trade Posters, |
| Trade Coupons, | Trade Price Lists, |
| Trade Designs, | Trade Prospectuses, |
| Trade Forms, | Trade Show Cards, |
| | Trade Wrappers. |

ORDER IN COUNCIL DATED 9 FEBRUARY 1920
(SR & O 1920 No 257)

*Under the Copyright Act 1911(1 & 2 Geo 5, c 46), further regulating copyright relations with the United States of America as regards works first published between 1 August 1914, and the termination of the War*

At the court at Buckingham Palace, the 9th day of February, 1920.

PRESENT,
The King's Most Excellent Majesty

Lord President                          Lord Colebrooke
Earl Curzon of Kedleston                Sir Frederick Ponsonby

Whereas by reason of conditions arising out of the war difficulties have been experienced by citizens of the United States of America in complying with the requirements of the Copyright Act 1911, as to first publication within the parts of His Majesty's dominions to which the Act extends of their works first published in the United States of America during the war:

And whereas His Majesty is advised that the Government of the United States of America has undertaken, upon issue of this Order, to extend the protection afforded by the United States Law of 18 December 1919, entitled 'An Act to amend sections 8 and 21 of the Copyright Act, approved 4 March 1909,' to British subjects:

And whereas by reason of the said undertaking of the Government of the United States of America His Majesty is satisfied that the said Government has made, or has undertaken to make, such provision as it is expedient to require for the protection of works first made or published between 1 August 1914, and the termination of the war in the parts of His Majesty's dominions to which this Order applies, and entitled to copyright under Part I of the Copyright Act 1911:

And whereas by the Copyright Act 1911 authority is conferred upon His Majesty to extend, by Order in Council, the protection of the said Act to certain classes of foreign works within any part of His Majesty's dominions, other than self-governing dominions, to which the said Act extends:

And whereas by reason of these premises it is desirable to provide protection within the said dominions for literary or artistic works first published in the United States of America between 1 August 1914, and the termination of the war which have failed to accomplish the formalities prescribed by the Copyright Act 1911, by reason of conditions arising out of the war:

Now, therefore, His Majesty, by and with the advice of His Privy Council, and by virtue of the authority conferred upon him by the Copyright Act 1911, is pleased to order, and it is hereby ordered, as follows:

**1.** The Copyright Act 1911, shall, subject to the provisions of the said Act and of this Order, apply to works first published in the United States of America between 1 August 1914, and the termination of the war, which have not been republished prior to the commencement of this Order in the parts of His Majesty's dominions to which this Order applies, in like manner as if they had been first published within the parts of His Majesty's dominions to which the said Act extends:

Provided that the enjoyment by any work of the rights conferred by the Copyright Act 1911 shall be conditional upon publication of the work in the dominion to which this Order relates not later than six months after the termination of the war, and shall commence from and after such publication, which shall not be colourable only, but shall be intended to satisfy the reasonable requirements of the public.

**2.** The provisions of section 15 of the Copyright Act 1911, as to the delivery of books to libraries, shall apply to works to which this Order relates upon their publication in the United Kingdom.

**3.** In the case of musical works to which this Order relates and provided that no contrivances by means of which the work may be mechanically performed have before the commencement of this Order been lawfully made, or placed on sale, within the parts of His Majesty's dominions to which this Order applies, copyright in the work shall include all rights conferred by the said Act with respect to the making of records, perforated rolls and other contrivances by means of which the work may be mechanically performed.

**4.** This Order shall apply to all His Majesty's dominions, colonies and possessions with the exception of those hereinafter named, that is to say:

> The Dominion of Canada;
> The Commonwealth of Australia;
> The Dominion of New Zealand;
> The Union of South Africa;
> Newfoundland.

**5.** Nothing in this Order shall be construed as depriving any work of any rights which have been lawfully acquired under the provisions of the Copyright Act 1911, or any Order in Council thereunder.

**6.** This Order shall take effect as from the 2nd day of February 1920, which day is in this Order referred to as the commencement of this Order.

And the Lords Commissioners of His Majesty's Treasury are to give the necessary orders accordingly.

## BRITISH MUSEUM REGULATIONS
(SR & O 1935 No 278)

*(Dated 12 October 1932, made by the Trustees of the British Museum under the British Museum Act 1932 (22 & 23 Geo 5, c 34) as to publications not required)*

The Trustees of the British Museum, being empowered under the British Museum Act 1932, by regulations to apply the said Act to publications of such classes as may be specified in such regulations being publications of the descriptions set out in the Schedule to the said Act and thereby to except certain publications from sub-section 1 of section 15 of the Copyright Act 1911, hereby make the following regulation within their said powers. The delivery by publishers of publications falling under the following categories is no longer required, unless a written demand for delivery of them or any of them is made by the Trustees—

Publications wholly or mainly in the nature of trade advertisements.

Registers of voters prepared under the Representation of the People Act 1918, as amended by any subsequent enactment.

Specifications of inventions prepared for the purposes of the Patents and Designs Act 1907, as amended by any subsequent enactment.

Publications wholly or mainly in the nature of time tables of passenger transport services, being publications prepared for local use.

Publications wholly or mainly in the nature of calendars. Publications wholly or mainly in the nature of blank forms of accounts, or blank forms of receipts, or other blank forms of a similar character.

Wall sheets printed with alphabets, mottoes, religious texts or other matter for the purpose of elementary instruction.

British Museum,
12 October 1932

## COPYRIGHT (UNITED STATES OF AMERICA) ORDER 1942
*(SR & O 1942 No 1579 as amended by SI 1950 No 1641)*

At the Court at Buckingham Palace, the 6th day of August, 1942

PRESENT,

The King's Most Excellent Majesty

| | |
|---|---|
| Lord President | Secretary Sir Archibald Sinclair |
| Lord Macmillan | Mr Williams |

Whereas by reason of conditions arising out of the war difficulties have been experienced by citizens of the United States of America in complying with the requirements of the Copyright Act 1911, as to first publication within the parts of His Majesty's dominions to which the Act extends of their works first published in the United States of America during the war:

And whereas His Majesty is advised that the Government of the United States of America has undertaken to grant such extension of time as may be deemed appropriate for the fulfilment of the conditions and formalities prescribed by the laws of the United States with respect to the works of British subjects first produced or published outside the United States and subject to copyright or to renewal of copyright under the laws of the United States including works subject to ad interim copyright:

And whereas by reason of the said undertaking of the Government of the United States of America His Majesty is satisfied that the said Government has made, or has undertaken to make, such provision as it is expedient to require for the protection of works first made or published during the period commencing on the 3rd day of September, 1939, and ending one year after the termination of the present war within the parts of His Majesty's dominions to which this Order applies and entitled to copyright under Part I of the Copyright Act 1911:

And whereas by the Copyright Act 1911, authority is conferred upon His Majesty to extend, by Order in Council, the protection of the said Act to certain classes of foreign works within any part of His Majesty's dominions, other than the self-governing dominions, to which the Act extends:

And whereas by reason of these premises it is desirable to provide protection within the parts of His Majesty's dominions to which this Order applies for literary or artistic works first published in the United States of America during the period commencing on the 3rd day of September, 1939, and ending one year after the termination of the present war which have failed to accomplish the formalities prescribed by the Copyright Act 1911, by reason of conditions arising out of the war:

Now, therefore, His Majesty, by and with the advice of His Privy Council, and by virtue of the authority conferred upon Him by the Copyright Act 1911, and of all other powers enabling Him in that behalf, is pleased to direct and doth hereby direct as follows:

**1.** The Copyright Act 1911, shall, subject to the provisions of the said Act and of this Order, apply to works first published in the United States of America during the period commencing on the 3rd day of September, 1939 [and ending on the 29th day of December 1950], which have not been republished in the parts of His Majesty's dominions to which this Order applies within fourteen days of the publication in the United States of America, in like manner as if they had been first published within the parts of His Majesty's dominion to which the said Act extends:

Provided that the enjoyment by any such work of the rights conferred by the Copyright Act 1911, shall be conditional upon publication of the work within the parts of His Majesty's dominions to which this Order relates [not later than the 28th day of December, 1950], and shall commence from and after such publication, which shall not be colourable only, but be intended to satisfy the reasonable requirements of the public.

**2.** The provisions of section 15 of the Copyright Act 1911, as to the delivery of books to libraries, shall apply to works to which this Order relates upon their publication in the United Kingdom.

**3.** Nothing in this Order shall be construed as depriving any work of any rights which have been lawfully acquired under the provisions of the Copyright Act 1911, or any Order in Council thereunder.

**4.** Where any person has, before the commencement of this Order, taken any action whereby he has incurred any expenditure or liability in connection with the reproduction or performance of any work which at the time was lawful, or for the purpose of or with a view to the reproduction or performance of a work at a time when such reproduction or performance would, but for the making of this Order, have been lawful, nothing in this Order shall diminish or prejudice any rights or interest arising from or in connection with such action which were subsisting and valuable at the said date, unless the person who by virtue of this Order becomes entitled to restrain such reproduction or performance agrees to pay such compensation as, failing agreement, may be determined by arbitration.

**5.** The Interpretation Act 1889, shall apply to the interpretation of this Order as if it were an Act of Parliament.

**6.** This Order may be cited as the Copyright (United States of America) Order 1942.

**7.** This Order shall come into operation on the date of its publication in the London Gazette, which day is in this Order referred to as the commencement of this Order. [The date of publication was 10 March 1944.]


COPYRIGHT (INDUSTRIAL DESIGNS) RULES 1957
(SI 1957 No 867)

*(Revoked by the Copyright (Industrial Process and Excluded Articles) (No 2) Order 1989 (SI 1989 No 1070), as from 1 August 1989)*

| | | |
|---|---|---|
| *Made* . . . . . . . . | *17 May 1957* |
| *Laid before Parliament* . . . . | *24 May 1957* |
| *Coming into operation* . . . . | *1 June 1957* |

The Board of Trade, in pursuance of the powers conferred upon them by section 36 of the Registered Designs Act 1949, and subsection (5) of section 10 of the Copyright Act 1956, hereby make the following rules—

*Industrial application of designs*

**1.** A design shall be taken to be applied industrially for the purposes of section 10 of the Copyright Act 1956, if it is applied—

(a) to more than fifty articles all of which do not together constitute a single set of articles as defined in subsection (1) of section 44 of the Registered Designs Act 1949; or

(b) to goods manufactured in lengths or pieces, other than hand-made goods.

*Interpretation*

**2.**—(1) Reference in these Rules to the application of a design to any articles or goods means the application of the design to those articles or goods by a process of printing or embossing or by any other process whatsoever, and shall be deemed to include a reference to the reproduction of the design on or in those articles or goods in the course of their production.

(2) The Interpretation Act 1889, shall apply to the interpretation of these Rules as it applies to the interpretation of an Act of Parliament, and as if these Rules and the Rules hereby revoked were Acts of Parliament.

*Revocation, citation and commencement*

**3.**—(1) The Copyright (Industrial Designs) Rules 1949, are hereby revoked.

(2) These Rules may be cited as the Copyright (Industrial Designs) Rules 1957, and shall come into operation on the 1st day of June, 1957.

COPYRIGHT (HONG KONG) ORDER 1972
(SI 1972 No 1724)

*(As amended by the Copyright (Hong Kong) (Amendment) Order 1979 (SI 1979 No 910), and the Copyright (Hong Kong) (Amendment) Order 1990 (SI 1990 No 588))*

| | | |
|---|---|---|
| *Made* . . . . . . . . | *14th November 1972* |
| *Laid before Parliament* . . . . | *20th November 1972* |
| *Coming into operation* . . . . | *12th December 1972* |

Her Majesty, by and with the advise of Her Privy Council, and by virtue of the Authority conferred upon Her by section 31 of the Copyright Act 1956 and of all other powers enabling Her in that behalf, is pleased to direct, and it is hereby directed, as follows—

**1.** This Order may be cited as the Copyright (Hong Kong) Order 1972 and shall come into operation on 12th December 1972.

**2.** The Interpretation Act 1889 shall apply to the interpretation of this Order as it applies to the interpretation of an Act of Parliament.

**3.** The provisions of the Copyright Act 1956 specified in Part I of Schedule 1 hereto shall extend to Hong Kong subject to the modifications specified in Part II of that Schedule.

**4.** The Copyright (International Organisations) Order 1957, as amended, the Copyright (Broadcasting Organisations) Order 1961, and the Copyright (International Conventions) Order 1972 (being Orders in Council made under Part V of the said Act) shall extend to Hong Kong subject, in the case of the last mentioned Order, to the modifications specified in Schedule 2 hereto.

### SCHEDULE 1

PART I

*Provisions of the Copyright Act 1956 extended to Hong Kong*

All the provisions of the Act, as amended by the Performers' Protection Acts 1958 and 1963, the *Films Act 1960* and the *Design Copyright Act 1968, except sections 23 to 30, 32, 34, 35, 42 and 44 and Schedules 4, 5 and 9* [**as amended by the Dramatic and Musical Performers' Protection Act 1958, the Films Act 1960, the Design Copyright Act 1968 and the Copyright (Amendment) Act 1971, except sections 28, *32*, 34, 35, 42 and 55 and Schedule 5.**]

*General note*
The words in bold were substituted for the words in italics by SI 1979 No 910, art 2; the number in bold italics was deleted by SI 1990 No 588, art 2.

PART II

*Modifications of the provisions extended*

*General Modifications*

1. In sections 7, 8(11) and 15(4), for references to the Board of Trade there shall be substituted references to the Governor in Council.
2. In sections 8(1) and 8(10), 10(2) and (3), 12(6), 21(1) and 21(6), 22(2) and 22(3), 43, 48(4) and 49(2) and paragraph 46 of Schedule 7, for 'the United Kingdom' there shall be substituted '**Hong Kong**'.

*Particular Modifications*

3. The provisions mentioned in the first column in the following table shall be modified in the manner specified in the second column.

| Provision | Modification |
|---|---|
| Section 8 | In subsections (2) and (4), for 'three-farthings' there shall be substituted 'five cents' and in subsection (2), for 'farthing' there shall be substituted 'cent'; |

for subsection (3) there shall be substituted the following—

'(3) If at any time by an order made under this section in its operation in the law of the United Kingdom any different rate of, or minimum amount of, royalty is prescribed either generally or in relation to any one or more classes of records, the provisions of this section shall be construed subject to the provisions of any such order as is for the time being in force, provided that any reference in such an order to any sum of money shall be construed as a reference to the equivalent amount in the currency of legal tender in Hong Kong as provided by any law of Hong Kong;'

in subsection (4)(a), all the words after the first reference to works shall be omitted.

| Section 10 | For subsection (5) there shall be substituted the following— |

'(5) For the purpose of this section a design shall be taken as being applied industrially if it is applied in the circumstances for the time being prescribed by rules made under this section and section 36 of the Registered Designs Act 1949 as extended by this section in the law of the United Kingdom.'.

| Section 13 | For subsection (3) there shall be substituted the following— |

'(3) Copyright subsisting in a cinematograph film by virtue of this section shall continue to subsist until the film is published and thereafter until the end of the period of fifty years from the end of the calendar year which includes the date of its first publication and shall then expire, or, if copyright subsists in the film by virtue only of the last preceding subsection, it shall continue to subsist as from the date of first publication until the end of the period of fifty years from the end of the calendar year which includes that date and shall then expire;'

in subsection (8), for 'any such film as is mentioned in paragraph (a) of subsection (1) of section 38 of the Films Act 1960 (which relates to newsreels)' there shall be substituted 'any film consisting wholly or mainly of photographs which, at the time they were taken, were means of communicating news',

subsection (11) shall be omitted.

Section 17    Subsection (6) shall be omitteD.

Section 18    In subsection (1), for the proviso there shall be substituted the following—

'Provided that if by virtue of section 5 of the Limitation Ordinance (Chapter 347) (which relates to limitation in cases of successive conversion and extinction of title of the owner of converted goods), the title of the owner of the copyright to such a copy or plate would (if he had then been the owner of the copy or plate) have been extinguished at the end of the period mentioned in that section, he shall not be entitled to any rights or remedies under this subsection in respect of any thing done in relation to that copy or plate after the end of that period;'

subsection (4) shall be omitted.

Section 21    In subsections (7) and (8), for the words 'forty shillings' and 'fifty pounds' there shall be substituted respectively 'five hundred dollars' and 'fifty thousand dollars' and for the words 'two months' there shall be substituted 'twelve months;'

subsection (10) shall be omitted.

Section 22    In subsection (1), for the 'Commissioners of Customs and Excise (in this section referred to as 'the Commissioners')' there shall be substituted ''the Director of Commerce and Industry' and, subject to the modifications to subsection (4) hereinafter provided, for subsequent references to the said Commissioners there shall be substituted references to the said Director;

in subsection (4) for 'the Commissioners' where those words first occur there shall be substituted 'the Governor in Council' and for 'the Commissioners consider' there shall be substituted 'the Governor in Council considers';

subsection (6) shall be omitted;

for subsection (7) there shall be substituted the following—

(7)    Where by virtue of this section the importation into Hong Kong of any copy of a work to which the section applies is prohibited, the importation into Hong Kong of such a copy shall, for the purposes only of the provisions of the Import and Export Ordinance (Chapter 60) providing for forfeiture, be deemed to be a contravention of that Ordinance.'

**Section 23**    **For subsection (2) there shall be substituted the following—**

**'(2)    The tribunal shall consist of a chairman who shall be a person qualified for appointment as a District Judge under section 5 of the District Court Ordinance (Chapter 336), and of not less than 2 nor more than 4 other members, all of whom shall be appointed from time to time by the Governor.;'**

**for subsections (5) and (6) there shall be substituted the following—**

**'(5)    There shall be a clerk to the tribunal who shall be appointed by the Governor. (6) The remuneration of the chairman and other members of the tribunal and of the clerk to the tribunal shall be determined by the Governor and shall be payable out of the general revenue of the Colony';**

**subsection (7) shall be omitted.**

**Section 24**    **For subsection (3)(c) there shall be substituted the following—**

**'(c) in relation to such licences as are mentioned in paragraph (c) of the last preceding subsection, means a licensee under the Television Ordinance (Chapter 52).'**

**Section 30**    **For subsection (6) there shall be substituted the following— (6) In this section 'the court' means the Court of Appeal of Hong Kong.']**

Section 31    Subsections (1) and (2) shall be omitted; in subsection (4), for 'the United Kingdom' there shall be substituted 'Hong Kong' and for 'in a country' there shall be substituted 'in the United Kingdom or in any country other than Hong Kong.'

**Section 32**    **In sub-section (1), for the words 'Her Majesty may by Order in Council', there shall be substituted 'The Governor may by Order'.**

**In sub-section (1)(a) and (c), for the words 'the United Kingdom,' there shall be substituted 'Hong Kong'.**

**In sub-section (1)(d), for the words 'laws of any part of the United Kingdom', there shall be substituted 'law of Hong Kong.'**

**In sub-section (1)(e), for the words 'the United Kingdom by the Corporation or the Authority,' there shall be substituted 'Hong Kong.'**

**In sub-section (2), the words 'in Council' shall be deleted.**

**In sub-section (2), for the words 'Her Majesty shall not make an Order in Council,' there shall be substituted 'The Governor shall not make an Order,' and for the words 'Her Majesty is satisfied,' there shall be substituted 'the Governor is satisfied'.]**

Section 33    For subsection (1) there shall be substituted the following—

'(1)   An organisation to which this section applies is one declared to be such by an Order in Council made under this section as part of the law of the United Kingdom which has been extended, in relation to that organisation, to Hong Kong.'.

Section 37    Subsection (4) shall be omitted.

Section 39    In subsection (8), for 'section three of the Crown Proceedings Act, 1947' there shall be substituted 'section 5 of the Crown Proceedings Ordinance (Chapter 300).'

Section 40    Subsection (3) shall be omitted; in subsection (4), for 'either of the two last preceding subsections' there shall be substituted 'the last preceding subsection', and 'or the programme to be transmitted, as the case may be' shall be omitted;

in subsection (5), the reference to a work shall be omitted.

Section 41    In subsection (7), for the definition of 'school' there shall be substituted '"school" has the same meaning as in the Education Ordinance (Chapter 279)'.

Section 46    Subsection (1) shall be omitted; in subsection (2), '(including any enactment of the Parliament of Northern Ireland)' shall be omitted.

Section 47    The whole section except subsection (4) shall be omitted; *in subsection (4), 'or rules' shall be omitted.*

Section 50    For subsection (2) there shall be substituted the following—

'(2)   Subject to the said transitional provisions the Copyright Act 1911 and the Copyright Order Confirmation (Mechanical Instruments: Royalties) Act 1928 are hereby repealed.'

Section 51    For subsection (2) there shall be substituted the following—

'(2)—(a)   Any provision of this Act empowering the Governor in Council to make regulations shall come into operation on the commencement of the Order in Council extending that provision to Hong Kong. (b) All the other provisions of this Act shall come into operation on 1st January 1973';

subsection (3) shall be omitted.

Schedule 1    In paragraph 2, for 'section seven of the Act of 1949' there shall be substituted 'section 2 of the United Kingdom Designs (Protection) Ordinance (Chapter 44)'.

| | |
|---|---|
| **Schedule 4** | **In paragraph 1(2), for 'Board of Trade, or, in the case of the chairman of the tribunal, to the Lord Chancellor,' there shall be substituted 'Governor;'** |

**in paragraph 1(3), for 'Board of Trade, or, in the case of the chairman of the tribunal, the Lord Chancellor,' there shall be substituted 'Governor;'**

**in paragraph 2, for 'Board of Trade, or, in the case of the chairman of the tribunal, the Lord Chancellor,' there shall be substituted 'Governor;'**

**in paragraph 6(1) for 'Lord Chancellor' there shall be substituted 'Chief Justice,' and subject to the approval of the Treasury,' shall be omitted;**

**for paragraph 6(2) there shall be substituted the following—**

**'(2) Any such rules may apply in relation to the tribunal any of the provisions of the Arbitration Ordinance (Chapter 341).'**

Schedule 7 *Paragraphs 25, 26, 40 and 41 shall be omitted.* [**Paragraphs 26, 40 and 41 shall be omitted.**]

*General note*
The words in italics in the entry relating to s 47 were deleted, the words in bold in the entry relating to Sch 7 were substituted for the words in italics, and the entries relating to ss 23, 24, 30, Sch 4 were inserted, by SI 1979 No 910, art 2. The entry relating to s 32 was inserted by SI 1990 No 588, art 2.

## SCHEDULE 2

*Modifications of the Copyright (International Conventions) Order 1972—*

(i) Articles 4 (other than paragraph (2)(b)) and 8 to 11 together with Schedules 4 to 7 shall be omitted.
(ii) In Article 3, for 'any part of the United Kingdom' there shall be substituted 'Hong Kong'.
(iii) In Schedule 2 the following dates shall be inserted respectively in the second column in relation to the countries mentioned in the following tables—

| | |
|---|---|
| Ghana | 22nd August 1962 |
| Kenya | 7th September 1962 |
| Malawi | 26th October 1965 |
| Mauritius | 12th March 1968 |
| Nigeria | 14th February 1962 |
| Zambia | 1st June 1965 |

Section 24
Section 30
Schedule 4

## COPYRIGHT (HONG KONG) (AMENDMENT) ORDER 1979
## (SI 1979 No 910)

| | | | |
|---|---|---|---|
| *Made* | . . . . | . . | *26th July 1979* |
| *Laid before Parliament* | . . | . . | *3rd August 1979* |
| *Coming into operation* | . . | . . | *24th August 1979* |

Whereas her Majesty, in pursuance of the Regency Acts 1937 to 1953, was pleased, by Letters Patent dated the 16th day of July 1979, to delegate to the six Councillors of State therein named or any two or more of them full power and authority during the period of Her Majesty's absence from the United Kingdom to summon and hold on Her Majesty's behalf Her Privy Council and to signify thereat Her Majesty's approval for anything for which Her Majesty's approval in Council is required.

Now, therefore, Her Majesty Queen Elizabeth The Queen Mother and His Royal Highness The Prince Charles, Prince of Wales, being authorised thereto by the said Letters Patent and in pursuance of the powers conferred by section 31(1) of the Copyright Act 1956 and all other powers enabling Her Majesty and by and with the advise of Her Majesty's Privy Council, do on Her Majesty's behalf order, and it is hereby ordered, as follows—

**1.**—(1) This Order may be cited as the Copyright (Hong Kong) (Amendment) Order 1979, and shall be construed as one with the Copyright (Hong Kong) Order 1972 (hereinafter referred to as 'the principal Order').

(2) The principal Order and this Order may be cited together as the Copyright (Hong Kong) Orders 1972 and 1979.

(3) This Order shall come into operation on 24th August 1979.

**2.** [This article amends the Copyright (Hong Kong)(Amendment) Order 1979 [SI 1972 No 1724] Schedule 1, Part I and Part II].


COPYRIGHT (INTERNATIONAL CONVENTIONS) ORDER 1979[1]
(SI 1979 No 1715)

> *Made* . . . . . . . . . . *19th December 1979*
> *Laid before Parliament* . . . . *3 January 1980*
> *Coming into operation* . . . . *24 January 1980*

Her Majesty, by and with the advice of Her Privy Council, and by virtue of the authority conferred upon her by sections 31, 32 and 47 of the Copyright Act 1956, and of all other powers enabling Her in that behalf, is pleased to order, and it is hereby ordered as follows—

PART I

*Citation, commencement and interpretation*

**1.** This Order may be cited as the Copyright (International Conventions) Order 1979, and shall come into operation on 24 January 1980.

**2.**—(1) In this Order—
'the Act' means the Copyright Act 1956; and 'material time' means—

  (i)  in relation to an unpublished work or subject-matter, the time at which such work or subject-matter was made or, if the making thereof extended over a period, a substantial part of that period;

  (ii) in relation to a published work or subject matter, the time of first publication.

PART II

*Protection for literary, dramatic, musical and artistic works, sound recordings, cinematograph films and published editions*

**3.** Subject to the following provisions of this Order, the provisions of Parts I and II of the Act (except section 14) and all the other provisions of the Act relevant to

---

1 The numbered footnotes (which are part of the text of this book, not the Order) indicate amendments to the previous (1972) Order which were consolidated in this Order, and amendments subsequent to the making of this Order.

those Parts shall in the case of any country mentioned in Schedules 1 or 2 hereto apply—

    (a)   in relation to literary, dramatic, musical or artistic works, sound recordings, cinematograph films or published editions first published in that country, as they apply to such works, recordings, films or editions first published in the United Kingdom;[2]

    (b)   in relation to persons who at any material time are citizens or subjects of, or domiciled or resident in, that country, as they apply to persons who at such time are British subjects or domiciled or resident in the United Kingdom;[2] and

    (c)   in relation to bodies incorporated under the laws of that country, as they apply to bodies incorporated under the laws of any part of the United Kingdom.[2]

**4.**—(1)  Subject to the following provisions of this Article, the relevant provisions of Schedule 7 to the Act shall have effect in relation to any work or other subject-matter in which copyright subsists by virtue of this Part of this Order as if for any references therein to the commencement of the Act or any of its provisions or to the date of the repeal of any provision of the Copyright Act 1911 or of any other enactment there were substituted references to 27 September 1957 (being the date on which the Copyright (International Conventions) Order 1957 came into operation).

    (2)  Subject to the following provisions of this Article, in the case of any country mentioned in Schedule 2 hereto in relation to which a date is specified in that Schedule—

    (a)   paragraph (1) of this Article shall have effect as if for the reference to 27 September 1957 there were substituted that date (if different); and

    (b)   copyright shall not subsist by virtue of this Part of this Order in any work or other subject-matter by reason only of its publication in such a country before the date so specified.

(3)  This Article shall not apply—

    (a)   in the case of **Bahamas**,[3] **Barbados**,[4] **Belize**,[5] **Cyprus**,[6] **Fiji**,[7] Ghana, Kenya, Malawi, **Malta**,[8] Mauritius, Nigeria, **St Vincent and the Grenadines**,[9] **Trinidad and Tobago**,[10] Zambia or **Zimbabwe**;[11] or

    (b)   to any work or subject-matter first published in the United States of America if immediately before 27 September 1957 copyright under the Copyright Act 1911 subsisted in such work or subject matter by virtue

---

2  Where this Order forms part of the law of dependent countries, see Sch 6, para 1, below.
3  Added by SI 1987 No 2060 on 25 December 1987.
4  See n 3, above.
5  Added by SI 1986 No 2235 on 27 January 1987.
6  See n 3, above.
7  See n 3, above.
8  See n 3, above.
9  Added by SI 1988 No 1855 on 24 November 1988.
10  Added by SI 1988 No 1307 on 24 August 1988.
11  See n 3, above.

of either an Order in Council dated 9 February 1920 regulating copyright relations with the United States of America or the Copyright (United States of America) Order 1942.*

**5.** The acts restricted by section 12 of the Act as applied by this Part of this Order shall not include—

(a)  causing the recording to be heard in public; or
(b)  broadcasting the recording;

except in the case of the countries mentioned in Schedule 3 to this Order.

**6.** Where any person has before the commencement of this Order incurred any expenditure or liability in connection with the reproduction or performance of any work or other subject-matter in a manner which at the time was lawful, or for the purpose of or with a view to the reproduction or performance of a work at a time when such reproduction or performance would, but for the making of this Order, have been lawful, nothing in this Part of this Order shall diminish or prejudice any right or interest arising from or in connection with such action which is subsisting and valuable immediately before the commencement of this Order unless the person who by virtue of this Part of this Order becomes entitled to restrain such reproduction or performance agrees to pay such compensation as, failing agreement, may be determined by arbitration.

**7.** Nothing in the provisions of the Act as applied by this Part of this Order shall be construed as reviving any right to make, or restrain the making of, or any right in respect of, translations, if such right has ceased before the commencement of this Order.

PART III

*Protection in respect of broadcasts*

**8.** The provisions of section 14 of the Act, so far as they relate to sound broadcasts and all the other provisions of the Act relevant thereto other than section 40(3), shall apply, in the case of each of the countries mentioned in Schedule 4 to this Order, in relation to sound broadcasts made from places in any such country by an organisation constituted in, or under the laws of, the country in which the broadcast is made as they apply in relation to sound broadcasts made from places in the United Kingdom by the British Broadcasting Corporation; so, however, that paragraphs 17 and 18 of Schedule 7 to the Act shall have effect as if for the references therein to the commencement of section 14 there were substituted references to the relevant date set out in the said Schedule 4 (being the date on which the provisions of section 14 of the Act so far as they relate to sound broadcasts were first applied in the case of that country).

**9.** The provisions of section 14 of the Act, so far as they relate to television broadcasts, and all the other provisions of the Act relevant thereto, other than section 37(4), section 40(3) and Schedule 5, shall apply, in the case of each of the countries mentioned in Schedule 5 to this Order, in relation to television broadcasts made from places in any such country by an organisation constituted in, or under the laws of, the country in which the broadcast was made as they apply in relation to television broadcasts made from places in the United Kingdom by the British

---

* SR & O 1942 No 1579, amended by SI 1950 No 1641.

Broadcasting Corporation or the Independent Broadcasting Authority; so, however, that—

(a) section 24(3)(c) of the Act shall have effect as if for the reference to the Corporation or the Authority or any organisation appointed by them there were substituted a reference to any owner or prospective owner of copyright in television broadcasts; and

(b) paragraphs 17 and 18 of Schedule 7 to the Act shall have effect as if for the references therein to the commencement of section 14 there were substituted references to the relevant date set out in Schedule 5 to this Order (being the date on which the provisions of section 14 of the Act so far as they relate to television broadcasts were first applied in the case of that country).

PART IV

*Extensions and revocations*

**10.** Parts I and II of this Order shall extend to the countries mentioned in Schedule 6 to this Order subject to the modifications mentioned in that Schedule and Part III shall extend to Gibraltar and Bermuda subject to the modifications mentioned in Schedule 7 to this Order.

**11.** The Orders mentioned in Schedule 8 to this Order are hereby revoked insofar as they form part of the law of the United Kingdom or any country mentioned in Schedule 6 to this Order.

## SCHEDULE 1

COUNTRIES OF THE BERNE COPYRIGHT UNION

*(The countries indicated with an asterisk[12] are also party to the Universal Copyright Convention.)*

Argentina*
Australia* (and Norfolk Island)
Austria*
Bahamas(*)[13]
Barbados[*][14]
Belgium*
Benin
Brazil*
Bulgaria(*)
Cameroon(*)
Canada*
Central African Empire[15]
Ceylon (Sri Lanka)
Chad
Chile*
Colombia*[16]
Congo (People's Republic)
Costa Rica*[17]
Cyprus
Czechoslovakia*

---

12 Asterisks shown in round brackets were added by Orders subsequent to the 1972 Order and asterisks in square brackets were added by orders subsequent to the 1979 Order.
13 Added by SI 1976 No 2153 on 14 January 1977.
14 Added by SI 1983 No 1708 on 19 December 1983.
15 Added by SI 1977 No 1632 on 9 November 1977.
16 Added by SI 1988 No 250 on 17 March 1988.
17 Added by SI 1978 No 1060 on 23 August 1978.

SCHEDULE 1—*cont.*

Denmark*
Egypt, Arab Republic of [18]
Fiji*
Finland*
France* (and French territories overseas)
Gabon
Federal Republic of Germany (and Berlin (West))* [19]
German Democratic Republic (and Berlin (East))[(*)][20]
Greece*
Hungary*
Iceland*
India*
Republic of Ireland*
Israel*
Italy*
Ivory Coast
Japan*
Lebanon*
Liberia* [21]
Libya [22]
Liechtenstein*
Luxembourg*
Madagascar
Mali
Malta*
Mauritania [23]
Mexico*
Monaco*
Morocco*
Netherlands* (and Netherlands Antilles)
New Zealand*
Niger
Norway*
Pakistan*
Peru* [24]
Philippines*
Poland*
Portugal* (including Portuguese provinces overseas)
Republic of Guinea[(*)][25]
Romania
Rwanda [26]
Senegal[(*)]
South Africa (and South West Africa)
Spain* (and its Colonies)
Sri Lanka (Ceylon)[(*)]
Surinam [27]
Sweden*
Switzerland*
Thailand
Togo [28]

---

18  Added by SI 1977 No 830 on 9 June 1977.
19  Words in brackets amended from '(and Land Berlin)' by SI 1973 No 772 on 21 May 1973.
20  Added by SI 1973 No 772 on 21 May 1973.
21  Added by SI 1989 No 157 on 8 March 1989.
22  Added by SI 1976 No 1784 on 25 November 1976.
23  Added by SI 1973 No 72 on 6 February 1973.
24  Added by SI 1988 No 1307 on 24 August 1988.
25  Added by SI 1980 No 1723 on 10 December 1980.
26  Added by SI 1984 No 549 on 10 May 1984.
27  Added by SI 1977 No 56 on 23 February 1977.
28  Added by SI 1975 No 431 on 16 April 1975.

SCHEDULE 1—*cont.*

Trinidad and Tobago[29]
Tunisia*
Turkey
United States of America* (and Guam, Panama Canal Zone, Puerto Rico and the Virgin Islands of the United States of America)[30]
Upper Volta[31]
Uruguay
Vatican City*
Venezuela*[32]
Yugoslavia*
Zaire
Zimbabwe[33]

# SCHEDULE 2

COUNTRIES PARTY TO THE UNIVERSAL COPYRIGHT CONVENTION BUT NOT MEMBERS OF THE BERNE UNION

| | |
|---|---|
| Algeria[34] | 28th August 1973 |
| Andorra | 27th September 1957 |
| Bangladesh[35] | 5th August 1975 |
| *Belize*[36] | *1st December 1982* |
| *Colombia*[37] | *18th June 1976* |
| [Costa Rica] | [27th September 1957] |
| Cuba | 27th September 1957 |
| Dominican Republic[38] | 8th May 1983 |
| Ecuador | 27th September 1957 |
| El Salvador[39] | 29th March 1979 |
| Ghana | — |
| Guatemala | 28th October 1964 |
| Haiti | 27th September 1957 |
| Kampuchea | 27th September 1957 |
| Kenya | — |
| Republic of Korea[40] | 1st October 1987 |
| Laos | 27th September 1957 |
| *Liberia*[41] | *27th September 1957* |
| Malawi | — |
| Mauritius | — |
| Nicaragua | 16th August 1961 |
| Nigeria | — |
| Panama | 17th October 1962 |
| Paraguay | 11th March 1962 |

---

29  See n 24, above.
30  See n 21, above.
31  Added by SI 1975 No 2193 on 24 January 1976.
32  See n 14, above.
33  See n 14, above.
34  Added by SI 1973 No 1751 on 31 October 1973; the date in relation to Algeria was substituted for the original date of 21 October 1973 by SI 1988 No 1855 on 24 November 1988.
35  Added by SI 1975 No 1837 on 12 December 1975.
36  Added by SI 1984 No 549 on 10 May 1984; the date in relation to Belize was subsequently revoked by SI 1986 No 2235 on 27 January 1987.
37  Added by SI 1976 No 1784 on 25 November 1976; deleted by SI 1988 No 250 on 17 March 1988.
38  See n 26, above.
39  Added by SI 1979 No 577 on 21 June 1979; the date in relation to El Salvador was substituted for the original date of 21 June 1979 by SI 1988 No 1855 on 24 November 1988.
40  Added by SI 1987 No 2060 on 25 December 1987.
41  Deleted by SI 1989 No 157 on 8 March 1989.

SCHEDULE 2—*cont.*

| | |
|---|---|
| *Peru*[42] | *16th October 1963* |
| St Vincent and the Grenadines[43] | — |
| Union of Soviet Socialist Republics[44] | 27th May 1973 |
| *United States of America (and Guam, Panama Canal Zone,* | *27th September 1957* |
| *Puerto Rico and the Virgin Islands of the United States of* | |
| *America)*[45] | |
| *Venezuela*[46] | *18th November 1966* |
| Zambia | — |

## SCHEDULE 3

COUNTRIES IN WHOSE CASE COPYRIGHT IN SOUND RECORDINGS INCLUDES EXCLUSIVE RIGHT TO PERFORM IN PUBLIC AND TO BROADCAST

Australia
Austria[47]
Barbados[48]
Brazil
Burkina[49]
Ceylon (Sri Lanka)
Chile[50]
Colombia[51]
People's Republic of Congo[52]
Costa Rica
Cyprus
Czechoslovakia
Denmark
Dominican Republic[53]
Ecuador
El Salvador
Federal Republic of Germany (and Berlin (West))[54]
Fiji
Finland[55]
France[56]
Guatemala[57]
India
Republic of Ireland
Italy
Israel
Luxembourg[58]
Mexico
Monaco[59]

---

42  Deleted by SI 1988 No 1307 on 24 August 1988.
43  Added by SI 1988 No 1855 on 24 November 1988.
44  Added by SI 1973 No 963 on 27 May 1973.
45  See n 41, above.
46  Deleted by SI 1983 No 1708 on 19 December 1983.
47  Added by SI 1973 No 1089 on 17 July 1973.
48  See n 26, above.
49  See n 43, above.
50  Added by SI 1974 No 1276 on 5 September 1974.
51  See n 22, above.
52  See n 43, above.
53  See n 43, above.
54  See n 19, above.
55  See n 26, above.
56  See n 40, above.
57  See n 13, above.
58  See n 43, above.
59  See n 43, above.

SCHEDULE 3—*cont.*

New Zealand
Niger[60]
Nigeria
Norway
Pakistan
Panama[61]
Paraguay
Peru[62]
Philippines[63]
Spain
Sri Lanka (Ceylon)
Sweden
Switzerland
Uruguay[64]

# SCHEDULE 4

COUNTRIES WHOSE ORGANISATIONS ARE PROTECTED IN RELATION TO SOUND BROADCASTS

| | |
|---|---|
| Austria[65] | 9th June 1973 |
| Barbados[66] | 18th September 1983 |
| Brazil[67] | 29th September 1965 |
| Burkina[68] | 14th January 1988 |
| Chile[69] | 5th September 1974 |
| Colombia[70] | 17th September 1976 |
| Congo (People's Republic)[71] | 18th May 1964 |
| Costa Rica[72] | 9th September 1971 |
| Czechoslovakia | 14th August 1964 |
| Denmark | 1st July 1965 |
| Dominican Republic[73] | 27th January 1987 |
| Ecuador[74] | 18th May 1964 |
| El Salvador[75] | 29th June 1979 |
| Federal Republic of Germany (and Berlin (West))[76] | 21st October 1966 |
| Fiji[77] | 11th April 1972 |
| Finland[78] | 21st October 1983 |
| France[79] | 3rd July 1987 |

---

60  See n 43, above.
61  See n 26, above.
62  See n 43, above.
63  Added by SI 1984 No 1987 on 21 January 1985.
64  Added by SI 1977 No 1256 on 24 August 1977.
65  See n 47, above; the date was substituted for the original date of 7 July 1973 by SI 1988 No 1855 on 24 November 1988.
66  See n 26, above.
67  The date was substituted for the original date of 5 November 1965 by SI 1988 No 1855 on 24 November 1988.
68  See n 43, above.
69  See n 50, above.
70  See n 22, above.
71  The date was substituted for the original date of 21 May 1964 as noted in n 67, above.
72  The date was substituted for the original date of 19 November 1971 as noted in n 67, above.
73  See n 43, above.
74  The date was substituted for the original date of 21 May 1964 as noted in n 67, above.
75  The date was substituted for the original date of 24 January 1980 as noted in n 67, above.
76  See n 19, above; the date was substituted for the original date of 18 November 1966 as noted in n 67, above.
77  The date was substituted for the original date of 31 May 1972 as noted in n 67, above.
78  See n 26, above.
79  See n 40, above.

SCHEDULE 4—*cont.*

| | |
|---|---|
| Guatemala[80] | 14th January 1977 |
| Republic of Ireland[81] | 19th September 1979 |
| Italy[82] | 8th April 1975 |
| Luxembourg[83] | 25th February 1976 |
| Mexico[84] | 18th May 1964 |
| Monaco[85] | 6th December 1985 |
| Niger[86] | 18th May 1964 |
| Norway[87] | 10th July 1978 |
| Panama[88] | 2nd September 1983 |
| Paraguay | 26th February 1970 |
| Peru[89] | 7th August 1985 |
| Philippines[90] | 25th September 1984 |
| Sweden[91] | 18th May 1964 |
| Uruguay[92] | 4th July 1977 |

## SCHEDULE 5

COUNTRIES WHOSE ORGANISATIONS ARE PROTECTED IN RELATION TO TELEVISION BROADCASTS

| | |
|---|---|
| Austria[93] | 9th June 1973 |
| Barbados[94] | 18th September 1983 |
| Belgium | 8th March 1968 |
| Brazil[95] | 29th September 1965 |
| Burkina[96] | 14th January 1988 |
| Chile[97] | 5th September 1974 |
| Colombia[98] | 17th September 1976 |
| Congo (People's Republic)[99] | 18th May 1964 |
| Costa Rica[100] | 9th September 1971 |
| Cyprus | 5th May 1970 |
| Czechoslovakia | 14th August 1964 |
| Denmark | 1st February 1962 |
| Dominican Republic[101] | 27th January 1987 |
| Ecuador[102] | 18th May 1964 |
| El Salvador[103] | 29th June 1979 |

---

80  See n 13, above.
81  The date was substituted for the original date of 24 January 1980 as noted in n 67, above.
82  See n 28, above.
83  The date was substituted for the original date of 18 March 1976 as noted in n 67, above.
84  The date was substituted for the original date of 21 May 1964 as noted in n 67, above.
85  See n 43, above.
86  The date was substituted for the original date of 21 May 1964 as noted in n 67, above.
87  The date was substituted for the original date of 23 August 1978 as noted in n 67, above.
88  See n 26, above.
89  See n 43, above.
90  See n 63, above.
91  The date was substituted for the original date of 21 May 1964 as noted in n 67, above.
92  The date was substituted for the original date of 21 May 1964 as noted in n 67, above.
93  See n 47, above; the date was susbstituted as noted in n 65, above.
94  See n 26, above.
95  See n 67, above; the date was substituted as noted in n 67, above.
96  See n 43, above.
97  See n 50, above.
98  See n 22, above.
99  See n 71, above.
100  See n 72, above.
101  See n 43, above.
102  See n 74, above.
103  See n 75, above.

SCHEDULE 5—*cont.*

| | |
|---|---|
| Federal Republic of Germany (and Berlin (West))[104] | 21st October 1966 |
| Fiji[105] | 11th April 1972 |
| Finland[106] | 21st October 1983 |
| France | 1st July 1961 |
| Guatemala[107] | I4th January 1977 |
| Republic of Ireland[108] | 19th September 1979 |
| Italy[109] | 8th April 1975 |
| Luxembourg[110] | 25th February 1976 |
| Mexico[111] | 18th May 1964 |
| Monaco[112] | 6th December 1985 |
| Niger[113] | 18th May 1964 |
| Norway | 10th August 1968 |
| Panama[114] | 2nd September 1983 |
| Paraguay | 26th February 1970 |
| Peru[115] | 7th August 1985 |
| Philippines[116] | 25th September 1984 |
| Spain | 19th November 1971 |
| Sweden | 1st July 1961 |
| Uruguay[117] | 4th July 1977 |

SCHEDULE 6[118]

COUNTRIES[119] TO WHICH PARTS I AND II OF THIS ORDER EXTEND

| | |
|---|---|
| [Bahama Islands][120] | [11th February 1963] |
| Bermuda | 6th December 1962 |
| *Belize*[121] | *16th October 1966* |
| British Indian Ocean Territory[122] | 21st November 1964 |
| British[123] Virgin Islands | 11th February 1963 |
| Cayman Islands | 4th June 1966 |
| Falkland Islands and its Dependencies | 10th October 1963 |
| Gibraltar | 1st October 1960 |
| Hong Kong | 12th December 1972 |
| Isle of Man | 31st May 1959 |
| Montserrat | 5th March 1966 |
| St Helena and its Dependencies | 10th October 1963 |

---

104 See n 19, above; the date was substituted as noted in n 76, above.
105 See n 77, above.
106 See n 26, above.
107 See n 13, above.
108 See n 81, above.
109 See n 28, above.
110 See n 83, above.
111 See n 84, above.
112 See n 43, above.
113 See n 86, above.
114 See n 26, above.
115 See n 43, above.
116 See n 63, above.
117 See n 64, above; the date was substituted as noted in n 92, above.
118 Insofar as this Order has been amended since 1972 (by the various Orders referred to in the footnotes) the precise terms of the amending Orders should be consulted for their effect (if any) on the laws of the dependencies listed in this Schedule.
119 Added by SI 1972 No 1724.
120 Deleted by SI 1976 No 2153 on 14 January 1977.
121 Formerly British Honduras; deleted by SI 1984 No 549 on 10 May 1984.
122 See n 26, above.
123 Changed from 'Virgin Islands' by SI 1975 No 431 on 16 April 1975.

SCHEDULE 6—*cont.*

*Modifications to this Order as extended*
1. Article 3 shall have effect as part of the law of any country to which it extends as if for references to the United Kingdom there were substituted references to the country in question.
2. Article 4 shall have effect as part of the law of any country to which it extends as if in paragraphs (1) and (3) there were substituted for '27th September 1957' the date indicated in relation to that country in the preceding provisions of this Schedule (being the date when the Act was first extended to that country).
3. Schedule 2 to this Order shall have effect as part of the law of any such country as if for any date in that Schedule which is earlier than the date mentioned in this Schedule in relation to the relevant country there were substituted that later date.

## SCHEDULE 7

MODIFICATIONS OF PART III OF, AND SCHEDULES 4 AND 5 TO, THIS ORDER IN ITS EXTENSION TO BERMUDA AND GIBRALTAR
1. (a) In Article 8 the words 'other than section 40(3)' shall be omitted;
   (b) In Article 9 the words 'other than section 37(4), section 40(3) and Schedule 5' shall be omitted.
2. Insofar as Part III is part of the law of Bermuda—
   (a) in Schedule 4 to this Order, the date mentioned in the second column shall be altered to 23rd August 1969 in relation to Brazil, Congo (People's Republic), Czechoslovakia, Denmark, Ecuador, Federal Republic of Germany (and Berlin (West)), Mexico, Niger and Sweden;
   *(b) in Schedule 5 the names of Belgium, Cyprus, France, Norway and Spain shall be omitted; and*
   *(c) the date mentioned in the second column shall be altered to 23rd August 1969 in relation to Brazil, Congo (People's Republic), Czechoslovakia, Denmark, Ecuador, Federal Republic of Germany (and Berlin West)), Mexico, Niger and Sweden.*
   **(b) in Schedule 5, the names of Belgium, Cyprus and Spain shall be omitted; and**
   **(c) the date mentioned in the second column in the said Schedule 5 shall be altered to—**
      **(i) 23rd August 1969, in relation to Brazil, Congo (People's Republic), Czechoslovakia, Denmark, Ecuador, Federal Republic of Germany (and Berlin (West)), Mexico, Niger and Sweden;**
      **(ii) 23rd August 1978, in relation to Norway;**
      **(iii) 3rd July 1987, in relation to France.**
3. Insofar as Part III is part of the law of Gibraltar—
   (a) in Schedule 4 to this Order the date mentioned in the second column shall be altered to 28th October 1966 in relation to Brazil, Congo (People's Republic), Czechoslovakia, Denmark, Ecuador, **Federal Republic of Germany (and Berlin (West))**, Mexico, Niger and Sweden;
   (b) in Schedule the date mentioned in the second column shall be altered to 28th October 1966 in relation to Brazil, Congo (People's Republic), Czechoslovakia, Denmark, Ecuador, **Federal Republic of Germany (and Berlin (West))**, France, Mexico, Niger and Sweden.

*General note*
Paras 2(b)(c) in bold substituted for the original paras (b), (c) by SI 1988, No 1855, art 2(f). Reference to Federal Republic of Germany (and Berlin (West)) in para 3 added by SI 1988 No 1855, art 2(g).

## SCHEDULE 8

ORDERS REVOKED

| Order | SI Number |
| --- | --- |
| The Copyright (International Conventions) Order 1972 . . . . . . | 1972/673 |
| The Copyright (International Conventions) (Amendment) Order 1973 . . | 1973/72 |
| The Copyright (International Conventions) (Amendment No 2) Order 1973 | 1973/772 |
| The Copyright (International Conventions) (Amendment No 3) Order 1973 | 1973/963 |
| The Copyright (International Conventions) (Amendment No 4) Order 1973 | 1973/1089 |
| The Copyright (International Conventions) (Amendment No 5) Order 1973 | 1973/1751 |
| The Copyright (International Conventions) (Amendment) Order 1974 . . | 1974/1276 |
| The Copyright (International Conventions) (Amendment) Order 1975 . . | 1975/431 |
| The Copyright (International Conventions) (Amendment No 2) Order 1975 | 1975/1837 |

SCHEDULE 8—cont.

| Order | SI Number |
|---|---|
| The Copyright (International Conventions) (Amendment No 3) Order 1975 | 1975/2193 |
| The Copyright (International Conventions) (Amendment) Order 1976 . . | 1976/227 |
| The Copyright (International Conventions) (Amendment No 2) Order 1976 | 1976/1784 |
| The Copyright (International Conventions) (Amendment No 3) Order 1976 | 1976/2153 |
| The Copyright (International Conventions) (Amendment) Order 1977 . . | 1977/56 |
| The Copyright (International Conventions) (Amendment No 2) Order 1977 | 1977/830 |
| The Copyright (International Conventions) (Amendment No 3) Order 1977 | 1977/1256 |
| The Copyright (International Conventions) (Amendment No 4) Order 1977 | 1977/1632 |
| The Copyright (International Conventions) (Amendment) Order 1978 . . | 1978/1060 |
| The Copyright (International Conventions) (Amendment) Order 1979 . . | 1979/577 |

## COPYRIGHT (TAIWAN) ORDER 1985
## (SI 1985 No 1777)

> *Made* . . . . . . . . *18th November 1985*
> *Laid before Parliament* . . . . *26th November 1985*
> *Coming into operation* . . . . *17th December 1985*

Whereas Her Majesty is satisfied that, in respect of the matters provided for in this Order, provison has been made under the laws of the territory of Taiwan whereby adequate protection will be given to owners of copyright under the Copyright Act 1956:

Now, therefore, Her Majesty, by and with the advice of Her Privy Council, and by virtue of the authority conferred on her by sections 32 and 47 of the said Act, is pleased to order, and it is hereby ordered, as follows:

**1.**—(1) This Order may be cited as the Copyright (Taiwan) Order 1985 and shall come into operation on 17th December 1985.

(2) In this Order—

'the Act' means the Copyright Act 1956: and
'material time' means—

(i) in relation to an unpublished work or subject matter, the time at which such work or subject matter was made, or, if the making thereof extended over a period, a substantial part of that period; and

(ii) in relation to a published work or subject matter, the time of first publication.

**2.** Subject to the following provisions of this Order, the provisions of Parts I and II of the Act (except sections 14 and 14A) and all of the other provisions of the Act relevant to those Parts shall in the case of the territory of Taiwan apply—

(a) in relation to literary, dramatic, musical or artistic works, sound recordings, cinematograph films or published editions first published in that territory as they apply to such works, recordings, films or editions first published in the United Kingdom;

(b) in relation to persons who at any material time are citizens or subjects of China, being citizens or subjects who at the same material time are resident or domiciled in the territory of Taiwan, as they apply to persons who at such time are British subjects within the meaning of the Act; and

(c) in relation to bodies incorporated under the laws of that territory, as they apply to bodies incorporated under the laws of any part of the United Kingdom.

**3.** The relevant provisions of Schedule 7 to the Act shall have effect in relation to any work or other subject matter in which copyright subsists by virtue of this Order as if for any references therein to the commencement of the Act or any of its provisions there were substituted references to 10th July 1985; and copyright shall not subsist by virtue of this Order in any work or other subject matter by reason only of its publication in the territory of Taiwan before that date.

**4.** The acts restricted by section 2(5)(f) of the Act as applied by this Order shall not include making a translation of the work.

**5.** Where any person has before the commencement of this Order incurred any expenditure or liability in connection with the reproduction or performance of any work or other subject matter in a manner which at the time was lawful, or for the purpose of or with a view to the reproduction or performance of a work at a time when such reproduction or performance would, but for the making of this Order have been lawful, nothing in this Order shall diminish or prejudice any right or interest arising from or in connection with such action which is subsisting and valuable immediately before the commencement of this Order unless the person who by virtue of this Order becomes entitled to restrain such reproduction or performance agrees to pay such compensation as, failing agreement, may be determined by arbitration.

COPYRIGHT (SINGAPORE) ORDER 1987
(SI 1987 No 940)

| | | | |
|---|---|---|---|
| *Made* | . . . . | . . | . . *8th May 1987* |
| *Laid before Parliament* | . . | . . | *17th June 1987* |
| *Coming into force* | . . | . . | *8th June 1987* |

Whereas Her Majesty is satisfied that, in respect of the matters provided for in this Order, provision has been made under the laws of Singapore whereby adequate provision will be given to owners of copyright under the Copyright Act 1956:

Now therefore, Her Majesty, by and with the advice of Her Privy Council, and by virtue of the authority conferred on Her by sections 31, 32 and 47 of the said Act, is pleased to order, and it is hereby ordered, as follows:

**1.** (1) This Order may be cited as the Copyright (Singapore) Order 1987 and shall come into force on 18th June 1987.

(2) In this Order—

'the Act' means the Copyright Act 1956; and
'material time' means—

(i) in relation to an unpublished work or subject-matter, the time at which such work or subject-matter was made or, if the making thereof extended over a period, a substantial part of that period; and

(ii) in relation to a published work or subject-matter, the time of first publication.

**2.** Subject to the following provisions of this Order, the provisions of Parts I and II of the Act and all the other provisions of the Act relevant to those Parts shall apply—

(a) in relation to literary, dramatic, musical or artistic works, sound recordings, cinematograph films or published editions first published in Singapore as they apply to such works, recordings, films or editions first published in the United Kingdom;

(b) in relation to persons who at any material time are resident in Singapore as they apply to persons who at such time are resident in the United Kingdom; and

(c) in relation to bodies incorporated under the laws of Singapore as they apply to bodies incorporated under the laws of any part of the United Kingdom.

**3.** The acts restricted by section 12 of the Act as applied by this Order shall not include causing the recording to be heard in public, broadcasting the recording or including it in a cable programme.

**4.** Where any person has before the commencement of this Order incurred any expenditure or liability in connection with the reproduction or performance of any work or other subject matter in a manner which at the time was lawful, or for the purpose of or with a view to the reproduction or performance of a work at a time when such reproduction or performance would, but for the making of this Order, have been lawful, nothing in this Order shall diminish or prejudice any right or interest arising from or in connection with such action which is subsisting and valuable immediately before the commencement of this Order unless the person who by virtue of this Order becomes entitled to restrain such reproduction or performance agrees to pay such compensation as, failing agreement, may be determined by arbitration.

**5.** This Order shall extend to the countries mentioned in the Schedule hereto, subject to the modification that article 2 above shall have effect as part of the law of any of those countries as if for references to the United Kingdom there were substituted references to the country in question.

## SCHEDULE

COUNTRIES TO WHICH THIS ORDER EXTENDS

British Indian Ocean Territory
British Virgin Islands
Cayman Islands
Falkland Islands
Falkland Islands Dependencies
Hong Kong
Isle of Man
Montserrat
St Helena
St Helena Dependencies (Ascension, Tristan da Cunha)

COPYRIGHT (SOUND RECORDINGS) (INDONESIA) ORDER 1988
(SI 1988 No 797)

| | |
|---|---|
| *Made* . . . . . . . . *27th April 1988* |
| *Laid before Parliament* . . . . *5th May 1988* |
| *Coming into force* . . . . *26th May 1988* |

Whereas Her Majesty in pursuance of the Regency Acts 1937 to 1953 was pleased, by Letters Patent dated the 28th day of March 1988, to delegate to the six Councillors of State therein named or any two or more of them full power and authority during the period of Her Majesty's absence from the United Kingdom to summon and hold on Her Majesty's behalf Her Privy Council and to signify thereat Her Majesty's approval for anything for which Her Majesty's approval in council is required:

And whereas Her Majesty Queen Elizabeth The Queen Mother and His Royal Highness The Prince Charles, The Prince of Wales, being authorised thereto by the said Letters Patent, are satisfied that, in respect of the matters provided for in this Order, provision will be made under the laws of Indonesia whereby adequate protection will be given to owners of copyright under the Copyright Act 1956:

Now, therefore, Her Majesty Queen Elizabeth The Queen Mother and His Royal Highness The Prince Charles, Prince of Wales, being authorised as aforesaid, and in pursuance of the powers conferred by sections 32 and 47 of the said Act of 1956, and by and with the advice of Her Majesty's Privy Council, do on Her Majesty's behalf order, and it is hereby ordered, as follows:

**1.** This Order may be cited as the Copyright (Sound Recordings) (Indonesia) Order 1988 and shall come into force on 26th May 1988.

**2.** Subject to Article 3 below, the provisions of section 12 of the Copyright Act 1956 and all the other provisions of that Act relevant to that section shall apply—

    (a)  in relation to sound recordings first published in Indonesia as they apply in relation to sound recordings first published in the United Kingdom; and

    (b)  in relation to every maker of a sound recording who—

        (i)  being an individual was, at the time when the recording was made, a citizen or subject of, or resident in, Indonesia, or

        (ii)  being a body corporate was, at the time when the recording was made, incorporated under the laws of Indonesia,

    as they apply in relation to individuals who at such a time were British subjects within the meaning of the said Act or resident in the United Kingdom and in relation to bodies incorporated under the laws of any part of the United Kingdom.

**3.** Where any person has before the commencement of this Order incurred any expenditure or liability in connection with—

    (a)  the making of a record embodying a sound recording, or

    (b)  causing a sound recording to be heard in public, or

    (c)  the broadcasting of a sound recording or its inclusion in a cable programme,

in a manner which at the time was lawful, or for the purpose of or with a view to the doing of any such act at a time when that act would, but for the making of this

Order, have been lawful, nothing in this Order shall diminish or prejudice any right or interest arising from or in connection with the incurring of that expenditure or liability which is subsisting and valuable immediately before the commencement of this Order unless the person who by virtue of this Order becomes entitled to restrain any such act as aforesaid agrees to pay such compensation as, failing agreement, may be determined by arbitration.

COPYRIGHT, DESIGNS AND PATENTS ACT 1988 (COMMENCEMENT No 1) ORDER 1989
(SI 1989 No 816)

*Made* . . . . . . . . *9th May 1989*

*(As amended by The Copyright, Designs and Patents Act 1988 (Commencement No 4) Order 1989 (SI 1989 No 1303))*

The Secretary of State , in exercise of the powers conferred upon him by section 305(3) of the Copyright, Designs and Patents Act 1988, hereby makes the following Order:

**1.** This Order may be cited as the Copyright, Designs and Patents Act 1988 (Commencement No 1) Order 1989.
**2.** The following provisions of the Copyright, Designs and Patents Act 1988 shall come into force on 1st August 1989:

Part I (copyright);
Part II (rights in performances);
Part III (design right);
Part IV (registered designs), except—

section 272 in so far as it relates to paragraph 21 of Schedule 3, and
section 273;

Part VI (patents), except—

sections 293 and 294, and
section 295 in so far as it relates to paragraphs 1 to 11 and 17 to 30 of Schedule 5;

Part VII (miscellaneous and general), except—

section 301,
section 303(1) in so far as it relates to paragraphs 15, 18(2) and 21 of Schedule 7, and
section 303(2) in so far as it relates to the references in Schedule 8 to section 32 of the Registered Designs Act 1949 and to the provisions of the Patents Act 1977, other than section 49(3) of, and paragraphs 1 and 3 of Schedule 5 to, that Act;
[**section 304(4) and (6)**]

Schedule 1 (copyright: transitional provisions and savings);
Schedule 2 (rights in performances: permitted acts);
Schedule 3 (minor and consequential amendments to the Registered Designs Act 1949), other than paragraph 21;

Schedule 5 (patents: miscellaneous amendments), other than paragraphs 1 to 11 and 17 to 30;
Schedule 7 (consequential amendments), other than paragraphs 15, 18(2) and 21;
Schedule 8 (repeals), except in so far as it relates to—

section 32 of the Registered Designs Act 1949, and
the provisions of the Patents Act 1977, other than section 49(3) of, and paragraphs 1 and 3 of Schedule 5 to, that Act.

*General note*
Words in bold added by SI 1989 No 1303, art 3.


COPYRIGHT, DESIGNS AND PATENTS ACT 1988 (COMMENCEMENT NO 2) ORDER 1989
(SI 1989 No 955)

*(As amended by the Copyright, Designs and Patents Act 1988 (Commencement No 3) Order 1989 (SI 1989 No 1032))*

*Made* . . . . . . . *9th June 1989*

The Secretary of State, in exercise of the powers conferred upon him by section 305(3) of the Copyright, Designs and Patents Act 1988 ('the Act'), hereby makes the following Order:

**1.** This Order may be cited as the Copyright, Designs and Patents Act 1988 (Commencement No 2) Order 1989.
**2.** The provisions of the Act specified in the Schedule to this Order (which, apart from this Order, come into force on 1st August 1989) shall come into force forthwith for the purpose only of enabling the making of subordinate legislation thereunder, by the authority shown in relation to those provisions, expressed to come into force on 1st August 1989.


### SCHEDULE

*PROVISIONS OF THE ACT COMING INTO FORCE FORTHWITH*

| Provision and Authority | Subject matter |
| --- | --- |
| *Regulations by the Secretary of State under sections 37(1), (2) and (4) and 38 to 43* | *Copying by librarians and archivists of prescribed libraries and archives.* |
| *Orders by the Secretary of State under—* | *Specification of material to be marked in* |
| *section 47(4)* | *relation to public inspection and copying of the same.* |
| *section 47(5)* | *Provisions relating to public inspection of material to apply to material or registers maintained by international organisations.* |
| *section 52(4)* | *Articles to be regarded as made by industrial process and excluded articles.* |

| | |
|---|---|
| *section 61* | *Recordings of folksongs for archival purposes for designated bodies.* |
| *section 74* | *Provision of subtitled copies of broadcasts and cable programmes for designated bodies.* |
| *section 75* | *Recordings for archives of designated class of broadcasts and cable programmes.* |
| *sections 100(4) and (5) and 196(4) and (5)* | *Prescribing the form of notice of seizure when infringing articles or illicit recordings are seized and detained.* |
| *Regulations by Commissioners of Customs and Excise under section 112(1), (2) and (3)* | *Prescribing the form of notices required under section 111 in respect of goods to be treated as prohibited goods.* |
| *Rules by the Lord Chancellor under sections 150, 152(2) and (3) and paragraph 34 of Schedule 1* | *Proceedings before the Copyright Tribunal.* |
| *Order in Council under—* | *Application of Part I of the Act to other* |
| *section 159* | *countries.* |
| *section 168(2)* | *Vesting of copyright in certain international organisations.* |
| *Order by Secretary of State under—* | *Descriptions of educational* |
| *section 174(1)(b)* | *establishments for the purposes of Part I of the Act.* |
| *section 174(2)* | *Application of provisions relating to educational establishments to certain teachers.* |
| *Order in Council under section 208(1)(a)* | *Designation of Convention countries enjoying reciprocal protection under Part II of the Act (performances).* |
| *Rules by Secretary of State under section 250* | *Proceedings before Comptroller under Part III of the Act (design right).* |
| *Order in Council under section 256(1)* | *Designation of countries enjoying reciprocal protection under Part III of the Act (design right).* |

## SCHEDULE

## PROVISIONS OF THE ACT COMING INTO FORCE FORTHWITH

| Provision and Authority | Subject matter |
|---|---|
| **Regulations by the Secretary of State under sections 37 and 38 to 43** | **Copying by librarians and archivists of prescribed libraries and archives.** |
| **Orders by the Secretary of State under—** | |
| **section 47** | **Specification of material to be marked in relation to public inspection and copying of the same, and application of provisions relating to public inspection of material to material or registers maintained by international organisations.** |
| **section 52** | **Articles to be regarded as made by industrial process and excluded articles.** |
| **section 61** | **Recordings of folksongs for archival purposes for designated bodies.** |
| **section 74** | **Provision of subtitled copies of broadcasts and cable programmes by designated bodies.** |
| **section 75** | **Recordings for archives of designated class of broadcasts and cable programmes.** |
| **sections 100 and 196** | **Prescribing the form of notice of seizure when infringing articles or illicit recordings are seized and detained.** |
| **Regulations by Commissioners of Customs and Excise under section 112** | **Prescribing the form of notices required under section 111 in respect of goods to be treated as prohibited goods.** |

| | |
|---|---|
| **Rules by the Lord Chancellor under sections 150, 152 and paragraph 34 of Schedule 1** | **Proceedings before the Copyright Tribunal.** |
| **Order in Council by Her Majesty under—** | |
| section 159 | **Application of Part I of the Act to other countries.** |
| section 168 | **Vesting of copyright in certain international organisations.** |
| **Order by Secretary of State under—** | |
| section 174 | **Descriptions of educational establishments for the purposes of Part I of the Act, and application of provisions relating to educational establishments to certain teachers.** |
| **Order in Council by Her Majesty under section 208** | **Designation of Convention countries enjoying reciprocal protection under Part II of the Act (performances).** |
| **Rules by Secretary of State under section 250** | **Proceedings before Comptroller under Part III of the Act (design right).** |
| **Order in Council under section 256** | **Designation of countries enjoying reciprocal protection under Part III of the Act (design right).** |

*General note*

The Schedule in italics was substituted for the Schedule in bold by SI 1989 No 1032, art 2.

## COPYRIGHT (INTERNATIONAL ORGANISATIONS) ORDER 1989
## (SI 1989 No 989)

| | |
|---|---|
| *Made* . . . . . . . . *13th June 1989* |
| *Laid before Parliament* . . . . *21st June 1989* |
| *Coming into force* . . . . *1st August 1989* |

Her Majesty, by virtue of the authority conferred upon Her by section 168(2) of the Copyright, Designs and Patents Act 1988, is pleased, by and with the advice of Her Privy Council, to order, and it is hereby ordered, as follows:

**1.** This Order may be cited as the Copyright (International Organisations) Order 1989 and shall come into force on 1st August 1989.

**2.** It is hereby declared to be expedient that section 168 of the Copyright, Designs and Patents Act 1988 (copyright vesting in certain international organisations) should apply to the United Nations, the Specialised Agencies of the United Nations and the Organisation of American States.

## COPYRIGHT AND RIGHTS IN PERFORMANCES (NOTICE OF SEIZURE) ORDER 1989
## (SI 1989 No 1006)

| | |
|---|---|
| *Made* . . . . . . . . *13th June 1989* |
| *Laid before Parliament* . . . . *26th June 1989* |
| *Coming into force* . . . . *1st August 1989* |

The Secretary of State, in exercise of the powers conferred upon him by section 100(4) and (5) and section 196(4) and (5) of the Copyright, Designs and Patents Act 1988 ('the Act'), hereby makes the following Order—

**1.** This Order may be cited as the Copyright and Rights in Performances (Notice of Seizure) Order 1989 and shall come into force on 1st August 1989.

**2.** The form set out in the Schedule to this Order is hereby prescribed for the notice required under section 100(4) and section 196(4), respectively, of the Act.

### SCHEDULE

THE COPYRIGHT AND RIGHTS IN PERFORMANCES (NOTICE OF SEIZURE) ORDER 1989

NOTICE OF SEIZURE

To Whom it May Concern

1. Goods in which you were trading have been seized. This notice tells you who carried out the seizure, the legal grounds on which this has been done and the goods which have been seized and detained. As required by the Copyright, Designs and Patents Act 1988, notice of the proposed seizure was given to the police station at (state address).

**Person carrying out seizure**
2. (State name and address)

*acting on the authority of (state name and address).

**Legal grounds for seizure and detention**
3. This action has been taken under *section 100/section 196 of the Act which (subject to certain conditions) permits a copyright owner, or a person having performing rights or recording rights, to

seize and detain infringing copies or illicit recordings found exposed or immediately available for sale or hire, or to authorise such seizure. The right to seize and detain is subject to a decision of the court under *section 114/section 204 of the Act (order as to disposal of goods seized and detained).

**Nature of the goods seized and detained**

*4. Infringing copies of works (within the meaning of section 27 of the Act)–(specify all articles seized)
Illicit recordings (within the meaning of section 197 of the Act)—(specify all articles seized)

Signed . . . . . . . . . . . . . . . . . . . . . . . . . Date . . . . . . . . . . . . . . . . .

*Delete as necessary


COPYRIGHT (RECORDINGS OF FOLKSONGS FOR ARCHIVES)
(DESIGNATED BODIES) ORDER 1989
(SI 1989 No 1012)

| | |
|---|---|
| *Made* . . . . . . . . | *. . 13th June 1989* |
| *Laid before Parliament* . . | *. . 26th June 1989* |
| *Coming into force* . . | *. . 1st August 1989* |

The Secretary of State, in exercise of the powers conferred upon him by section 61 of the Copyright, Designs and Patents Act 1988 ('the Act'), and upon being satisfied that the bodies designated by this Order are not established or conducted for profit, hereby makes the following Order—

**1.** This Order may be cited as the Copyright (Recordings of Folksongs for Archives) (Designated Bodies) Order 1989 and shall come into force on 1st August 1989.

**2.** Each of the bodies specified in the Schedule to this Order is designated as a body for the purposes of section 61 of the Act.

**3.**—(1) For the purposes of section 61(3) of the Act the conditions specified in paragraph (2) of this article are prescribed as the conditions which must be met for the making and supply, by the archivist of an archive maintained by a body designated by this Order, of a copy of a sound recording made in reliance on section 61(1) of the Act and included in such archive.

(2) The prescribed conditions are—

(a) that the person requiring a copy satisfies the archivist that he requires it for purposes of research or private study and will not use it for any other purpose, and

(b) that no person is furnished with more than one copy of the same recording.


SCHEDULE

1. The Archive of Traditional Welsh Music, University College of North Wales.
2. The Centre for English Cultural Tradition and Language.
3. The Charles Parker Archive Trust (1982).
4. The European Centre for Traditional and Regional Cultures.
5. The Folklore Society.
6. The Institute of Folklore Studies in Britain and Canada.
7. The National Museum of Wales, Welsh Folk Museum.
8. The National Sound Archive, the British Library.
9. The North West Sound Archive.
10. The Sound Archives, British Broadcasting Corporation.
11. Ulster Folk and Transport Museum.
12. The Vaughan Williams Memorial Library, English Folk Dance and Song Society.

## COPYRIGHT (SUB-TITLING OF BROADCASTS AND CABLE PROGRAMMES) (DESIGNATED BODY) ORDER 1989
### (SI 1989 No 1013)

| | |
|---|---|
| *Made* .. .. .. | *.. 13th June 1989* |
| *Laid before Parliament* .. | *.. 4th July 1989* |
| *Coming into force* .. | *.. 1st August 1989* |

The Secretary of State, in exercise of the powers conferred upon him by section 74 of the Copyright, Designs and Patents Act 1988 ('the Act'), and upon being satisfied that the body designated by this Order is not established or conducted for profit, hereby makes the following Order—

**1.** This Order may be cited as the Copyright (Sub-titling of Broadcasts and Cable Programmes) (Designated Body) Order 1989 and shall come into force on 1st August 1989.

**2.** The National Sub-titling Library for Deaf People is designated as a body for the purposes of section 74 of the Act.

## COPYRIGHT, DESIGNS AND PATENTS ACT 1988 (COMMENCEMENT NO 3) ORDER 1989
### (SI 1989 No 1032)

| | |
|---|---|
| *Made* .. .. .. | *.. 20th June 1989* |

The Secretary of State, in exercise of the powers conferred upon him by section 305(3) of the Copyright Designs and Patents Act 1988 ('the Act'), hereby makes the following Order—

**1.** This Order may be cited as the Copyright, Designs and Patents Act 1988 (Commencement No 3) Order 1989.

**2.** The Copyright, Designs and Patents Act 1988 (Commencement No 2) Order 1989 [SI 1989 No 955] is amended by substituting for the Schedule thereto the Schedule set out in the Schedule to this Order.

### SCHEDULE

[This Schedule substitutes SI 1989 No 955, Schedule].

## COPYRIGHT (APPLICATION OF PROVISIONS RELATING TO EDUCATIONAL ESTABLISHMENTS TO TEACHERS) (NO 2) ORDER 1989
### (SI 1989 No 1067)

| | |
|---|---|
| *Made* .. .. .. | *.. 26th June 1989* |
| *Laid before Parliament* .. | *.. 4th July 1989* |
| *Coming into force* .. | *.. 1st August 1989* |

The Secretary of State, in exercise of his powers conferred upon him by section 174(2) of the Copyright, Designs and Patents Act 1988 ('the Act'), hereby makes the following order:

**1.** This Order may be cited as the Copyright (Application of Provisions relating to Educational Establishments to Teachers) (No 2) Order 1989 and shall come into force on 1st August 1989.

**2.** Sections 35 and 36 of the Act (which provide for educational use of recordings of broadcasts and cable programmes and copying of passages from published works in which copyright subsists) and sections 137 to 141 of the Act (which provide for reprographic copying of works under licence) shall apply in relation to teachers who are employed by a local education authority to give instruction elsewhere to pupils who are unable to attend an educational establishment.

**3.** The Copyright (Application of Provisions relating to Educational Establishments to Teachers) Order 1989 is hereby revoked [SI 1989 No 1007].

## COPYRIGHT (EDUCATIONAL ESTABLISHMENTS) (NO 2) ORDER 1989 (SI 1989 No 1068)

> *Made* . . . . . . . . *26h June 1989*
> *Laid before Parliament* . . . . *4th July 1989*
> *Coming into force* . . . . *1st August 1989*

The Secretary of State, in exercise of his powers conferred upon him by section 174(1)(b) of the Copyright, Designs and Patents Act 1988 ('the Act'), hereby makes the following order:

**1.** This Order may be cited as the Copyright (Educational Establishments) (No 2) Order 1989 and shall come into force on 1st August 1989.

**2.** The description of educational establishments mentioned in the Schedule to this Order are specified for the purposes of Part I of the Act.

**3.** The Copyright (Educational Establishments) Order 1989 [SI 1989 No 1008] is hereby revoked.

### SCHEDULE

1. Any university empowered by Royal Charter or Act of Parliament to award degrees and any college, or institution in the nature of a college, in such a university.

2. Any institution providing further education within the meaning of section 1(5)(*b*) of the Education (Scotland) Act 1980 and any educational establishment (other than a school) within the meaning of section 135(1) of that Act.

3. Any institution providing further education within the meaning of article 5(*c*) of the Education and Libraries (Northern Ireland) Order 1986 and any college of education within the meaning of that Order.

4. Any institution the sole or main purpose of which is to provide further education within the meaning of section 41 of the Education Act 1944 or higher education within the meaning of section 120 of the Education Reform Act 1988, or both.

5. Any theological college.

## COPYRIGHT (INDUSTRIAL PROCESS AND EXCLUDED ARTICLES) (NO 2) ORDER 1989 (SI 1989 No 1070)

> *Made* . . . . . . . . *26th June 1989*
> *Laid before Parliament* . . . . *4th July 1989*
> *Coming into force* . . . . *1st August 1989*

The Secretary of State, in exercise of his powers conferred upon him by section 52(4) of the Copyright, Designs and Patents Act 1988 ('the Act'), hereby makes the following order—

**1.** This Order may be cited as the Copyright (Industrial Process and Excluded Articles) (No 2) Order 1989 and shall come into force on 1st August 1989.

**2.** An article is to be regarded for the purposes of section 52 of the Act (limitation of copyright protection for design derived from artistic work) as made by an industrial process if—

(a) it is one of more than fifty articles which—
    (i) all fall to be treated for the purposes of Part I of the Act as copies of a particular artistic work, but
    (ii) do not all together constitute a single set of articles as defined in section 44(1) of the Registered Designs Act 1949; or
(b) it consists of goods manufactured in lengths or pieces, not being hand-made goods.

**3.**—(1) There are excluded from the operation of section 52 of the Act—

(a) works of sculpture, other than casts or models used or intended to be used as models or patterns to be multiplied by any industrial process;
(b) wall plaques, medals and medallions; and
(c) printed matter primarily of a literary or artistic character, including book jackets, calendars, certificates, coupons, dress-making patterns, greetings cards, labels, leaflets, maps, plans, playing cards, postcards, stamps, trade advertisements, trade forms and cards, transfers and similar articles.

(2) Nothing in article 2 of this Order shall be taken to limit the meaning of 'industrial process' in paragraph (1)(a) of this article.

**4.** The Copyright (Industrial Designs) Rules 1957 [SI 1957 No 867] and the Copyright (Industrial Process and Excluded Articles) Order 1989 [SI 1989 No 1010] are hereby revoked.

COPYRIGHT (MATERIAL OPEN TO PUBLIC INSPECTION)
(INTERNATIONAL ORGANISATIONS) ORDER 1989
(SI 1989 No 1098)

> *Made*     . .    . .     . .   . . *29th June 1989*
> *Laid before Parliament*   . .    . . *10th July 1989*
> *Coming into operation*    . .    . . *1st August 1989*

The Secretary of State, in exercise of his powers conferred upon him by section 47(5) of the Copyright, Designs and Patents Act 1988, hereby makes the following order:

**1.** This Order may be cited as the Copyright (Material Open to Public Inspection) (International Organisations) Order 1989 and shall come into force on 1st August 1989.

**2.** Subsections (1) to (3) of section 47 of the Copyright, Designs and Patents Act 1988 apply, subject to the modifications set out in article 3 below, to material made open to public inspection by—

(a) the European Patent Office under the Convention on the Grant of European Patents; and

(b) the World Intellectual Property Organisation under the Patent Co-operation Treaty;

as they apply in relation to material open to public inspection pursuant to a statutory requirement or to a statutory register.

**3.** Subsections (1) to (3) of the said section 47 shall be modified by the substitution for the words 'the appropriate person', in each place where they occur, of the words 'the Comptroller-General of Patents, Designs and Trade Marks'.


COPYRIGHT (MATERIAL OPEN TO PUBLIC INSPECTION) (MARKING OF COPIES OF MAPS) ORDER 1989
(SI 1989 No 1099)

*Made* . . . . . . *29th June 1989*
*Laid before Parliament* . . . . *10th July 1989*
*Coming into force* . . . . *1st August 1989*

The Secretary of State, in exercise of his powers conferred upon him by section 47(4) of the Copyright, Designs and Patents Act 1988, hereby makes the following order:

**1.** This Order may be cited as the Copyright (Material Open to Public Inspection) (Marking of Copies of Maps) Order 1989 and shall come into force on 1st August 1989.

**2.** Subsections (2) and (3) of section 47 of the Copyright, Designs and Patents Act 1988 shall, in the case of a map which is open to public inspection pursuant to a statutory requirement, or is on a statutory register, apply only to copies of the map marked in the following manner—

'This copy has been made by or with the authority of (insert the name of the person required to make the map open to public inspection or the person maintaining the register) pursuant to section 47 of the Copyright, Designs and Patents Act 1988 ('the Act'). Unless the Act provides a relevant exception to copyright, the copy must not be copied without the prior permission of the copyright owner.'


COPYRIGHT TRIBUNAL RULES 1989
(SI 1989 No 1129)

*(As amended by the Copyright Tribunal Rules (Amendment) Regulations 1991 (SI 1991 No 201), and the Copyright Tribunal Rules (Amendment) Regulations 1992 (SI 1992 No 467))*

*Made* . . . . . . *4th July 1989*
*Laid before Parliament* . . . . *10th July 1989*
*Coming into force* . . . . *1st August 1989*

The Lord Chancellor in exercise of the powers conferred upon him by sections 150 and 152(2) and (3) of, and paragraph 34 of Schedule 1 to, the Copyright,

Designs and Patents Act 1988, after consultation with the Lord Advocate, with the approval of the Treasury as to the fees chargeable under these Rules in respect of proceedings before the Copyright Tribunal, and after consultation with the Council of Tribunals and Inquiries Act 1971, hereby makes the following Rules:

## Preliminary

### Citation and commencement

**1.** These Rules may be cited as the Copyright Tribunal Rules 1989 and shall come into force on 1st August 1989.

### Interpretation

**2.**—(1) In these Rules, unless the context otherwise requires—

'the Act' means the Copyright, Designs and Patents Act 1988;
**['the 1990 Act' means the Broadcasting Act 1990;]**
'applicant' means a person or organisation who has made a reference or application to the Tribunal;
'the Chairman' means the Chairman of the Tribunal or a deputy chairman or any other member of the Tribunal appointed to act as chairman;
'costs', in relation to proceedings in Scotland, means 'expenses';
'credentials' means—

    (a) the validity of an organisation's claim to be representative of a class of persons, or

    (b) the possession by an intervener of a substantial interest in the matter in dispute;

'intervener' means a person or organisation who has applied under rule *7, 23, 26, 30, 33, 37, 41 or 44* [**7, 23, 26, 26D, 30, 33, 37, 41, 41D, or 44**] to be made a party to proceedings;
'the office' means the office for the time being of the Tribunal;
'proceedings' means proceedings in respect of a reference or an application before the Tribunal;
**['programme service' has the meaning given to it by section 201 of the 1990 Act]**
'the Secretary' means the Secretary for the time being of the Tribunal; and
'the Tribunal' means the Copyright Tribunal.

(2) A rule or schedule referred to by number means the rule or schedule so numbered in these Rules; a form referred to by number means a form in Schedule 3 so numbered, and a requirement in these Rules for the service of a notice in a specified form shall be taken to have been complied with if the service of the notice is in a form which is substantially in accordance with the form so specified.

*General note*
The definitions 'the 1990 Act' and 'programme service' were inserted and the figures in bold in the definition 'intervener' were substituted for those in italics by SI 1991 No 201, r 2(a).

### References and applications with respect to Licensing Schemes

**Commencement of proceedings (Forms 1 & 2)**

**3.**—(1) Proceedings in relation to a reference or an application with respect to a licensing scheme shall be commenced by the service on the Secretary by the applicant of a notice—

(a) in Form 1 in the case of a reference under section 118, 119, or 120 of the Act,

(b) in Form 2 in the case of an application for the grant of a licence or a review of the Tribunal's order under section 121 or 122 of the Act,

together with a statement of the applicant's case.

(2) As soon as practicable after receipt of the notice, the Secretary shall serve a copy of the same (with a copy of the applicant's statement) on the operator of the licensing scheme named in the notice and, in the case of a further reference under section 120 of the Act or an application for a review of an order under section 122 of the Act, as the case may be, on every person who was a party to the proceedings when the order of the Tribunal was made.

(3) In the case of a reference under section 118 of the Act the Tribunal shall, as soon as practicable after the receipt of the applicant's notice, decide whether to entertain the reference and may for that purpose, at its discretion, allow representations in writing to be made by the applicant or the operator of the scheme or both and if, after considering the reference and representations (if any), the Tribunal—

(a) decides to entertain the reference, it shall give such directions as to the taking of any steps required or authorised under these Rules, or as to any further matter (including any order as to costs) as the Tribunal thinks fit, and

(b) declines to entertain the reference, it shall direct that no further proceedings shall be taken by any party in connection with the reference, otherwise than in relation to any order for costs which the Tribunal may make under rule 48.

(4) The decision of the Tribunal shall be in writing and shall include a statement of its reasons, and the Secretary shall serve a copy thereof on the applicant and the operator of the licensing scheme.

**Application for special leave (Form 3)**

**4.**—(1) An application under section 120 of the Act for the special leave of the Tribunal on a further reference under that section or an application under section 122 of the Act for the special leave of the Tribunal to review its order under that section shall be made by the service on the Secretary by the applicant of a notice in Form 3, together with a statement of the grounds for the application. The applicant shall serve a copy of the notice and statement on every person who was a party to the reference or application on which the Tribunal made the last previous order with respect to the licensing scheme.

(2) Within 14 days of the service upon him of such notice, any such party may make representations in writing to the Tribunal regarding the application for

special leave, and he shall serve a copy of any such representations on the applicant and inform the Secretary of the date of such service.

(3) The Tribunal, after considering the application and any representations and, if it considers necessary, after having given the applicant and any such party who has made such representations an opportunity of being heard, shall grant or dismiss the application (with such order as to costs) as it may think fit, and if it grants the application it may give such directions as to the taking of any steps required or authorised under these Rules, or as to any further matter as the Tribunal thinks fit.

(4) The decision of the Tribunal shall be in writing and shall include a statement of its reasons, and the Secretary shall serve a copy thereof on the applicant and any party who made representations.

## Advertisement of reference or application

**5.**—(1) Except where the Tribunal has declined to entertain a reference under section 118 of the Act, or the Chairman in any other case otherwise directs, the Secretary shall give notice by advertisement in such manner as the Chairman may think fit of every reference or application under section 118, 119, 120, 121 or 122 of the Act.

(2) An advertisement shall state—

(a) the names and addresses of the applicant and any organisation or person on whom a copy of the notice of reference or application has been served in accordance with rule 3;
(b) the nature of the reference or application;
(c) the time, not being less than 21 days from the date of publication of the advertisement, within which—
   (i) an objection to the applicant's credentials may be made in accordance with rule 6, and
   (ii) any other organisation or person may apply to the Tribunal to be made a party to the proceedings in accordance with rule 7.

## Objections to applicant's credentials (Form 4)

**6.**—(1) Any organisation or person intending to object to the applicant's credentials shall, within the time specified under rule 5(2)(c), serve on the Secretary a notice of objection in Form 4:

Provided that the Tribunal or the Chairman may give leave, subject to such conditions as the Tribunal or Chairman may think fit, to serve such notice notwithstanding the expiration of the time specified under that rule.

(2) If notice of objection to the applicant's credentials has been served on the Secretary in accordance with this rule or if the Tribunal intends to make such objection of its own motion, the Secretary shall, on the expiration of the time specified in the advertisement under rule 5(2)(c), serve upon every party to the proceedings a notice of the same, and the proceedings shall (unless the Tribunal or the Chairman shall otherwise direct on the grounds that no reasonable cause of objection has been disclosed) be stayed from the date of such notice until further order.

(3) As soon as practicable after service of the notice under paragraph (2) above, the Chairman shall give directions for the making of representations in writing for the purpose of the consideration by the Tribunal of the objection. After consideration of the representations by the Tribunal the Chairman may, if he thinks

fit, give the applicant, any objector and any other party an opportunity of being heard at a hearing to be appointed by the Chairman.

(4) If, after considering the objection and any written or oral representations, the Tribunal is not satisfied of the applicant's credentials, it shall direct that no further proceedings shall be taken by any party in connection with the reference or application, otherwise than in relation to any order for costs which the Tribunal may make under rule 48.

(5) If, after considering the objection and any written or oral representations, the Tribunal is satisfied of the applicant's credentials it shall direct that the reference or application shall proceed and the Tribunal or the Chairman may give such consequential directions as to the taking of any steps required or authorised under these Rules, or as to any further matter as the Tribunal or Chairman may think fit.

(6) When the Tribunal has arrived at its decision on the objection, or where the objection has been withdrawn or is not proceeded with, the Secretary shall serve notice of the same on every party to the proceedings.

### Intervener's application (Form 5)

**7.**—(1) An application to the Tribunal by a person or organisation to be made a party to a reference or an application referred to in rule 3 may be made by serving on the Secretary, within the time specified under rule 5(2)(c), a notice of intervention in Form 5, together with a statement of his interest:

Provided that the Tribunal or the Chairman may give leave, subject to such conditions as the Tribunal or Chairman may think fit, to serve such notice notwithstanding the expiration of the time specified under that rule.

(2) As soon as practicable after receipt of a notice served under this rule the Secretary shall—

(a) serve a copy of the notice on every other party to the proceedings, and
(b) serve on the intervener a copy of the applicant's reference or application and statement of case, together with any other notice of intervention which has been served upon him.

### Objections to intervener's credentials (Form 6)

**8.**—(1) Any party intending to object to an intervener's credentials shall, within 14 days of being served with a copy of the notice of intervention under rule 7, serve on the Secretary a notice of objection in Form 6.

(2) The Secretary shall, as soon as practicable after receipt of any notice of objection, serve on every other party to the proceedings a copy of the same.

(3) If the Tribunal intends of its own motion to object to an intervener's credentials, the Secretary shall, on the expiration of the time specified under rule 5(2)(c), serve on the intervener and every other party notice of that intention with a statement of the Tribunal's reasons for the objection.

(4) An objection to an intervener's credentials shall not, subject to any direction to the contrary that the Chairman may give under rule 11(2)(vii), operate as a stay of the proceedings and shall be considered by the Tribunal at the same time as the reference or application in question.

### Written response by operator of scheme or intervener

**9.**—(1) Except where otherwise directed under rule 3(3)(a), the operator of the licensing scheme shall, within 28 days of the service on him of a copy of the applicant's statement of case in accordance with rule 3(2), serve on the Secretary a written answer to the applicant's statement setting out his case.

(2) Within 21 days of the expiration of the time specified under rule 5(2)(c), an intervener shall serve on the Secretary a statement of the case he intends to make.

(3) The Secretary shall serve a copy of such case or answer on every other party to the proceedings within 10 days of the receipt thereof.

### Amendment of statement of case and answer

**10.**—(1) Subject to paragraph (3) of this rule, a party may at any time amend his statement of case or answer by serving on the Secretary the amended statement or answer.

(2) On being served with an amended statement of case or answer, the Secretary shall as soon as practicable serve a copy thereof on every other party.

(3) No amended statement of case or answer shall, without the leave of the Chairman, be served after such date as the Chairman may direct under rule 11(2)(iii).

### Chairman's directions

**11.**—(1) Upon the expiration of the time specified by rule 9(2) for the service on the Secretary of a statement of case or answer, the Chairman shall appoint a date and place for the attendance of the parties for the purpose of his giving directions as to the further conduct of the proceedings, and the Secretary shall serve on every party and every person whose application under rule 7(1) has not been determined not less than 21 days' notice of such date and place.

(2) On the appointed day, the Chairman shall afford every party attending the appointment an opportunity of being heard and, after considering any representations made orally or in writing, give such directions as he thinks fit with a view to the just, expeditious and economical disposal of the proceedings and, without prejudice to the generality of the foregoing, may give directions as to—

  (i)  the date and place of any oral hearing requested by any party or which the Chairman for any reason considers necessary, and the procedure (including the number of representatives each party may appoint for the purpose of such hearing) and the timetable (including the allocation of time for the making of representations by each party) to be followed at such a hearing;

  (ii)  the procedure to be followed with regard to the submission and exchange of written arguments;

(iii) the date after which no amended statement of case or answer may be served without leave;

(iv) the preparation and service by each party, or any one party if all other parties agree, of a schedule setting out the issues to be determined by the Tribunal and brief particulars of the contentions of each party in relation thereto;

  (v)  the admission of any facts or documents, and the discovery and inspection of documents;

(vi) the giving of evidence on affidavit; and

(vii) the consideration by the Tribunal of whether any objection made to an intervener's credentials under rule 8 shall operate as a stay of the proceedings.

(3) The Chairman may postpone or adjourn to a later date to be appointed by

him the giving of any directions under this rule and, at any time after directions have been given under this rule the Chairman may, whether or not any application on that behalf has been made under rule 12, give such further directions as he may think fit.

(4) If any party fails to comply with any direction given or order made under this rule or rule 12, the Chairman may, without prejudice to the making of any order under rule 53, give such consequential directions as may be necessary and may order such a party to pay any costs occasioned by his default.

### Application for directions

**12.**—(1) A party may, at any stage of the proceedings, apply to the Tribunal for directions with respect to any issue or other matter in the proceedings and, except where the Tribunal (whether generally or in any particular case) otherwise directs or these Rules otherwise provide, every such application shall be disposed of by the Chairman.

(2) The application shall be made by the service of a notice on the Secretary (stating the grounds upon which it is made) and, unless the notice is accompanied by the written consent of all parties to the proceedings, the party making the application shall serve a copy of the application on every other party to the proceedings and inform the Secretary of the date of such service.

(3) Any party who objects to the application may, within 7 days after being served with the copy thereof, serve a notice of objection (stating the grounds of objection) on the Secretary and he shall serve a copy of the same on the applicant and any other party to the proceedings and inform the Secretary of the date of such service.

(4) After considering the application and any objection thereto and, if he considers necessary, after having given all parties concerned an opportunity of being heard, the Chairman may make such order in the matter as he thinks fit and give such consequential directions as may be necessary.

### Consolidation of proceedings

**13.** Where there is pending before the Tribunal more than one reference under section 118, 119, or 120 of the Act, or more than one application under section 121 or 122 of the Act relating to the same licensing scheme, the Chairman may if he thinks fit, either of his own motion or on an application made under rule 12, order that some or all of the references or applications, as the case may be, shall be considered together, and may give such consequential directions as may be necessary:

Provided that the Chairman shall not make an order under this rule of his own motion without giving all parties concerned a reasonable opportunity of objecting to the proposed order.

### Procedure and evidence at hearing

**14.**—(1) Every party to a reference or application which is considered at an oral hearing before the Tribunal shall be entitled to attend the hearing, to address the Tribunal, to give evidence and call witnesses.

(2) Except where the Tribunal or the Chairman otherwise orders in the case of an application for directions under rule 12, the hearing shall be in public.

(3) Evidence before the Tribunal shall be given orally or, if the parties so agree or the Tribunal or the Chairman so orders, by affidavit, but the Tribunal may at

any stage of the proceedings require the personal attendance of any deponent for examination and cross-examination.

## Representation and rights of audience

**15.**—(1) Subject to paragraph (5) of this rule, a party may at any stage of the proceedings appoint some other person to act as agent for him in the proceedings.

(2) The appointment of an agent shall be made in writing and shall not be effective until notice thereof has been served on the Secretary, and a copy of the same has been served on every other party and the Secretary informed of the date of such service.

(3) Only one agent shall be appointed to act for a party at any one time.

(4) For the purpose of service on a party of any document, or the taking of any step required or authorised by these Rules, an agent appointed by a party shall be deemed to continue to have authority to act for such a party until the Secretary and every other party has received notice of the termination of his appointment.

(5) A party or an agent appointed by him under paragraph (1) of this rule may be represented at any hearing, whether before the Tribunal or the Chairman, by a barrister, or in Scotland an advocate, or a solicitor, or by any other person allowed by the Tribunal or the Chairman to appear on his behalf or may, save in the case of a corporation or unincorporated body, appear in person.

## Withdrawal of reference or application

**16.**—(1) The applicant may withdraw his reference or application made under rule 3 at any time before it has been finally disposed of by serving a notice thereof on the Secretary, but such withdrawal shall be without prejudice to the Tribunal's power to make an order as to the payment of costs incurred up to the time of service of the notice. The applicant shall serve a copy of the notice on every other party to the proceedings and inform the Secretary of the date of such service.

(2) Any party to the proceedings upon whom a copy of the notice of withdrawal is served under this rule may, within 14 days of such service, apply to the Tribunal for an order that, notwithstanding such withdrawal, such reference or application should proceed to be determined by the Tribunal, and if the Tribunal decides, at its discretion, to proceed with such reference or application it may for that purpose substitute such party as the applicant to the proceedings and give such consequential directions as may be necessary.

## Decision of Tribunal

**17.** The final decision of the Tribunal on a reference or an application made under rule 3 shall be given in writing and shall include a statement of the Tribunal's reasons and, where on any further reference or application for review of the Tribunal's order under section 120 or 122 of the Act the Tribunal has varied the licensing scheme, there shall be annexed to the decision a copy of the scheme as so varied, and the Secretary shall as soon as practicable serve on every party to the proceedings a copy of the Tribunal's decision.

## Publication of decision

**18.** The Secretary shall cause a copy of the Tribunal's decision to be made available at the office for public inspection during office hours and, if the Chairman so directs, shall cause to be advertised, in such manner as the Chairman thinks fit, short particulars of the decision.

**Effective date of order**

**19.** Except where the operation of the order is suspended under rule 42 or 43, the order of the Tribunal shall take effect from such date, and shall remain in force for such period, as shall be specified in the order.

**References and applications with respect to licensing by licensing bodies commencement of proceedings (Forms 7 & 8)**

**20.**—(1) Proceedings with respect to licensing by licensing bodies shall be commenced by the service on the Secretary by the applicant of a notice—

(a) in Form 7 in the case of a reference under section 125 or 126 of the Act,
(b) in Form 8 in the case of an application for a review of an order under section 127 of the Act,

together with a statement of the applicant's case.

(2) As soon as practicable after receipt of the notice, the Secretary shall serve a copy of the same (with a copy of the applicant's statement) on the licensing body named in the notice under paragraph (1)(*a*) above, and in the case of an application for review of an order under section 127, on any person named in the notice under paragraph (1)(b) above.

(3) In the case of a reference under section 125 of the Act the Tribunal shall, as soon as practicable after the receipt of the applicant's notice, decide whether to entertain the reference and may for that purpose, at its discretion, allow representations in writing to be made by the applicant or the licensing body or both and if, after considering the reference and representations (if any) the Tribunal—

(a) decides to entertain the reference, it shall give such directions as to the taking of any steps required or authorised under these Rules, or as to any further matter (including any order as to costs) as the Tribunal thinks fit, and
(b) declines to entertain the reference, it shall direct that no further proceedings shall be taken by any party in connection with the reference, otherwise than in relation to any order for costs which the Tribunal may make under rule 48.

(4) The decision of the Tribunal shall be in writing and shall include a statement of its reasons, and the Secretary shall serve a copy thereof on the applicant and the licensing body.

**Application for special leave (Form 3)**

**21.**—(1) An application under section 127(2) of the Act for the special leave of the Tribunal for the review of its order under that section shall be made by the service on the Secretary by the applicant of a notice in Form 3 together with a statement of the grounds for the application. The applicant shall serve a copy of the notice and statement on every person who was a party to the reference on which the Tribunal made the last previous order with respect to the licence.

(2) Within 14 days of the service upon him of such notice, any such party may make representations in writing to the Tribunal regarding the application for special leave, and he shall serve a copy of any such representations on the applicant and inform the Secretary of the date of such service.

(3) The Tribunal, after considering the application and any representations and, if it considers necessary, after having given the applicant and any such party who has made such representations an opportunity of being heard, shall grant or dismiss the application (with such order as to costs) as it may think fit, and if it grants the application it may give such directions as to the taking of any steps required or authorised under these Rules or as to any further matter as the Tribunal thinks fit.

(4) The decision of the Tribunal shall be in writing and shall include a statement of its reasons, and the Secretary shall serve a copy thereof on the applicant and on any party who made representations.

### Procedure, and decision of Tribunal

**22.**—(1) Except where otherwise directed under rule 20(3), the licensing body or other person shall, within 21 days of the service of the notice under rule 20(2), serve on the Secretary his written answer to the applicant's statement, and shall serve a copy of the same on the applicant and inform the Secretary of the date of such service.

(2) Rules 10 to 16 shall apply to proceedings in respect of a reference or application under rules 20 and 21 as they apply to proceedings in respect of a reference or an application under rule 3.

(3) The final decision of the Tribunal on a reference or an application under rule 20 shall be given in writing and shall include a statement of the Tribunal's reasons and there shall be annexed to the decision a copy of the order and, where the Tribunal has varied a previous order, a copy of that order as varied.

(4) The Secretary shall as soon as practicable serve on every party to the proceedings a copy of the Tribunal's decision. Rules 18 and 19 shall apply with regard to the publication and the effective date of the decision.

### Intervener's application (Forms 5 & 6)

**23.**—(1) A person or organisation who claims to have a substantial interest in proceedings in respect of a reference or an application under rule 20 may apply to the Tribunal to be made a party to that reference or application by serving on the Secretary a notice of intervention in Form 5, together with a statement of his interest.

(2) As soon as practicable after receipt of a notice under this rule the Secretary shall—

(a) serve a copy of the notice on every other party to the proceedings, and
(b) serve on the intervener a copy of the applicant's reference or application and statement of case, together with any other notice of intervention which has been served on him.

(3) Within 14 days of the service upon him of the notice, a party intending to object to an intervener's credentials shall serve on the Secretary a notice of objection in Form 6 and shall serve a copy of the same on the intervener and inform the Secretary of the date of such service.

(4) The Tribunal, after considering the intervener's application and any objection to his credentials and, if it considers necessary, after having given the intervener and any party who has served a notice of objection an opportunity of being heard, shall, if satisfied of the substantial interest of the intervener, grant the application and may thereupon give such directions or further directions as to the taking of any steps required or authorised under these Rules or as to any further

matter as may be necessary to enable the intervener to participate in the proceedings as a party.

(5) Subject to any direction to the contrary that the Chairman may give under rule 11(2)(vii) an objection to an intervener's credentials shall not operate as a stay of proceedings and shall be considered by the Tribunal at the same time as the reference or application in question.

### Appeals Against Orders made by the Secretary of State

### Commencement of appeal proceedings (Forms 9 & 10)

**24.** An appeal to the Tribunal under section 139 of the Act against an order made by the Secretary of State may be made within 6 weeks of the making of the order or such further period as the Tribunal may allow—

(a) in the case of an order under section 137 of the Act, by the service by the copyright owner on the Secretary of a notice in Form 9, together with a statement of his case, and by serving a copy thereof on the licensing body and any person or organisation who was given notice under that section; and

(b) in the case of an order under section 138, by the copyright owner or any person or organisation who was given notice under that section and who made representations, by the service on the Secretary of a notice in Form 10, together with a statement of his case, and by serving a copy thereof on any other person or organisation who made representations under that section.

### Procedure, and decision of Tribunal

**25.**—(1) Within 21 days of the service of the notice upon him under this rule a person or organisation shall serve on the Secretary a written answer to the appellant's statement setting out his case, and shall serve a copy thereof on the appellant and any other person served with notice under this rule and inform the Secretary of the date of such service.

(2) Rules 10 to 16 shall apply to proceedings in respect of an appeal under rule 24 as they apply to proceedings in respect of an application under rule 3.

(3) The final decision of the Tribunal on an appeal under rule 24 shall be given in writing and shall include a statement of the Tribunal's reasons and, where the Tribunal varies any previous order or makes any other order, there shall be annexed to the decision a copy of that order as varied or, as the case may be, that other order; and the Secretary shall as soon as practicable serve on every party to the appeal a copy of the Tribunal's decision. Rules 18 and 19 shall apply with regard to the publication and the effective date of the decision.

### Intervener's application (Forms 5 & 6)

**26.** A person or organisation who claims to have a substantial interest in proceedings in respect of an appeal under rule 24 may, in accordance with rule 23, apply to the Tribunal to be made a party and that rule shall apply to proceedings in respect of such an application as it applies to proceedings in respect of an application under rule 20.

### Applications and references with respect to use as of right of sound recordings in broadcasts and cable programme services

**Commencement of proceedings (Forms 10A, 10B & 10C)**
**26A.**—(1) Proceedings with respect to use as of right of sound recordings in broadcasts or cable programme services shall be commenced by the service on the Secretary by the applicant of a notice—

(a) in Form 10A in the case of an application to settle terms of payment under section 135D of the Act,

(b) in Form 10B in the case of a reference under section 135E of the Act,

(c) in Form 10C in the case of an application for a review of an order under section 135F of the Act,

together with a statement of the applicant's case.

(2) As soon as practicable after receipt of the notice, the Secretary shall serve a copy of the same (with a copy of the applicant's statement) on the licensing body named in the notice and, in the case of an application for review of an order under section 135F, on every person who was a party to the proceedings when the original order of the Tribunal was made.

(3) Except where the Chairman otherwise directs, the Secretary shall give notice by advertisement in such manner as the Chairman may think fit of every reference or application under section 135D, 135E or 135F of the Act.

*General note*
This rule was added by SI 1991 No 201, r 2(b).

**Application for special leave (Form 3)**
**26B.**—(1) An application under section 135F(2) of the Act for the special leave of the Tribunal for the review of its order under that section shall be made by the service on the Secretary by the applicant of a notice in Form 3 together with a statement of the grounds for the application. The applicant shall serve a copy of the notice and statement on every person who was a party to the application or reference on which the Tribunal made the last previous order with respect to the licence.

(2) Within 14 days of the service upon him of such notice, any such party may make representations in writing to the Tribunal regarding the application for special leave, and he shall serve a copy of any such representations on the applicant and inform the Secretary of the date of such service.

(3) The Tribunal, after considering the application and any representations and, if it considers necessary, after having given the applicant and any such party who has made such representations an opportunity of being heard, shall grant or dismiss the application (with such order as to costs) as it may think fit, and if it grants the application it may give such directions as to the taking of any steps required or authorised under these Rules or as to any further matter as the Tribunal thinks fit.

(4) The decision of the Tribunal shall be in writing and shall include a statement of its reasons, and the Secretary shall serve a copy thereof on the applicant and on any party who made representations.

*General note*
This rule was added by SI 1991 No 201, r 2(b).

**Procedure, and decision of Tribunal**
**26C.**—(1) Within 21 days of the service of the notice under rule 26A, the licensing body or other person shall serve on the Secretary his written answer to the applicant's statement, and shall serve a copy of the same on the applicant and inform the Secretary of the date of such service.

(2) Rules 10 to 16 shall apply to proceedings in respect of a reference or application under rules 26A and 26B as they apply to proceedings in respect of a reference or an application under rule 3.

(3) The final decision of the Tribunal on a reference or an application under rule 26A shall be given in writing and shall include a statement of the Tribunal's reasons and there shall be annexed to the decision a copy of the order and, where the Tribunal has varied a previous order, a copy of that order as varied.

(4) The Secretary shall as soon as practicable serve on every party to the proceedings a copy of the Tribunal's decision. Rule 18 shall apply with regard to the publication of the decision.

*General note*
This rule was added by SI 1991 No 201, r 2(b).

**Intervener's application (Forms 5 & 6)**
**26D.** A person or organisation who claims to have a substantial interest in proceedings in respect of a reference or an application under rule 26A may, in accordance with rule 23, apply to the Tribunal to be made a party to that reference or application and that rule shall apply to proceedings in respect of such an application as it applies to proceedings in respect of an application under rule 20.

*General note*
This rule was added by SI 1991 No 201, r 2(b).

### Application to settle the royalty or other sum payable

**Commencement of proceedings (Forms 11 & 12)**
**27.** Proceedings in relation to an application under section 142 of the Act shall be commenced by the service on the Secretary by the copyright owner or the person claiming to be treated as licensed by him—

(a) of a notice in Form 11, in the case of an application under subsection (1) of that section to settle the royalty or other sum payable in pursuance of section 66 of the Act, and

(b) of a notice in Form 12, in the case of an application under subsection (3) of that section for a variation of an order of the Tribunal made under subsection (2) of that section,

together with a statement of the applicant's case, and by serving a copy thereof on the other party.

**Application for special leave (Form 3)**
**28.**—(1) An application under section 142(4) of the Act for the special leave of the Tribunal for a variation of an order under that section shall be made by the service on the Secretary by the applicant of a notice in Form 3, together with a

statement of the grounds for the application, and by serving a copy thereof on the other party.

(2) Within 14 days of the service upon him of a copy of the notice under this rule, the other party may make representations in writing to the Tribunal regarding the application for special leave, and he shall serve a copy of any such representations on the applicant and inform the Secretary of the date of such service.

(3) The Tribunal, after considering the application and any representations and, if it considers necessary, after having given the applicant and any such party who has made such representations an opportunity of being heard, shall grant or dismiss the application (with such order as to costs) as it may think fit, and if it grants the application it may give such directions as to the taking of any steps required or authorised under these Rules or as to any further matter as the Tribunal thinks fit.

(4) The decision of the Tribunal shall be in writing and shall include a statement of its reasons, and the Secretary shall serve a copy thereof on the applicant and on every party who made representations.

### Procedure, and decision of Tribunal

**29.**—(1) Within 21 days of the service of the notice under rule 27 the other party shall serve on the Secretary his written answer to the applicant's statement, and shall serve a copy of the same on the applicant and inform the Secretary of the date of such service.

(2) Rules 10 to 16 shall apply to proceedings in respect of an application under rules 27 and 28 as they apply to proceedings in respect of an application under rule 3.

(3) The final decision of the Tribunal on an application under rule 27 shall be given in writing and shall include a statement of the Tribunal's reasons, and there shall be annexed to the decision a copy of the order and where the Tribunal has varied a previous order, a copy of that order as varied; and the Secretary shall as soon as practicable serve on every party to the proceedings a copy of the Tribunal's decision. Rules 18 and 19 shall apply with regard to the publication and the effective date of the decision.

### Intervener's application (Forms 5 & 6)

**30.** A person or organisation who claims to have a substantial interest in proceedings in respect of an application under rule 27 may, in accordance with rule 23, apply to the Tribunal to be made a party and that rule shall apply to proceedings in respect of such an application as it applies to proceedings in respect of an application under rule 20.

### Application to settle terms of licence as of right

### Commencement of proceedings (Form 13)

**31.** Proceedings in relation to an application by a person requiring a licence in the circumstances described in section 144(4) of the Act shall be commenced by the service on the Secretary by the applicant of a notice in Form 13 with a statement of the terms required and the reasons for the same, and he shall serve a copy of the same on the copyright owner.

### Procedure, and decision of Tribunal

**32.**—(1) Within 21 days of the service of the notice under rule 31, the copyright owner may serve on the Secretary his written answer setting out the grounds of his objection and the terms of the licence which he considers the Tribunal should settle, and shall serve a copy of the same on the applicant and inform the Secretary of the date of such service.

(2) Rules 10 to 16 shall apply to proceedings in respect of an application under rule 31 as they apply to proceedings in respect of an application under rule 3.

(3) The final decision of the Tribunal on an application under rule 31 shall be given in writing and shall include a statement of the Tribunal's reasons, and the Secretary shall as soon as practicable serve on every party to the proceedings a copy of the Tribunal's decision. Rule 18 shall apply with regard to the publication of the decision.

### Intervener's application (Forms 5 & 6)

**33.** A person or organisation who claims to have a substantial interest in proceedings in respect of an application under rule 31 may, in accordance with rule 23, apply to the Tribunal to be made a party and that rule shall apply to proceedings in respect of such an application as it applies to proceedings in respect of an application under rule 20.

## Application for Tribunal's consent on behalf of performer

### Commencement of proceedings (Form 14)

**34.** Proceedings under section 190 of the Act for the Tribunal's consent on behalf of the performer to the making of a recording from a previous recording of a performance shall be commenced by the service by the applicant on the Secretary of a notice in Form 14 together with a statement—

(a) where the identity or whereabouts of the performer cannot be ascertained, of the inquiries made by him in that respect and the result of those inquiries, or

(b) where the identity or whereabouts of the performer are known, of the grounds on which the applicant considers that the performer's withholding of consent is unreasonable, and by serving a copy thereof on the performer.

### Inquiries by Tribunal

**35.**—(1) Where a notice has been served in accordance with rule 34(a), the Tribunal shall, after requiring of the applicant such further particulars as it may consider necessary, cause to be served on such persons as it considers are likely to have relevant information with regard to the identity or the whereabouts of the performer a notice seeking such information, and at the same time cause to be published, in such publications as it considers appropriate and at such intervals as it may determine, a notice setting out brief particulars of the application and requesting information on the identity or whereabouts of the performer.

(2) On the expiration of 28 days from the date of the publication of the notice, or the date of publication of the last such notice, the Tribunal may, on being satisfied that the identity or whereabouts of the performer cannot be ascertained, make an order giving its consent on such terms as it thinks fit.

### Procedure, and decision of Tribunal

**36.**—(1) Within 21 days of the service of the notice under rule 34(b), the performer may serve on the Secretary his answer setting out his case and of the grounds for his withholding of consent, and shall serve a copy of the same on the applicant and inform the Secretary of the date of such service.

(2) Rules 10 to 16 shall apply to proceedings in respect of an application under rule 34(b) as they apply to proceedings in respect of an application under rule 3.

(3) The final decision of the Tribunal on an application under rule 34 shall be given in writing and shall include a statement of the Tribunal's reasons and where the Tribunal has, in default of an agreement between the applicant and the performer, made an order as to the payment to be made to the performer in consideration of the consent given on his behalf by the Tribunal, there shall be annexed to the decision a copy of that order; and the Secretary shall as soon as practicable serve on every party to the proceedings a copy of the Tribunal's decision. Rules 18 and 19 shall apply with regard to the publication and the effective date of the decision.

### Intervener's application (Forms 5 & 6)

**37.** A person or organisation who claims to have a substantial interest in proceedings in respect of an application under rule 34 may, in accordance with rule 23, apply to the Tribunal to be made a party, and that rule shall apply to proceedings in respect of such an application as it applies to proceedings in respect of an application under rule 20.

### Application for Tribunal's determination of royalty payable to the Hospital for Sick Children

### Commencement of proceedings (Forms 15 & 16)

**38.** Proceedings under paragraph 5 of Schedule 6 to the Act for the determination of the royalty or other remuneration to be paid to the Hospital for Sick Children shall be commenced by the service on the Secretary by the applicant of a notice—

(a) in Form 15, in the case of an application under paragraph 5(1) of Schedule 6 to the Act, and
(b) in Form 16, in the case of an application for a review of an order under paragraph 5(2) of that Schedule,

together with a statement of the applicant's case, and by serving a copy thereof on the other party.

### Application for special leave (Form 3)

**39.**—(1) An application for the special leave of the Tribunal for the review of an order under paragraph 5(3) of Schedule 6 to the Act shall be made by serving on the Secretary a notice in Form 3 together with a statement of the grounds for the application, and by serving a copy thereof on the person who was a party to the proceedings when the order of the Tribunal was made.

(2) Within 14 days of the service upon him of a copy of the notice under this rule, the other party may make representations in writing to the Tribunal regarding the application for special leave, and he shall serve a copy of any such representations on every other party to the proceedings and inform the Secretary of the date of such service.

(3) The Tribunal, after considering the application and any representations and, if it considers necessary, after having given the applicant and any such party who has made such representations an opportunity of being heard, shall grant or dismiss the application (with such order as to costs) as it may think fit, and if it grants the

application it may give such directions as to the taking of any steps required or authorised under these Rules or as to any further matter as the Tribunal thinks fit.

(4) The decision of the Tribunal shall be in writing and shall include a statement of its reasons, and the Secretary shall serve a copy thereof on the applicant and on any party who made representations.

### Procedure, and decision of Tribunal

**40.**—(1) Within 21 days of the service of the notice under rule 38, the other party shall serve on the Secretary a written answer to the applicant's statement, and shall serve a copy of the same on the applicant and inform the Secretary of the date of such service.

(2) Rules 10 to 16 shall apply to proceedings in respect of an application under rules 38 and 39 as they apply to proceedings in respect of an application under rule 3.

(3) The final decision of the Tribunal on an application under rule 38 shall be given in writing and shall include a statement of the Tribunal's reasons and where the Tribunal has varied a previous order there shall be annexed to the decision a copy of that order as varied; and the Secretary shall as soon as practicable serve on every party to the proceedings a copy of the Tribunal's decision. Rule 18 shall apply with regard to the publication of the decision.

### Intervener's application (Forms 5 & 6)

**41.** A person or organisation who claims to have a substantial interest in proceedings in respect of an application under rule 38 may, in accordance with rule 23, apply to the Tribunal to be made a party and that rule shall apply to proceedings in respect of such an application as it applies to proceedings in respect of an application under rule 20.

### Use of information as of right application to settle terms of payment

### Commencement of proceedings (Forms 16A & 16B)

**41A.**—(1) Proceedings under Schedule 17 to the 1990 Act for the settlement of terms of payment to be made by a publisher to a person providing a programme service shall be commenced by the service on the Secretary by the applicant of a notice—

- (a) **in Form 16A, in the case of an application under paragraph 5(1) of Schedule 17 to the 1990 Act,**
- (b) **in Form 16B, in the case of an application for a review of an order under paragraph 6(1) of that Schedule,**

together with a statement of the applicant's case.

(2) As soon as practicable after receipt of the notice, the Secretary shall serve a copy of the same (with a copy of the applicant's statement) on the person providing the programme service named in the notice and, in the case of an application for review of an order under paragraph 6(1) of Schedule 17 to the 1990 Act, on every person who was a party to the proceedings when the original order of the Tribunal was made.

(3) Except where the Chairman otherwise directs, the Secretary shall give notice by advertisement in such manner as the Chairman may think fit of every reference or application under paragraph 5(1) or 6(1) of Schedule 17 to the 1990 Act.

**Application for special leave (Form 3)**
**41B.**—(1) An application for the special leave of the Tribunal for the review of an order under paragraph 6(2) of Schedule 17 to the 1990 Act shall be made by serving on the Secretary a notice in Form 3, together with a statement of the grounds for the application. The applicant shall serve a copy of the notice and statement on every person who was a party to the application when the order of the Tribunal was made.

(2) Within 14 days of the service upon him of a copy of the notice under that rule, the other party may make representations in writing to the Tribunal regarding the application for special leave, and he shall serve a copy of any such representations on every other party to the proceedings and inform the Secretary of the date of such service.

(3) The Tribunal, after considering the application and any representations and, if it considers necessary, after having given the applicant and any such party who has made representations an opportunity of being heard, shall grant or dismiss the application for special leave (with such order as to costs) as it may think fit, and if it grants the application it may give such directions as to the taking of any steps required or authorised under these Rules or as to any further matter as the Tribunal thinks fit.

(4) The decision of the Tribunal shall be in writing and shall include a statement of its reasons, and the Secretary shall serve a copy thereof on the applicant and on any party who made representations.

*General note*
This rule was added by SI 1991 No 201, r 2(c).

**Procedure and decision of Tribunal**
**41C.**—(1) Within 21 days of the service of the notice under rule 41A, the other party shall serve on the Secretary a written answer to the applicant's statement, and shall serve a copy of the same on the applicant and inform the Secretary of the date of service.

(2) Rules 10 to 16 shall apply in respect of an application under rules 41A and 41B as they apply to proceedings in respect of an application under rule 3.

(3) The final decision of the Tribunal on an application under rule 41A shall be given in writing and shall include a statement of the Tribunal's reasons, and there shall be annexed to the decision a copy of the order and where the Tribunal has varied a previous order, a copy of that order as varied, and the Secretary shall as soon as practicable serve on every party to the proceedings a copy of the Tribunal's decision. Rule 18 shall apply with regard to the publication of the decision.

*General note*
This rule was added by SI 1991 No 201, r 2(c).

**Intervener's application (Forms 5 & 6)**
**41D.** A person or organisation who claims to have a substantial interest in the proceedings in respect of any application under rule 41A may, in accordance with rule 23, apply to the Tribunal to be made a party to that application and

**that rule shall apply to proceedings in respect of such an application as it applies to proceedings in respect of an application under rule 20.**

*General note*
This rule was added by SI 1991 No 201, r 2(c).

## Appeal to the court from decision of tribunal and suspension of tribunal's orders

### Notice of appeal (Form 17)

**42.**—(1) An appeal to the High Court or, in the case of proceedings of the Tribunal in Scotland, to the Court of Session under section 152 of the Act on a point of law arising from a decision of the Tribunal shall be brought within 28 days of the date of the decision of the Tribunal or within such further period as the court may, on an application to it, allow.

(2) A party so appealing to the court on a point of law shall as soon as may be practicable serve on the Secretary a notice in Form 17 of such an appeal, and shall serve a copy thereof on every person who was a party to the proceedings giving rise to that decision.

(3) Where an appeal has been lodged with the court, the Tribunal shall not make any further order on the reference or application which is the subject of the appeal until the court has given its decision thereon.

(4) On receipt of the notice of appeal by the Secretary the Tribunal may of its own motion suspend the operation of any order contained in its decision, and shall, if an order is so suspended, cause notice of the same to be served on every person affected by the suspension and may, if it thinks fit, cause notice of the suspension to be published in such manner as it may direct.

### Application for suspension of order (Form 18)

**43.**—(1) A party to the proceedings may, pending the determination of an appeal under rule 42, apply to the Tribunal to suspend the operation of an order made by it by serving on the Secretary a notice in Form 18 within 7 days of the receipt of the decision of the Tribunal together with a statement of the grounds for suspension, and he shall serve a copy of the same on every person who was a party to the proceedings giving rise to that decision and inform the Secretary of the date of such service.

(2) Within 14 days of the service of the notice under paragraph (1) above a party may serve on the Secretary a statement setting out the grounds of his objection to the applicant's case, and shall serve a copy of the same on every person who was a party to the proceedings giving rise to the decision and inform the Secretary of the date of such service.

(3) Rules 10 to 16 shall apply to proceedings in respect of an application under this rule as they apply to proceedings in respect of an application under rule 3.

(4) Where the Tribunal, after consideration of the application and any representations, refuses an application to suspend the operation of its order, the Secretary shall as soon as practicable serve on every party to the proceedings a copy of the Tribunal's decision together with a statement of the Tribunal's reasons for refusal.

(5) Where any order of the Tribunal has been suspended upon the application of a party to the proceedings or by the court the Secretary shall serve notice of the suspension on all parties to the proceedings, and if particulars of the order have

been advertised shall cause notice of the suspension to be advertised in the same manner, and rule 18 shall apply with regard to the publication of the decision.

### Intervener's application (Forms 5 & 6)

**44.** A person or organisation who claims to have a substantial interest in proceedings in respect of an application under rule 43 may, in accordance with rule 23, apply to the Tribunal to be made a party, and that rule shall apply to proceedings in respect of such an application as it applies to proceedings in respect of an application under rule 20.

### Effect of suspension of order

**45.** If the operation of any order is suspended under rule 42 or 43, then, while the order remains suspended, sections 123 and 128 of the Act shall not have effect in relation to the order.

## Miscellaneous and general

### Application of Arbitration Acts

**46.** The provisions of sections 12, 14, 17 and 26 of the Arbitration Act 1950 (which are set out in Part 1 of Schedule 2), shall apply in the case of proceedings before the Tribunal in England and Wales, and the provisions of sections 13, 14, 16, 21 and 24 of, and paragraphs 4, 5 and 8 of Schedule 1 to, the Arbitration Act (Northern Ireland) 1937 (which are set out in Part 2 of Schedule 2), shall apply in the case of proceedings before the Tribunal in Northern Ireland, as those provisions respectively apply to an arbitration where no contrary intention is expressed in the arbitration agreement.

### Enforcement of Tribunal's orders in Scotland

**47.** Any decision of the Tribunal may be enforced in Scotland in like manner as a recorded decree arbitral.

### Costs

**48.**—(1) The Tribunal may, at its discretion, at any stage of the proceedings make any order it thinks fit in relation to the payment of costs by one party to another in respect of the whole or part of the proceedings.

(2) Any party against whom an order for costs is made shall, if the Tribunal so directs, pay to any other party a lump sum by way of costs, or such proportion of the costs as may be just, and in the last mentioned case the Tribunal may assess the sum to be paid or may direct that it be assessed by the Chairman, or taxed by a taxing officer of the Supreme Court or the Supreme Court of Northern Ireland or by the Auditor of the Court of Session.

### Fees

**49.** The fees specified in Schedule 1 shall be payable in respect of the matters therein mentioned.

### Service of documents

**50.**—(1) Any notice or other document required by these Rules to be served on any person may be sent to him by pre-paid post at his address for service, or, where no address for service has been given, at his registered office, principal place of business or last known address, and every notice or other document required to be served on the Secretary may be sent by pre-paid post to the Secretary at the office.

(2) Service of any notice or document on a successor in title or successor in interest of a party to any proceedings shall be effective if served or sent to him in accordance with this rule.

(3) Any notice or other document required to be served on a licensing body or organisation which is not a body corporate may be sent to the secretary, manager or other similar officer.

(4) The Tribunal or the Chairman may direct that service of any notice or other document be dispensed with or effected otherwise than in the manner provided by these Rules.

(5) Service of any notice or document on a party's solicitor or agent shall be deemed to be service on such party, and service on a solicitor or agent acting for more than one party shall be deemed to be service on every party for whom such a solicitor or agent acts.

## Notice of intention to exercise right

**50A.** *Notice of an intention to exercise rights conferred by section 135C of the Act or paragraph 4 of Schedule 17 to the 1990 Act to be given to the Tribunal under section 135B(3)(a) of the Act and paragraph 3(2)(a) of Schedule 17 to the 1990 Act may be effected by service on the Secretary of such notice and rule 50(1) shall apply to such service as it applies to any notice required to be served on the Secretary by these Rules.*

*General note*

This rule was inserted in error by SI 1991 No 201 with effect from 1st March 1991 and was revoked by SI 1992 No 467 on 4th March 1992.

## Time

**51.**—(1) Except in the case of the time limit imposed under rule 42(1), the time for doing any act may (whether it has already expired or not) be extended—

(a) with the leave of the Tribunal or the Chairman, or
(b) by the consent in writing of all parties, except where the Tribunal or Chairman has fixed the time by order or, if the time is prescribed by these Rules, has directed that it may not be extended or further extended without leave.

(2) A party in whose favour time is extended by consent under paragraph (1)(b) above shall, as soon as may be practicable after the necessary consents have been obtained, serve notice thereof on the Secretary.

(3) Where the last day for the doing of any act falls on a day on which the office is closed and by reason thereof the act cannot be done on that day, it may be done on the next day on which the office is open.

## Office hours

**52.** The office shall be open between 10.00am and 4.00pm Monday to Friday, excluding Good Friday, Christmas Day and any day specified or proclaimed to be a bank holiday under section 1 of the Banking and Financial Dealings Act 1971.

## Failure to comply with directions

**53.** If any party fails to comply with any direction given, in accordance with these Rules, by the Tribunal or the Chairman, the Tribunal may, if it considers that the justice of the case so requires, order that such party be debarred from taking any further part in the proceedings without leave of the Tribunal.

## Power of Tribunal to regulate procedure
**54.** Subject to the provisions of the Act and these Rules, the Tribunal shall have power to regulate its own procedure.

## Transitional provisions and revocation of previous Rules
**55.**—(1) In relation to any proceedings which are pending under Part IV of the Copyright Act 1956 when these Rules come into force, these Rules shall apply subject to such modifications as the Tribunal or the Chairman may, in the circumstances, consider appropriate.

(2) The Perfoming Right Tribunal Rules 1965, and the Performing Right Tribunal (Amendment) Rules 1971 [SI 1971 No 636] are hereby revoked, but without prejudice to anything done thereunder.

### SCHEDULE 1

#### TABLE OF FEES

| | |
|---|---|
| *(1) On serving notice in Forms 1, 2, 7, 8, 12, 14, 15 or 16.* | *£30* |
| *(2) On serving notice in Forms 3, 4, 5, 6, 9, 10, 11, 13, 17 or 18.* | *£15* |
| *(3) On every application for directions under rule 12.* | *£10* |

### SCHEDULE 1

#### TABLE OF FEES

| | |
|---|---|
| **(1)  On serving notice in Forms 1, 2, 7, 8, 10A, 10B, 12, 14, 15, 16 or 16A.** | **£30** |
| **(2)  On serving notice in Forms 3, 4, 5, 6, 9, 10, 10C, 11, 13, 16B, 17 or 18.** | **£15** |
| **(3)  On every application for directions under rule 12.** | **£10** |

*General note*
The Schedule in bold was substituted for the original Schedule 1 by SI 1991 No 201, r 3.

### SCHEDULE 2

PROVISIONS OF ARBITRATION ACTS

PART 1

Provisions of the Arbitration Act 1950 which apply in the case of proceedings before the Tribunal in England and Wales

Sections 12, 14, 17 and 26 shown below—

**Conduct of proceedings, witnesses, &c**
12.—(1) Unless a contrary intention is expressed therein, every arbitration agreement shall, where such a provision is applicable to the reference, be deemed to contain a provision that the parties to the reference, and all persons claiming through them respectively, shall, subject to any legal objection, submit to be examined by the arbitrator or umpire, on oath or affirmation, in relation to the matters in dispute, and shall, subject as aforesaid, produce before the arbitrator or umpire all documents within their possession or power respectively which may be required or called for, and do all other things which during the proceedings on the reference the arbitrator or umpire may require.

(2) Unless a contrary intention is expressed therein, every arbitration agreement shall, where such a provision is applicable to the reference, be deemed to contain a provision that the witnesses on the reference shall, if the arbitrator or umpire thinks fit, be examined on oath or affirmation.

(3) An arbitrator or umpire shall, unless a contrary intention is expressed in the arbitration agreement, have power to administer oaths to, or take the affirmations of, the parties to and witnesses on a reference under the agreement.

(4) Any party to a reference under an arbitration agreement may sue out a writ of subpoena ad testificandum or a writ of subpoena duces tecum, but no person shall be compelled under any such writ to produce any document which he could not be compelled to produce on the trial of an action, and the High Court or a judge thereof may order that a writ of subpoena ad testificandum or of subpoena duces tecum shall issue to compel the attendance before an arbitrator or umpire of a witness wherever he may be within the United Kingdom.

(5) The High Court or a judge thereof may also order that a writ of habeas corpus ad testificandum shall issue to bring up a prisoner for examination before an arbitrator or umpire.

(6) The High Court shall have, for the purpose of and in relation to a reference, the same power of making orders in respect of—

(a)   security for costs;

(b)   discovery of documents and interrogatories;

(c)   the giving of evidence by affidavit;

(d)   examination on oath of any witness before an officer of the High Court or any other person, and the issue of a commission or request for the examination of a witness out of the jurisdiction;

(e)   the preservation, interim custody or sale of any goods which are the subject matter of the reference;

(f)   securing the amount in dispute in the reference;

(g)   the detention, preservation or inspection of any property or thing which is the subject of the reference or as to which any question may arise therein, and authorising for any of the purposes aforesaid any persons to enter upon or into any land or building in the possession of any party to the reference, or authorising any samples to be taken or any observation to be made or experiment to be tried which may be necessary or expedient for the purpose of obtaining full information or evidence; and

(h)   interim injunctions or the appointment of a receiver;

as it has for the purpose of and in relation to an action or matter in the High Court:

Provided that nothing in this subsection shall be taken to prejudice any power which may be vested in an arbitrator or umpire of making orders with respect to any of the matters aforesaid.

### Interim awards

14. Unless a contrary intention is expressed therein, every arbitration agreement shall, where such a provision is applicable to the reference, be deemed to contain a provision that the arbitrator or umpire may, if he thinks fit, make an interim award, and any reference in this Part of this Act to an award includes a reference to an interim award.

### Power to correct slips

17. Unless a contrary intention is expressed in the arbitration agreement, the arbitrator or umpire shall have power to correct in an award any clerical mistake or error arising from any accidental slip or omission.

### Enforcement of award

26.—(1) An award on an arbitration agreement may, by leave of the High Court or a judge thereof, be enforced in the same manner as a judgment or order to the same effect, and where leave is so given, judgment may be entered in terms of the award.

(2) If—

(a)   the amount sought to be recovered does not exceed the county court limit; and

(b)   a county court so orders,

it shall be recoverable (by execution issued from the county court or otherwise) as if payable under an order of that court and shall not be enforceable under subsection (1) above.

(3) An application to the High Court under this section shall preclude an application to a county court and an application to a county court under this section shall preclude an application to the High Court.

(4) In subsection (2)(*a*) above 'the county court limit' means the amount which for the time being is the county court limit for the purposes of section 16 of the County Courts Act 1984 (money recoverable by statute).

PART 2

Provisions of the Arbitration Act (Northern Ireland) 1937 which apply in the case of proceedings before the Tribunal in Northern Ireland.

**A.** Sections 13, 14, 16, 21 and 24 shown below—

### Powers of arbitrators
13. The arbitrators or umpire acting under a reference in an arbitration agreement shall, unless the arbitration agreement or the reference thereunder expresses a contrary intention, have power to administer oaths to or take the affirmations of the parties and witnesses appearing, and to correct in an award any clerical mistake or error arising from any accidental slip or omission.

### Attendance of witnesses
14. Any party to a reference under an arbitration agreement may sue out a writ of subpoena ad testificandum, or a writ of subpoena duces tecum, but no person shall be compelled under any such writ to produce any document which he could not be compelled to produce on the trial of an action:

Provided that no writ shall issue under this section unless the arbitrator has entered on the reference or has been called on to act by notice in writing from a party to the reference and has agreed to do so.

### Entry of judgment in terms of award
16. An award on a reference under an arbitration agreement may, by leave of the court, be entered as a judgment in terms of the award, and shall thereupon have the same force and effect as a judgment or order of the court.

### Additional powers of court
21.—(1) The court shall have, for the purpose of and in relation to a reference, the same power of making orders in respect of any of the matters set out in the Second Schedule to this Act as it has for the purpose of and in relation to an action or matter in the court:

Provided that nothing in the foregoing provision shall be taken to prejudice any power which may be vested in an arbitrator or umpire of making orders with respect to any of the matters aforesaid.

(2) Where relief by way of interpleader is granted and it appears to the court that the claims in question are matters to which an arbitration agreement, to which the claimants are parties, applies, the court may direct the issue between the claimants to be determined in accordance with the agreement.

(3) Where an application is made to set aside an award the court may order that any money made payable by the award shall be brought into court or otherwise secured pending the determination of the application.

### Additional powers to compel attendance of witnesses
24.—(1) The court may order that a writ of subpoena ad testificandum or of subpoena duces tecum shall issue to compel the attendance of a witness before any referee, arbitrator or umpire.

(2) The court may also order that a writ of habeas corpus ad testificandum shall issue to bring up a prisoner for examination before any referee, arbitrator or umpire.

**B.** First Schedule (provisions to be implied in arbitration agreements), paragraphs 4, 5 and 8 shown below—

4. The parties to the reference and all persons claiming through them respectively shall, subject to any legal objection, submit to be examined by the arbitrators or umpire on oath or affirmation in relation to the matters in dispute and shall, subject as aforesaid, produce before the arbitrators or umpire all books, deeds, papers, accounts, writings and documents within their possession or power respectively which may be required or called for, and do all other things which during the proceedings on the reference the arbitrators or umpire may require.
5. The witnesses on the reference shall, if the arbitrators or umpire think fit, be examined on oath or affirmation.
8. The arbitrators or umpire may, if they think fit, make an interim award.

**C.** Second Schedule (matters in respect of which court may make orders) referred to in section 21(1), shown below—

1. Security for costs.
2. Discovery of documents and interrogatories.
3. The giving of evidence by affidavit.

4. Examination on oath of any witnesses before an officer of the court or any other person, and the issue of a commission or request for the examination of a witness out of the jurisdiction.

5. The preservation, interim custody, or sale, of any goods which are the subject matter of the reference.

6. Securing the amount in dispute in the reference.

7. The detention, preservation or inspection of any property or thing which is the subject of the reference or as to which any question may arise therein, and authorising for any of the purposes aforesaid any persons to enter upon or into any land or building in the possession of any party to the reference, or authorising any samples to be taken or any observation to be made or experiment to be tried which may be necessary or expedient for the purpose of obtaining full information or evidence.

8. Interim injunctions or the appointment of a receiver.

## SCHEDULE 3

FORM 1

COPYRIGHT, DESIGNS AND PATENTS ACT 1988: COPYRIGHT TRIBUNAL: NOTICE OF REFERENCE UNDER SECTION 118, 119 OR 120

To,

The Secretary to the Tribunal
1. TAKE NOTICE that

*Whereas
(state name and address of *organisation*) ('the Applicant'), being representative of persons claiming that they require licences (describe case(s) for which licence is required) to which the licensing scheme proposed (specified below) would apply;

*Whereas
*(state name and address of *person*) ('the Applicant') claims that a licence (describe case for which licence is required) is required
*(state name and address of *organisation*) ('the Applicant'), being representative of persons claiming that they require licences (describe case(s) for which licence is required)
to which the licensing scheme (specified below) applies;

*Whereas
*(state name and address of *operator of scheme*) ('the Applicant'), is the operator of the scheme (specified below)
*(state name and address of *person*) ('the Applicant') claims that a licence (describe case for which licence is required) is required to which the licensing scheme (specified below) applies
*(state name and address of *organisation*) ('the Applicant'), being representative of persons claiming that they require licences (describe case(s) for which licence is required) to which the licensing scheme (specified below) applies;
the Applicant hereby refers to the Tribunal the licensing scheme, particulars of which are—
(state name and address of operator of scheme and the scheme) .. .. .. .. .. .. .. .. .. as confirmed/varied (Delete whichever is inappropriate) by the Tribunal by an Order dated .. .. .. and bearing the reference number .. .. .. ..

2. The Applicant is an organisation representing (here give particulars of the persons whom the Applicant claims to represent and the grounds on which it claims to represent them).

3. There is delivered herewith a statement of the Applicant's case.

4. All communications about this reference should be addressed to

(the Applicant at the address shown above)

(name and address of Applicant's solicitor/agent).

Signed .. .. .. .. .. .. .. .. ..

Status of signatory .. .. .. .. .. .. .. .. .. .. (Applicant, an officer of Applicant, solicitor or agent)

Date .. .. .. .. .. .. .. .. ..

*Delete whichever is inappropriate

FORM 2

COPYRIGHT, DESIGNS AND PATENTS ACT 1988: COPYRIGHT TRIBUNAL: NOTICE OF
APPLICATION UNDER SECTION 121 OR 122

To,
The Secretary to the Tribunal
1. TAKE NOTICE that

*(name and address of person)
*(name and address of operator of licensing scheme)
('the Applicant') hereby applies to the Tribunal in connection with the licensing scheme (specified
below)—
*being in a case covered by the scheme, for the grant of a licence in connection with the scheme which
the operator of the scheme has *refused/failed to grant or procure the grant within a reasonable time
*being a case excluded from the scheme, the operator of the scheme has *refused/failed to grant or
procure the grant within a reasonable time/has proposed terms for a licence which are unreasonable

*for a review of its Order dated .. .. .. .. .. and bearing the reference number .. .. .. .. ..

2. The particulars of the licensing scheme are (name and address of operator of scheme and the case
covered or excluded by the scheme).

3. Description of the case for which a licence is required .. .. .. .. ..

4. There is delivered herewith a statement of the Applicant's case.

5. All communications about this reference should be addressed to

*(the Applicant at the address shown above)

*(name and address of Applicant's solicitor/agent).

Signed .. .. .. .. .. .. .. ..

Status of signatory .. .. .. .. .. .. .. .. .. (Applicant, an officer of Applicant, solicitor or agent)

Date .. .. .. .. .. .. .. ..

*Delete whichever is inappropriate

**FORM 3**

**BROADCASTING ACT 1990: COPYRIGHT, DESIGNS AND PATENTS ACT 1988:
COPYRIGHT TRIBUNAL: APPLICATION FOR SPECIAL LEAVE UNDER SECTION
120, 122, 127, 135F OR 142 OR SCHEDULE 6, PARAGRAPH 5 OF THE ACT OR
SCHEDULE 17, PARAGRAPH 6 OF THE 1990 ACT**

**To,**
**The Secretary to the Tribunal**

**1. TAKE NOTICE that (name and address of person, organisation, operator of licensing scheme,
licensing body, publisher or person providing a programme service) ('the Applicant') hereby
applies for the special leave of the Tribunal**

| | |
|---|---|
| **Application under s 120(2)** | **\*to refer again to the Tribunal the licensing scheme which was \*confirmed/varied by the Tribunal by an order** |
| **Application under s 122(2)** | **\*to review its order as to entitlement to licence** |
| **Application under s 127(2)** | **\*to review its order as to licence** |
| **Application under s 142(4) or Schedule 6, paragraph 5(3)** | **\*to review its order as to royalty or other sum/remuneration payable** |
| **Application under s 135F(2)** | **\*to review its order as to terms of payment** |
| **Application under s 135F(2)** | **\*to review its order as to reasonableness of a \*condition/requirement for information** |

| | |
|---|---|
| Application under | *to review its order as to terms of payment |
| Schedule 17, | |
| paragraph 6(2) of | |
| 1990 Act | |

dated .. .. .. .. and bearing reference number .. .. .. .. .. .. .. .. .. .. .. .. .. .. .. .. .. .. .. .. .. .

2. There is delivered herewith a statement of the grounds for the application.

3. A copy of this Notice, together with the statement, *has been/will be served on (date of service) on every person who was a party to the proceedings to which the above order of the Tribunal relates, namely (specify names and addresses of parties).

4. All communications about this application should be addressed to
   *(the Applicant at the address shown above)
   *(name and address of Applicant's solicitor/agent).

Signed .. .. .. .. .. .. .. .. .. ..

Status of signatory .. .. .. .. .. .. .. .. .. .. (Applicant, an officer of Applicant, solicitor or agent)

Date .. .. .. .. .. .. .. .. .. ..

*Delete whichever is inappropriate

*General note*
This form was substituted by SI 1991 No 201, r 4(a), Schedule, Part I.

FORM 4

COPYRIGHT, DESIGNS AND PATENTS ACT 1988: COPYRIGHT TRIBUNAL: NOTICE OF OBJECTION TO APPLICANT'S CREDENTIALS

To,
The Secretary to the Tribunal
1. TAKE NOTICE that in connection with the proceedings commenced by notice of *reference/application dated .. .. .. served by (name of Applicant) (name and address of party making objection) ('the Objector'), being
*(*a person/an organisation on whom a copy of the aforementioned notice was served on (date of service))
*(an intervener by virtue of a notice of intervention served on (date of service))
objects to the Applicant's credentials.

2. The Objector's grounds for the objection are as follows (state grounds).
4. All communications about this objection should be addressed to

*(the Objector at the address shown above)
*(name and address of Objector's solicitor/agent).

Signed .. .. .. .. .. .. .. .. .. ..

Status of signatory .. .. .. .. .. .. .. .. .. .. (Objector, an officer of Objector, solicitor or agent)

Date .. .. .. .. .. .. .. .. .. ..

*Delete whichever is inappropriate

**FORM 5**

**BROADCASTING ACT 1990: COPYRIGHT, DESIGNS AND PATENTS ACT 1988: COPYRIGHT TRIBUNAL: NOTICE OF INTERVENTION**

**To,**
**The Secretary to the Tribunal**
**1. TAKE NOTICE that (name and address of intervener) ('the Intervener') wishes to be made a party to the proceedings commenced by notice of *reference/application/appeal dated .. .. .. .. .. .. .. .. .. ..**
**\*(which was advertised in (name of publication and date of issue)).**

**2. The Intervener has a substantial interest in the matter for the following reasons (state reasons).**

**3. All communications about this reference should be addressed to**

**\*(the Intervener at the address shown above)**

**\*(name and address of Intervener's solicitor/agent).**

**Signed .. .. .. .. .. .. .. .. .. ..**

**Status of signatory .. .. .. .. .. .. .. .. .. .. (Intervener, an officer of Intervener, solicitor or agent)**

**Date .. .. .. .. .. .. .. .. .. ..**

**\*Delete whichever is inappropriate**

*General note*
This form was substituted by SI 1991 No 201, r 4(a), Schedule, Part I.

## FORM 6

**BROADCASTING ACT 1990: COPYRIGHT, DESIGNS AND PATENTS ACT 1988: COPYRIGHT TRIBUNAL: NOTICE OF OBJECTION TO INTERVENER'S CREDENTIALS**

**To,**
**The Secretary to the Tribunal**
**1. TAKE NOTICE that in connection with \*proceedings commenced by notice of \*reference/application dated .. .. .. served by (name of Applicant), and with the notice of intervention given by (name of Intervener) dated .. .. .. (name and address of party making objection) ('the Objector'), being**
**\*(the Applicant)**
**\*(the licensing body named in the notice of \*reference/application)**
**\*(person providing a programme service named in the notice of \*reference/application)**
**\*(\*a person/an organisation on whom the notice of \*reference/application was served)**
**\*(an intervener in the proceedings by virtue of a notice of intervention served on (date of service))**
**objects to the Intervener's credentials.**

**2. The Objector's grounds for the objection are as follows (state grounds).**

**3. All communications about this reference should be addressed to**
**\*(the Objector at the address shown above)**
**\*(name and address of Objector's solicitor/agent).**

**Signed .. .. .. .. .. .. .. .. .. ..**

**Status of signatory .. .. .. .. .. .. .. .. .. .. (Objector, an officer of Objector, solicitor or agent).**

**Date .. .. .. .. .. .. .. .. .. ..**

**\*Delete whichever is inappropriate**

*General note*
This form was substituted by SI 1991 No 201, r 4(a), Schedule, Part I.

FORM 7

COPYRIGHT, DESIGNS AND PATENTS ACT 1988: COPYRIGHT TRIBUNAL: NOTICE OF REFERENCE UNDER SECTION 125 OR 126

To,
The Secretary to the Tribunal
1. TAKE NOTICE that (name and address of prospective licensee or licensee) ('the Applicant'),
Reference under s 125
*(being the prospective licensee under the terms of a licence to be granted by (name and address of licensing body))
Reference under s 126
*(being a licensee under a licence granted by (name and address of licensing body), which licence is due to expire *by effluxion of time/as a result of a notice given by the licensing body on .. .. .. .. .. .. ..)

hereby—
*(refer to the Tribunal the terms on which the licensing body proposes to grant the licence)
*(apply to the Tribunal on the ground that it is unreasonable that the licence should cease to be in force).

2. There is delivered herewith a statement of the Applicant's case.

3. All communications about this reference should be addressed to
*(the Applicant at the address shown above)
*(name and address of Applicant's solicitor/agent).

Signed .. .. .. .. .. .. .. .. .. ..

Status of signatory .. .. .. .. .. .. .. .. .. .. (Applicant, an officer of Applicant, solicitor or agent)

Date .. .. .. .. .. .. .. .. .. ..

(*Delete whichever is inappropriate)

## FORM 8

COPYRIGHT, DESIGNS AND PATENTS ACT 1988: COPYRIGHT TRIBUNAL: NOTICE OF APPLICATION FOR REVIEW OF ORDER UNDER SECTION 127

To,
The Secretary to the Tribunal
1. TAKE NOTICE that (name and address of licensing body or person seeking review) ('the Applicant') hereby applies to the Tribunal for a review of its Order dated .. .. .. and bearing the reference number .. .. .. .. relating to the licence granted *to/by (name and address of licensee or licensing body).

2. There is delivered herewith a statement of the Applicant's case.

3. All communications about this application should be addressed to
*(the Applicant at the address shown above)
*(name and address of Applicant's solicitor/agent).

Signed .. .. .. .. .. .. .. .. ..

Status of signatory .. .. .. .. .. .. .. .. .. .. (Applicant, an officer of Applicant, solicitor or agent)

Date .. .. .. .. .. .. .. .. .. ..

*Delete whichever is inappropriate

## FORM 9

COPYRIGHT, DESIGNS AND PATENTS ACT 1988: COPYRIGHT TRIBUNAL: NOTICE OF APPEAL UNDER SECTION 139 AGAINST ORDER UNDER SECTION 137

To,
The Secretary to the Tribunal
1. TAKE NOTICE that (name and address of appellant) ('the Appellant'), being the owner of the copyright in (describe the work) which is the subject of an Order by the Secretary of State under section 137 of the Act dated .. .. .. and bearing the reference number .. .. .. (a copy of which is attached) hereby appeals to the Tribunal against that Order.

2. There is delivered herewith a statement of the Appellant's case.

3. A copy of this Notice, together with the statement, has been/will (Delete whichever is inappropriate) be served on (date of service) on the licensing body and any person or organisation who was given notice under section 137(3), namely (specify names and addresses of parties).

4. All communications about this appeal should be addressed to
*(the Appellant at the address shown above)
*(name and address of Appellant's solicitor/agent).

Signed .. .. .. .. .. .. .. ..

Status of signatory .. .. .. .. .. .. .. .. .. (Appellant, an officer of Appellant, solicitor or agent)

Date .. .. .. .. .. .. .. ..

*Delete whichever is inappropriate

FORM 10

COPYRIGHT, DESIGNS AND PATENTS ACT 1988: COPYRIGHT TRIBUNAL: NOTICE OF APPEAL UNDER SECTION 139 AGAINST ORDER UNDER SECTION 138

To,
The Secretary to the Tribunal
1. TAKE NOTICE that (name and address of appellant) ('the Appellant'), being
*(the owner of the copyright in (describe the work))
*(*a person/an organisation who was given notice under section 138(3)) and made representations in accordance with section 138(4))
hereby appeals to the Tribunal against the Order by the Secretary of State dated .. .. .. .. .. .. and bearing the reference number .. .. .. .. (a copy of which is attached).

2. There is delivered herewith a statement of the Appellant's case.

3. A copy of this Notice, together with the statement, *has been/will be served on (date of service) on every person or organisation who made representations under section 138, namely (specify names and addresses of parties).

4. All communications about this appeal should be addressed to
*(the Appellant at the address shown above)
*(name and address of Appellant's solicitor/agent).

Signed .. .. .. .. .. .. .. ..

Status of signatory .. .. .. .. .. .. .. .. .. (Appellant, an officer of Appellant, solicitor or agent)

Date .. .. .. .. .. .. .. ..

*Delete whichever is inappropriate

**FORM 10A**

**COPYRIGHT, DESIGNS AND PATENTS ACT 1988: COPYRIGHT TRIBUNAL: NOTICE OF APPLICATION UNDER SECTION 135D**

**To,**
**The Secretary to the Tribunal**
**1. TAKE NOTICE that (name and address of prospective licensee or licensee) ('the Applicant') being a person intending to avail himself of the right to include sound recordings in a *broadcast/and/cable programme service for which (name and address of licensing body) could *grant/procure the grant of a licence,**
***having given notice to the Tribunal on (date on which notice was given) of the intention to exercise that right; and the date on which it was proposed to begin to do so, namely ( ),**
***who herewith gives notice to the Tribunal of the intention to exercise that right; and of the date on which it is proposed to begin to do so, namely ( ),**
**hereby applies to the Tribunal to settle the terms as to payment for including sound recordings in a *broadcast/and/cable programme service.**

**2. There is delivered herewith a statement of the Applicant's case.**

**3. All communications about this application should be addressed to**
***(the Applicant at the address shown above)**
***(name and address of Applicant's solicitor/agent).**

**Signed .. .. .. .. .. .. .. ..**

**Status of signatory .. .. .. .. .. .. .. .. (Applicant, an officer of Applicant, solicitor or agent)**

**Date .. .. .. .. .. .. .. ..**

***Delete whichever is inappropriate**

*General note*
This form was added by SI 1991 No 201, r 4(b), Schedule, Part II.

**FORM 10B**

**COPYRIGHT, DESIGNS AND PATENTS ACT 1988: COPYRIGHT TRIBUNAL: NOTICE OF REFERENCE UNDER SECTION 135E**

To,

The Secretary to the Tribunal

1. TAKE NOTICE that (name and address of person making reference) ('the Applicant') being a person who
*has given notice to the Copyright Tribunal on (date on which notice was given) of his intention to exercise
*has exercised
the right to include sound recordings in a *broadcast/and/cable programme service,
*having been given notice of (a) condition(s) as to the inclusion in a *broadcast/and/cable programme service by:
*having been required to provide information to:
(name and address of licensing body),hereby refers to the Tribunal the question whether
*the condition(s) (setting out condition objected to) is a reasonable condition
*the information (setting out item objected to) can reasonably be required to be provided.

2. There is delivered herewith a statement of the Applicant's case.
3. All communications about this reference should be addressed to
*(the Applicant at the address shown above)
*(name and address of Applicant's solicitor/agent).

Signed .. .. .. .. .. .. .. ..

Status of signatory .. .. .. .. .. .. .. .. .. (Applicant, an officer of Applicant, solicitor or agent)

Date .. .. .. .. .. .. .. ..

*Delete whichever is inappropriate

*General note*
This form was added by SI 1991 No 201, r 4(b), Schedule, Part II.

**FORM 10C**

**COPYRIGHT, DESIGNS AND PATENTS ACT 1988: COPYRIGHT TRIBUNAL: NOTICE OF APPLICATION FOR REVIEW OF ORDER UNDER SECTION 135F**

To,
The Secretary to the Tribunal

1. TAKE NOTICE that (name and address of licensing body or person seeking review) ('the Applicant') hereby applies to the Tribunal for a review of its order dated .. .. .. .. .. .. and bearing the reference number .. .. .. ..
*in respect of the settlement of the terms as to payment for including sound recordings in a *broadcast/and/cable programme service payable to (name and address of licensing body)
*in respect of the reasonableness of *a condition(s)/requirement to provide information to (name and address of licensing body).

2. There is delivered herewith a statement of the Applicant's case.

3. All communications about this application should be addressed to
*(the Applicant at the address shown above)
*(name and address of Applicant's solicitor/agent).

Signed .. .. .. .. .. .. .. ..

Status of signatory .. .. .. .. .. .. .. .. .. (Applicant, an officer of Applicant, solicitor or agent)

Date .. .. .. .. .. .. .. ..

*Delete whichever is inappropriate

*General note*
This form was added by SI 1991 No 201, r 4(b), Schedule, Part II.

FORM 11

COPYRIGHT, DESIGNS AND PATENTS ACT 1988: COPYRIGHT TRIBUNAL: NOTICE OF APPLICATION TO SETTLE ROYALTY OR OTHER SUM PAYABLE UNDER SECTION 142

To,
The Secretary to the Tribunal
1. TAKE NOTICE that (name and address of applicant) ('the Applicant'), being
*(the owner of the copyright in (describe the works))
*(The person claiming to be treated as licensed by the owner of the copyright in (describe the works))
hereby applies to the Tribunal to settle the royalty or other sum payable in pursuance of section 66 of the Act.

2. There is delivered herewith a statement of the Applicant's case with respect to the royalty or other sum payable.

3. A copy of this Notice, together with the statement, *has been/will be served on (date of service) on (state name and address of other party).

4. All communications about this application should be addressed to
*(the Applicant at the address shown above)
*(name and address of Applicant's solicitor/agent).

Signed .. .. .. .. .. .. .. ..

Status of signatory .. .. .. .. .. .. .. .. (Applicant, an officer of Applicant, solicitor or agent)

Date .. .. .. .. .. .. .. ..

*Delete whichever is inappropriate

FORM 12

COPYRIGHT, DESIGNS AND PATENTS ACT 1988: COPYRIGHT TRIBUNAL: NOTICE OF APPLICATION FOR REVIEW OF ORDER UNDER SECTION 142(3)

To,
The Secretary to the Tribunal
1. TAKE NOTICE that
*(state name and address of owner of copyright)
*(state name and address of person claiming to be treated as licensed by the owner of copyright)

('the Applicant') hereby applies to the Tribunal for a review of its Order dated .. .. .. .. and bearing the reference number .. .. .. in respect of the settlement of the royalty or other sum payable to (name and address of owner of copyright in respect of the work).

2. There is delivered herewith a statement of the Applicant's case.

3. A copy of this Notice, together with the statement, *has been/will be served on (date of service) on the party (state name and address of other party).

4. All communications about this application should be addressed to
*(the Applicant at the address shown above)
*(name and address of Applicant's solicitor/agent).

Signed .. .. .. .. .. .. .. ..

Status of signatory .. .. .. .. .. .. .. .. .. (Applicant, an officer of Applicant, solicitor or agent)

Date .. .. .. .. .. .. .. ..

*Delete whichever is inappropriate

FORM 13

COPYRIGHT, DESIGNS AND PATENTS ACT 1988: COPYRIGHT TRIBUNAL: NOTICE OF APPLICATION TO SETTLE TERMS OF LICENCE OF RIGHT UNDER SECTION 144

To,
The Secretary to the Tribunal
1. TAKE NOTICE that (name and address of applicant) ('the Applicant'), hereby applies to the Tribunal to settle the terms of a licence available by virtue of section 144 of the Act in respect of (describe the works).

2. There is delivered herewith a statement setting out the terms required by the Applicant and the reasons for the same.

3. A copy of this Notice, together with the statement, has been/will be (Delete whichever is inappropriate) served on (date of service) on the copyright owner, namely (state name and address of owner of copyright in the work).

4. All communications about this reference should be addressed to
*(the Applicant at the address shown above)
*(name and address of Applicant's solicitor/agent).

Signed .. .. .. .. .. .. .. ..

Status of signatory .. .. .. .. .. .. .. .. (Applicant, an officer of Applicant, solicitor or agent)

Date .. .. .. .. .. .. .. ..

*Delete whichever is inappropriate

FORM 14

COPYRIGHT, DESIGNS AND PATENTS ACT 1988: COPYRIGHT TRIBUNAL: NOTICE OF APPLICATION FOR TRIBUNAL'S CONSENT ON BEHALF OF PERFORMER UNDER SECTION 190

To,
The Secretary to the Tribunal
1. TAKE NOTICE that (name and address of applicant) ('the Applicant') wishes to make a recording from a previous recording of (specify performance)
*(the identity or whereabouts of the performer(s) of which cannot be ascertained by reasonable inquiry)
*(the performer(s) of which unreasonably withhold his/their consent)
hereby applies to the Tribunal for its consent to the recording.

2. There is delivered herewith a statement setting out—
*(the inquiries made by the Applicant as to the identity or whereabouts of the performer(s) and the result of those inquiries)
*(the grounds on which the Applicant considers that the withholding of consent is unreasonable).

3. (A copy of the Applicant's statement, *has been/will be served on (date of service) on the performer(s) (state name(s) and address(es) of performer(s)).

4. All communications about this reference should be addressed to
*(the Applicant at the address shown above)
*(name and address of Applicant's solicitor/agent).

Signed .. .. .. .. .. .. .. ..

Status of signatory .. .. .. .. .. .. .. .. (Applicant, an officer of Applicant, solicitor or agent)

Date .. .. .. .. .. .. .. ..

*Delete whichever is inappropriate

*Appendix 2*

FORM 15

COPYRIGHT, DESIGNS AND PATENTS ACT 1988: COPYRIGHT TRIBUNAL: NOTICE OF APPLICATION FOR TRIBUNAL'S DETERMINATION OF ROYALTY PAYABLE UNDER PARAGRAPH 5(1) OF SCHEDULE 6

To,
The Secretary to the Tribunal
1. TAKE NOTICE that
*(the Trustees of The Hospital for Sick Children)
*(state name and address of person)
('the Applicant') hereby applies to the Tribunal to settle the royalty or other remuneration payable in respect of the *public performance/commercial publication/broadcasting/inclusion in a cable programme service of the *whole/part of 'Peter Pan' or its adaptation.

2. There is delivered herewith a statement of the Applicant's case.

3. A copy of this Notice, together with the statement, *has been/will be served on (date of service) on *the other party (state name and address of other party)/the Trustees of The Hospital for Sick Children.

4. All communications about this application should be addressed to
*(the Applicant at the address shown above)
*(name and address of Applicant's solicitor/agent).

Signed .. .. .. .. .. .. .. ..

Status of signatory .. .. .. .. .. .. .. .. (Applicant, an officer of Applicant, solicitor or agent)

Date .. .. .. .. .. .. .. ..

*Delete whichever is inappropriate

FORM 16

COPYRIGHT, DESIGNS AND PATENTS ACT 1988: COPYRIGHT TRIBUNAL: NOTICE OF APPLICATION FOR REVIEW OF ORDER UNDER PARAGRAPH 5(2) OF SCHEDULE 6

To,
The Secretary to the Tribunal
1. TAKE NOTICE that
*(the Trustees of The Hospital for Sick Children)
*(state name and address of person)
('the Applicant') hereby applies to the Tribunal for a review of its Order dated .. .. .. and bearing the reference number .. .. .. in respect of the determination of the royalty or other remuneration payable to the Trustees of The Hospital for Sick Children.

2. There is delivered herewith a statement of the Applicant's case.

3. A copy of this Notice, together with the statement, *has been/will be served on (date of service) on *the other party (state name and address of other party)/the Trustees of The Hospital for Sick Children.

4. All communications about this application should be addressed to
*(the Applicant at the address shown above)
*(name and address of Applicant's solicitor/agent).

Signed .. .. .. .. .. .. .. ..

Status of signatory .. .. .. .. .. .. .. .. (Applicant, an officer of Applicant, solicitor or agent)

Date .. .. .. .. .. .. .. ..

*Delete whichever is inappropriate

**FORM 16A**

**BROADCASTING ACT 1990: COPYRIGHT, DESIGNS AND PATENTS ACT 1988:
COPYRIGHT TRIBUNAL: NOTICE OF APPLICATION UNDER SECTION 176 OF, AND
PARAGRAPH 5 OF SCHEDULE 17 TO, THE BROADCASTING ACT 1990**

To,
The Secretary to the Tribunal
1. TAKE NOTICE that (name and address of publisher) ('the Applicant') being a person
intending to exercise the right to be treated as if he had at all material times been the holder of
a licence granted by (name and address of person) *providing/treated as providing (name of
programme service) authorising him to publish copyright information relating to the titles of the
programmes which are to be, or may be, included in the service and the times of their inclusion
('the act restricted by copyright'),
*having given notice to the Tribunal on ( ) of the intention to exercise that right and the date on
which it was proposed to begin to do so, namely ( ),
*who herewith gives notice to the Tribunal of the intention to exercise that right and of the date
on which it is proposed to begin to do so, namely ( ),
hereby applies to the Tribunal to settle the terms of payment for doing the act restricted by
copyright.

2. There is delivered herewith a statement of the Applicant's case.

3. All communications about this application should be addressed to
*(the Applicant at the address shown above)
*(name and address of Applicant's solicitor/agent).

Signed .. .. .. .. .. .. .. ..

Status of signatory .. .. .. .. .. .. .. .. (Applicant, an officer of Applicant, solicitor or agent)

Date .. .. .. .. .. .. .. ..

*Delete whichever is inappropriate


*General note*
This form was added by SI 1991 No 201, r 4(b), Schedule, Part II.


**FORM 16B**

**BROADCASTING ACT 1990: COPYRIGHT, DESIGNS AND PATENTS ACT 1988:
COPYRIGHT TRIBUNAL: NOTICE OF APPLICATION FOR REVIEW OF ORDER
UNDER SECTION 176 OF, AND PARAGRAPH 6(1) OF SCHEDULE 17 TO, THE
BROADCASTING ACT 1990**

To,
The Secretary to the Tribunal
1. TAKE NOTICE that
*(name and address of person) providing (name of programme service)
*(name and address of publisher)
seeking review ('the Applicant') hereby applies to the Tribunal for a review of its order dated .. ..
.. .. and bearing the reference number .. .. .. .. .. in respect of the settlement of the terms of payment
for exercising the right to publish copyright information relating to titles of programmes which
are to be or may be included in the programme service and the times of their inclusion.

2. There is delivered herewith a statement of the Applicant's case.

3. All communications about this application should be addressed to
*(the Applicant at the address shown above)
*(name and address of Applicant's solicitor/agent).

Signed .. .. .. .. .. .. .. ..

Status of signatory .. .. .. .. .. .. .. .. (Applicant, an officer of Applicant, solicitor or agent)

Date .. .. .. .. .. .. .. ..

*Delete whichever is inappropriate

*General note*
This form was added by SI 1991 No 201, r 4(b), Schedule, Part II.

FORM 17

COPYRIGHT, DESIGNS AND PATENTS ACT 1988: COPYRIGHT TRIBUNAL: NOTICE OF APPEAL ON POINT OF LAW UNDER SECTION 152

To,
The Secretary to the Tribunal
1. TAKE NOTICE that (name and address of appellant) ('the Applicant'), being a party to the proceedings on the *reference/application/appeal intends to appeal to the *High Court/Court of Session against the decision of the Tribunal dated .. .. .. and bearing the reference number .. .. .. on the following point(s) of law—
(state point(s) of law).

2. (A copy of this Notice, *has been/will be served on (date of service) on every person or organisation who was a party to the proceedings, namely (specify names and addresses of parties).

3. All communications about this appeal should be addressed to
*(the Appellant at the address shown above)
*(name and address of Applicant's solicitor/agent).

Signed .. .. .. .. .. .. .. ..

Status of signatory .. .. .. .. .. .. .. .. (Appellant, an officer of Appellant, solicitor or agent)

Date .. .. .. .. .. .. .. ..

*Delete whichever is inappropriate

FORM 18

COPYRIGHT, DESIGNS AND PATENTS ACT 1988: COPYRIGHT TRIBUNAL: NOTICE OF APPLICATION TO SUSPEND ORDER OF TRIBUNAL

To,
The Secretary to the Tribunal
1. TAKE NOTICE that (name and address of applicant) ('the Applicant'), being a party to the proceedings on the *reference/application/appeal (specify the proceedings) hereby applies to the Tribunal for the suspension of the operation of the Order of the Tribunal dated .. .. .. and bearing the reference number .. .. .. ..

2. There is delivered herewith a statement setting out the grounds for suspension—
(state grounds for suspension).

3. A copy of this Notice, together with the statement, *has been/will be served on (date of service) on every person or organisation who was a party to the proceedings, namely (specify names and addresses of parties).

4. All communications about this application should be addressed to
*(the Applicant at the address shown above)
*(name and address of Applicant's solicitor/agent).

Signed .. .. .. .. .. .. .. ..

Status of signatory .. .. .. .. .. .. .. .. (Applicant, an officer of Applicant, solicitor or agent)

Date .. .. .. .. .. .. .. ..

*Delete whichever is inappropriate

COPYRIGHT (CUSTOMS) REGULATIONS 1989
(SI 1989 No 1178)

| | | |
|---|---|---|
| *Made* .. .. .. .. | | *10th July 1989* |
| *Laid before Parliament* .. | .. | *11th July 1989* |
| *Coming into force* .. | .. | *1st August 1989* |

The Commissioners of Customs and Excise, in exercise of the powers conferred on them by section 112(1), (2) and (3) of the Copyright, Designs and Patent Act 1988 and of all other powers enabling them in that behalf, hereby make the following Regulations:

**1.** These Regulations may be cited as the Copyright (Customs) Regulations 1989 and shall come into force on 1st August 1989.

**2.**—(1) Notice given under section 111(1) of the Copyright, Designs and Patents Act 1988 shall be in the form set out in Schedule 1 or a form to the like effect approved by the Commissioners; and a separate notice shall be given in respect of each work.

(2) Notice given under section 111(3) of that Act shall be in the form set out in Schedule 2 or a form to the like effect approved by the Commissioners; and a separate notice shall be given in respect of each work and in respect of each expected importation into the United Kingdom.

(3) In regulations 3 to 9 'notice' means a notice given under either of those subsections.

**3.** The notice shall contain full particulars of the matters specified therein and shall contain a declaration by the signatory that the information given by him in the notice is true.

**4.** A fee of £30 (plus value added tax) in respect of the notice shall be paid to the Commissioners at the time it is given.

**5.** The person giving the notice shall furnish to the Commissioners a copy of the work specified in the notice at the time the notice is given and at that time or at the time the goods to which the notice relates are imported shall furnish to them such evidence as they may reasonably require to establish—

(a)  his ownership of the copyright in such work;
(b)  that goods detained are infringing copies; or
(c)  that a person who has signed the notice as agent is duly authorised.

**6.** The person giving the notice shall give security or further security within such time and in such manner, whether by bond or by deposit of a sum of money, as the Commissioners may require, in respect of any liability or expense which they may incur in consequence of the notice by reason of the detention of any article or anything done to an article detained.

**7.** In every case, whether any security or further security is given or not, the person who has given the notice shall keep the Commissioners indemnified against all such liability and expense as is mentioned in regulation 6.

**8.** The person giving the notice shall notify the Commissioners in writing of any change in the ownership of the copyright in the work specified in the notice or other change affecting the notice within fourteen days of such change.

**9.** The notice shall be deemed to have been withdrawn—

(a) as from the expiry of fourteen days from any change in ownership of the copyright specified in the notice, whether notified to the Commissioners in accordance with regulation 8 or not; or

(b) if the person giving the notice has failed to comply with any requirement of these Regulations.

**10.** [Revokes the Copyright (Customs) Regulations 1957, SI 1957 No 875 and the Copyright (Customs) (Amendment) Regulations 1982, SI 1982 No 766].

SCHEDULE 1

**Notice under The Copyright, Designs & Patents Act 1988 requesting infringing copies of a literary, dramatic or musical work to be treated as prohibited goods**

**Please read these notes before completing this notice.**

1. This notice may only be given by the owner of the copyright in a published literary, dramatic or musical work or a person acting on his behalf. A separate notice must be given for each work.

2. The period specified in part 1 shall not exceed 5 years and shall not extend beyond the period for which copyright is to subsist.

3. A fee of £30 (plus VAT) is payable. Please enclose a cheque for the required amount made payable to 'Commissioners of Customs and Excise'.

4. A copy of the work specified in part 2 should be enclosed.

5. The person who has given the notice shall keep the Commissioners of Customs and Excise indemnified against any liability or expense which they may incur as a result of detaining any article or anything done to an article detained because of this notice. You may need to provide the Commissioners with security to cover this indemnity. You will be informed when this is required.

**6. Part 3 is not obligatory, but please give as many details as possible.**

**Part 1.**

I.................................................................................................................................. give notice that

Full name of signatory in BLOCK LETTERS

..............................................................................................................................................

Name and address of Owner of Copyright

..............................................................................................................................................

..............................................................................................................................................

is the owner of the copyright in the work specified below which subsists under the Copyright, Designs and Patents Act 1988 and I request that any infringing copies of the said work be treated as prohibited goods for a period starting

on.................................... and ending on ................................

**Part 2.**

**Particulars of work**

Title:..........................................................................................................................................

..............................................................................................................................................

Full name of author/authors:........................................................................................................

..............................................................................................................................................

Date copyright expires:.............................................

**Part 3.**

**Details of expected importation**

    a)   Date of importation ............................................................................................................

    b)   Place of customs declaration ...........................................................................................

    c)   Place of unloading ............................................................................................................

    d)   Country of origin ..............................................................................................................

    e)   Country from which goods consigned ...........................................................................

    f)   Bill of lading/airway bill/consignment reference number ..........................................

    g)   Name of ship/aircraft flight number/vehicle registration number .............................

    h)   Name and address of importer/consignee .......................................................................

             .............................................................................................................................................

    i)   Tariff classification and commodity code ......................................................................

**Part 4.**

**Declaration**

I declare that the information given by me in this notice is true.

Signature ....................................................................     Date ................................................

(*Owner of copyright/authorised agent)

*Delete as necessary

**Part 5.**

Please send the completed notice, enclosing fee and a copy of the work, to—

HM Customs and Excise
CDB3(B)
Dorset House
Stamford Street
LONDON SE1 9PS

## SCHEDULE 2

**Notice under The Copyright, Designs & Patents Act 1988 requesting infringing copies of a sound recording or film to be treated as prohibited goods**

**Please read these notes before completing this notice.**

1. This notice may only be given by the owner of the copyright in a sound recording or film or a person acting on his behalf. A separate notice must be given in respect of each work and each expected importation of infringing copies of the work.
2. A fee of £30 (plus VAT) is payable. Please enclose a cheque for the required amount made payable to 'Commissioners of Customs and Excise'.
3. A copy of the work specified in part 2 should be enclosed.
4. The person who has given the notice shall keep the Commissioners of Customs and Excise indemnified against any liability or expense which they may incur as a result of detaining any article or anything done to an article detained because of this notice. You may need to provide the Commissioners with security to cover this indemnity. You will be informed when this is required.
**5. Part 4 is not obligatory, but please give as many details as possible.**

**Part 1.**

I.................................................................................................................................... give notice that

Full name of signatory in BLOCK LETTERS

......................................................................................................................................

Name and address of Owner of Copyright

......................................................................................................................................

......................................................................................................................................

is the owner of the copyright in the work specified below which subsists under the Copyright, Designs and Patents Act 1988 and that infringing copies of the work are expected to be imported into the United Kingdom and I request that these copies be treated as prohibited goods.

**Part 2.**

**Particulars of work**

Title .........................................................................................................................................

......................................................................................................................................

Label, marking or statement borne by work: .........................................................................

......................................................................................................................................

Date copyright expires: ...........................................................................................................

**Part 3.**

**Expected arrival in United Kingdom**

Date ..............................................................

Place ........................................................................................................................................

**Part 4.**

**Details of expected importation**

a)   Place of customs declaration .......................................................................................

b)   Place of unloading .........................................................................................................

c)   Country of origin ...........................................................................................................

d)   Country from which goods consigned .........................................................................

e)   Bill of lading/airway bill/consignment reference number ...........................................

f)   Name of ship/aircraft flight number/vehicle registration number ..............................

g)   Name and address of importer/consignee ....................................................................

    ..........................................................................................................................................

h)   Tariff classification and commodity code ....................................................................

**Part 5.**

**Declaration**

I declare that the information given by me in this notice is true.

Signature ......................................................................          Date ....................................

(*Owner of copyright/authorised agent)

*Delete as necessary

**Part 6.**

Please send the completed notice, enclosing fee and a copy of the work, to—

HM Customs and Excise
CDB3(B)
Dorset House
Stamford Street
LONDON SE1 9PS

COPYRIGHT (LIBRARIANS AND ARCHIVISTS) (COPYING OF
COPYRIGHT MATERIAL) REGULATIONS 1989
(SI 1989 No 1212)

| Made | .. | .. | .. | .. | *14th July 1989* |
| Laid before Parliament | .. | | .. | *18th July 1989* |
| Coming into force | | .. | .. | *1st August 1989* |

The Secretary of State, in exercise of the powers conferred upon him by sections
37(1), (2) and (4) and 38 to 43 of the Copyright, Designs and Patents Act 1988,
hereby makes the following Regulations:

**Citation and commencement**
**1.** These Regulations may be cited as the Copyright (Librarians and Archivists)
(Copying of Copyright Material) Regulations 1989 and shall come into force on
1st August 1989.

**Interpretation**
**2.** In these Regulations—

'the Act' means the Copyright, Designs and Patents Act 1988;
'the archivist' means the archivist of a prescribed archive;
'the librarian' means the librarian of a prescribed library;
'prescribed archive' means an archive of the descriptions specified in paragraph
    (4) of regulation 3 below;
'prescribed library' means a library of the descriptions specified in paragraphs
    (1), (2) and (3) of regulation 3 below.

**Descriptions of libraries and archives**
**3.**—(1) The descriptions of libraries specified in Part A of Schedule 1 to these
Regulations are prescribed for the purposes of section 38 and 39 of the Act:
    Provided that any library conducted for profit shall not be a prescribed library
for the purposes of those sections.
    (2) All libraries in the United Kingdom are prescribed for the purposes of
sections 41, 42 and 43 of the Act as libraries the librarians of which may make
and supply copies of any material to which those sections relate.
    (3) Any library of a description specified in Part A of Schedule 1 to these
Regulations which is not conducted for profit and any library of the description
specified in Part B of that Schedule which is not conducted for profit are prescribed
for the purposes of sections 41 and 42 of the Act as libraries for which copies of
any material to which those sections relate may be made and supplied by the
librarian of a prescribed library.
    (4) All archives in the United Kingdom are prescribed for the purposes of
sections 42 and 43 of the Act as archives which may make and supply copies of
any material to which those sections relate and any archive within the United
Kingdom which is not conducted for profit is prescribed for the purposes of
section 42 of the Act as an archive for which copies of any material to which that
section relates may be made and supplied by the archivist of a prescribed archive.
    (5) In this regulation 'conducted for profit', in relation to a library or archive,
means a library or archive which is established or conducted for profit or which
forms part of, or is administered by, a body established or conducted for profit.

**Copying by librarian of article or part of published work**
**4.** —(1) For the purposes of sections 38 and 39 of the Act the conditions specified in paragraph (2) of this regulation are prescribed as the conditions which must be complied with when the librarian of a prescribed library makes and supplies a copy of any article in a periodical or, as the case may be, of a part of a literary, dramatic or musical work from a published edition to a person requiring the copy.
(2) The prescribed conditions are—

(a) that no copy of any article or any part of a work shall be supplied to the person requiring the same unless—
  (i) he satisfies the librarian that he requires the copy for purposes of research or private study and will not use it for any other purpose; and
  (ii) he has delivered to the librarian a declaration in writing, in relation to that article or part of a work, substantially in accordance with Form A in Schedule 2 to these Regulations and signed in the manner therein indicated;
(b) that the librarian is satisfied that the requirement of such person and that of any other person—
  (i) are not similar, that is to say, the requirements are not for copies of substantially the same article or part of a work at substantially the same time and for substantially the same purpose; and
  (ii) are not related, that is to say, he and that person do not receive instruction to which the article or part of the work is relevant at the same time and place;
(c) that such person is not furnished—
  (i) in the case of an article, with more than one copy of the article or more than one article contained in the same issue of a periodical; or
  (ii) in the case of a part of a published work, with more than one copy of the same material or with a copy of more than a reasonable proportion of any work; and
(d) that such person is required to pay for the copy a sum not less than the cost (including a contribution to the general expenses of the library) attributable to its production.

(3) Unless the librarian is aware that the signed declaration delivered to him pursuant to paragraph (2)(a)(ii) above is false in a material particular, he may rely on it as to the matter he is required to be satisfied on under paragraph (2)(a)(i) above before making or supplying the copy.

**Copying by librarian to supply other libraries**
**5.**—(1) For the purposes of section 41 of the Act the conditions specified in paragraph (2) of this regulation are prescribed as the conditions which must be complied with when the librarian of a prescribed library makes and supplies to another prescribed library a copy of any article in a periodical or, as the case may be, of the whole or part of a published edition of a literary, dramatic or musical work required by that other prescribed library.
(2) The prescribed conditions are—

(a) that the other prescribed libarary is not furnished with more than one copy of the article or of the whole or part of the published edition; or

(b) that, where the requirement is for a copy of more than one article in the same issue of a periodical, or for a copy of the whole or part of a published edition, the other prescribed library furnishes a written statement to the effect that it is a prescribed library and that it does not know, and could not by reasonable inquiry ascertain, the name and address of a person entitled to authorise the making of the copy; and

(c) that the other prescribed library shall be required to pay for the copy a sum not less than the cost (including a contribution to the general expenses of the library) attributable to its production.

### Copying by librarian or archivist for the purposes of replacing items in a permanent collection

**6.**—(1) For the purposes of section 42 of the Act the conditions specified in paragraph (2) of this regulation are prescribed as the conditions which must be complied with before the librarian or, as the case may be, the archivist makes a copy from any item in the permanent collection of the library or archive in order to preserve or replace that item in the permanent collection of that library or archive or in the permanent collection of another prescribed library or archive.

(2) The prescribed conditions are—

(a) that the item in question is an item in the part of the permanent collection maintained by the library or archive wholly or mainly for the purposes of reference on the premises of the library or archive, or is an item in the permanent collection of the library or archive which is available on loan only to other libraries or archives;

(b) that it is not reasonably practicable for the librarian or archivist to purchase a copy of that item to fulfil the purpose under section 42(1)(a) or (b) of the Act;

(c) that the other prescribed library or archive furnishes a written statement to the effect that the item has been lost, destroyed or damaged and that it is not reasonably practicable for it to purchase a copy of that item, and that if a copy is supplied it will only be used to fulfil the purpose under section 42(1)(b) of the Act; and

(d) that the other prescribed library or archive shall be required to pay for the copy a sum not less than the cost (including a contribution to the general expenses of the library or archive) attributable to its production.

### Copying by librarian or archivist of certain unpublished works

**7.**—(1) For the purposes of section 43 of the Act the conditions specified in paragraph (2) of this regulation are prescribed as the conditions which must be complied with in the circumstances in which that section applies when the librarian or, as the case may be, the archivist makes and supplies a copy of the whole or part of a literary, dramatic or musical work from a document in the library or archive to a person requiring the copy.

(2) The prescribed conditions are—

(a) that no copy of the whole or part of the work shall be supplied to the person requiring the same unless—

    (i) he satisfies the librarian or archivist that he requires the copy for purposes of research or private study and will not use it for any other purpose; and

415

(ii) he has delivered to the librarian or, as the case may be, the archivist a declaration in writing, in relation to that work, substantially in accordance with Form B in Schedule 2 to these Regulations and signed in the manner therein indicated;

(b) that such person is not furnished with more than one copy of the same material; and

(c) that such person is required to pay for the copy a sum not less than the cost (including a contribution to the general expenses of the library or archive) attributable to its production.

(3) Unless the librarian or archivist is aware that the signed declaration delivered to him pursuant to paragraph (2)(a)(ii) above is false in a material particular, he may rely on it as to the matter he is required to be satisfied on under paragraph (2)(a)(i) above before making or supplying the copy.

## Revocations

**8.** The Regulations mentioned in Schedule 3 to these Regulations are hereby revoked.

SCHEDULE 1

PART A

1. Any library administered by—

(a) a library authority within the meaning of the Public Libraries and Museums Act 1964 in relation to England and Wales;

(b) a statutory library authority within the meaning of the Public Libraries (Scotland) Act 1955, in relation to Scotland;

(c) an Education and Library Board within the meaning of the Education and Libraries (Northern Ireland) Order 1986, in relation to Northern Ireland.

2. The British Library, the National Library of Wales, the National Library of Scotland, the Bodleian Library, Oxford and the University Library, Cambridge.

3. Any library of a school within the meaning of section 174 of the Act and any library of a description of educational establishment specified under that section in the Copyright (Educational Establishments) (No 2) Order 1989.

4. Any parliamentary library or library administered as part of a government department, including a Northern Ireland department, or any library conducted for or administered by an agency which is administered by a Minister of the Crown.

5. Any library administered by—

(a) in England and Wales, a local authority within the meaning of the Local Government Act 1972, the Common Council of the City of London or the Council of the Isles of Scilly;

(b) in Scotland, a local authority within the meaning of the Local Government (Scotland) Act 1973;

(c) in Northern Ireland, a district council established under the Local Government Act (Northern Ireland) 1972.

6. Any other library conducted for the purpose of facilitating or encouraging the study of bibliography, education, fine arts, history, languages, law, literature, medicine, music, philosophy, religion, science (including natural and social science) or technology, or administered by any establishment or organisation which is conducted wholly or mainly for such a purpose.

PART B

Any library outside the United Kingdom which is conducted wholly or mainly for the purpose of facilitating or encouraging the study of bibliography, education, fine arts, history, languages, law, literature, medicine, music, philosophy, religion, science (including natural and social science) or technology.

## SCHEDULE 2

FORM A

DECLARATION: COPY OF ARTICLE OR PART OF PUBLISHED WORK

To:

The Librarian of ................................................................................................................ Library

[Address of Library]

Please supply me with a copy of:

*the article in the periodical, the particulars of which are [ ............................................................]

*the part of the published work, the particulars of which are [ .......................................................]

required by me for the purposes of research or private study.

2. I declare that—

    (a)   I have not previously been supplied with a copy of the same material by you or any other librarian;

    (b)   I will not use the copy except for research or private study and will not supply a copy of it to any other person; and

    (c)   to the best of my knowledge no other person with whom I work or study has made or intends to make, at or about the same time as this request, a request for substantially the same material for substantially the same purpose.

3. I understand that if the declaration is false in a material particular the copy supplied to me by you will be an infringing copy and that I shall be liable for infringement of copyright as if I had made the copy myself.

Name ...........................................................        †Signature ..................................

Address .......................................................        Date ...........................................................

..................................................................

..................................................................

..................................................................

*Delete whichever is inappropriate.

†This must be the personal signature of the person making the request. A stamped or typewritten signature, or the signature of an agent, is NOT acceptable.

FORM B

DECLARATION: COPY OF WHOLE OR PART OF UNPUBLISHED WORK

To:

The *Librarian/Archivist of ....................................... *Library/Archive

[Address of Library/Archive]

Please supply me with a copy of:

the *whole/following part [particulars of part] of the [particulars of the unpublished work] required by me for the purposes of research or private study.

2. I declare that—

    (a)   I have not previously been supplied with a copy of the same material by you or any other librarian or archivist;

    (b)   I will not use the copy except for research or private study and will not supply a copy of it to any other person; and

    (c)   to the best of my knowledge the work had not been published before the document was deposited in your *library/archive and the copyright owner has not prohibited copying of the work.

3. I understand that if the declaration is false in a material particular the copy supplied to me by you will be an infringing copy and that I shall liable for infringement of copyright as if I had made the copy myself.

Name ............................................................    †Signature ................................

Address ......................................................    Date ........................................

....................................................................

....................................................................

\*Delete whichever is inappropriate.

†This must be the personal signature of the person making the request. A stamped or typewritten signature, or the signature of an agent, is NOT acceptable.

## SCHEDULE 3

REVOCATIONS

| Number | Title |
|---|---|
| SI 1957/868 | The Copyright (Libraries) Regulations 1957 |
| SI 1989/1009 | The Copyright (Copying by Librarians and Archivists) Regulations 1989 |
| SI 1989/1069 | The Copyright (Copying by Librarians and Archivists) (Amendment) Regulations 1989 |

# COPYRIGHT, DESIGNS AND PATENTS ACT 1988 (ISLE OF MAN) (NO 2) ORDER 1989
# (SI 1989 No 1292)

> *Made* . . . . . . . . *28th July 1989*
> *Coming into force* . . . . *1st August 1989*

Her Majesty, in pursuance of section 304(4) and (6) of the Copyright, Designs and Patents Act 1988, is pleased, by and with the advice of Her Privy Council, to order, and it is hereby ordered, as follows:

**1.** This Order may be cited as the Copyright, Designs and Patents Act 1988 (Isle of Man) (No 2) Order 1989 and shall come into force on 1st August 1989.

**2.**—(1) The following provisions of the Copyright, Designs and Patents Act 1988 shall extend to the Isle of Man subject to the exceptions and modifications specified in paragraphs (2) and (3) below—

    (a) Part IV (*registered designs*), except section 272 (so far as that section relates to paragraph 21 of Schedule 3) and section 273;

    (b) section 300 (*fraudulent application or use of trade marks an offence*);

    (c) Schedule 3 (*registered designs: minor and consequential amendments*), except paragraph 21, and

    (d) paragraphs 12 to 16 of Schedule 5 (*patents: miscellaneous amendments*).

    (2) Any reference in any of those provisions to an Act of Parliament or to a provision of such an Act shall be construed, unless the contrary intention appears, as a reference to that Act or provision as it has effect in the Isle of Man.

(3) Without prejudice to paragraph (2) above, sections 58A to 58D of the Trade Marks Act 1938 inserted by section 300 shall have effect subject to the exceptions and modifications specified in the Schedule to this Order.

**3.** The following provisions of the Copyright, Designs and Patents Act 1988 shall extend to the Isle of Man—

(a) section 303 (*consequential amendments and repeals*), so far as it relates to the provisions specified in paragraphs (*b*) and (*c*) below;

(b) paragraphs 5, 20, 22 and 23 of Schedule 7, and

(c) Schedule 8, so far as it relates to—

    (i) the Registered Designs Act 1949 (except section 32 of that Act), and

    (ii) section 49(3) of, and paragraphs 1 and 3 of Schedule 5 to, the Patents Act 1977.

**4.** The Copyright, Designs and Patents Act 1988 (Isle of Man) Order 1989 [SI 1989 No 981] is hereby revoked.

## SCHEDULE

EXCEPTIONS AND MODIFICATIONS SUBJECT TO WHICH PROVISIONS OF THE TRADE MARKS ACT 1938 HAVE EFFECT IN THE ISLE OF MAN

1. In section 58A(4)(b), for 'indictment' substitute 'information'.

2.—(1) In section 58B(2), for paragraphs (a) and (b) substitute 'when he is orally charged or is served with a summons or information'.

    (2) In section 58B(3), omit '(or, in Scotland, the Lord Advocate or procurator-fiscal)'.

    (3) For section 58B(4) substitute—

    '**(4) An appeal lies from an order made under this section by a court of summary jurisdiction to Her Majesty's High Court of Justice of the Isle of Man.**'.

    (4) Omit section 58B(6).

3.—(1) In section 58C(4), for the words from 'or under' onwards substitute '**or an order for delivery up could be made under section 21(9) of the Copyright Act 1956.**'.

    (2) Omit section 58C(5).

4. Omit section 58D.

COPYRIGHT, DESIGNS AND PATENTS ACT 1988
(COMMENCEMENT NO 4) ORDER 1989
(SI 1989 No 1303)

*Made* . . . . . . *27th July 1989*

The Secretary of State, in exercise of the powers conferred upon him by section 305(3) of the Copyright, Designs and Patents Act 1988, hereby makes the following order.

**1.** This Order may be cited as the Copyright, Designs and Patents Act 1988 (Commencement No 4) Order 1989.

**2.** Section 304(4) and (6) of the Copyright, Designs and Patents Act 1988 ('the 1988 Act') shall come into force on 28th July 1989.

**3.** In article 2 of the Copyright, Designs and Patents Act 1988 (Commencement No 1) Order 1989 [SI 1989 No 816] there shall be added to the list of the provisions of Part VII of the 1988 Act which do not come into force on 1st August 1989 a reference to section 304(4) and (6).

THE COPYRIGHT, DESIGNS AND PATENTS ACT 1988 (GUERNSEY) ORDER 1989 (SI 1989 No 1997)

| | |
|---|---|
| *Made* . . . . . . . . | *1st November 1989* |
| *Coming into force* . . . . . . | *1st December 1989* |

At the Court at Buckingham Palace, the 1st day of November 1989
Present,
The Queen's Most Excellent Majesty in Council

Her Majesty, in pursuance of section 304(5) of the Copyright, Designs and Patents Act 1988(a), is pleased, by and with the advice of Her Privy Council, to order, and it is hereby ordered, as follows:

**1.** This Order may be cited as the Copyright, Designs and Patents Act 1988 (Guernsey) Order 1989 and shall come into force on 1st December 1989.
**2.** Sections 297 to 299 of the Copyright, Designs and Patents Act 1988 (fraudulent reception of transmissions) shall extend to the Bailiwick of Guernsey with the exceptions and modifications specified in the Schedule to this Order.

*G I de Deney*
Clerk of the Privy Council

SCHEDULE

Article 2
EXCEPTIONS AND MODIFICATIONS IN THE EXTENSION OF SECTIONS 297 TO 299 OF THE COPYRIGHT, DESIGNS AND PATENTS ACT 1988 TO THE BAILIWICK OF GUERNSEY

1.   Any reference to an enactment shall be construed, unless the contrary intention appears, as a reference to it as it has effect in the Bailiwick of Guernsey.
2.  In section 297(1), after 'United Kingdom' there shall be inserted 'or Bailiwick of Guernsey'.
3.  In section 298 —

    (a)   in subsection (1)(a) and (b), after 'United Kingdom' there shall be inserted 'or Bailiwick of Guernsey';
    (b)   in subsection (3), for '99 or 100 (delivery up or seizure of certain articles)' there shall be substituted '7 of the Copyright Act 1911(a) (rights of owner against persons possessing or dealing with infringing copies etc)', and
    (c)   for subsections (4) to (6) there shall be substituted the following subsection:

        '(4) In section 8 of the Copyright Act 1911 (exemption of innocent infringer from liability to pay damages etc) as it applies to proceedings for infringement of the rights conferred by this section, the references to the defendant not being aware of the existence of the copyright in the work, and to his not being aware and having no reasonable ground for suspecting that copyright subsisted in the work, shall be construed respectively as references to his not being aware, and to his not being aware and having no reasonable ground for suspecting, that his acts infringed the rights conferred by this section.'.

4.   In section 299—

(a)   in subsection (1)(a), after 'United Kingdom' there shall be inserted 'and Bailiwick of Guernsey';

(b)   in subsection (2), for 'United Kingdom' whenever occurring there shall be substituted 'Bailiwick of Guernsey';

(c)   subsection (3) shall be omitted, and

(d)   in subsection (5), for '(copyright)' there shall be substituted 'of this Act as it has effect in England and Wales.'.


## FRAUDULENT RECEPTION OF TRANSMISSIONS (GUERNSEY) ORDER 1989
## (SI 1989 No 2003)

| | |
|---|---|
| *Made* . . . . . . | *1st November 1989* |
| *Laid before Parliament* . . . . | *8th November 1989* |
| *Coming into force* . . . . | *1st December 1989* |

Whereas it appears to Her Majesty that provision will be made under the laws of the Bailiwick of Guernsey giving adequate protection to persons making charges for programmes included in broadcasting or cable programme services provided from the United Kingdom and for encrypted transmissions sent from the United Kingdom:

**1.** This Order may be cited as the Fraudulent Reception of Transmissions (Guernsey) Order 1989 and shall come into force on 1st December 1989.

**2.** Section 297 of the Copyright, Designs and Patents Act 1988 applies in relation to programmes included in broadcasting or cable programme services provided from a place in the Bailiwick of Guernsey, and section 298 of the said Act applies in relation to such programmes and to encrypted transmissions of any other description provided or sent from a place in the Bailiwick of Guernsey.


## COPYRIGHT (HONG KONG) (AMENDMENT) ORDER 1990
## (SI 1990 No 588)

| | |
|---|---|
| *Made* . . . . . . | *14th March 1990* |
| *Laid before Parliament* . . . . | *22nd March 1990* |
| *Coming into force* . . . . | *12th April 1990* |

Her Majesty in pursuance of the powers conferred by section 31 of the Copyright Act 1956 and all other powers enabling Her in that behalf, is pleased, by and with the advice of Her Privy Council, to order, as follows—

**1.**—(1)   This Order may be cited as the Copyright (Hong Kong) (Amendment) Order 1990 and shall be construed as one with the Copyright (Hong Kong) Orders 1972 and 1979 (hereinafter referred to as 'the principal Order').

(2)   The principal Order and this Order may be cited together as the Copyright (Hong Kong) Orders 1972 to 1990.

(3)   This Order shall come into force on 12th April 1990.

**2.** This article amends the Copyright (Hong Kong ) Order 1972 [SI 1972 No 1724 Sch 1, Parts I, II].

COPYRIGHT (CERTIFICATION OF LICENSING SCHEME FOR
EDUCATIONAL RECORDING OF BROADCASTS AND CABLE
PROGRAMMES) (EDUCATIONAL RECORDING AGENCY LIMITED)
ORDER 1990
(SI 1990 No 879)

*(As amended by the Copyright (Certification Of Licensing Scheme For Educational
Recording Of Broadcasts And Cable Programmes) (Educational Recording Agency
Limited) Order 1992 (SI 1992 No 211 (superseded by SI 1993 No 193)), the
Copyright (Certification Of Licensing Scheme For Educational Recording Of
Broadcasts And Cable Programmes) (Educational Recording Agency Limited)
Order 1993 (SI 1993 No 193), the Copyright (Certification Of Licensing Scheme
For Educational Recording Of Broadcasts And Cable Programmes) (Educational
Recording Agency Limited) Order 1994 (SI 1994 No 247))*

*Made* . . . . . . *5th April 1990*

Whereas the Educational Recording Agency Limited, whose registered office is
at Hanover Square, London W1R OBE has applied to the Secretary of State to
certify, for the purposes of section 35 of the Copyright, Designs and Patents Act
1988 ('the Act'), a licensing scheme to be operated by it:

And whereas the Secretary of state is satisfied that the scheme enables the works
to which it relates to be identified with sufficient certainty by persons likely to
require licences and that it sets out clearly the charges (if any) payable and the
other terms on which licences will be granted:

Now, therefore, the Secretary of State, in exercise of the powers conferred upon
him by section 143(2) and (3)(a) of the Act, hereby makes the following Order—

**1.** This Order may be cited as the Copyright (Certification of Licensing Scheme
for Educational Recording of Broadcasts and Cable Programmes) (Educational
Recording Agency Limited) Order 1990.

**2.** The licensing scheme set out in the Schedule to this Order is certified for the
purposes of section 35 of the Act (recording by educational establishments of
broadcasts or cable programmes).

**3.** The certification under article 2 above shall, for the purposes of section 35 of
the Act, come into operation on 30th May 1990.

SCHEDULE

THE EDUCATIONAL RECORDING AGENCY LIMITED LICENSING SCHEME

1. The Educational Recording Agency Limited (to be known as ERA) has been established to operate
a Licensing Scheme for the purposes of section 35 of the Copyright, Designs and Patents Act 1988
('the Act').

2. The Licensing Scheme set out hereunder shall apply to any school as defined in section 174 of the
Act and any other description of educational establishment as may be specified by order of the Secretary
of State under that section ('Educational Establishment').

3. The copyright works covered by a Licence granted under the Licensing Scheme are the works in
respect of which the Licensor Members of ERA (or persons represented by the Licensor Members)
own or control the right to cause or authorise the recording of such copyright works by Educational
Establishments for the educational purposes of that Establishment.

4. The Licensor Members of ERA and the works in respect of which the relevant rights are generally
owned or controlled by such Licensors will be specified in Licences issued as follows—

| | |
|---|---|
| AUTHOR'S LICENSING AND COLLECTING SOCIETY LIMITED ('ALCS') | Those literary and dramatic works which are owned by or controlled by persons represented by ALCS and which are included in any broadcast or cable programme. |
| BBC ENTERPRISES LIMITED | The broadcasts of the British Broadcasting Corporation and all those copyright works of the British Broadcasting Corporation which are included in any broadcast or cable programme. |
| *CHANNEL FOUR TELEVISION COMPANY LIMITED ('Channel 4')*<br><br>**CHANNEL FOUR TELEVISION CORPORATION ('Channel 4')** | The copyright works of Channel 4 including any broadcasts made by Channel 4 itself and the films and sound recordings comprising television programmes which are commissioned by Channel 4 and broadcast on the *Fourth Channel* **television broadcasting service known as Channel 4** or otherwise included in any broadcast or cable programme. |
| DESIGN AND ARTISTS COPYRIGHT SOCIETY LIMITED ('DACS') | Those artistic works which are owned or controlled by persons represented by DACS and which are included in any broadcast or cable programme. |
| THE BRITISH PHONOGRAPHIC INDUSTRY LIMITED ('BPI') | Those sound recordings which are owned or controlled by persons represented by BPI and which are included in any broadcast or cable programme. |
| INDEPENDENT TELEVISION ASSOCIATION ('ITV Association') | The copyright works of members of the ITV Association including any broadcasts made by one or more members of the ITV Association themselves and the films and sound recordings comprising television programmes made or commissioned by such members and those copyright works which have been contributed to those programmes by employees of any ITV Company and which are included in any broadcast or cable programme. |
| MECHANICAL COPYRIGHT PROTECTION SOCIETY LIMITED ('MCPS') | Those musical works and sound recordings which are owned or controlled by members of MCPS and entrusted by its members to MCPS and which are included in any broadcast or cable programme. |
| SIANEL PEDWAR CYMRU ('S4C') | The copyright works of S4C including any broadcasts made by S4C itself and those films and sound recordings comprising television programmes which are commissioned by S4C and broadcast on the *Welsh Fourth Channel* television broadcasting service known as S4C] or otherwise included in any broadcast or cable programme. |

*However, Licences under the ERA Licensing Scheme shall not authorise the recording of Open University or Open College programmes.* **However, Licences under the ERA Licensing Scheme shall not authorise the recording of Open University programmes.** If the Licensee is in any doubt as to whether a Licence covers a particular right or a particular copyright work the Licensee shall be entitled to contact ERA who shall be obliged within a reasonable time (by one of the Licensor Members) to confirm whether or not a particular right or work is owned by one of the Licensors.

5. No recording or copying under any Licence shall be made except by or on behalf of the Licensee and any such recording or copying shall be made either—

  (a)   on the premises of the Educational Establishment by or under the direct supervision of a teacher or employee of the Licensee; or

  (b)   at the residence of a teacher employed by the Licensee by that teacher; or

  (c)   at the premises of a third party authorised by the Licensee to make recordings or copies on behalf of the Licensee under written contractual terms and conditions which prevent the retention of any recordings or copies by that third party or any other third party unless ERA shall have expressly agreed that a specific third party may retain any recordings or copies for subsequent use only by authorised Licensees of ERA in accordance with the provisions of the Licensing Scheme.

6. Licensees shall be required to ensure that all recordings or copies made under a Licence are marked with the date and title of the recording, and with a statement in clear and bold lettering that 'this recording is to be used only for educational purposes' or such other wording or prohibition as ERA shall reasonably require from time to time.

7. Licensees may be required to undertake and maintain at the request of ERA details of television or radio programmes or any part or parts of such programmes which are recorded and the number of copies of such recordings made under a Licence. In addition, Licensees may be required to maintain further records and answer questionnaires or surveys as ERA may reasonably require to monitor and administer proper operation of the Licensing Scheme.

8. ERA shall be entitled to inspect and have access to all records that Licensees are required to maintain under the above provisions, and further have access to all recordings and copies of copyright works made by a Licensee under the terms of a Licence granted, in order to inspect the same to check compliance with the Licence.

*9. Licences shall operate for such period or periods as may from time to time be specified or agreed with ERA*

  [**9.(a)   Licences may be granted for such period or periods as may from time to time be specified by or agreed with ERA**

  **(b)   The Licence fee shall be calculated by reference to the period for which it is granted and to the tariff applicable in respect of that period.**

  **(c)   Licence fees for periods of less than one year shall be calculated on a pro-rata basis.**]

10. *The annual tariff for Licences, applicable from the date of operation of the certification of the Licensing Scheme and calculated on a full time and full time equivalents per capita basis by type of Educational Establishment, shall be—*

  *(a)   Primary/Preparatory Educational Establishments (including Preparatory Schools)—15p per student.*

  *(b)   Secondary Educational Establishments (including Sixth Form Colleges)—30p per student.*

  *(c)   Educational Establishments of Further Education—50p per student.*

  *(d)   Educational Establishments of Higher Education (including Higher Education Colleges, Polytechnics and Universities)—£1.00 per student.*

  *(e)   Other Educational Establishments designated from time to time by the Secretary of State—a fee related to the above by type.*

*The annual tariff for Licences in respect of the categories listed in (i) to (v) below shall be calculated on a full time and full time equivalents per capita basis by type of Educational Establishment as follows:*

  *(a)   in respect of Licences granted prior to the 6th April 1992 as set out in column A below;*

  *(b)   in respect of Licences granted on or after the 6th April 1992 as set out in column B below.*

| | A<br>*per student* | B<br>*per student* |
|---|---|---|
| *(i)   Primary/Preparatory Educational Establishments (including Preparatory Schools)* | *15p* | *17p* |
| *(ii)   Secondary Educational Establishments (including Sixth Form Colleges)* | *30p* | *35p* |
| *(iii)   Educational Establishments of Further Education* | *50p* | *58p* |
| *(iv)   Educational Establishments of Higher Education (including Higher Education Colleges, Polytechnics and Universities)* | *£1.00* | *£1.15* |
| *(v)   other Educational Establishments designated from time to time by the Secretary of State* | *a fee related to the above by type* | *a fee related to the above by type* |

*For Licences taking effect on or after 1st April 1993 the annual tariff, when calculated on a full-time and full-time equivalents per capita basis by type of Educational Establishment, shall be—*

   *(a)   Primary/Preparatory Educational Establishments (including Preparatory Schools)—18p per student.*

   *(b)   Secondary Educational Establishments—36p per student.*

   *(c)   Educational Establishments of Further Education (including Sixth Form Colleges)—60p per student.*

   *(d)   Educational Establishments of Higher Education (including Higher Education Colleges and Universities)—£1.20 per student.*

   *(e)   Other Educational Establishments designated from time to time by the Secretary of State—a fee related to the above by type.*

**(a) For licences taking effect on or after 1st April 1994 but on or before 31st March 1995, the annual tariff, when calculated on a full-time and full-time equivalents per capita basis by type of Educational Establishment, shall be—**

   **(i)   Primary/Preparatory Educational Establishments (including Preparatory Schools)—18p per student.**

   **(ii)   Secondary Educational Establishments—37p per student.**

   **(iii)   Educational Establishments of Further Education (including sixth form colleges)—61p per student.**

   **(iv)   Educational Establishments of Higher Education (including Higher Education Colleges and Universities)—£1.22 per student.**

   **(v)   Other Educational Establishments designated from time to time by the Secretary of State—a fee related to the above by type.**

**(b) for licences taking effect on or after 1st April 1995, the annual tariff, when calculated on a full-time and full-time equivalents per capita basis by type of Educational Establishment, shall be—**

   **(i)   Primary/Preparatory Educational Establishments (including Preparatory Schools)—19p per student.**

   **(ii)   Secondary Educational Establishments—38p per student.**

   **(iii)   Educational Establishments of Further Education (including sixth form colleges)—63p per student.**

   **(iv)   Educational Establishments of Higher Education (including Higher Education Colleges and Universities)—£1.25 per student.**

   **(v)   Other Educational Establishments designated from time to time by the Secretary of State—a fee related to the above by type.**

*NOTE 1*

Under the Licensing Scheme discounted rates below the above tariff may be negotiated covering large user groups and may form part of Licences agreed to operate for more than one year.

*NOTE 2*

An individual Educational Establishment not covered by a blanket discount arrangement of the type referred to in NOTE 1 above which does not wish to avail itself of the entire repertoire available under an ERA Licence, will, on signing a declaration to the relevant effect, be granted a licence by ERA with a current zero tariff. A Licence granted on this basis will entitle the individual Educational Establishment to record only that part of the ERA repertoire included in broadcasts by the BBC and ITV Companies which are designated as educational.

11. Licensees shall pay agreed Licence Fees together with any VAT or other Government tax which may be applicable from time to time in addition to such Licence Fee on such date or dates as may be from time to time required by ERA.

12. ERA shall be entitled to terminate Licences granted—

   (a)   if Licence Fees are not paid when due—provided that ERA shall have given to a Licensee such period of notice as ERA may from time to time reasonably include in the terms of Licences issued;

   (b)   for any other substantial breach of the conditions of Licence; and

   (c)   if a Licensee becomes insolvent.

13. If punctual payment of agreed Licence Fees is not made, ERA shall be entitled to charge interest on amounts unpaid at such reasonable rate as ERA may from time to time require.

14. If a Licence is terminated by ERA it shall be entitled to require a Licensee to delete all recordings or copies made by the Educational Establishment to which the Licence formerly related.

15. If a Licensee is in breach of the terms of a Licence and ERA incurs costs and expenses either in monitoring and discovering any breach of the terms of a Licence or in enforcing the conditions of any Licence, the Licensee shall be required to indemnify ERA in respect of any such costs and expenses so incurred.

16. Licensees shall be required to take all reasonable steps to comply with reasonable recommendations of ERA to ensure that rights granted by a Licence are not exceeded or abused by teachers, employees, pupils or other persons.

17. Licences issued shall be governed by and interpreted in accordance with the law of England.

*General note*

In para 4, the first and second words in bold were substituted by SI 1993 No 193, art 2(a), and the final words in bold were substituted by SI 1994 No 247, art 2(a). Para 9 was substituted by SI 1993 No 193, art 2(b). Para 10 has been substituted by SI 1992 No 211, SI 1993 No 193, and SI 1994 No 247, art 2(b).


## COPYRIGHT, DESIGNS AND PATENTS ACT 1988 (COMMENCEMENT NO 5) ORDER 1990 (SI 1990 No 1400)

*Made* . . . . . . . . *10th July 1990*

The Secretary of State, in exercise of the powers conferred upon him by section 305(3) of the Copyright, Designs and Patents Act 1988, hereby makes the following Order:

**1.** This Order may be cited as the Copyright, Designs and Patents Act 1988 (Commencement No 5) Order 1990.

**2.** The following provisions of the Copyright, Designs and Patents Act 1988 shall come into force on 13th August 1990—

(a) in Part IV (registered designs)—
section 272 in so far as it relates to paragraph 21 of Schedule 3, and section 273;

(b) Part V (patent agents and trade mark agents) save in so far as article 3 below otherwise provides;

(c) in Part VI (patents)—
section 295 in so far as it relates to paragraph 27 of Schedule 5;

(d) in Part VII (miscellaneous and general)—
section 303(1) in so far as it relates to paragraphs 15, 18(2) and 21 of Schedule 7, and
section 303(2) in so far as it relates to the references in Schedule 8 to—
section 32 of the Registered Designs Act 1949, and sections 84, 85, 104, the words 'within the meaning of section 104 above' in section 105, sections 114 and 115, section 123(2)(k), and the definition of 'patent agent' in section 130(1), of the Patents Act 1977;

(e) in Schedule 3 (minor and consequential amendments to the Registered Designs Act 1949) paragraph 21;

(f) Schedule 4;

(g) in Schedule 5 (patents: miscellaneous amendments), paragraph 27;

(h) in Schedule 7 (consequential amendments), paragraphs 15, 18(2) and 21;

(i) in Schedule 8 (repeals) the references to—
section 32 of the Registered Designs Act 1949, and sections 84, 85, 104, the words 'within the meaning of section 104 above' in section 105, sections 114 and 115, section 123(2)(k), and the definition of 'patent agent' in section 130(1), of the Patents Act 1977.

**3.** For the purpose only of making rules expressed to come into force on or after 13th August 1990, any provision of Part V of the Copyright, Designs and Patents Act 1988 conferring power to make rules shall come into force forthwith.

## COPYRIGHT (MATERIAL OPEN TO PUBLIC INSPECTION) (MARKING OF COPIES OF PLANS AND DRAWINGS) ORDER 1990 (SI 1990 No 1427)

| | |
|---|---|
| *Made* . . . . . . . . | *16th July 1990* |
| *Laid before Parliament* . . . . | *3rd July 1990* |
| *Coming into force* . . . . | *15th August 1990* |

The Secrtary of State, in exercise of the powers conferred upon him by sections 47(4) of the Copyright, Designs and Patents Act 1988, hereby makes the following Order—

**1.** This Order may be cited as the Copyright (Material Open to Public Inspection) (Marking of Copies of Plans and Drawings) Order 1990 and shall come into force on 15th August 1990.

**2.** Subsection (2) of section 47 of the Copyright, Designs and Patents Act 1988 shall, in the case of a plan or drawing which is open to public inspection pursuant to a statutory requirement, apply only to copies of the plan or drawing marked in the following manner—

'This copy has been made by or with the authority of (insert the name of the person required to make the plan or drawing open to public inspection) pursuant to section 47 of the Copyright, Designs and Patents Act 1988. Unless that Act provides a relevant exception to copyright, the copy must not be copied without the prior permission of the copyright owner.'

## COPYRIGHT, DESIGNS AND PATENTS ACT 1988 (ISLE OF MAN) ORDER 1990 (SI 1990 No 1505)

| | |
|---|---|
| *Made* . . . . . . . . | *24th July 1990* |
| *Coming into force* . . . . | *13th August 1990* |

Her Majesty, in pursuance of section 304(4) and (6) of the Copyright, Designs and Patents Act 1988, is pleased, by and with the advice of Her Privy Council, to order, and it is hereby ordered, as follows:

**1.** This Order may be cited as the Copyright, Designs and Patents Act 1988 (Isle of Man) Order 1990 and shall come into force on 13th August 1990.

**2.** The following provisions of the Copyright, Designs and Patents Act 1988 shall extend to the Isle of Man subject to the exceptions and modifications specified in the Schedule to this Order—

(a) section 272, so far as it relates to paragraph 21 of Schedule 3, and that paragraph *(registered designs: minor and consequential amendments)*;
(b) section 273 and Schedule 4 *(text of Registered Designs Act 1949 as amended)*;
(c) Part V *(patent agents and trade mark agents)*;
(d) paragraph 27 of Schedule 5 *(patents: miscellaneous amendments)*.

**3.** Section 303(2) of and Schedule 8 to the Copyright, Designs and Patents Act 1988 shall extend to the Isle of Man so far as they relate to the repeal of—

(a) section 32 of the Registered Designs Act 1949, and
(b) the following provisions of the Patents Act 1977—
    (i) sections 84 and 85;
    (ii) section 104;
    (iii) in section 105, the words 'within the meaning of section 104 above';
    (iv) sections 114 and 115;
    (v) section 123(2)(k), and
    (vi) in section 130(1), the definition of 'patent agent'.

## SCHEDULE

EXCEPTIONS AND MODIFICATIONS IN THE EXTENSION OF PROVISIONS OF THE COPYRIGHT, DESIGNS AND PATENTS ACT 1988 TO THE ISLE OF MAN

1. Any reference to an Act of Parliament or to a provision of such an Act shall be construed, unless the contrary intention appears, as a reference to that Act or provision as it has effect in the Isle of Man.
2. Schedule 4 shall have effect as if the text of the Registered Designs Act 1949 contained therein were the text of that Act as modified by the Registered Designs Act 1949 (Isle of Man) Order 1989.
3.—(1) Part V shall have effect subject to the following provisions of this paragraph.

(2) In section 278—

(a) in subsection (1), for 'solicitor' and 'solicitors' there shall be substituted respectively 'advocate' and 'advocates';
(b) in subsection (2), for the words from 'the enactments' to the end there shall be substituted 'section 1 of the Legal Practitioners Registration Act 1986 (an Act of Tynwald) (which restricts the use of certain expressions in reference to persons not qualified to act as advocates)', and
(c) subsection (3) shall be omitted.

(3) In section 280—

(a) in subsection (2), for 'England, Wales or Northern Ireland' and 'solicitor' there shall be substituted respectively 'the Isle of Man' and 'advocate', and
(b) subsection (4) shall be omitted.

(4) In section 284—

(a) in subsection (2), for 'England, Wales or Northern Ireland' and 'solicitor' there shall be substituted respectively 'the Isle of Man' and 'advocate', and
(b) subsection (4) shall be omitted.

(5) Section 285(2)(b) shall be omitted.

COPYRIGHT (STATUS OF FORMER DEPENDENT TERRITORIES)
ORDER 1990
(SI 1990 No 1512)

| | |
|---|---|
| *Made* . . . . . . . . | *24th July 1990* |
| *Laid* . . . . . . . . | *1st August 1990* |
| *Coming into force* . . . . | *22nd August 1990* |

Her Majesty, in pursuance of section 37(1) and (2)(b) of Schedule 1 to the Copyright, Designs and Patents Act 1988 ('the Act'), is pleased, by and with the advice of Her Privy Council, to order, and it is hereby ordered, as follows—

**1.** This Order may be cited as the Copyright (Status of Former Dependent Territories) Order 1990 and shall come into force on 22nd August 1990.

**2.** It is hereby declared for the purposes of paragraph 37(1) of Schedule 1 to the Act (copyright status of former dependent territories) that immediately before the commencement of Part I of the Act on 1st August 1989 each of the countries specified in Schedule 1 to this Order was a country to which the Copyright Act 1956 extended or was treated as such a country by virtue of paragraph 39(2) of Schedule 7 to that Act (countries to which the Copyright Act 1911 extended or was treated as extending).

**3.** It is hereby declared that each of the countries specified in Schedule 2 to this Order shall cease to be treated as a country to which Part I of the Act extends for the purposes of sections 154 to 156 of the Act (qualification for copyright protection) by reason of the fact that the provisions of the Copyright Act 1956 or, as the case may be, the Copyright Act 1911, which extended there as part of the law of that country have been repealed or amended.

SCHEDULE 1

Countries to which the Copyright Act 1956 extended or was treated as extending immediately before 1st August 1989:

Antigua
Botswana
Dominica
Gambia
Grenada
Guyana
Jamaica
Kiribati
Lesotho
St Christopher-Nevis
St Lucia
Seychelles
Solomon Islands
Swaziland
Tuvalu
Uganda

## SCHEDULE 2

Countries ceasing to be treated as countries to which Part I of the Copyright, Designs and Patents Act 1988 extends:

Botswana
Seychelles
Solomon Islands
Uganda

## COPYRIGHT, DESIGNS AND PATENTS ACT 1988 (COMMENCEMENT NO 6) ORDER 1990
## (SI 1990 No 2168)

*Made* . . . . . . . . . . *1st November 1989*

The Secretary of State, in exercise of the powers conferred upon him by section 305(3) of the Copyright, Designs and Patents Act 1988, hereby makes the following Order—

**1.** This Order may be cited as the Copyright, Designs and Patents Act 1988 (Commencement No 6) Order 1990.

**2.** The following provisions of the Copyright, Designs and Patents Act 1988 shall come into force on 7th January 1991—

(a) in Part VI (patents), save in so far as article 3 below otherwise provides— section 295 in so far as it relates to paragraphs 1 to 11, 17 to 23, 25, 26, 28 and 30 of Schedule 5;

(b) in Part VII (miscellaneous and general), section 303(2) in so far as it relates to the references in Schedule 8 to— section 14(4) and (8), paragraph (b) and the word 'and' preceding it in section 28(3), section 28(5) to (9), sections 72(3) and 88, the words '88(6) and (7)' in section 130(7) of, and paragraphs 2, 7 and 8 of Schedule 5 to, the Patents Act 1977;

(c) in Schedule 5 (patents: miscellaneous amendments), save in so far as article 3 below otherwise provides— paragraphs 1 to 11, 17 to 23, 25, 26, 28 and 30;

(d) in Schedule 8 (repeals) the references to— section 14(4) and (8), paragraph (b) and the word 'and' preceding it in section 28(3), section 28(5) to (9), sections 72(3) and 88, the words '88(6) and (7)' in section 130(7) of, and paragraphs 2, 7 and 8 of Schedule 5 to, the Patents Act 1977.

**3.** For the purposes only of making rules expressed to come into force on or after 7th January 1991, any amendment to the Patents Act 1977 effected by a provision referred to in article 2(a) and (c) above which confers power to make rules or prescribe anything shall come into force forthwith.

COPYRIGHT (ISLE OF MAN) (REVOCATION) ORDER 1992
(SI 1992 No 1306)

| | |
|---|---|
| *Made* . . . . . . *4th June 1992* |
| *Coming in to force* . . . . *1st July 1992* |

At the Court at Buckingham Palace, the 4th day of June 1992
Present,
The Queen's Most Excellent Majesty in Council

Whereas it appears to Her Majesty that provision with respect to copyright has been made in the law of the Isle of Man otherwise than by extending the provisions of Part I of the Copyright, Designs and Patents Act 1988(a);

Now, therefore, Her Majesty, in pursuance of paragraph 36(3) of Schedule 1 to that Act, is pleased, by and with the advice of Her Privy Council, to order, and it is hereby ordered, as follows:

**1.** This Order may be cited as the Copyright (Isle of Man) (Revocation) Order 1992 and shall come into force on 1st July 1992.

**2.** The Copyright (Isle of Man) Order 1986 [SI 1986 No 1299] is hereby revoked.


COPYRIGHT (APPLICATION TO THE ISLE OF MAN) ORDER 1992
(SI 1992 No 1313)

| | |
|---|---|
| *Made* . . . . . . | *4th June 1992* |
| *Laid before Parliament* . . . . | *9th June 1992* |
| *Coming into force* . . . . | *1st July 1992* |

Whereas Her Majesty is satisfied that, in respect of the classes of works to which this Order relates, provision has been or will be made under the laws of the Isle of Man giving adequate protection to the owners of copyright under Part I of the Copyright, Designs and Patents Act 1988:

Now, therefore, Her Majesty, in pursuance of section 159 of the said Act, is pleased, by and with the advice of Her Privy Council, to order, and it is hereby ordered, as follows:

**1.** This Order may be cited as the Copyright (Application to the Isle of Man) Order 1992 and shall come into force on 1st July 1992.

**2.** Sections 153 to 156 of the Act (qualification for copyright protection) apply in relation to:

(a) persons who are domiciled or resident in the Isle of Man as they apply to persons who are domiciled or resident in the United Kingdom;

(b) bodies incorporated under the law of the Isle of Man as they apply in relation to bodies incorporated under the law of a part of the United Kingdom;

(c) works first published in the Isle of Man as they apply in relation to works first published in the United Kingdom; and

(d) broadcasts made from, or cable programmes sent from, the Isle of Man as they apply in relation to broadcasts made from, or cable programmes sent from, the United Kingdom.

COPYRIGHT (COMPUTER PROGRAMS) REGULATIONS 1992
(SI 1992 No 3233)

> *Made* . . . . . . . . *16th December 1992*
> *Coming into force* . . . . *1st January 1993*

Whereas a draft of the following Regulations has been approved by resolution of each House of Parliament:

Now, therefore, the Secretary of State, being a Minister designated for the purposes of section 2(2) of the European Communities Act 1972 in relation to measures relating to the protection by copyright of computer programmes, in exercise of the powers conferred by section 2(2) and (4) of the said Act 1972, hereby makes the following Regulations—

**Citation, commencement and extent**
**1.**—(1) These Regulations may be cited as the Copyright (Computer Programs) Regulations 1992 and shall come into force on 1st January 1993.

(2) These Regulations extend to Northern Ireland.
**2.** The Copyright, Designs and Patents Act 1988 shall be amended as follows.

*Amendments of Part I (copyright) of the Copyright, Designs and Patents Act 1988*

**'Literary work' extended to include preparatory design material for a computer program**
**3.** [This regulation amends Copyright, Designs and Patents Act 1988, s 3(1)].

**Restriction of infringement by issue of copies of computer programs within the Community**
**4.** [This regulation amends Copyright, Designs and Patents Act 1988, s 18(2) and adds s 18(3)].

**Meaning of 'adaptation' in relation to a computer program**
**5.** [This regulation amends Copyright, Designs and Patents Act 1988, s 21].

**Meaning of 'infringing copy'**
**6.** [This regulation amends Copyright, Designs and Patents Act 1988, s 27(3) and adds s 27(3A)].

**Exclusion of decompilation of computer programs from fair dealing**
**7.** [This regulation adds Copyright, Designs and Patents Act 1988, s 29(4).

**New permitted acts in relation to computer programs**
**8.** [This regulation adds Copyright, Designs and Patents Act 1988, ss 50A, 50B, 50C].
**9.** [This regulation amends Copyright, Designs and Patents Act 1988, s 179].

## Amendments of Part VII (miscellaneous and general) of the Copyright, Designs and Patents Act 1988

### Devices designed to circumvent copy-protection applied to computer programs

**10.** [This regulation adds Copyright, Designs and Patents Act 1988, s 296(2A)].

### Avoidance of certain terms relating to computer programs

**11.** [This regulation adds Copyright, Designs and Patents Act 1988, s 296A].

## Transitional provisions and savings

### Computer programs created before 1st January 1993

**12.**—(1) Subject to paragraph (2), the amendments of the Copyright, Designs and Patents Act 1988 made by these Regulations apply in relation to computer programs created before 1st January 1993 as they apply to computer programs created on or after that date.

(2) Nothing in these Regulations affects any agreement or any term or condition of an agreement where the agreement, term or condition is entered into before 1st January 1993.

COPYRIGHT (RECORDING FOR ARCHIVES OF DESIGNATED CLASS
OF BROADCASTS AND CABLE PROGRAMMES) (DESIGNATED
BODIES) ORDER 1993
(SI 1993 No 74)

| | |
|---|---|
| *Made* . . . . . . | *18th January 1993* |
| *Laid before Parliament* | . . *21st January 1993* |
| *Coming into force* . . | . . *12th February 1993* |

The Secretay of State, in exercise of the powers conferred upon him by section 75 of the Copyright, Designs and Patent Act 1988 ('the Act'), and upon being satisfied that the bodies designated by this Order are not established or conducted for profit, hereby makes the following Order:

**1.** This Order may be cited as the Copyright (Recording for Archives of Designated Class of Broadcasts and Cable Programmes) (Designated Bodies) Order 1993 and shall come into force on 12th February 1993.

**2.** Each of the bodies specified in the Schedule to this Order is designated as a body for which a recording of a broadcast or cable programme of the class designated by article 3 below, or a copy thereof, may be made for the purpose of placing the same in any archive maintained by it.

**3.** All broadcasts other than encrypted transmissions and all cable programmes are designated as a class for the purposes of section 75 of the Act.

**4.** The Copyright (Recording for Archives of Designated Class of Broadcasts and Cable Programmes) (Designated Bodies) Order 1991 [SI 1991 No 1116] is hereby revoked.

SCHEDULE

DESIGNATED BODIES
The British Film Institute
The British Library
The British Medical Association
The British Music Information Centre
The Imperial War Museum
The Music Performance Research Centre
The National Library of Wales
The Scottish Film Council

COPYRIGHT (CERTIFICATION OF LICENSING SCHEME FOR
EDUCATIONAL RECORDING OF BROADCASTS AND CABLE
PROGRAMMES) (EDUCATIONAL RECORDING AGENCY LIMITED)
(AMENDMENT) ORDER 1993
(SI 1993 No 193)

*Made* . . . . . . *27th January 1993*
*Coming into force* . . . . *1st April 1993*

Whereas by virtue of the Copyright (Certification of Licensing Scheme for
Educational Recording and Broadcasts and Cable Programmes) (Educational
Recording Agency Limited) Order 1990 ('the Principal Order') the Secretary of
State certified for the purposes of section 35 of the Copyright, Designs and
Patents Act 1988 ('the Act') the licensing scheme set out in the Schedule to the
Principle Order, being a scheme operated by the Educational Recording Agency
Limited;

And whereas the Principal Order was amended by the Copyright (Certification
of Licensing Scheme for Educational Recording of Broadcasts and Cable
Programmes) (Educational Recording Agency Limited) (Amendment) Order
1992;

And whereas the Educational Recording Agency Limited has applied to the
Secretary of State for the Principle Order (as amended) to be further amended in
accordance with article 2 of this Order;

Now, therefore, the Secretary of State, in exercise of the powers conferred upon
him by section 143 of the Act makes the following Order:

**1.** This Order may be cited as the Copyright (Certification of Licensing Scheme
for Educational Recording of Broadcasts and Cable Programmes) (Educational
Recording Agency Limited) (Amendment) Order 1993 and shall come into force
on 1st April 1993.

**2.** (This article amends The Copyright (Certification of Licensing Scheme for
Educational Recording of Broadcasts and Cable Programmes) (Educational
Recording Agency Limited) Order 1990 [SI 1990 No 879, Schedule, paras 4, 9,
10]).

## COPYRIGHT (APPLICATION TO OTHER COUNTRIES) ORDER 1993 (SI 1993 No 942)

*As amended by The Copyright (Application to Other Countries) (Amendment) Order 1994 [SI 1994 No 263]*

| | |
|---|---|
| *Made* . . . . . . | *31st March 1993* |
| *Laid before Parliament* . . | *13th April 1993* |
| *Coming into force* . . . . | *4th May 1993* |

Whereas Her Majesty is satisfied that provision has been or will be made—

(a) in respect of literary, dramatic, musical and artistic works, films and typographical arrangements of published editions, under the law of Uganda,

(b) in respect of sound recordings, under the laws of Bangladesh, Ghana, Malawi and Thailand,

(c) in respect of broadcasts, under the laws of Malawi,

giving adequate protection to the owners of copyright under Part I of the Copyright, Designs and Patents Act 1988:

Now, therefore, Her Majesty, by and with the advice of Her Privy Council, and by virtue of the authority conferred upon Her by section 159 of the said Act, is pleased to order, and it is hereby ordered as follows—

**1.**—(1) This Order may be cited as the Copyright (Application to Other Countries) Order 1993 and shall come into force on 4th May 1993.

(2) In this Order—

'the Act' means the Copyright, Designs and Patents Act 1988, and

'first published' shall be construed in accordance with section 155(3) of the Act.

**2.**—(1) In relation to literary, dramatic, musical and artistic works, films and the typographical arrangements of published editions, sections 153, 154 and 155 of the Act (qualification for copyright protection) apply in relation to—

(a) persons who are citizens or subjects of a country specified in Schedule 1 to this Order or are domiciled or resident there as they apply to persons who are British citizens or are domiciled or resident in the United Kingdom;

(b) bodies incorporated under the law of such a country as they apply in relation to bodies incorporated under the law of a part of the United Kingdom; and

(c) works first published in such a country as they apply in relation to works first published in the United Kingdom;

but subject to paragraph (2) and article 5 below.

(2) Copyright does not subsist—

(a) in a literary, dramatic, musical or artistic work by virtue of section 154 of the Act as applied by paragraph (1) above (qualification by reference to author) if it was first published—

    (i) before 1st June 1957 (commencement of Copyright Act 1956), or

    (ii) before 1st August 1989 (commencement of Part I of the Act) and at the material time (as defined in section 154(4)(b) of the Act) the author was not a relevant person; or

(b) in any work by virtue of paragraph (1) above if—

    (i) a date is, or dates are, specified in Schedule 1 to this Order in respect of the only country or countries relevant to the work for the purposes of paragraph (1) above, and

    (ii) the work was first published before that date or (as the case may be) the earliest of those dates;

and for the purposes of sub-paragraph (a)(ii) of this paragraph, a 'relevant person' is a Commonwealth citizen, a British protected person, a citizen or subject of any country specified in Schedule 1 to this Order, or a person resident or domiciled in the United Kingdom, another country to which the relevant provisions of Part I of the Act extend or (subject to article 5 below) a country specified in Schedule 1 to this Order.

(3) Where copyright subsists in a work by virtue of paragraph (1) above, the whole of Part I of the Act (including Schedule 1 to the Act) applies in relation to the work, save that in relation to an artistic work consisting of the design of a typeface—

(a) section 54(2) (articles for producing material in particular typeface) does not apply,

(b) section 55 (making such articles not an infringement) applies as if the words in subsection (2) from the beginning to 'marketed' were omitted, and

(c) paragraph 14(5) of Schedule 1 (transitional provision) does not apply,

and subject also to articles 5 and 7 below.

**3.** In relation to sound recordings, article 2 above shall apply as it applies in relation to films, subject to the following modifications—

(a) sections 19, 20, 26 and 107(3) of the Act (infringement by playing in public, broadcasting or inclusion in a cable programme service and related provisions) apply only if—

    (i) at least one of the countries relevant to the work for the purposes of article 2(1) above is specified in Schedule 2 to this Order, or

    (ii) the sound recording in question is a film sound-track accompanying a film; *and*

(b) *paragraph (1) of article (2) shall (subject to article 5 below) apply as if Indonesia were specified in Schedule 1 to this Order.*

*General note*
Words in italics revoked by the Copyright (Application to Other Countries) (Amendment) Order 1994, SI 1994 No 263, art 2(a).

**4.**—(1) In relation to broadcasts, sections 153, 154 and 156 of the Act (qualification for copyright protection) apply in relation to—

(a) persons who are citizens or subjects of a country specified in Schedule 3 to this Order or are domiciled or resident there as they apply to persons who are British citizens or are domiciled or resident in the United Kingdom;

(b) bodies incorporated under the law of such a country as they apply in relation to bodies incorporated under the law of a part of the United Kingdom; and

(c) broadcasts made from such a country as they apply to broadcasts made from the United Kingdom;

but subject to paragraphs (2) and (3) and article 5 below.

(2) If the only country or countries relevant to a broadcast for the purposes of paragraph (1) above are identified in Schedule 3 to this Order by the words 'television only', copyright subsists in the broadcast only if it is a television broadcast.

(3) Copyright does not subsist in a broadcast by virtue of paragraph (1) above if it was made before the relevant date.

(4) Where copyright subsists in a broadcast by virtue of paragraph (1) above, the whole of Part I of the Act (including Schedule 1 to the Act) applies in relation to the broadcast, save that for the purposes of section 14(2) (duration of copyright in repeats)—

(a) a broadcast shall be disregarded if it was made before the relevant date, and
(b) a cable programme shall be disregarded if it was included in a cable programme service before the later of the relevant date and 1st January 1985;

and subject also to article 7 below.

(5) For the purposes of paragraphs (3) and (4) above, the 'relevant date' is the date or (as the case may be) the earliest of the dates specified in Schedule 3 to this Order in respect of the country or countries relevant to the broadcast for the purposes of paragraph (1) above, being (where different dates are specified for television and non-television broadcasts) the date appropriate to the type of broadcast in question.

(6) *In respect of Singapore* **In respect of Indonesia and Singapore**, this article applies in relation to cable programmes as it applies in relation to broadcasts, subject to article 5 below.

*General note*
In para (6), the words in bold were added and the words in italics deleted by the Copyright (Application to other Countries) Amendment Order 1994, SI 1994 No 263, art 2(b).

**5.** Schedule 4 to this Order shall have effect so as to modify the application of this Order in respect of certain countries.

**6.** Nothing in this Order shall be taken to derogate from the effect of paragraph 35 of Schedule 1 to the Act (continuation of existing qualification for copyright protection).

**7.**—(1) This article applies in any case in which—

(a) a work was made before 1st August 1989 (commencement of Part I of the Act) and copyright under the Copyright Act 1956 did not subsist in it when it was made, or
(b) a work is made on or after 1st August 1989 and copyright under the Act does not subsist in it when it is made,

but copyright subsequently subsists in it by virtue of article 2(1), 3 or 4(1) above.

(2) Where in any such case a person incurs or has incurred any expenditure or liability in connection with, for the purpose of or with a view to the doing of an act which at the time is not or was not an act restricted by any copyright in the work, the doing, or continued doing, of that act after copyright subsequently subsists in the work by virtue of article 2(1), 3 or 4(1) above shall not be an act restricted by the copyright unless the owner of the copyright or his exclusive licensee (if any) pays such compensation as, failing agreement, may be determined by arbitration.

**8.**—The Orders listed in Schedule 5 to this Order are hereby revoked.

## SCHEDULE

### COUNTRIES ENJOYING PROTECTION IN RESPECT OF ALL WORKS EXCEPT BROADCASTS AND CABLE PROGRAMMES

(The countries specified in this Schedule either are parties to the Berne Copyright Convention and/or the Universal Copyright Convention or otherwise give adequate protection under their law.)

**Albania**
Algeria (28th August 1973)
Andorra (27th September 1957)
Argentina
Australia (including Norfolk Island)
Austria
Bahamas
Bangladesh
Barbados
Belgium
Belize
Benin
Bolivia *(22nd March 1990)*
**Bosnia–Herzegovina**
Brazil
Bulgaria
Burkina Faso
Cameroon
Canada
Central African Republic
Chad
Chile
China
Colombia
Congo
Costa Rica
Cote d'Ivoire
Croatia
Cuba (27th September 1957)
Cyprus, Republic of
*Czechoslovakia*
**Czech Republic**
Denmark (including Greenland and the Faeroe Islands)
Dominican Republic (8th May 1983)
Ecuador
Egypt
El Salvador *(29 March 1979)*
Fiji
Finland
France (including all Overseas Departments and Territories)
Gabon
Gambia
Germany
Ghana
Greece
Guatemala (28th October 1964)
Guinea, Republic of
Guinea-Bissau
Haiti (27th September 1957)
Holy See
Honduras
Hungary
Iceland
India
**Indonesia**
Ireland, Republic of

438

Israel
Italy
**Jamaica**
Japan
Kampuchea (27th September 1957)
**Kazakhstan (25th December 1991)**
Kenya
Korea, Republic of (1st October 1987)
Laos (27th September 1957)
Lebanon
Lesotho
Liberia
Libya
Liechtenstein
Luxembourg
**Macedonia**
Madagascar
Malawi
Malaysia
Mali
Malta
Mauritania
Mauritius
Mexico
Monaco
Morocco
**Namibia**
Netherlands (including Aruba and the Netherlands Antilles)
New Zealand
Nicaragua (16th August 1961)
Niger
Nigeria
Norway
Pakistan
Panama (17th October 1962)
Paraguay
Peru
Philippines
Poland
Portugal
Romania
**Russian Federation (25th December 1991)**
Rwanda
**Saint Lucia**
St. Vincent and the Grenadines
Senegal
Singapore
**Slovak Republic**
Slovenia
South Africa
Soviet Union (27th May 1973)
Spain
Sri Lanka
Suriname
Sweden
Switzerland
Taiwan, territory of (10th July 1985)
**Tajikistan (25th December 1991)**
Thailand
Togo
Trinidad and Tobago
Tunisia
Turkey

Uganda (20th July 1964)
United States of America (including Puerto Rico and all territories and possessions)
Uruguay
Venezuela
Yugoslavia
Zaire
Zambia
Zimbabwe

*General note*
Words in bold were inserted and words in italics were revoked by the Copyright (Application to Other Countries) (Amendment) Order 1994, SI 1994 No 263, art 2(c).

## SCHEDULE 2

COUNTRIES ENJOYING FULL PROTECTION FOR SOUND RECORDINGS

(The countries specified in this Schedule either are parties to the Rome Convention for the Protection of Performers, Producers of Phonograms and Broadcasting Organisations or otherwise give adequate protection under their law.)

Argentina
Australia (including Norfolk Island)
Austria
Bangladesh
Barbados
**Bolivia**
Brazil
Burkina Faso
Chile
Colombia
Congo
Costa Rica
*Czechoslovakia*
**Czech Republic**
Denmark (including Greenland and the Faeroe Islands)
Dominican Republic
Ecuador
El Salvador
Fiji
Finland
France (including all Overseas Departments and Territories)
Germany
Ghana
Greece
Guatemala
Honduras
India
Indonesia
Ireland, Republic of
Italy
Japan
Lesotho
Luxembourg
Malawi
Malaysia
Mexico
Monaco
**Netherlands**
New Zealand
Niger
**Nigeria**
Norway

Pakistan
Panama
Paraguay
Peru
Philippines
**Slovak Republic**
Spain
Sweden
**Switzerland**
Taiwan, territory of
Thailand
Uruguay

*General note*
Words in bold were inserted and the word in italics were revoked by the Copyright (Application to Other Countries) (Amendment) Order 1994, SI 1994 No 263, art 2(d).

## SCHEDULE 3

COUNTRIES ENJOYING PROTECTION IN RESPECT OF BROADCASTS

(The countries specified in this Schedule either are parties to the Rome Convention for the Protection of Performers, Producers of Phonograms and Broadcasting Organisations and/or the European Agreement on the Protection of Television Broadcasts or otherwise give adequate protection under their law.)

Argentina (2nd March 1992)
Australia (30th September 1992)
Austria (9th June 1973)
Barbados (18th September 1983)
Belgium (8th March 1968—television only)
**Bolivia (24th November 1993)**
Brazil (29th September 1965)
Burkina Faso (14th January 1988)
Chile (5th September 1974)
Colombia (17th September 1976)
Congo (18th May 1964)
Costa Rica (9th September 1971)
Cyprus, Republic of (5th May 1970—television only)
*Czechoslovakia (14th August 1964)*
**Czech Republic (1st January 1993)**
Denmark (including Greenland and the Faeroe Islands) (1st February 1962—television; 1st July 1965—non-television)
Dominican Republic (27th January 1987)
Ecuador (18th May 1964)
El Salvador (29th June 1979)
Fiji (11th April 1972)
Finland (21st October 1983)
France (including all Overseas Departments and Territories) (1st July 1961—television; 3rd July 1987—non-television)
Germany (21st October 1966)
Greece (6th January 1993)
Guatemala (14th January 1977)
Honduras (16th February 1990)
**Indonesia (1st June 1957)**
Ireland, Republic of (19th September 1979)
Italy (8th April 1975)
Japan (26th October 1989)
Lesotho (26th January 1990)
Luxembourg (25th February 1976)
Malawi (22nd June 1989)
Malaysia (1st June 1957)

Mexico (18th May 1964)
Monaco (6th December 1985)
**Netherlands (7th October 1993)**
Niger (18th May 1964)
**Nigeria (29th October 1993)**
Norway (10th August 1968—television; 10th July 1978—non-television)
Panama (2nd September 1983)
Paraguay (26th February 1970)
Peru (7th August 1985)
Philippines (25th September 1984)
Singapore (1st June 1957)
**Slovak Republic (1st January 1993)**
Spain (19th November 1971—television; 14th November 1991—non-television)
Sweden (1st July 1961—television; 18th May 1964—non-television)
**Switzerland (24th September 1993)**
Uruguay (4th July 1977)

*General note*
Words in bold were inserted and words in italics were revoked by the Copyright (Application to Other Countries) (Amendment) Order 1994, SI 1994 No 263, art 2(e).

## SCHEDULE 4

MODIFICATIONS

*1. In respect of Indonesia, article 2(1)(a) above as applied by article 3(b) above shall apply as if the reference to persons domiciled in Indonesia were omitted.*
**1. In respect of Indonesia—**
   (a) **subparagraph (c) of article 2(1) shall not apply except as applied by article 3(a) in relation to sound recordings, and**
   (b) **in the application of article 4(3) above in relation to cable programmes by virtue of article 4(6), the relevant date is 1st January 1985.**
2. In respect of Singapore—
   (a) articles 2(1)(a) and (2) and 4(1)(a) above shall apply as if the references to persons domiciled in Singapore were omitted, and
   (b) in the application of article 4(3) above in relation to cable programmes by virtue of article 4(6), the relevant date is 1st January 1985.
3. In respect of the territory of Taiwan—
   (a) article 2(1)(a) and (2) above shall apply as if the reference to persons domiciled or resident in the territory of Taiwan were limited to such persons who are also citizens or subjects of China, and
   (b) in the application of Part I of the Act by virtue of article 2(3) above, subsection (1) of section 21 (infringement by making adaptation) applies as if subsection (3)(a)(i) of that section (translation of literary of dramatic work) were omitted.

*General note*
Para 1 was substituted by the Copyright (Application to Other Countries) (Amendment) Order 1994, SI 1994 No 263, art 2(f).

## SCHEDULE 5

ORDERS IN COUNCIL REVOKED

| *Number* | *Title* |
|---|---|
| SI 1989/1293 | The Copyright (Application to Other Countries) (No 2) Order 1989 |
| SI 1989/2415 | The Copyright (Application to Other Countries) (No 2) (Amendment) Order 1989 |
| SI 1990/2153 | The Copyright (Application to Other Countries) (No 2) (Amendment) Order 1990 |

COPYRIGHT (CERTIFICATION OF LICENSING SCHEME FOR
EDUCATIONAL RECORDING OF BROADCASTS) (OPEN UNIVERSITY
EDUCATIONAL ENTERPRISES LIMITED) ORDER 1993
(SI 1993 No 2755)

| | |
|---|---|
| *Made* . . . . . . *4th November 1993* | |
| *Coming into force* . . . . *1st January 1994* | |

Whereas by virtue of the Copyright (Certification of Licensing Scheme for Educational Recording of Broadcasts ) (Open University Educational Enterprises Limited) Order 1990 the Secretary of State certified for the purposes of section 35 of the Copyright, Designs and Patents Act 1988 ('the Act') the licensing scheme set out in the Schedule to that Order('the 1990 scheme'), being a scheme operated by Open University Educational Enterprises Limited;

And whereas the Educational Enterprises Limited has applied to the Secretary of State to certify a new licensing scheme to be operated by it to replace the 1990 scheme;

And whereas the Secretary of State, is satisfied that the new scheme enables the works to which it relates to be identified with sufficient certainty by persons likely to require licences and that it sets out clearly the charges (if any) payable and the other terms on which licences will be granted;

Now, therefore, the Secretary of State, in exercise of powers conferred upon him by section 143 of the Act, hereby makes the following Order:

**1.** This Order may be cited as the Copyright (Certification of Licensing Scheme for Educational Recording of Broadcasts) (Open University Educational Enterprises Limited) Order 1993 and shall come into force on 1st January 1994.

**2.** The licensing scheme set out in the Schedule to this Order is certified for the purposes of section 35 of the Act (recording by educational establishments of broadcasts or cable programmes).

**3.** The certification under article 2 above shall for the purposes of section 35 of the Act come into operation on 1st January 1994.

**4.** The Copyright ( Certification of Licensing Scheme for Educational Recording of Broadcasts)(Open University Educational Enterprises Limited) Order 1990 [SI 1990 No 2008] is hereby revoked.

SCHEDULE

OPEN UNIVERSITY EDUCATIONAL ENTERPRISES LIMITED LICENSING SCHEME

Open University Educational Enterprises Limited holds an exclusive right under copyright to licence the recording off air of all Open University television programmes in the United Kingdom by educational establishments and operates a licensing scheme for the off air recording of designated television programmes.

The scheme set out hereunder is operated for the purposes of section 35 of the Copyright, Designs and Patents Act 1988 in respect of recording of broadcasts by educational establishments and replaces the scheme scheduled to the Copyright (Certification of Licensing Scheme for Educational Recording of Broadcasts) (Open University Educational Enterprises Limited) Order 1990 ('the 1990 Scheme').

The educational establishments to which the licensing scheme applies are schools and further and higher educational establishments.

The charges payable under the licences are set out:

    (a)   in respect of schools, in Appendix A to the licensing scheme;

    (b)   subject to paragraph (c), in respect of further and higher educational establishments, in Appendix B to the licensing scheme;

*Appendix 2*

(c)   where a licensee under the licensing scheme is an educational establishment which was a sixth form college licensee under the 1990 scheme, in Appendix A to the licensing scheme.

*The Open University Licensed Off Air Recording Scheme for Schools and Further and Higher Educational Establishments*
Licences shall be issued in accordance with the terms set out below.

DEFINITIONS

In the Scheme and the Appendices the following expressions have the meanings set opposite them:

| | |
|---|---|
| School: | Any school as defined in section 174 of the Copyright, Designs and Patents Act 1988 and any further educational establishment defined as a sixth form college under the 1990 scheme, which was also a licensee, and charged as such a college, under that scheme; |
| Educational establishment: | Any further or higher educational establishment as defined in section 174 of the Copyright, Designs and Patents Act 1988 and any other description of such educational establishment as may be specified by order of the Secretary of State under that section (except for any further educational establishment defined as a sixth form college under the 1990 scheme, which was also a licensee and charged as such a college under that scheme); |
| Licence fee: | The fee payable by schools calculated in accordance with Open University Educational Enterprises Limited's scale of fees set out in Appendix A for the use of designated programmes in accordance with the terms of the licence for a period up to twelve months from the date of the licence unless or until the licence is terminated pursuant to Clauses 2 or 6 thereof; |
| Programme fee: | The fee payable by educational establishments calculated in accordance with Open University Educational Enterprises Limited's scale of programme fees as set out in Appendix B for the use of a designated programme in accordance with the terms of the licence for a period of up to twelve months from the date of its recording unless or until the licence is terminated pursuant to Clauses 2 or 6 thereof; |
| Designated programmes: | The broadcast television programmes which shall be those broadcast by the British Broadcasting Corporation or other broadcasting organisations on behalf of The Open University and as listed in the broadcast schedule published annually by Open University Educational Enterprises Limited; |
| Record off air: | To record by the use of any available playback device on video tape a transmission by broadcast or diffusion of television programmes to be received by television or similar receiving device; and |
| Educational purposes: | The showing of recordings of designated programmes exclusively in teaching, training or study as part of a formal or informal course of instruction undertaken or carried out by the licensee for non profit making purposes and where no charge is made on any person for the purposes of viewing the designated programmes, including the loan of recordings to bona fide students for such purposes. |

1. GRANT
The school or the educational establishment (hereinafter referred to as 'the Licensee') shall warrant that it is a school or educational establishment, as the case may be, and Open University Educational Enterprises Limited shall grant to the licensee on the terms set out below a non-exclusive licence to record off air designated programmes for educational purposes.

2. TERM
The licence shall continue from the date of issue for a period of twelve months and shall be automatically renewed for further periods of twelve months unless or until terminated in accordance with Clause 6, or by either side giving to the other not less than one calendar month's notice in writing, in the case of Educational Establishments, to expire on the date of the anniversary of any twelve month period.

444

3. WARRANTIES AND OBLIGATIONS OF OPEN UNIVERSITY EDUCATIONAL ENTERPRISES LIMITED

(1) *Warranties*

Open University Educational Enterprises Limited warrants that it is duly appointed by the relevant copyright owners and/or broadcasting organisations to act as licensor on their behalf and it has full power and authority to grant the rights set out herein.

(2) *Obligations*

Open University Educational Enterprises Limited shall publish a broadcast schedule annually.

4. OBLIGATIONS OF THE LICENSEE

The licensee shall:

(1) ensure that all recording off air is made by a lecturer, instructor, teacher or other suitably qualified person appointed for the purpose by the licensee;

(2) ensure that recordings of the designated programmes are not edited, cut or amended in any way without prior written permission of Open University Educational Enterprises Limited and are not shown or disclosed or passed into the possession of any third party and are not removed from the direct control of the licensee;

(3) ensure that the recorded designated programmes are used for educational purposes only and the licensee shall not itself or through its employees or agents, sell, lend, hire or otherwise use or dispose of recordings of designated programmes other than in accordance with the terms of the licence and shall prevent any third party from duplicating, selling, lending, hiring or otherwise using or disposing of recordings of the designated programmes;

(4) where the licensee is an educational establishment, make up, retain and keep made up such detailed and accurate records as may be required by Open University Educational Enterprises Limited of the designated programmes recorded and in particular shall complete the log sheets provided by or approved in writing by Open University Educational Enterprises Limited;

(5) affix to each recording in a prominent place and shall not obscure, remove, alter or deface a label which shall include the title of the designated programme and the date upon which it was recorded;

(6) where the licensee is an educational establishment, return to Open University Educational Enterprises Limited all duly completed log sheets on dates specified by Open University Educational Enterprises Limited to a maximum number of three times in each twelve month licence period and on termination of the licence;

(7) subject to paragraph (8) below, erase any and all recordings of the designated programmes in existence at the expiration of the licence period or upon termination of the licence whichever shall be the sooner and shall supply to Open University Educational Enterprises Limited a certificate of erasure within 28 days of such expiration or termination;

(8) if the licence period is automatically continued without interruption for a further period of twelve months pursuant to Clause 2 the licensee may at its option and subject to paragraph (7) retain recordings of designated programmes:

    (a) where the licensee is a school, for the following twelve month period and subject always to the proper licence fee therefor being paid;

    (b) where the licensee is an educational establishment, provided such programmes remain entered into the log for the following twelve month period and subject always to the proper recording fees therefor being paid.

5. CONSIDERATION

In consideration for the licence:

(1) where the licensee is a school,

    (a) the licensee shall pay Open University Educational Enterprises Limited (inclusive of VAT) the fee set out in Appendix A;

    (b) Licence fees payable under paragraph (1)(a) shall be paid within thirty days of the date of the invoice whenever sent to the licensee by Open University Educational Enterprises Limited;

(2) where the licensee is an educational establishment,

    (a) the licensee shall pay Open University Educational Enterprises Limited (inclusive of VAT) the fees set out in Appendix B;

    (b) fees payable under paragraph (2)(a) shall be calculated by Open University Educational

Enterprises Limited annually and shall be paid within thirty days of the date of the invoice whenever sent to the licensee by Open University Educational Enterprises Limited;

(c) the licensee shall permit its records and accounts to be examined upon reasonable notice in writing from Open University Educational Enterprises Limited by Open University Educational Enterprises Limited's properly appointed representative at Open University Educational Enterprises Limited's expense to verify the records and payments for which provision is made in the licence.

## 6. TERMINATION

Open University Educational Enterprises Limited shall at its option be entitled by notice in writing to the licensee to terminate the licence forthwith in any of the following events that is to say if the licensee shall:

(1) fail to promptly account and make payments thereunder or shall fail to perform any other obligation required of it thereunder and the licensee shall not have cured or remedied such failure within 14 (fourteen) days of a request from Open University Educational Enterprises Limited (time being of the essence);

(2) adopt a resolution for its winding up (otherwise than for the purpose of and followed by an amalgamation or reconstruction) or if a petition is presented for the appointment of an administrator or if a receiver or an adminstrative receiver is appointed in respect of, or an encumbrancer takes possession of, the whole or any part of its undertaking or assets or if the licensee is unable to pay its debts within the meaning of section 123 of the Insolvency Act 1986;

(3) cease to carry on the business or function as a school or an educational establishment, as the case may be.

## 7. ALTERATIONS TO AGREEMENT

Any alteration or variation to the licence shall not be valid or enforceable unless recorded in writing and signed by an authorised signatory of each party.

## 8. ASSIGNMENT

The licence is specific to the licensee and the licensee shall not assign the benefits or the obligations of the Licence.

## 9. EXPENSES

Save as otherwise expressed all expenses of and incidental to the fulfilment of the licence shall be borne by the party incurring such expense.

## 10. FORCE MAJEURE

Neither party to the licence shall be liable in any way for any delays or failure to perform its obligations thereunder resulting from any cause beyond its reasonable control.

## 11. NOTICE

Any notice or other communication required to be given (whether required to be given in writing or otherwise) shall be given by post, cable, telex or facsimile copy addressed to the party to receive such notice at its address for service being its address contained in the licence or such other address as shall have been notified to the other for the purpose of the licence. Any notice given by post shall be deemed to have been served at the expiration of three days after it is posted. Any notice given by cable, telex or facsimile copy shall be deemed to have been served (at the sender's address for service) on the date on which it was despatched.

## 12. INDEMNITY

The licensee will indemnify and at all times keep Open University Educational Enterprises Limited fully indemnified against all actions, proceedings, claims, costs and damages whatsoever made against or incurred by Open University Educational Enterprises Limited in consequence of any breach or non-performance by the licensee, its employees or agents of any of the covenants contained in the licence.

446

13. LAW OF ENGLAND

The law of England shall govern the licence.

## APPENDIX A
### THE OPEN UNIVERSITY LICENSED OFF AIR RECORDING SCHEME
### SCALE OF LICENCE FEES FOR SCHOOLS

CATEGORY 1A:   Licence fee per annum for primary schools £28 per annum (plus VAT)

CATEGORY 1B:   Licence fee per annum for secondary schools and sixth form colleges £78 per annum (plus VAT)

## APPENDIX B
### THE OPEN UNIVERSITY LICENSED OFF AIR RECORDING SCHEME
### SCALE OF FEES FOR FURTHER AND HIGHER EDUCATIONAL ESTABLISHMENTS

Scale of Fees per annum for colleges of further education, colleges of higher education, polytechnics, universities and certain other individual educational institutions

| Number of recordings | Fee per annum or part thereof | Unit cost per additional recordings |
|---|---|---|

Under 5 recordings will be charged at £19.36 per recording

| Number of recordings | Fee per annum or part thereof | Unit cost per additional recordings |
|---|---|---|
| 5 | £96.80 | |
| 6–9 | | £19.36 |
| 10 | £155.25 | |
| 11–14 | | £15.48 |
| 15 | £212.55 | |
| 16–24 | | £14.20 |
| 25 | £322.65 | |
| 26–49 | | £12.90 |
| 50 | £594.75 | |
| 51–74 | | £11.88 |
| 75 | £865.75 | |
| 76–99 | | £11.50 |
| 100 | £1,128.50 | |
| 101–124 | | £11.30 |
| 125 | £1,355.40 | |
| 126–149 | | £10.86 |
| 150 | £1,552.50 | |
| 151–199 | | £10.38 |
| 200 | £1,934.60 | |
| 201–249 | | £9.68 |
| 250 | £2,328.70 | |
| 251–299 | | £9.30 |
| 300 | £2,651.10 | |
| 301–399 | | £8.88 |
| 400 | £3,290.00 | |
| 401–499 | | £8.22 |
| 500 | £3,869.20 | £7.15 |

VAT IS ADDITIONAL

Please note that the FEES relate to EACH EPISODE of a series. Thus a series of six programmes will attract six programme fees.

These fees apply to those programmes which are retained for use. A FREE 28 day period for PREVIEW purposes ONLY is allowed to assess suitability.

COPYRIGHT (CERTIFICATION OF LICENSING SCHEME FOR
EDUCATIONAL RECORDING OF BROADCASTS AND CABLE
PROGRAMMES) (EDUCATIONAL RECORDING AGENCY LIMITED)
(AMENDMENT) ORDER 1994
(SI 1994 No 247)

> *Made* . . . . . . *2nd February 1994*
> *Coming into force* . . . . *1st April 1994*

Whereas by virtue of the Copyright (Certification of Licensing Scheme for
Educational Recording and Broadcasts and Cable Programmes) (Educational
Recording Agency Limited) Order 1990 ('the Principal Order') the Secretary of
State certified for the purposes of section 35 of the Copyright, Designs and Patents
Act 1988 ('the Act') the licensing scheme set out in the Schedule to the Principle
Order, being a scheme operated by the Educational Recording Agency Limited;

And whereas the Principal Order was amended by the Copyright (Certification
of Licensing Scheme for Educational Recording of Broadcasts and Cable
Programmes) (Educational Recording Agency Limited) (Amendment) Order
1992 and the Copyright (Certification of Licensing Scheme for Educational
Recording of Broadcasts and Cable Programmes) (Educational Recording Agency
Limited) (Amendment) Order 1993;

And whereas the Educational Recording Agency Limited has applied to the
Secretary of State for the Principle Order (as amended) to be further amended in
accordance with article 2 of this Order;

Now, therefore, the Secretary of State, in exercise of the powers conferred upon
him by section 143 of the Act makes the following Order—

**1.** This Order may be cited as the Copyright (Certification of Licensing Scheme
for Educational Recording of Broadcasts and Cable Programmes) (Educational
Recording Agency Limited) (Amendment) Order 1994 and shall come into force
on 1st April 1994.
**2.** This article amends The Copyright Certification of Licensing Scheme for
Educational Recording of Broadcasts and Cable Programmes) (Educational
Recording Agency Limited) Order 1990[SI 1990 No 879, Schedule, paras 4, 10].


PERFORMANCES (RECIPROCAL PROTECTION) (CONVENTION
COUNTRIES) ORDER 1994
(SI 1994 No 264)

> *Made* . . . . . . *8th February 1994*
> *Laid before Parliament* . . *18th February 1994*
> *Coming into force* . . . . *11th March 1994*

Her Majesty, by virtue of the authority conferred upon Her by section 208(1)(a)
of the Copyright, Designs and Patents Act 1988 is pleased, by and with the
advice of Her Privy Council, to order, and it is hereby ordered, as follows:

**1.** This Order may be cited as the Performances (Reciprocal Protection)
(Convention Countries) Order 1994 and shall come into force on 11th March 1994.
**2.** The following countries are hereby designated as enjoying reciprocal protection
under Part II of the Copyright, Designs and Patents Act 1988 (rights in
performances)—

Argentina
Australia
Austria
Barbados
Bolivia
Brazil
Burkina Faso
Chile
Columbia
Congo
Costa Rica
Czech Republic
Denmark (including Greenland and the Faeroe Islands)
Dominican Republic
Ecuador
El Salvador
Fiji
Finland
France (including all Overseas Departments and Territories)
Germany
Greece
Guatemala
Honduras
Ireland, Republic of
Italy
Japan
Lesotho
Luxembourg
Mexico
Monaco
Netherlands
Niger
Nigeria
Norway
Panama
Paraguay
Peru
Philippines
Spain
Slovak Republic
Sweden
Switzerland
Uruguay

**3.** The Performances (Reciprocal Protection) (Convention Countries) Order 1993, SI 1993 No 943 is hereby revoked.

# Part B  Public Lending Right

## PUBLIC LENDING RIGHT ACT 1979 (COMMENCEMENT) ORDER 1980
## (SI 1980 No 83 )

| | |
|---|---|
| *Made* . . . . | *. . 22nd January 1980* |
| *Laid before Parliament* | *. . 31st January 1980* |
| *Coming into force* . . | *. . 21st February 1980* |

In exercise of the power conferred by section 5(3) of the Public Lending Right Act 1979 and vested in me, I hereby make the following Order—

**1.** This Order may be cited as the Public Lending Right Act 1979 (Commencement) Order 1980 and shall come into operation on 21st February 1980.
**2.** The Public Lending Right Act 1979 shall come into force on 1st March 1980.

## PUBLIC LENDING RIGHT SCHEME 1982 (COMMENCEMENT)
## ORDER 1982
## (SI 1982 No 719)

| | |
|---|---|
| *Made* . . . . . . | *17th May 1982* |
| *Laid before Parliament* . . | *1st June 1982* |
| *Coming into force* . . . . | *24th June 1982* |

**1.** This Order may be cited as the Public Lending Right Scheme 1982 (Commencement) Order 1982 and shall come into operation on 14th June 1982.
**2.**—(1) The Scheme set out in the Appendix hereto, which has been approved by a resolution of each House of Parliament, shall come into force in the manner hereinafter provided.

(2) [This sub-paragraph provides that the provisions of the original scheme came into force as follows: Pts I, II, IV, Sch 2 and Sch 3, Pt I, came into force on 14th June 1982; Pt III and Sch 1 came into force on 1st September 1982; and Pt V, Sch 3, Pt II and Sch 4 came into force on 1st July 1983].

*General note*
This scheme is printed as set out in Appendix 2 of the Public Lending Right Scheme 1982 (Commencement of Variations) Order 1990 (SI 1990 No 2360), as amended by the Public Lending Right Scheme 1982 (Commencement of Variations) Order 1991 (SI 1991 No 2618), and the Public Lending Right Scheme 1982 (Commencement of Variations) Order 1993 (SI 1993 No 3049). The Scheme as set out in that Appendix came into force on 27th December 1990, but see the general notes below as to the coming into force of any amendments thereto.

## APPENDIX 2

## PUBLIC LENDING RIGHT SCHEME 1982
## Arrangement of scheme

# PUBLIC LENDING RIGHT SCHEME 1982

## PART I
## TITLE AND INTERPRETATION

### Citation and extent
**1.** This Scheme may be cited as the Public Lending Right Scheme 1982, and shall extend to the whole of the United Kingdom.

### General definitions
**2.**—(1) In this Scheme, except where the context otherwise requires, the following expressions have the meanings hereby respectively assigned to them, that is to say—

'the Act' means the Public Lending Right Act 1979;

'author', in relation to an eligible book, means a person who is, or one of a number of persons who are, treated as such by article 4;

'eligible author', in relation to an eligible book, means an author of that book who is an eligible person;

'eligible book' has the meaning assigned thereto by article 6;

'eligible person', in relation to an author, has the meaning assigned thereto by article 5;

'financial year' means a period of twelve months ending on the 31st March;

'identifying number' means the number entered in the Register in pursuance of article 8(1)(a)(iv);

'local library authority' has the meaning assigned thereto by section 5(2) of the Act;

'posthumously eligible book' has the meaning assigned thereto by article 6A;

'posthumously eligible person' has the meaning assigned thereto by article 5A;
'the Registrar' and 'the Register' have the meanings assigned thereto by
section 5(2) of the Act;
'registered interest' means the interest (being the whole or a share thereof), in
the Public Lending Right in respect of a particular book, shown on the
Register as belonging to a particular person, and 'registered owner' means
the person for the time being so registered;
'the registry' means the place at which the Register is for the time being
maintained in pursuance of article 7;
'sampling year' has the meaning assigned thereto by article 36.

(2) In this Scheme, except where the context otherwise requires, any reference
to an article or to a Part or to a Schedule shall be construed as a reference to an
article contained in, or to a Part of or a Schedule to, this Scheme, as the case may
be, and any reference in any article to a paragraph shall be construed as a reference
to a paragraph in that article.

### Delivery of documents and service of notice
**3.** Unless the context otherwise requires, any requirement in this Scheme for—

(a) a document or an application to be delivered at the registry or produced to
the Registrar or for notice to be given to him, shall be satisfied if the same
is either—

   (i) delivered in person at the registry between the hours of 11 am and
   3 pm on a working day; or
   (ii) sent through the post by recorded delivery;

(b) a local library authority or a registered owner to be notified of any matter
shall be satisfied if such notification is sent through the post.

### PART II
### BOOKS AND AUTHORS ELIGIBLE UNDER THE SCHEME

### Authors
**4.**—(1) Subject to paragraph (2), a person shall be treated as an author of a book
for the purpose of this Scheme if he is either—

(a) a writer of the book, including without prejudice to the generality of that
expression,

   (i) a translator thereof, and
   (ii) an editor or compiler thereof, who in either case has contributed
   more than ten per cent of the contents of the book or more than ten
   pages of the contents, whichever is the less, **or who is entitled to
   a royalty payment from the publisher in respect of the book**; or
*(b) an illustrator thereof, which for this purpose includes the author of a
photograph (within the meaning of section 48 of the Copyright Act 1956).*
**(b) is evidenced by his entitlement to a royalty payment from the publisher
in respect of the book; or**
**(c) in the case of a book without a title page, is evidenced—**

   **(i) by his being named elsewhere in the book and in the view of the
   Registrar his contribution to the book was such that he would
   have merited a mention on the title page had there been one, or**

   **(ii) by his entitlement to a royalty payment from the publisher in respect of the book, or**

 **(d) is evidenced by a statement, signed by all the other authors of the book in respect of whom the fact that they are authors of the book is evidenced in accordance with paragraphs (a) to (c), that his contribution to the book was such that it is appropriate that he should be treated as an author of the book and the Registrar is satisfied that it is appropriate so to treat him.**

(2) Notwithstanding paragraph (1), a person shall not be treated as an author of a book unless the fact that he is an author within the meaning of paragraph (1)—

 (a) is evidenced by his being named on the title page of the book; or

 (b) in the case of a person treated as an author by virtue of paragraph (1)(a)(i), is evidenced as aforesaid or, if the translated text amounts to at least half of the book's contents, by his being named on the cover or the title page verso of the book.

*General note*

The words in bold in para (1)(a)(ii) were inserted, and paras (b)-(d) were substituted for the original para (b), by SI 1991 No 2618, with effect from 18th December 1991.

### Eligible persons

**5.**—(1) For the purposes of the Scheme, and in relation to each application by a person relating to an eligible book, the applicant is an eligible person if he is an author (within the meaning of article 4) of that book who at the date of the application has his only or principal home in one of the countries specified in Schedule 5, or, if he has no home, has been present in one of those countries for not less than twelve months out of the preceding twenty-four months.

(2) In this Article 'principal home', in the case of a person having more than one home means that one of those homes at which he has been for the longest aggregate period during the twenty-four months immediately preceding the application for registration.

### Posthumously eligible persons

**5A.** For the purposes of the Scheme, and in relation to each application relating to a posthumously eligible book, an author who is dead is a posthumously eligible person if, had he been an applicant for first registration of Public Lending Right in relation to that book at the date of his death, he would have been an eligible person in accordance with article 5.

### Eligible books

**6.**—(1) For the purposes of this Scheme, an eligible book is a book (as defined in paragraph (2)) the sole author, or at least one of the authors, of which is an eligible person; and there shall be treated as a separate book—

 (a) each volume of a work published in two or more volumes, and

 (b) each new edition of a book.

(2) In paragraph (1) 'book' means a printed and bound publication (including a paper-back edition) but does not include—

 (a) a book bearing, in lieu of the name of an author who is a natural person, the name of a body corporate or an unincorporated association;

(b) *a book with four or more authors, but for the purpose of this sub-paragraph a translator, editor or compiler shall not be treated as an author of the book unless each of his co-authors is a translator, editor or compiler;*

(c) a book which is wholly or mainly a musical score;

(d) a book the copyright of which is vested in the Crown;

(e) a book which has not been offered for sale to the public;

(f) a serial publication including, without prejudice to the generality of that expression, a newspaper, magazine, journal or periodical; or

(g) a book in respect of which an application for first registration of Public Lending Right has not been made before 30th June 1991 and which does not have an International Standard Book Number.

*General note*
Para (b) was deleted by SI 1991 No 2618, with effect from 18th December 1991.

## Posthumously eligible books

**6A.** For the purposes of the Scheme, a book is a posthumously eligible book if—

(a) it is a book within the meaning of article 6(2),

(b) the sole author, or at least one of the authors, of the book is a posthumously eligible person, and

(c) the book is either—

(i) published within one year before or ten years after the date of that person's death and that person had made a successful application during his lifetime for registration of Public Lending Right or of an eligible author's share of the Right in respect of at least one other book, or

(ii) a book which consists of or incorporates a work of that person which had previously been the constituent of or incorporated in a book in relation to which that person had made such an application as aforesaid.

PART III
REGISTRATION OF PUBLIC LENDING RIGHT
THE REGISTER

## The Register

**7.** The Registrar shall establish and maintain a Public Lending Right Register at such place as the Secretary of State may from time to time determine, and upon each such determination notice shall be published in the London Gazette, the Edinburgh Gazette and the Belfast Gazette, of such place and the time of the commencement of registration thereat.

## The content of the Register

**8.**—(1) The Register shall contain—

(a) particulars of each book in respect of which Public Lending Right subsists, including—

(i) the title of the book;

(ii) the name or names of the persons appearing on the title page as the authors thereof,

(iii) the true identity of an author if different from (ii) above;

(iv) a number for that book, determined by, or in accordance with arrangements made by, the Registrar;

(b) the name and address of each person entitled to the Right in respect of each such book and, if more than one, the share of each such person in such Right.

(2) The Registrar shall also keep at the registry an index whereby all entries in the Register can readily be traced, and for this purpose 'index' includes any device or combination of devices serving the purpose of an index.

### Registration

**9.**—(1) Public Lending Right in respect of a book may, and may only, be registered if—

(a) the book is an eligible book and application in that behalf is made in accordance with articles 14 and 17, or

(b) the book is a posthumously eligible book and application in that behalf is made in accordance with articles 14A and 17B.

(2) Subject to paragraph (3), an eligible author's share of the Public Lending Right in respect of an eligible book with two or more authors (including any who are not eligible persons) may, and may only, be registered on application in that behalf made in accordance with articles 14 and 17.

(3) The share of the Public Lending Right in such a book as is mentioned in paragraph (2) of an author who was not an eligible person at the time when application was first made for the registration of the share of the Right of any co-author may, and may only, be registered if—

(a) he has become and remains an eligible person, and

(b) application in that behalf is made in accordance with Articles 14 and 17.

(4) A posthumously eligible person's share of the Public Lending Right in respect of a posthumously eligible book with two or more authors (including any who are not eligible persons) may, and may only, be registered on application made in accordance with articles 14A and 17B.

### Shares in Public Lending Right

**9A.**—(1) Subject to the following paragraphs an eligible person's registered share of Public Lending Right in respect of a book of which he is author shall be the whole of that Right or, where a book has two or more authors (including any who are not eligible persons), such share of the Public Lending Right as may be specified in accordance with article 17(1)(c) in the application for first registration of the Right.

(2) A translator's share of Public Lending Right in respect of a book shall be thirty per cent of that Right, or if there is more than one translator (including any who are not eligible persons), an equal share of thirty per cent, but this paragraph shall not apply where a translator is an author of the book in another capacity unless he makes an application in accordance with article 17(1)(c)(ii).

(3) An editor's or compiler's share of Public Lending Right in respect of a book shall be

(a) twenty per cent of that Right, or

(b) if he satisfies the Registrar that he has contributed more than twenty per cent of the contents of the book, the percentage equal to the percentage contribution, or

(c) if there is more than one editor or compiler (including any who are not eligible persons), an equal share of twenty per cent or the higher percentage attributable to the editors or compilers in accordance with sub-paragraph (b).

(4) An illustrator's share of Public Lending Right in respect of a book, and each eligible person's share of Public Lending Right in respect of a book with two or more authors (including any who are not eligible persons) none of whom is an illustrator, translator or editor or compiler, shall not exceed fifty per cent of that Right unless the Registrar is satisfied that any share exceeding fifty per cent which is specified in accordance with article 17(1)(c) in the application for first registration of the Right or in accordance with Article 17(2) in the application for first registration of an eligible author's share of the Right is reasonable in relation to that author's contribution.

(5) Where a book has two or more authors (including any who are not eligible persons) and the Registrar is satisfied that one or more of them is dead or cannot be traced at the date of application despite all reasonable steps having been taken to do so, the Public Lending Right shall be apportioned amongst all the authors (including any who are not eligible persons)

(a) by attributing to each author the same share of Public Lending Right as has been attributed to that author in respect of any other book by the same authors or, if there has been more than one such other book, the most recent book by those authors in respect of which Public Lending Right has been registered, if the Registrar is satisfied that there has been no significant change in the respective contributions of the authors;

(b) where sub-paragraph (a) does not apply, equally, subject to

    (i) the prior application of paragraphs (2), (3) and (7), and

    (ii) where the book is illustrated,

        (aa) the attribution of twenty per cent of the Public Lending Right to the illustrator, or

        (bb) if he satisfies the Registrar that he has contributed more than twenty per cent of the contents of the book, the attribution of the percentage equal to that percentage contribution, or

        (cc) if there is more than one illustrator (including any who are not eligible persons), the attribution of an equal share of twenty per cent or the higher percentage attributable to illustrators in accordance with sub-paragraph (bb).

(6) Where paragraph (5)(b)(ii) applies an illustrator who is also an author of a book in another capacity shall, in addition to any share of Public Lending Right to which he is entitled under that paragraph, be entitled to any further share of the Right which is attributable to him as author in that other capacity.

(7) Where all the persons (including the personal representatives of a posthumously eligible person) amongst whom the Public Lending Right would otherwise be apportioned equally in accordance with paragraph (5)(b) jointly notify the Registrar in writing that they wish the Right to be apportioned in a manner other than equally, the apportionment specified by them shall apply if the Registrar is satisfied that it is reasonable in that case.

(8) Where all the authors who are party to an application under article 17(1)(c)

and who are entitled under paragraphs (2), (3), and (5)(b)(ii) to a share of a percentage of Public Lending Right in respect of the relevant book specify in accordance with article 17(1)(c) that the said percentage shall be apportioned in a manner other than that provided for by those paragraphs the specified apportionment shall apply if the Registrar is satisfied that it is reasonable in that case.

### Dealings to be effected only on the Register

**10.** No Public Lending Right in respect of a particular book shall subsist and no transmission of a registered interest shall be effective until such Right or such transmission has been entered in the Register by the Registrar.

### Register to be conclusive

**11.** The Register shall be conclusive as to whether Public Lending Right subsists in respect of a particular book and also as to the persons (if any) who are for the time being entitled to the Right.

### Amendment of the Register

**12.** The Register may be amended pursuant to an Order of a Court of competent jurisdiction or by the decision of the Registrar in any of the following cases—

(a) in any case and at any time with the consent of the registered owner or owners of the Right in respect of a particular book;
(b) where a Court of competent jurisdiction or the Registrar is satisfied that an entry in the Register has been obtained by fraud;
(c) where a decision of a Court of competent jurisdiction affects any interest in an eligible book and, in consequence thereof, the Registrar is of the opinion that amendment of the Register is required;
(d) where two or more persons are erroneously registered as being entitled to the same interest in Public Lending Right in respect of a particular book;
(e) where an entry erroneously relates to a book which is not an eligible book;
(f) in any other case where by reason of any error or omission in the Register, or by reason of any entry made under a mistake, it appears to the Registrar just to amend the Register.

### Payments consequent upon amendment

**13.** The person who, as a result of an amendment of the Register pursuant to article 12 or 17A, becomes the registered owner of a registered interest shall be entitled to the payment of Public Lending Right in respect of that interest from the date upon which the Register was amended.

*Procedure for registration*

### Forms of application

**14.** Any application required under this Scheme other than an application required under article 14A—

(a) for first registration of Public Lending Right of an eligible author's share of the Right;
(b) for the transfer of a registered interest, or
(c) for renunciation of a registered interest,

shall be made in writing to the Registrar and provide the information specified in Part I, II or III of Schedule 1 (as the case may be) in such form as he may from time to time require.

### Forms of application in respect of posthumously eligible books

**14A.** An application under article 17B for first registration of Public Lending Right, or of a posthumously eligible person's share of the Right, in relation to a posthumously eligible book shall be made in writing to the Registrar and shall provide in such form as he may from time to time require

(a) the information specified in paragraphs 1 to 4 of Part I of Schedule 1 other than the address specified in paragraph 4,

(b) a statement signed by the personal representatives of the posthumously eligible person that the conditions as to eligibility in articles 5A and 6A are satisfied, and

(c) in the case of a work by more than one author, a statement signed as aforesaid that the posthumously eligible person in relation to whom the application is being made was translator, editor or compiler or illustrator of the book and that the claim to Public Lending Right in respect thereof is limited to the percentage prescribed in article 9A(2), (3) or (5)(b)(ii) or that the other author, or one of the other authors, of the work is a translator and that the claim to Public Lending Right in respect thereof is limited to that share or to a share of that share to which the translator is not entitled,

and shall be accompanied, when the personal representatives have not previously made an application under article 17B in relation to that posthumously eligible person, by

(i) the probate, letters of administration or confirmation of executors of the posthumously eligible person in relation to whom the application is being made, and

(ii) a certificate signed by a Member of Parliament, Justice of the Peace, Minister of Religion, lawyer, bank officer, school teacher, police officer, doctor or other person accepted by the Registrar as being of similar standing and stating that he had known the posthumously eligible person in relation to whom the application is being made for at least two years before the date of his death, that he was not related to him and that to the best of his knowledge the contents of the statement referred to in paragraph (b) are true.

### Recording of receipt of application

**15.** The Registrar shall record the date upon which each application for first registration is received by him.

### Completion of registration

**16.** (1) When the Registrar is satisfied as to the eligibility of a book for registration and as to the persons entitled to Public Lending Right in respect of that book and, if more than one, of their respective shares therein, the registration shall be completed and, as regards a first registration of the Right, each registration shall be effective as from the day the application was recorded by the Registrar as having been received by him.

(2) On completion of a registration the Registrar shall issue to any person so entered in the Register as having an interest in the Public Lending Right in respect

of the book to which the entry relates, an acknowledgement of registration in the form of a copy of the relevant entry, indicating therein the date from which the entry takes effect.

## First registration

### Application for first registration
**17.**—(1) An application for first registration of Public Lending Right in respect of an eligible book—

(a) shall satisfy the requirements of article 14 and be made by delivery at the registry;

(b) shall be made by an eligible author, and

(c) where the book has two or more authors (including any who are not eligible persons), shall specify the proposed shares of each of them and for that purpose each of those authors who is alive at the date of application shall be a party to the application, unless

    (i) the Registrar is satisfied that he cannot be traced, despite all reasonable steps having been taken to do so, or

    (ii) the application is made by the translator or editor or compiler of the book and he specifies that he is making the application only in his capacity as such, or

    (iii) any author of the book who is not a party to the application is a translator and the application specifies that it relates only to that share of Public Lending Right in the book to which the translator is not entitled, or

    (iv) the application is made by an author of the book and he specifies that he is making the application otherwise than wholly or partly in the capacity of translator, editor, or compiler of the book, and—

        (aa) there is at the date of the application an effective agreement or arrangement between each person who is an author of the book (including any author who is not an eligible person or who does not wish to register);

        (bb) each such person is a party to the agreement or arrangement otherwise than wholly or partly in the capacity of translator, editor or compiler of the book; and

        (cc) the agreement or arrangement relates to the apportionment of shares of Public Lending Right in the book or, where there is any eligible person who would be entitled to a share of the Right by virtue of being a translator, editor, or compiler, to the apportionment of shares in such proportion of the Right as would remain after taking account of any such entitlement.

(2) An application for first registration of an eligible author's share of Public Lending Right in respect of an eligible book with two or more authors (including any who are not eligible persons)—

(a) shall satisfy the requirements of article 14 and be made by delivery at the registry,

(b) shall be made by the author concerned, and

    (c)  shall, when made by an author otherwise than wholly or partly in the capacity of translator, editor or compiler of the book, satisfy the requirements of paragraph (1)(c)(iv).

(3) Anything which falls to be done by an author under this article shall, if he is not of full age, be done by his parent or guardian and that parent or guardian shall be recorded in the Register as the person to whom are payable sums in respect of any registered interest of the author until such time as a transfer of the registration into the author's own name has been recorded in pursuance of article 25.

### Transitional provisions for translators, editors and compilers

**17A.**—(1) Where an application for first registration of Public Lending Right in respect of a book was made before 28th December 1984 and a translator, editor or compiler thereof would have been party to the said application if it had been made on or after that date he may, if he is an eligible person, make an application for the registered shares of the Right to be revised.

(2) Subject to the following paragraphs, the provisions of this Scheme shall apply to an application under paragraph (1) as though it were an application for first registration of Public Lending Right.

(3) Where a successful application is made under paragraph (1)—

    (a)  the applicant's share of the Public Lending Right shall be that prescribed in article 9A(2) or (3) as the case may be, and

    (b)  the relevant shares of his co-authors, one to another, shall remain unaltered, unless all the authors who were party to the original application before 28th December 1984 are party to the application under paragraph (1) and specify an apportionment of their shares in a different manner and the Registrar is satisfied that such apportionment is reasonable.

(4) Where a successful application is made in accordance with paragraph (1) the Registrar shall amend the Register accordingly.

### Application for first registration in respect of posthumously eligible books

**17B.** An application for first registration of Public Lending Right in respect of a posthumously eligible book and an application for first registration of a posthumously eligible person's share of Public Lending Right in respect of such a book with two or more authors (including any who are not eligible persons)—

    (a)  shall satisfy the requirements of article 14A and be made by delivery at the registry, and

    (b)  shall be made by the personal representatives of the posthumously eligible person concerned.

### Evidence required in connection with the applications

**18.** The Registrar may require the submission of evidence to satisfy him that—

    (a)  a book is an eligible book,

    (b)  a person applying as author for the first registration of Public Lending Right, or the registration of a share of the Right, is in fact the author of that book and is an eligible person,

    (c)  any co-author who is not a party to an application for first registration of Public Lending Right is dead or cannot be traced despite all reasonable steps having been taken to do so, and

(d) where such an application as is mentioned in article 17(1)(c)(iv) has been made in accordance with paragraph (1) or (2) of that article—

> (i) there is such an agreement or arrangement as is mentioned in article 17(1)(c)(iv), and
>
> (ii) the share of Public Lending Right of the person making the application is as specified in that agreement or arrangement,

and may for the purpose of obtaining any such evidence require a statutory declaration to be made by any person.

## *Subsequent dealings with public lending right*

### Public Lending Right to be transmissible

**19.** A registered interest shall be transmissible by assignment or assignation, by testamentary disposition or by operation of law, as personal or movable property, so long, as regards a particular book, as the Right in respect of that book is capable of subsisting.

### Period during which the Right may be transferred

**20.** The duration of Public Lending Right in respect of any book and the period during which there may be dealings therein shall be from the date of the book's first publication (or, if later, the beginning of the sampling year in which application is made for it to be registered) until fifty years have elapsed since the end of the sampling year in which the author died or, if the book is registered as the work of more than one author, as regards dealings in the share of the Right attributable to that author, the end of the year in which that author died.

### Whole interest to be assigned

**21.** (1) The disposition of Public Lending Right, after the first registration thereof, shall, as respects each registered interest in any book, be for the whole of that interest.

(2) On such disposition the interest may be registered in the name of joint owners, being not more than four in number and all being of full age, but in such case the senior only shall be deemed, for the purposes of the Scheme, to be the registered owner; seniority shall be determined by the order in which names stand in the Register.

(3) Subject to articles 29 and 30, no notice of any trusts, expressed, implied or constructive, shall be entered on the Register or be receivable by the Registrar.

### Applications for transfer

**22.** Every application for registration of a transfer of Public Lending Right shall satisfy the requirements of article 14 and be made by delivery at the registry.

### Stamp duty

**23.**—(1) An application for transfer shall bear the proper Inland Revenue stamp impressed thereon to show that all duty payable (if any) in respect of the transaction has been paid.

(2) Where an application for transfer is submitted or the purpose of giving effect to a transaction under a deed or other instrument on which the Inland Revenue stamp has already been impressed, such stamped instrument shall, before

completion of the registration, be produced to the Registrar to show that all duty payable (if any) in respect of the transaction has been paid.

**Proof of author's existence**
**24.** It shall be a condition of registration of every transfer that the transferee provides, and gives an undertaking to the Registrar in future to provide at such intervals and in such form as the Registrar may require, evidence that the author is still alive, or, as the case may be, evidence of the author's death.

**Registration by an author on attainment of full age**
**25.** An author whose interest is, pursuant to article 17(3), registered in the name of his parent or guardian may, on attaining full age, make application to the Registrar in accordance with articles 21 to 23, so far as they are applicable, for the transfer of the registration of the Right into his own name, and until such transfer has been recorded the Registrar shall be entitled to remit any sums due in respect of the Right to such parent or guardian.

*Transmission on death*

**Registration of personal representatives**
**26.** On production of the probate, letters of administration, or confirmation of executors of a registered owner, the personal representatives named in such probate, letters or confirmation shall, on production of the same to the Registrar, be registered as owner in place of the deceased owner with the addition of the words 'executor or executrix (or administrator or administratrix) of [name] deceased'.

**Transfer by personal representatives**
**27.** The personal representatives registered under the preceding article may transfer the interest of the deceased owner, such transfer being in accordance with articles 21 to 24 or such provisions thereof as are applicable in the circumstances of the case.

*Transfer on bankruptcy, liquidation or sequestration*

**Registration of Official Receiver, Official Assignees or Judicial Factor**
**28.**—(1) On the production to the Registrar of an office copy of an Order of a Court having jurisdiction in bankruptcy adjudging a registered owner bankrupt or directing the estate of a deceased registered owner to be administered in accordance with an order under section 421 of the Insolvency Act 1986 or section 21 of the Bankruptcy Amendment Act (Northern Ireland) 1929, together with a certificate signed by the Official Receiver or Official Assignee, as the case may be, that any registered interest in the name of the bankrupt registered owner, or deceased registered owner, is part of his property divisible amongst his creditors, the Official Receiver or the Official Assignee may be registered as the registered owner in place of the bankrupt or deceased registered owner.

(2) Where there is produced to the Registrar a certified copy of an Order of a Court having competent jurisdiction in Scotland awarding sequestration of the estate of a registered owner (including a deceased registered owner) and appointing a judicial factor the Registrar shall on receipt of such a copy enter in the Register the name of the judicial factor as registered owner with the addition of the words 'judicial factor in the estate of [name]'.

**Registration of Trustee in Bankruptcy in place of Official Receiver, Assignees in Bankruptcy or Judicial Factor**
**29.**—(1) Where the Official Receiver or the Official Assignee has been registered as registered owner and some other person is subsequently appointed trustee, or, in Northern Ireland, a creditor's assignee is appointed, the trustee or the assignee may be registered as registered owner in place of the Official Receiver, or the Official Assignee, on production of an office copy of the certificate by the Department of Trade of his appointment as trustee, or in Northern Ireland an office copy of the certificate under section 90 of the Bankruptcy (Ireland) Amendment Act 1872 or of the certificate of the vesting of the estate and effects of the registered owner in the assignee.

(2) Where a judicial factor has been registered as an owner in terms of article 28(2) and some other person is subsequently elected as a trustee on behalf of the creditors of the former registered owner, the Registrar, on receipt of the notification of such election and of sufficient evidence to demonstrate that that person has been so elected, shall enter in the Register the name of the trustee as registered owner with the addition of the words 'trustee in the estate of [name]'.

(3) If the Official Receiver or the Official Assignee has not been entered on the Register under article 28(1) the trustee or the assignee may be registered as registered owner on production of office copies of the Order adjudging the registered owner bankrupt and the appropriate certificate referred to in paragraph (1) with a certificate signed by the trustee or the assignee that the registered interest is part of the property of the bankrupt divisible amongst his creditors.

(4) If a judicial factor has not been entered in the Register as owner under article 28(2) the Registrar shall, on receipt of the certified copy of an Order of a Court under article 28(2) together with the notification and evidence referred to in paragraph (2), enter in the Register as registered owner the name of the duly elected trustee with the addition of the words 'trustee in the estate of [name]'.

**Registration of a trust under a Scheme of Arrangement or an Arrangement under the control of the Court**
**30.**—(1) If any registered interest is vested in a trustee under the provisions of a Scheme of Arrangement approved by a Court having jurisdiction in bankruptcy, the Official Receiver or other trustee may be registered as owner in like manner as a trustee in bankruptcy upon production of an office copy of the Scheme of Arrangement, a certificate signed by the Official Receiver, or such other trustee, that the registered interest was part of the property vested in him under the provisions of the Scheme, and in the case of a trustee other than the Official Receiver, an office copy of the certificate by the Department of Trade of his appointment as trustee.

(2) If any registered interest of an arranging debtor who is a registered owner is vested in the Official Assignee alone or jointly with other persons under section 349 of the Irish Bankrupt and Insolvent Act 1857, the Official Assignee and such other persons (if any) may be registered as owner in his place on production of an office copy of the Order of the Court approving and confirming the resolution or agreement referred to in the said section with a certificate by the Official Assignee identifying the arranging debtor named in the Order of the Court with the registered owner endorsed thereon and a certificate signed by the Official Assignee and other such person (if any) that the registered interest was part of the property vested under the resolution or agreement.

(3) If, as regards Scotland, a registered owner—

(a) has entered into a deed of arrangement for behoof of his creditors, the Registrar shall, on receiving a certified copy of the Order of the Court approving such arrangement, enter on the Register as owner the name of the person who is under the said deed of arrangement to receive any payments due to the owner (where that person is not the registered owner at the date of approval of the arrangement);

(b) has entered into a private trust deed or composition contract for behoof of his creditors, the trustee under such deed or contract may make an application, accompanied by such evidence as the Registrar may require, for transmission of the registered interest into his name as such trustee; and on receipt of such an application the Registrar shall make the appropriate entry in the Register.

## Liquidation of a company

**31.** In the liquidation of a company in which an interest in Public Lending Right is vested, any resolution or order appointing a liquidator may be filed and referred to on the Register, and, when so registered, shall be deemed to be in force until it is cancelled or superseded on the Register.

## Renunciation

**32.**—(1) On making application in that behalf which satisfies the requirements of article 14, the registered owner of a registered interest may absolutely and unconditionally renounce that interest as provided in paragraph (2).

(2) Such renunciation may, as to extent, be in respect of either the whole or a half share of the registered interest and may be effective for all time, or in respect of such financial years as shall be specified by the registered owner.

(3) An application for renunciation shall bear the proper Inland Revenue stamp impressed thereon.

(4) The Registrar shall as at the date from which the renunciation is to have effect amend the Register—

(a) in the case of a renunciation for all time of the whole of the registered interest by removing from the Register the entry relating to the registered owner and, if that interest represents the whole of the Public Lending Right in a book, the entry relating to that book; or

(b) in all other cases, by noting against the relevant entry in the Register the extent of the renunciation and the period during which it is effective.

(5) Immediately upon the amendment of the Register as provided in paragraph (4), any sum due by way of Public Lending Right which, apart from the renunciation would become payable to the registered owner by 31st March in any year falling within the period to which the renunciation applies, shall cease to be so payable.

## *General*

## Neglected applications for registration

**33.** Where in the case of any application for first or any subsequent registration an applicant has failed to provide within three months information requested by the Registrar, notice may be given to the applicant that the application will be treated as abandoned unless the information is duly furnished within a time (not being less than one month) determined by the Registrar and specified in the notice; and if, at the expiration of that time, the information so requested is not furnished, the application may be treated as abandoned.

**Removal of entries from the Register**
**34.** Where the Registrar, pursuant to section 4(5) of the Act, directs the removal from the Register of any entry relating to a book in whose case no sum has become due by way of Public Lending Right for a period of at least ten years, any subsequent application for the entry to be restored to the Register may be made only by the person who, at the date of the removal of the entry, was the registered owner, or by his legal personal representatives.

**Copies of entries in the Register**
**35.**—(1) The Registrar shall not supply a copy of any entry in the Register otherwise than to—

- (a) a registered owner, as regards any entry which relates to his registered interest; or
- (b) such other person as the registered owner may direct, but if the entry in question also relates to other registered owners, only with the consent of all such owners.

(2) The Registrar may require a payment of a fee for supplying a copy of an entry in the Register, not exceeding £5 in respect of each such entry.

PART IV
ASCERTAINMENT OF THE NUMBER OF LOANS OF BOOKS

**Special definitions**
**36.** In this Part, unless the context otherwise requires—
'copy' means an individual copy of a particular book, and 'copy number' means a number which distinguishes the copy to which it is applied from other copies of the same book in the same library;
'group', in relation to service points, means a group specified in Schedule 2;
'library' has the meaning assigned to it by section 3(4) of the Act;
'loans' means loans whereby books are lent out from a service point to individual borrowers, and includes loans of books not normally held at that service point;
'mobile library service point' means a service point which is taken about from place to place;
'month' means one of the twelve months in the calendar year;
'operative sampling point' means a sampling point at which loans are for the time being required to be recorded in pursuance of article 40(1);
'ordinary service point' means a service point from which fewer than 500,000 loans were made during the preceding period of twelve months;
'participating period', in relation to a sampling point, means the period commencing on the date on which the local library authority having responsibility for it receives from the Registrar notice of designation pursuant to article 38(6) and ending on the date specified in a notice given thereunder as the date upon which it is to cease to act as a sampling point;
'principal service point', in relation to a library authority, means any of the following—

(a) whichever of the service points for which that authority is responsible is the service point from which the greatest number of loans were made during the preceding period of twelve months;

(b) any service point for which that authority is responsible, the number of loans from which during the preceding period of twelve months was not less than three-quarters of the number of loans made from the service point referred to in paragraph (a) during the same period;

(c) any other such service point from which 500,000 or more loans were made during the aforesaid period;

and 'principal service points' means every service point which is a principal service point in relation to any library authority;

'sampling point' means any principal service point, ordinary service point or mobile library service point, or any number of such points in relation to any local library authority, which has been designated, for the time being, by the Registrar under article 38;

'sampling year' means the period of twelve months ending on 30th June;

'service point' means a place from which books comprised in a library are lent out to the public at large.

### Number of loans to be ascertained by means of a sample

**37.** The number of occasions on which a book is lent out shall be determined by means of a sample of the lendings of that book from particular service points, designated in accordance with the provisions of this Part; and for the purpose of the sample, service points shall be classified into groups, according to local library authority areas, specified in Schedule 2.

### Designation of sampling points

**38.**—(1) Such local library authorities as the Registrar may require shall, not later than 30th September in each year, furnish to the Registrar lists, as at 31st March of that year, of all their principal, ordinary and mobile service points. The Registrar shall, not later than 31st December of that year, designate in accordance with paragraph (5) those service points which are to be operative sampling points or which are to be included in operative sampling points as from the beginning of the ensuing sampling year.

(1A) The Registrar may, at any time after he has designated a sampling point in accordance with paragraph (1), discontinue the designation of that point and designate a new sampling point, such discontinuance and new point to take effect from 1st January in the ensuing sampling year. Notice of discontinuance and designation pursuant to this paragraph shall be given in accordance with paragraph (5).

(2) The Registrar shall so exercise his powers under this article as to secure, subject to paragraph (4), that—

(a) at all times there shall be not less than 30 operative sampling points comprising—

(i) five points falling within not less than three local library authority areas in Group A and five points falling within not less than four local library authority areas in Group D in Schedule 2,

(ii) four points falling within not less than three local library authority areas in each of Groups B, C and E in Schedule 2,

      (iii) three points falling within not less than three local library authority areas in each of Groups F and G in Schedule 2, and

      (iv) two points falling within not less than two local library authority areas in Group H in Schedule 2;

(b) at all times the operative sampling points falling within each Group in Schedule 2 shall include, subject to paragraph (3), a principal service point and an ordinary service point;

(c) at all times one of the three operative sampling points falling within Group F in Schedule 2 shall be with the County of Dyfed or that of Gwynedd or the Districts of Colwyn or Glyndwr in the County of Clwyd;

(d) at all times one of the three operative sampling points falling within Group G in Schedule 2 shall be outside the Metropolitan Districts of Edinburgh and Glasgow;

(e) no operative sampling point shall consist only of a mobile library service point other than an operative sampling point falling within the County of Dyfed, or that of Gwynedd or the Districts of Colwyn or Glyndwr in the County of Clwyd;

(f) during each sampling year at least eight operative sampling points shall be replaced by new such points; and

(g) no operative sampling point shall remain as such for a continuous period of more than four years.

(3) The relevant local library authority shall notify the Registrar of any change in the categorisation of a sampling point which consists of a single principal, ordinary or mobile service point but the Registrar shall not be required by paragraph (2)(a) to discontinue the designation of the point as a sampling point before the expiry of the sampling year in which he receives such notice or, if that year has less than six months to run, before the expiry of the next following sampling year.

For the purposes of this paragraph and of paragraph (2)(a), a change in the categorisation of a sampling point shall be disregarded if it is occasioned by an increase or decrease of less than 10 per cent in the number of loans made therefrom.

(4) The local library authority shall notify the Registrar of any decision to close a service point which is or is included in a sampling point and the date on which the closure takes effect but, if it is not reasonably practicable for the Registrar to satisfy the requirements of paragraph (2) before the closure takes effect, those requirements shall be treated as satisfied if satisfied as soon as is reasonably practicable thereafter.

(5) The Registrar shall give to the local library authority responsible for a sampling point—

(a) for the purposes of designating that point under paragraphs (1) or (1A), notice in writing of such designation specifying the period ending on 31st December or 30th June, in any sampling year for which he intends the point to be an operative sampling point;

(b) for the purpose of discontinuing that point as a sampling point, not less than six months notice in writing of such discontinuance.

### Provision by libraries of recording facilities
**39.** Upon receipt of a notice under article 38(6)(a) a local library authority shall—

(a) arrange for every book which may be lent out from the sampling point to which the designation refers to be marked, in such form as the Registrar may require, with its identifying number and (where more than one copy may be lent out) copy number, and shall notify the Registrar at such time and in such manner as he may direct of the number of books so marked; and

(b) acquire, in accordance with arrangements approved by the Registrar, such equipment (including computer programs) as may be necessary to enable the authority to comply with the provisions of article 40 regarding the furnishing of information to the Registrar.

### Duty to record lendings
**40.**—(1) A local library authority which has received a notice under article 38(6)(a) shall, for such period as is specified in the notice, record every occasion on which a copy of a book is lent out to the public from the sampling point to which the notice refers and shall furnish to the Registrar, in such form and at such intervals as he may direct, details of such lendings, including the identifying number and any copy number of the copy in question.

(2) For the purpose of this article each volume of a work published in two or more volumes shall be treated as a separate book.

### Provision of book loan data
**41.** Each local library authority shall submit to the Registrar, in such form, at such intervals and in respect of such periods as he may direct, a return of the total number of occasions on which the books comprised in all its collections were the subject of loans.

### Method of determining the number of notional loans
**42.**—(1) The Registrar shall, from the details of loans furnished to him by local library authorities pursuant to the provisions of this Part (upon the accuracy of which the Registrar shall be entitled to rely), calculate, in accordance with paragraph (2), the number of notional loans of each book in respect of which Public Lending Right subsists in each sampling year.

(2) The number of notional loans of each book made during a sampling year shall be the aggregate of the number of notional loans of that book made in all groups; and the number of notional loans for a group shall be determined in accordance with the following formula—

Total notional loans in the group = A/B x C

Where—

A represents the number of loans of that book recorded during the sampling year at the operative sampling points in that group;

B represents the total number of loans of books made to the public during the sampling year from the operative sampling point in that group; and

C represents the aggregate of the loans of all books made to the public from all libraries (within the meaning of section 3(4) of the Act) in the area of the group during the financial year ending in the sampling year in question, or, as regards any particular library for which loan data relating to that financial year is not available to the Registrar, the most recent financial year for which he has such data.

(3) For the purposes of paragraph (2)—

(a) Groups A, B and C in Schedule 2 shall be treated as one group;

(b) if on any occasion on which any details of lendings at a particular sampling point which consists of a single service point are furnished to the Registrar in accordance with article 40 and record loans of a copy of a book in excess of an average of one loan for each period of five days covered by the details, the loans in excess of that average shall be disregarded; and

(c) the Registrar may disregard any loan of a book made after 30th June 1991 from a sampling point if a local library authority, on the first occasion after 30th June 1991 on which it reports, in accordance with article 40, a loan of that book from that sampling point, does not specify an International Standard Book Number in respect of the book, and the book is not registered at the time of such report.

### Reimbursement of local library authorities

**43.**—(1) The Registrar shall, subject to the provisions of this article and article 44, reimburse to local library authorities the net expenditure incurred by them in giving effect to this Scheme.

(2) It shall be the duty of local library authorities to keep proper accounts and records in respect of the expenditure (including overhead expenses) incurred by them in giving effect to this Scheme and the Registrar may withhold payment to a local library authority, in whole or in part, until such time as such authority has furnished to him sufficient evidence as to the amount of the expenditure so incurred.

### Expense incurred in respect of sampling points

**44.**—(1) Without prejudice to the generality of article 43(2) each local library authority to which a notice has been given under article 38(6)(a) shall submit to the Registrar at such time and in such form as he may require estimates of the net expenditure to be incurred in giving effect to this Scheme at the sampling point or points specified in such notice.

(2) Such local library authority may from time to time during the participating period submit to the Registrar claims in respect of the expenditure incurred, or estimated to have been incurred by it, and the Registrar shall be entitled to rely upon the accuracy of such claims and to make payments on account of the expenditure incurred by that authority in giving effect to the Scheme.

(3) The total amount payable by way of reimbursement to such local library authority shall be finally determined by the Registrar after examination of such audited financial statements and such books, records, documents, and accounts relating thereto as he may require; and any balance found after such final determination to be due by or to the Registrar in account with the local library authority in question shall be paid to or recovered from such local library authority.

(4) In reckoning the net expenditure for the purposes of this article and of article 43, the following shall be deducted from the gross expenditure incurred by a local library authority in connection with a sampling point—

(a) any sum received in connection with the disposal (by sale, lease or otherwise) of any property or equipment purchased pursuant to paragraph (b) of article 39;

(b) any sum which it might reasonably be expected would have been received on such a disposal (whether or not there has been a disposal of the property or equipment in question);

(c) any insurance monies received in respect of the loss or destruction of or damage to any such property or equipment;

(d) an amount representing the appropriate proportion of the net cost (whether by way of purchase, lease, or otherwise) of any property or equipment which is used by a local library authority partly in connection with this Scheme and partly for other purposes not connected therewith:

Provided that where deductions are made under both sub-paragraphs (a) and (b) in respect of the same property or equipment, the aggregate deductions thereunder shall not exceed whichever is the greater of the sums mentioned in those sub-paragraphs.

(5) In determining the amount finally to be paid to or recovered from a local library authority pursuant to paragraph (3), account shall be taken of any expenditure reasonably incurred by that authority in discontinuing the sampling point.

### PART V
### CALCULATION AND PAYMENT OF PUBLIC LENDING RIGHT

**Determination of the sum due in respect of Public Lending Right**
**46.**—(1) For any financial year, the sum due by way of Public Lending Right in respect of a registered interest to the registered owner thereof shall be ascertained by reference to—

(a) the product of the number of notional loans attributable to that interest (calculated in accordance with paragraph (4)) and *1.37p 1.81p* **2.00p**, and

(b) the aggregate amount of that product and the like products in the case of all other registered interests which initially were registered interests of the same author or were interests registered by the personal representatives of the same author.

(2) Subject to paragraph (3) the sum so due for the financial year shall be—

(a) except where the following sub-paragraph applies, the product mentioned in paragraph (1)(a);

(b) if the aggregate amount mentioned in paragraph (1)(b) exceeds £6,000, the product of

$x/y$ and £6,000 where—

x is the number of notional loans attributable to the interest in question, and y is the aggregate of that number and the number of notional loans attributable to all other registered interests which initially were registered interests of the same author or were interests registered by the personal representatives of the same author.

(3) If the aggregate of the amounts determined in accordance with paragraph (2) in respect of each registered interest of the registered owner thereof is less than £1, the sum due in respect of the registered interest shall be nil.

(4) For the purposes of paragraphs (1) and (2)(b), the number of notional loans attributable to any registered interest in any financial year shall be calculated by ascertaining, in accordance with article 42(2), the number of notional loans of the book to which it relates which were made during the sampling year ending in that financial year, and shall be—

(a) if the registered interest represents the whole of the Public Lending Right in respect of that book, the total notional loans of the book in question;

(b) if the registered interest relates only to a share of the Public Lending Right in respect of that book, such proportion of the total notional loans of the book as the registered interest bears to the whole of the Public Lending Right in that book, fractions of a loan being disregarded;

(c) if the Right in respect of that registered interest has been renounced in part, such proportion of the notional loans attributable to the registered interest under sub-paragraph (a) or (b), as the case may be, which the unrenounced share bears to the whole of the registered interest, fractions of a loan being disregarded;

(d) nil, if the Right in respect of the registered interest has been wholly renounced for the financial year in question.

(5) For the purposes of paragraphs (1) and (2)(b), the references to interests which were initially registered interests of the same author include interests which, in pursuance of article 17(3), were registered in the name of his parent or guardian.

*General note*
The figure in bold in para (1)(a) was substituted by SI 1991 No 2618, with effect from 18th December 1991 by SI 1992 No 3049, with effect from 30th December 1992, and by SI 1993 No 3049, with effect from 30th December 1993.

## Persons to whom the payment is due
**47.** The person entitled to the Public Lending Right in respect of any registered book in any financial year shall be the registered owner thereof as at 30th June of that year.

## Right to be claimed
**48.**—(1) No payment shall be made in respect of Public Lending Right unless that Right has been claimed by or on behalf of the person for the time being entitled.

(2) A claim in respect of the Right may be made for—

(a) a specified period;

(b) an unspecified period determinable by not less than three months written notice of termination given to the Registrar by or on behalf of the person for the time being entitled to the Right.

(3) A claim shall automatically lapse in the event of any change of ownership recorded on the Register, subsequent to first registration thereof, in respect of the Right to which the claim relates.

## Notification of entitlement and payment of sums due under the Scheme
**49.**—(1) Any sum payable by way of Public Lending Right in respect of a registered interest, for any financial year, shall (unless sooner paid) fall due for payment on the last day of that year.

(2) Any such sum may be paid by cheque or warrant sent through the post directed to the registered address of the registered owner or, in the case of joint owners, to the registered address of the senior owner (as defined in article 21(2)), or to such person and to such address as the owner or joint owners may direct by a written payment mandate to the Registrar, delivered at the registry, in the form set out in Schedule 4 or a form to the like effect; every such cheque or warrant shall be made payable to the order of the person to whom it is sent and any one of two or more joint owners may give a good receipt for any money due to them under this Scheme.

(3) The Registrar shall at the end of each financial year, or as soon as is reasonably practicable thereafter, inform each registered owner to whom a sum is payable by way of Public Lending Right in respect of that year, by notice posted to his registered address of—

(a)  the notional number of lendings for that year of each book in respect of which he is a registered owner; and
(b)  the amount of such sum.

(4) If, after the Registrar has notified the registered owner as provided in paragraph (3), the cheque or warrant for the sum referred to therein is not presented for payment and thereby lapses—

(a)  there shall be no further duty on the part of the Registrar to take steps to trace the registered owner and it shall be the responsibility of such owner to make application to the Registrar for payment; and
(b)  if at the end of six years from the date upon which a payment in respect of Public Lending Right becomes due no such application has been made by the person entitled thereto, the entitlement to such payment shall lapse.

(5) At the request of a registered owner to whom no notice is required to be given under paragraph (3) in respect of any financial year, the Registrar shall supply to him particulars (calculated in accordance with article 42) of the number of notional loans during the sampling year ending in that financial year of any book in respect of which he is the registered owner, provided the request is made no later than six months after the end of that financial year.

**Power to call for information**
**50.** The Registrar may at any time require a statutory declaration or other sufficient evidence that an author or any registered owner is alive and is the person to whom money is payable under this Scheme, and may withhold payment until such declaration or evidence as he may require is produced.

**Interest**
**51.** No sum determined to be due under this Scheme shall carry interest.

SCHEDULE 1

INFORMATION TO BE PROVIDED IN CONNECTION WITH APPLICATIONS

PART I

APPLICATION FOR FIRST REGISTRATION

Each application shall provide the Registrar, in such form as he may from time to time require, with the following—
1. The title of the book to which the application relates.
2. *The name of every person named on the title page as author (within the meaning of article 4).*
**2. The name of every author (within the meaning of article 4) and the evidence on which each author relies for the purpose of being treated as an author in accordance with article 4(2).**
3. The true identity (if different from 2 above) of each such person, and his address.
4. The International Standard Book Number (if any) of the book.
5. A statement signed by each applicant that in each case the conditions as to eligibility specified in Part II of the Scheme are satisfied at the date of application, accompanied, when the applicant has not previously made an application under article 17 of this Scheme, by a certificate signed by a Member of Parliament, Justice of the Peace, Minister of Religion, lawyer, bank officer, school teacher, police officer, doctor or other person accepted by the Registrar as being of similar standing and stating that

he has known the applicant for at least two years, that he is not related to the applicant and that to the best of his knowledge the contents of the statement by the applicant are true.

6. In the case of a work by more than one author—

(a) a statement signed by all the authors who are alive and can be traced at the date of application specifying—

(i) the agreed share in the Public Lending Right of each author, and

(ii) whether any author is translator, editor, compiler or, if any author is dead or untraced at the date of application, illustrator of the book and, if so, whether he is also an author of the book in another capacity, or

(b) a statement by the applicant that he is a translator, editor or compiler of the book and that his claim to the Public Lending Right in respect thereof is limited to the percentage prescribed in article 9A(2) or (3) as the case may be, or

(c) where one of the authors of the work is a translator, a statement signed by the other author or, if more than one, all the other authors who are alive can be traced at the date of application specifying—

(i) that another author of the book who is not a party to the application is a translator,

(ii) that the claim to Public Lending Right in respect thereof is limited to that share to which the translator is not entitled, and

(iii) here there is more than one author other than the translator

(aa) the agreed share of each such author in that share of the Public Lending Right to which the translator is not entitled, and

(bb) whether any such author is editor or compiler or, if any such author is dead or untraced at the date of application, illustrator of the book and, if so, whether he is also an author of the book in another capacity, or

(d) where such an application as is mentioned in paragraph (1)(c)(iv) of article 17 is made in accordance with paragraph (1) or (2) of that article, a statement specifying the names of all the other persons whether or not party to such agreement or arrangement as is mentioned in paragraph (1)(c)(iv) of article 17, who are eligible for a share of Public Lending Right in respect of the book.

7. Where an editor or compiler of a book wishes to claim, or claim an equal share of more than twenty per cent of the Public Lending Right in accordance with article 9A(3), particulars indicating evidence of the percentage that he has, or where there are two or more editors or compilers that they have jointly, contributed to the contents of the book.

8. In the case of an author not of full age, a declaration by the applicant that he is the parent or guardian, as the case may be, of the author, and a copy of the author's birth certificate.

*General note*
Para 2 was substituted by SI 1991 No 2618, with effect from 18th December 1991.

## PART II

### APPLICATION FOR TRANSFER OF REGISTERED INTEREST

Each application shall provide the Registrar, in such form as he may from time to time require, with the following—

1. The title of the book.
2. The International Standard Book Number (if any) of the book.
3. The name and address of the transferor.
4. The name and address of the transferee.
5. An undertaking by the transferee to furnish to the Registrar, whenever so required, proof that the author is still alive.

## PART III
### APPLICATION FOR RENUNCIATION OF REGISTERED INTEREST

Each application shall provide the Registrar, in such form as he may from time to time require, with the following—

1. The name and address of the person renouncing.
2. The title of the book to which the renunciation relates.
3. The International Standard Book Number (if any) of the book.
4. The extent of the Right being renounced.
5. The period in respect of which the Right is renounced.

## SCHEDULE 2

GROUPING SERVICE POINTS

Service points shall be grouped according to local library authority areas as follows—

GROUP A

Those within the areas of the following non-metropolitan counties—

| | | |
|---|---|---|
| Bedfordshire | Essex | Oxfordshire |
| Berkshire | Hertfordshire | Suffolk |
| Buckinghamshire | Kent | Surrey |
| Cambridgeshire | Norfolk | West Sussex |
| East Sussex | Northamptonshire | |

GROUP B

Those within the areas of the following non-metropolitan counties—

| | | |
|---|---|---|
| Avon | Hampshire | Somerset |
| Cornwall | Hereford & Worcester | Staffordshire |
| Devon | The Isle of Wight | Warwickshire |
| Dorset | The Isles of Scilly | Wiltshire |
| Gloucestershire | Shropshire | |

GROUP C

Those within the areas of the following non-metropolitan counties—

| | | |
|---|---|---|
| Cheshire | Humberside | North Yorkshire |
| Cleveland | Lancashire | Nottinghamshire |
| Cumbria | Leicestershire | |
| Derbyshire | Lincolnshire | |
| Durham | Northumberland | |

GROUP D

Those within the areas of the metropolitan districts of England.

GROUP E

Those within the area of Greater London.

GROUP F

Those in Wales.

GROUP G

Those in Scotland.

GROUP H

Those in Northern Ireland.

## SCHEDULE 4

PAYMENT MANDATE

'Please forward, until further notice, all sums that may from time to time become due to me/us or the survivor(s) of us by way of Public Lending Right to [here state full name and address of the bank, firm or person to whom payments are to be sent] or[where payment is to be made to Bank] to such other Branch of that Bank as the Bank may from time to time request. Your compliance with this request shall discharge the Registrar's liability in respect of such sums.'

Date .................................      Signature ...........................................

                                   Name ................................................
                                   (Block Capitals)

                                   Address ...........................................

## SCHEDULE 5

SPECIFIED COUNTRIES

Federal Republic of Germany
United Kingdom

## PUBLIC LENDING RIGHT SCHEME 1982 (COMMENCEMENT OF VARIATIONS) ORDER 1990
## (SI 1990 No 2360)

*Made*      . .      . .      . .      *26th November 1990*
*Laid before Parliament*    . .      *6th December 1990*
*Coming into force*   . .      . .      *27th December 1990*

Whereas the Public Lending Right Scheme 1982 ('the Scheme') was brought into force on 14th June 1982;

Whereas the Scheme has been varied

And whereas the Lord President of the Council has, after consultation with representatives of authors and library authorities and of others who appear likely to be affected, further varied the scheme;

Now therefore, the Lord President of the Council, in exercise of the powers conferred by section 3(7) of the Public Lending Right Act 1979 and now vested in him, hereby makes the following order—

**1.** This Order may be cited as the Public Lending Right Scheme 1982 (Commencement of Variations) Order 1990.

**2.** The variations in the Public Lending Right Scheme 1982 which were made on 26th November 1990 by the Lord President of the Council and are set out in Appendix 1 to this Order shall come into force on 27th December 1990; and accordingly on and after that date that Scheme has effect as set out in Appendix 2 to this Order.

*General note*
Appendices 1 and 2 not printed here. See the Public Lending Right Scheme 1982 (Commencement) Order 1982, SI 1982 No 719 for the variations.

PUBLIC LENDING RIGHT (INCREASE OF LIMIT) ORDER 1993
(SI 1993 No 799)

> *Made* . . . . . . *15th March 1993*
> *Coming into force* . . . . *1st April 1993*

Whereas a draft of this order has been laid before the House of Commons in accordance with section 2(3) of the Public Lending Right Act 1979 and has been approved by a resolution of that House;

Now, therefore, the Secretary of State, in exercise of the powers conferred by the said section 2(3) and now vested in him, and with the consent of the Treasury, hereby makes the following Order—

**1.** This Order may be cited as the Public Lending Right (Increase of Limit) Order 1993 and shall come into force on 1st April 1993.

**2.** The limit on the sums to be paid under section 2(2) of the Public Lending Right Act 1979 out of money provided by Parliament into the Central Fund to satisfy the liabilities of any one financial year of the Fund shall, in respect of any financial year beginning after 31st March 1993, be increased to £5 million less the total of any sums paid in that year, out of money so provided, under paragraph 2 of the Schedule to that Act (pay, pension, etc of Registrar).

# Part C   Registered Designs

DESIGN RULES 1949
(SI 1949 No 2368)

| | | | |
|---|---|---|---|
| *Made* | . . | . . | *16th December 1949* |
| *Laid before Parliament* | . . | | *22 December 1949* |
| *Coming into operation* | . . | | *. . 2 January 1950* |

By virtue of the provisions of the Registered Designs Act 1949, the Board of Trade do hereby make the following Rules—

## *Short title and commencement*

**1.** These Rules may be cited as the Designs Rules 1949, and shall come into operation on the 2nd day of January, 1950.

## *Application for registration*

**13.** Where it is desired to register the same design in respect of more than one article, a separate application shall be made in respect of each article. In that case each application shall be numbered separately, and shall be treated as a separate and distinct application.

**14.**—(1) Every application shall state the article to which the design is to be applied, and that the applicant claims to be the proprietor thereof.

   (2) Except in the case of an application to register a design to be applied to a textile article, to wallpaper or to lace, the application shall further be accompanied by a statement of the features of the design for which novelty is claimed.

**15.** The applicant shall, if required by the Registrar in any case so to do, indorse on each of the representations of one or more articles, or consists of a registered design with modifications or variations not sufficient to alter the character or substantially to affect the identity thereof, and it is desired to claim the protection of section 4 for such application, it shall contain the number or numbers of the registration or registrations already affected.

**16.** If the application is for the registration of a design which has already been registered in respect of one or more articles, or consists of a registered design with modifications or variations not sufficient to alter the character or substantially to affect the identity thereof, and it is desired to claim the protection of Section 4 for such application, it shall contain the number or numbers of the registration or registrations already effected.

**24.** Where a portrait of Their Majesties or of any member of the Royal Family, or a reproduction of the armorial bearings, insignia, orders of chivalry, decorations or flags of any country, city, borough, town, place, society, body corporate, institution or person appears on a design, the Registrar, before proceeding to register the design, shall, if he so requires, be furnished from such official or other person as appears to the Registrar to be entitled to give consent, and in default of such consent he may refuse to register the design.

**25.** Where the name or portrait of a living person appears on a design, the Registrar shall be furnished, if he so requires, with consent from such person before proceeding to register the design. In the case of a person recently dead the Registrar may call for consent from his personal representative before proceeding with the registration of a design on which the name or portrait of the deceased person appears.

## *Designs excluded from registration under section 1(4)*

**26.** There shall be excluded from registration under the Act designs to be applied to any of the following articles, namely—

(1) works of sculpture other than casts or models used or intended to be used as models or patterns to be multiplied by any industrial process;

(2) wall plaques and medals;

(3) printed matter primarily of a literary or artistic character, including book-jackets, calendars, certificates, coupons, dressmaking patterns, greetings cards, leaflets, maps, plans, postcards, stamps, trade advertisements, trade forms, and cards, transfers, and the like.

REGISTERED DESIGNS APPEAL TRIBUNAL RULES 1950
(SI 1950 No 430)

*(As amended by the Registered Designs Appeal Tribunal (Amendment) Rules 1970 (SI 970 No 1075))*

| | | | |
|---|---|---|---|
| *Made* | . . | . . | . . | *23rd March 1950* |
| *Coming into force* | . . | | . . | *1st April 1950* |

I, the Honourable George Harold Lloyd-Jacob, Knight, the Judge of the High Court nominated by the Lord Chancellor to be the Appeal Tribunal constituted under section 28 (2) of the Registered Designs Act 1949 do, by virtue of section 28 (8) of the Act and all other powers enabling me in this behalf, hereby make the following Rules—

*1. Any person who desires to appeal to the Registered Designs Appeal Tribunal from a decision of the Comptroller General of Patents, Designs, and Trade Marks (in these Rules referred to as 'the Registrar') in any case in which a right of appeal is given by the Registered Designs Act 1949 (in these Rules referred to as 'the Act') shall, within 14 days from the date of the decision, file with the registrar of the Appeal Tribunal, Room 174, Royal Courts of Justice, London, WC2, a notice in the form set out in the Schedule hereto)*

**1.—(1) Any person who desires to appeal to the Registered Designs Appeal Tribunal from a decision of the Comptroller-General of Patents, Designs and Trade Marks (in these Rules referred to as 'the Registrar') in any case in which a right of appeal is given by the Registered Designs Act 1949 (in these Rules referred to as 'the Act') shall file with the registrar of the Appeal Tribunal at the Royal Courts of Justice, London, a notice of appeal in the form set out in the schedule to these Rules.**

(2) The notice of appeal shall be filed—

(a) in the case of a decision on a matter of procedure, within 14 days after the date of the decision; and

(b) in any other case, within six weeks after the date of the decision.

(3) The Registrar may determine whether any decision is on a matter of procedure and any such determination shall itself be a decision on a matter of procedure.

*General note*
This rule was substituted by SI 1970 No 1075, r 2.

**2.** The appellant shall *send a copy of the notice of appeal* **within two days of filing the notice of appeal send a copy thereof** to the Registrar and to any person who appeared, or gave notice of opposition, on the proceedings before the Registrar.

*General note*
The words in bold were substituted for the words in italics by SI 1970 No 1075, r 3.

**3.** On receiving the notice of appeal the Registrar shall forthwith transmit to the registrar of the Appeal Tribunal all the papers relating to the matter which is the subject of the appeal.

**4.** *No appeal shall be entertained of which notice is not given within 14 days from the date of the decision appealed against, or within such further time as the Registrar may allow (upon request received before the expiration of the said 14 days) except by leave of the Appeal Tribunal.*

**4. Except by leave of the Appeal Tribunal, no appeal shall be entertained unless notice of appeal has been given within the period specified in rule 1(2) or within such further time as the Registrar may allow upon request made to him prior to the expiry of that period.**

*General note*
This rule was substituted by the Registered Designs Appeal Tribunal (Amendment) Rules 1950 [SI 1970 No 1075, r 4.]

**5.** The registrar of the Appeal Tribunal shall give to the appellant and the Registrar and to any opposing party not less than seven days' notice of the time and place appointed for the hearing of the appeal, unless the Appeal Tribunal expressly directs that shorter notice may be given.

**5A.—(1) A party to an appeal before the Appeal Tribunal may appear and be heard either in person or by a patent agent, a solicitor, or counsel.**

**(2) In this Rule—**

> **'counsel' means a member of the Bar of England or Wales or of Northern Ireland or a member of the Faculty of Advocates in Scotland; and**
> **'patent agent' has the same meaning as it has in the Patents Act 1949.**

*General note*
This rule was inserted by the Registered Designs Appeal Tribunal (Amendment) Rules 1950 [SI 1970 No 1075, r 5.]

**6.** The evidence used on appeal to the Appeal Tribunal shall be the same as that used before the Registrar and no further evidence shall be given, except with the leave of the Appeal Tribunal given upon application made for that purpose.

**7.** The regulations applicable to the filing of documentary evidence on proceedings before the Registrar shall apply to documentary evidence filed on an appeal to the Appeal Tribunal.

**8.** The Appeal Tribunal may, at the request of any party, order the attendance at the hearing for the purpose of cross-examination of any person who has made a declaration in the matter to which the appeal relates.

**9.** Any person requiring the attendance of a witness for cross-examination shall tender to the witness whose attendance is required a reasonable sum for conduct money.

**10.** The Appeal Tribunal may, in awarding costs, either fix the amount thereof or direct by whom and in what manner the amount of the costs is to be ascertained.

**11.** If any costs awarded are not paid within fourteen days after the amount thereof has been fixed or ascertained, or within such shorter period as may be directed by the Appeal Tribunal, the party to whom the costs are payable may apply to the Appeal Tribunal for an order for payment under the provisions of section 28(5) of the Act.

**12.** Any notice or other document required to be filed with or sent to the registrar of the Appeal Tribunal under these Rules may be sent by prepaid letter through the post.

**13.** The Interpretation Act 1889, shall apply to the interpretation of these Rules as it applies to the interpretation of an Act of Parliament.

**14.** These Rules may be cited as the Registered Designs Appeal Tribunal Rules 1950, and shall come into force on the first day of April, 1950.

SCHEDULE

*Notice of Appeal*

IN THE MATTER OF AN APPLICATION BY

FOR REGISTRATION (OR CANCELLATION OF REGISTRATION OR FOR A COMPULSORY LICENCE IN RESPECT) OF A DESIGN NO......................................................

I/We *(a)(Here insert name(s) and full address(s) of appellant(s)*

of

hereby give notice of appeal to the Appeal Tribunal from the decision of the *(b) here insert 'Comptroller-General' or 'Officer acting for Comptroller-General' as the case may be*

dated the                    day of                    19

whereby he *(c) State concisely the decision appealed against*

Signature *(d) To be signed by the appellant personally or by his duly authorised representative*

Address

Date

*Note—This notice must be sent to the registrar of the Registered Designs Appeal Tribunal, Room 174, Royal Courts of Justice, London, WC2, and must bear an impressed judicature fee stamp for £3. An unstamped copy of the notice must be sent to the Comptroller-General of Patents, Designs and Trade Marks at the Patent Office, 25, Southampton Buildings, London, WC2, and to any opponent(s).*

**Note—This notice must be sent to the Registrar of the Registered Designs Appeal Tribunal, Royal Courts of Justice, London, WC2A 2LL, and must bear an impressed judicature fee stamp for £6. An unstamped copy of the notice must be sent to the Comptroller-General of Patents, Designs and Trade Marks at the Patent Office, 25 Southampton Buildings, London, WC2, and to any person who appeared or gave notice of opposition on the proceedings from which the appeal is brought, within the period prescribed by the Registered Designs Appeal Tribunal Rules'.**

*General note*
The Note to this Schedule was substituted by the Registered Designs Appeals Tribunal (Amendment) Rules [SI 1970 No 1075, r 6.]

## REGISTERED DESIGNS APPEAL TRIBUNAL (FEES) ORDER 1973
(SI 1973 No 165)

> *Made* . . . . . . *1st February 1973*
> *Coming into operation.* . . . *1st March 1973*

The Lord Chancellor, the Judges of the Supreme Court and the Treasury, in exercise of the powers and authorities vested in them respectively by section 28(3) of the Registered Designs Act 1949, section 213 of the Supreme Court of Judicature (Consolidation) Act 1925 and section 2 of the Public Offices Fees Act 1879, do hereby, according as the provisions of the said enactments respectively authorise and require them, make, advise, consent to and concur in the following Order—

**1.**—(1) This Order may be cited as the Registered Designs Appeal Tribunal (Fees) Order 1973 and shall come into operation on 1st March 1973.

(2) In this Order, unless the context otherwise requires—

'Appeal Tribunal' means the Appeal Tribunal constituted under section 28(2) of the Registered Designs Act 1949, as amended by section 24 of the Administration of Justice Act 1969;

'Registrar' means the Registrar of the Appeal Tribunal;

a rule referred to by number means the rule so numbered in the Registered Designs Appeal Tribunal Rules 1950, as amended.

(3) The Interpretation Act 1889 shall apply to the interpretation of this Order as it applies to the interpretation of an Act of Parliament.

**2.** A fee of £6 shall be taken on the filing of every notice of appeal to the Appeal Tribunal under rule 1(1).

**3.** The fee fixed by this Order shall be taken in cash or, if the Registrar so permits, by cheque and the notice of appeal filed with the Registrar shall be marked by or on his behalf showing the amount of the fee and the date of its receipt.

**4.** Where it appears to the Lord Chancellor that the payment of any fee fixed by this Order would, owing to the exceptional circumstances of the particular case, involve undue hardship, the Lord Chancellor may reduce or remit the fee in that case.

**5.** The Patents and Registered Designs Appeal Tribunal Fees Order 1970 [SI 1970 No 529], insofar as it relates to the Appeal Tribunal is revoked.


## REGISTERED DESIGNS ACT 1949 (ISLE OF MAN) ORDER 1989
(SI 1989 No 982)

> *Made* . . . . . . *13th June 1989*
> *Coming into force* . . . . *1st August 1989*

Her Majesty, in pursuance of section 47 of the Registered Designs Act 1949, is pleased, by and with the advice of Her Privy Council, to order, and it is hereby ordered, as follows:

**1.** This Order may be cited as the Registered Designs Act 1949 (Isle of Man) Order 1989 and shall come into force on 1st August 1989.

**2.** The Registered Designs Act 1949 shall, as it has effect in the Isle of Man, be subject to the modifications specified in the Schedule to this Order.

SCHEDULE

MODIFICATIONS SUBJECT TO WHICH THE REGISTERED DESIGNS ACT 1949 HAS
EFFECT IN THE ISLE OF MAN

1.—(1) Any reference to an Act of Parliament (including the Registered Designs Act 1949) or to a provision of such an Act shall be construed, unless the contrary intention appears, as a reference to that Act or provision as it has effect in the Isle of Man.

(2) Notwithstanding section 47, any reference to the United Kingdom which occurs in the expression 'His Majesty's Government in the United Kingdom' does not include the Isle of Man.

(3) References to the Crown include the Crown in right of the Government of the Isle of Man.

(4) References to a Government department shall be construed as including references to a Department of the Government of the Isle of Man, and in relation to such a Department references to the Treasury shall be construed as references to the Treasury of the Isle of Man.

2. For section 27 substitute—

'27. In this Act 'the court' means Her Majesty's High Court of Justice of the Isle of Man.'.

3. In section 28(5), for paragraphs (a) and (b) substitute 'in the Isle of Man, in the same way as an execution issued out of the court'.

4. In section 30(2), for paragraphs (a) and (b) substitute 'in the Isle of Man, in the same way as an execution issued out of the court'.

5. In section 33(1)(a), for 'indictment' substitute 'information'.

6. In section 34(a), for 'indictment' substitute 'information'.

7. In section 44, after subsection (1) insert—

(1A) References in this section to the Copyright, Designs and Patents Act 1988 are to that Act as it has effect in England and Wales.'.

8. Omit sections 45 and 46.

*Appendix 2*

## REGISTERED DESIGNS RULES 1989
## (SI 1989 No 1105)

*(As amended by the Registered Designs (Amendment) Rules 1990 (SI 1990 No 1456))*

|  |  |  |
|---|---|---|
| *Made* . . . . . . | *29th June 1989* |
| *Laid before Parliament* . . | *10th July 1989* |
| *Coming into force* . . . . | *1st August 1989* |

**Arrangement of rules**

Preliminary

The Secretary of State, in the exercise of the powers conferred upon him by sections 1(5), 3(1), (4) and (6), 5(2), 6(6), 8(3), 8A(1) and (3), 11(1), 17(1), (5) and (6), 18(1), 19(1) and (2), 20(3), and (4), 22(2), 29, 30(1) and (3), 31, 32(1)and (1A), 39(1) and 44(1) of the Registered Designs Act 1949 and after consultation with the Council on Tribunals pursuant to section 10(1) of the Tribunals and Inquiries Act 1971, hereby makes the following Rules:

## *Preliminary*

### Citation and commencement
**1.** These Rules may be cited as the Registered Designs Rules 1989 and shall come into force on 1st August 1989.

### Interpretation
**2.** In these Rules, unless the context otherwise requires—

> 'the Act' means the Registered Designs Act 1949 and 'section' means a section of the Act;
> 'convention application' means an application in the United Kingdom under section 14;
> 'Journal' means the Official Journal (Patents) published by the Comptroller-General of Patents, Designs and Trade Marks under the Patents Act 1977;
> 'register' means the register of designs kept under section 17;
> 'specimen' means an article with the design applied to it;

'textile article' means textile and plastics piece goods, handkerchiefs, shawls and such other classes of articles of a similar character as the registrar may from time to time decide, for which the protection required is limited to features of pattern and ornament only;

'United Kingdom' includes the Isle of Man.

**3.** (Revokes the Designs Rules 1984, [SI 1984 No 1989] the Designs (Amendment) Rules 1987, [SI 1987 No 287] and the Designs (Amendment) Rules 1988,[SI 1988 No 2088]).

## Forms
**4.**—(1) The forms mentioned in these Rules are those set out in Schedule 1 to these Rules.

(2) A requirement under these Rules to use a form set out in Schedule 1 to these Rules is satisfied by the use either of a replica of that form or of a form which contains the information required by the form set out in the said Schedule and which is acceptable to the registrar.

## *Documents*

### Size and presentation of documents
**5.** Subject to any directions that may be given by the registrar in any particular case, all applications, notices, papers having representations affixed, and other documents filed under the Act or these Rules shall be upon strong paper and, except where otherwise required, on one side only, of a size approximately 297 mm by 210 mm (11¾ inches by 8¼ inches) or approximately 330 mm by 200 mm to 210 mm (13 inches by 8 inches to 8¼ inches) and having on the left hand part thereof a margin of approximately 50 mm (2 inches).

### Signature of documents
**6.**—(1) This rule applies to any notice, application or other document required or authorised by the Act or these Rules to be given, made or filed at the Patent Office and such a notice, application or other document is referred to in the following paragraphs of this rule as a 'document'.

(2) A document filed by or on behalf of a firm which is concerned in any proceedings to which these Rules relate as principal and not as an agent shall contain the names of all the partners in full and shall be signed by all the partners, by any partner stating that he signs on behalf of the firm (or, in the case of a firm formed under the law of Scotland, by any partner in the firm's name) or by any other person who satisfies the registrar that he is authorised to sign the document.

(3) A document signed for or on behalf of a body corporate shall be signed by a director or the secretary or other principal officer of the body or by any other person who satisfies the registrar that he is authorised to sign the document.

(4) A document signed for or on behalf of an unincorporated body or association of persons other than a firm may be signed by any person who satisfies the registrar that he is authorised to sign the document.

### Service of documents
**7.** Any notice, application or other document sent to the Patent Office by posting it in the United Kingdom shall be deemed to have been given, made or filed at the time when the letter containing it would be delivered in the ordinary course of post.

## *Address*

### Address for service
**8.**—(1) Every person concerned in any proceedings to which these Rules relate and every person registered as proprietor of, or as having an interest in, a registered design shall furnish to the registrar an address for service in the United Kingdom and that address may be treated for all purposes connected with such proceedings or such registered design as the address of that person.

(2) Such address shall, in the case of a registered proprietor, be entered on the register as the address for service of such proprietor.

### Failure to provide address for service
**9.** Where an address for service in the United Kingdom has not been furnished to the registrar by an applicant in any proceedings to which these Rules relate, the registrar need not proceed with the examination of the application until such an address has been furnished to him.

## *Agents*

### Appointment of agents
**10.**—(1) Unless the registrar otherwise directs in any particular case, anything required or authorised by these Rules to be done by or in relation to any person may be done by, or in relation to, his agent.

(2) Where after a person has become a party to proceedings before the registrar he appoints an agent for the first time, or appoints one agent in substitution for another, the newly appointed agent shall file Designs Form 1A in duplicate on or before the first occasion when he acts as agent.

## *Applications for registration*

### *Recognition of agents*
*11. The registrar may refuse to recognise as agent in respect of any business under the Act—*

*(a)  any individual whose name has been erased from, and not restored to, the register of patents agents kept in pursuance of rules made under the Patents Act 1977 or who is for the time being suspended from acting as a patent agent; or*

*(b)  any person who is found by the Secretary of State to have beeen convicted of any offence or to have been guilty of any such misconduct as, in the case of an individual registered in the register of patents agents aforesaid, would render him liable to have his name erased from it; or*

*(c)  any company or firm, if any person whom the registrar could refuse to recognise as agent in respect of any business under the Act is acting as a director or manager of the company or is a partner in the firm.*

*General note*
This rule was revoked by The Registered Designs (Amendment) Rules 1990 [SI 1990 No 1456.]

### Form for applications
**12.** Applications to register designs shall be made on Designs Form 2A.

## Application for same design in respect of more than one article

**13.** Where it is desired to register the same design in respect of more than one article other than sets of articles, a separate application shall be made in respect of each article and each application shall be numbered separately and shall be treated as a separate and distinct application.

## Article to which design is applied

**14.**—(1) Every application shall state the article to which the design is to be applied and that the applicant claims to be the proprietor of the design in relation to that article.

(2) If any question arises as to whether an article to which a design is to be applied is made substantially of lace or as to whether a design to be applied to a textile article consists substantially of checks or stripes, it shall be decided by the registrar.

## Statement of novelty on representations or specimens

**15.**—(1) Except in the case of an application to register the pattern or ornament of a design to be applied to a textile article, to wallpaper or similar wall covering or to lace or to sets of textile articles or lace, a statement satisfactory to the registrar of the features of the design for which novelty is claimed shall appear on each representation or specimen of the design.

(2) The statement referred to in paragraph (1) above shall appear on the front of the first sheet only of each representation or specimen (except where the registrar is satisfied that this is impracticable in which case it shall appear in a place satisfactory to the registrar) and it shall be separate from any other statement or disclaimer.

## Registration of same design in respect of other articles, etc

**16.** If the application is for the registration of a design which has already been registered or applied for in respect of one or more articles, or consists of a design already registered or applied for with modifications or variations not sufficient to alter the character or substantially to affect the identity thereof, and it is desired to claim the protection of section 4 for such application, it shall contain the number or numbers of the registration or registrations already effected or the application or applications already made.

## *Representations and specimens*

## Supply of representations and specimens

**17.** Except as regards applications for registration of designs to be applied to sets of articles, there shall be furnished in connection with an application four identical representations of the design, in a form satisfactory to the registrar, or four specimens. Where representations are supplied the registrar may at any time before registration require specimens or additional representations.

## Representations and specimens for sets of articles

**18.**—(1) There shall be furnished in connection with an application for the registration of a design to be applied to a set of articles five identical representations of the design in a form satisfactory to the registrar, or five specimens.

(2) The representations shall show the design as applied to each different article included in the set.

## Size and presentation of representations

**19.**—(1) Each representation of the design, whether to be applied to a single article or to a set of articles, shall be upon paper of the size prescribed by rule 5 above and not on cardboard, and shall appear on one side only of the paper. The figure or figures shall be placed in an upright position on the sheet except where the registrar is satisfied that it is impracticable. When more figures than one are shown, these shall where reasonably practicable be on one and the same sheet, and each shall be designated perspective view, front view, side view, plan or otherwise as the case may be.

(2) Each sheet shall bear in the top left hand corner the name of the applicant and in the top right hand corner the number of sheets comprising the representation and the consecutive number of each sheet.

## Drawings or tracings

**20.** When the representations furnished are drawings or tracings they shall be in ink and if on tracing cloth or tracing paper shall be mounted on paper of the size prescribed by rule 5 above.

## Replacement of specimens by representations

**21.** When specimens are furnished and are not, in the registrar's opinion, of a kind which can be conveniently mounted in a flat position by means of an adhesive upon paper or by stitching on linen-backed sheets of paper of the size prescribed by rule 5 above and stored without damage to other documents, representations shall be furnished in place of specimens.

## Words, letters or numerals

**22.** In an application where words, letters or numerals appear in the design, the registrar may require that a disclaimer of any right to their exclusive use shall appear on each representation or specimen.

## Repeating surface patterns

**23.** Each representation or specimen of a design which consists of a repeating surface pattern shall show the complete pattern and a sufficient portion of the repeat in length and width, and shall not be of less size than 180 mm by 130 mm (7 inches by 5 inches).

## Use of portrait of a member of the Royal Family or armorial bearings, etc

**24.** Where a portrait of Her Majesty or of any member of the Royal Family, or a reproduction of the armorial bearings, insignia, orders of chivalry, decorations or flags of any country, city, borough, town, place, society, body corporate, institution or person appears on a design, the registrar, before proceeding to register the design, shall, if he so requires, be furnished with a consent to the registration and use of such portrait or reproduction from such official or other person as appears to the registrar to be entitled to give consent, and in default of such consent he may refuse to register the design.

## Use of portrait of living or recently dead person

**25.** Where the name or portrait of a living person appears on a design, the registrar shall be furnished, if he so requires, with consent from such person before proceeding to register the design and, in the case of a person recently dead, the registrar may call for consent from his personal representative before proceeding with the registration of a design on which the name or portrait of the deceased person appears.

## *Designs excluded from registration under section 1(5)*

### Exclusion of designs to be applied to certain articles

**26.**—There shall be excluded from registration under the Act designs to be applied to any of the following articles, namely—

(1) works of sculpture, other than casts or models used or intended to be used as models or patterns to be multiplied by any industrial process;

(2) wall plaques, medals and medallions;

(3) printed matter primarily of a literary or artistic character, including book jackets, calendars, certificates, coupons, dress-making patterns, greetings cards, labels, leaflets, maps, plans, playing cards, postcards, stamps, trade advertisements, trade forms and cards, transfers and similar articles.

## *Convention applications*

### Declarations

**27.** An application for registration under section 14 shall contain a declaration that the application in a convention country upon which the applicant relies is the first application made in a convention country in respect of the design, whether by the applicant or by any person of whom he claims to be the personal representative or assignee, and shall specify the convention country in which such foreign application was made, or is to be deemed under section 14(4) to have been made, and the official date thereof.

### Copies and translations

**28.**—(1) In addition to the representations or specimens filed with every convention application there shall be filed with the application, or within three months thereafter, a copy of the representation of the design filed or deposited in respect of the first application in a convention country, duly certified by the authority with which it was filed or otherwise verified to the satisfaction of the registrar.

(2) If any certificate or other document relating to the application is in a language other than English, a translation thereof into English verified to the satisfaction of the registrar as corresponding to the original text shall be annexed thereto.

## *Procedure on receipt of application*

### Statement of objections by registrar

**29.** If upon consideration there appears to the registrar to be any objection to the application, a statement of those objections shall be sent to the applicant in writing, and unless within two months thereafter the applicant applies for a hearing or makes observations in writing on those objections, he shall be deemed to have withdrawn his application.

**Decision of registrar to be communicated in writing**
**30.** If the applicant applies for a hearing, the decision of the registrar at the hearing shall be communicated to the applicant in writing, together with an indication in general terms of the grounds for that decision.

**Appeal from registrar's decision**
**31.** If the applicant desires to appeal from the registrar's decision, he shall within one month from the date of the decision apply to the registrar, upon Designs Form 7, requesting him to state in writing the grounds of, and the materials used by him in arriving at, his decision. Upon receipt of such application, the registrar shall send to the applicant a statement as aforesaid in writing and the date when the statement is sent shall be deemed to be the date of the registrar's decision for the purpose of an appeal.

*Certificate of registration*

**Form of certificate**
**32.** The certificate of registration of a design shall be in the form set out in Schedule 2 to these Rules, provided always that, in the case of a design which is registered under the provisions of section 4 in association with a design which has been previously registered, the certificate shall contain a statement that the design has been registered in association with that previously registered design.

**Copy of certificate**
**33.** An application under section 18(2) for a copy of a certificate of registration shall be made on Designs Form 6 and, where the original certificate has been lost, destroyed or otherwise cannot be produced, shall be accompanied by evidence setting out in full and verifying the circumstances in which the original certificate was lost, destroyed or cannot be produced. An application for a copy of a certificate made for any other reason shall be accompanied by a statement as to why the applicant considers it expedient for a copy to be furnished to him and shall be supported by such evidence as the registrar shall require.

*Novelty of designs*

**Deemed application date under section 3(4)**
**34.**—(1) For the purpose of deciding whether a design is new the registrar may direct—

    (a) that an application for the registration of a design, which has been amended in such a way that the appearance of the design has been altered significantly, shall be treated as having been made on the date on which it was so amended; or

    (b) that, where an application for the registration of a design disclosed more than one design and has been amended so as to exclude one or more designs from the application, a subsequent application for the registration of a design so excluded made by the person who made the earlier application or his successor in title shall be treated as having been made on the date on which the earlier application was made or is treated as having been made, provided always that the later application is filed before the end of the period provided by rule 36 below for the completion of the earlier application (including any extension of time allowed under the said rule 36) or the date on which the certificate of registration of the design which is the subject of the earlier application (as amended) is granted, whichever is the earlier.

(2) Nothing in paragraph (1)(a) of this rule shall be taken to limit the discretion of the registrar to decline to accept an amendment of an application for the registration of a design.

### Industrial application of designs
**35.** A design shall be regarded for the purposes of section 6 as 'applied industrially' if it is applied—

(a) to more than fifty articles which do not all together constitute a single set of articles as defined in section 44(1); or
(b) to goods manufactured in lengths or pieces, not being hand-made goods.

## *Non-completion*

### Time limits
**36.** The time prescribed for the purposes of section 3(6), which relates to non-completion of an application, shall be twelve months from the date of the application:

Provided that the application may be completed at any time after twelve months but within fifteen months of the date aforesaid, if a request for an extension of time is made on Designs Form 8 accompanied by the prescribed fee.

## *Death of applicant*

### Substitution
**37.** In the case of the death of any applicant for the registration of a design after the date of his application, and before registration of the design has been effected, the registrar may, on being satisfied of the applicant's death, enter in the register, in place of the name and address of such deceased applicant, the name and address of the person owning the design, on such ownership being proved to the satisfaction of the registrar.

## *Extension of duration of right in registered design*

### Extension for further periods of five years
**38.**—(1) An application for extension of the period for which the right in a registered design subsists for a further period of five years shall be made on Designs Form 9A not more than three months before the expiry of the period of five years immediately preceding that further period.

(2) On receipt of the prescribed extension fee accompanied by Designs Form 9A, duly completed, the registrar shall issue a certificate of extension of the period for which the right in the registered design subsists.

### Notice of expiry of the right in a registered design
**39.**—(1) Where the right in a registered design has expired under section 8(3), the registrar shall, not later than six weeks after the date on which the right expired (and if an application for extension of the period for which the right subsists has

still not been received by the registrar), send to the registered proprietor of the design a notice of that fact.

(2) This rule does not apply to the right in a design registered in pursuance of an application made before 1st August 1989.

### Late extensions
**40.** An application for extension of the period for which the right in a registered design subsists for a further period of five years made during the period of six months immediately following the end of a five year period shall be made on Designs Form 9A.

### Restoration of lapsed right in a design under section 8A
**41.**—(1) An application under section 8A may be made within twelve months from the date on which the right in the registered design expired.

(2) Any such application shall be made on Designs Form 29 and shall be supported by evidence in support of the statements made in that application.

(3) The registrar shall enter in the register notice of the application and shall publish such notice in the Journal.

(4) If, upon consideration of the evidence, the registrar is not satisfied that a case for an order under section 8A has been made out, he shall notify the applicant accordingly and, unless within two months the applicant requests to be heard in the matter, the registrar shall refuse the application.

(5) If the applicant requests a hearing within the time allowed, the registrar shall, after giving the applicant an opportunity of being heard, determine whether the application shall be allowed or refused.

(6) If the registrar decides to allow the application, he shall notify the applicant accordingly and require him to file Designs Form 30, together with Designs Form 9A, duly completed, and the amount of the unpaid extension fee and the prescribed restoration fee, upon receipt of which the registrar shall order the restoration of the right in the design and advertise the fact in the Journal.

(7) If the registrar decides to refuse the application he shall notify the applicant accordingly, giving written reasons for his decision if so required by the applicant.

(8) This rule does not apply to the right in a design registered in pursuance of an application made before 1st August 1989.

### *Registration of assignments, etc*

### Procedure for application for registration
**42.**—(1) An application under section 19(1) or (2) for the registration of the title of any person becoming entitled by assignment, transmission or operation of law to a registered design or to a share in a registered design, or becoming entitled as mortgagee, licensee or otherwise to any interest in a registered design shall be made on Designs Form 12A.

(2) Application may be made on Designs Form 12A for entry in the register of notification of any other transaction, event or document purporting to affect the proprietorship of a registered design.

### Filing of certified copies
**43.** A certified copy of any document which is referred to in an application under rule 42 above shall be filed with the application.

**Particulars to be provided**
**44.** An application under rule 42(1) above shall contain the name and address of the person claiming or stated to be entitled together with full particulars of the transaction, event or document under which title is claimed or given.

**Cancellation of claim to be mortgagee or licensee**
**45.** Where the name of a person is entered in the register as mortgagee or licensee, such person may on making an application for the purpose on Designs Form 12A have a note entered in the register that he no longer claims to be mortgagee or licensee, as the case may be.

**Alteration of name or address**
**46.**—(1) A request by any person upon the alteration of his name for that alteration to be entered in the register or on any application or other document filed at the Patent Office shall be made on Designs Form 16.

(2) Before acting on a request to alter a name, the registrar may require such proof of the alteration as he thinks fit.

(3) A request by any person for the alteration or correction of his address or address for service entered in the register or on any application or other document filed at the Patent Office shall be made in writing.

(4) Where any person files a form under these Rules and on that form he specifies as his address or address for service an address which differs from the address or address for service (as the case may be) which he has previously furnished to the registrar, he shall be deemed, in relation to the design to which the form relates, to have made a request in writing under paragraph (3) above in respect of any address or address for service of his (as the case may be) entered in the register and on any application or other document filed at the Patent Office.

(5) If the registrar is satisfied that the request to alter a name, address or address for service may be allowed, he shall cause the register, application or other document to be altered accordingly.

*Correction of errors*

**Request for correction**
**47.** Where a person interested desires, under the provisions of section 21, to correct an error, he shall make his request on Designs Form 18 (unless the error relates to his address or address for service).

*Discretionary powers*

**Exercise of discretionary powers of registrar**
**48.**—(1) Without prejudice to any provisions of the Act or these Rules requiring the registrar to hear any party to proceedings under the Act, or to give any such party an opportunity to be heard, the registrar shall, before exercising any discretion vested in him by or under the Act adversely to any party to a proceeding before him, give that party an opportunity to be heard.

(2) The registrar shall give that party at least fourteen days' notice of the time when he may be heard unless that party consents to shorter notice.

## *Dispensation power*

### Registrar's power to dispense from Rules
**49.** Where under these Rules any person is required to do any act or thing, or any document or evidence is required to be produced or filed and it is shown to the satisfaction of the registrar that from any reasonable cause that person is unable to do that act or thing, or that document or evidence cannot be produced or filed the registrar may, upon the production of such evidence and subject to such terms as he thinks fit, dispense with the doing of any such act or thing, or the production or filing of that document or evidence.

## *Amendments*

### Registrar's power to allow amendments and rectify irregularities in procedure
**50.** If the registrar thinks fit any document or drawing or other representation of a design may be amended, and any irregularity in procedure may be rectified, on such terms as the registrar may direct.

## *Extension of time*

### Registrar's power to extend times prescribed by Rules
**51.** The times or periods prescribed by these Rules for doing any act or taking any proceeding thereunder, other than the period prescribed in rule 41(1) above, may be extended by the registrar if he thinks fit, upon such notice and upon such terms as he may direct, and such extension may be granted although the time or period for doing such act or taking such proceeding has already expired.

## *Application for compulsory licence under section 10 or cancellation of registration of design under section 11(2) or (3)*

### Procedure for application
**52.**—(1) An application for the grant of a compulsory licence under section 10 or for the cancellation of the registration of a design under section 11(2) or (3) shall be made on Designs Form 25A. Such application shall be accompanied by a copy thereof and a statement in duplicate setting out fully the nature of the applicant's interest and the facts upon which he relies.

(2) A copy of the application and the statement of case shall be sent by the registrar to the registered proprietor.

### Opposition by registered proprietor
**53.** If the registered proprietor desires to oppose the application he shall, within such time as the registrar may allow, file a counter-statement fully setting out the grounds on which the application is to be opposed and shall send to the applicant a copy thereof.

### Evidence of applicant
**54.** The applicant may, within such time as the registrar may allow after receipt of the counter-statement, file evidence in support of his case and shall send to the registered proprietor a copy of any evidence so filed.

**Evidence of registered proprietor and evidence in reply**
**55.**—(1) Within such time as the registrar may allow, the registered proprietor may file evidence in support of his case and shall send to the applicant a copy thereof.

(2) Following receipt of the copy from the registered proprietor and within such time as the registrar may allow, the applicant may file evidence confined to matters strictly in reply and shall send to the registered proprietor a copy thereof.

**Prohibition on further evidence**
**56.** No further evidence shall be filed by either party except by leave or direction of the registrar.

**Procedure for hearing**
**57.**—(1) On completion of the evidence, if any, or at such other time as he may see fit, the registrar shall appoint a time for the hearing of the case, and shall give the parties at least fourteen days' notice of the appointment.

(2) If either party desires to be heard he shall give notice in writing of that fact to the registrar and the registrar may refuse to hear a party who has not given him such notice prior to the date of the hearing.

(3) The hearing before the registrar of any dispute between two or more parties relating to any matter in connection with a registered design shall be in public unless the registrar, after consultation with those parties to the dispute who appear in person or are represented at the hearing, otherwise directs.

(4) Nothing in this rule shall prevent a member of the Council on Tribunals or of its Scottish Committee from attending a hearing in his capacity as such.

*Cancellation under section 11(1)*

**Request for cancellation**
**58.** Where the registered proprietor of a design desires to cancel his registration, he shall request such cancellation on Designs Form 19.

*Licences of right*

**Application to settle terms of licence of right**
**59.**—(1) An application to settle the terms of a licence under section 11A(4) of the Act or section 266(2) of the Copyright, Designs and Patents Act 1988 shall be made on Designs Form 31 and shall be accompanied by a copy thereof and a statement in duplicate setting out the terms of the licence which the applicant requires the registrar to settle.

(2) Within fourteen days of the receipt of Designs Form 31 the registrar shall send a copy of it, together with a copy of the applicant's statement, to the registered proprietor.

(3) The registered proprietor shall, if he does not agree to the terms of the licence set out in the applicant's statement, within six weeks of the receipt of the copies referred to in paragraph (2) above serve a notice of objection on the registrar with a statement setting out the grounds of his objection and at the same time shall serve a copy of the same on the applicant.

(4) Within four weeks of the receipt of the notice of objection the applicant may serve on the registrar a counter-statement, and at the same time shall serve a copy of the same on the registered proprietor.

(5) No amended statement or further statement shall be served by either party except by leave or direction of the registrar.

(6) The registrar may give such directions as he may think fit with regard to the subsequent procedure.

## *Costs*

### Costs of proceedings

**60.**—(1) The registrar may, in any proceedings before him under the Act, by order award to any party such costs as he may consider reasonable, and direct how and by what parties they are to be paid.

(2) In the event of an application for the grant of a compulsory licence or for the cancellation of the registration of a design being uncontested by the registered proprietor, the registrar in deciding whether costs should be awarded to the applicant shall consider whether proceedings might have been avoided if reasonable notice had been given by the applicant to the registered proprietor before the application was filed.

### Security for costs

**61.**—(1) If a person neither resides nor carries on business in the United Kingdom or another member State of the European Economic Community, the registrar may require him to give security for the costs of any application or appeal falling within section 30(3).

(2) In default of such security being given, the registrar, in the case of an application, or the Appeal Tribunal, in the case of an appeal, may treat the application or appeal as abandoned.

## *Evidence before registrar*

### Evidence

**62.**—(1) Where under these Rules evidence may be filed, it shall be by statutory declaration or affidavit.

(2) The registrar may if he thinks fit in any particular case take oral evidence in lieu of or in addition to such evidence and shall allow any witness to be cross-examined on his statutory declaration, affidavit or oral evidence, unless he directs otherwise.

(3) The registrar shall in relation to the examination of witnesses on oath and the discovery and production of documents have all the powers of an official referee of the Supreme Court.

(4) The rules applicable to the attendance of witnesses before such a referee shall apply in relation to the attendance of witnesses in proceedings before the registrar.

### Form and content of statutory declaration or affidavit

**63.**—(1) The statutory declarations and affidavits required by these Rules, or used in any proceedings thereunder, shall be headed in the matter or matters to which they relate, and shall be divided into paragraphs consecutively numbered, and each paragraph shall, so far as possible, be confined to one subject.

(2) Every statutory declaration or affidavit shall state the description and true place of abode of the person making the same, and shall be written, typed, lithographed or printed.

**Making and subscription of statutory declaration or affidavit**
**64.**—(1) Any statutory declaration or affidavit filed under the Act or these Rules shall be made and subscribed as follows—

(a) in the United Kingdom, before any justice of the peace or any commissioner or other officer authorised by law in any part of the United Kingdom to administer an oath for the purpose of any legal proceedings;

(b) in any other part of Her Majesty's dominions or in the Republic of Ireland, before any court, judge, justice of the peace or any officer authorised by law to administer an oath there for the purpose of any legal proceedings; and

(c) elsewhere, before a British Minister, or person exercising the functions of a British Minister, or a Consul, Vice-Consul or other person exercising the functions of a British Consul or before a notary public, judge or magistrate.

(2) Any document purporting to have affixed, impressed or subscribed thereto or thereon the seal or signature of any person authorised by paragraph (1) above to take a declaration may be admitted by the registrar without proof of the genuineness of the seal or signature, or of the official character of the person or his authority to take the declaration.

**Registrar's power to require documents, information or evidence**
**65.** At any stage of any proceedings before the registrar, he may direct that such documents, information or evidence as he may require shall be filed within such period as he may fix.

*Advisers*

**Registrar's power to appoint advisers**
**66.** The registrar may appoint an adviser to assist him in any proceedings before the registrar and shall settle the question or instructions to be submitted or given to such adviser.

*Inspection of register and documents*

**Inspection by public**
**67.** The register (or the material on the register) and the material available for inspection pursuant to section 22 shall be made available for inspection by the public on payment of the prescribed fee between the hours of 10.00 am and 4.00 pm on weekdays, other than Saturdays and days which are specified as excluded days for the purposes of section 39.

**Direction by registrar under section 5(1)**
**68.** Where the registrar has given a direction under section 5(1) prohibiting or restricting the publication of a design, the representation or specimen of the design and any such evidence as is mentioned in section 5(2)(b) shall not be open to public inspection while such direction remains in force.

**Prohibition on inspection under section 22(2)**
**69.** The period under section 22(2) during which a design shall not be open to inspection, except as provided in that section, shall be, as regards designs to be

applied to textile articles, three years and as regards designs to be applied to wallpaper and similar wall covering and lace, two years from the date of the registration thereof.

## *Searches*

### Procedure when registration number known
**70.** Where any person desires to obtain the information which he is entitled to obtain under section 23 and can furnish the registration number of the design, he shall make his request on Designs Form 20 and the registrar shall thereafter furnish him with the information aforesaid.

### Procedure when registration number unknown or general search
**71.** The registrar shall, upon a request for the purpose made on Designs Form 21, accompanied by a representation or specimen (in duplicate) of the design applied to an article, cause such search as may be reasonably practicable to be made among registered designs and state whether the design as applied to that article appears to be identical with, or closely to resemble, any registered design applied to that or any other article, and shall furnish such information as can properly be given.

## *Certificates and copies supplied by registrar*

### Certificates supplied by registrar
**72.** Upon request made on Designs Form 23 and payment of the appropriate fee—

    (a)  the registrar shall supply a certified copy of an entry in the register or a certified extract from the register; and

    (b)  the registrar may supply—

        (i)  a certified copy of any representation, specimen or document kept in the Patent Office or a certified extract from any such document; or

        (ii)  a certificate for the purposes of section 17(9).

### Copies supplied by registrar
**73.** Upon request and payment of the appropriate fee—

    (a)  the registrar shall supply an uncertified copy of an entry in the register or an uncertified extract from the register; and

    (b)  the registrar may supply an uncertified copy of any representation or document kept in the Patent Office or an uncertified extract from any such document.

## *Hours of business and excluded days*

### Hours of business
**74.** The Patent Office shall be deemed to be closed at the following hours for the transaction of business of the classes specified—

    (a)  on weekdays, other than Saturdays, at midnight for the filing of applications, forms and other documents, and at 4.00 pm for all other business,

    (b)  on Saturdays, at 1.00 pm for the filing of new applications for the registration of designs which are not convention applications.

**Excluded days**

**75.**—(1) The following shall be excluded days for all purposes under the Act:

    (a) all Sundays;

    (b) Good Friday and Christmas Day;

    (c) any day specified as or proclaimed to be a bank holiday in England in or under section 1 of the Banking and Financial Dealings Act 1971;

    (d) any Saturday immediately preceded by a day falling within sub-paragraph (b) or (c) above.

(2) Saturdays not falling within paragraph (1) above shall be excluded days for all purposes except the filing of new applications for the registration of designs which are not convention applications.

**Calculation of times or periods**

**76.**—(1) Where, on any day, there is—

    (a) a general interruption or subsequent dislocation in the postal services of the United Kingdom, or

    (b) an event or circumstances causing an interruption in the normal operation of the Patent Office,

the registrar may certify the day as being one on which there is an 'interruption' and, where any period of time specified in the Act or these Rules for the giving, making or filing of any notice, application or other document expires on a day so certified the period shall be extended to the first day next following (not being an excluded day) which is not so certified.

(2) Any certificate of the registrar given pursuant to this rule shall be posted in the Patent Office.

(3) Where in connection with an application for the registration of a design the period of time referred to in rule 34(1)(b) above or the period of six months after the opening of an exhibition referred to in section 6(2) ends on a day which is certified by the registrar for the purposes of paragraph (1) above or which is an excluded day for the purposes of section 39, the application shall be treated as having been made within the relevant period if it is made on the first following day which is neither so certified nor an excluded day.

(4) If in any particular case the registrar is satisfied that the failure to give, make or file any notice, application or other document within—

    (a) any period of time specified in the Act or these Rules for such giving, making or filing,

    (b) the period of six months specified in section 6(2) or 14(1), or

    (c) the period of time referred to in rule 34(1)(b) above,

was wholly or mainly attributable to a failure or undue delay in the postal services in the United Kingdom, the registrar may, if he thinks fit—

    (i) in the case of a period of time falling within sub-paragraph (a) above, extend the period so that it ends on the day of the receipt by the addressee of the notice, application or other document (or, if the day of such receipt is an excluded day, on the first following day which is not an excluded day), or

    (ii) in the case of the said periods of six months or the period of time referred to in rule 34(1)(b) above, determine that the application shall be treated as having been made within the relevant period,

in each case upon such notice to other parties and upon such terms as he may direct.

501

## *Orders of the court*

### Service of application on registrar
**77.** Where application to the court under section 20 for rectification of the register has been made, the applicant shall forthwith serve an office copy of the application on the registrar, who shall enter a notice of the application in the register.

### Filing of order with registrar
**78.** Where an order has been made by the court in any case under the Act, the person in whose favour such order has been made shall forthwith file Designs Form 28 accompanied by an office copy of the order. The register shall, if necessary, thereupon be rectified by the making of any entry therein or the variation or deletion of any entry therein.

## SCHEDULE

## GENERAL FORMS

**List of Forms**

| | |
|---|---|
| 1A | Appointment or change of agent. |
| 2A | Application for registration of a design. |
| 6 | Application for a copy of a certificate of registration of a design. |
| 7 | Request to the registrar for statement of grounds of decision under rule 31. |
| 8 | Request for extension of time to complete an application for the registration of a design. |
| 9A | Application to extend period of protection. |
| 12A | Application to register an assignment, licence, mortgage or other event affecting the rights in a registered design. |
| 16 | Application to record alteration of name. |
| 18 | Request for correction of error. |
| 19 | Request by proprietor of design to cancel registration. |
| 20 | Request for information under section 23 on supply of registration number. |
| 21 | Request for search when registration number is not supplied. |
| 23 | Request for certificate of the registrar. |
| 25A | Application for grant of a compulsory licence under section 10 or for cancellation of the registration under section 11(2) or (3). |
| 28 | Notification of order of the court. |
| 29 | Application for restoration of a lapsed right in a design. |
| 30 | Fee for restoration of a registered design. |
| 31 | Application for settlement of the terms of a licence of right. |

# Patent Office
### The

**Designs Form 1A**

**Appointment or
Change of Agent**

For Official Use

Registered
Designs Act 1949

## Notes

Please file this form in duplicate.
Please type, or write in dark ink using
BLOCK LETTERS. A fee is not required
for this form.

Rule 10 of the Registered Designs
Rules 1989 is the main rule governing
the completion and filing of this form.

This form may be used for more than
one design if the same authorisation
has been given. If you do not have
enough space, please use a separate
sheet of paper.

This form is for use only where, after a
person has become a party to
proceedings before the Registrar he
appoints an agent for the first time or
appoints one agent in substitution for
another.

This form is to be completed by the
newly appointed agent and filed in
duplicate. Where the agent has been
appointed in substitution for another,
the duplicate will be sent to the
original agent.

Please mark correct box.

**Please sign here** ➤

1. Your reference.

2. Please give Design Application or Registered Design number(s)

3. Please give full name and address of applicant or registered proprietor.
Name

Address

Postcode

ADP number (if known)

4. Please give your name and address in the United Kingdom.
Name

Address

Postcode

ADP number (if known)

5. Have you been authorised to act in all matters relating to the above
application/registered design?

Yes  No

If 'No' please give details of the extent of your appointment.

6. I declare that I/we have been appointed by the person(s) named at 3
above to act as agent as detailed in 5 above.

Signed ———————————————————— Date ——————

day  month  year

Revised 1989

503

The
**Patent
Office**

**Designs Form 2A**

**Application for
Registration of a
Design**

For Official Use

Registered
Designs Act 1949

## Notes

Please type, or write in dark ink using BLOCK LETTERS. For details of prescribed fees please contact the Designs Registry at the Patent Office.

Rules 6, 12 to 14 and 16 of the Registered Designs Rules 1989 are the main rules governing the completion and filing of this form.

If you do not have enough space, please use a separate sheet of paper.

❷ Please enter the names of each applicant. Names of individuals should be entered in full and the surname or family name should be underlined. The names of all partners in a firm must be given in full. Corporate bodies should be designated by their corporate name.

❹ Applicants resident abroad **must** provide a United Kingdom address.

❺ Please mark appropriate box(es). For a definition of textile articles please see Rule 2 of the Registered Design Rules 1989.

❻ Please name concisely the specific article as shown in the representations for which protection is required.

1. Your reference.

2. Please give full name(s) and address(es) of applicant(s).

Name

Address

Postcode

ADP number (if known)

3. If you are a corporate body please give country of incorporation.

State of incorporation (if appropriate)

4. Please give the name of your agent (if applicable).

Please give an address for service in the United Kingdom to which all correspondence will be sent.

Postcode

ADP number (if known)

5. Are you applying for registration of a design applied to:

a single article? ☐

or to a set of articles? ☐

Is the design to be applied to:

a single article made substantially of lace or is it a design consisting substantially of checks or stripes to be applied to a single textile article? ☐

or to any other article? ☐

6. What article is the design to be applied to?

Revised 1989    Please turn over ⇌

This form should be accompanied by **four** (**five** in respect of a set of articles) identical representations or specimens of the design. Except in the case of an application for a design applied to lace, a textile article or wallpaper (or similar wall covering) each representation or specimen should carry a statement of the features of the design for which novelty is claimed. If words, letters or numerals appear in the design, the Registrar will normally require a disclaimer of any right to their exclusive use to appear on each representation or specimen.

**❾** An application claiming priority under Section 14 of the Registered Designs Act 1949 must be filed in the UK within 6 months of the first filing of the design in any Convention country.

**❿** This part only applies if the application is made by virtue of Section 14 of the Registered Designs Act 1949.

Please enter details of instrument. For example, Deed of Assignment, with name(s) and date(s)

7. If an identical design has been previously registered or applied for in the United Kingdom in respect of another article please give its Design number.

8. If the design possesses modifications or variations not sufficient to alter the character or substantially to affect the identity of a design already registered or applied for in the United Kingdom please enter that design's number.

9. If you wish to claim priority from a previous application filed in a Convention country so that this application is treated as made on the date of the previous application, please give:

Name of country

Date of previous application _____

day   month   year

10. If the original application in the Convention country was made by someone other than yourself please explain how your right to apply for registration in the United Kingdom was acquired. (If this information is not given at the time of filing this form it must be supplied prior to registration of the design.)

## Declaration

This application is made to register the design shown in the representation(s) or specimen attached. I declare that the applicant claims to be the proprietor of the design in relation to the article specified at part 6 overleaf and to be the owner of any design right that exists in this design. I also declare in respect of any entry at part 9 above that the application made in the Convention country upon which the applicant relies is the first application made for registration of the design in a Convention country.

**Please sign here** ➤

Signed _____ Date _____

day   month   year

This application form must be signed by one of the following:

● The applicant.

● A partner or other person authorised to act on behalf of a firm.

● A director or secretary or authorised signatory of a corporate body.

● The applicant's authorised agent.

## Reminder

Have you attached

representations or specimens of the design? ☐

any continuation sheet if appropriate? ☐

Does the statement of novelty appear on the first sheet of each representation or specimen? ☐
(not applicable for textiles, lace or wallpaper)

the prescribed fee? ☐

505

### The Patent Office

### Registered Designs Act 1949

## Designs Form 6

## Application for a copy of Certificate of Registration of a Design

For Official Use

## Notes

Please type, or write in dark ink using BLOCK LETTERS. For details of prescribed fees please contact the Designs Registry at the Patent Office.

Rule 33 of the Registered Designs Rules 1989 is the main rule governing the completion and filing of this form.

Please mark correct box

1. Your reference.

2. Please give Registered Design number.

3. Please give full name of applicant for certificate.

ADP number (if known)

4. The original certificate

has been lost ☐

has been destroyed ☐

cannot be produced ☐

or

A copy of the original certificate is requested for other reasons which are set out in the accompanying statement. ☐

5. Please state your interest in the design.

6. Please give a name and address in the United Kingdom to which the certificate is to be sent.
Name

Address

Postcode

ADP number (if known)

**Please sign here ➤**

This form must be accompanied by evidence setting out in full and verifying the circumstances in which the original certificate of registration was lost or destroyed or cannot be produced ( if this is the case ) and by a representation or specimen of the design identical with that attached to the original Certificate of Registration.

Signed ———————————— Date ————

day   month   year

## Reminder

Have you attached

evidence of circumstances? ☐

representation? ☐

the prescribed fee? ☐

Revised 1989

**The Patent Office**

Registered
Designs Act 1949

**Designs Form 7**

**Request to the Registrar for Statement of Grounds of Decision under Rule 31**

For Official Use

**Notes**

Please type, or write in dark ink using BLOCK LETTERS. For details of prescribed fees please contact the Designs Registry at the Patent Office.

Rule 31 of the Registered Designs Rules 1989 is the main rule governing the completion and filing of this form.

1. Your reference.

2. Please give Design Application number.

3. Please give full name of applicant for the design.

ADP number (if known)

4. Please give a name and address for service in the United Kingdom to which all correspondence will be sent.
Name

Address

Postcode

ADP number (if known)

5a. Date of hearing        Date _____
day month year

5b. Date of Registrar's decision   Date _____
day month year

**Please sign here** ➤ Signed _____ Date _____
day month year

This form must be accompanied by the prescribed fee.

Revised 1989

507

**The Patent Office**

Registered
Designs Act 1949

**Designs Form 8**

**Request for extension of time to complete an Application for the Registration of a Design**

For Official Use

**Notes**

Please type, or write in dark ink using BLOCK LETTERS. For details of prescribed fees please contact the Designs Registry at the Patent Office.

Rule 36 of the Registered Designs Rules 1989 is the main rule governing the completion and filing of this form.

The initial twelve month period for completion of an application may be extended, by up to three months on payment of the prescribed fee.

1. Your reference.

2. Please give Design Application number.

3. Please give full name of the applicant for the design.

ADP number (if known)

4. Please give a name and address for service in the United Kingdom to which all correspondence will be sent.
Name

Address

Postcode

ADP number (if known)

5. I/We request the extension of the period available for the completion of the application for registration of this design.
The period of time extension required is

Please mark correct box

one month ☐

two months ☐

three months ☐

**Please sign here** ➤ Signed _____ Date _____
day month year

This form must be accompanied by the prescribed fee.

Revised 1989

The
Patent
Office

Registered
Designs Act 1949

**Designs Form 9A**

**Application to
extend period of
protection.**

For Official Use

## Notes

Please type, or write in dark ink using BLOCK LETTERS. For details of prescribed fees please contact the Designs Registry at the Patent Office.

Rules 38 and 40 of the Registered Designs Rules 1989 are the main rules governing the completion and filing of this form.

Please mark correct box

❹ Each period for which the right subsists is normally five years. However, in the case of an associated design registered under Section 4 of the Registered Designs Act 1949 the right will expire when the right in the original design expires. The extended period may thus be less than the full five years.

❺ The period for making the application may be extended by up to six months provided that the fee is paid within the period being purchased.

❻ The extension fee must be paid together with any additional fee for late application.

**Please sign here** ➤

1. Your reference.

2. Please give Registered Design number.

3. Please give full name of registered proprietor.

ADP number (if known)

4. I/We apply for an extension for

a second period ☐

or a third period ☐

5. Please complete this part if the application for extension is late.

number of additional months required ☐

6. Please give details of fees paid

Extension of period  £ ☐

Additional fee for late application (if necessary)  £ ☐

7. Please give a name and address in the United Kingdom to which the certificate of extension will be sent.
Name

Address

Postcode

ADP number (if known)

Signed —————————————— Date ———
day   month   year

This form must be accompanied by the prescribed fee(s)

Revised 1989

## The Patent Office

**Designs Form 12A**
**Application to register an assignment, licence mortgage or other event affecting the rights in a Registered Design**

Registered
Designs Act 1949

For Official Use

### Notes

Please type, or write in dark ink using BLOCK LETTERS. For details of prescribed fees please contact the Designs Registry at the Patent Office.

Rules 42 to 45 of the Registered Designs Rules 1989 are the main rules governing the completion and filing of this form.

This form may be used for more than one design if the same change is made.

If you do not have enough space, please use a separate sheet of paper.

1. Your reference.

2. Please give Registered Design number(s).

3. Please give name of the registered proprietor.

ADP number (if known)

4. Please give full name and address of the person gaining an interest or claiming an interest has ceased.
Name

Address

Postcode

ADP number (if known)

**5** Examples are an assignment, a licence, a mortgage, or probate.

A certified copy establishing the transaction, event or document must be forwarded for retention with this form

5. Please give details of the transaction, event or document affecting any interest in the design together with its date and the names of all parties involved.

If 'Yes' please mark box.

Do you require an entry in the Register showing you no longer claim any interest in a mortgage or licence?

6. Please give a name and address for service in the United Kingdom to which all correspondence will be sent.
Name

Address

Postcode

ADP number (if known)

Revised 1989

Please turn over ⇆

Please mark correct box.

7. Does the address for service entered at part 6 apply to:-

all matters concerned with the registered design? ☐

only those matters dealt with by this application? ☐

❽ Complete this part only when the name and address differs from that entered at part 4.

8. Please give the full name and address of the person making this application.

Name

Address

Postcode

ADP number (if known)

## Declaration

I/We declare that where design right exists in the design(s) mentioned in this application, the person(s) entitled to any interest which the applicant is seeking to register by this application is/are also entitled to the corresponding interest in the design right(s).

**Please sign here** ➤

Signed ———————————— Date ————

day   month   year

## Reminder

Have you attached

a certified copy of the document under which the change is made? ☐

any continuation sheet if appropriate? ☐

the prescribed fee? ☐

511

## The Patent Office

Registered
Designs Act 1949

**Designs Form 16**

**Application to record alteration of name**

For Official Use

### Notes

Please type, or write in dark ink using BLOCK LETTERS. For details of prescribed fees please contact the Designs Registry at the Patent Office.

Rule 46 of the Registered Designs Rules 1989 is the main rule governing the completion and filing of this form.

This form may be used for more than one design if the same alteration is made. One fee is charged for each design affected. If you do not have enough space, please use a separate sheet of paper.

❺ Evidence of the alteration must be provided - for example a copy of the Certificate of Incorporation.

❻ An address for service in the United Kingdom must be supplied.

1. Your reference.

2. Please give Design Application or Registered Design number(s).

3. Please give full name(s) of applicant(s) for registration of the design /registered proprietor(s) as currently on the register/in the application for registration.

ADP number (if known)

4. Please give the name to be altered.

ADP number (if known)

5. Please give the new name (and address if appropriate) to be recorded.
Name

Address

Postcode

ADP number (if known)

6. Please give a name and address for service in the United Kingdom to which all correspondence will be sent.
Name

Address

Postcode

ADP number (if known)

**Please sign here** ➤ Signed ——————————————— Date _____
day   month   year

Please enter number of applications/registrations to be amended.

This form must be accompanied by the prescribed fee.
Revised 1989

512

The
Patent
Office

**Designs Form 18**

**Request for
Correction of
Error**

Registered
Designs Act 1949

For Official Use

## Notes

Please type, or write in dark ink using BLOCK LETTERS. For details of prescribed fees please contact the Designs Registry at the Patent Office.

Rule 47 of the Registered Designs Rules 1989 is the main rule governing the completion and filing of this form.

❸ For the interest state whether applicant for registration or proprietor of design or state other interest as appropriate.

❹ This form should be accompanied by a statutory declaration or other suitable evidence stating the circumstances in which the error occurred.

Please mark correct box

This form may be used for more than one design if the same error has been made. One fee is charged for each design affected. If you do not have enough space please use a separate sheet of paper.

**Please sign here** ➤

1. Your reference.

2. Please give Design Application or Registered Design number(s).

3. Please give the full name of the person requesting the correction and state his interest in the matter.
Name

ADP number (if known)
Interest

4. Please give details of the error to be corrected.

Is the error to be corrected in the

application? ☐

representation? ☐

register? ☐

5. Please give a name and address for service in the United Kingdom to which all correspondence will be sent.
Name

Address

Postcode

ADP number (if known)

Signed —————————————— Date ————
day   month   year

Please enter the number of applications or
registrations to be amended. ☐

## Reminder

Have you attached      evidence in support of error correction? ☐

the prescribed fee? ☐

Revised 1989

**The Patent Office**
<u></u>

Registered
Designs Act 1949

**Designs Form 19**

**Request by Proprietor of Design to Cancel Registration**

For Official Use

## Notes

Please type, or write in dark ink using BLOCK LETTERS. A fee is not required for this form.

Rule 58 of the Registered Designs Rules 1989 is the main rule governing the completion and filing of this form.

1. Your reference.

2. Please give Registered Design number.

3. Please give full name of registered proprietor(s).

ADP number (if known)

4. Please give a name and address for service in the United Kingdom to which all correspondence will be sent.
Name

Address

Postcode

ADP number (if known)

5. It is requested that the registration of this Design be cancelled.

**Please sign here** ➤  Signed ———————————————— Date ——————
day   month   year

Revised 1989

**The Patent Office**

Registered
Designs Act 1949

**Designs Form 20**

**Request for information under Section 23 on supply of Registration number**

For Official Use

### Notes

Please type, or write in dark ink using BLOCK LETTERS. For details of prescribed fees please contact the Designs Registry at the Patent Office.

Rule 70 of the Registered Designs Rules 1989 is the main rule governing the completion and filing of this form.

1. Your reference.

2. Please give Registered Design number.

3. Please give full name and address in the United Kingdom to which the information is to be sent.
Name

Address

Postcode

ADP number (if known)

**Please sign here** ➤ Signed _____ Date _____
day   month   year

This form must be accompanied by the prescribed fee.

Revised 1989

515

### The Patent Office

**Designs Form 21**

**Request for search when Registration Number is not supplied**

Registered
Designs Act 1949

**For Official Use**

**Notes**

Please type, or write in dark ink using BLOCK LETTERS. For details of prescribed fees please contact the Designs Registry at the Patent Office.

Rule 71 of the Registered Designs Rules 1989 is the main rule governing the completion and filing of this form.

❷ Please enter the address in the United Kingdom to which the result of the search is to be sent.

❸ Please enter the name of the article, as shown in the representations, or specimen which must be supplied in duplicate and attached to this form.

This form can only be used to obtain a search for a single design.

1. Your reference.

2. Please give full name and address of applicant for search.
Name

Address

Postcode

Telephone number

ADP number (if known)

3. Please make a search in respect of the design shown in the attached representations ( or specimen) applied to a

I/We apply for information on whether the design appears to be identical with, or closely resembles any registered design, and if so,

• in respect of what articles

• whether any extension of the period of right in the registered design has been granted

• the date of registration

• the name and address of the registered proprietor

**Please sign here** ➤ Signed ——————————————— Date ———
day month year

**Reminder**

Have you attached

a representation or specimen in duplicate? ☐

the prescribed fee? ☐

Revised 1989

# The Patent Office

**Designs Form 23**

**Request for Certificate of the Registrar**

For Official Use

Registered
Designs Act 1949

## Notes

Please type, or write in dark ink using BLOCK LETTERS and use a separate form for each design.

Rule 72 of the Registered Designs Rules 1989 is the main rule governing the completion and filing of this form.

This form may be used to obtain certificates, certified copies and certified extracts.

For certificates sealed and attached to documents please use part 5. For certificates impressed on documents please use part 6. The current prescribed fees for each type of certificate may be obtained from the Designs Registry at the Patent Office.

1. Your reference.

2. Please give Design Application or Registered Design number.

3. Please give the name of the applicant(s)/registered proprietor(s) of the design.

ADP number (if known)

4. Please give full name and address in the United Kingdom of the person to whom the certificate(s) will be sent.

Name

Address

Postcode

ADP number (if known)

**5. Certificates Sealed and Attached to Documents**

❺ Please mark appropriate box to indicate what the Registrar is requested to certify.

What is the Registrar requested to certify?

Number required

the particulars of the design as originally filed

the particulars of the design as registered

other, including certificates under section 17(9) (please specify)

Please describe any special requirements. If you do not have enough space please use a separate sheet of paper.

Is the certificate required for

Please mark

legal proceedings?

obtaining a registration abroad?

something else? (please specify)

Revised 1989

Please turn over ↩

517

**❻** Do not complete part 6 if only the certificate(s) provided under part 5 are required.

Under part 6 the certificate is impressed by means of a rubber stamp and the document is embossed by the seal of the Patent Office.

## 6. Certificates Impressed on Documents

Please indicate which document(s) you want certified

Number required

register entry ☐

representation of design ☐

statement of novelty (if separate from representation) ☐

other documents (please specify) ☐
↓

**❼** Items supplied for certification must be identical to the corresponding document on the official file.

## 7. General

Are the documents to be certified enclosed?

Yes ☐   No ☐

If 'No', the Registry will, if possible, prepare photocopies.

If you have any special delivery/collection instructions please give details.

**Please sign here** ➤

Signed —————————————— Date ——————
day   month   year

This form must be accompanied by the prescribed fee.

The
Patent
Office

Registered
Designs Act 1949

**Designs Form 25A
Application for grant
of a Compulsory
Licence under
Section 10 or for
Cancellation of the
registration under
Section 11(2) or (3)**

For Official Use

## Notes

Please type, or write in dark ink using BLOCK LETTERS. For details of prescribed fees please contact the Designs Registry at the Patent Office.

Rule 52 of the Registered Designs Rules 1989 is the main rule governing the completion and filing of this form.

1. Your reference.

2. Please give Registered Design number.

3. Please give full name and address of applicant for compulsory licence or for cancellation.
Name

Address

Postcode

ADP number (if known)

4. Please give a name and address for service in the United Kingdom to which all correspondence will be sent.
Name

Address

Postcode

ADP number (if known)

Please mark correct box

❺ This form must be filed in duplicate together with a statement in duplicate setting out fully the nature of the applicant's interest, and facts on which he/she relies.

5. I/We apply for the grant of a compulsory licence in respect of the design.

or  I/We apply for the cancellation of the registration of the design on the grounds that:

**Please sign here** ➤ Signed ——————————— Date ———————
day   month   year

## Reminder

Have you attached     a duplicate copy of this form?

the statement of case in duplicate?

the prescribed fee?

Revised 1989

519

### The Patent Office

**Registered Designs Act 1949**

**Designs Form 28**

**Notification of Order of the Court**

For Official Use

**Notes**

Please type, or write in dark ink using BLOCK LETTERS.

A fee is not required for this form.

Rule 78 of the Registered Design Rules 1989 is the main rule governing the completion and filing of this form.

❸ Please enter the name of the proprietor of the Design as entered on the Register of Designs immediately prior to the issue of the Order.

❻ The Registrar will rectify the Register as necessary.

1. Your reference.

2. Please give Registered Design number.

3. Please give full name of registered proprietor.

ADP number (if known)

4. Please give the name and address of the person in whose favour the Order has been made.
Name

Address

Postcode

ADP number (if known)

5. Please give a name and address for service in the United Kingdom to which all correspondence will be sent.
Name

Address

Postcode

ADP number (if known)

6. An office copy of the Order of the Court accompanies this form. Please briefly state the effect of the Order.

**Please sign here** ➤ Signed ——————————————— Date ———————
day month year

Revised 1989

## The
## Patent
## Office

Registered
Designs Act 1949

**Designs Form 29**

**Application for
Restoration of a
lapsed right in a
Design**

For Official Use

### Notes

Please type, or write in dark ink using
BLOCK LETTERS. For details of
prescribed fees please contact the
Designs Registry at the Patent Office.

Rule 41 of the Registered Designs
Rules 1989 is the main rule governing
the completion and filing of this form.

❹ If you do not have enough space,
please use a separate sheet of paper.
Supporting evidence must be
provided.

❺ Please complete this only if the
applicant is not also the registered
proprietor.

1. Your reference.

2. Please give Registered Design number.

3. Please give full name of registered proprietor(s).

ADP number (if known)

4. Please give your reasons for applying for restoration.

5. Please give applicant's name and address (see note).
Name

Address

Postcode

ADP number (if known)

Please state your interest in the Registered Design.

6. Please give a name and address for service in the United Kingdom to
which all correspondence will be sent.
Name

Address

Postcode

ADP number (if known)

**Please sign here** ➤ Signed ——————————————— Date ———————
day   month   year

This form must be accompanied by the prescribed
fee.

Issued 1989

521

### The Patent Office

**Designs Form 30**

**Fee for Restoration of a Registered Design**

Registered Designs Act 1949

For Official Use

**Notes**

Please type, or write in dark ink using BLOCK LETTERS. For details of prescribed fees please contact the Designs Registry at the Patent Office.

Rule 41 of the Registered Designs Rules 1989 is the main rule governing the completion and filing of this form.

1. Your reference.

2. Please give Registered Design number.

3. Please give full name of the registered proprietor(s).

ADP number (if known)

4. Please give a name and address for service in the United Kingdom to which all correspondence will be sent.
Name

Address

Postcode

ADP number (if known)

**Please sign here** ➤ Signed _____ Date _____
day   month   year

**Reminder**

This form must be accompanied by the unpaid extension fee and the prescribed restoration fee.

Have you attached

completed Designs Form 9A and extension fee?  ☐

the prescribed restoration fee?  ☐

Issued 1989

The
**Patent
Office**

**Designs Form 31**

**Application for
settlement of the
terms of a
Licence of Right**

Registered Designs
Act 1949
Copyright, Designs
and Patents Act
1988

For Official Use

### Notes

Please type, or write in dark ink using
BLOCK LETTERS. For details of
prescribed fees please contact the
Design Registry at the Patent Office.

Rule 59 of the Registered Designs
Rules 1989 is the main rule governing
the completion and filing of this form.

1. Your reference.

2. Please give Registered Design number.

3. Please give full name and address of applicant.
Name

Address

Postcode

ADP number (if known)

4. Please give a name and address for service in the United Kingdom to
which all correspondence will be sent.
Name

Address

Postcode

ADP number (if known)

Only the person acquiring the licence
can apply.

Application is made to the Registrar for settlement of the terms of a
licence of right to be granted under this Registered Design.

**Please sign here** ➤ Signed ——————————— Date ————
day month year

### Reminder
Have you attached

a duplicate copy of this form? ☐

the statement of terms in duplicate? ☐

the prescribed fee? ☐

Issued 1989

523

PATENT AGENTS (NON-RECOGNITION OF CERTAIN AGENTS BY COMPTROLLER) RULES 1990
(SI 1990 No 1454)

| | | | |
|---|---|---|---|
| *Made* | . . | . . | *18th July 1990* |
| *Coming into force* . . | | . . | *13th August 1990* |

The Secretary of State, in the exercise of the powers conferred upon him by section 281 of the Copyright, Designs and Patents Act 1988, and after consultation with the Council on Tribunals in accordance with section 10(1) of the Tribunals and Inquiries Act 1971, hereby makes the following Rules—

**1.** These Rules may be cited as the Patent Agents (Non-recognition of Certain Agents by Comptroller) Rules 1990 and shall come into force on 13th August 1990.

**2.**—In these Rules—

'the Act' means the Copyright, Designs and Patents Act 1988;
'the Comptroller' means the Comptroller-General of Patents, Designs and Trade Marks;
'the register' means the register of patent agents required to be kept pursuant to rules made under section 275 of the Act.

**3.** The Comptroller is hereby authorised to refuse to recognise as agent in respect of any business under the Patents Act 1949, the Registered Designs Act 1949 or the Patents Act 1977—

(a) a person who has been convicted of an offence under section 88 of the Patents Act 1949, section 114 of the Patents Act 1977 or section 276 of the Act;

(b) an individual whose name has been erased from and not restored to the register on the ground of misconduct;

(c) a person who is found by the Secretary of State to have been guilty of such conduct as would, in the case of an individual registered in the register, render him liable to have his name erased from the register on the ground of misconduct;

(d) a partnership or body corporate of which one of the partners or directors is a person whom the Comptroller could refuse to recognise under paragraph (a), (b) or (c) above.


REGISTERED DESIGNS (FEES) RULES 1992
(SI 1992 No 617)

| | | | |
|---|---|---|---|
| *Made* | . . | . . | *10th March 1992* |
| *Laid before Parliament* | | . . | *11th March 1992* |
| *Coming into force* . . | | . . | *11th May 1992* |

The Secretary of State, in exercise of the powers conferred upon him by sections 36, 40 and 44(1) of the Registered Designs Act 1949, of the power conferred upon him by the Department of Trade and Industry (Fees) Order 1988, and of all other powers enabling him in that behalf, after consultation with the Council on Tribunals pursuant to section 10(1) of the Tribunals Inquiries Act 1971 and with the consent of the Treasury pursuant to the said section 40, hereby makes the following Rules—

**1.**—(1) These Rules may be cited as the Registered Designs (Fees) Rules 1992 and shall come into force on 11th May 1992.

(2) The Registerd Design (Fees) Rules 1991[SI 1991 No 1628 ] are hereby revoked.

**2.** These Rules shall be construed as one with the Registered Designs Rules 1989.

**3.** The fees to be paid in respect of any matters arising under the Registered Designs Act 1949 shall be those specified in the Schedule to these Rules; and in any case where a form specified in the Schedule as the corresponding form in relation to any matter is required by the Registered Designs Rules 1989 to be used, that form or any alternative form accepted by the registrar under rule 4(2) of those Rules shall be accompanied by the fee, if any, specified in respect of that matter.

SCHEDULE

FEES PAYABLE

(In this Schedule references to a section are to that section of the Registered Designs Act 1949 and references to a rule are to that rule in the Registered Designs Rules 1989.)

| Number of corresponding Designs | Item | Amount £ |
|---|---|---|
| 1A | Appointment or change of agent | — |
| 2A | On application to register one design to be applied to a single article not falling within the next item | 60 |
| 2A | On application to register one design to be applied to a single article made substantially of lace or a design consisting substantially of checks or stripes to be applied to a single textile article | 35 |
| 2A | On application to register one design to be applied to a set of articles | 90 |
| 6 | On application for a copy of certificate of registration of a design | 22 |
| 7 | On request to the registrar for statement of grounds of decision under rule 31 | 65 |
| 8 | On request for extension of time to complete an application for the registration of a design— | |
| | by one month | 18 |
| | by two months | 36 |
| | by three months | 54 |
| 9A | On application to extend period of protection— | |
| | for second period | 130 |
| | for third period | 210 |
| 9A | Additional fee payable under section 8(4) in respect of extra time for making application for extension of period of protection— | |
| | Additional time not exceeding one month | 18 |
| | Each succeeding month (not exceeding six months) | 18 |
| 12A | On application under rule 42 to enter subsequent proprietorship, etc and on application under rule 45 by mortgagee or licensee for entry that he no longer claims to be such— | |
| | One design and any additional design similarly affected— | 55 |

| | | |
|---|---|---:|
| 16 | On application to record alteration of name— | — |
| 18 | On request under section 21 for correction of error— | |
| | One design and any additional design—same error— | 55 |
| 19 | On request by proprietor of design to cancel registration | — |
| 20 | On request for information under section 23 on supply of registration number | |
| 21 | On request for search when registration number is not supplied | 25 |
| 23 | On request for certificate of the registrar— | |
| | Sealed and attached to document | 22 |
| | By impression on document | 16 |
| 25A | On application for grant of a compulsory licence under section 10 or for cancellation of the registration under section 11(2) or (3) | — |
| 28 | On notification of order of the court | — |
| 29 | On application for restoration of a lapsed right in a design | 120 |
| 30 | On provision of fee for restoration of a registered design | 120 |
| 31 | On application for settlement of the terms of a licence of right | — |
| | Inspection in person without provision of copy of register or design where inspection is permitted other than inspection under section 22(2)— | — |
| | On request for uncertified copy or extract under rule 73— | |
| | In respect of each design | 3 |

## DESIGNS (CONVENTION COUNTRIES) ORDER 1993
## (SI 1993 No 1257)

| | | |
|---|---|---|
| *Made* . . . . | | *12th May 1993* |
| *Coming into force* . . . . | | *14th June 1993* |

Her Majesty, in exercise of powers conferred upon Her by section 13(1) of the Registered Designs Act 1949, is pleased, by and with the advice of Her Privy Council, to order, and it is hereby ordered, as follows:

**1.** This Order may be cited as the Designs (Convention Countries) Order 1993 and shall come into force on 14th June 1993.

**2.** Belarus, Croatia, the Czech Republic, Kazakhstan, the Slovak Republic, Slovenia, the Russian Federation and the Ukraine are convention countries for the purposes of all the provisions of the Registered Designs Act 1949.

LIST OF CONVENTION COUNTRIES FOR THE PURPOSES
OF RDA 49, s 13
The list of countries declared to be convention countries (as of 14 June 1993) is:

| | | | |
|---|---|---|---|
| Algeria | Germany | Monaco | Uganda |
| Argentina | Ghana | Mongolia (People's | Ukraine |
| Australia | Greece | Republic) | USA |
| Austria | Guinea | Morocco | Uruguay |
| Bahamas | Guinea - Bissau | Netherlands | Vatican (Holy See) |
| Bangladesh | Haiti | New Zealand | Vietnam |
| Barbados | Hong Kong | Niger | Yugoslavia |
| Belarus | Hungary | Nigeria | Zaire |
| Belgium | Iceland | Norway | Zambia |
| Benin | India | Pakistan | Zimbabwe |
| Brazil | Indonesia | Philippines | |
| Bulgaria | Iran | Poland | |
| Burkina Faso | Iraq | Portugal | |
| Burundi | Ireland | Romania | |
| Cameroon | Israel | Russian Federation | |
| Canada | Italy | Rwanda | |
| Central African | Ivory Coast | San Marino | |
|   Republic | Japan | Senegal | |
| Chad | Jordan | Singapore | |
| Chile | Kazakhstan | Slovak Republic | |
| China (People's | Kenya | Slovenia | |
|   Republic) | Korea (South) | South Africa | |
| Congo | Lebanon | Spain | |
| Croatia | Lesotho | Sri Lanka | |
| Cuba | Libya | Sudan | |
| Cyprus | Liechtenstein | Surinam | |
| Czech Republic | Luxembourg | Swaziland | |
| Czechoslovakia | Madagascar | Sweden | |
| Denmark | Malawi | Switzerland | |
| Dominican Republic | Malaysia | Syria | |
| Egypt | Mali | Tanzania | |
| Finland | Malta | Togo | |
| France | Mauritania | Trinidad and Tobago | |
| Gabon | Mauritius | Tunisia | |
| Gambia | Mexico | Turkey | |

SUMMARY OF DESIGNS REGISTRY OFFICE PRACTICE RELATING TO
THE SIGNIFICANCE OF COLOUR IN THE REGISTRATION OF
INDUSTRIAL DESIGNS

**1. General**
The Office practice concerning the part played by colour in design registration is
based on the understanding that on the reported authorities, whilst colour may
form an element in a design, colour of colouring as such does not constitute design:
ie, that, unless the change of colour creates a new pattern of ornament, registration
will be refused.

**2. Monochrome representations**
In the large majority of cases the representations filed in support of a design
application comprise monochrome drawings or photographs, any pattern or
ornament on the article being represented by means of shading the various areas
in tones of grey corresponding to the tonal density of the colours thus represented.

### 3. Coloured representations of specimens

In a relatively small number of cases applicants file coloured representations or specimens in support of an application, together with a statement of novelty worded to the effect that 'The feature of the design for which novelty is claimed is the pattern or ornament created by the tonal contrast of the colours applied to the article as shown in the representations.' Whilst the application is in some doubt as to the validity of such a claim, the application is accepted for registration, provided that the design possesses the necessary substantial novelty.

### 4. Colour-coded representations

The official records show that in at least one instance the Office has accepted monochrome drawn representations in which the coloured areas on the article have been indicated and identified by means of stippling and hatching, a colour key identifying the actual colour of each of those areas being provided on the representation.

### 5. Contemporaneous applications

Circumstances have arisen where an applicant has filed more than one application on the same day for a number of designs which differ one from the other only in the particular combination and disposition of the colours adopted for each design. Similarly, occasions have arisen where an applicant has filed two applications on the same day, each application being supported by monochrome representations, the only difference between the representations being that, whereas the represent-ations for one application show, for example, a pattern formed by white stars on a black background, the representations or the other application show an otherwise identical pattern with the polarity reversed, ie, black stars on a white background.

As however these contemporaneous applications cannot anticipate one another and cannot be said to be identical if the designs which form the subject of the applications possess the necessary novelty they have been accepted for registration accordingly.

### 6. Anticipations

When making a search among prior registered designs and/or trade publications, etc in order to test the novelty of a design, circumstances may arise where the design which is the subject of the search differs from a prior published or registered design only in the matter of tonal variation (in the case of monochrome representations) or colour variation (in the case of coloured representations or specimens) of certain elements forming the pattern or ornament.

Again, if the novelty claim relating to the design being searched is for the pattern or ornament of the article or for the shape or configuration and pattern or ornament of the article and in the opinion of the Office no new pattern or ornament has been created, ie, the differences in the pattern or ornament are not substantial, an objection to registration would be raised against the application accordingly.

### 7. Conclusion

It is difficult, if not impossible, to lay down hard and fast rules as to the degree of difference which alteration of colour or colours within a pattern or ornament may impart to a design and each application must be judged on its own merits. For example, the degree of difference may to some extent depend upon the comparative simplicity or complexity of the designs being considered. However, it may be said that, generally speaking, alteration of colour or colours in a design which is in other respects not substantially different from a prior design would be regarded by the Office as being in the nature of a variant commonly known in the trade and would not in itself impart the substantial novelty necessary to substantiate a valid registration.

# Part D    Unregistered Designs/Semiconductor Topographies

SEMICONDUCTOR PRODUCTS (PROTECTION OF TOPOGRAPHY)
REGULATIONS 1987
(SI 1987 No 1497)

| | |
|---|---|
| *Made* . . . . . . *20th August 1987* | |
| *Laid before Parliament* . . *1st September 1987* | |
| *Coming into force* . . . . *7th November 1987* | |

The Secretary of State, being designated for the purposes of section 2(2) of the European Communities Act 1972 in relation to the conferment and protection of exclusive rights in the topographies of semiconductor products, in exercise of the powers conferred on him by the said section 2(2) hereby makes the following Regulations:

**1.** These Regulations may be cited as the Semiconductor Products (Protection of Topography) Regulations 1987 and shall come into force on 7th November 1987.
**2.**—(1)In these Regulations—

'semiconductor product' means an article the purpose, or one of the purposes, of which is the performance of an electronic function and which consists of two or more layers, at least one of which is composed of semiconducting material and in or upon one or more of which is fixed a pattern appertaining to that or another function;
'topography' means the design, however expressed, of any of the following:

(a) the pattern fixed, or intended to be fixed, in or upon a layer of a semiconductor product;
(b) the pattern fixed, or intended to be fixed, in or upon a layer of material in the course of, and for the purpose of, the manufacture of a semiconductor product;
(c) the arrangement of the layers of a semiconductor product in relation to one another;

'topography right' has the meaning given in regulation 4(1) below and, unless the context otherwise requires, references to topography right are references to topography right subsisting in a topography.

(2) For the purposes of these Regulations, the creation of a topography occurs upon its first expression in a form from which it can be reproduced.
(3) For the purposes of these Regulations, and subject to paragraph (4) below, the commercial exploitation of a topography is the sale or hire, or the offer or exposure for sale or hire, of—

(a) a reproduction of the whole or a substantial part of the topography, or
(b) a semiconductor product incorporating such a reproduction,

being (except for the purposes of Regulation 3(2) below) lawful exploitation by or with the licence or consent of the owner of topography right in the topography or of any predecessor in title of the owner.

(4) No account shall be taken of any commercial exploitation which is subject to an obligation of confidence in respect of information about the topography exploited unless either—

(a) the topography has been commercially exploited on a previous occasion (whether or not subject to an obligation of confidence), or

(b) the obligation is imposed at the behest of the Crown, or of the government of any country outside the United Kingdom, for the protection of security in connection with the production of arms, munitions or war material.

(5) For the purposes of these Regulations, no account shall be taken of any offer for sale or hire the acceptance of which would lead to an agreement to sell or hire but not yet an actual sale or hire.

**3.**—(1) Where a topography is original and its creator is a qualified person or, in the case of a topography created in the course of employment or pursuant to commission, the employer or commissioner is a qualified person, topography right shall, subject to Regulation 8 below, subsist in the topography in favour of the creator, employer or commissioner, as the case may be.

(2) If paragraph (1) above does not apply, topography right shall subsist where—

(a) the topography is original;

(b) the first commercial exploitation of the topography in the world occurs within the territory of a member state;

(c) the person so exploiting the topography is a qualified person; and

(d) that person at the time of that exploitation has been exclusively authorised to exploit the topography commercially in every member state by, as the case may be, the creator, his employer or the commissioner of the topography or, as the case may be, by a person lawfully claiming through the creator, employer or commissioner;

and in such a case topography right shall, subject to regulation 8 below, subsist in the topography in favour of that person.

(3) A topography is original if it satisfies the requirements of being—

(a) the result of the creator's own intellectual effort (or of the combined intellectual efforts of the creators if there are more than one), and

(b) not commonplace among creators of topographies or manufacturers of semiconductor products,

or if it consists of a combination of elements in which the combination itself satisfies those requirements, irrespective of whether the several elements do.

(4) For the purposes of this regulation, a person is a qualified person if—

(a) being an individual he is a British citizen or a citizen or subject of another member state or has his habitual residence in the United Kingdom, Gibraltar or another member state, or

(b) being a firm or a body corporate it has a place of business within the United Kingdom, Gibraltar or another member state at which substantial business activity is carried on,

or if he falls within one of the additional classes of qualified persons set out in Part I of Schedule 1 to these Regulations.

(5) In determining whether, for the purposes of paragraph (4)(b) above or Schedule 1 below, a person has a place of business within any territory at which

substantial business activity is carried on, no account shall be taken of dealings in goods which are at all material times outside that territory.

(6) For the purposes of this regulation, a topography is created in the course of employment or pursuant to commission if it is created in the course of the creator's employment under a contract of service or apprenticeship or pursuant to a contract (other than a contract of service or apprenticeship) under which a person other than the creator commissions the creation of the topography and pays or agrees to pay for it in money or money's worth, unless in either case the contract provides to the contrary; and 'employer' and 'commissioner' shall be construed accordingly.

**4.**—(1) Topography right is, subject to paragraph (2) below, the exclusive right to make a reproduction of the whole or a substantial part of the topography or deal in such a reproduction or a semiconductor product incorporating such a reproduction; and a person deals in a reproduction or a semiconductor product if he sells or hires it, offers or exposes it for sale or hire or imports it into the United Kingdom for the purpose of selling or hiring it.

(2) Paragraph (1) above shall not apply in respect of—

(a) the making of any reproduction privately for non-commercial purposes;
(b) the making of any reproduction for the purpose of analysing or evaluating the topography or analysing, evaluating or teaching the concepts, processes, systems or techniques embodied in it;
(c) dealing in any reproduction or product after it has been sold or hired within—

　(i) the United Kingdom by or with the licence of the owner of topography right in the topography, or
　(ii) the territory of any other member state or of Gibraltar by or with the consent of the person, or one of the persons, for the time being entitled to import it into or sell or hire it within that territory;

(d) any act restricted by copyright in the topography as an artistic work within the meaning of the Copyright Act 1956.

**5.** Topography right shall commence upon the creation of the topography or, in a case falling within regulation 3(2) above, upon its first commercial exploitation, and shall cease—

(a) at the end of the tenth year after the end of the year in which it was first commercially exploited anywhere in the world, or
(b) if it is not commercially exploited anywhere in the world within a period of fifteen years commencing with its creation, at the end of that period.

**6.**—(1) Topography right is infringed, subject to paragraphs (2) and (3) below, by any person who, in the United Kingdom, during the subsistence of the right and without the licence of the owner of the right, does or authorises any other person to do any act within the exclusive right provided for in regulation 4(1) above.

(2) Topography right in one original topography is not infringed by creating another original topography as a result of an analysis or evaluation falling within regulation 4(2)(b) above, making a reproduction of that other topography or dealing in such a reproduction or a semiconductor product incorporating such a reproduction.

(3) Topography right is not infringed by dealing in a reproduction or a semiconductor product if the person dealing in it does not know, and has no reasonable

grounds to believe, that the dealing is an infringement.

**7.**—(1)Infringement of topography right shall be actionable at the suit of the owner of the right and, subject to paragraphs (2) and (3) below, in any action for such an infringement all such relief, by way of damages, injunction, accounts or otherwise, shall be available to the plaintiff as is available in any corresponding proceedings in respect of infringement of other proprietary rights.

(2) Where in an action for infringement of topography right it is proved or admitted that an infringement was committed (other than by dealing in a reproduction or a semiconductor product) but that at the time of the infringement the defendant did not know, and had no reasonable grounds to believe, that topography right subsisted in the topography, the plaintiff shall not be entitled to any damages against the defendant in respect of the infringement, but shall be entitled to an account of profits in respect of the infringement whether any other relief is granted or not.

(3) Where in an action for infringement of topography right it is proved or admitted that an infringement was committed by dealing in a reproduction or a semiconductor product but that the defendant's acquisition of the reproduction or product was innocent, the plaintiff shall not be entitled to any relief against the defendant in respect of the infringement other than damages, and any damages awarded shall be limited to an amount which, in the opinion of the court, would have been a reasonable royalty payment under a licence had one been granted by the plaintiff to the defendant in respect of the acts constituting the infringement.

(4) For the purposes of paragraph (3) above, the defendant's acquisition was innocent if at the time of acquiring the reproduction or product he did not know, and had no reasonable grounds to believe, that dealing in it in the United Kingdom would be an infringement, or if—

    (a)  his title to the reproduction or product was derived, directly or indirectly, from a person who, at the time that he acquired it, did not know, and had no reasonable grounds to believe, that dealing in it in the United Kingdom would be an infringement, and

    (b)  the disposal of the reproduction or product by that person either—

        (i)   would have been an infringment of topography right but for regulation 6(3) above, or

        (ii)  was an infringement in respect of which paragraph (3) above applied, or

        (iii) occurred within the territory of a member state other than the United Kingdom or in Gibraltar and could not have been prevented because of Article 5(6) of Council Directive 87/54/EEC on the legal protection of topographies of semiconductor products.

(5) In this regulation, 'action' includes a counterclaim, and references to the plaintiff and to the defendant in an action shall be construed accordingly; and in the application of this regulation to Scotland, 'injunction' means an interdict, 'accounts' means count, reckoning and payment, 'an account of profits' means an accounting and payment of profits, 'plaintiff' means pursuer and 'defendant' means defender.

**8.**—(1) For the purposes of these Regulations, the owner of topography right is the person who for the time being is actually entitled to it or will become entitled to it upon the creation of the topography (where the topography has not yet been created) or upon the subsistence of topography right in the topography (where the right does not yet subsist in it).

(2) The owner of topography right may assign it (or his prospective entitlement to it) by instrument in writing signed by him or on his behalf; and topography right (and the prospective entitlement to it) is transmissible by testamentary disposition or operation of law as personal or moveable property.

(3) A licence granted by the owner in respect of topography right shall be binding upon all his successors in title in respect of it except for subsequent purchasers in good faith for valuable consideration without actual or constructive notice of the licence and persons deriving title from such purchasers; and where the owner of topography right is not such a purchaser in good faith and does not derive title from such a purchaser, references in these Regulations to the licence of the owner include the licence of a predecessor in title of the owner.

**9.**—(1) The acts restricted by the copyright in an artistic work in accordance with section 3(5) of the Copyright Act 1956 shall exclude—

(a) the reproduction of a topography in three dimensions;
(b) the reproduction of a topography in two dimensions—

    (i) in the course of, and for the purposes of, the manufacture of a semi-conductor product, or
    (ii) where the making of the thing from which the reproduction is immediately taken is, by virtue of this paragraph, not an act restricted by copyright; and

(c) the publication of any such reproduction as is mentioned in subparagraph (a) or (b) above or its inclusion in a television broadcast or a cable programme.

(2) Schedule 2 to these Regulations shall have effect for the purpose of modifying other legislation.

**10.**—(1) These Regulations shall not apply in respect of any topography created before 7th November 1987.

(2) Regulation 9(1) above shall not apply in respect of any artistic work made before 7th November 1987.

### SCHEDULE 1

ADDITIONAL CLASSES OF QUALIFIED PERSONS

PART I

DESCRIPTIONS OF ADDITIONAL CLASSES

1. British Dependent Territory citizens.
2. Citizens and subjects of any country specified in Part II below.
3. Habitual residents of any country specified in Part II below, the Isle of Man, the Channel Islands or any colony.
4. Firms and bodies corporate formed under the law of, or of any part of, the United Kingdom, Gibraltar, another member state or any country specified in Part II below with a place of business within any country so specified at which substantial business activity is carried on.

PART II

SPECIFIED COUNTRIES

United States of America.

SCHEDULE 2

CONSEQUENTIAL MODIFICATION OF LEGISLATION

1. The provisions specified in Table A below shall apply as if references therein to copyright, or to copyright in a work, extended to topography right, and as if references therein to a work in which copyright subsists extended to a topography in which topography right subsists.

**Table A**

| *Act* | *Section or Schedule* |
|---|---|
| Patents, Designs, Copyright and Trade Marks (Emergency) Act 1939 | Sections 1 and 2 |
| Crown Proceedings Act 1947 | Section 3 |
| Defence Contracts Act 1958 | Section 6(2) |
| Restrictive Trade Practices Act 1976 | Schedule 3, paragraph 5A |
| Unfair Contract Terms Act 1977 | Schedule 1, paragraph 1(c) |
| Judicature (Northern Ireland) Act 1978 | Section 94A(5) |
| State Immunity Act 1978 | Section 7(b) |
| Supreme Court Act 1981 | Section 72(5) and Schedule 1 paragraph 1(i) |
| Companies Act 1985 | Sections 396(1)(j) and 410(4)(c)(vi) |
| Law Reform (Miscellaneous Provisions) (Scotland) Act 1985 | Section 15(5) |

2. The provisions specified in Table B below shall apply as if there were inserted at the end of each thereof the words, 'or of any topography right'.

**Table B**

| *Act* | *Section or Schedule* |
|---|---|
| Patents Act 1949 | Section 47(1) |
| Registered Designs Act 1949 | Schedule 1, paragraph 2(1) |
| Post Office Act 1969 | Schedule 10, paragraphs 8(1) and 18(1) |
| Patents Act 1977 | Section 57(1) |
| British Telecommunications Act 1981 | Schedule 5, paragraphs 9(1) and 19(1) |

3. Subject to any Order made by virtue of subsection (1)(a) of section 3 of the Northern Ireland Constitution Act 1973 after the making of these Regulations, topography right shall not be a transferred matter for the purposes of that Act but shall for the purposes of subsection (2) of that section be treated as specified in Schedule 3 to that Act.


DESIGN RIGHT (SEMICONDUCTOR TOPOGRAPHIES)
REGULATIONS 1989
(SI 1989 No 1100)

*(As amended by the Design Right (Semiconductor Topographies) (Amendment) Regulations 1993 (SI 1993 No 2497), which superseded the amendments previously made by the Design Right (Semiconductor Topographies) (Amendment) Regulations 1989 (SI 1989 No 2147), the Design Right (Semiconductor Topographies) (Amendment) Regulations 1990 (SI 1990 No 1003), the Design Right (Semiconductor Topographies) (Amendment) Regulations 1991 (SI 1991 No 2237), the Design Right (Semiconductor Topographies) (Amendment) Regulations 1992 (SI 1992 No 400))*

| | |
|---|---|
| *Made* . . . . . . | *29th June 1989* |
| *Coming into force* . . . . | *1st August 1989* |

**Citation and commencement**

Whereas a draft of the following Regulations has been approved by the resolution of each House of Parliament:

Now, therefore, the Secretaty of State, being designated for the purposes of section 2(2) of the European Communities Act 1972 in relation to the conferment and protection of exclusive rights in the topographies of semiconductor products, in exercise of the powers conferred on him by the said section 2(2) hereby makes the following Regulations:

**1.** These Regulations may be cited as the Design Right (Semiconductor Topographies) Regulations 1989 and shall come into force on 1st August 1989.

### Interpretation

**2.** —(1) In these Regulations—

    'the Act' means the Copyright, Designs and Patents Act 1988;

    'semiconductor product' means an article the purpose, or one of the purposes, of which is the performance of an electronic function and which consists of two or more layers, at least one of which is composed of semiconducting material and in or upon one or more of which is fixed a pattern appertaining to that or another function; and

    'semiconductor topography' means a design within the meaning of section 213(2) of the Act which is a design of either of the following:

(a) the pattern fixed, or intended to be fixed, in or upon—

    (i) a layer of a semiconductor product, or

    (ii) a layer of material in the course of and for the purpose of the manufacture of a semiconductor product, or

(b) the arrangement of the patterns fixed, or intended to be fixed, in or upon the layers of a semiconductor product in relation to one another.

(2) Except where the context otherwise requires, these Regulations shall be construed as one with Part III of the Act (design right).

### Application of Copyright, Designs and Patents Act 1988, Part III

**3.** In its application to a design which is a semiconductor topography, Part III of the Act shall have effect subject to regulations 4 to 9 below.

### Qualification

**4.**—(1) Section 213(5) of the Act has effect subject to paragraphs (2) to (4) below.

(2) Part III of the Act has effect as if for section 217 of the Act there was substituted the following:

'**217.**—(1) In this Part—

'qualifying individual' means a citizen or subject of, or an individual habitually resident in, a qualifying country; and

'qualifying person' means—

(a) a qualifying individual,

(b) a body corporate or other body having legal personality which has in any qualifying country or in Gibraltar a place of business at which substantial business activity is carried on, or

(c) a person who falls within one of the additional classes set out in Part I of the Schedule to the Design Right (Semiconductor Topographies) Regulations 1989.

(2) References in this Part to a qualifying person include the Crown and the government of any other qualifying country.

(3) In this section 'qualifying country' means—

(a)  the United Kingdom, or

(b)  another member State of the European Economic Community.

(4) The reference in the definition of 'qualifying individual' to a person's being a citizen or subject of a qualifying country shall be construed in relation to the United Kingdom as a reference to his being a British citizen.

(5) In determining for the purpose of the definition of 'qualifying person' whether substantial business activity is carried on at a place of business in any country, no account shall be taken of dealings in goods which are at all material times outside that country.'.

(3) Where a semiconductor topography is created in pursuance of a commission or in the course of employment and the designer of the topography is, by virtue of section 215 of the Act (as substituted by regulation 5 below), the first owner of design right in that topography, section 219 of the Act does not apply and section 218(2) to (4) of the Act shall apply to the topography as if it had not been created in pursuance of a commission or in the course of employment.

(4) Section 220 of the Act has effect subject to regulation 7 below and as if for subsection (1) there was substituted the following:

'**220.**—(1) A design which does not qualify for design right protection under section 218 or 219 (as modified by regulation 4(3) of the Design Right (Semiconductor Topographies) Regulations 1989) or under the said regulation 4(3) qualifies for design right protection if the first marketing of articles made to the design—

(a)  is by a qualifying person who is exclusively authorised to put such articles on the market in every member State of the European Economic Community, and

(b)  takes place within the territory of any member State.';

and subsection (4) of section 220 accordingly has effect as if the words 'in the United Kingdom' were omitted.

## Ownership of design right

**5.** Part III of the Act has effect as if for section 215 of the Act there was substituted the following:

'**215.**—(1)  The designer is the first owner of any design right in a design which is not created in pursuance of a commission or in the course of employment.

(2)  Where a design is created in pursuance of a commission, the person commissioning the design is the first owner of any design right in it subject to any agreement in writing to the contrary.

(3)  Where, in a case not falling within subsection (2) a design is created by an employee in the course of his employment, his employer is the first owner of any design right in the design subject to any agreement in writing to the contrary.

(4)  If a design qualifies for design right protection by virtue of section 220

(as modified by regulation 4(4) of the Design Right (Semiconductor Topographies) Regulations 1989), the above rules do not apply and, subject to regulation 7 of the said Regulations, the person by whom the articles in question are marketed is the first owner of the design right.'.

## Duration of design right

**6.**—(1) Part III of the Act has effect as if for section 216 of the Act there was substituted the following:

'**216.**—The design right in a semiconductor topography expires—

(a) ten years from the end of the calendar year in which the topography or articles made to the topography were first made available for sale or hire anywhere in the world by or with the licence of the design right owner, or

(b) if neither the topography nor articles made to the topography are so made available within a period of fifteen years commencing with the earlier of the time when the topography was first recorded in a design document or the time when an article was first made to the topography, at the end of that period.'.

(2) Subsection (2) of section 263 of the Act has effect as if the words 'or a semiconductor topography' were inserted after the words 'in relation to an article'.

(3) The substitute provision set out in paragraph (1) above has effect subject to regulation 7 below.

## Confidential information

**7.** In determining, for the purposes of section 215(4), 216 or 220 of the Act (as modified by these Regulations), whether there has been any marketing, or anything has been made available for sale or hire, no account shall be taken of any sale or hire, or any offer or exposure for sale or hire, which is subject to an obligation of confidence in respect of information about the semiconductor topography in question unless either—

(a) the article or semiconductor topography sold or hired or offered or exposed for sale or hire has been sold or hired on a previous occasion (whether or not subject to an obligation of confidence), or

(b) the obligation is imposed at the behest of the Crown, or of the government of any country outside the United Kingdom, for the protection of security in connection with the production of arms, munitions or war material.

## Infringement

**8.**—(1) Section 226 of the Act has effect as if for subsection (1) there was substituted the following:

'**226**—(1) Subject to subsection (1A), the owner of design right in a design has the exclusive right to reproduce the design—

(a) by making articles to that design, or

(b) by making a design document recording the design for the purpose of enabling such articles to be made.

(1A) Subsection (1) does not apply to—

(a) the reproduction of a design privately for non-commercial aims; or

(b) the reproduction of a design for the purpose of analysing or evaluating the design or analysing, evaluating or teaching the concepts, processes, systems or techniques embodied in it.'.

(2) Section 227 of the Act does not apply if the article in question has previously been sold or hired within—

(a) the United Kingdom by or with the licence of the owner of design right in the semiconductor topography in question, or

(b) the territory of any other member State of the European Economic Community or the territory of Gibraltar by or with the consent of the person for the time being entitled to import it into or sell or hire it within that territory.

(3) Section 228(6) of the Act does not apply.

(4) It is not an infringement of design right in a semiconductor topography to—

(a) create another original semiconductor topography as a result of an analysis or evaluation of the first topography or of the concepts, processes, systems or techniques embodied in it, or

(b) reproduce that other topography.

(5) Anything which would be an infringement of the design right in a semiconductor topography if done in relation to the topography as a whole is an infringement of the design right in the topography if done in relation to a substantial part of the topography.

## Licences of right
**9.** Section 237 of the Act docs not apply.

## Revocation and transitional provisions
**10.**—(1)The Semiconductor Products (Protection of Topography) Regulations 1987 [SI 1987 No 1497] are hereby revoked.

(2) Sub-paragraph (1) of paragraph 19 of Schedule 1 to the Act shall not apply in respect of a semiconductor topography created between 7th November 1987 and 31st July 1989.

(3) In its application to copyright in a semiconductor topography created before 7th November 1987, sub-paragraph (2) of the said paragraph 19 shall have effect as if the reference to sections 237 to 239 were a reference to sections 238 and 239; and sub-paragraph (3) of that paragraph accordingly shall not apply to such copyright.

## SCHEDULE
### ADDITIONAL CLASSES OF QUALIFYING PERSONS

### PART I
### DESCRIPTIONS OF ADDITIONAL CLASSES

**1. British Dependent Territory citizens.**

**2. Citizens and subjects of any country specified in Part II below.**

**3. Habitual residents of any country specified in Part II below, the Isle of Man, the Channel Islands or any colony.**

**4. Firms and bodies corporate formed under the law of, or of any part of, the United Kingdom, Gibraltar, another member State of the European Economic Community or any country specified in Part II below with a place of business within any country so specified at which substantial business activity is carried on.**

*Appendix 2*

## PART II

### SPECIFIED COUNTRIES: CITIZENS, SUBJECTS, HABITUAL RESIDENTS, BODIES CORPORATE AND OTHER BODIES HAVING LEGAL PERSONALITY

**Australia**
**Austria**
**Finland**
**French overseas territories (French Polynesia; French Southern and Antarctic Territories; Mayotte; New Caledonia and dependencies; Saint-Pierre and Miquelon; Wallis and Futuna Islands)**
**Iceland**
**Japan**
**Liechtenstein**
**Norway**
**Sweden**
**Switzerland**
**United States of America.**

*General note*
The Schedule was substituted by the Design Right (Semiconductor Topographies)(Amendment) Regulations 1993 [ SI 1993 No 2497.] Previous amendments to the Schedule made by SI 1989 No 2147, 1990 No 1003, 1991 No 2237 and 1992 No 400 have been superseded and are not printed here.


## DESIGN RIGHT (PROCEEDINGS BEFORE COMPTROLLER) RULES 1989 (SI 1989 No 1130)

*(As amended by the Design Right (Proceedings before Comptroller) (Amendment) Rules 1990 (SI 1990 No 1453, the Design Right (Proceedings before Comptroller) (Amendment) (No 2) Rules 1990 (SI 1990 No 1699) (superseded by SI 1992 No 615), and the Design Right (Proceedings before Comptroller) (Amendment) Rules 1992 (SI 1992 No 615))*

| | |
|---|---|
| *Made* . . . . . . | *4th July 1989* |
| *Laid before Parliament* . . | *10 th July 1989* |
| *Coming into force* . . . . | *1st August 1989* |

The Secretary of State, in exercise of the powers conferred upon him by section 250 of the Copyright Designs and Patents Act 1988 with the consent of the Treasury pursuant to subsection (3) of that section as to the fees prescribed under these rules, and after consultation with the Council on Tribunals in accordance with section 10(1) of the Tribunal and Inquiries Act 1971 hereby makes the following Rules—

### Citation and commencement
**1.** These Rules may be cited as the Design Right (Proceedings before Comptroller) Rules 1989 and shall come into force on 1st August 1989.

### Interpretation
**2.**—(1) In these Rules, unless the context otherwise requires—

'the Act' means the Copyright, Designs and Patents Act 1988;

'applicant' means a person who has referred a dispute or made an application to the Comptroller;

'application' means an application to the Comptroller to settle or vary the terms of a licence of right or to adjust the terms of a licence'

'dispute' means a dispute as to any of the matters referred to in rule 3(1); and

'proceedings' means proceedings before the Comptroller in respect of a dispute or application.

(2) A rule or schedule referred to by number means the rule or schedule so numbered in these Rules; and a requirement under these Rules to use a form set out in Schedule 1 is satisfied by the use either of a replica of that form or of a form which contains the information required by the form set out in the said Schedule and which is acceptable to the Comptroller.

## Proceedings in respect of a dispute

**3.**—(1) Proceedings under section 246 of the Act in respect of a dispute as to—

(a)  the subsistence of design right,

(b)  the term of design right, or

(c)  the identity of the person in whom design right first vested,

shall be commenced by the service by the applicant on the Comptroller of a notice in Form 1 in Schedule 1. There shall be served with that notice a statement in duplicate setting out the name and address of the other party to the dispute (hereinafter in this rule referred to as the respondent), the issues in dispute, the applicant's case and the documents relevant to his case.

(2) Within 14 days of the receipt of the notice the Comptroller shall send a copy of the notice, together with a copy of the applicant's statement, to the respondent.

(3) Within 28 days of the receipt by him of the documents referred to in paragraph (2) above, the respondent shall serve on the Comptroller a counter-statement and shall at the same time serve a copy of it on the applicant. Such counter-statement shall set out full particulars of the grounds on which he contests the applicant's case, any issues on which he and the applicant are in agreement and the documents relevant to his case.

(4) Within 21 days of the service on him of the counter-statement, the applicant may serve a further statement on the Comptroller setting out the grounds on which he contests the respondent's case, and shall at the same time serve a copy of it on the respondent.

(5) No amended statement or further statement shall be served by either party except by leave or direction of the Comptroller.

**4.**—(1) The Comptroller shall give such directions as to the further conduct of proceedings as he considers appropriate.

(2) If a party fails to comply with any direction given under this rule, the Comptroller may in awarding costs take account of such default.

**5.**—(1) Unless the Comptroller otherwise directs, all evidence in the proceedings shall be by statutory declaration or affidavit.

(2) Where the Comptroller thinks fit in any particular case to take oral evidence in lieu of or in addition to evidence by statutory declaration or affidavit he may so direct and, unless he directs otherwise, shall allow any witness to be cross-examined on his evidence.

(3) A party to the proceedings who desires to make oral representations shall

so notify the Comptroller and the Comptroller shall, unless he and the parties agree to a shorter period, give at least 14 days' notice of the time and place of the hearing to the parties.

(4) If a party intends to refer at a hearing to any document not already referred to in the proceedings, he shall, unless the Comptroller and the other party agree to a shorter period, give 14 days' notice of his intention, together with particulars of every document to which he intends to refer, to the Comptroller and the other party.

(5) At any stage of the proceedings the Comptroller may direct that such documents, information or evidence as he may require shall be filed within such time as he may specify.

(6) The hearing of any proceedings, or part of proceedings, under this rule shall be in public, unless the Comptroller, after consultation with the parties, otherwise directs.

**6.**—(1) Any party to the proceedings may appear in person or be represented by counsel or a solicitor (of any part of the United Kingdom) or, subject to paragraph (4) below, a patent agent or any other person whom he desires to represent him.

(2) Anything required or authorised by these Rules to be done by or in relation to any person may be done by or in relation to his agent.

(3) Where after a person has become a party to the proceedings he appoints an agent for the first time or appoints an agent in substitution for another, the newly appointed agent shall give written notice of his appointment to the Comptroller and to every other party to the proceedings.

(4) The Comptroller may refuse to recognise as such an agent in respect of any proceedings before him—

    (a) a person who has been convicted of an offence under section 88 of the Patents Act 1949 or section 114 of the Patents Act 1977 [or section 276 of the Act];

    (b) any individual whose name has been erased from and not restored to, or who is suspended from, the register of patent agents (kept in pursuance of rules made under the Patents Act 1977 [section 275 of the Act]) on the ground of misconduct;

    (c) a person who is found by the Secretary of State to have been guilty of such conduct as would, in the case of an individual registered in the register of patent agents, render him liable to have his name erased from the register on the ground of misconduct;

    (d) a partnership or body corporate of which one of the partners or directors is a person whom the Comptroller could refuse to recognise under sub-paragraphs (a), (b) or (c) above.

*General note*
In para (4), the first words in square brackets were inserted and the second words in square brackets were substituted by the Design Right (Proceedings before Comptroller)(Amendment) Rules 1990 [SI 1990 No 1453.]

**7.**—(1) A person who claims to have a substantial interest in a dispute in respect of which proceedings have been commenced may apply to the Comptroller to be made a party to the dispute in Form 2 in Schedule 1, supported by a statement of his interest. He shall serve a copy of his application, together with his statement, on every party to the proceedings.

(2) The Comptroller shall, upon being satisfied of the substantial interest of that

person in the dispute, grant the application and shall give directions or further directions under rule 4(1) as may be necessary to enable that person to participate in the proceedings as a party to the dispute.

**8.** A party (including a person made a party to the proceedings under rule 7) may at any time before the Comptroller's decision withdraw from the proceedings by serving a notice to that effect on the Comptroller and every other party to the proceedings, but such withdrawal shall be without prejudice to the Comptroller's power to make an order as to the payment of costs incurred up to the time of service of the notice.

**9.** After hearing the party or parties desiring to be heard, or if none of the parties so desires, then without a hearing, the Comptroller shall decide the dispute and notify his decision to the parties, giving written reasons for his decision if so required by any party.

**Proceedings in respect of application to settle terms of licence of right or adjust terms of licence**

**10.**—(1) Proceedings in respect of an application to the Comptroller—

(a)  under section 247 of the Act, to settle the terms of a licence available as of right by virtue of section 237 or under an order under section 238 of the Act, or

(b)  under paragraph 19(2) of Schedule 1 to the Act, to settle the terms of a licence available as of right in respect of a design recorded or embodied in a design document or model before 1st August 1989, or

(c)  brought by virtue of paragraph 19(5) of Schedule 1 to the Act, to adjust the terms of a licence granted before 1st August 1989 in respect of a design referred to in sub-paragraph (b) above,

shall be commenced by the service by the applicant on the Comptroller of a notice in Form 3 in Schedule 1.

(2) There shall be served with the notice a statement in duplicate setting out—

(a)  in the case of an application referred to in paragraph (1)(a) or (b) above, the terms of the licence which the applicant requires the Comptroller to settle and, unless the application is one to which rule 13 relates, the name and address of the owner of the design right or, as the case may be, the copyright owner of the design;

(b)  in the case of an application referred to in paragraph (1)(c) above, the date and terms of the licence and the grounds on which the applicant requires the Comptroller to adjust those terms and the name and address of the grantor of the licence.

(3) Within 14 days of the receipt of the notice the Comptroller shall send a copy of it, together with a copy of the applicant's statement, to the person (hereinafter in this rule referred to as the respondent) shown in the application as the design right owner, copyright owner or grantor of the licence, as appropriate.

(4) Within 6 weeks of the receipt by him of the notice sent under paragraph (3) above the respondent shall, if he does not agree to the terms of the licence required by the applicant to be settled or, as the case may be, adjusted, serve a notice of objection on the Comptroller with a statement setting out the grounds of his objection and at the same time shall serve a copy of the same on the applicant.

(5) Within 4 weeks of the receipt of the notice of objection the applicant may

serve on the Comptroller a counter-statement and at the same time serve a copy of it on the respondent.

(6) No amended statement or further statement shall be served by either party except by leave or direction of the Comptroller.

**11.** Rules 4, 5, 6 and 8 shall apply in respect of proceedings under rule 10 as they apply in respect of proceedings under rule 3.

**12.** After hearing the party or parties desiring to be heard, or if none of the parties so desires, then without a hearing, the Comptroller shall decide the application and notify his decision to the parties, giving written reasons for his decision if so required by any party.

## Settlement of terms where design right owner unknown

**13.**—(1) Where a person making an application under rule 10(1)(a) or (b) is unable (after making such inquiries as he considers reasonable) to discover the identity of the design right owner or, as the case may be, the copyright owner, he shall serve with his notice under that rule a statement to that effect, setting out particulars of the inquiries made by him as to the identity of the owner of the right and the result of those inquiries.

(2) The Comptroller may require the applicant to make such further inquiries into the identity of the owner of the right as he thinks fit and, may for that purpose, require him to publish in such a manner as the Comptroller considers appropriate particulars of the application.

(3) The Comptroller shall, upon being satisfied from the applicant's statement or the further inquiries made under paragraph (2) above that the identity of the owner of the right cannot be discovered, consider the application and settle the terms of the licence.

## Proceedings in respect of application by design right owner to vary terms of licence

**14.**—(1) Where the Comptroller has, in settling the terms of the licence under rule 13, ordered that the licence shall be free of any obligation as to royalties or other payments, the design right owner or copyright owner (as the case may be) may serve on the Comptroller a notice in Form 4 in Schedule 1 applying for the terms of the licence to be varied from the date of his application. There shall be served with the notice a statement in duplicate setting out the particulars of the grounds for variation and the terms required to be varied.

(2) Within 14 days of the receipt of the notice the Comptroller shall send a copy of the notice, together with the design right or copyright owner's statement, to the applicant under rule 10 (hereinafter in this rule referred to as the licensee).

(3) The licensee shall, if he does not agree to the terms as required to be varied by the design right or copyright owner, within 6 weeks of the receipt of the notice serve notice of objection on the Comptroller with a statement setting out the grounds of his objection and at the same time shall serve a copy on the design right or copyright owner, as the case may be.

(4) Within 4 weeks of the receipt of the notice of objection the design right or copyright owner may serve on the Comptroller a counter-statement, and at the same time shall serve a copy of it on the licensee.

(5) No amended statement or further statement shall be served by either party except by leave or direction of the Comptroller.

**15.** Rules 4, 5, 6 and 8 shall apply in respect of proceedings under rule 14 as they apply in respect of proceedings under rule 3.

**16.** After hearing the party or parties desiring to be heard, or if none of the parties so desires, then without a hearing, the Comptroller shall decide the application and notify his decision to the parties, giving written reasons for his decision if so required by any party.

**General**

**17.** Any document filed in any proceedings may, if the Comptroller thinks fit, be amended, and any irregularity in procedure may be rectified by the Comptroller on such terms as he may direct.

**18.**—(1) Any statutory declaration or affidavit filed in any proceedings shall be made and subscribed as follows—

    (a)  in the United Kingdom, before any justice of the peace or any commissioner or other officer authorised by law in any part of the United Kingdom to administer an oath for the purpose of any legal proceedings;

    (b)  in any other part of Her Majesty's dominions or in the Republic of Ireland, before any court, judge, justice of the peace or any officer authorised by law to administer an oath there for the purpose of any legal proceedings; and

    (c)  elsewhere, before a British Minister, or person exercising the functions of a British Minister, or a Consul, Vice-Consul or other person exercising the functions of a British Consul or before a notary public, judge or magistrate.

(2) Any document purporting to have fixed, impressed or subscribed thereto or thereon the seal or signature of any person authorised by paragraph (1) above to take a declaration may be admitted by the Comptroller without proof of the genuineness of the seal or signature or of the official character of the person or his authority to take the declaration.

(3) In England and Wales, the Comptroller shall, in relation to the giving of evidence (including evidence on oath), the attendance of witnesses and the discovery and production of documents, have all the powers of a judge of the High Court, other than the power to punish summarily for contempt of court.

(4) In Scotland, the Comptroller shall, in relation to the giving of evidence (including evidence on oath), have all the powers which a Lord Ordinary of the Court of Session has in an action before him, other than the power to punish summarily for contempt of court, and, in relation to the attendance of witnesses and the recovery and production of documents, have all the powers of the Court of Session.

**19.** The Comptroller may appoint an adviser to assist him in any proceedings and shall settle the question or instructions to be submitted or given to such an adviser.

**20.**—(1) The times or periods prescribed by these Rules for doing any act or taking any proceedings thereunder may be extended by the Comptroller if he thinks fit, upon such notice and upon such terms as he may direct, and such extension may be granted although the time for doing such act or taking such proceedings has already expired.

(2) Where the last day for the doing of any act falls on a day on which the Patent Office is closed and by reason thereof the act cannot be done on that day, it may be done on the next day on which the Office is open.

**21.** For the purposes of these Rules the Patent Office shall be open Monday to Friday—

    (a)  between 10.00 a.m. and midnight, for the filing of applications, forms and other documents, and

    (b)  between 10.00 a.m. and 4.00 p.m. for all other purposes,

excluding Good Friday, Christmas Day and any day specified or proclaimed to be a bank holiday under section 1 of the Banking and Financial Dealings Act 1971.

**22.**—(1) The Comptroller may, in respect of any proceedings, by order award such costs or, in Scotland, such expenses as he considers reasonable and direct how, to what party and from what parties they are to be paid.

(2) Where any applicant or a person making an application under rule 7 neither resides nor carries on business in the United Kingdom or another member State of the European Economic Community the Comptroller may require him to give security for the costs or expenses of the proceedings and in default of such security being given may treat the reference or application as abandoned.

**23.**—(1) Every person concerned in any proceedings to which these Rules relate shall furnish to the Comptroller an address for service in the United Kingdom, and that address may be treated for all purposes connected with such proceedings as the address of the person concerned.

(2) Where any document or part of a document which is in a language other than English is served on the Comptroller or any party to proceedings or filed with the Comptroller in pursuance of these Rules, it shall be accompanied by a translation into English of the document or part, verified to the satisfaction of the Comptroller as corresponding to the original text.

**24.** The fees specified in Schedule 2 shall be payable in respect of the matters there mentioned.

**The Patent Office**

**Design Right Form 1**

**Reference of dispute to Comptroller**

For Official Use

Copyright, Designs & Patents Act 1988

**Notes**

Please type or write in dark ink using BLOCK LETTERS. For details of prescribed fees please contact the Patent Office.

Rule 3 of the Design Right (Proceedings before Comptroller) Rules 1989 is the main rule governing the completion and filing of this form.

This form must be filed together with a statement in duplicate setting out the matters referred to in Rule 3(1).

1. Your reference

2. Please give full name and address of person making the reference.
Name

Address

Postcode

ADP number (if known)

3. Please give an address for service in the United Kingdom to which all correspondence will be sent.
Name

Address

Postcode

ADP number (if known)

❶ Identification may be made by providing drawings, photographs or other identifying material.

4. Please identify the design which is the subject of the proceedings.

Please mark correct box (es)

5. The dispute to be settled is in respect of :-

the subsistence of the design right ☐

the term of the design right ☐

the identity of the person in whom design right first vested ☐

6. Please give the name and address of the other party to the dispute.
Name

Address

Postcode

ADP number (if known)

**Please sign here** ➤ Signed _____ Date _____
day   month   year

**Reminder**
Have you attached          the statement of case in duplicate? ☐

the prescribed fee? ☐

Issued   1989

**The Patent Office**

**Design Right Form 2**

**Application to be made a party to proceedings.**

For Official Use

Copyright, Designs
& Patents Act 1988

**Notes**

Please type or write in dark ink using BLOCK LETTERS. For details of prescribed fees please contact the Patent Office.

Rule 7 of the Design Right (Proceedings before Comptroller) Rules 1989 is the main rule governing the completion and filing of this form.

A statement to show your substantial interest in the dispute in respect of which proceedings have been commenced must accompany this form. You must also serve a copy of the form and statement on every party to the proceedings.

1. Your reference

2. Please give full name and address of person applying to be made a party to dispute.
Name

Address

Postcode

ADP number (if known)

3. Please give an address for service in the United Kingdom to which all correspondence will be sent.
Name

Address

Postcode

ADP number (if known)

4. Please identify the proceedings relating to the dispute in which you claim to have a substantial interest.

**Please sign here ➤**    Signed _____ Date _____

day   month   year

**Reminder**
Have you attached          a statement of your interest? ☐

the prescribed fee? ☐

Issued   1989

**The Patent Office**

Copyright, Designs
& Patents Act 1988

**Design Right Form 3**

**Application to settle terms of Licence of Right or to adjust terms of Licence granted before 1st August 1989**

**For Official Use**

**Notes**

Please type or write in dark ink using BLOCK LETTERS. For details of prescribed fees please contact the Patent Office.

Rules 10 and 13 of the Design Right (Proceedings before Comptroller) Rules 1989 are the main rules governing the completion and filing of this form.

This form must be filed, by the person requiring the settlement or adjustment of the licence, together with a statement in duplicate setting out the terms required. Where the applicant has been unable to discover the identity of the design right or copyright owner a statement must also be filed setting out the particulars of and result of the inquiries made to try to identify the owner.

❶ Identification may be made by providing drawings, photographs or other identifying material.

❺ If part 6(a) of this form applies, give the name and address of the design right or copyright owner (if known). If part 6(b) applies give the name and address of the grantor of the licence in question.

Please mark correct box

**Please sign here ➤**

**Important note**
This form is **not** for use by the design right or copyright owner.

1. Your reference

2. Please give full name and address of applicant.
Name

Address

Postcode
ADP number (if known)

3. Please give an address for service in the United Kingdom to which all correspondence will be sent.
Name

Address

Postcode
ADP number (if known)

4. Please identify the design which is the subject of these proceedings.

5. Please give the name and address of the respondent (see note 5).
Name

Address

Postcode
ADP number (if known)

6. Application is made to the Comptroller:
(a) to settle the terms of a licence for the design which is available as of right by virtue of:     Section 237 ☐

an order under Section 238 ☐

paragraph 19(2) of Schedule 1 ☐

(b) to adjust terms of a licence under paragraph 19(5) of Schedule 1 ☐

Signed _____  Date _____
                                              day   month   year

**Reminder**
Have you attached     the prescribed fee? ☐

the statement in duplicate of the terms required ? ☐

a statement of inquiries made to identify the design right or copyright owner (if inquiries unsuccessful)? ☐

Issued   1989

# The Patent Office

Copyright, Designs
& Patents Act 1988

**Design Right Form 3**

**Application to settle terms of Licence of Right or to adjust terms of Licence granted before 1st August 1989**

| For Official Use |
| --- |

## Notes

Please type or write in dark ink using BLOCK LETTERS. For details of prescribed fees please contact the Patent Office.

Rules 10 and 13 of the Design Right (Proceedings before Comptroller) Rules 1989 are the main rules governing the completion and filing of this form.

This form must be filed, by the person requiring the settlement or adjustment of the licence, together with a statement in duplicate setting out the terms required. Where the applicant has been unable to discover the identity of the design right or copyright owner a statement must also be filed setting out the particulars of and result of the inquiries made to try to identify the owner.

❶ Identification may be made by providing drawings, photographs or other identifying material.

❺ If part 6(a) of this form applies, give the name and address of the design right or copyright owner (if known). If part 6(b) applies give the name and address of the grantor of the licence in question.

Please mark correct box

**Please sign here** ➤

**Important note**
This form is **not** for use by the design right or copyright owner.

---

1. Your reference

2. Please give full name and address of applicant.
Name

Address

Postcode
ADP number (if known)

3. Please give an address for service in the United Kingdom to which all correspondence will be sent.
Name

Address

Postcode
ADP number (if known)

4. Please identify the design which is the subject of these proceedings.

5. Please give the name and address of the respondent (see note 5).
Name

Address

Postcode
ADP number (if known)

6. Application is made to the Comptroller:
(a) to settle the terms of a licence for the design which is available as of right by virtue of:    Section 237 ☐

an order under Section 238 ☐

paragraph 19(2) of Schedule 1 ☐

(b) to adjust terms of a licence under paragraph 19(5) of Schedule 1 ☐

Signed _____ Date _____
day month year

**Reminder**
Have you attached    the prescribed fee? ☐

the statement in duplicate of the terms required ? ☐

a statement of inquiries made to identify the design right or copyright owner (if inquiries unsuccessful)? ☐

Issued   1989

DESIGN RIGHT (RECIPROCAL PROTECTION) (NO 2) ORDER 1989
(SI 1989 No 1294)

*Made* . . . . . . *28th July 1989*
*Laid before Parliament* . . . . *31st July 1989*
*Coming into force* . . . . . . *1st August 1989*

Whereas, it appears to Her Majesty that the laws of the countries mentioned in article 2 of this Order provide adequate protection for British Designs:

Now, therefore, Her Majesty, by virtue of the authority conferred upon Her by section 256(1) of the Copyright Designs and Patents Act 1988, is pleased, by and with the advice of Her Privy Council, to order, and it is hereby ordered, as follows:

**1.** This Order may be cited as the Design Right (Reciprocal Protection) (No 2) Order 1989 and shall come into force on 1st August 1989.

**2.** The following countries are hereby designated as enjoying reciprocal protection under Part III of the Copyright, Designs and Patents Act 1988 (design right)—

Anguilla
Bermuda
British Indian Ocean Territory
British Virgin Islands
Cayman Islands
Channel Islands
Falklands Islands
Gibraltar
Hong Kong
Isle of Man
Montserrat
New Zealand
Pitcairn, Henderson, Ducie and Oeno Islands
St Helena and Dependencies
South Georgia and the South Sandwich Islands
Turks and Caicos Islands.

**3.** The Design Right (Reciprocal Protection) Order 1989[ SI 1989 No 990] is hereby revoked.

# PART E  MISCELLANEOUS

HIGH COURT AND COUNTY COURTS JURISDICTION ORDER 1991
(SI 1991 No 724)

*Made* . . . . . . . . *9th March 1991*
*Coming into force.* . . . . . *1st July 1991*

The Lord Chancellor, in exercise of the powers conferred upon him by sections 1
and 120 of the Courts and Legal Services Act 1990, having consulted as required
by section 1(9) of that Act, hereby makes the following Order a draft of which
has, in accordance with section 120(4) of that Act, been laid before and approved
by the resolution of each House of Parliament—

**Title and commencement**
**1.** This Order may be cited as the High Court and County Courts Jurisdiction Order
1991 and shall come into force on 1st July 1991.

**Jurisdiction**
**2.**—(1) A county court shall have jurisdiction under—

(sub-paras (a)-(m))
(n)  sections 99, 102(5), 114, 195, 204, 230, 231 and 235(5) of the Copyright,
Designs and Patents Act 1988, and
(sub-para (o))

whatever the amount involved in the proceedings and whatever the value of any
fund or asset connected with the proceedings.

**Allocation—Trial**
**7.**—(1)–(4)
(5) The High Court and the county courts, when considering whether to exercise
their powers under section 40(2), 41(1) or 42(2) of the County Courts Act 1984
(Transfer) shall have regard to the following criteria—

(a)  the financial substance of the action, including the value of any counter-
claim,
(b)  whether the action is otherwise important and, in particular, whether it
raises questions of importance to persons who are not parties or questions
of general public interest,
(c)  the complexity of the facts, legal issues, remedies or procedures involved,
and
(d)  whether transfer is likely to result in a more speedy trial of the action,

but no transfer shall be made on the grounds of sub-paragraph (d) alone.

PATENTS COUNTY COURT (DESIGNATION AND JURISDICTION)
ORDER 1994
(SI 1994 No 1609)

| | |
|---|---|
| *Made* . . . . . . *17th June 1994* | |
| *Coming into force.* . . . . . *1th July 1994* | |

The Lord Chancellor, in exercise of the powers conferred on him by section 287 of the Copyright, Designs and Patents Act 1988, hereby makes the following Order—

**Citation and commencement**
**1.** This Order may be cited as the Patents County Court (Designation and Jurisdiction) Order 1994 and shall come into force on 11th July 1994.

**Designation as Patents County Court**
**2.** The Central London County Court is hereby designated as a patents county court.
**3.** As a patents county court, the Central London County Court shall have jurisdiction, subject to article 4 below, to hear and determine any action or matter relating to patents or designs over which the High Court would have jurisdiction, together with any claims or matters ancillary to, or arising from, such proceedings.
**4.** The jurisdiction conferred by article 3 above shall not include jurisdiction to hear appeals from the comptroller.

**Discontinuance and transitional provision**
**5.**—(1) The Edmonton County Court shall cease to be a patents county court and accordingly the Patents County Court (Designation and Jurisdiction) Order 1990 is hereby revoked.

(2) The patents county court at the Central London County Court shall have jurisdiction in proceedings commenced in the patents county court at the Edmonton County Court before the coming into force of this Order.


RULES OF THE SUPREME COURT (REVISION) 1965
(SI 1965 No 1776)

| | |
|---|---|
| *Made* . . . . . . *30th September 1965* | |
| *Coming into force.* . . . . . *1st October 1966* | |

ORDER 93
APPLICATIONS AND APPEALS TO HIGH COURT UNDER VARIOUS ACTS:
CHANCERY DIVISION

**[Applications under section 114, 204 or 231 of the Copyright, Designs and Patents Act 1988**

**24.**—(1) Where an application is made under section 114, 204 or 231 of the Copyright, Designs and Patents Act 1988, the applicant shall serve notice of the application on all persons so far as reasonably ascertainable having an interest in the copy or other article which is the subject of the application, including any person in whose favour an order could be made in respect of the copy or other article under any of the said sections of the Act of 1988 or under section 58C of the Trade Marks Act 1938.

(2) An application under the said section 114, 204 or 231 shall be made by originating summons or, if it is made in a pending action, by summons or motion in that action.]

*General note*
This rule was inserted by SI 1989 No 1307, r 19, as from 1 September 1989.

ORDER 104
THE PATENTS ACTS 1949 TO 1961 AND 1977; THE REGISTERED DESIGNS ACT 1949 TO 1971; THE DEFENCE CONTRACTS ACT 1958

RULES 1, 2, 21, 22, 23

*(The original Order 104 was renumbered as Order 105 and new Order 104 was inserted by the Rules of the Supreme Court (Amendment No 3) 1978, SI 1978 No 579, coming into force on 1st June 1978. This Order is printed as amended by the Rules of the Supreme Court (Amendment No 2) 1986, SI 1986 No 1187).*

**[Definitions**
**1.** In this Order—
'the 1949 Act' means the Patents Act 1949;
'the 1977 Act' means the Patents Act 1977;
'the comptroller' means the Comptroller-General of Patents, Designs and Trade Marks;
'the Court', without prejudice to Order 1, rule 4(2), means the Patents Court;
'existing patent' means a patent mentioned in section 127(2)(a) or (c) of the 1977 Act;
'the journal' means the journal published pursuant to rules made under section 123(6) of the 1977 Act;
'1977 Act patent' means a patent under the 1977 Act;
'patent' means an existing patent or a 1977 Act patent.]

*General note*
Original Order 104 renumbered as Order 105 and new Order 104 inserted by the Rules of the Supreme Court (Amendment No 3) 1978, SI 1978 No 579, r 12.

**[Assignment of proceedings**
**2.**—(1) All proceedings in the High Court under the Patents Acts 1949 to 1961 and 1977, the Registered Designs Acts 1949 to 1961 and the Defence Contracts Act 1958, and all proceedings for the determination of a question or the making of a declaration relating to a patent under the inherent jurisdiction of the High Court, shall be assigned to the Chancery Division and taken by the Court.

(2) Nothing in Order 4, rule 1, shall apply in relation to any proceedings mentioned in paragraph (1) but every writ, summons, petition, notice, pleading, affidavit or other document relating to such proceedings must be marked in the top left-hand corner with the words 'Patents Court'.]

*General note*
See the note to Order 104, r 1.

## [Proceedings for determination of certain disputes

**21.**—(1) The following proceedings must be begun by originating motion, that is to say—

    (a) proceedings for the determination of any dispute referred to the Court under—

        (i) section 48 of the 1949 Act or section 58 of the 1977 Act;

        (ii) paragraph 3 of Schedule 1 to the Registered Designs Act 1949, or

       (iii) section 4 of the Defence Contracts Act 1958;

    (b) any application under section 45(3) of the 1977 Act.

(2) There must be at least 10 clear days between the serving of notice of a motion under this rule and the day named in the notice for hearing the motion.

(3) On the hearing of a motion under this rule the Court shall give such directions for the further conduct of the proceedings as it thinks necessary or expedient and, in particular, directions for the service of particulars and as to the manner in which the evidence shall be given and as to the date of the hearing.]

*General note*
See the note to Order 104, r 1. This rule was originally rule 16 and was renumbered as rule 21 by the Rules of the Supreme Court (Amendment No 2) 1986, SI 1986 No 1187, r 15(5), (7).

## [Application for rectification of register of patents or designs

**22.**—(1) An application to the Court for an order that the register of patents or the register of designs be rectified must be made by originating motion, except where it is made in a petition for the revocation of a patent or by way of counterclaim in proceedings for infringement or by originating summons in proceedings for an order under section 51 of the Trustee Act 1925.

(2) Where the application relates to the register of patents, the applicant shall forthwith serve an office copy of the application on the comptroller, who shall be entitled to appear and to be heard on the application.]

*General note*
See the note to Order 104, r 1. This rule was originally rule 17 and was renumbered as rule 22 by the Rules of the Supreme Court (Amendment No 2) 1986, SI 1986 No 1187, r 15(5), (7).

## [Counterclaim for rectification of register of designs

**23.**—(1) Where in any proceedings a claim is made for relief for infringement of the copyright in a registered design, the party against whom the claim is made may in his defence put in issue the validity of the registration of that design or may counterclaim for an order that the register of designs be rectified by cancelling or varying the registration or may do both those things.

(2) A party to any such proceedings who in his pleading (whether a defence or counterclaim) disputes the validity of the registration of a registered design must serve with the pleading particulars of the objections to the validity of the registration on which he relies in support of the allegation of invalidity.

(3) A party to any such proceedings who counterclaims for an order that the register of designs be rectified must serve on the comptroller a copy of the counterclaim together with a copy of the particulars mentioned in paragraph (2); and the comptroller shall be entitled to take such part in the proceedings as he thinks fit but need not serve a defence or other pleading unless ordered to do so by the Court.]

*General note*
See the note to Order 104, r 1. This rule was originally rule 18 and was renumbered as rule 123 by the Rules of the Supreme Court (Amendment No 2) 1986, SI 1986 No 1187, r 15(5), (7).

COUNTY COURT RULES 1981
(SI 1981 No 1687)

|  |  |  |  |  |  |  |
|---|---|---|---|---|---|---|
| *Made* | . . | . . | . . | . . | *16th April 1981* | |
| *Coming into force.* | . | . . | . . | *.1st September 1982* | |

ORDER 48A
PATENTS AND DESIGNS

*(Order 48A was inserted by the County Court (Amendment No 2) Rules 1990 (SI 1990 No 1495) and came into force on 3rd September 1990)*

### Application and interpretation
**1.**—(1) This Order applies to proceedings in respect of which patents county courts have jurisdiction under section 287(1) of the 1988 Act.

(2) In this Order—

'The 1988 Act' means the Copyright, Designs and Patents Act 1988;

'patents county court' means a county court designated as a patents county court under section 287(1) of the 1988 Act;

'patents judge' means a person nominated under section 291(1) of the 1988 Act as the patents judge of a patents county court.

### Patents judge
**2.**—(1) Subject to paragraph (2), proceedings to which this Order applies shall be dealt with by the patents judge.

(2) When an interlocutory matter needs to be dealt with urgently and the patents judge is not available, the matter may be dealt with by another judge.

### Commencement
**3.** Every summons, notice, pleading, affidavit or other document relating to proceedings to which this Order applies must be marked in the top left hand corner with the words 'patents county court'.

### Pleadings
**4.**—(1) Every summons issued in accordance with rule 3 above shall be endorsed with or accompanied by a statement of case.

(2) Where a claim is made by the plaintiff in respect of the infringement of a patent, the statement of case shall give full particulars of the infringement relied on, setting out—

(a) which of the claims in the specification of the patent are alleged to be infringed; and

(b) in respect of each claim alleged to be infringed the grounds relied on in support of the allegations that such claim has been infringed; and all facts, matters and arguments relied on as establishing those grounds, including at least one example of each type of infringement alleged.

(3) Where, in any proceedings, the validity of a patent is put in issue, the statement of case shall give particulars of the objections to the validity of the patent which are relied on; and in particular shall explain the relevance of every citation to each claim, with identification of the significant parts of each citation, and shall give all facts, matters and arguments which are relied on for establishing the invalidity of the patent.

(5) Every statement of case shall be signed—

(a)  by the plaintiff, if he sues in person; or
(b)  by the plaintiff's solicitor in his own name or the name of his firm;

and shall state the plaintiff's address for service.

(6) Where a defendant wishes to serve a defence to any claim he shall serve it, together with any counterclaim including a statement of case under paragraph (2) or (3) above, upon the plaintiff within 42 days of service upon him of the summons.

(7) Where a party wishes to serve a reply or a defence to counterclaim, he shall do so within 28 days of the service of the previous pleading upon him.

(8) Pleadings will close seven days after the expiry of the time for service of a reply.

(9) No time limit mentioned in this rule may be extended more than once (and then by no more than 42 days) save by order of the court; and such order shall, in the first place, be applied for in writing, whereupon the judge shall either grant the application, refuse it or order a hearing.

(10) The parties to proceedings shall notify the court of any agreed extension of any time limit mentioned in this rule.

**Service**
**5.**—(1) In their application to proceedings to which this Order applies, rules 10 and 13 of Order 7 shall apply as if—

(a)  before the words 'an officer' in paragraph (1)(b) of each rule there were inserted the words 'the plaintiff or'; and
(b)  in paragraph (4) of rule 10 (and in that paragraph as applied by rule 13) after the words 'sent by post' there were inserted the words 'by an officer of the court'.

(2) Where a pleading is served which refers to any document, the party serving the pleading must also serve with it a copy of any such document together with an English translation of any foreign language text, certified as being accurate.

**Interrogatories and notices to admit facts**
**6.**—(1)

(a)  Interrogatories under Order 14, rule 11, and
(b)  a notice to admit facts under Order 20, rule 2,

may not be served without the leave of the court unless (in the case of a notice to admit facts) it is served within 14 days of the close of pleadings; and accordingly those provisions of Order 14, rule 11 (and of the RSC which are applied by that rule) which relate only to interrogatories without order shall not apply to proceedings under this Order.

(2) An application for leave to serve interrogatories or a notice to admit facts may only be made on notice at the preliminary consideration under rule 8.

### Scientific advisors, assessors and patent office reports

**7.**—(1) The court may at any time, on or without the application of any party—

(a) appoint scientific advisers or assessors to assist the court; or

(b) order the Patent Office to inquire into and report on any question of fact or opinion.

(2) RSC Order 104, rule 15 shall apply to the appointment of a scientific adviser under this rule.

(3) Where the court appoints an assessor under this rule without the application of a party, paragraphs (3) and (6) of Order 13, rule 11 shall apply, and paragraph (4) of that rule shall apply with the omission of the words from 'the applicant shall' to 'and thereupon' inclusive.

### Preliminary consideration

**8.**—(1) Within fourteen days of the close of pleadings, all parties shall file and serve an application for directions, signed by the person settling it.

(2) Each application for directions shall:

(a) summarise the outstanding issues in the proceedings;

(b) summarise the further steps necessary to prove the applicant's contentions in the proceedings and prepare his case for a hearing;

(c) give full particulars of any experiments the applicant intends to conduct, stating the facts which he intends to prove by them and the date by which he will submit a written report of the results; and

(d) set out all orders and directions the applicant will ask for at the preliminary consideration of the action.

(3) As soon as is practicable after receipt of each party's application for directions, the proper officer shall set a date for the preliminary consideration.

(4) On the preliminary consideration the judge may, with or without the application of any party and either after a consideration of the papers or having adjudicated upon a point of law strike out any point raised in the proceedings.

(5) On the preliminary consideration, the judge shall give such directions as are necessary to prepare the proceedings for hearing and in particular shall consider and (where appropriate) give directions in respect of each or any of the following matters, namely—

(a) the witnesses who may be called;

(b) whether their evidence should be given orally or in writing or any combination of the two;

(c) the exchange of witness statements;

(d) the provision of Patent Office Reports;

(e) the use of assessors at the hearing;

(f) transfer to the High Court;

(g) reference to the Court of Justice of the European Communities;

(h) applications for discovery and inspection;

(i) applications for leave under rule 6 above; and

(j) written reports of the results of any experiments of which particulars have been given under rule 8(2)(c).

### General modification of county court rules

**9.** In their application to proceedings to which this Order applies, county court rules shall be subject to the following modifications—

(a) Order 3 rules 3(1) and (2)(c) shall have effect as if for the words 'particulars of claim' there are substituted the words 'statement of case';

(b) in Order 3, rule 3(2)(a), the words from 'and in the case' to 'return day' inclusive shall be omitted;

(c) Order 3, rule 3(3) shall not apply;

(d) Order 6, rule 7 shall not apply;

(e) Order 9 shall not apply, with the exception of Order 9 rule 19, which shall apply to every defence or counterclaim delivered under rule 4(6) above as it applies to those delivered under Order 9, rule 2.

### Application of Rules of the Supreme Court

**10.**—(1) RSC Order 104, rule 3 shall apply to applications by a patentee or the proprietor of a patent intending to apply under section 30 of the Patents Act 1949 or section 75 of the Patents Act 1977 for leave to amend his specification, save that references therein to an application by motion shall be construed, for the purposes of an application to a patents county court, as an application on notice to the patents judge.

(2) RSC Order 104, rule 17 shall apply to actions to which this Order applies, with the omission of the words 'by originating summons'.

(3) RSC Order 104, rule 16(3), rule 20 and rule 23 shall apply to actions to which this Order applies.

## GENERAL NOTICE GEN (93) 2: CROWN AND PARLIAMENTARY COPYRIGHT

### Scope and purpose

**1.** This note states the practice to be followed with regard to Crown and Parliamentary copyright, as defined by the Copyright, Designs and Patents Act 1988 (published by HMSO, ISBN 0 10 544888 5).

### References

**2.** This note supersedes General Notice GEN 90/23, which is now withdrawn.

**3.** The Copyright, Designs and Patents Act 1988 came into effect on 1 August 1989 and replaced the Copyright Act 1956 and the Copyright (Computer Software) Amendment Act 1985.

### Summary of points

**4.** A summary of the advice contained in this note is as follows:

(i) All applications received by departments for permission to reproduce Crown copyright material not converted by a specific delegated authority should be referred to HMSO's Copyright Section (see paragraph 8).

(ii) Conditions relating to the reproduction of parliamentary copyright items published by HMSO are similar to those for Crown copyright material. All applications to reproduce this material should be referred to HMSO's Copyright Section (see paragraph 9).

(iii) For copyright purposes, official material is divided into six categories (see paragraph 110).

(iv)   Considerable freedom is allowed in the reproduction of material in the first three categories listed in paragraph 11 within guidelines issued by HMSO (see paragraphs 12–13).

(v)   Any department wishing to reproduce Parliamentary material not published by HMSO should apply to the officials of the relevant House (see paragraph 14).

(vi)   Fees should be levied for the reproduction for commercial purposes of non-parliamentary material (see paragraph 15).

(vii)   The administration of Crown copyright relating to charts and Ordnance Survey maps is subject to special delegation arrangements (see paragraph 16).

(viii)   If a work is commissioned, first copyright normally rests with the author or his employer (see paragraph 18).

(ix)   The Central Computer and Telecommunications Agency provides advice in cases where computer software is commissioned (see paragraph 19).

(x)   Advice on the levying of fees is set out in paragraphs 21–23.

(xi)   Any apparent infringement of Crown or parliamentary copyright should be reported to HMSO (see paragraph 24).

## Background

**5.** The 1988 Act revises the definition in the 1956 Act of Crown copyright and, in addition, introduces a new category of Parliamentary copyright. In the Act, copyright is defined as a 'property right', which means that it should be dealt with like any other property, which could include licensing or outright sale to a third party, or prohibition of use by a third party, for breach of which the owner can seek legal damages.

**6.** Copyright covers a wide variety of material, published and unpublished, including books, reports, photographs, drawings and computer programs. In general, the first owner of copyright is the creator or author of the work or his employer, although there are some exceptions to this. The most notable exceptions are in the fields of Crown and parliamentary copyright.

**7.** Under the 1956 Act, the copyright in works commissioned by a Government Department was generally claimed for the Crown on the grounds that:

(i)   the work in question was 'made by or under the direction or control of Her Majesty or a Government department'; or

(ii)   because the work was first published by the Crown.

Under the 1988 Act, however, Crown copyright only covers those works 'made by Her Majesty or by an officer or servant of the Crown in the course of his duties'. Consequently, if an author or consultant is hired by a Department to produce a work, the copyright in that work would normally rest with the author (or his employer) and not the commissioner. If, therefore, it is necessary for the Crown to hold the copyright in a particular commissioned work, then this should be made a specific condition of contract with the author or consultant. The 1988 Act also covers computer works which are defined by the Act as 'literary works' and are accorded, with some exceptions, the same status as, for example, a novel or a textbook.

## Reproduction of official material

**8.** The rights in respect of all Crown copyright and other copyrights belonging to the Crown are administered by HMSO. The unique authority to do so is granted

by Her Majesty to the Controller of HMSO by means of Royal Letters Patents. All applications received by departments for permission to reproduce official material not known to be covered by a specific delegated authority to a Department should be referred to HMSO's Copyright Section, who will normally take account of the views of the department of origin of the material before authorising its use.
**9.** Under the 1988 Act, authority for Parliamentary copyright lies with the Clerk of the Parliaments for House of Lords material and with the Speaker of the House of Commons for Commons material. For those Parliamentary items which HMSO publishes, the Controller of HMSO administers Parliamentary copyright. The conditions relating to the reproduction of this Parliamentary copyright material will be similar to those for Crown copyright.
**10.** In cases where a published version of a Crown or Parliamentary copyright work is available, departments should obtain the required number of official copies rather than engage in multiple or extensive photocopying.

**Classes of official material for copyright purposes**
**11.** For copyright purposes, official material may be divided into the following categories:

(i) Statutory material, including Bills and Acts of Parliament, Statutory Rules and Orders, and Statutory Instruments.;
(ii) The Official Report of the House of Lords and House of Commons Debates (Hansard), Lord's Minutes, the Vote Bundle, Commons Order-books and Commons Statutory Instrument Lists;
(iii) Other Parliamentary papers published by HMSO, including Reports of Select Committees of both Houses;
(iv) Other Parliamentary material not published by HMSO;
(v) Non-Parliamentary material comprising all papers of Government Departments and Crown bodies–both published and unpublished–not contained in other classes.
(vi) Charts and navigational material published by the Ministry of Defence (Hydrographic department) and maps and other items in all media published by Ordnance Survey.

**12.** Considerable freedom is allowed in the reproduction of material in the first three categories, within guidelines issued by HMSO through the Publishers Association, the Library Association and other outlets (copies are available from HMSO's Copyright Section on request). Nevertheless, all Crown rights in respect of this material are reserved and will be asserted in cases such as those where the material would be reproduced in an undesirable context or where the reproduction of the whole or part of the material falls outside the conditions specified in HMSO's guidelines, or where its reproduction could result in a significant loss of sales of official publications. All departments have a responsibility to ensure that Crown (and parliamentary) copyright is not being used illegally. However, any action to enforce the Crown's rights in copyright matters would be taken in consultation with HMSO.
**13.** Copies of Acts of Parliament, Statutory Rules and Orders and Statutory Instruments, other than those reproduced by the order of HMSO, do not have the legal standing of officially published versions produced by HMSO. Any organisation or individual wishing to reproduce the Official Report of Parliamentary Debates (Hansard) should be warned that, even though these may be verbatim reports of speeches as reported in the Official Report, it will not have

the same rights of privilege in proceedings for defamation as those enjoyed by the Official Report. Reproducing all or part of the Official Report for advertising purposes is not permitted.

**14.** All applications for reproduction of material falling in the fourth category should be referred to the officials of the relevant House (see addresses at paragraph 27).

**15.** The fifth category comprises a wide range of Government material, including many items which explain the operation of Acts of Parliament, or make available the results of research, and other activities of Departments. It is desirable that this information should be widely known, but official publication is the usual channel for this purpose and, subject to the exercise of the discretions described in paragraph 22 below, there is no reason why free reproduction should be allowed of this kind of material for commercial purposes. The exercise of the Crown's copyright is also necessary to protect official material from misuse by unfair or misleading selection, undignified association, or undesirable use for advertising purposes. The rights of the Crown will therefore normally be enforced for material in this category. Acknowledgment of source and of the permission of the Controller of HMSO should be given, and suitable fees levied for reproduction.

**16.** The administration of Crown copyright relating to material in the sixth category, charts and Ordnance Survey maps, is subject to appropriate arrangements for delegation between the Controller of HMSO and the Ministry of Defence (Hydrographic Department) and Ordnance Survey.

**17.** In the reproduction of copyright material not belonging to the Crown, departments should ensure that they abide by the terms of the Copyright, Designs and Patents Act 1988.

**18.** If a work is commissioned by a Department or other Crown body, first copyright, in the normal course of events, would rest with the author, artist, photographer, composer or creator of the work or with this employer and not with the commissioner. If, therefore, it is considered necessary for the Crown to hold copyright in a particular commissioned or similar work, this must be negotiated as a specific condition within the commissioning agreement. For practical purposes, the decision as to whether or not copyright should be claimed for the Crown on commissioned work will rest with the commissioning body, but the general benefit to the Crown of acquiring rights in commissioned works should always be borne in mind. Rights thus acquired in commissioned works should bear the usual 'Crown copyright' line as with works 'made by Her Majesty or by an officer or servant of the Crown in the course of his duties'. Care should be taken in acquiring such rights for the Crown rather than for a named individual or postholder. In the latter case, the copyright may not be the Crown's and therefore the Crown would be unable to assert or defend its rights with regard to the material in question.

**19.** In cases where computer software is commissioned (specifically defined by the 1988 Act as 'literary work'), the copyright should remain the property of the software developer where the Crown's intention is generally to acquire use of the software rather than to buy the software outright for further exploitation. This is the normal policy advocated by the Central Computer and Telecommunications Agency (CCTA). CCTA provide guidance on how Crown requirements are best met in this situation and also offer appropriate contract terms to use where it is seen as essential to acquire rights for the Crown.

**20.** Departments (or other Crown bodies) should consult HMSO's Copyright Section before concluding any agreement to publish through a private publisher material whose copyright is held by the Crown or is the responsibility of the Controller of HMSO. An exception is the material specified at paragraph 23. Departments or other Crown bodies should also take into account the Tradeable Information guidelines issued by the Department of Trade and Industry.

**Fees**

**21.** In assessing fees payable to the Crown in respect of all categories of official material, the Controller will consider the value of the material to the applicant and the extent which commercial or private reproduction will affect the revenue from sales of official publications. The Controller can use his discretion to waive or reduce fees in appropriate circumstances.

**22.** The Controller will waive or reduce fees in respect of applications for use of material for professional, technical or scientific purposes where profit is not a primary purpose of reproduction. Consideration of reduction or remission of fees will also be given to reproduction in works of scholarship, in the journals of learned societies and similar non-profit making bodies, for educational purposes and in other cases where the need for the fullest dissemination of official information is paramount and the commercial or other aspects are relatively unimportant.

**23.** In this connection all Departments and other Crown bodies are now hereby given the right to authorise the publication of papers in learned journals and in the Proceedings of Conferences and Seminars, provided that the source is acknowledged and that the copyright in the work is not assigned to the publisher concerned. In these particular cases, fees may be waived or reduced at the discretion of the authorising Department or other Crown body in line with paragraph 22 above. In the case of any doubts, reference should be made to HMSO's Copyright Section.

**Infringement of Crown and Parliamentary Copyright**

**24.** Any apparent infringement of Crown or Parliamentary copyright or other copyright held by the Crown which comes to the notice of a Department or other Crown body should be reported to HMSO's Copyright Section or in the case of Ordnance Survey maps etc, to the Ordnance Survey. Consideration will then be given to further action, including the possibility of legal proceedings.

**Action**

**25.** Departments are asked to ensure that the arrangements set out in this note are brought to the attention of all staff concerned. Departments should also be aware that HMSO issue other guidance material on Crown and parliamentary copyright and copies can be readily obtained on application to HMSO's Copyright Section at the address given below.

**Contacts**

**26.** HMSO has produced a useful guide to copyright entitled:
'Copyright–a brief guide for Government Departments', which is available on request from HMSO's Copyright Section. HMSO staff will also be pleased to assist with any problems or queries which Departments may have in relation to copyright matters.

**⚜HMSO**

Your reference

Our reference  PU 15/108

Date      November 1989

St Crispins
Duke Street
Norwich
NR3 1PD

Telephone
0603 69
GTN 3014 "

Switchboard
0603 622211
Fax 0603 695582

Dear Librarian

## PHOTOCOPYING CROWN AND PARLIAMENTARY COPYRIGHT PUBLICATIONS

### Introduction

1.  This letter revises HMSO's earlier 'Dear Librarian' letter of August 1985 in the light of the Copyright, Designs & Patents Act 1988 (ISBN 0 10 544888 5, available from HMSO). it is intended to clarify the circumstances in which it is necessary to seek prior permission before photocopying Crown and Parliamentary copyright material.   In recognition of the unique nature of much of this material, considerable freedom is allowed in its reproduction but within the guidance described below.

2.  Under the Copyright, Designs & Patents Act 1988, a new category of "Parliamentary copyright" was introduced.   It should be noted that HMSO administers Parliamentary copyright on behalf of the House of Lords and the House of Commons in those Parliamentary works published by HMSO but Parliamentary copyright material **NOT** published by HMSO will be administered by officials of the relevant House of Parliament.

3.  For the purposes of defining conditions for reproduction, Crown and Parliamentary copyright material can be divided into the following broad categories:

    (a)  Statutory Publications, including Bills and Acts of Parliament, Statutory Rules and Orders, and Statutory Instruments;

    (b)  The Official Report of the House of Lords and House of Commons Debates (Hansard), Lords' Minutes, the Vote Bundle, Commons Order-Books and Commons Statutory Instruments List;

    (c)  Other Parliamentary papers published by HMSO, including Reports of Select Committees of both Houses;

    (d)  Other Parliamentary material not published by HMSO;

    (e)  Non-Parliamentary publications, comprising all papers of Government Departments - both published and unpublished - not contained in other categories;

*competing through quality*

564

2.

(f)   Charts and Navigational publications published by the MOD (Hydrographic Department) and maps and other publications in all media published by the Ordnance Survey.

4.   This letter is primarily concerned with <u>published</u> Crown and Parliamentary copyright material.  The photocopying of unpublished material that is subject to Crown or Parliamentary copyright may also require prior permission and unless alternative arrangements are displayed at the site where the material is held, application should be made to HMSO with regard to the Crown copyright material, at the address shown at paragraph 25, or to the appropriate House of Parliament in respect of unpublished Parliamentary copyright material, at the address shown at paragraph 26.

5.   The position regarding the photocopying of published material in the six categories is set out below.

## Statutory Publications (category 3(a) above)

6.   There is no objection to the photocopying of extracts of up to 30% of the whole publication;  it is not necessary to seek permission before doing so and no fees are levied.

7.   Permission is not normally granted for the photocopying of longer extracts (ie of 30% or more of the whole text) or the complete text of Bills or Acts within six months of publication by HMSO.  Similarly, permission is not normally granted for the photocopying of longer extracts or the complete text of Statutory Rules, Orders or Instruments within three months of publication by HMSO.  Under exceptional circumstances permission may be granted within the embargo periods but formal application to HMSO is required and a fee may be levied.

8.   Outside the embargo periods, these publications may be photocopied without applying for permission and no fees are levied.

## The Official Reports and House business papers (category 3(b) above)

9.   There is no objection to the photocopying of these publications.  No fees are levied and no prior permission is required.

10.   Any person or body using unofficial reports of proceedings in Parliament, even though they are photocopies of verbatim reports of speeches as reported in the Official Report, may not enjoy as extensive privilege in proceedings for defamation as the full Official Report would enjoy.

11.   Reproduction from the Official Reports in connection with advertising is not permitted.

## Other Parliamentary papers published by HMSO (category 3(c) above)

12.   There is no objection to the photocopying of BRIEF extracts - which, for this category, may be defined as up to 5% of the whole publication;  it is not necessary to seek permission before doing so and no fees are levied.

13.   Permission is not normally granted for the photocopying of longer extracts (ie of 5% or more of the whole text) or the complete text within six months of the date of publication by HMSO.  Under exceptional circumstances permission may be granted within this embargo period, but formal application to HMSO is required and a fee may be levied.

3.

14. Outside the embargo period these publications may be photocopied without applying for permission and no fees are levied.

## Parliamentary papers not published by HMSO (category 3(d) above)

15. This Parliamentary copyright material is administered by officials of the relevant House and application for its use should be made to the relevant address at paragraph 26 below.

## Non-Parliamentary publications (category 3(e) above)

16. This category covers a wide range of material published by HMSO and by Government Departments and Crown bodies. Unless otherwise stated on the publication, applications are required for permission to photocopy both extracts and complete texts. A fee, calculated according to the number of pages copied, will normally be levied. The exception to this is where free Departmentally produced information publications are for any reason unobtainable, when permission for photocopying is not required. Users of such photocopies should always check on the currency of the information in the publication.

17. Users registered by the Copyright Licensing Agency (CLA) need not apply for permission to make photocopies of material in this category providing the copying is within the terms of the CLA licence.

## Charts and Navigational publications published by the MOD (Hydrographic Department) and maps and other publications in all media published by the Ordnance Survey (category 3 (f) above)

18. The administration of Crown copyright relating to publications in this category is subject to appropriate arrangements for delegation between the Controller of HMSO and the MOD (Hydrographic Department) and Ordnance Survey. Application for permission to photocopy such material should be made to MOD (Hydrographic Department) or Ordnance Survey - as appropriate - at the addresses in paragraph 27.

## General

19. It is not intended that the above guidance should in any way conflict with any statutory rights. In case of doubt, further clarification should be sought from HMSO at the address in paragraph 25, or, as the case may be, from the appropriate House at the address in paragraph 26.

20. Although permission is not currently required for photocopying defined classes of material in some circumstances (as detailed above), all Crown and Parliamentary rights in respect of copyright are reserved and will be asserted in cases considered by the Controller of HMSO or the appropriate House as exceptional.

21. The commercial reproduction, photocopying or microcopying of Crown and Parliamentary copyright material is not covered by this letter and is subject to separate licensing arrangements. Similarly, where it is proposed to make multiple copies or to undertake systematic or repeated copying, application must be made to HMSO or, as the case may be, to the appropriate House, unless the copying is undertaken within the terms of a licence granted by the Copyright Licensing Agency (in which case the conditions of the licence will apply), or if the copying is of material described at paragraph 22 below.

22. Multiple, systematic or repeated copying may be undertaken of the following material without seeking permission before doing so and no fees are levied:

4.

(i)   Statutory publications - extracts of up to 30% of the publication; longer extracts or the complete text if outside the embargo period (see paragraph 7).

(ii)  The Official Reports and other House business papers - no restrictions, but see paragraphs 10 and 11.

(iii) Other Parliamentary papers published by HMSO - brief extracts of up to 5% of the publication.

23.   Photocopies of Crown and Parliamentary copyright material in all classes are not permitted to be misused by unfair or misleading selection, undignified association or undesirable use for advertising purposes. In cases of doubt, application must be made to HMSO or, as the case may be, to the appropriate House at the address below.

24.   Librarians should be aware of Statutory Instrument 1989/1212, the Copyright (Librarians and Archivists)(Copying of Copyright Material) Regulations 1989, ISBN 0 11 0972120 and available from HMSO.

## Contact

25.   Unless otherwise stated above (or on the publication concerned), the address for all applications for permission to photocopy Crown and published Parliamentary copyright material - and for all enquiries about this letter - is as follows:

Her Majesty's Stationery Office
Copyright Section (P6)
St Crispins
Duke Street
NORWICH      NR3 1PD

Tel: 0603 695506      (Direct Dialling)
Fax: 0603 695582

26.   Enquiries regarding reproduction of Parliamentary material not published by HMSO should be directed to:

Chief Clerk              or    Clerk of the Journals
Journal Office                 Journal Office
House of Lords                 House of Commons
LONDON      SW1A 0PW           LONDON      SW1A 0AA

Tel: 01 219 3187/3327          Tel: 01 219 3315/3320

27.   Other useful addresses are:

Copyright Branch               Hydrographic Department
Ordnance Survey                Finance Section
Romsey Road                    Ministry of Defence
Maybush                        TAUNTON
SOUTHAMPTON   SO9 4DH          Somerset   TA1 2DN

Tel: 0703 792302               Tel: 0823 337900 Ext 337

Yours faithfully

CHRIS PENN
Director
Publications Division

NB:   This letter may be freely reproduced.

**HMSO**

Your reference

Our reference  PU 15/108

Date  November 1989

St Crispins
Duke Street
Norwich
NR3 1PD

Telephone
0603 69
GTN 3014 "

Switchboard
0603 622211
Fax 0603 695582

Dear Publisher

## REPRODUCTION OF CROWN AND PARLIAMENTARY COPYRIGHT MATERIAL

### Introduction

1.   This letter revises HMSO's earlier 'Dear Publisher' letter of August 1985 in the light of the Copyright, Designs and Patents Act 1988 (ISBN 0 10 544888 5, available from HMSO).   It is intended to clarify the circumstances in which publishers should seek permission before undertaking the reproduction of Crown and Parliamentary copyright material.   In recognition of the unique nature of much of this material, considerable freedom is allowed in its reproduction but within the guidance described below.

2.   Under the Copyright, Designs and Patents Act 1988, a new category of "Parliamentary copyright" was introduced.   It should be noted that HMSO administers Parliamentary copyright on behalf of the House of Lords and the House of Commons in those Parliamentary works published by HMSO but Parliamentary copyright material **NOT** published by HMSO will be administered by officials of the relevant House of Parliament.

3.   For the purposes of defining conditions for reproduction, Crown and Parliamentary copyright material can be divided into the following broad categories:

   (a)   Statutory material, including Bills and Acts of Parliament, Statutory Rules and Orders, and Statutory Instruments;

   (b)   The Official Report of the House of Lords and House of Commons Debates (Hansard), Lords' Minutes, the Vote Bundle, Commons Order-Books and Commons Statutory Instrument Lists;

   (c)   Other Parliamentary papers published by HMSO, including Reports of Select Committees of both Houses;

   (d)   Other Parliamentary material not published by HMSO;

   (e)   Non-Parliamentary works, comprising all papers of Government Departments - both published and unpublished - not contained in other categories;

*competing through quality*

2.

(f)    Charts and Navigational publications published by the MOD (Hydrographic Department) and maps and other publications in all media published by the Ordnance Survey.

### Statutory Material (Category 3(a) above)

4.    There is no objection to the reproduction of extracts (defined for these purposes as being up to 30% of the original publication) provided that the source is acknowledged.  Permission is not required unless the official publication is to be used as camera-ready copy.

5.    The reproduction of longer extracts (defined for these purposes as being 30% or more of the original publication) or the complete text is NOT NORMALLY ALLOWED during the following embargo periods:

(i)    Bills and Acts of Parliament            -    6 months from date of publication;

(ii)   Statutory Instruments, Orders and Rules    -    3 months from date of publication.

However, these restrictions will be waived if the texts are reproduced as part of a book or journal containing SUBSTANTIAL annotations to the text or commentary on it.  Permission is not then required unless the official publication is to be used as camera-ready copy.  The source should be acknowledged as either Crown or Parliamentary copyright, whichever is appropriate.

6.    Outside the embargo periods, there is no objection to the reproduction of this material, and permission is not then required unless the official publication is to be used as camera-ready copy.  The source should be acknowledged as either Crown or Parliamentary copyright, whichever is appropriate.

### The Official Reports and House business papers (category 3(b) above)

7.    Reproduction is not allowed in connection with advertising.

8.    Otherwise, the publications may be reproduced freely.  Permission is not required unless the official publication is to be used as camera-ready copy or the extracts form a substantial part of the reproduction.  However, please note that:

(i)    the source must be acknowledged as Parliamentary copyright and extracts must be reproduced verbatim;

(ii)   any person or body publishing unofficial reports of proceedings in Parliament, even though they are verbatim reports of speeches as reported in the Official Report, may not enjoy as extensive privilege in proceedings for defamation as the full Official Report would enjoy.

### Other Parliamentary Papers published by HMSO (category 3(c) above)

9.    There is no objection to the reproduction of BRIEF extracts - which, for this category, may be defined as up to 5% of the whole publication;  it is not necessary to seek permission before doing so and no fees are levied.  The source should be acknowledged.

10.   Longer extracts, or the whole publication, must not be reproduced without the permission of Her Majesty's Stationery Office.  The conditions of publication are the subject of formal permission and normally any such permissions would not allow reproduction until 6 months after the date of publication by HMSO.

3.

#### Other Parliamentary material not published by HMSO (category 3(d) above)

11.     This Parliamentary copyright material is administered by officials of the relevant House and application for its use should be made to the appropriate address at paragraph 21.

#### Non-Parliamentary material (category 3(e) above)

12.     This category covers a wide range of material published by HMSO and by Government Departments and Crown bodies. It also covers unpublished material. Neither the whole text nor extracts in this category should be reproduced without the permission of HMSO, or of departments and bodies having delegated authority to grant such permission. The conditions of publication are the subject of formal agreement.

#### Charts and Navigational publications published by the MOD (Hydrographic Department) and maps and other publications in all media published by the Ordnance Survey

13.     The administration of Crown copyright relating to publications in this category is subject to appropriate arrangements for delegation between the Controller of HMSO and the MOD (Hydrographic Department) and Ordnance Survey. Applications for permission to reproduce such material should be made to MOD (Hydrographic Department) or Ordnance Survey - as appropriate - at the addresses in paragraph 22 and not to HMSO. (Please note that Ordnance Survey maps, map extracts or redrawn maps must not be reproduced without Ordnance Survey permission).

#### Camera-Ready Copy

14.     As already described, permission is required for the use of the official text as camera-ready copy. Such permission will not normally be refused - subject to the general conditions outlined above relating to embargo periods, etc - but a fee will be charged.

#### General

15.     The guidance contained in this letter is intended to apply to printed reproduction and to publication within the United Kingdom only. All rights relating to reproduction outside the UK and to reproduction in other media are reserved. Publishers intending to reproduce Crown or Parliamentary copyright material outside the UK or in media other than print (eg microform or computer media) must therefore seek HMSO clearance in advance.

16.     The Royal Arms and official printing and publishing imprints should not be reproduced. Copies of Acts of Parliament, Statutory Rules and Orders and Statutory Instruments, other than those reproduced by or by the order of Her Majesty's Stationery Office, must not purport to be published by Authority.

17.     The reproduction of Crown or Parliamentary copyright material so as to result in unfair or misleading selection, undignified association, or undesirable use for advertising purposes is not permitted. In cases of doubt, application must be made to HMSO at the address at paragraph 20 or, as the case may be, to the relevant House at the address in paragraph 21.

18.     Although this letter provides the current working guidelines for the reproduction of defined classes of material, all Crown and Parliamentary rights in respect of copyright are reserved and will be asserted in cases considered by the Controller of HMSO or by the relevant House as exceptional.

4.

19.  This letter is primarily addressed to publishers, but it also covers the arrangements for any wide-scale reproduction of Crown or Parliamentary copyright material including, for example, by professional bodies.

## Contact

20.  Further advice may be obtained from:

Her Majesty's Stationery Office
Copyright Section (P6)
St Crispins
Duke Street
NORWICH      NR3 1PD

Tel: 0603 695506 (Direct dialling)
Fax: 0603 695582

21.  Enquiries regarding the reproduction of Parliamentary material not published by HMSO should be directed to:

| Chief Clerk | or | Clerk of the Journals |
|---|---|---|
| Journal Office | | Journal Office |
| House of Lords | | House of Commons |
| LONDON      SW1A 0PW | | LONDON      SW1A 0AA |
| | | |
| Tel: 01 219 3187/3327 | | Tel: 01 219 3315/3320 |

22.  Other useful addresses are:

| Copyright Branch | Hydrographic Department |
|---|---|
| Ordnance Survey | Finance Section |
| Romsey Road | Ministry of Defence |
| Maybush | TAUNTON |
| SOUTHAMPTON      SO9 4DH | Somerset      TA1 2DN |
| | |
| Tel: 0703 792302 | Tel: 0823 337900 Ext 337 |

Yours faithfully

CHRIS PENN
Director
Publications Division

N.B.  This letter may be freely reproduced.

# Appendix 3

# Legislation relating to works made before 1 July 1912

ENGRAVING COPYRIGHT ACT 1734
(8 Geo 2 c 13)

*An Act for the encouragement of the arts of designing, engraving, and etching historical and other prints, by vesting the properties thereof in the inventors and engravers during the time therein mentioned.*

**1.** That from and after the twenty-fourth day of June, which shall be in the year of our Lord one thousand seven hundred and thirty five, every person who shall invent and design, engrave, etch, or work in mezzotinto or chiaro oscuro, or from his own works and invention shall cause to be designed and engraved, etched, or worked in mezzotinto or chiaro oscuro, any historical or other print or prints, shall have the sole right and liberty of printing and reprinting the same for the term of fourteen years, to commence from the day of the first publishing thereof, which shall be truly engraved with the name of the proprietor on each plate, and printed on every such print or prints; and that if any print-seller or other person whatsoever, from and after the said twenty-fourth day of June one thousand seven hundred and thirty five, within the time limited by his Act, shall engrave, etch, or work as aforesaid, or in any other manner copy and sell, or cause to be engraved, etched, or copied and sold, in whole or in part, by varying, adding to, or diminishing from the main design, or shall print, reprint, or import for sale, or cause to be printed, reprinted, or imported for sale, any such print or prints, or any parts thereof, without the consent of the proprietor or proprietors thereof first had and obtained in writing, signed by him or them respectively in the presence of two or more credible witnesses, or, knowing the same to be so printed or reprinted without the consent of the proprietor or proprietors, shall publish, sell, or expose to sale or otherwise, or in any other manner dispose of, or cause to be published, sold, or exposed to sale or otherwise, or in any other manner disposed of, any such print or prints without such consent first had and obtained as aforesaid, then such offender or offenders shall forfeit the plate or plates on which such print or prints are or shall be copied, and all and every sheet or sheets (being part of or whereon such print or prints are or shall be so copied or printed) to the proprietor or proprietors of such original print or prints, who shall forthwith destroy and damask the same; and further, that every such offender or offenders shall forfeit five shillings for every print which shall be found in his, her, or their custody, either printed or published and exposed to sale, or otherwise disposed of contrary to the true intent and meaning of this Act, the one moiety thereof to the King's most excellent Majesty, his heirs and successors, and the other moiety thereof to any person or persons that shall sue for the same, to be recovered in any of his Majesty's courts of record at Westminster, by action of debt, bill, plaint, or information, in which no wager of law, essoign, privilege, or protection, or more than one imparlance shall be allowed.

## ENGRAVING COPYRIGHT ACT 1766
(7 Geo 3 c 38)

*An Act to amend and render more effectual an Act made in the eighth year of the reign of King George the Second, for encouragement of the arts of designing, engraving, and etching historical and other prints . . .*

**1.** That from and after the first day of January one thousand seven hundred and sixty seven, all and every person and persons who shall invent or design, engrave, etch, or work in mezzotinto or chiaro oscuro, or from his own work, design, or invention shall cause or procure to be designed, engraved, etched, or worked in mezzotinto or chiaro oscuro, any historical print or prints, or any print or prints of any portrait, conversation, landscape, or architecture, map, chart, or plan, or any other print or prints whatsoever, shall have and are hereby declared to have the benefit and protection of the said Act and this Act under the restrictions and limitations herein after-mentioned.

**2.** And . . . from and after the said first day of January one thousand seven hundred and sixty seven, all and every person and persons who shall engrave, etch, or work in mezzotinto or chiaro oscuro, or cause to be engraved, etched, or worked any print taken from any picture, drawing, model, or sculpture, either ancient or modern, shall have and are hereby declared to have the benefit and protection of the said Act and this Act for the term herein after-mentioned, in like manner as if such print had been graved or drawn from the original design of such graver, etcher, or draftsman; and if any person shall engrave, print, and publish, or import for sale any copy of any such print contrary to the true intent and meaning of this and the said former Act, every such person shall be liable to the penalties contained in the said Act, to be recovered as therein and hereinafter is mentioned.

**7.** And . . . the sole right and liberty of printing and reprinting intended to be secured and protected by the said former Act and this Act, shall be extended, continued, and be vested in the respective proprietors for the space of twenty-eight years to commence from the day of the first publishing of any of the works respectively herein-before and in the said former Act mentioned.

## PRINTS COPYRIGHT ACT 1776
(17 Geo 3 c 57)

*An Act for more effectually securing the property of prints to inventers and engravers, by enabling them to sue for and recover penalties in certain cases.*

**1.** That from and after the twenty-fourth day of June one thousand seven hundred and seventy seven, if any engraver, etcher, printseller or other person shall, within the time limited by the aforesaid Acts or either of them, engrave, etch or work or cause or procure to be engraved, etched or worked, in mezzotinto or chiaro oscuro or otherwise, or in any other manner copy in the whole or in part, by varying, adding to or diminishing from the main design, or shall print, reprint or import for sale, or cause or procure to be printed, reprinted or imported for sale, or shall publish, sell or otherwise dispose of, or cause or procure to be published, sold or otherwise disposed of, any copy or copies of any historical print or prints, or any print or prints of any portrait, conversation, landscape or architecture, map, chart or plan, or any other print or prints whatsoever, which hath or have been or shall be engraved, etched, drawn or designed in any part of Great Britain, without the express consent of the proprietor or proprietors thereof first had and obtained in writing signed by him, her or them respectively, with his, her or their own hand or hands, in the presence of and attested by two or more credible witnesses, then every such proprietor or proprietors shall and may, by and in a special action upon the case to be brought against the person or persons so offending, recover such damages as a jury on the trial of such action, or on the execution of a writ of inquiry thereon, shall give or assess, together with double costs of suit.


## SCULPTURE COPYRIGHT ACT 1814
(54 Geo 3 c 56)

*An Act to amend and render more effectual an Act of His present Majesty for encouraging the art of making new models and casts of busts and other things therein mentioned, and for giving further encouragement to such arts.*
[18th May 1814]

**1.** That from and after the passing of this Act every person or persons who shall make or cause to be made any new and original sculpture, or model, or copy, or cast of the human figure or human figures, or of any bust or busts, or of any part or parts of the human figure, clothed in drapery or otherwise, or of any animal or animals, or of any part or parts of any animal combined with the human figure or otherwise, or of any subject being matter of invention in sculpture, or of any alto or basso-relievo representing any of the matters or things herein-before mentioned, or any cast from nature of the human figure, or of any part or parts of the human figure, or of any cast from nature of any animal, or of any part or parts of any animal, or of any such subject containing or representing any of the matters and things herein-before mentioned, whether separate or combined, shall have the sole right and property of all and in every such new and original sculpture, model, copy, and cast of the human figure or human figures, and of all and in every such bust or busts, and of all and in every such part or parts of the human figure, clothed in drapery or otherwise, and of all and in every such new and original sculpture, model, copy, and cast representing any animal or animals, and of all and in every such work representing any part or parts of any animal combined with the human figure or otherwise, and of all and in every such new and original sculpture, model, copy, and cast of any subject, being matter of invention in sculpture, and of all and in every such new and original sculpture, model, copy, and cast in alto or basso-relievo representing any of the matters or things herein-before mentioned, and of every such cast from nature, for the term of fourteen years from first putting forth or publishing the same; provided in all and in every case the proprietor or proprietors do cause his, her, or their name or names, with the date, to be put on all and every such new and original sculpture, model, copy, or cast, and on every such cast from nature, before the same shall be put forth or published.

**6.** Provided always, . . . that from and immediately after the expiration of the said term of fourteen years, the sole right of making and disposing of such new and original sculpture, or model, or copy, or cast of any of the matters or things herein-before mentioned, shall return to the person or persons who originally made or caused to be made the same, if he or they shall be then living, for the further term of fourteen years, . . .

## DRAMATIC COPYRIGHT ACT 1833
(3 & 4 Will 4 c 15)

*An Act to amend the laws relating to dramatic literary property.*

[10th June 1833]

**1.** That from and after the passing of this Act the author of any tragedy, comedy, play, opera, farce, or any other dramatic piece of entertainment, composed, and not printed and published by the author thereof or his assignee, or which hereafter shall be composed and not printed or published by the author thereof or his assignee, or the assignee of such author, shall have as his own property the sole liberty of representing, or causing to be represented, at any place or places of dramatic entertainment whatsoever, in any part of the United Kingdom of Great Britain and Ireland, in the Isles of Man, Jersey, and Guernsey, or in any part of the British Dominions, any such production as aforesaid, not printed and published by the author thereof or his assignee, and shall be deemed and taken to be the proprietor thereof; and that the author of any such production, printed and published within ten years before the passing of this Act by the author thereof or his assignee, or which shall hereafter be so printed and published, or the assignee of such author, shall, from the time of passing this Act, or from the time of such publication respectively, until the end of twenty-eight years from the day of such first publication of the same, and also, if the author or authors, or the survivor of the authors, shall be living at the end of that period, during the residue of his natural life, have as his own property the sole liberty of representing, or causing to be represented, the same at any such place of dramatic entertainment as aforesaid, and shall be deemed and taken to be the proprietor thereof: Provided nevertheless, that nothing in this Act contained shall prejudice, alter, or affect the right or authority of any person to represent or cause to be represented, at any place or places of dramatic entertainment whatsoever, any such production as aforesaid, in all cases in subject, being matter of invention in sculpture, and of all and in every such new and original sculpture, model, copy, and cast in alto or basso-relievo representing any of the matters or things herein-before mentioned, and of every such cast from nature, for the term of fourteen years from first putting forth or publishing the same; provided in all and in every case the proprietor or proprietors do cause his, her, or their name or names, with the date, to be put on all and every such new and original sculpture, model, copy, or cast, and on every such cast from nature, before the same shall be put forth or published.

PRINTS AND ENGRAVINGS COPYRIGHT (IRELAND) ACT 1836
(6 & 7 Will 4 c 59)

*An Act to extend the protection of copyright in prints and engravings to Ireland.*
[13th August 1836]

**2.** And be it further enacted, that from and after the passing of this Act, if any engraver, etcher, print-seller, or other person shall, within the time limited by the aforesaid recited Acts, engrave, etch, or publish, or cause to be engraved, etched, or published, any engraving or print of any description whatever, either in whole or in part, which may have been or which shall hereafter be published in any part of Great Britain or Ireland, without the express consent of the proprietor or proprietors thereof first had and obtained in writing, signed by him, her, or them respectively, with his, her, or their own hand or hands, in the presence of and attested by two or more credible witnesses, then every such proprietor shall and may, by and in a separate action upon the case, to be brought against the person so offending in any court of law in Great Britain or Ireland, recover such damages as a jury on the trial of such action or on the execution of a writ of inquiry thereon shall give or assess, together with double costs of suit.

COPYRIGHT ACT 1842
(5 & 6 Vict c 45)

*An Act to amend the law of copyright.*                           [1st July 1842]

**2.** And be it enacted, that in the construction of this Act the word 'book' shall be construed to mean and include every volume, part or division of a volume, pamphlet, sheet of letter-press, sheet of music, map, chart, or plan separately published; that the words 'dramatic piece' shall be construed to mean and include every tragedy, comedy, play, opera, farce, or other scenic, musical, or dramatic entertainment; that the word 'copyright' shall be construed to mean the sole and exclusive liberty of printing or otherwise multiplying copies of any subject to which the said word is herein applied; that the words 'personal representative' shall be construed to mean and include every executor, administrator, and next of kin entitled to administration; that the word 'assigns' shall be construed to mean and include every person in whom the interest of an author in copyright shall be vested, whether derived from such author before or after the publication of any book, and whether acquired by sale, gift, bequest, or by operation of law, or otherwise; that the words 'British Dominions' shall be construed to mean and include all parts of the United Kingdom of Great Britain and Ireland, the Islands of Jersey and Guernsey, all parts of the East and West Indies, and all the colonies, settlements, and possessions of the Crown which now are or hereafter may be acquired; and that whenever in this Act, in describing any person, matter, or thing, the word importing the singular number or the masculine gender only is used, the same shall be understood to include and to be applied to several persons as well as one person, and females as well as males, and several matters or things as well as one matter or thing, respectively, unless there shall be something in the subject or context repugnant to such construction.

**3.** And be it enacted, that the copyright in every book which shall after the passing of this Act be published in the lifetime of its author shall endure for the natural life of such author, and for the further term of seven years, commencing at the time of his death, and shall be the property of such author and his assigns: Provided always, that if the said term of seven years shall expire before the end of forty-two years from the first publication of such book, the copyright shall in that case endure for such period of forty-two years; and that the copyright in every book which shall be published after the death of its author shall endure for the term of forty-two years from the first publication thereof, and shall be the property of the proprietor of the author's manuscript from which such book shall be first published, and his assigns.

**18.** And be it enacted, that when any publisher or other person shall, before or at the time of the passing of this Act, have projected, conducted, and carried on, or shall hereafter project, conduct, and carry on, or be the proprietor of any encyclopædia, review, magazine, periodical work, or work published in a series of books or parts, or any book whatsoever, and shall have employed or shall employ any persons to compose the same, or any volumes, parts, essays, articles, or portions thereof, for publication in or as part of the same, and such work, volumes, parts, essays, articles, or portions shall have been or shall hereafter be composed under such employment, on the terms that the copyright therein shall belong to such proprietor, projector, publisher, or conductor, and paid for by such proprietor, projector, publisher, or conductor, the copyright in every such encyclopædia, review, magazine, periodical work, and work published in a series of books or parts, and in every volume, part, essay, article, and portion so composed and paid for, shall be the property of such proprietor, projector, publisher, or other conductor, who shall enjoy the same rights as if he were the actual author thereof, and shall have such term of copyright therein as is given to the authors of books by this Act; except only that in the case of essays, articles, or portions forming part of and first published in reviews, magazines, or other periodical works of a like nature, after the term of twenty-eight years from the first publication thereof respectively the right of publishing the same in a separate form shall revert to the author for the remainder of the term given by this Act: Provided always, that during the term of twenty-eight years the said proprietor, projector, publisher, or conductor shall not publish any such essay, article, or portion separately or singly without the consent previously obtained of the author thereof, or his assigns: Provided also, that nothing herein contained shall alter or affect the right of any person who shall have been or who shall be so employed as aforesaid to publish any such composition in a separate form, who by any contract, express or implied, may have reserved or may hereafter reserve to himself such right; but every author reserving, retaining, or having such right shall be entitled to the copyright in such composition when published in a separate form, according to this Act, without prejudice to the right of such proprietor, projector, publisher, or conductor as aforesaid.

**20.** And whereas an Act was passed in the third year of the reign of His late Majesty, to amend the law relating to dramatic literary property, and it is expedient to extend the term of the sole liberty of representing dramatic pieces given by that Act to the full time by this Act provided for the continuance of copyright: And whereas it is expedient to extend to musical compositions the benefits of that Act, and also of this Act; be it therefore enacted, that the provisions of the said Act of His late Majesty, and of this Act, shall apply to musical compositions, and that the sole liberty of representing or performing, or causing or permitting to be represented or performed, any dramatic piece or musical composition, shall endure and be the property of the author thereof, and his assigns, for the term in this Act provided for the duration of copyright in books; and the provisions herein-before enacted in respect of the property of such copyright, and of registering the same, shall apply to the liberty of representing or performing any dramatic piece or musical composition, as if the same were herein expressly re-enacted and applied thereto, save and except that the first public representation or performance of any dramatic piece or musical composition shall be deemed equivalent, in the construction of this Act, to the first publication of any book: Provided always, that in case of any dramatic piece or musical composition in manuscript, it shall be sufficient for the person having the sole liberty of representing or performing, or causing to be represented or performed the same, to register only the title thereof, the name and place of abode of the author or composer thereof, the name and place of abode of the proprietor thereof, and the time and place of its first representation or performance.

**22.** And be it enacted, that no assignment of the copyright of any book consisting of or containing a dramatic piece or musical composition shall be holden to convey to the assignee the right of representing or performing such dramatic piece or musical composition, unless an entry in the said registry book shall be made of such assignment, wherein shall be expressed the intention of the parties that such right should pass by such assignment.

## INTERNATIONAL COPYRIGHT ACT 1844
(7 & 8 Vict c 12)

**19.** And be it enacted, that neither the author of any book, nor the author or composer of any dramatic piece or musical composition, nor the inventor, designer, or engraver of any print, nor the maker of any article of sculpture, or of such other work of art as aforesaid, which shall after the passing of this Act be first published out of Her Majesty's Dominions, shall have any copyright therein respectively, or any exclusive right to the public representation or performance thereof, otherwise than such (if any) as he may become entitled to under this Act.

## INTERNATIONAL COPYRIGHT ACT 1852
(15 Vict c 12)

**14.** It is hereby declared, that the provisions of the said Acts [the Engraving Copyrights Acts] are intended to include prints taken by lithography or any other mechanical process by which prints or impressions of drawings or designs are capable of being multiplied indefinitely, and the said Acts shall be construed accordingly.

## FINE ARTS COPYRIGHT ACT 1862
(25 & 26 Vict c 68)

*An Act for amending the law relating to copyright in works of the fine arts, and for repressing the commission of fraud in the production and sale of such works.* [29th July 1862]

**1.** The author, being a British subject or resident within the Dominions of the Crown, of every original painting, drawing, and photograph which shall be or shall have been made either in the British Dominions or elsewhere, and which shall not have been sold or disposed of before the commencement of this Act, and his assigns, shall have the sole and exclusive right of copying, engraving, reproducing, and multiplying such painting or drawing, and the design thereof, or such photograph, and the negative thereof, by any means and of any size, for the term of the natural life of such author, and seven years after his death; provided that when any painting or drawing, or the negative of any photograph, shall for the first time after the passing of this Act be sold or disposed of, or shall be made or executed for or on behalf of any other person for a good or a valuable consideration, the person so selling or disposing of or making or executing the same shall not retain the copyright thereof, unless it be expressly reserved to him by agreement in writing, signed, at or before the time of such sale or disposition, by the vendee or assignee of such painting or drawing, or of such negative of a photograph, or by the person for or on whose behalf the same shall be so made or executed, but the copyright shall belong to the vendee or assignee of such painting or drawing, or of such negative of a photograph, or to the person for or on whose behalf the same shall have been made or executed; nor shall the vendee or assignee thereof be entitled to any such copyright, unless, at or before the time of such sale or disposition, an agreement in writing, signed by the person so selling or disposing of the same, or by his agent duly authorized, shall have been made to that effect.


INTERNATIONAL COPYRIGHT ACT 1886
(49 & 50 Vict c 33)

*An Act to amend the law respecting international and colonial copyright.*
[25th June 1886]

**2.** The following provisions shall apply to an Order in Council under the International Copyright Acts:—
(1) The order may extend to all the several foreign countries named or described therein:
(2) The order may exclude or limit the rights conferred by the International Copyright Acts in the case of authors who are not subjects or citizens of the foreign countries named or described in that or any other order, and if the order contains such limitation and the author of a literary or artistic work first produced in one of those foreign countries is not a British subject, nor a subject or citizen of any of the foreign countries so named or described, the publisher of such work, unless the order otherwise provides, shall for the purpose of any legal proceedings in the United Kingdom for protecting any copyright in such work be deemed to be entitled to such copyright as if he were the author, but this enactment shall not prejudice the rights of such author and publisher as between themselves:
(3) The International Copyright Acts and an order made thereunder shall not confer on any person any greater right or longer term of copyright in any work than that enjoyed in the foreign country in which such work was first produced.

**3.**—(2) Where a work produced simultaneously in the United Kingdom, and in some foreign country or countries is by virtue of an Order in Council under the International Copyright Acts deemed for the purpose of copyright to be first produced in one of the said foreign countries, and not in the United Kingdom, the copyright in the United Kingdom shall be such only as exists by virtue of production in the said foreign country, and shall not be such as would have been acquired if the work had been first produced in the United Kingdom.

**5.**—(2) Provided that if after the expiration of ten years, or any other term prescribed by the order, next after the end of the year in which the work, or in the case of a book published in numbers each number of the book, was first produced, an authorised translation in the English language of such work or number has not been produced, the said right to prevent the production in and importation into the United Kingdom of an unauthorised translation of such work shall cease.

**6.** Where an Order in Council is made under the International Copyright Acts with respect to any foreign country, the author and publisher of any literary or artistic work first produced before the date at which such order comes into operation shall be entitled to the same rights and remedies as if the said Acts and this Act and the said order had applied to the said foreign country at the date of the said production: Provided that where any person has before the date of the publication of an Order in Council lawfully produced any work in the United Kingdom, nothing in this section shall diminish or prejudice any rights or interests arising from or in connexion with such production which are subsisting and valuable at the said date.

**8.**—(1) The Copyright Acts shall, subject to the provisions of this Act, apply to a literary or artistic work first produced in a British possession in like manner as they apply to a work first produced in the United Kingdom.

ORDER IN COUNCIL (ADOPTING BERNE CONVENTION)
*Dated* 2 *December 1887*
At the Court at Windsor, the 28th day of November, 1887.

Whereas a Convention, of which an English translation is set out in the First Schedule to this Order, has been concluded between Her Majesty the Queen of the United Kingdom of Great Britain and Ireland, and the foreign countries named in this Order, with respect to the protection to be given by copyright to the authors of literary and artistic works:

And whereas the ratifications of the said Convention were exchanged on the 5th day of September, 1887, between Her Majesty the Queen and the Governments of the foreign countries following, that is to say:

Belgium, France, Germany, Haiti, Italy, Spain, Switzerland, Tunis:

And whereas Her Majesty in Council is satisfied that the foreign countries named in this Order have made such provisions as it appears to Her Majesty expedient to require for the protection of authors of works first produced in Her Majesty's dominions.

Now, therefore, Her Majesty, by and with the advice of Her Privy Council, and by virtue of the authority committed to Her by the International Copyright Acts 1844 to 1886, doth order, and it is hereby ordered, as follows:—

**1.** The Convention as set out in the First Schedule to this Order, shall, as from the commencement of this Order, have full effect throughout Her Majesty's dominions, and all persons are enjoined to observe the same.

**2.** This Order shall extend to the foreign countries following, that is to say:

Belgium, France, Germany, Hayti, Italy, Spain, Switzerland, Tunis.

And the above countries are in this Order referred to as the foreign countries of the Copyright Union, and those foreign countries together with Her Majesty's Dominions, are in this Order referred as the countries of the Copyright Union.

**3.** The author of a literary or artistic work which, on or after the commencement of this Order, is first produced in one of the foreign countries of the Copyright Union shall, subject as in this Order and in the International Copyright Acts 1845 to 1886, mentioned, have as respects that work throughout Her Majesty's dominions the same right of copyright, including any right capable of being conferred by an Order in Council under section 2 or section 5 of the International Copyright Act 1844, or under any other enactment, as if the work had been first produced in the United Kingdom, and shall have such right during the same period: Provided that the author of a literary or artistic work shall not have any greater right or longer term of copyright therein, than that which he enjoys in the country in which the work is first produced. The author of any literary or artistic work first produced before the commencement of this Order shall have the rights and remedies to which he is entitled under section 6 of the International Copyright Act 1886.

**4.** The rights conferred by the International Copyright Acts 1844 to 1886, shall, in the case of a literary or artistic work first produced in one of the foreign countries of the Copyright Union by an author who is not a subject or citizen of any of the said foreign countries, be limited as follows, that is to say, the author shall not be entitled to take legal proceedings in Her Majesty's dominions for protecting any copyright in such work, but the publisher of such work shall, for the purpose of any legal proceedings in Her Majesty's dominions for protecting any copyright in such work, be deemed to be entitled to such copyright as if he were the author, but without prejudice to the rights of such author and publisher as between themselves.

**5.** A literary or artistic work first produced simultaneously in two or more countries of the Copyright Union shall be deemed for the purpose of copyright to have been first produced in that one of those countries in which the term of copyright in such work is shortest.

**6.** Section 6 of the International Copyright Act 1852, shall not apply to any dramatic piece to which protection is extended by virtue of this Order.

**7.** The Orders mentioned in the Second Schedule to this Order are hereby revoked. Provided that neither such revocation nor anything else in this Order shall prejudicially affect any right acquired or accrued before the commencement of this Order, by virtue of any Order hereby revoked, and any person entitled to such right shall continue to be entitled thereto, and to the remedies for the same, in like manner as if this Order had not been made.

**8.** This Order shall be construed as if it formed part of the International Copyright Act 1886.

**9.** This Order shall come into operation on the 6th day of December, 1887, which day is in this Order referred to as the commencement of this Order.

And the Lords Commissioners of Her Majesty's Treasury are to give the necessary orders accordingly.

BERNE CONVENTION

## Copyright Convention

Convention for protecting effectually and in as uniform a manner as possible the rights of authors over their literary and artistic works, made on the 5th of September, 1887, between Her Majesty The Queen of the United Kingdom of Great Britain and Ireland, Empress of India; His Majesty the German Emperor, King of Prussia; His Majesty the King of the Belgians: Her Majesty the Queen Regent of Spain, in the name of His Catholic Majesty the King of Spain; the President of the French Republic; the President of the Republic of Haiti; His Majesty the King of Italy; the Federal Council of the Swiss Federation; His Highness the Bey of Tunis.

(The following is an English translation of the Convention, with the omission of the formal beginning and end.)

*Article* 1

The contracting States are constituted into a Union for the protection of the rights of authors over their literary and artistic works.

*Article* 2

Authors of any of the countries of the Union, or their lawful representatives, shall enjoy in the other countries for their works, whether published in one of those countries or unpublished, the rights which the respective laws do now or may hereafter grant to natives.

The enjoyment of these rights is subject to the accomplishment of the conditions and formalities prescribed by law in the country of origin of the work, and cannot exceed in the other countries the term of protection accorded in the said country of origin.

The country of origin of the work is that in which the work is first published, or if such publication takes place simultaneously in several countries of the Union, that one of them in which the shortest term of protection is accorded by law.

For unpublished works the country to which the author belongs is considered the country of origin of the work.

*Article* 3

The stipulations of the present Convention apply equally to the publishers of literary and artistic works published in one of the countries of the Union, but of which the authors belong to a country which is not a party to the Union.

*Article* 4

The expression 'literary and artistic works' comprehends books, pamphlets, and all other writings; dramatic or dramatico-musical works, musical compositions with or without words; works of design, painting, sculpture, and engraving; lithographs, illustrations, geographical charts, plans, sketches, and plastic works relative to geography, topography, architecture, or science in general; in fact every production whatsoever in the literary, scientific, or artistic domain which can be published by any mode of impression or reproduction.

*Article 5*

Authors of any of the countries of the Union, or their lawful representatives, shall enjoy in the other countries exclusive rights of making or authorizing the translation of their works until the expiration of ten years from the publication of the original work in one of the countries of the Union.

For works published in incomplete parts ('livraisons') the period of ten years commences from the date of publication of the last part of the original work.

For works composed of several volumes, as well as for bulletins or collections ('cahiers') published by literary or scientific societies or by a private person, each volume, bulletin, or collection, is, with regard to the period of ten years, considered as a separate work.

In the cases provided for by the present article, and for the calculation of the period of protection, the 31st December of the year in which the work was published is admitted as the date of publication.

*Article 6*

Authorized translations are protected as original works. They consequently enjoy the protection stipulated in Articles 2 and 3 as regards their unauthorized reproduction in the countries of the Union.

It is understood that in the case of a work for which the translating right has fallen into the public domain, the translator cannot oppose the translation of the same work by other writers.

*Article 7*

Articles from newspapers or periodicals published in any of the countries of the Union may be reproduced in the original or in translation in the other countries of the Union, unless the authors or publishers have expressly forbidden it. For periodicals it is sufficient if the prohibition is made in a general manner at the beginning of each number of the periodical.

This prohibition cannot in any case apply to articles of political discussion, or to the reproduction of news of the day or current topics.

*Article 8*

As regards the liberty of extracting portions from literary or artistic works for use in publications destined for educational or scientific purposes, or for chresto-mathies, the matter is to be decided by the legislation of the different countries of the Union, or by special arrangements existing or to be concluded between them.

*Article 9*

The stipulations of Article 2 apply to the public representation of dramatic or dramatico-musical works whether such works be published or not.

Authors of dramatic or dramatico-musical works, or their lawful representatives, are during the existence of their exclusive right of translation, equally protected against the unauthorized public representation of their works.

The stipulations of Article 2 apply equally to the public performance of unpublished musical works, or of published works in which the author has expressly declared on the title-page or commencement of the work that he forbids the public performance.

*Article 10*

Unauthorized indirect appropriations of a literary or artistic work, of various kinds, such as *adaptations, arrangements of music*, &c, are specially included among the illicit reproductions to which the present Convention applies, when they are only a reproduction of a particular work, in the same form, or in another form, with non-essential alterations, additions, or abridgments, so made as not to confer the character of a new original work.

It is agreed that in the application of the present article, the tribunals of the various countries of the Union, will, if there is occasion, conform themselves to the provisions of their respective laws.

*Article* 11

In order that the authors of works protected by the present Convention shall, in the absence of proof to the contrary, be considered as such, and be consequently admitted to institute proceedings against pirates before the Courts of the various countries of the Union, it will be sufficient that their name be indicated on the work in the accustomed manner.

For anonymous or pseudonymous works, the publisher whose name is indicated on the work is entitled to protect the rights belonging to the author. He is, without other proof, reputed the lawful representative of the anonymous or pseudonymous author.

It is, nevertheless, agreed that the tribunals may, if necessary, require the production of a certificate from the competent authority to the effect that the formalities prescribed by law in the country of origin, have been accomplished, as contemplated in Article 2.

*Article* 14

Under the reserves and conditions to be determined by common agreement, the present Convention applies to all works which at the moment of its coming into force have not yet fallen into the public domain in the country of origin.

*Article* 18

Countries which have not become parties to the present Convention, and which grant by their domestic law protection of rights secured by this Convention, shall be admitted to accede thereto on request to that effect.

Such accession shall be notified in writing to the Government of the Swiss Confederation, who will communicate it to all the other countries of the Union.

Such accession shall imply full adhesion to all the clauses and admission to all the advantages provided by the present Convention.

*Article* 19

Countries acceding to the present Convention shall also have the right of acceding thereto at any time for their Colonies or foreign possessions.

They may do this either by a general declaration comprehending all their Colonies or possessions within the accession, or, by specially naming those comprised therein, or by simply indicating those which are excluded.

*Final protocol*

(2) As regards Article 9 it is agreed that those countries of the Union whose legislation implicitly includes choreographic works amongst dramatico-musical works, expressly admit the former works to the benefits of the Convention concluded this day.

It is, however, understood that questions which may arise on the application of this clause shall rest within the competence of the respective tribunals to decide.

(4) The common agreement alluded to in Article 14 of the Convention, is established as follows:—

The application of the Convention to works which have not fallen into the public domain at the time when it comes into force, shall operate according to the stipulations on this head which may be contained in special Conventions either existing or to be concluded.

In the absence of such stipulations between any countries of the Union, the respective countries shall regulate, each for itself, by its domestic legislation, the manner in which the principle contained in Article 14 is to be applied.

SECOND SCHEDULE

ORDERS IN COUNCIL REVOKED

Orders in Council of the dates named below for securing the privileges of copyright in her Majesty's Dominions to authors of works of literature and the fine arts and dramatic pieces, and musical compositions first produced in the following countries, namely:—

| Foreign Countries | Date of Order |
|---|---|
| Prussia . . . . . | 27 Aug 1846. |
| Saxony. . . . . . | 26 Sept 1846. |
| Brunswick . . . . . | 24 April 1847. |
| The States of the Thuringian Union . . . . . } | 10 Aug 1847. |
| Hanover . . . . . | 30 Oct 1847. |
| Oldenburg . . . . . | 11 Feb 1848. |
| France . . . . . | 10 Jan 1852. |
| Anhalt-Dessau, and Anhalt-Bernbourg . . . } | 11 Mar 1853. |
| Hamburg . . . . { | 25 Nov 1853. 8 July 1855. |
| Belgium . . . . . | 8 Feb 1855. |
| Prussia, Saxony, Saxe-Weimar . . | 19 Oct 1855. |
| Spain . . . . . | 24 Sept 1857 and 20 Nov 1880. |
| The States of Sardinia . . . . | 4 Feb 1861. |
| Hesse Darmstadt . . . . | 5 Feb 1862. |
| Italy . . . . | 9 Sept 1885. |
| German Empire . . . . | 24 Sept 1886. |

The Order in Council of 5th August, 1875, revoking the application of s 6 of 15 & 16 Vict c 12, to dramatic pieces referred to in the Order in Council of 10th January, 1852, with reference to works first published in France.

## ADDITIONAL ACT OF PARIS 1896

*Article* 1

The International Convention of the 9th September, 1886, is modified as follows:

(1) *Art* 2—The first paragraph of Art 2 shall run as follows:

'Authors who are subjects or citizens of any of the countries of the Union, or their lawful representatives, shall enjoy in the other countries for their works, whether unpublished, or first published in one of those countries, the rights which the respective laws do now or may hereafter grant to natives.'

A fifth paragraph is added in these terms:

'Posthumous works shall be included among those to be protected.'
(2) *Art 3*—Art 3 shall run as follows:
'Authors not being subjects or citizens of one of the countries of the Union, who first publish or cause to be first published, their literary or artistic works in one of those countries, shall enjoy, in respect of such works, the protection granted by the Berne Convention, and by the present Additional Act.'
(3) *Art 5*—The first paragraph of Art 5 shall run as follows:
'Authors who are subjects or citizens of any of the countries of the Union, or their lawful representatives, shall enjoy in the other countries the exclusive right of making or authorising the translation of their works during the entire term of their right over the original work. Nevertheless, the exclusive right of translation shall cease to exist if the author shall not have availed himself of it, during a term of ten years from the date of the first publication of the original work, by publishing or causing to be published in one of the countries of the Union, a translation in the language for which protection is to be claimed.'
(4) *Art 7*—Art 7 shall run as follows:
'Serial stories, including tales, published in the newspapers or periodicals of one of the countries of the Union, may not be reproduced, in original or translation, in the other countries, without the sanction of the authors or of their lawful representatives.

'This stipulation shall apply equally to other articles in newspapers or periodicals, when the authors or editors shall have expressly declared in the newspaper or periodical itself in which they shall have been published that reproduction is forbidden. In the case of periodicals it shall be sufficient if such prohibition is indicated in general terms at the beginning of each number.

'In the absence of prohibition such articles may be reproduced on condition that the source is indicated.

'The prohibition cannot in any case apply to articles of political discussion, to news of the day, or to miscellaneous information.'


TREATY BETWEEN GREAT BRITAIN AND AUSTRIA-HUNGARY
**Convention for the establishment of international copyright**
(Vienna, 24 April 1893)


*Article* 1
Authors of literary or artistic works and their legal representatives, including publishers, shall enjoy reciprocally, in the dominions of the High Contracting Parties, the advantages which are, or may be, granted by law there for the protection of works of literature or art.

Consequently, authors of literary or artistic works which have been first published in the dominions of one of the High Contracting Parties, as well as their legal representatives, shall have in the dominions of the other High Contracting Party the same protection and the same legal remedy against all infringement of their rights, as if the work had been first published in the country where the infringement may have taken place.

In the same manner, the authors of literary or artistic works, and their legal representatives, who are subjects of one of the High Contracting Parties, or who reside within its dominions, shall in the dominions of the other Contracting Party enjoy the same protection and the same legal remedies against all infringements of their rights as though they were subjects of, or residents in, the State in which the infringement may have taken place. These advantages shall only be reciprocally guaranteed to authors and their legal representatives when the work in question is also protected by the laws of the State where the work was first published, and the duration of protection in the other country shall not exceed that which is granted to authors and their legal representatives in the country where the work was first published.

### Article 2

The right of translation forming part of the copyright, the protection of the right of translation, is assumed under the conditions laid down by this Convention. If ten years after the expiry of the year in which a work to be protected in Her Majesty's dominions on the basis of this Convention has appeared, no translation in English has been published, the right of translating the work into English shall no longer within those dominions exclusively belong to the author.

In the case of a book published in numbers, the aforesaid period of ten years shall commence at the end of the year in which each number is published.

### Article 3

Authorised translations are protected as original works. They consequently enjoy the full protection granted by this Convention. It is understood that in the case of a work for which the translating right has fallen into the public domain, the translator cannot oppose the translation of the same work by other writers.

### Article 4

The expression 'literary or artistic works' comprehends books, pamphlets, and all other writings; dramatic or dramatico-musical works, musical compositions, with or without words; works of design, painting, sculpture, and engraving; lithographs, illustrations, geographical charts, plans, sketches, and plastic works relating to geography, topography, architecture, or science in general; in fact, every production whatsoever in the literary, scientific, or artistic domain which can be published by any mode of impression or reproduction.

### Article 5

In the British Empire, and in the Kingdoms and States represented in the Austrian Reichsrath, the enjoyment of the rights secured by the present Convention is subject only to the accomplishment of the conditions and formalities prescribed by the law of that State in which the work is first published; and no further formalities or conditions shall be required in the other country.

Consequently, it shall not be necessary that a work which has obtained legal protection in one country should be registered, or copies thereof deposited in the other country in order that the remedies against infringement may be obtained which are granted in the other country to works first published there.

In the dominions of the Hungarian Crown the enjoyment of these rights is subject, however, to the accomplishment of the conditions and formalities prescribed by the laws and regulations both of Great Britain and of Hungary.

### Article 6

In order that the authors of works protected by the present Convention shall, in the absence of proof to the contrary, be considered as such, and be, consequently, admitted to institute proceedings in respect of the infringement of copyright before the Courts of the other State, it will suffice that their name be indicated on the work in the accustomed manner.

The Tribunals may, however, in case of doubt, require the production of such further evidence as may be required by the laws of the respective countries.

For anonymous or pseudonymous works, the publisher whose name is indicated on the work is entitled to protect the rights belonging to the author. He is, without other proof, reputed the legal representative of the anonymous or pseudonymous author, until the latter or his legal representative has declared and proved his rights.

*Article* 8

The provisions of the present Convention shall be applied to literary or artistic works produced prior to the date of its coming into effect, subject, however, to the limitations prescribed by the following regulations:

(b)  In the United Kingdom of Great Britain and Ireland—

The author and publisher of any literary or artistic work first produced before the date at which this Convention comes into effect shall be entitled to all legal remedies against infringement; provided that where any person has, before the date of the publication of the Order in Council putting this Convention into effect, lawfully produced any work in the United Kingdom, any rights or interest arising from or in connection with such production, which are subsisting and valuable at the said date, shall not be diminished or prejudiced.

# Appendix 4

# International conventions

BERNE CONVENTION FOR THE PROTECTION OF LITERARY AND
ARTISTIC WORKS
(Paris Act, 24 July 1971)

The countries of the Union, being equally animated by the desire to protect, in as
effective and uniform a manner as possible, the rights of authorities in their literary
and artistic works, recognising the importance of the work of the Revision
Conference held at Stockholm in 1967,

Have resolved to revise the Act adopted by the Stockholm Conference, while
maintaining without change Articles 1 to 20 and 22 to 26 of that Act.
Consequently, the undersigned Plenipotentiaries, have presented their full powers,
recognised as in good and due form, have agreed as follows:

*Article 1*

The countries to which this Convention applies constitute a Union for the
protection of the rights of authors in their literary and artistic works.

*Article 2*

(1) The expression 'literary and artistic works' shall include every production in
the literary, scientific and artistic domain, whatever may be the mode or form of
its expression, such as books, pamphlets and other writings; lectures, addresses,
sermons and other works of the same nature; dramatic or dramatico-musical
works; choreographic works and entertainments in dumb show; musicial
compositions with or without words; cinematographic works to which are
assimilated works expressed by a process analogous to cinematography; works of
drawing, painting, architecture, sculpture, engraving and lithography; photographic works to which are assimilated works expressed by a process analogous
to photography; works of applied art; illustrations, maps, plans, sketches and three-
dimensional works relative to geography, topography, architecture or science.

(2) It shall, however, be a matter for legislation in the countries of the Union
to prescribe that works in general or any specified categories of works shall not
be protected unless they have been fixed in some material form.

(3) Translations, adaptations, arrangements of music and other alterations of a
literary or artistic work shall be protected as original works without prejudice to
the copyright in the original work.

(4) It shall be a matter for legislation in the countries of the Union to determine the protection to be granted to official texts of a legislative, administrative and legal nature, and to official translations of such texts.

(5) Collections of literary or artistic works such as encyclopaedias and anthologies which, by reason of the selection and arrangement of their contents, constitute intellectual creations shall be protected as such, without prejudice to the copyright in each of the works forming part of such collections.

(6) The works mentioned in this Article shall enjoy protection in all countries of the Union. This protection shall operate for the benefit of the author and his successors in title.

(7) Subject to the provisions of Article 7(4) of this Convention, it shall be a matter for legislation in the countries of the Union to determine the extent of the application of their laws to works of applied art and industrial designs and models, as well as the conditions under which such works, designs and models shall be protected. Works protected in the country of origin solely as designs and models shall be entitled in another country of the Union only to such special protection as is granted in that country to designs and models; however, if no such special protection is granted in that country, such works shall be protected as artistic works.

(8) The protection of this Convention shall not apply to news of the day or to miscellaneous facts having the character of mere items of press information.

## Article 2bis

(1) It shall be a matter for legislation in the countries of the Union to exclude, wholly or in part, from the protection provided by the preceding Article political speeches and speeches delivered in the course of legal proceedings.

(2) It shall also be a matter for legislation in the countries of the Union to determine the conditions under which lectures, addresses and other works of the same nature which are delivered in public may be reproduced by the press, broadcast, communicated by the public by wire and made the subject of public communication as envisaged in Article 11bis(1) of this Convention, when such use is justified by the informatory purpose.

(3) Nevertheless, the author shall enjoy the exclusive right of making a collection of his works mentioned in the preceding paragraphs.

## Article 3

(1) The protection of this Convention shall apply to:

(a) authors who are nationals of one of the countries of the Union, for their works, whether published or not;
(b) authors who are not nationals of one of the countries of the Union, for their works first published in one of those countries, or simultaneously in a country outside the Union and in a country of the Union.

(2) Authors who are not nationals of one of the countries of the Union but who have their habitual residence in one of them shall, for the purposes of this Convention, be assimilated to nationals of that country.

(3) The expression 'published works' means works published with the consent of their authors, whatever may be the means of manufacture of the copies provided that the availability of such copies has been such as to satisfy the reasonable

requirements of the public, having regard to the nature of the work. The performance of a dramatic, dramatico-musical, cinematographic or musical work, the public recitation of a literary work, the communication by wire or the broadcasting of literary or artistic works, the exhibition of a work of art and the construction of a work of architecture shall not constitute publication.

(4) A work shall be considered as having been published simultaneously in several countries if it has been published in two or more countries within thirty days of its first publication.

*Article 4*

The protection of this Convention shall apply, even if the conditions of Article 3 are not fulfilled, to:

- (a) authors of cinematographic works the maker of which has his headquarters or habitual residence in one of the countries of the Union;
- (b) authors of works of architecture erected in a country of the Union or of other artistic works incorporated in a building or other structure located in a country of the Union.

*Article 5*

(1) Authors shall enjoy, in respect of works for which they are protected under this Convention, in countries of the Union other than the country of origin, the rights which their respective laws do now or may hereafter grant to their nationals, as well as the rights specially granted by this Convention.

(2) The enjoyment and the exercise of these rights shall not be subject to any formality; such enjoyment and such exercise shall be independent for the existence of protection in the country of origin of the work. Consequently, apart from the provisions of this Convention, the extent of protection, as well as the means of redress afforded to the author to protect his rights, shall be governed exclusively by the laws of the country where protection is claimed.

(3) Protection in the country of origin is governed by domestic law. However, when the author is not a national of the country of origin of the work for which he is protected under this Convention, he shall enjoy in that country the same rights as national authors.

(4) The country of origin shall be considered to be:

- (a) in the case of works first published in a country of the Union, that country; in the case of works published simultaneously in several countries of the Union which grant different terms of protection, the country whose legislation grants the shortest term of protection;
- (b) in the case of works published simultaneously in a country outside the Union and in a country of the Union, the latter country;
- (c) in the case of unpublished works or of works first published in a country outside the Union, without simultaneous publication in a country of the Union, the country of the Union of which the author is a national, provided that:

    - (i) when these are cinematographic works the maker of which has his headquarters or his habitual residence in the country of the Union, the country of origin shall be that country, and

(ii) when these are works of architecture erected in a country of the Union or other artistic works incorporated in a building or other structure located in a country of the Union, the country of origin shall be that country.

### *Article 6*

(1)   Where any country outside the Union fails to protect in an adequate manner the works of authors who are nationals of one of the countries of the Union, the latter country may restrict the protection given to the works of authors who are, at the date of the first publication thereof, nationals of the other country and are not habitually resident in one of the countries of the Union. If the country of first publication avails itself of this right, the other countries of the Union shall not be required to grant to works thus subjected to special treatment a wider protection than that granted to them in the country of first publication.

(2)  No restrictions introduced by virtue of the preceding paragraph shall affect the rights which an author may have acquired in respect of a work published in a country of the Union before such restrictions were put into force.

(3) The countries of the Union which restrict the grant of copyright in accordance with this Article shall give notice thereof to the Director General of the World Intellectual Property Organisation (hereinafter designated as the Director General) by a written declaration specifying the countries in regard to which protection is restricted, and the restrictions to which rights of authors who are nationals of those countries are subjected. The Director General shall immediately communicate this declaration to all the countries of the Union.

### *Article 6*bis

(1)  Independently of the authors economic rights, and even after the transfer of the said rights, the author shall have the right to claim authorship of the work and to object to any distortion, mutilation or other modification of, or other derogatory action in relation to, the said work, which would be prejudicial to his honour or reputation.

(2)  The rights granted to the author in accordance with the preceding paragraph shall, after his death, be maintained, at least until the expiry of the economic rights, and shall be exercisable by the persons or institutions authorised by the legislation of the country where protection is claimed. However, those countries whose legislation, at the moment of their ratification of or accession to this Act, does not provide for the protection after the death of the author of all the rights set out in the preceding paragraph may provide that some of these rights may, after his death, cease to be maintained.

(3)  The means of redress for safeguarding the rights granted by this Article shall be governed by the legislation of the country where protection is claimed.

### *Article 7*

(1)  The term of protection granted by this Convention shall be the life of the author and fifty years after his death.

(2)  However, in the case of cinematographic works, the countries of the Union may provide that the term of protection shall expire fifty years after the work has been made available to the public with the consent of the author, or, failing such

an event within fifty years from the making of such a work, fifty years after the making.

(3) In the case of anonymous or pseudonymous works, the term of protection granted by this Convention shall expire fifty years after the work has been lawfully made available to the public. However, when the pseudonym adopted by the author leaves no doubt as to his identity, the term of protection shall be that provided in paragraph (1). If the author of an anonymous or pseudonymous work discloses his identity during the above-mentioned period, the term of protection applicable shall be that provided in paragraph (1). The countries of the Union shall not be required to protect anonymous or pseudonymous works in respect of which it is reasonable to presume that their author has been dead for fifty years.

(4) It shall be a matter for legislation in the countries of the Union to determine the term of protection of photographic works and that of works of applied art in so far as they are protected as artistic works; however, this term shall last at least until the end of a period of twenty-five years from the making of such a work.

(5) The term of protection subsequent to the death of the author and the terms provided by paragraphs (2), (3) and (4) shall run from the date of death or of the event referred to in those paragraphs, but such terms shall always be deemed to begin on the first of January of the year following the death or such event.

(6) The countries of the Union may grant a term of protection in excess of those provided by the preceding paragraphs.

(7) Those countries of the Union bound by the Rome Act of this Convention which grant, in their national legislation in force at the time of signature of the present Act, shorter terms of protection than those provided for in the preceding paragraphs shall have the right to maintain such terms when ratifying or acceding to the present Act.

(8) In any case the term shall be governed by the legislation of the country where protection is claimed; however, unless the legislation of that country otherwise provides, the term shall not exceed the term fixed in the country of origin of the work.

## Article 7bis

The provisions of the preceding Article shall also apply in the case of a work of joint authorship, provided that the terms measured from the death of the author shall be calculated from the death of the last surviving author.

## Article 8

Authors of literary and artistic works protected by this Convention shall enjoy the exclusive right of making and of authorising the translation of their works throughout the term of protection of their rights in the original works.

## Article 9

(1) Authors of literary and artistic works protected by this Convention shall have the exclusive right of authorising the reproduction of these works, in any manner or form.

(2) It shall be a matter for legislation in the countries of the Union to permit the reproduction of such works in certain special cases, provided that such reproduction does not conflict with a normal exploitation of the work and does not unreasonably prejudice the legitimate interests of the author.

(3) Any sound or visual recording shall be considered as a reproduction for the purposes of this Convention.

*Article 10*

(1) It shall be permissible to make quotations from a work which has already been lawfully made available to the public, provided that their making is compatible with fair practice, and their extent does not exceed that justified by the purpose, including quotations from newspaper articles and periodicals in the form of press summaries.

(2) It shall be a matter for legislation in the countries of the Union, and for special agreements existing or to be concluded between them, to permit the utilisation, to the extent justified by the purpose, of literary or artistic works by way of illustration in publications, broadcasts or sound or visual recordings for teaching, provided such utilisation is compatible with fair practice.

(3) Where use is made of works in accordance with the preceding paragraphs of this Article, mention shall be made of the source, and of the name of the author if it appears thereon.

*Article 10*bis

(1) It shall be a matter for legislation in the countries of the Union to permit the reproduction by the press, the broadcasting or the communication to the public by wire of articles published in newspapers or periodicals on current economic, political or religious topics, and of broadcast works of the same character, in cases in which the reproduction, broadcasting or such communication thereof is not expressly reserved. Nevertheless, the source must always be clearly indicated; the legal consequences of a breach of this obligation shall be determined by the legislation of the country where protection is claimed.

(2) It shall also be a matter for legislation in the countries of the Union to determine the conditions under which, for the purpose of reporting current events by means of photography, cinematography, broadcasting or communication to the public by wire, literary or artistic works seen or heard in the course of the event may, to the extent justified by the informatory purpose, be reproduced and made available to the public.

*Article 11*

(1) Authors of dramatic, dramatico-musical and musical works shall enjoy the exclusive right of authorising:

   (i)  the public performance of their works, including such public performance by any means or process;

   (ii)  any communication to the public of the performance of their works.

(2) Authors of dramatic or dramatico-musical works shall enjoy, during the full term of their rights in the original works, the same rights with respect to translations thereof.

*Article 11*bis

(1) Authors of literary and artistic works shall enjoy the exclusive right of authorising:

(i)    the broadcasting of their works or the communication thereof to the public by any other means of wireless diffusion of signs, sounds or images;

(ii)   any communication to the public by wire or by rebroadcasting of the broadcast of the work, when this communication is made by an organisation other than the original one;

(iii)  the public communication by loudspeaker or any other analogous instrument transmitting, by signs, sounds or images, the broadcast of the work.

(2) It shall be a matter for legislation in the countries of the Union to determine the conditions under which the rights mentioned in the preceding paragraph may be exercised, but these conditions shall apply only in the countries where they have been prescribed. They shall not in any circumstances be prejudicial to the moral rights of the author, nor to his right to obtain equitable remuneration which, in the absence of agreement, shall be fixed by competent authority.

(3) In the absence of any contrary stipulation, permission granted in accordance with paragraph (1) of this Article shall not imply permission to record, by means of instruments recording sounds or images, the work broadcast. It shall, however, be a matter for legislation in the countries of the Union to determine the regulations for ephemeral recordings made by a broadcasting organisation by means of its own facilities and used for its own broadcasts. The preservation of these recordings in official archives may, on the ground of their exceptional documentary character, be authorised by such legislation.

*Article 11*ter

(1) Authors of literary works shall enjoy the exclusive right of authorising:

(i)    the public recitation of their works, including such public recitation by any means or process;

(ii)   any communication to the public of the recitation of their works.

(2) Authors of literary works shall enjoy, during the full term of their rights in the original works, the same rights with respect to translations thereof.

*Article 12*

Authors of literary or artistic works shall enjoy the exclusive right of authorising adaptations, arrangements and other alterations of their works.

*Article 13*

(1) Each country of the Union may impose for itself reservations and conditions on the exclusive right granted to the author of a musical work and to the author of any words, the recording of which together with the musical work has already been authorised by the latter, to authorise the sound recording of that musical work, together with such words, if any; but all such reservations and conditions shall apply only in the countries which have imposed them and shall not, in any circumstances, be prejudicial to the rights of these authors to obtain equitable remuneration which, in the absence of agreement, shall be fixed by competent authority.

(2) Recordings of musical works made in a country of the Union in accordance

with Article 13(3) of the Conventions signed at Rome on June 2, 1928, and at Brussels on June 26, 1948, may be reproduced in that country without the permission of the author of the musical work until a date two years after that country becomes bound by this Act.

(3) Recordings made in accordance with paragraphs (1) and (2) of this Article and imported without permission from the parties concerned into a country where they are treated as infringing recordings shall be liable to seizure.

## Article 14

(1) Authors of literary or artistic works shall have the exclusive right of authorising:

    (i)  the cinematographic adaptation and reproduction of these works, and the distribution of the works thus adapted or reproduced;

    (ii)  the public performance and communication to the public by wire of the works thus adapted or reproduced.

(2) The adaptation into any other artistic form of a cinematographic production derived from literary or artistic works shall, without prejudice to the authorisation of the author of the cinematographic production, remain subject to the authorisation of the authors of the original works.

(3) The provisions of Article 13(1) shall not apply.

## Article 14bis

(1) Without prejudice to the copyright in any work which may have been adapted or reproduced a cinematographic work shall be protected as an original work. The owner of copyright in a cinematographic work shall enjoy the same rights as the author of an original work, including the rights referred to in the preceding Article.

(2)(a) Ownership of copyright in a cinematographic work shall be a matter for legislation in the country where protection is claimed.

(b) However, in the countries of the Union which, by legislation, include among the owners of copyright in a cinematographic work authors who have brought contributions to the making of the work, such authors, if they have undertaken to bring such contributions, may not, in the absence of any contrary or special stipulation, object to the reproduction, distribution, public performance, communication to the public by wire, broadcasting or any other communication to the public, or to the subtitling or dubbing of texts, of the work.

(c) The question whether or not the form of the undertaking referred to above should, for the application of the preceding subparagraph (b), be in a written agreement or a written act of the same effect shall be a matter for the legislation of the country where the maker of the cinematographic work has his headquarters or habitual residence. However, it shall be a matter for the legislation of the country of the Union where protection is claimed to provide that the said undertaking shall be in a written agreement or a written act of the same effect. The countries whose legislation so provides shall notify the Director General by means of a written declaration, which will be immediately communicated by him to all the other countries of the Union.

(d) By contrary or special stipulation is meant any restrictive condition which is relevant to the aforesaid undertaking.

(3) Unless the national legislation provides to the contrary, the provisions of

paragraph (2)(b) above shall not be applicable to authors of scenarios, dialogues and musical works created for the making of the cinematographic work, or to the principal director thereof. However, those countries of the Union whose legislation does not contain rules providing for the application of the said paragraph (2)(b) to such director shall notify the Director General by means of a written declaration, which will be immediately communicated by him to all the other countries of the Union.

*Article 14ᵗᵉʳ*

(1)  The author, or after his death the persons or institutions authorised by national legislation, shall, with respect to original works of art and original manuscripts of writers and composers, enjoy the inalienable right to an interest in any sale of the work subsequent to the first transfer by the author of the work.

(2)  The protection provided by the preceding paragraph may be claimed in a country of the Union only if legislation in the country to which the author belongs so permits, and to the extent permitted by the country where this protection is claimed.

(3)  The procedure for collection and the amounts shall be matters for determination by national legislation.

*Article 15*

(1)  In order that the author of a literary or artistic work protected by this Convention shall, in the absence of proof to the contrary, be regarded as such, and consequently be entitled to institute infringement proceedings in the countries of the Union, it shall be sufficient for his name to appear on the work in the usual manner. This paragraph shall be applicable even if this name is a pseudonym, where the pseudonym adopted by the author leaves no doubt as to his identity.

(2)  The person or body corporate whose name appears on a cinematographic work in the usual manner shall, in the absence of proof to the contrary, be presumed to be the maker of the said work.

(3)  In the case of anonymous and pseudonymous works, other than those referred to in paragraph (1) above, the publisher whose name appears on the work shall, in the absence of proof to the contrary, be deemed to represent the author, and in this capacity he shall be entitled to protect and enforce the authors rights. The provisions of this paragraph shall cease to apply when the author reveals his identity and establishes his claim to authorship of the work.

(4)(a)  In the case of unpublished works where the identity of the author is unknown, but where there is every ground to presume that he is a national of a country of the Union, it shall be a matter for legislation in that country to designate the competent authority which shall represent the author and shall be entitled to protect and enforce his rights in the countries of the Union.

(b)  Countries of the Union which make such designation under the terms of this provision shall notify the Director General by means of a written declaration giving full information concerning the authority thus designated. The Director General shall at once communicate this declaration to all other countries of the Union.

## Article 16

(1) Infringing copies of a work shall be liable to seizure in any country of the Union where the work enjoys legal protection.

(2) The provisions of the preceding paragraph shall also apply to reproductions coming from a country where the work is not protected, or has ceased to be protected.

(3) The seizures shall take place in accordance with the legislation of each country.

## Article 17

The provisions of this Convention cannot in any way affect the right of the Government of each country of the Union to permit, to control, or to prohibit, by legislation or regulation, the circulation, presentation, or exhibition of any work ˀr production in regard to which the competent authority may find it necessary to exercise that right.

## Article 18

(1) This Convention shall apply to all works which, at the moment of its coming into force, have not yet fallen into the public domain in the country of origin through the expiry of the term of protection.

(2) If, however, through the expiry of the term of protection which was previously granted, a work has fallen onto the public domain of the country where protection is claimed, that work shall not be protected anew.

(3) The application of this principle shall be subject to any provisions contained in special conventions to that effect existing or to be concluded between countries of the Union. In the absence of such provisions, the respective countries shall determine, each in so far as it is concerned, the conditions of application of this principle.

(4) The preceding provisions shall also apply in the case of new accessions to the Union and to cases in which protection is extended by the application of Article 7 or by the abandonment of reservations.

## Article 19

The provisions of this Convention shall not preclude the making of a claim to the benefit of any greater protection which may be granted by legislation in a country of the Union.

## Article 20

The Governments of the countries of the Union reserve the right to enter into special agreements among themselves, in so far as such agreements grant to authors more extensive rights than those granted by the Convention, or contain other provisions not contrary to this Convention. The provisions of existing agreements which satisfy these conditions shall remain applicable.

## Article 21

(1) Special provisions regarding developing countries are included in the Appendix.

(2) Subject to the provisions of Article 28(1)(b), the Appendix forms an integral part of this Act.

*Article 22*

(1)(a) The Union shall have an Assembly consisting of those countries of the Union which are bound by Articles 22 to 26.

(b) The Government of each country shall be represented by one delegate, who may be assisted by alternate delegates, advisors, and experts.

(c) The expenses of each delegation shall be borne by the Government which has appointed it.

(2)(a) The Assembly shall:

(i) deal with all matters concerning the maintenance and development of the Union and the implementation of this Convention;

(ii) give directions concerning the preparation for conferences of revision to the International Bureau of Intellectual Property (hereinafter designated as the International Bureau) referred to in the Convention Establishing the World Intellectual Property Organisation (hereinafter designated as the Organisation), due account being taken of any comments made by those countries of the Union which are not bound by Articles 22 to 26;

(iii) review and approve the reports and activities of the Director General of the Organisation concerning the Union, and give him necessary instructions concerning matters within the competence of the Union;

(iv) elect the members of the Executive Committee of the Assembly;

(v) review and approve the reports and activities of its Executive Committee, and give instructions to such Committee;

(vi) determine the programme and adopt the triennial budget of the Union, and approve its final accounts;

(vii) adopt the financial regulations of the Union;

(viii) establish such committees of experts and working groups as may be necessary for the work of the Union;

(ix) determine which countries not members of the Union and which intergovernmental and international non-governmental organisations shall be admitted to its meetings as observers;

(x) adopt amendments to Articles 22 to 26;

(xi) take any other appropriate action designed to further the objectives of the Union;

(xii) exercise such other functions as are appropriate under this Convention;

(xiii) subject to its acceptance, exercise such rights as are given to it in the Convention establishing the Organisation.

(b) With respect to matters which are of interest also to other Unions administered by the Organisation, the Assembly shall make its decisions after having heard the advice of the Coordination Committee of the Organisation.

(3)(a) Each country member of the Assembly shall have one vote.

(b) One-half of the countries members of the Assembly shall constitute a quorum.

(c) Notwithstanding the provisions of subparagraph (b), if, in any session, the number of countries represented is less than one-half but equal to or more than one-third of the countries members of the Assembly, the Assembly may make decisions but, with the exception of decisions concerning its own procedure, all

601

such decisions shall take effect only if the following conditions are fulfilled. The International Bureau shall communicate the said decisions to the countries members of the Assembly which were not represented and shall invite them to express in writing their vote or abstention within a period of three months from the date of the communication. If, at the expiration of this period, the number of countries having thus expressed their vote or abstention attains the number of countries which was lacking for attaining the quorum in the session itself, such decisions shall take effect provided that at the same time the required majority still obtains.

(d) Subject to the provisions of Article 26(2), the decisions of the Assembly shall require two-thirds of the votes cast.

(e) Abstentions shall not be considered as votes.

(f) A delegate may represent, and vote in the name of, one country only.

(g) Countries of the Union not members of the Assembly shall be admitted to its meetings as observers.

(4)(a) The Assembly shall meet once in every third calendar year in ordinary session upon convocation by the Director General and, in the absence of exceptional circumstances, during the same period and at the same place as the General Assembly of the Organisation.

(b) The Assembly shall meet in extraordinary session upon convocation by the Director General, at the request of the Executive Committee or at the request of one-fourth of the countries members of the Assembly.

(5) The Assembly shall adopt its own rules of procedure.

*Article 23*

(1) The Assembly shall have an Executive Committee.

(2)(a) The Executive Committee shall consist of countries elected by the Assembly from among countries members of the Assembly. Furthermore, the country on whose territory the Organisation has its headquarters shall, subject to the provisions of Article 25(7)(b), have an *ex officio* seat on the Committee.

(b) The Government of each country member of the Executive Committee shall be represented by one delegate, who may be assisted by alternate delegates, advisors, and experts.

(c) The expenses of each delegation shall be borne by the Government which has appointed it.

(3) The number of countries members of the Executive Committee shall correspond to one-fourth of the number of countries members of the Assembly. In establishing the number of seats to be filled, remainders after division by four shall be disregarded.

(4) In electing the members of the Executive Committee, the Assembly shall have due regard to an equitable geographical distribution and to the need for countries party to the Special Agreements which might be established in relation with the Union to be among the countries constituting the Executive Committee.

(5)(a) Each member of the Executive Committee shall serve from the close of the session of the Assembly which elected it to the close of the next ordinary session of the Assembly.

(b) Members of the Executive Committee may be re-elected, but not more than two-thirds of them.

(c) The Assembly shall establish the details of the rules governing the election and possible re-election of the members of the Executive Committee.

(6)(a) The Executive Committee shall:

(i)   prepare the draft agenda of the Assembly;

(ii)  submit proposals to the Assembly respecting the draft programme and triennial budget of the Union prepared by the Director General;

(iii) approve, within the limits of the programme and the triennial budget, the specific yearly budgets and programmes prepared by the Director General;

(iv)  submit, with appropriate comments, to the Assembly the periodical reports of the Director General and the yearly audit reports on the accounts;

(v)   in accordance with the decisions of the Assembly and having regard to circumstances arising between two ordinary sessions of the Assembly, take all necessary measures to ensure the execution of the program of the Union by the Director General;

(vi)  perform such other functions as are allocated to it under this Convention.

(b) With respect to matters which are of interest also to other Unions administered by the Organisation, the Executive Committee shall make its decisions after having heard the advice of the Coordination Committee of the Organisation.

(7)(a) The Executive Committee shall meet once a year in ordinary session upon convocation by the Director General, preferably during the same period and at the same place as the Coordination Committee of the Organisation.

(b) The Executive Committee shall meet in extraordinary session upon convocation by the Director General, either on his own initiative, or at the request of its Chairman or one-fourth of its members.

(8)(a) Each country member of the Executive Committee shall have one vote.

(b) One-half of the members of the Executive Committee shall constitute a quorum.

(c) Decisions shall be made by a simple majority of the votes cast.

(d) Abstentions shall not be considered as votes.

(e) A delegate may represent, and vote in the name of, one country only.

(9) Countries of the Union not members of the Executive Committee shall be admitted to its meetings as observers.

(10) The Executive Committee shall adopt its own rules of procedure.

*Article 24*

(1)(a) The administrative tasks with respect to the Union shall be performed by the International Bureau, which is a continuation of the Bureau of the Union united with the Bureau of the Union established by the International Convention,for the Protection of Industrial Property.

(b) In particular, the International Bureau shall provide the secretariat of the various organs of the Union.

(c) The Director General of the Organisation shall be the chief executive of the Union and shall represent the Union.

(2) The International Bureau shall assemble and publish information concerning the protection of copyright. Each country of the Union shall promptly communicate to the International Bureau all new laws and official texts concerning the protection of copyright.

(3) The International Bureau shall publish a monthly periodical.

(4) The International Bureau shall, on request, furnish information to any country of the Union on matters concerning the protection of copyright.

(5) The International Bureau shall conduct studies, and shall provide services, designed to facilitate the protection of copyright.

(6) The Director General and any staff member designated by him shall participate, without the right to vote, in all meetings of the Assembly, the Executive Committee and any other committee of experts or working group. The Director General, or a staff member designated by him, shall be *ex officio* secretary of these bodies.

(7)(a) The International Bureau shall, in accordance with the directions of the Assembly and in cooperation with the Executive Committee, make the preparations for the conferences of revision of the provisions of the Convention other than Articles 22 to 26.

(b) The International Bureau may consult with intergovernmental and international non-governmental organisations concerning preparations for conferences of revision.

(c) The Director General and persons designated by him shall take part, without the right to vote, in the discussions at these conferences.

(8) The International Bureau shall carry out any other tasks assigned to it.

*Article 25*

(1)(a) The Union shall have a budget.

(b) The budget of the Union shall include the income and expenses proper to the Union, its contribution to the budget of expenses common to the Unions, and, where applicable, the sum made available to the budget of the Conference of the Organisation.

(c) Expenses not attributable exclusively to the Union but also to one or more other Unions administered by the Organisation shall be considered as expenses common to the Unions. The share of the Union in such common expenses shall be in proportion to the interest the Union has in them.

(2) The budget of the Union shall be established with due regard to the requirements of coordination with the budgets of the other Unions administered by the Organisation.

(3) The budget of the Union shall be financed from the following sources:

    (i)   contributions of the countries of the Union;
    (ii)  fees and charges due for services performed by the International Bureau in relation to the Union;
    (iii) sale of, or royalties on, the publications of the International Bureau concerning the Union;
    (iv) gifts, bequests, and subventions;
    (v)  rents, interests, and other miscellaneous income.

(4)(a) For the purpose of establishing its contribution towards the budget, each country of the Union shall belong to a class, and shall pay its annual contributions on the basis of a number of units fixed as follows:

| | |
|---|---|
| Class I | 25 |
| Class II | 20 |
| Class III | 15 |
| Class IV | 10 |
| Class V | 5 |
| Class VI | 3 |
| Class VIII | 1 |

(b) Unless it has already done so, each country shall indicate, concurrently with depositing its instrument of ratification or accession, the class to which it wishes to belong. Any country may change class. If it chooses a lower class, the country must announce it to the Assembly at one of its ordinary sessions. Any such change shall take effect at the beginning of the calendar year following the session.

(c) The annual contribution of each country shall be an amount in the same proportion to the total sum to be contributed to the annual budget of the Union by all countries as the number of its units is to the total of the units of all contributing countries.

(d) Contributions shall become due on the first of January of each year.

(e) A country which is in arrears in the payment of its contributions shall have no vote in any of the organs of the Union of which it is a member if the amount of its arrears equals or exceeds the amount of the contributions due from it for the preceding two full years. However, any organ of the Union may allow such a country to continue to exercise its vote in that organ if, and as long as, it is satisfied that the delay in payment is due to exceptional and unavoidable circumstances.

(f) If the budget is not adopted before the beginning of a new financial period, it shall be at the same level as the budget of the previous year, in accordance with the financial regulations.

(5) The amount of the fees and charges due for services rendered by the International Bureau in relation to the Union shall be established, and shall be reported to the Assembly and the Executive Committee, by the Director General.

(6)(a) The Union shall have a working capital fund which shall be constituted by a single payment made by each country of the Union. If the fund becomes insufficient, an increase shall be decided by the Assembly.

(b) The amount of the initial payment of each country to the said fund or of its participation in the increase thereof shall be a proportion of the contribution of that country for the year in which the fund is established or the increase decided.

(c) The proportion and the terms of payment shall be fixed by the Assembly on the proposal of the Director General and after it has heard the advice of the Coordination Committee of the Organisation.

(7)(a) In the headquarters agreement concluded with the country on the territory of which the Organisation has its headquarters, it shall be provided that, whenever the working capital fund is insufficient, such country shall grant advances. The amount of these advances and the conditions on which they are granted shall be the subject of separate agreements, in each case, between such country and the Organisation. As long as it remains under the obligation to grant advances, such country shall have an *ex officio* seat on the Executive Committee.

(b) The country referred to in subparagraph (a) and the Organisation shall each have the right to denounce the obligation to grant advances, by written notification. Denunciation shall take effect three years after the end of the year in which it has been notified.

(8) The auditing of the accounts shall be effected by one or more of the countries of the Union or by external auditors, as provided in the financial regulations. They shall be designated with their agreement, by the Assembly.

*Article 26*

(1) Proposals for the amendment of Articles 22, 23, 24, 25, and the present Article, may be initiated by any country member of the Assembly, by the Executive Committee, or by the Director General. Such proposals shall be communicated by the Director General to the member countries of the Assembly at least six months in advance of their consideration by the Assembly.

(2) Amendments of the Articles referred to in paragraph (1) shall be adopted by the Assembly. Adoption shall require three-fourths of the votes cast, provided that any amendment of Article 22, and of the present paragraph, shall require four-fifths of the votes cast.

(3) Any amendment to the Articles referred to in paragraph (1) shall enter into the force one month after written notifications of acceptance, effected in accordance with their respective constitutional processes, have been received by the Director General from three-fourths of the countries members of the Assembly at the time it adopted the amendment. Any amendment to the said Articles thus accepted shall bind all the countries which are members of the Assembly at the time the amendment enters into force, or which become members thereof at a subsequent date, provided that any amendment increasing the financial obligations of countries of the Union shall bind only those countries which have notified their acceptance of such amendment.

## Article 27

(1) This Convention shall be submitted to revision with a view to the introduction of amendments designed to improve the system of the Union.

(2) For this purpose, conferences shall be held successively in one of the countries of the Union among the delegates of the said countries.

(3) Subject to the provisions of Article 26 which apply to the amendment of Articles 22 to 26, any revision of this Act, including the Appendix, shall require the unanimity of the votes cast.

## Article 28

(1)(a) Any country of the Union which has signed this Act may ratify it, and, if it has not signed it, may accede to it. Instruments of ratification or accession shall be deposited with the Director General.

(b) Any country of the Union may declare in its instrument of ratification or accession that its ratification or accession shall not apply to Articles 1 to 21 and the Appendix, provided that, if such country has previously made a declaration under Article VI(1) of the Appendix, then it may declare in the said instrument only that its ratification or accession shall not apply to Articles 1 to 20.

(c) Any country of the Union which, in accordance with subparagraph (b), has excluded provisions therein referred to from the effects of its ratification or accession may at any later time declare that it extends the effects of its ratification or accession to those provisions. Such declaration shall be deposited with the Director General.

(2)(a) Articles 1 to 21 and the Appendix shall enter into force three months after both of the following two conditions are fulfilled:

(i)   at least five countries of the Union have ratified or acceded to this Act without making a declaration under paragraph (1)(b),

(ii)  France, Spain, the United Kingdom of Great Britain and Northern Ireland, and the United States of America have become bound by the Universal Copyright Convention as revised at Paris on July 24, 1971.

(b) The entry into force referred to in subparagraph (a) shall apply to those countries of the Union which, at least three months before the said entry into force, have deposited instruments of ratification or accession not containing a declaration under paragraph (1)(b).

(c) With respect to any country of the Union not covered by subparagraph (b) and which ratifies or accedes to this Act without making a declaration under paragraph (1)(b), Articles 1 to 21 and the Appendix shall enter into force three months after the date on which the Director General has notified the deposit of the relevant instrument of ratification or accession, unless a subsequent date has been indicated in the instrument deposited. In the latter case, Articles 1 to 21 and the Appendix shall enter into force with respect to that country on the date thus indicated.

(d) The provisions of subparagraphs (a) to (c) do not affect the application of Article VI of the Appendix.

(3) With respect to any country of the Union which ratifies or accedes to this Act with or without a declaration made under paragraph (1)(b), Articles 22 to 38 shall enter into force three months after the date on which the Director General has notified the deposit of the relevant instrument of ratification or accession, unless a subsequent date has been indicated in the instrument deposited. In the latter case, Articles 22 to 38 shall enter into force with respect to that country on the date thus indicated.

## *Article 29*

(1) Any country outside the Union may accede to this Act and thereby become party to this Convention and a member of the Union. Instruments of accession shall be deposited with the Director General.

(2)(a) Subject to subparagraph (b), this Convention shall enter into force with respect to any country outside the Union three months after the date on which the Director General has notified the deposit of its instrument of accession, unless a subsequent date has been indicated in the instrument deposited. In the latter case, this Convention shall enter into force with respect to that country on the date thus indicated.

(b) If the entry into force according to subparagraph (a) precedes the entry into force of Articles 1 to 21 and the Appendix according to Article 28(2)(a), the said country shall, in the meantime, be bound, instead of by Articles 1 to 21 and the Appendix, by Articles 1 to 20 of the Brussels Act of this Convention.

## *Article 29*bis

Ratification of or accession to this Act by any country not bound by Articles 22 to 38 of the Stockholm Act of this Convention shall, for the sole purposes of Article 14(2) of the Convention establishing the Organisation, amount to a ratification of or accession to the said Stockholm Act with the limitation set forth in Article 28(1)(b)(i) thereof.

## *Article 30*

(1) Subject to the exceptions permitted by paragraph (2) of this Article, by Article 28(1)(b), by Article 33(2), and by the Appendix, ratification or accession shall automatically entail acceptance of all the provisions and admission to all the advantages of this Convention.

(2)(a) Any country of the Union ratifying or acceding to this Act may, subject to Article V(2) of the Appendix retain the benefit of the reservation it has previously formulated on condition that it makes a declaration to that effect at the time of the deposit of its instrument of ratification or accession.

(b) Any country outside the Union may declare, in acceding to this Convention and subject to Article V(2) of the Appendix, that it intends to substitute, temporarily at least, for Article 8 of this Act concerning the right of translation, the provisions of Article 5 of the Union Convention of 1886, as completed at Paris in 1896, on the clear understanding that the said provisions are applicable only to translations into a language in general use in the said country. Subject to Article 1(6)(b) of the Appendix, any country has the right to apply, in relation to the right of translation of works whose country of origin is a country availing itself of such a reservation, a protection which is equivalent to the protection granted by the latter country.

(c) Any country may withdraw such reservations at any time by notification addressed to the director General.

## Article 31

(1) Any country may declare in its instrument of ratification or accession, or may inform the Director General by written notification at any time thereafter, that this Convention shall be applicable to all or part of those territories, designated in the declaration or notification, for the external relations of which it is responsible.

(2) Any country which has made such a declaration or given such a notification may, at any time, notify the Director General that this Convention shall cease to be applicable to all or part of such territories.

(3)(a) Any declaration made under paragraph (1) shall take effect on the same date as the ratification or accession in which it was included, and any notification given under that paragraph shall take effect three months after its notification by the Director General.

(b) Any notification given under paragraph :(2) shall take effect twelve months after its receipt by the Director General.

(4) This Article shall in no way be understood as implying the recognition or tacit acceptance by a country of the Union of the factual situation concerning a territory to which this Convention is made applicable by another country of the Union by virtue of a declaration under paragraph (1).

## Article 32

(1) This Act shall, as regards relations between the countries of the Union, and to the extent that it applies, replace the Berne Convention of September 9, 1886, and the subsequent Acts of revision. The Acts previously in force shall continue to be applicable, in their entirety or to the extent that this Act does not replace them by virtue of the preceding sentence, in relations with countries of the Union which do not ratify or accede to this Act.

(2) Countries outside the Union which become party to this Act shall, subject to paragraph (3), apply it with respect to any country of the Union not bound by this Act or which, although bound by this Act, has made a declaration pursuant to Article 28(1)(b). Such countries recognize that the said country of the Union, in its relations with them:

(i) may apply the provisions of the most recent Act by which it is bound, and
(ii) subject to Article I(6) of the Appendix, has the right to adapt the protection to the level provided for by this Act.

(3) Any country which has availed itself of any of the faculties provided for in the Appendix may apply the provisions of the Appendix relating to the faculty or faculties of which it has availed itself in its relations with any other country of the Union which is not bound by this Act, provided that the latter country has accepted the application of the said provisions.

*Article 33*

(1) Any dispute between two or more countries of the Union concerning the interpretation or application of this Convention, not settled by negotiation, may, by any one of the countries concerned, brought before the International Court of Justice by application in conformity with the Statute of the Court, unless the countries concerned agree on some other method of settlement. The country bringing the dispute before the Court shall inform the International Bureau; the International Bureau shall bring the matter to the attention of the other countries of the Union.

(2) Each country may, at the time it signs this Act or deposits its instrument of ratification or accession, declare that it does not consider itself bound by the provisions of paragraph (1). With regard to any dispute between such country and any other country of the Union, the provisions of paragraph (1) shall not apply.

(3) Any country having made a declaration in accordance with the provisions of paragraph (2) may, at any time, withdraw its declaration by notification addressed to the Director General.

*Article 34*

(1) Subject to Article 29[bis], no country may ratify or accede to earlier Acts of this Convention once Articles 1 to 21 and the Appendix have entered into force.

(2) Once Articles 1 to 21 and the Appendix have entered into force, no country may make a declaration under Article 5 of the Protocol Regarding Developing Countries attached to the Stockholm Act.

*Article 34*

(1) Subject to Article 29[bis], no country may ratify or accede to earlier Acts of this Convention once Articles 1 to 21 and the Appendix have entered into force.

(2) Once Articles 1 to 21 and the Appendix have entered into force, no country may make a declaration under Article 5 of the Protocol Regarding Developing Countries attached to the Stockholm Act.

*Article 35*

(1) This Convention shall remain in force without limitation as to time.

(2) Any country may denounce this Act by notification addressed to the Director General. Such denuciation shall constitute also denunciation of all earlier Acts and shall affect only the country making it, the Convention remaining in full force and effect as regards the other countries of the Union.

(3) Denunciation shall take effect one year after the day on which the Director General has received the notification.

(4) The right of denunciation provided by this Article shall not be exercised by any country before the expiration of five years from the date upon which it becomes a member of the Union.

*Article 36*

(1) Any country party to this Convention undertakes to adopt, in accordance with its constitution, the measures necessary to ensure the application of this Convention.

(2) It is understood that, at the time a country becomes bound by this Convention, it will be in a position under its domestic law to give effect to the provisions of this Convention.

*Article 37*

(1)(a) This Act shall be signed in a single copy in the French and English languages and, subject to paragraph (2), shall be deposited with the Director General.

(b) Official texts shall be established by the Director General, after consultation with the interested Governments, in the Arabic, German, Italian, Portuguese and Spanish languages, and such other languages as the Assembly may designate.

(c) In case of differences of opinion on the interpretation of the various texts, the French text shall prevail.

(2) This Act shall remain open for signature until 31 January, 1972. Until that date, the copy referred to in paragraph (1)(a) shall be deposited with the Government of the French Republic.

(3) The Director General shall certify and transmit two copies of the signed text of this Act to the Governments of all countries of the Union and, on request, to the Government of any other country.

(4) The Director General shall register this Act with the Secretariat of the United Nations.

(5) The Director General shall notify the Governments of all countries of the Union of signatures, deposits of instruments of ratification or accession and any declarations included in such instruments or made pursuant to Articles 28(1)(c), 30(2)(a) and (b), and 33(2), entry into force of any provisions of this Act, notifications of denunciation, and notifications pursuant to Articles 30(2)(c), 31(1) and (2), 33(3), and 38(1), as well as the Appendix.

*Article 38*

(1) Countries of the Union which have not ratified or acceded to this Act and which are not bound by Articles 22 to 26 of the Stockholm Act of this Convention may, until April 26, 1975, exercise, if they so desire, the rights provided under the said Articles as if they were bound by them. Any country desiring to exercise such rights shall give written notification to this effect to the Director General; this notification shall be effective on the date of its receipt. Such countries shall be deemed to be members of the Assembly until the said date.

(2) As long as all the countries of the Union have not become members of the Organisation, the International Bureau of the Organisation shall also function as the Bureau of the Union, and the Director General as the Director of the said Bureau.

(3) Once all the countries of the Union have become Members of the Organisation, the rights, obligations, and property, of the Bureau of the Union shall devolve on the International Bureau of the Organisation.

## APPENDIX

Special Provisions Regarding Developing Countries

*Article 1*

(1)   Any country regarded as a developing country in conformity with the established practice of the General Assembly of the United Nations which ratifies or accedes to this Act, of which this Appendix forms an integral part, and which, having regard to its economic situation and its social or cultural needs does not consider itself immediately in a position to make provision for the protection of all the rights as provided for in this Act, may, by a notification deposited with the Director General at the time of depositing its instrument of ratification or accession or, subject to Article V(1)(c), at any time thereafter, declare that it will avail itself of the faculty provided for in Article II, or of the faculty provided for in Article III, or of both of those faculties. It may, instead of availing itself of the faculty provided for in Article II, make a declaration according to Article V(1)(a).

(2)(a)  Any declaration under paragraph (1) notified before the expiration of the period of ten years from the entry into force of Articles 1 to 21 and this Appendix according to Article 28(2) shall be effective until the expiration of the said period. Any such declaration may be renewed in whole or in part for periods of ten years each by a notification deposited with the Director General not more than fifteen months and not less than three months before the expiration of the ten-year period then running.

(b)  Any declaration under paragraph (1) notified after the expiration of the period of ten years from the entry into force of Articles 1 to 21 and this Appendix according to Article 28(2) shall be effective until the expiration of the ten-year period then running. Any such declaration may be renewed as provided for in the second sentence of subparagraph (a).

(3)  Any country of the Union which has ceased to be regarded as a developing country as referred to in paragraph (1) shall no longer be entitled to renew its declaration as provided in paragraph (2), and, whether or not it formally withdraws its declaration, such country shall be precluded from availing itself of the faculties referred to in paragraph (1) from the expiration of the ten-year period then running or from the expiration of a period of three years after it has ceased to be regarded as a developing country, whichever period expires later.

(4)  Where, at the time when the declaration made under paragraph (1) or (2) ceases to be effective, there are copies in stock which were made under a licence granted by virtue of this Appendix, such copies may continue to be distributed until their stock is exhausted.

(5)  Any country which is bound by the provisions of this Act and which has deposited a declaration or a notification in accordance with Article 31(1) with respect to the application of this Act to a particular territory, the situation of which can be regarded as analogous to that of the countries referred to in paragraph (1), may, in respect of such territory, make the declaration referred to in paragraph (1) and the notification of renewal referred to in paragraph (2). As long as such declaration or notification remains in effect, the provisions of this Appendix shall be applicable to the territory in respect of which it was made.

(6)(a)  The fact that a country avails itself of any of the faculties referred to in paragraph (1) does not permit another country to give less protection to works of which the country of origin is the former country than it is obliged to grant under Articles 1 to 20.

(b) The right to apply reciprocal treatment provided for in Article 30(2)(b), second sentence, shall not, until the date on which the period applicable under Article 1(3) expires, be exercised in respect of works the country of origin of which is a country which has made a declaration according to Article V(1)(a).

*Article II*

(1) Any country which has declared that it will avail itself of the faculty provided for in this Article shall be entitled, so far as works published in printed or analogous forms of reproduction are concerned, to substitute for the exclusive right of translation provided for in Article 8 a system of non-exclusive and non-transferable licences, granted by the competent authority under the following conditions and subject to Article IV.

(2)(a) Subject to paragraph (3), if, after the expiration of a period of three years, or of any longer period determined by the national legislation of the said country, commencing on the date of the first publication of the work, a translation of such work has not been published in a language in general use in that country by the owner of the right of translation, or with his authorisation, any national of such country may obtain a licence to make a translation of the work in the said language and publish the translation in printed or analogous forms of reproduction.

(b) A licence under the conditions provided for in this Article may also be granted if all the editions of the translation published in the language concerned are out of print.

(3)(a) In the case of translations into a language which is not in general use in one or more developed countries which are members of the Union, a period of one year shall be substituted for the period of three years referred to in paragraph (2)(a).

(b) Any country referred to in paragraph (1) may, with the unanimous agreement of the developed countries which are members of the Union and in which the same language is in general use, substitute, in the case of translations into that language, for the period of three years referred to in paragraph (2)(a) a shorter period as determined by such agreement but not less than one year. However, the provisions of the foregoing sentence shall not apply where the language in question is English, French or Spanish. The Director General shall be notified of any such agreement by the Governments which have concluded it.

(4)(a) No licence obtainable after three years shall be granted under this Article until a further period of six months has elapsed, and no licence obtainable after one year shall be granted under this Article until a further period of nine months has elapsed

   (i) from the date on which the applicant complies with the requirements mentioned in Article IV(1), or

   (ii) where the identity or the address of the owner of the right of translation is unknown, from the date on which the applicant sends, as provided for in Article IV(2), copies of his application submitted to the authority competent to grant the licence.

(b) If, during the said period of six or nine months, a translation in the language in respect of which the application was made is published by the owner of the right of translation or with his authorisation, no licence under this Article shall be granted.

(5) Any licence under this Article shall be granted only for the purpose of teaching, scholarship or research.

(6) If a translation of a work is published by the owner of the right of translation or with his authorisation at a price reasonably related to that normally charged in the country for comparable works, any licence granted under this Article shall terminate if such translation is in the same language and with substantially the same content as the translation published under the licence. Any copies already made before the licence terminates may continue to be distributed until their stock is exhausted.

(7) For works which are composed mainly of illustrations, a licence to make and publish a translation of the text and to reproduce and publish the illustrations may be granted only if the conditions of Article III are also fulfilled.

(8) No licence shall be granted under this Article when the author has withdrawn from circulation all copies of his work.

(9)(a) A licence to make a translation of a work which has been published in printed or analogous forms of reproduction may also be granted to any broadcasting organisation having its headquarters in a country referred to in paragraph (1), upon an application made to the competent authority of the country by the said organisation, provided that all the following conditions are met:

(i)   the translation is made from a copy made and acquired in accordance with the laws of the said country;

(ii)  the translation is only for use in broadcasts intended exclusively for teaching or for the dissemination of the results of specialised technical or scientific research to experts in a particular profession;

(iii) the translation is used exclusively for the purposes referred to in condition (ii) through broadcasts made lawfully and intended for recipients on the territory of the said country, including broadcasts made through the medium of sound or visual recordings lawfully and exclusively made for the purpose of such broadcasts;

(iv)  all uses made of the translation are without any commercial purpose.

(b) Sound or visual recordings of a translation which was made by a broadcasting organisation under a licence granted by virtue of this paragraph may, for the purposes and subject to the conditions referred to in subparagraph (a) and with the agreement of that organisation, also be used by any other broadcasting organisation having its headquarters in the country whose competent authority granted the licence in question.

(c) Provided that all of the criteria and conditions set out in subparagraph (a) are met, a licence may also be granted to a broadcasting organisation to translate any text incorporated in an audio-visual fixation where such fixation was itself prepared and published for the sole purpose of being used in connection with systematic instructional activities.

(d) Subject to subparagraphs (a) to (c), the provisions of the preceding paragraphs shall apply to the grant and exercise of any licence granted under this paragraph.

*Article III*

(1)   Any country which has declared that it will avail itself of the faculty provided for in this Article shall be entitled to substitute for the exclusive right of reproduction provided for in Article 9 a system of non-exclusive and non-transferable licences, granted by the competent authority under the following conditions and subject to Article IV.

(2)(a) If, in relation to a work to which this Article applies by virtue of paragraph (7), after the expiration of

(i) the relevant period specified in paragraph (3), commencing on the date of first publication of a particular edition of the work, or
(ii) any longer period determined by national legislation of the country referred to in paragraph (1), commencing on the same date,

copies of such edition have not been distributed in that country to the general public or in connection with systematic instructional activities, by the owner of the right of reproduction or with his authorisation, at a price reasonably related to that normally charged in the country for comparable works, any national of such country may obtain a licence to reproduce and publish such edition at that or a lower price for use in connection with systematic instructional activities.

(b) A licence to reproduce and publish an edition which has been distributed as described in subparagraph (a) may also be granted under the conditions provided for in this Article if, after the expiration of the applicable period, no authorised copies of that edition have been on sale for a period of six months in the country concerned to the general public or in connection with systematic instructional activities at a price reasonably related to that normally charged in the country for comparable works.

(3) The period referred to in paragraph (2)(a)(i) shall be five years, except that

(i) for works of the natural and physical sciences, including mathematics, and of technology, the period shall be three years;
(ii) for works of fiction, poetry, drama and music, and for art books, the period shall be seven years.

(4)(a)  No licence obtainable after three years shall be granted under this Article until a period of six months has elapsed

(i) from the date on which the applicant complies with the requirements mentioned in Article IV(1), or
(ii) where the identity or the address of the owner of the right of reproduction is unknown, from the date on which the applicant sends, as provided for in Article IV(2), copies of his application submitted to the authority competent to grant the licence.

(b)  Where licences are obtainable after other periods and Article IV(2) is applicable, no licence shall be granted until a period of three months has elapsed from the date of the dispatch of the copies of the application.

(c) If, during the period of six or three months referred to in subparagraphs (a) and (b), a distribution as described in paragraph 2(a) has taken place, no licence shall be granted under this Article.

(d) No licence shall be granted if the author has withdrawn from circulation all copies of the edition for the reproduction and publication of which the licence has been applied for.

(5) A licence to reproduce and publish a translation of a work shall not be granted under this Article in the following cases:

(i) where the translation was not published by the owner of the right of translation or with his authorisation, or

(ii) where the translation is not in a language in general use in the country in which the licence is applied for.

(6) If copies of an edition of a work are distributed in the country referred to in paragraph (1) to the general public or in connection with systematic instructional activities, by the owner of the right of reproduction or with his authorisation, at a price reasonably related to that normally charged in the country for comparable works, any licence granted under this Article shall terminate if such edition is in the same language and with substantially the same content as the edition which was published under the said licence. Any copies already made before the licence terminates may continue to be distributed until their stock is exhausted.

(7)(a) Subject to subparagraph (b), the works to which this Article applies shall be limited to works published in printed or analogous forms of reproduction.

(b) This Article shall also apply to the reproduction in audio-visual form of lawfully made audio-visual fixations including any protected works incorporated therein and to the translation of any incorporated text into a language in general use in the country in which the licence is applied for, always provided that the audio-visual fixations in question were prepared and published for the sole purpose of being used in connection with the systematic instructional activities.

## Article IV

(1) A licence under Article II or Article III may be granted only if the applicant, in accordance with the procedure of the country concerned, establishes either that he has requested, and has been denied, authorisation by the owner of the right to make and publish the translation or to reproduce and publish the edition, as the case may be, or that, after due diligence on his part, he was unable to find the owner of the right. At the same time as making the request, the applicant shall inform any national or international information centre referred to in paragraph (2).

(2) If the owner of the right cannot be found, the applicant for a licence shall send, by registered airmail, copies of his application, submitted to the authority competent to grant the licence, to the publisher whose name appears on the work and to any national or international information centre which may have been designated, in a notification to that effect deposited with the Director General, by the Government of the country in which the publisher is believed to have his principal place of business.

(3) The name of the author shall be indicated on all copies of the translation or reproduction published under a licence granted under Article II or Article III. The title of the work shall appear on all such copies. In the case of a translation, the original title of the work shall appear in any case on all the said copies.

(4)(a) No licence granted under Article II or Article III shall extend to the export of copies, and any such licence shall be valid only for publication of the translation or of the reproduction, as the case may be, in the territory of the country in which it has been applied for.

(b) For the purposes of subparagraph (a), the notion of export shall include the sending of copies from any territory to the country which, in respect of that territory, has made a declaration under Article I(5).

(c) Where a governmental or other public entity of a country which has granted a licence to make a translation under Article II into a language other than English, French or Spanish sends copies of a translation published under such licence to another country, such sending of copies shall not, for the purposes of subparagraph (a), be considered to constitute export if all of the following conditions are met:

(i) the recipients are individuals who are nationals of the country whose competent authority has granted the licence, or organisations grouping such individuals;

(ii) the copies are to be used only for the purpose of teaching, scholarship or research;

(iii) the sending of the copies and their subsequent distribution to recipients is without any commercial purpose; and

(iv) the country to which the copies have been sent has agreed with the country whose competent authority has granted the licence to allow the receipt, or distribution, or both, and the Director General has been notified of the agreement by the Government of the country in which the licence has been granted.

(5) All copies published under a licence granted by virtue of Article II or Article III shall bear a notice in the appropriate language stating that the copies are available for distribution only in the country or territory to which the said licence applies.

(6)(a) Due provision shall be made at the national level to ensure

(i) that the licence provides, in favour of the owner of the right of translation or of reproduction, as the case may be, for just compensation that is consistent with standards of royalties normally operating on licences freely negotiated between persons in the two countries concerned, and

(ii) payment and transmittal of the compensation: should national currency regulations intervene, the competent authority shall make all efforts, by the use of international machinery, to ensure transmittal in internationally convertible currency or its equivalent.

(b) Due provision shall be made by national legislation to ensure a correct translation of the work, or an accurate reproduction of the particular edition, as the case may be.

## Article V

(1)(a) Any country entitled to make a declaration that it will avail itself of the faculty provided for in Article II may, instead, at the time of ratifying or acceding to this Act:

(i) if it is a country to which Article 30(2)(a) applies, make a declaration under that provision as far as the right of translation is concerned;

(ii) if it is a country to which Article 30(2)(a) does not apply, and even if it is not a country outside the Union, make a declaration as provided for in Article 30(2)(b), first sentence.

(b) In the case of a country which ceases to be regarded as a developing country as referred to in Article I(1), a declaration made according to this paragraph shall be effective until the date on which the period applicable under Article I(3) expires.

(c) Any country which has made a declaration according to this paragraph may not subsequently avail itself of the faculty provided for in Article II even if it withdraws the said declaration.

(2) Subject to paragraph (3), any country which has availed itself of the faculty provided for in Article II may not subsequently make a declaration according to paragraph (1).

(3) Any country which has ceased to be regarded as a developing country as referred to in Article 1(1) may, not later than two years prior to the expiration of the period applicable under Article 1(3), make a declaration to the effect provided for in Article 30(2)(b), first sentence, notwithstanding the fact that it is not a country outside the Union. Such declaration shall take effect at the date on which the period applicable under Article 1(3) expires.

*Article VI*

(1) Any country of the Union may declare, as from the date of this Act, and at any time before becoming bound by Articles 1 to 21 and this Appendix:

(i) if it is a country which, were it bound by Articles 1 to 21 and this Appendix, would be entitled to avail itself of the faculties referred to in Article I(1), that it will apply the provisions of Article II or of Article III or of both to works whose country of origin is a country which, pursuant to (ii) below, admits the application of those Articles to such works, or which is bound by Articles 1 to 21 and this Appendix; such declaration may, instead of referring to Article II, refer to Article V;

(ii) that it admits the application of this Appendix to works of which it is the country of origin by countries which have made a declaration under (i) above or a notification under Article I.

(2) Any declaration made under paragraph (1) shall be in writing and shall be deposited with the Director General. The declaration shall become effective from the date of its deposit.

UNIVERSAL COPYRIGHT CONVENTION
(as revised at Paris on 24 July 1971)

The Contracting States.

Moved by the desire to ensure in all countries copyright protection of literary, scientific and artistic works,

Convinced that a system of copyright protection appropriate to all nations of the world and expressed in a universal convention, additional to, and without impairing international systems already in force, will ensure respect for the rights of the individual and encourage the development of literature, the sciences and the arts,

Persuaded that such a universal copyright system will facilitate a wider dissemination of works of the human mind and increase international understanding,

Have resolved to revise the Universal Copyright Convention as signed at Geneva on 6 September 1952 (hereinafter called 'the 1952 Convention'), and consequently,

Have agreed as follows:

## Article I

Each Contracting State undertakes to provide for the adequate and effective protection of the rights of authors and other copyright proprietors in literary, scientific and artistic works, including writings, musical, dramatic and cinematographic works, and paintings, engravings and sculpture.

## Article II

(1) Published works of nationals of any Contracting State and works first published in that State shall enjoy in each other Contracting State the same protection as that other State accords to works of its nationals first published in its own territory, as well as the protection specially granted by this Convention.

(2) Unpublished works of nationals of each Contracting State shall enjoy in each other Contracting State the same protection as that other State accords to unpublished works of its own nationals, as well as the protection specially granted by this Convention.

(3) For the purpose of this Convention any Contracting State may, by domestic legislation, assimilate to its own nationals any person domiciled in that State.

## Article III

(1) Any Contracting State which, under its domestic law, requires as a condition of copyright, compliance with formalities such as deposit, registration, notice, notarial certificates, payment of fees or manufacture or publication in that Contracting State, shall regard these requirements as satisfied with respect to all works protected in accordance with this Convention and first published outside its territory and the author of which is not one of its nationals, if from the time of the first publication all the copies of the work published with the authority of the author or other copyright proprietor bear the symbol © accompanied by the name of the copyright proprietor and the year of first publication placed in such manner and location as to give reasonable notice of claim of copyright.

(2) The provisions of paragraph 1 shall not preclude any Contracting State from requiring formalities or other conditions for the acquisition and enjoyment of copyright in respect of works first published in its territory or works of its nationals wherever published.

(3) The provisions of paragraph 1 shall not preclude any Contracting State from providing that a person seeking judicial relief must, in bringing the action, comply with procedural requirements, such as that the complainant must appear through domestic counsel or that the complainant must deposit with the court or an administrative office, or both, a copy of the work involved in the litigation; provided that failure to comply with such requirements shall not affect the validity of the copyright, nor shall any such requirement be imposed upon a national of another Contracting State if such requirement is not imposed on nationals of the State in which protection is claimed.

(4) In each Contracting State there shall be legal means of protecting without formalities the unpublished works of nationals of other Contracting States.

(5) If a Contracting State grants protection for more than one term of copyright and the first term is for a period longer than one of the minimum periods prescribed in Article IV, such State shall not be required to comply with the provisions of paragraph 1 of this Article in respect of the second or any subsequent term of copyright.

*Article IV*

(1) The duration of protection of a work shall be governed, in accordance with the provisions of Article II and this Article, by the law of the Contracting State in which protection is claimed.

(2)(a) The term of protection for works protected under this Convention shall not be less than the life of the author and twenty-five years after his death. However, any Contracting State which, on the effective date of this Convention in that State, has limited this term for certain classes of works to a period computed from the first publication of the work, shall be entitled to maintain these exceptions and to extend them to other classes of works. For all these classes the term of protection shall not be less than twenty-five years from the date of first publication.

(b) Any Contracting State which, upon the effective date of this Convention in that State, does not compute the term of protection upon the basis of the life of the author, shall be entitled to compute the term of protection from the date of the first publication of the work or from its registration prior to publication, as the case may be, provided the term of protection shall not be less than twenty-five years from the date of the first publication or from its registration prior to publication, as the case may be.

(c) If the legislation of a Contracting State grants two or more successive terms of protection, the duration of the first term shall not be less than one of the minimum periods specified in subparagraphs (a) and (b).

(3) The provisions of paragraph 2 shall not apply to photographic works or to works of applied art; provided, however, that the term of protection in those Contracting States which protections photographic works, or works of applied art in so far as they are protected as artistic works, shall not be less than ten years for each of said classes of work.

(4)(a) No Contracting State shall be obliged to grant protection to a work for a period longer than that fixed for the class of works to which the work in question belongs, in the case of unpublished works by the law of the Contracting State of which the author is a national, and in the case of published works by the law of the Contracting State in which the work has been first published.

(b) For the purposes of the application of subparagraph (a), if the law of any Contracting State grants two or more successive terms of protection the period of protection of that State shall be considered to be the aggregate of those terms. However, if a specified work is not protected by such State during the second or any subsequent term for any reason, the other Contracting States shall not be obliged to protect it during the second or any subsequent term.

(5) For the purposes of the application of paragraph 4, the work of a national of a Contracting State, first published in a non-Contracting State, shall be treated as though first published in the Contracting State of which the author is a national.

(6) For the purposes of the application of paragraph 4, in case of simultaneous publication in two or more Contracting States, the work shall be treated as though first published in the State which affords the shortest term; any work published in two or more Contracting States within thirty days of its first publication shall be considered as having been published in said Contracting States.

*Article IV*bis

(1) The rights referred to in Article I shall include the basic rights ensuring the author's economic interests, including the exclusive rights to authorise reproduction by any means, public performance and broadcasting. The provisions

of this Article shall extend to works protected under this Convention either in their original form or in any form recognisably derived from the original.

(2) However, any Contracting State may, by its domestic legislation, make exceptions that do not conflict with the spirit and the provisions of this Convention, to the rights mentioned in paragraph 1 of this Article. Any State whose legislation so provides, shall nevertheless accord a reasonable degree of effective protection to each of the rights to which exception has been made.

*Article V*

(1) The rights referred to in Article I shall include the exclusive right of the author to make, publish and authorise the making and publication of translations of works protected under this Convention.

(2) However, any Contracting State may, by its domestic legislation, restrict the right of translation of writings, but only subject to the following provisions:

(a) If, after the expiration of a period of seven years from the date of the first publication of a writing, a translation of such writing has not been published in a language in general use in the Contracting State, by the owner of the right of translation or with his authorisation, any national of such Contracting State may obtain a non-exclusive licence from the competent authority thereof to translate the work into that language and publish the work so translated.

(b) Such national shall in accordance with the procedure of the State concerned, establish either that he has requested, and been denied, authorisation by the proprietor of the right to make and publish the translation, or that, after due diligence on his part, he was unable to find the owner of the right. A licence may also be granted on the same conditions if all previous editions of a translation in a language in general use in the Contracting State are out of print.

(c) If the owner of the right of translation cannot be found, then the applicant for a licence shall send copies of his application to the publisher whose name appears on the work and, if the nationality of the owner of the right of translation is known, to the diplomatic or consular representative of the State of which such owner is a national, or to the organisation which may have been designated by the government of that State. The licence shall not be granted before the expiration of a period of two months from the date of dispatch of the copies of the application.

(d) Due provision shall be made by domestic legislation to ensure to the owner of the right of translation a compensation which is just and conforms to international standards, to ensure payment and transmittal of such compensation and to ensure a correct translation of the work.

(e) The original title and the name of the author of the work shall be printed on all copies of the published translation. The licence shall be valid only for publication of the translation in the territory of the Contracting State where it has been applied for. Copies so published may be imported and sold in another Contracting State if a language in general use in such other State is the same language as that into which the work has been so translated, and if the domestic law in such other State makes provision for such licences and does not prohibit such importation and sale. Where the foregoing conditions do not exist, the importation and sale of such copies in a Contracting State shall be governed by its domestic law and its agreements. The licence shall not be transferred by the licensee.

(f) The licence shall not be granted when the author has withdrawn from circulation all copies of the work.

*Article V*bis

(1) Any Contracting State regarded as a developing country in conformity with the established practice of the General Assembly of the United Nations may, by a notification deposited with the Director-General of the United Nations Educational, Scientific and Cultural Organisation (hereinafter called 'the Director-General') at the time of its ratification, acceptance or accession or thereafter, avail itself of any or all of the exceptions provided for in Articles V *ter* and V *quater*.

(2) Any such notification shall be effective for ten years from the date of coming into force of this Convention, or for such part of that ten-year period as remains at the date of deposit of the notification, and may be renewed in whole or in part for further periods of ten years each, if not more than fifteen or less than three months before the expiration of the relevant ten-year period, the Contracting State deposits a further notification with the Director-General. Initial notifications may also be made during these further periods of ten years in accordance with the provisions of this Article.

(3) Notwithstanding the provisions of paragraph 2, a Contracting State that has ceased to be regarded as a developing country as referred to in paragraph I shall no longer be entitled to renew its notification made under the provisions of paragraph 1 or 2, and whether or not it formally withdraws the notification such State shall be precluded for availing itself of the exemptions provided for in Articles V *ter* and V *quarter* at the end of the current ten-year period, or at the end of the three years after it has ceased to be regarded as a developing country, whichever period expires later.

(4) Any copies of a work already made under the exceptions provided for in Articles V *ter* and V *quater* may continue to be distributed after the expiration of the period for which notifications under this Article were effective until their stock in exhausted.

(5) Any Contracting State that has deposited a notification in accordance with Article XIII with respect to the application of this Convention to a particular country or territory, the situation of which can be regarded as analogous to that of the States referred to in paragraph 1 of this Article, may also deposit notifications and renew them in accordance with the provisions of this Article with respect to any such country or territory. During the effective period of such notifications, the provisions of Articles V *ter* and V *quater* may be applied with respect to such country or territory. The sending of copies from the country or territory to the Contracting States shall be considered as export within the meaning of Articles V *ter* and V *quater*.

*Article V*ter

(1)(a) Any Contracting State to which Article V *bis* (1) applies may substitute for the period of seven years provided for in Article V (2) a period of three years or any longer period prescribed by its legislation. However, in the case of a translation into a language not in general use in one or more of the developed countries that are party to this Convention or only the 1952 Convention, the period shall be one year instead of three.

(b) A Contracting State to which Article V *bis* (1) applies may, with the unaminous agreement of the developed countries party to this Convention or only the 1952 Convention and in which the same language is in general use, substitute, in the case of translation into that language, for the period of three years provided for in subparagraph (a) another period as determined by such agreement but not shorter than one year. However, this subparagraph shall not apply where the language in question is English, French or Spanish. Notification of any such agreement shall be made to the Director-General.

(c) The licence may only be granted if the applicant, in accordance with the procedure of the State concerned, establishes either that he has requested, and been denied, authorisation by the owner of the right of translation, or that, after due diligence on his part, he was unable to find the owner of the right. At the same time as he makes his request he shall inform either the International Copyright Information Centre established by the United Nations Educational, Scientific and Cultural Organisation or any national or regional information centre which may have been designated in a notification to that effect deposited with the Director-General by the government of the State in which the publisher is believed to have his principal place of business.

(d) If the owner of the right of translation cannot be found, the applicant for a licence shall send, by registered airmail, copies of his application to the publisher whose name appears on the work and to any national or regional information centre as mentioned in subparagraph (c). If no such centre is notified he shall also send a copy to the international copyright information centre established by the United Nations Educational, Scientific and Cultural Organisation.

(2)(a) Licences obtainable after three years shall not be granted under this Article until a further period of six months has elapsed and licences obtainable after one year until a further period of nine months has elapsed. The further period shall begin either from the date of the request for permission to translate mentioned in paragraph 1(c) or, if the identity or address of the owner of the right of translation is not known, from the date of dispatch of the copies of the application for a licence mentioned in paragraph 1(d).

(b) Licences shall not be granted if a translation has been published by the owner of the right of translation or with his authorisation during the said period of six months or nine months.

(3) Any licence under this Article shall be granted only for the purpose of teaching, scholarship or research.

(4)(a) Any licence granted under this Article shall not extend to the export of copies and shall be valid only for publication in the territory of the Contracting State where it has been applied for.

(b) Any copy published in accordance with a licence granted under this Article shall bear a notice in the appropriate language stating that the copy is available for distribution only in the Contracting State granting the licence. If the writing bears the notice specified in Article III(1) the copies shall bear the same notice.

(c) The prohibition of export provided for in subparagraph (a) shall not apply where a governmental or other public entity of a State which was granted a licence under this Article to translate a work into a language other than English, French or Spanish sends copies of a translation prepared under such licence to another country if:

    (i)  the recipients are individuals who are nationals of the Contracting State granting the licence, or organisations grouping such individuals;

    (ii)  the copies are to be used only for the purpose of teaching, scholarship or research;

    (iii) the sending of the copies and their subsequent distribution to recipients is without the object of commercial purpose; and

(iv) the country to which the copies have been sent has agreed with the Contracting State to allow the receipt, distribution or both and the Director-General has been notified of such governments which have concluded it.

(5) Due provision shall be made at the national level to ensure:

(a) that the licence provides for just compensation that is consistent with the standards of royalties normally operating in the case of licences freely negotiated between persons in the two countries concerned; and

(b) payment and transmittal of the compensation; however, should national currency regulations intervene, the competent authority shall make all efforts, by the use of international machinery, to ensure transmittal in internationally convertible currency or its equivalent.

(6) Any licence granted by a Contracting State under this Article shall terminate if a translation of the work in the same language with substantially the same content as the edition in respect of which the licence was granted is published in the said State by the owner of the right of translation or with his authorisation, at a price reasonably related to that normally charged in the same State for comparable works. Any copies already made before the licence is terminated may continue to be distributed until their stock is exhausted.

(7) For works which are composed mainly of illustrations a licence to translate the text and to reproduce the illustrations may be granted only if the conditions of Article V *quater* are also fulfilled.

(8) (a) A licence to translate a work protected under this Convention, published in printed or analogous forms of reproduction, may also be granted to a broadcasting organisation having its headquarters in a Contracting State to which Article V *bis* (1) applies, upon an application made in that State by the said organisation under the following conditions:

(i) the translation is made from a copy made and acquired in accordance with the laws of the Contracting State;

(ii) the translation is for use only in broadcasts intended exclusively for teaching or for the dissemination of the results of specialised technical or scientific research to experts in a particular profession;

(iii) the translation is used exclusively for the purposes set out in condition (ii), through broadcasts lawfully made which are intended for recipients on the territory of the Contracting State, including broadcasts made through the medium of sound or visual recording lawfully and exclusively made for the purpose of such broadcasts;

(iv) sound or visual recordings of the translation may be exchanged only between broadcasting organisations having their headquarters in the Contracting State granting the licence; and

(v) all uses made of the translation are without any commercial purpose.

(b) Provided all of the criteria and conditions set out in subparagraph (a) are met, a licence may also be granted to a broadcasting organisation to translate any text incorporated in an audio-visual fixation which was itself prepared and published for the sole purpose of being used in connection with systematic instructional activities.

(c) Subject to subparagraphs (a) and (b), the other provisions of this Article shall apply to the grant and exercise of the licence.

(9) Subject to the provisions of this Article, any licence granted under this Article shall be governed by the provisions of Article V, and shall continue to be governed by the provisions of Article V and of this Article, even after the seven-year period provided for in Article V(2) has expired. However, after the said period has expired, the licensee shall be free to request that the said licence by replaced by a new licence governed exclusively by the provisions of Article V.

## Article V^quater

(1) Any Contracting State to which Article V *bis* (1) applies may adopt the following provisions:

(a) If, after the expiration of (i) the relevant period specified in subparagraph (c) commencing from the date of first publication of a particular edition of a literary, scientific or artistic work referred to in paragraph 3, or (ii) any longer period determined by national legislation of the State, copies of such edition have not been distributed in that State to the general public or in connexion with systematic instructional activities at a price reasonably related to that normally charged in the State for comparable works, by the owner of the right of reproduction or with his authorisation, any national of such State may obtain a non-exclusive licence from the competent authority to publish such edition at that or a lower price for use in connexion with systematic instructional activities. The licence may only be granted if such national, in accordance with the procedure of the State concerned, establishes either that he has requested, and has been denied, authorisation by the proprietor of the right to publish such work, or that, after due diligence on his part, he was unable to find the owner of the right. At the same time as he makes his request he shall inform either the international copyright information centre established by the United Nations Educational, Scientific and Cultural Organisation or any national or regional information centre referred to in subparagraph (d).

(b) A licence may also be granted on the same conditions if, for a period of six months, no authorised copies of the edition in question have been on sale in the State concerned to the general public or in connexion with systematic instructional activities at a price reasonably related to that normally charged in the State for comparable works.

(c) The period referred to in subparagraph (a) shall be five years except that:

  (i)   for works of the natural and physical sciences, including mathematics, and of technology, the period shall be three years;
  (ii)  for works of fiction, poetry, drama, and music, and for art books, the period shall be seven years.

(d) If the owner of the right of reproduction cannot be found, the applicant for a licence shall send, by registered airmail, copies of his application to the publisher whose name appears on the work and to any national or regional information centre identified as such in a notification deposited with the Director-General by the State in which the publisher is believed to have his principal place of business. In the absence of any such notification, he shall also send a copy to the international copyright information centre established by the United Nations Educational, Scientific and Cultural Organisation. The licence shall not be granted before the expiration of a period of three months from the date of dispatch of the copies of the application.

(e) Licences obtainable after three years shall not be granted under this Article:

(i)  'until a period of six months has elapsed from the date of the request for permission referred to in subparagraph (a) or, if the identity or address of the owner of the right of reproduction is unknown, from the date of the dispatch of the copies of the application for a licence referred to in subparagraph (d);

(ii) if any such distribution of copies of the edition as is mentioned in subparagraph (a) has taken place during that period.

(f) The name of the author and the title of the particular edition of the work shall be printed on all copies of the published reproduction. The licence shall not extend to the export of copies and shall be valid only for publication in the territory of the Contracting State where it has been applied for. The licence shall not be transferable by the licensee.

(g) Due provision shall be made by domestic legislation to ensure an accurate reproduction of the particular edition in question.

(h) A licence to reproduce and publish a translation of a work shall not be granted under this Article in the following cases:

(i)  where the translation was not published by the owner of the right of translation or with his authorisation;

(ii) where the translation is not in a language in general use in the State with power to grant the licence.

(2) The exceptions provided for in paragraph 1 are subject to the following additional provisions:

(a) Any copy published in accordance with a licence granted under this Article shall bear a notice in the appropriate language stating that the copy is available for distribution only in the Contracting State to which the said licence applies. If the edition bears the notice specified in Article III(1), the copies shall bear the same notice.

(b) Due provision shall be made at the national level to ensure:

(i)  that the licence provides for just compensation that is consistent with standards of royalties normally operating in the case of licences freely negotiated between persons in the two countries concerned; and

(ii) payment and transmittal of the compensation; however, should national currency regulations intervene, the competent authority shall make all efforts, by the use of international machinery, to ensure transmittal in the international convertible currency or its equivalent.

(c) Whenever copies of an edition of a work are distributed in the Contracting State to the general public or in connexion with systematic instructional activities, by the owner of the right of reproduction or with his authorisation, at a price reasonably related to that normally charged in the State for comparable works, any licence granted under this Article shall terminate if such edition is in the same language and is substantially the same in content as the edition published under licence. Any copies already made before the licence is terminated may continue to be distributed until their stock is exhausted.

(d) No licence shall be granted when the author has withdrawn from circulation all copies of the edition in question.

(3)(a) Subject to subparagraph (b), the literary, scientific or artistic works to which this Article applies shall be limited to works published in printed or analogous forms of reproduction.

(b) The provisions of this Article shall also apply to reproduction in audio-visual form of lawfully made audio-visual fixations including any protected works incorporated therein and to the translation of any incorporated text into a language in general use in the State with power to grant the licence; always provided that the audio-visual fixations in question were prepared and published for the sole purpose of being used in connexion with systematic instructional activities.

*Article VI*

Publication, as used in this Convention, means the reproduction in tangible form .nd the general distribution to the public of copies of a work from which it can be read or otherwise visually perceived.

*Article VII*

This Convention shall not apply to works or rights in works which, at the effective date of this Convention in a Contracting State where protection is claimed, are permanently in the public domain in the said Contracting State.

*Article VIII*

(1) This Convention, which shall bear the date of 24 July 1971, shall be deposited with the Director-General and shall remain open for signature by all States party to the 1952 Convention for a period of 120 days after the date of this Convention. It shall be subject to ratification or acceptance by the signatory States.

(2) Any State which has not signed this Convention may accede thereto.

(3) Ratification, acceptance or accession shall be effected by the deposit of an instrument to that effect with the Director-General.

*Article IX*

(1) This Convention shall come into force three months after the deposit of twelve instruments of ratification, acceptance or accession.

(2) Subsequently, this Convention shall come into force in respect of each State three months after that State has deposited its instrument of ratification, acceptance or accession.

(3) Accession to this Convention by a State not party to the 1952 Convention shall also constitute accession to that Convention; however, if its instrument of accession is deposited before this Convention comes into force, such State may make its accession to the 1952 Convention conditional upon the coming into force of this Convention. After the coming into force of this Convention, no State may accede solely to the 1952 Convention.

(4) Relations between States party to this Convention and States that are party only to the 1952 Convention, shall be governed by the 1952 Convention. However, any State party only to the 1952 Convention may, by a notification deposited with the Director-General, declare that it will admit the application of the 1971 Convention to works of its nationals or works first published in its territory by all States party to this Convention.

*Article X*

(1) Each Contracting State undertakes to adopt, in accordance with its Constitution, such measures as are necessary to ensure the application of this Convention.

(2) It is understood that at the date this Convention comes into force in respect of any State, that State must be in a position under its domestic law to give effect to the terms of this Convention.

*Article XI*

(1) An Intergovernmental Committee is hereby established with the following duties:

(a) to study the problems concerning the application and operation of the Universal Copyright Convention;

(b) to make preparation for periodic revisions of this Convention;

(c) to study any other problems concerning the international protection of copyright, in co-operation with the various interested international organisations, such as the United Nations Educational, Scientific and Cultural Organisation, the International Union for the Protection of Literary and Artistic Works and the Organisation of American States;

(d) to inform States party to the Universal Copyright Convention as to its activities.

(2) The Committee shall consist of the representatives of eighteen States party to this Convention or only to the 1952 Convention.

(3) The Committee shall be selected with due consideration to a fair balance of national interests on the basis of geographical location, population, languages and stage of development.

(4) The Director-General of the United Nations Educational, Scientific and Cultural Organisation, the Director-General of the World Intellectual Property Organisation and the Secretary-General of the Organisation of American States, or their representatives, may attend meetings of the Committee in an advisory capacity.

*Article XII*

The Intergovernmental Committee shall convene a conference for revision whenever it deems necessary, or at the request of at least ten States party to this Convention.

*Article XIII*

(1) Any Contracting State may, at the time of deposit of its instrument of ratification, acceptance or accession, or at any time thereafter, declare by notification addressed to the Director-General that this Convention shall apply to all or any of the countries or territories for the international relations of which it is responsible and this Convention shall thereupon apply to the countries or territories named in such notification after the expiration of the term of three months provided for in Article IX. In the absence of such notification, this Convention shall not apply to any such country or territory.

(2) However, nothing in this Article shall be understood as implying the recognition or tacit acceptance by a Contracting State of the factual situation

concerning a country or territory to which this Convention is made applicable by another Contracting State in accordance with the provisions of this Article.

## Article XIV

(1) Any Contracting State may denounce this Convention in its own name or on behalf of all or any of the countries or territories with respect to which a notification has been given under Article XIII. The denunciation shall be made by notification addressed to the Director-General. Such denunciation shall also constitute denunciation of the 1952 Convention.

(2) Such denunciation shall operate only in respect of the State or of the country or territory on whose behalf it was made and shall not take effect until twelve months after the date of receipt of the notification.

## Article XV

A dispute between two or more Contracting States concerning the interpretation or application of this Convention, not settled by negotiation, shall, unless the States concerned agree on some other method of settlement, be brought before the International Court of Justice for determination by it.

## Article XVI

(1) This Convention shall be established in English, French and Spanish. The three texts shall be signed and shall be equally authoritative.

(2) Official texts of this Convention shall be established by the Director-General, after consultation with the governments concerned, in Arabic, German, Italian and Portuguese.

(3) Any Contracting State or group of Contracting States shall be entitled to have established by the Director-General other texts in the language of its choice by arrangement with the Director-General.

(4) All such texts shall be annexed to the signed texts of this Convention.

## Article XVII

(1) This Convention shall not in any way affect the provisions of the Berne Convention for the Protection of Literary and Artistic Works or membership in the Union created by that Convention.

(2) In application of the foregoing paragraph, a declaration has been annexed to the present Article. This declaration is an integral part of this Convention for the States bound by the Berne Convention on 1 January 1951, or which have or may become bound to it at a later date. The signature of this Convention by such States shall also constitute signature of the said declaration, and ratification, acceptance or accession by such States shall include the Declaration, as well as this Convention.

## Article XVIII

This Convention shall not abrogate multilateral or bilateral copyright conventions or arrangements that are or may be in effect exclusively between two or more American Republics. In the event of any difference either between the provisions of such existing conventions or arrangements and the provisions of this Convention, or between the provisions of this Convention and those of any new convention or arrangement which may be formulated between two or more American Republics after this Convention comes into force, the convention or arrangement most recently formulated shall prevail between the parties thereto. Rights in works acquired in any Contracting State under existing conventions or arrangements before the date this Convention comes into force in such State shall not be affected.

## Article XIX

This Convention shall not abrogate multilateral or bilateral conventions or arrangements in effect between two or more Contracting States. In the event of any difference between the provisions of such existing conventions or arrangements and the provisions of this Convention, the provisions of this Convention shall prevail. Rights in works acquired in any Contracting State under existing conventions or arrangements before the date on which this Convention comes into force in such State shall not be affected. Nothing in this Article shall affect the provisions of Articles XVII and XVIII.

## Article XX

Reservations to this Convention shall not be permitted.

## Article XXI

(1) The Director-General shall send duly certified copies of this Convention to the States interested and to the Secretary-General of the United Nations for registration by him.

(2) He shall also inform all interested States of the ratifications, acceptances and accessions which have been deposited, the date on which this Convention comes into force, the notifications under this Convention, and denunciations under Article XIV.

## Appendix declaration relating to article XVII

The States which are members of the International Union for the Protection of Literary and Artistic Works (hereinafter called 'the Berne union') and which are signatories to this Convention,

Desiring to reinforce their mutual relations on the basis of the said Union and to avoid any conflict which might result from the co-existence of the Berne Convention and the Universal Copyright Convention,

Recognising the temporary need of some States to adjust their level of copyright protection in accordance with their stage of culture, social and economic development,

Have, by common agreement, accepted the terms of the following declaration:

(a) Except as provided by paragraph (b), works which, according to the Berne Convention, have as their country of origin a country which has withdrawn from the Berne Union after 1 January 1951, shall not be protected by the Universal Copyright Convention in the countries of the Berne Union;

(b) Where a Contracting State is regarded as a developing country in conformity with the established practice of the General Assembly of the United Nations, and has deposited with the Director-General of the United Nations Educational, Scientific and Cultural Organisation, at the time of its withdrawal from the Berne Union, a notification to the effect that it regards itself as a developing country, the provisions of paragraph (a) shall not be applicable as long as such State may avail itself of the exceptions provided for by this Convention in accordance with Article V *bis*;

(c) The Universal Copyright Convention shall not be applicable to the relationships among countries of the Berne Union in so far as it relates to the protection of works having as their country of origin, within the meaning of the Berne Convention, a country of the Berne Union.

## Resolution concerning article XI

The Conference for Revision of the Universal Copyright Convention,
Having considered the problems relating to the Intergovernmental Committee provided for in Article XI of this Convention, to which this resolution is annexed, resolves that:

(1) At its inception, the Committee shall include representatives of the twelve States members of the Intergovernmental Committee established under Article XI of the 1952 Convention and the resolution annexed to it, and in addition, representatives of the following States: Algeria, Australia, Japan, Mexico, Senegal and Yugoslavia.

(2) Any States that are not party to the 1952 Convention and have not acceded to this Convention before the first ordinary session of the Committee following the entry into force of this Convention shall be replaced by other States to be selected by the Committee at its first ordinary session in conformity with the provisions of Article XI(2) and (3).

(3) As soon as this Convention comes into force the Committee as provided for in paragraph 1 shall be deemed to be constituted in accordance with Article XI of this Convention.

(4) A session of the Committee shall take place within one year after the coming into force of this Convention; thereafter the Committee shall meet in ordinary session at intervals of not more than two years.

(5) The Committee shall elect its Chairman and two Vice-Chairmen. It shall establish its Rules of Procedure having regard to the following principles:

(a) the normal duration of the term of office of the members represented on the Committee shall be six years with one-third retiring every two years, it being however understood that, of the original terms of office, one-third shall expire at the end of the Committee's second ordinary session which will follow the entry into force of this Convention, a further third at the end of its third ordinary session, and the remaining third at the end of its fourth ordinary session.

(b) The rules governing the procedure whereby the Committee shall fill vacancies, the order in which terms of membership expire, eligibility for re-election, and election procedures, shall be based upon a balancing of the needs for continuity of membership and rotation of representation, as well as the considerations set out in Article XI(3). Expresses the wish that the United Nations Educational, Scientific and Cultural Organisation provide its Secretariat.

In faith whereof the undersigned, having deposited their respective full powers, have signed this Convention.

Done at Paris, this twenty-fourth day of July 1971, in a single copy.

*Protocol 1*

*Annexed to the Universal Copyright Convention as revised at Paris on 24 July 1971 concerning the application of that Convention to works of Stateless persons and refugees*

The State party hereto, being also party to the Universal Copyright Convention as revised at Paris on 24 July 1971 (hereinafter called 'the 1971 Convention'),

Have accepted the following provisions:

(1) Stateless persons and refugees who have their habitual residence in a State party to this Protocol shall, for the purposes of the 1971 Convention, be assimilated to the nationals of that State.

(2)(a) This Protocol shall be signed and shall be subject to ratification or acceptance, or may be acceded to, as if the provisions of Article VIII of the 1971 Convention applied hereto.

(b) This Protocol shall enter into force in respect of each State, on the date of deposit of the instrument of ratification, acceptance or accession of the State concerned or on the date of entry into force of the 1971 Convention with respect to such State, whichever is the later.

(c) On the entry into force of this Protocol in respect of a State not party to Protocol 1 annexed to the 1952 Convention, the latter Protocol shall be deemed to enter into force in respect of such State.

In faith whereof the undersigned, being duly authorised thereto, have signed this Protocol.

Done at Paris, this twenty-fourth day of July 1971, in the English, French and Spanish languages, the three texts being equally authoritative, in a single copy which shall be deposited with the Director-General of the United Nations Educational, Scientific and Cultural Organisation. The Director-General shall send certified copies to the signatory States, and to the Secretary-General of the United Nations for registration.

*Protocol 2*

*Annexed to the Universal Copyright Convention as revised at Paris on 24 July 1971 concerning the application of that Convention to the works of certain international organisations*

The States party hereto, being also party to the Universal Copyright Convention as revised at Paris on 24 July 1971 (hereinafter called 'the 1971 Convention'),

Have accepted the following provisions:

(1)(a) The protection provided for in Article II(1)) of the 1971 Convention shall apply to works published for the first time by the United Nations, by the Specified Agencies in relationship there with, or by the Organisations of American States.

(b) Similarly, Article II(2) of the 1971 Convention shall apply to the said organisation or agencies.

(2)(a) This Protocol shall be signed and shall be subject to ratification or acceptance, or may be acceded to, as if the provisions of Article VIII of the 1971 Convention applied hereto.

(b) This Protocol shall enter into force for each State on the date of deposit of the instrument of ratification, acceptance or accession of the State concerned or on the date of entry into force of the 1971 Convention with respect to such State, whichever is the later.

In faith whereof the undersigned, being duly authorised thereto, have signed this Protocol.

Done at Paris, this twenty-fourth day of July 1971, in the English, French and Spanish languages, the three text being equally authoritative, in a single copy which shall be deposited with the Director-General of the United Nations Educational, Scientific and Cultural Organisation. The Director-General shall send certified copies to the signatory States, and to the Secretary-General of the United Nations for registration.

## INTERNATIONAL CONVENTION FOR THE PROTECTION OF PERFORMERS, PRODUCERS OF PHONOGRAMS AND BROADCASTING ORGANISATIONS (ROME, 26 OCTOBER 1961)

The Contracting States, moved by the desire to protect the rights of performers, producers of phonograms, and broadcasting organisations,
Have agreed as follows:

*Article 1*

Protection granted under this Convention shall leave intact and shall in no way affect the protection of copyright in literary and artistic works. Consequently, no provision of this Convention may be interpreted as prejudicing such protection.

*Article 2*

1. For the purposes of this Convention, national treatment shall mean the treatment accorded by the domestic law of the Contracting State in which protection is claimed:

    (a)  to performers who are its nationals, as regards performance taking place, broadcast, or first fixed, on its territory;

    (b)  to producers of phonograms who are its nationals, as regards phonograms first fixed or first published on its territory;

    (c)  to broadcasting organisations which have their headquarters on its territory, as regards broadcasts transmitted from transmitters situated on its territory.

2. National treatment shall be subject to the protection specifically guaranteed, and the limitations specifically provided for, in this Convention.

*Article 3*

For the purposes of this Convention:

    (a)  'Performers' means actors, singers, musicians, dancers, and other persons who act, sing, deliver, declaim, play in, or otherwise perform literary or artistic works;

    (b)  'Phonogram' means any exclusively aural fixation of sounds of a performance or of other sounds;

(c) 'Producer of phonograms' means the person who, or the legal entity which, first fixes the sounds of a performance or other sounds;

(d) 'Publication' means the offering of copies of a phonogram to the public in reasonable quantity;

(e) 'Reproduction' means the making of a copy or copies of a fixation;

(f) 'Broadcasting' means the transmission by wireless means for public reception of sounds or of images and sounds;

(g) 'Rebroadcasting' means the simultaneous broadcasting by one broadcasting organisation of the broadcast of another broadcasting organisation.

*Article 4*

Each Contracting State shall grant national treatment to performers if any of the following conditions is met:

(a) the performance takes place in another Contracting State;

(b) the performance is incorporated in a phonogram which is protected under Article 5 of this Convention;

(c) the performance, not being fixed on a phonogram, is carried by a broadcast which is protected by Article 6 of this Convention.

*Article 5*

1. Each Contracting State shall grant national treatment to producers of phonograms if any of the following conditions is met:

(a) the producer of the phonogram is a national of another Contracting State (criterion of nationality);

(b) the first fixation of the sound was made in another Contracting State (criterion of fixation);

(c) the phonogram was first published in another Contracting State (criterion of publication).

2. If a phonogram was first published in a non-Contracting State but if it was also published, within thirty days of its first publication, in a Contracting State (simultaneous publication), it shall be considered as first published in the Contracting State.

3. By means of a notification deposited with the Secretary-General of the United Nations, any Contracting State may declare that it will not apply the criterion of publication or, alternatively, the criterion of fixation. Such notification may be deposited at the time of ratification, acceptance or accession, or at any time thereafter; in one last case, it shall become effective six months after it has been deposited.

*Article 6*

1. Each Contracting State shall grant national treatment to broadcasting organisations if either of the following conditions is met:

(a) the headquarters of the broadcasting organisation is situated in another Contracting State.

(b) the broadcast was transmitted from a transmitter situated in another Contracting State.

2. By means of a notification deposited with the Secretary-General of the United Nations, any Contracting State may declare that it will protect broadcasts only if the headquarters of the broadcasting organisation is situated in another Contracting State and the broadcast was transmitted from a transmitter situated in the same Contracting State. Such notification may be deposited at the time of ratification, acceptance or accession, or at any time thereafter; in the last case, it shall become effective six months after it has been deposited.

*Article 7*

1. The protection provided for performers by this Convention shall include the possibility of preventing:

(a) the broadcasting and the communication to the public, without their consent, of their performance, except where the performance used in the broadcasting or the public communication is itself already a broadcast performance or is made from a fixation;

(b) the fixation, without their consent, of their unfixed performance;

(c) the reproduction, without their consent, of a fixation of their performance:

(i) if the original fixation itself was made without their consent;

(ii) if the reproduction is made for purposes different from those for which the performers gave their consent;

(iii) if the original fixation was made in accordance with the provisions of Article 15, and the reproduction is made for purposes different from those referred to in those provisions.

2.—(1) If broadcasting was consented to by the performers it shall be a matter for the domestic law of the Contracting State where protection is claimed to regulate the protection against rebroadcasting, fixation for broadcasting purposes, and the reproduction of such fixation for broadcasting purposes.

(2) The terms and conditions governing the use by broadcasting organisations of fixations made for broadcasting purposes shall be determined in accordance with the domestic law of the Contracting State where protection is claimed.

(3) However, the domestic law referred to in sub-paragraphs (1) and (2) of this paragraph shall not operate to deprive performers of the ability to control, by contract, their relations with broadcasting organisations.

*Article 8*

Any Contracting State may, by its domestic laws and regulations, specify the manner in which performers will be represented in connexion with the exercise of their rights if several of them participate in the same performance.

*Article 9*

Any Contracting State may, by its domestic laws and regulations, extend the protection provided for in this Convention to artistes who do not perform literary or artistic works.

*Article 10*

Producers of phonograms shall enjoy the right to authorise or prohibit the direct or indirect reproduction of their phonograms.

*Article 11*

If, as a condition of protecting the rights of producers of phonograms, or of performers, or both, in relation to phonograms, a Contracting State, under its domestic law, requires compliance with formalities, these shall be considered as fulfilled if all the copies in commerce of the published phonogram or their containers bear a notice consisting of the symbol ℗, accompanied by the year date of the first publication, placed in such a manner as to give reasonable notice of claim of protection; and if the copies or their containers do not identify the producer or the licensee of the producer (by carrying his name, trade mark or other appropriate designation), the notice shall also include the name of the owner of the rights of the producer; and, furthermore, if the copies or their containers do not identify the principal performers the notice shall also include the name of the person who, in the country in which the fixation was effected, owns the rights of such performers.

*Article 12*

If a phonogram published for commercial purposes, or a reproduction of such phonogram, is used directly for broadcasting or for any communication to the public, a single equitable remuneration shall be paid by the user to the performers, or to the producers of the phonograms, or to both. Domestic law may, in the absence of agreement between these parties, lay down the conditions as to the sharing of this remuneration.

*Article 13*

Broadcasting organisations shall enjoy the right to authorise or prohibit :

    (a)  the rebroadcasting of their broadcasts;
    (b)  the fixation of their broadcasts;
    (c)  the reproduction

        (i)  of fixations, made without their consent, of their broadcasts;
        (ii)  of fixations, made in accordance with the provisions of Article 15, of their broadcasts if the reproduction is made for purposes different from those referred to in those provisions;

    (d)  the communication to the public of their television broadcasts if such communication is made in places accessible to the public against payment of an entrance fee; it shall be a matter for the domestic law of the State where protection of this right is claimed to determine the conditions under which it may be exercised.

*Article 14*

The term of protection to be granted under this Convention shall last at least until the end of a period of twenty years computed from the end of the year in which:

  (a) the fixation was made—for phonograms and for performances incorporated therein;
  (b) the performance took place—for performances not incorporated in phonograms;
  (c) the broadcast took place—for broadcasts.

*Article 15*

1. Any Contracting State may, in its domestic laws and regulations, provide for exceptions to the protection guaranteed by this Convention as regards:

  (a) private use;
  (b) use of short excerpts in connexion with the reporting of current events;
  (c) ephemeral fixation by a broadcasting organisation by means of its own facilities and for its own broadcasts;
  (d) use solely for the purposes of teaching or scientific research.

2. Irrespective of paragraph 1 of this Article, any Contracting State may, in its domestic laws and regulations, provide for the same kinds of limitations with regard to the protection of performers, producers and phonograms and broadcasting organisations as it provides for, in its domestic laws and regulations, in connexion with the protection of copyright in literary and artistic works. However, compulsory licences may be provided for only to the extent to which they are compatible with the Convention.

*Article 16*

1. Any State, upon becoming party to this Convention, shall be bound by all the obligations and shall enjoy all the benefits thereof. However a State may at any time, in a notification deposited with the Secretary—General of the United Nations, declare that:

  (a) as regards Article 12:
      (i) it will not apply the provisions of that Article;
      (ii) it will not apply the provisions of that Article in respect of certain uses;
      (iii) as regards phonograms the producer of which is not a national of another Contracting State, it will not apply that Article;
      (iv) as regards phonograms the producer of which is a national of another Contracting State, it will limit the protection provided for by that Article to the extent to which, and to the term for which, the latter State grants protection to phonograms first fixed by a national of the State making the declaration; however, the fact that the Contracting State of which the producer is a national does not grant the protection to the same beneficiary or beneficiaries as the State making the declaration shall not be considered as a difference in the extent of the protection;
  (b) as regards Article 13, it will not apply item (d) of that Article; if a Contracting State makes such a declaration, the other Contracting States shall not be obliged to grant the right referred to in Article 13, item (d), to broadcasting organisations whose headquarters are in that State.

2. If the notification referred to in paragraph 1 of this Article is made after the date of the deposit of the instrument of ratification, acceptance or accession, the declaration will become effective six months after it has been deposited.

*Article 17*

Any State which, on 26 October 1961, grants protection to producers of phonograms solely on the basis of the criterion of fixation may, by a notification deposited with the Secretary-General of the United Nations at the time of ratification, acceptance or accession, declare that it will apply, for the purposes of Article 5, the criterion of fixation alone and, for the purposes of paragraph 1(a)(iii) and (iv) of Article 16, the criterion of fixation instead of the criterion of nationality.

*Article 18*

Any State which has deposited a notification under paragraph 3 of Article 5, paragraph 2 of Article 6, paragraph 1 of Article 16 or Article 17, may, by a further notification deposited with the Secretary-General of the United Nations, reduce its scope or withdraw it.

*Article 19*

Notwithstanding anything in this Convention, once a performer has consented to the incorporation of his performance in a visual or audio-visual fixation, Article 7 shall have no further application.

*Article 20*

1. This Convention shall not prejudice rights acquired in any Contracting State before the date of coming into force of this Convention for that State.
2. No Contracting State shall be bound to apply the provisions of this Convention to performances or broadcasts which took place, or to phonograms which were fixed, before the date of coming into force of this Convention for that State.

*Article 21*

The protection provided for in this Convention shall not prejudice any protection otherwise secured to performers, producers of phonograms and broadcasting organisations.

*Article 22*

Contracting States reserve the right to enter into special agreements among themselves in so far as such agreements grant to performers, producers of phonograms or broadcasting organisations more extensive rights than those granted by this Convention or contain other provisions not contrary to this Convention.

*Article 23*

This convention shall be deposited with the Secretary-General of the United Nations. It shall be open until June 30, 1962, for signature by any State invited to the Diplomatic Conference on the International Protection of Performers,

Producers of Phonograms and Broadcasting Organisations which is a party to the Universal Copyright Convention or a member of the International Union for the Protection of Literary and Artistic Works.

*Article 24*

1. This Convention shall be subject to ratification or acceptance by the signatory States.

2. This Convention shall be open for accession by any State invited to the Conference referred to in Article 23, and by any State Member of the United Nations, provided that in either case such state is a party to the Universal Copyright Convention or a member of the International Union for the Protection of Literary and Artistic Works.

3. Ratification, acceptance or accession shall be effected by the deposit of an instrument to that effect with the Secretary-General of the United Nations.

*Article 25*

1. This Convention shall come into force three months after the date of deposit of the sixth instrument of ratification, acceptance or accession.

2. Subsequently, this Convention shall come into force in respect of each State three months after the date of deposit of its instrument or ratification, acceptance or accession.

*Article 26*

1. Each Contracting State undertakes to adopt, in accordance with its Constitution, the measures necessary to ensure the application of this Convention.

2. At the time of deposit of its instrument of ratification, acceptance or accession, each State must be in a position under its domestic law to give effect to the terms of this Convention.

*Article 27*

1. Any State may, at the time of ratification, acceptance or accession, or at any time thereafter, declare by notification addressed to the Secretary-General of the United Nations that this Convention shall extend to all or any of the territories for whose international relations it is responsible, provided that the Universal Copyright Convention or the International Convention for the Protection of Literary and Artistic Works applies to the territory or territories concerned. This notification shall take effect three months after the date of its receipt.

2. The notifications referred to in paragraph 3 of Article 5, paragraph 2 of Article 6, paragraph 2 of Article 16 and Articles 17 and 18, may be extended to cover all or any of the territories referred to in paragraph 1 of this Article.

*Article 28*

1. Any Contracting State may denounce this Convention, on its own behalf, or on behalf of all or any of the territories referred to in Article 27.

2. The denunciation shall be effected by a notification addressed to the Secretary-General of the United Nations and shall take effect twelve months after the date of receipt of the notification.

3. The right of denunciation shall not be exercised by a Contracting State before

the expiry of a period of five years from the date on which the Convention came into force with respect to that State.

4. A Contracting State shall cease to be a party to this Convention from that time when it is neither a party to the Universal Copyright Convention nor a member of the International Union for the Protection of Literary and Artistic Works.

5. This Convention shall cease to apply to any territory referred to in Article 27 from that time when neither the Universal Copyright Convention nor the International Convention for the Protection of Literary and Artistic Works applies to that territory.

*Article 29*

1. After this Convention has been in force for five years, any Contracting State may, by notification addressed to the Secretary-General of the United Nations, request that a conference by convened for the purpose of revising the Convention. The Secretary-General shall notify all Contracting States of this request. If, within a period of six months following the date of notification by the Secretary-General of the United Nations, not less than one half of the Contracting States notify him of their concurrence with the request, the Secretary-General shall inform the Director-General of the International Labour Office, the Director-General of the United Nations Educational, Scientific and Cultural Organisation and the Director of the Bureau of the International Union for the Protection of Literary and Artistic Works, who shall convene a revision conference in co-operation with the Inter-governmental Committee provided for in Article 32.

2. The adoption of any revision of this Convention shall require an affirmative vote by two-thirds of the States attending the revision conference, provided that this majority includes two-thirds of the States which, at the time for the revision conference, are parties to the Convention.

3. In the event of adoption of a Convention revising this Convention in whole or in part, and unless the revising Convention provides otherwise:

(a) this Convention shall cease to be open to ratification, acceptance or accession as from the date of entry into force of the revising Convention;

(b) this Convention shall remain in force as regards relations between or with Contracting States which have not become parties to the revising Convention.

*Article 30*

Any dispute which may arise between two or more Contracting States concerning the interpretation or application of this Convention and which is not settled by negotiation shall, at the request of any one of the parties to the dispute, be referred to the International Court of Justice for decision, unless they agree to another mode of settlement.

*Article 31*

Without prejudice to the provisions of paragraph 3 of Article 5, paragraph 2 of Article 6, paragraph 1 of Article 16 and Article 17, no reservation may be made to this Convention.

*Article 32*

1. An Intergovernmental Committee is hereby established with the following duties:

  (a) to study questions concerning the applications and operation of this Convention; and
  (b) to collect proposals and to prepare documentation for possible revision of this Convention.

2. The Committee shall consist of representatives of the Contracting States, chosen with due regard to equitable geographical distribution. The number of members shall be six if there are twelve Contracting States or less, nine if there are thirteen to eighteen Contracting States and twelve if there are more than eighteen Contracting States.

3. The Committee shall be consituted twelve months after the Convention comes into force by an election organised among the Contracting States, each of which shall have one vote, by the Director-General of the International Labour Office, the Director-General of the United Nations Educational, Scientific and Cultural Organisation and the Director of the Bureau of the International Union for the Protection of Literary and Artistic Works, in accordance with rules previously approved by a majority of all Contracting States.

4. The Committee shall elect its Chairman and officers. It shall establish its own rules of procedure. These rules shall in particular provide for the future operation of the Committee and for a method of selecting its members for the future in such a way as to ensure rotation among the various Contracting States.

5. Officials of the International Labour Office, the United Nations Educational, Scientific and Cultural Organisation and the Bureau of the International Union for the Protection of Literary and Artistic Works, designated by the Directors-General and the Director thereof, shall constitute the Secretariat of the Committee.

6. Meetings of the Committee, which shall be convened whenever a majority of its members deems it necessary, shall be held successively at the headquarters of the International Labour Office, the United Nations Educational, Scientific and Cultural Organisation and the Bureau of the International Union for the Protection of Literary and Artistic Works.

7. Expenses of members of the Committee shall be borne by their respective Governments.

*Article 33*

1. The present Convention is drawn up in English, French and Spanish, the three texts being equally authentic.

2. In addition, official texts of the present Convention shall be drawn up in German, Italian and Portuguese.

*Article 34*

1. The Secretary-General of the United Nations shall notify the States invited to the Conference referred to in Article 23 and every State Member of the United Nations, as well as the Director-General of the International Labour Office, the Director-General of the United Nations Educational, Scientific and Cultural

Organisation and the Director of the Bureau of the International Union for the Protection of Literary and Artistic Works:

    (a)  of the deposit of each instrument of ratification, acceptance or accession;

    (b)  of the date of entry into force of the Convention;

    (c)  of all notifications, declarations or communications provided for in this Convention;

    (d)  if any of the situations referred to in paragraphs 4 and 5 of Article 28 arise.

2. The Secretary-General of the United Nations shall also notify the Director-General of the International Labour Office, the Director-General of the United Nations Educational, Scientific and Cultural Organisation and the Director of the Bureau of the International Union for the Protection of Literary and Artistic Works of the requests communicated to him in accordance with Article 29, as well as of any communication received from the Contracting States concerning the revision of the Convention.

*General note*

Cmnd 2425. Ratified by the United Kingdom 30 October 1963. Entered into force 18 May 1964. The United Kingdom ratification was accompanied by the following declaration:

(1) in respect of Article 5(1)(b) and in accordance with Article 5(3) of the Convention, the United Kingdom will not apply, in respect of phonograms, the criterion of fixation;

(2) in respect of Article 6(1) and in accordance with Article 6(2) of the Convention, the United Kingdom will protect broadcasts only if the headquarters of the broadcasting organisation is situated in another Contracting State and the broadcast was transmitted from a transmitter situated in the same Contracting State;

(3) in respect of Article 12 and in accordance with Article 16(1) of the Convention,

    (a)  the United Kingdom will not apply the provisions of Article 12 in respect of the following uses:

        (i)  the causing of a phonogram to be heard in public at any premises where persons reside or sleep, as part of the amenities provided exclusively or mainly for residents or inmates therein except where a special charge is made for admission to the part of the premises where the phonogram is to be heard,

        (ii)  the causing of a phonogram to be heard in public as part of the activities of, or for the benefit of, a club, society or other organisation which is not established or conducted for profit and whose main objects are charitable or are otherwise concerned with the advancement of religion, education or social welfare, except where a charge is made for admission to the place where the phonogram is to be heard, and any of the proceeds of the charge are applied otherwise than for the purpose of the organisation;

    (b)  as regards phonograms the producer of which is not a national of another Contracting State or as regards phonograms the producer of which is a national of a Contracting State which has made a declaration under Article 16(1)(a)(i) stating that it will not apply the provisions of Article 12, the United Kingdom will not grant the protection provided for by Article 12, unless, in either event, the phonogram has been first published in a Contracting State which has made no such declaration.

## PARIS CONVENTION FOR THE PROTECTION OF INDUSTRIAL PROPERTY OF 20 MARCH 1883

(As revised at Brussels on 14 December 1900, at Washington on 2 June 1911, at the Hague on 6 November 1925, at London on 2 June 1934, at Lisbon on 31 October 1958, and at Stockholm on 14 July 1967.)

*Article 1*

[Establishment of the Union; Scope of Industrial Property]*

---

\* Articles have been given titles to facilitate their identification. There are no titles in the signed (French) text.

(1)  The countries to which this Convention applies constitute a Union for the protection of industrial property.

(2)  The protection of industrial property has as its object patents, utility models, industrial designs, trademarks, service marks, trade names, indications of source or appellations of origin, and the repression of unfair competition.

(3)  Industrial property shall be understood in the broadest sense and shall apply not only to industry and commerce proper, but likewise to agricultural and extractive industries and to all manufactured or natural products, for example, wines, grain, tobacco leaf, fruit, cattle, minerals, mineral waters, beer, flowers, and flour.

(4)  Patents shall include the various kinds of industrial patents recognized by the laws of the countries of the Union, such as patents of importation, patents of improvement, patents and certificates of addition, etc.

*Article 2*
[National Treatment for Nationals of Countries of the Union]

(1) Nationals of any country of the Union shall, as regards the protection of industrial property, enjoy in all the other countries of the Union the advantages that their respective laws now grant, or may hereafter grant, to nationals; all without prejudice to the rights specially provided for by this Convention. Consequently, they shall have the same protection as the latter, and the same legal remedy against any infringement of their rights, provided that the conditions and formalities imposed upon nationals are complied with.

(2) However, no requirement as to domicile or establishment in the country where protection is claimed may be imposed upon nationals of countries of the Union for the enjoyment of any industrial property rights.

(3) The provisions of the laws of each of the countries of the Union relating to judicial and administrative procedure and to jurisdiction, and to the designation of an address for service or the appointment of an agent, which may be required by the laws on industrial property are expressly reserved.

*Article 3*
[Same Treatment for Certain Categories of Persons as for Nationals of Countries of the Union]

Nationals of countries outside the Union who are domiciled or who have real and effective industrial or commercial establishments in the territory of one of the countries of the Union shall be treated in the same manner as nationals of the countries of the Union.

*Article 4*
[A to I. *Patents, Utility Models, Industrial Designs, Marks, Inventors' Certificates:* Right of Priority—G. *Patents:* Division of the Application]

A.—(1) Any person who has duly filed an application for a patent, or for the registration of a utility model, or of an industrial design, or of a trademark, in one of the countries of the Union, or his successor in title, shall enjoy, for the purpose of filing in the other countries, a right of priority during the periods hereinafter fixed.

(2) Any filing that is equivalent to a regular national filing under the domestic legislation of any country of the Union or under bilateral or multilateral treaties

concluded between countries of the Union shall be recognized as giving rise to the right of priority.

(3) By a regular national filing is meant any filing that is adequate to establish the date on which the application was filed in the country concerned, whatever may be the subsequent fate of the application.

B.—Consequently, any subsequent filing in any of the other countries of the Union before the expiration of the periods referred to above shall not be invalidated by reason of any acts accomplished in the interval, in particular, another filing, the publication or exploitation of the invention, the putting on sale of copies of the design, or the use of the mark, and such acts cannot give rise to any third-party right or any right of personal possession. Rights acquired by third parties before the date of the first application that serves as the basis for the right of priority are reserved in accordance with the domestic legislation of each country of the Union.

C.—(1) The periods of priority referred to above shall be twelve months for patents and utility models, and six months for industrial designs and trademarks.

(2) These periods shall start from the date of filing of the first application; the day of filing shall not be included in the period.

(3) If the last day of the period is an official holiday, or a day when the Office is not open for the filing of applications in the country where protection is claimed, the period shall be extended until the first following working day.

(4) A subsequent application concerning the same subject as a previous first application within the meaning of paragraph (2), above, filed in the same country of the Union, shall be considered as the first application, of which the filing date shall be the starting point of the period of priority, if, at the time of filing the subsequent application, the said previous application has been withdrawn, abandoned, or refused, without having been laid open to public inspection and without leaving any rights outstanding, and if it has not yet served as a basis for claiming a right of priority. The previous application may not thereafter serve as a basis for claiming a right of priority.

D.—(1) Any person desiring to take advantage of the priority of a previous filing shall be required to make a declaration indicating the date of such filing and the country in which it was made. Each country shall determine the latest date on which such declaration must be made.

(2) These particulars shall be mentioned in the publications issued by the competent authority, and in particular in the patents and the specifications relating thereto.

(3) The countries of the Union may require any person making a declaration of priority to produce a copy of the application (description, drawings, etc) previously filed. The copy, certified as correct by the authority which received such application, shall not require any authentication, and may in any case be filed, without fee, at any time within three months of the filing of the subsequent application. They may require it to be accompanied by a certificate from the same authority showing the date of filing, and by a translation.

(4) No other formalities may be required for the declaration of priority at the time of filing the application. Each country of the Union shall determine the consequences of failure to comply with the formalities prescribed by this Article, but such consequences shall in no case go beyond the loss of the right of priority.

(5) Subsequently, further proof may be required.

Any person who avails himself of the priority of a previous application shall be required to specify the number of that application; this number shall be published as provided for by paragraph (2), above.

E.—(1) Where an industrial design is filed in a country by virtue of a right of priority based on the filing of a utility model, the period of priority shall be the same as that fixed for industrial designs.

(2) Furthermore, it is permissible to file a utility model in a country by virtue of a right of priority based on the filing of a patent application, and vice versa.

F.—No country of the Union may refuse a priority or a patent application on the ground that the applicant claims multiple priorities, even if they originate in different countries, or on the ground that an application claiming one or more priorities contains one or more elements that were not included in the application or applications whose priority is claimed, provided that, in both cases, there is unity of invention within the meaning of the law of the country.

With respect to the elements not included in the application or applications whose priority is claimed, the filing of the subsequent application shall give rise to a right of priority under ordinary conditions.

G.—(1) If the examination reveals that an application for a patent contains more than one invention, the applicant may divide the application into a certain number of divisional applications and preserve as the date of each the date of the initial application and the benefit of the right of priority if any.

(2) The applicant may also, on his own initiative, divide a patent application and preserve as the date of each divisional application the date of the initial application and the benefit of the right of priority, if any. Each country of the Union shall have the right to determine the conditions under which such division shall be authorized.

H.—Priority may not be refused on the ground that certain elements of the invention for which priority is claimed do not appear among the claims formulated in the application in the country of origin, provided that the application documents as a whole specifically disclose such elements.

I.—(1) Applications for inventors' certificates filed in a country in which applicants have the right to apply at their own option either for a patent or for an inventor's certificate shall give rise to the right of priority provided for by this Article, under the same conditions and with the same effects as applications for patents.

(2) In a country in which applicants have the right to apply at their own option either for a patent or for an inventor's certificate, an applicant for an inventor's certificate shall, in accordance with the provisions of this Article relating to patent applications, enjoy a right of priority based on an application for a patent, a utility model, or an inventor's certificate.

*Article 5*
[D. *Patents, Utility Models, Marks, Industrial Designs:* Marking]

D.—No indication or mention of the patent, of the utility model, of the registration of the trademark, or of the deposit of the industrial design, shall be required upon the goods as a condition of recognition of the right of protection.

*Article 5^{bis}*
[*All Industrial Property Rights:* Period of Grace for the Payment of Fees for the Maintenance of Rights; *Patents:* Restoration]

(1) A period of grace of not less than six months shall be allowed for the payment of the fees prescribed for the maintenance of industrial property rights, subject, if the domestic legislation so provides, to the payment of a surcharge.

*Article 5$^{quinquies}$*
[*Industrial Designs*]

Industrial designs shall be protected in all the countries of the Union.

*Article 11*
[*Inventions, Utility Models, Industrial Designs, Marks:* Temporary Protection at Certain International Exhibitions]

(1) The countries of the Union shall, in conformity with their domestic legislation, grant temporary protection to patentable inventions, utility models, industrial designs, and trademarks, in respect of goods exhibited at official or officially recognized international exhibitions held in the territory of any of them.

(2) Such temporary protection shall not extend the periods provided by Article 4. If, later, the right of priority is invoked, the authorities of any country may provide that the period shall start from the date of introduction of the goods into the exhibition.

(3) Each country may require, as proof of the identity of the article exhibited and of the date of its introduction, such documentary evidence as it considers necessary.

*Article 12*
[*Special National Industrial Property Services*]

(1) Each country of the Union undertakes to establish a special industrial property service and a central office for the communication to the public of patents, utility models, industrial designs, and trademarks.

(2) This service shall publish an official periodical journal. It shall publish regularly:

   (*a*)  the names of the proprietors of patents granted, with a brief designation of the inventions patented;
   (*b*)  the reproductions of registered trademarks.

*Article 13*
[Assembly of the Union]

(1)(*a*) The Union shall have an Assembly consisting of those countries of the Union which are bound by Articles 13 to 17.

   (*b*) The Government of each country shall be represented by one delegate, who may be assisted by alternate delegates, advisors, and experts.

   (*c*) The expenses of each delegation shall be borne by the Government which has appointed it.

(2)(*a*) The Assembly shall:

   (i)    deal with all matters concerning the maintenance and development of the Union and the implementation of this Convention;
   (ii)   give directions concerning the preparation for conferences of revision to the International Bureau of Intellectual Property (hereinafter designated as 'the International Bureau') referred to in the Convention establishing the World Intellectual Property Organization (hereinafter designated as 'the Organization'), due account being taken of any comments made by those countries of the Union which are not bound by Articles 13 to 17;

    (iii)   review and approve the reports and activities of the Director-General of the Organization concerning the Union, and give him all necessary instructions concerning matters within the competence of the Union;

    (iv)   elect the members of the Executive Committee of the Assembly;

    (v)   review and approve the reports and activities of its Executive Committee, and give instructions to such Committee;

    (vi)   determine the program and adopt the triennial budget of the Union, and approve its final accounts;

    (vii)   adopt the financial regulations of the Union;

    (viii)   establish such committees of experts and working groups as it deems appropriate to achieve the objectives of the Union;

    (ix)   determine which countries not members of the Union and which intergovernmental and international nongovernmental organizations shall be admitted to its meetings as observers;

    (x)   adopt amendments to Articles 13 to 17;

    (xi)   take any other appropriate action designed to further the objectives of the Union;

    (xii)   perform such other functions as are appropriate under this Convention;

    (xiii)   subject to its acceptance, exercise such rights as are given to it in the Convention establishing the Organization.

(*b*) With respect to matters which are of interest also to other Unions administered by the Organization, the Assembly shall make its decision after heaving heard the advice of the Coordination Committee of the Organization.

(3)(*a*) Subject to the provisions of subparagraph (*b*), a delegate may represent one country only.

(*b*) Countries of the Union grouped under the terms of a special agreement in a common office possessing for each of them the character of a special national service of industrial property as referred to in Article 12 may be jointly represented during discussions by one of their number.

(4) (*a*) Each country member of the Assembly shall have one vote.

(*b*) One-half of the countries members of the Assembly shall constitute a quorum.

(*c*) Notwithstanding the provisions of subparagraph (*b*), if, in any session, the number of countries represented is less than one-half but equal to or more than one-third of the countries members of the Assembly, the Assembly may make decisions but, with the exception of decisions concerning its own procedure, all such decisions shall take effect only if the conditions set forth hereinafter are fulfilled. The International Bureau shall communicate the said decisions to the countries members of the Assembly which were not represented and shall invite them to express in writing their vote or abstention within a period of three months from the date of the communication. If, at the expiration of this period, the number of countries having thus expressed their vote or abstention attains the number of countries which was lacking for attaining the quorum in the session itself, such decision shall take effect provided that at the same time the required majority still obtains.

(*d*) Subject to the provisions of Article 17(2), the decisions of the Assembly shall require two-thirds of the votes cast.

(*e*) Abstentions shall not be considered as votes.

(5)(*a*) Subject to the provisions of subparagraph (*b*), a delegate may vote in the name of one country only.

(*b*) The countries of the Union referred to in paragraph (3)(*b*) shall, as a general rule, endeavor to send their own delegations to the sessions of the Assembly. If, however, for exceptional reasons, any such country cannot send its own delegation, it may give to the delegation of another such country the power to vote in its name, provided that each delegation may vote by proxy for one country only. Such power to vote shall be granted in a document signed by the Head of State or the competent Minister.

(6) Countries of the Union not members of the Assembly shall be admitted to the meetings of the latter as observers.

(7)(*a*) The Assembly shall meet once in every third calendar year in ordinary session upon convocation by the Director-General and, in the absence of exceptional circumstances, during the same period and at the same place as the General Assembly of the Organization.

(*b*) The Assembly shall meet in extraordinary session upon convocation by the Director-General, at the request of the Executive Committee or at the request of one-fourth of the countries members of the Assembly.

(8) The Assembly shall adopt its own rules of procedure.

## *Article 14*
[Executive Committee]

(1) The Assembly shall have an Executive Committee.

(2)(*a*) The Executive Committee shall consist of countries elected by the Assembly from among countries members of the Assembly. Furthermore, the country on whose territory the Organization has its headquarters shall, subject to the provisions of Article 16(7)(*b*), have an *ex officio* seat on the Committee.

(*b*) The Government of each country member of the Executive Committee shall be represented by one delegate, who may be assisted by alternate delegates, advisors, and experts.

(*c*) The expenses of each delegation shall be borne by the Government which has appointed it.

(3) The number of countries members of the Executive Committee shall correspond to one-fourth of the number of countries members of the Assembly. In establishing the number of seats to be filled, remainders after division by four shall be disregarded.

(4) In electing the members of the Executive Committee, the Assembly shall have due regard to an equitable geographical distribution and to the need for countries party to the Special Agreements established in relation with the Union to be among the countries constituting the Executive Committee.

(5)(*a*) Each member of the Executive Committee shall serve from the close of the session of the Assembly which elected it to the close of the next ordinary session of the Assembly.

(*b*) Members of the Executive Committee may be re-elected, but only up to a maximum of two-thirds of such members.

(*c*) The Assembly shall establish the details of the rules governing the election and possible re-election of the members of the Executive Committee.

(6)(*a*) The Executive Committee shall:

(i) prepare the draft agenda of the Assembly;
(ii) submit proposals to the Assembly in respect of the draft program and triennial budget of the Union prepared by the Director-General;
(iii) approve, within the limits of the program and the triennial budget, the specific yearly budgets and programs prepared by the Director-General;

(iv) submit, with the appropriate comments, to the Assembly the periodical reports of the Director-General and the yearly audit reports on the accounts;

(v) take all necessary measures to ensure the execution of the program of the Union by the Director-General, in accordance with the decisions of the Assembly and having regard to circumstances arising between two ordinary sessions of the Assembly;

(vi) perform such other functions as are allocated to it under this Convention.

(*b*) With respect to matters which are of interest also to other Unions administered by the Organization, the Executive Committee shall make its decisions after having heard the advice of the Coordination Committee of the Organization.

(7)(*a*) The Executive Committee shall meet once a year in ordinary session upon convocation by the Director-General, preferably during the same period and at the same place as the Coordination Committee of the Organization.

(*b*) The Executive Committee shall meet in extraordinary session upon convocation by the Director-General, either on his own initiative, or at the request of its Chairman or one-fourth of its members.

(8)(*a*) Each country member of the Executive Committee shall have one vote.

(*b*) One-half of the members of the Executive Committee shall constitute a quorum.

(*c*) Decisions shall be made by a simple majority of the votes cast.

(*d*) Abstentions shall not be considered as votes.

(*e*) A delegate may represent, and vote in the name of, one country only.

(9) Countries of the Union not members of the Executive Committee shall be admitted to its meeting as observers.

(10) The Executive Committee shall adopt its own rules of procedure.

## Article 15
[International Bureau]

(1)(a) Administrative tasks concerning the Union shall be performed by the International Bureau, which is a continuation of the Bureau of the Union united with the Bureau of the Union established by the International Convention for the Protection of Literary and Artistic Works.

(*b*) In particular, the International Bureau shall provide the secretariat of the various organs of the Union.

(*c*) The Director-General of the Organization shall be the chief executive of the Union and shall represent the Union.

(2) The International Bureau shall assemble and publish information concerning the protection of industrial property. Each country of the Union shall promptly communicate to the International Bureau all new laws and official texts concerning the protection of industrial property. Furthermore, it shall furnish the International Bureau with all the publications of its industrial property service of direct concern to the protection of industrial property which the International Bureau may find useful in its work.

(3) The International Bureau shall publish a monthly periodical.

(4) The International Bureau shall, on request, furnish any country of the Union with information on matters concerning the protection of industrial property.

(5) The International Bureau shall conduct studies, and shall provide services, designed to facilitate the protection of industrial property.

(6) The Director-General and any staff member designated by him shall participate, without the right to vote, in all meetings of the Assembly, the Executive Committee, and any other committee of experts or working group. The Director-General, or a staff member designated by him, shall be *ex officio* secretary of these bodies.

(7)(*a*) The International Bureau shall, in accordance with the directions of the Assembly and in cooperation with the Executive Committee, make the preparations for the conferences of revision of the provisions of the Convention other than Articles 13 to 17.

(*b*) The International Bureau may consult with intergovernmental and international non-governmental organizations concerning preparations for conferences of revision.

(*c*) The Director-General and persons designated by him shall take part, without the right to vote, in the discussions at these conferences.

(8) The International Bureau shall carry out any other tasks assigned to it.

*Article 16*
[Finances]

(1)(*a*) The Union shall have a budget.

(*b*) The budget of the Union shall include the income and expenses proper to the Union, its contribution to the budget of expenses common to the Unions, and, where applicable, the sum made available to the budget of the Conference of the Organization.

(*c*) Expenses not attributable exclusively to the Union but also to one or more other Unions administered by the Organization shall be considered as expenses common to the Unions. The share of the Union in such common expenses shall be in proportion to the interest the Union has in them.

(2) The budget of the Union shall be established with due regard to the requirements of coordination with the budgets of the other Unions administered by the Organization.

(3) The budget of the Union shall be financed from the following sources:

    (i)   contributions of the countries of the Union;

    (ii)  fees and charges due for services rendered by the International Bureau in relation to the Union;

    (iii) sale of, or royalties on, the publications of the International Bureau concerning the Union;

    (iv) gifts, bequests, and subventions;

    (v)  rents, interests, and other miscellaneous income.

(4)(*a*) For the purpose of establishing its contribution towards the budget, each country of the Union shall belong to a class, and shall pay its annual contributions on the basis of a number of units fixed as follows:

| | |
|---|---|
| Class I | 25 |
| Class II | 20 |
| Class III | 15 |
| Class IV | 10 |
| Class V | 5 |
| Class VI | 3 |
| Class VII | 1 |

(*b*) Unless it has already done so, each country shall indicate, concurrently with depositing its instrument of ratification or accession, the class to which it wishes to belong. Any country may change class. If it chooses a lower class, the country must announce such change to the Assembly at one of its ordinary sessions. Any such change shall take effect at the beginning of the calendar year following the said session.

(*c*) The annual contribution of each country shall be an amount in the same proportion to the total sum to be contributed to the budget of the Union by all countries as the number of its units is to the total of the units of all contributing countries.

(*d*) Contributions shall become due on the first of January of each year.

(*e*) A country which is in arrears in the payment of its contributions may not exercise its right to vote in any of the organs of the Union of which it is a member if the amount of its arrears equals or exceeds the amount of the contributions due from it for the preceding two full years. However, any organ of the Union may allow such a country to continue to exercise its right to vote in that organ if, and as long as, it is satisfied that the delay in payment is due to exceptional and unavoidable circumstances.

(*f*) If the budget is not adopted before the beginning of a new financial period, it shall be at the same level as the budget of the previous year, as provided in the financial regulations.

(5) The amount of the fees and charges due for services rendered by the International Bureau in relation to the Union shall be established, and shall be reported to the Assembly and the Executive Committee, by the Director-General.

(6)(*a*) The Union shall have a working capital fund which shall be constituted by a single payment made by each country of the Union. If the fund becomes insufficient, the Assembly shall decide to increase it.

(*b*) The amount of the initial payment of each country to the said fund or of its participation in the increase thereof shall be a proportion of the contribution of that country for the year in which the fund is established or the decision to increase it is made.

(*c*) The proportion and the terms of payment shall be fixed by the Assembly on the proposal of the Director-General and after it has heard the advice of the Coordination Committee of the Organization.

(7)(*a*) In the headquarters agreement concluded with the country on the territory of which the Organization has its headquarters, it shall be provided that, whenever the working capital fund is insufficient, such country shall grant advances. The amount of these advances and the conditions on which they are granted shall be the subject of separate agreements, in each case, between such country and the Organization. As long as it remains under the obligation to grant advances, such country shall have an *ex officio* seat on the Executive Committee.

(*b*) The country referred to in subparagraph (*a*) and the Organization shall each have the right to denounce the obligation to grant advances, by written notification. Denunciation shall take effect three years after the end of the year in which it has been notified.

(8) The auditing of the accounts shall be effected by one or more of the countries of the Union or by external auditors, as provided in the financial regulations. They shall be designated, with their agreement, by the Assembly.

*Article 17*
[Amendment of Articles 13 to 17]

(1) Proposals for the amendment of Articles 13, 14, 15, 16, and the present Article,

may be initiated by any country member of the Assembly, by the Executive Committee, or by the Director-General. Such proposals shall be communicated by the Director-General to the member countries of the Assembly at least six months in advance of their consideration by the Assembly.

(2) Amendments to the Articles referred to in paragraph (1) shall be adopted by the Assembly. Adoption shall require three-fourths of the votes cast, provided that any amendment to Article 13, and to the present paragraph, shall require four-fifths of the votes cast.

(3) Any amendment to the Articles referred to in paragraph (1) shall enter into force one month after written notifications of acceptance, effected in accordance with their respective constitutional processes, have been received by the Director-General from three-fourths of the countries members of the Assembly at the time it adopted the amendment. Any amendment to the said Articles thus accepted shall bind all the countries which are members of the Assembly at the time the amendment enters into force, or which become members thereof at a subsequent date, provided that any amendment increasing the financial obligations of countries of the Union shall bind only those countries which have notified their acceptance of such amendment.

## Article 18
[Revision of Articles 1 to 12 and 18 to 30]

(1) This Convention shall be submitted to revision with a view to the introduction of amendments designed to improve the system of the Union.

(2) For that purpose, conferences shall be held successively in one of the countries of the Union among the delegates of the said countries.

(3) Amendments to Articles 13 to 17 are governed by the provisions of Article 17.

## Article 19
[Special Agreements]

It is understood that the countries of the Union reserve the right to make separately between themselves special agreements for the protection of industrial property, in so far as these agreements do not contravene the provisions of this Convention.

## Article 20
[Ratification or Accession by Countries of the Union; Entry Into Force]

(1)(*a*) Any country of the Union which has signed this Act may ratify it, and, if it has not signed it, may accede to it. Instruments of ratification and accession shall be deposited with the Director-General.

(*b*) Any country of the Union may declare in its instrument of ratification or accession that its ratification or accession shall not apply:

(i) to Articles 1 to 12, or
(ii) to Articles 13 to 17.

(*c*) Any country of the Union which, in accordance with subparagraph (*b*), has excluded from the effects of its ratification or accession one of the two groups of Articles referred to in that subparagraph may at any later time declare that it extends the effects of its ratification or accession to that group of Articles. Such declaration shall be deposited with the Director-General.

(2)(*a*) Articles 1 to 12 shall enter into force, with respect to the first ten countries of the Union which have deposited instruments of ratification or accession without making the declaration permitted under paragraph (1)(*b*)(i), three months after the deposit of the tenth such instrument of ratification or accession.

(*b*) Articles 13 to 17 shall enter into force, with respect to the first ten countries of the union which have deposited instruments of ratification or accession without making the declaration permitted under paragraph (1)(*b*)(ii), three months after the deposit of the tenth such instrument of ratification or accession.

(*c*) Subject to the initial entry into force, pursuant to the provisions of subparagraphs (*a*) and (*b*), of each of the two groups of Articles referred to in paragraph (1)(*b*)(i) and (ii), and subject to the provisions of paragraph (1)(*b*), Articles 1 to 17 shall, with respect to any country of the Union, other than those referred to in subparagraphs (*a*) and (*b*), which deposits an instrument of ratification or accession or any country of the Union which deposits a declaration pursuant to paragraph (1)(*c*), enter into force three months after the date of notification by the Director-General of such deposit, unless a subsequent date has been indicated in the instrument or declaration deposited. In the latter case, this Act shall enter into force with respect to that country on the date thus indicated.

(3) With respect to any country of the Union which deposits an instrument of ratification or accession, Articles 18 to 30 shall enter into force on the earlier of the dates on which any of the groups of Articles referred to in paragraph (1)(*b*) enters into force with respect to that country pursuant to paragraph (2)(*a*, (*b*), or (*c*).

*Article 21*
[Accession by Countries Outside the Union; Entry Into Force]

(1) Any country outside the Union may accede to this Act and thereby become a member of the Union. Instruments of accession shall be deposited with the Director-General.

(2)(*a*) With respect to any country outside the Union which deposits its instrument of accession one month or more before the date of entry into force of any provisions of the present Act, this Act shall enter into force, unless a subsequent date has been indicated in the instrument of accession, on the date upon which provisions first enter into force pursuant to Article 20(2)(*a*) or (*b*); provided that:

(i) if Articles 1 to 12 do not enter into force on that date, such country shall, during the interim period before the entry into force of such provisions, and in substitution therefor, be bound by Articles 1 to 12 of the Lisbon Act,

(ii) if Articles 13 to 17 do not enter into force on that date, such country shall, during the interim period before the entry into force of such provisions, and in substitution therefor, be bound by Articles 13 and 14(3), (4), and (5) of the Lisbon Act.

If a country indicates a subsequent date in its instrument of accession, this Act shall enter into force with respect to that country on the date thus indicated.

(*b*) With respect to any country outside the Union which deposits its instrument of accession on a date which is subsequent to, or precedes by less than one month, the entry into force of one group of Articles of the present Act, this Act shall, subject to the proviso of subparagraph (*a*), enter into force three months after the date on which its accession has been notified by the Director-General, unless a subsequent date has been indicated in the instrument of accession. In the latter case, this Act shall enter into force with respect to the country on the date thus indicated.

(3) With respect to any country outside the Union which deposits its instrument of accession after the date of entry into force of the present Act in its entirety, or less than one month before such date, this Act shall enter into force three months after the date on which its accession has been notified by the Director-General, unless a subsequent date has been indicated in the instrument of accession. In the latter case, this Act shall enter into force with respect to that country on the date thus indicated.

*Article 22*
[Consequences of Ratification or Accession]

Subject to the possibilities of exceptions provided for in Articles 20(1)(*b*) and 28(2), ratification or accession shall automatically entail acceptance of all the clauses and admission to all the advantages of this Act.

*Article 23*
[Accession to Earlier Acts]

After the entry into force of this Act in its entirety, a country may not accede to earlier Acts of this Convention.

*Article 24*
[Territories]

(1) Any country may declare in its instrument of ratification or accession, or may inform the Director-General by written notification any time thereafter, that this Convention shall be applicable to all or part of those territories, designated in the declaration or notification, for the external relations of which it is responsible.

(2) Any country which has made such a declaration or given such a notification may, at any time, notify the Director-General that this Convention shall cease to be applicable to all or part of such territories.

(3)(*a*) Any declaration made under paragraph (1) shall take effect on the same date as the ratification or accession in the instrument of which it was included, and any notification given under such paragraph shall take effect three months after its notification by the Director-General.

(*b*) Any notification given under paragraph (2) shall take effect twelve months after its receipt by the Director-General.

*Article 25*
[Implementation of the Convention on the Domestic Level]

(1) Any country party to this Convention undertakes to adopt, in accordance with its constitution, the measures necessary to ensure the application of this Convention.

(2) It is understood that, at the time a country deposits its instrument of ratification or accession, it will be in a position under its domestic law to give effect to the provisions of this Convention.

*Article 26*
[Denunciation]

(1) This Convention shall remain in force without limitation as to time.

(2) Any country may denounce this Act by notification addressed to the Director-General. Such denunciation shall constitute also denunciation of all earlier Acts and shall affect only the country making it, the Convention remaining in full force and effect as regards the other countries of the Union.

(3) Denunciation shall take effect one year after the date on which the Director-General has received the notification.

(4) The right of denunciation provided by this Article shall not be exercised by any country before the expiration of five years from the date upon which it becomes a member of the Union.

*Article 27*
[Application of Earlier Acts]

(1) The present Act shall, as regards the relations between the countries to which it applies, and to the extent that it applies, replace the Convention of Paris of March 20, 1883, and the subsequent Acts of revision.

(2)(*a*) As regards the countries to which the present Act does not apply, or does not apply in its entirety, but to which the Lisbon Act of October 31 1958, applies, the latter shall remain in force in its entirety or to the extent that the present Act does not replace it by virtue of paragraph (1).

(*b*) Similarly, as regards the countries to which neither the present Act, nor portions thereof, nor the Lisbon Act applies, the London Act of June 2, 1934, shall remain in force in its entirety or to the extent that the present Act does not replace it by virtue of paragraph (1).

(*c*) Similarly, as regards the countries to which neither the present Act, nor portions thereof, nor the Lisbon Act, nor the London Act applies, the Hague Act of November 6, 1925, shall remain in force in its entirety or to the extent that the present Act does not replace it by virtue of paragraph (1).

(3) Countries outside the Union which become party to this Act shall apply it with respect to any country of the Union not party to this Act or which, although party to this Act, has made a declaration pursuant to Article 20(1)(*b*)(i). Such countries recognize that the said country of the Union may apply, in its relations with them, the provisions of the most recent Act to which it is party.

*Article 28*
[Disputes]

(1) Any dispute between two or more countries of the Union concerning the interpretation or application of this Convention, not settled by negotiation, may, by any one of the countries concerned, be brought before the International Court of Justice by application in conformity with the Statute of the Court, unless the countries concerned agree on some other method of settlement. The country bringing the dispute before the Court shall inform the International Bureau; the International Bureau shall bring the matter to the attention of the other countries of the Union.

(2) Each country may, at the time it signs this Act or deposits its instrument of ratification or accession, declare that it does not consider itself bound by the provisions of paragraph (1). With regard to any dispute between such country and any other country of the Union, the provisions of paragraph (1) shall not apply.

(3) Any country having made a declaration in accordance with the provisions of paragraph (2) may, at any time, withdraw its declaration by notification addressed to the Director-General.

*Article 29*
[Signatures, Languages, Depositary Functions]

(1)(*a*) This Act shall be signed in a single copy in the French language and shall be deposited with the Government of Sweden.

(*b*) Official texts shall be established by the Director-General, after consultation with the interested Governments, in the English, German, Italian, Portuguese, Russian and Spanish languages, and such other languages as the Assembly may designate.

(*c*) In case of differences of opinion on the interpretation of the various texts, the French text shall prevail.

(2) This Act shall remain open for signature at Stockholm until January 13, 1968.

(3) The Director-General shall transmit two copies, certified by the Government of Sweden, of the signed text of this Act to the Governments of all countries of the Union and, on request, to the Government of any other country.

(4) The Director-General shall register this Act with the Secretariat of the United Nations.

(5) The Director-General shall notify the Governments of all countries of the Union of signatures, deposits of instruments of ratification or accession and any declarations included in such instruments or made pursuant to Article 20(1)(*c*), entry into force of any provisions of this Act, notifications of denunciation, and notifications pursuant to Article 24.

*Article 30*
[Transitional Provisions]

(1) Until the first Director-General assumes office, references in this Act to the International Bureau of the Organization or to the Director-General shall be deemed to be references to the Bureau of the Union or its Director respectively.

(2) Countries of the Union not bound by Articles 13 to 17 may, until five years after the entry into force of the Convention establishing the Organization, exercise, if they so desire, the rights provided under Articles 13 to 17 of this Act as if they were bound by those Articles. Any country desiring to exercise such rights shall give written notification to that effect to the Director-General; such notification shall be effective from the date of its receipt. Such countries shall be deemed to be members of the Assembly until the expiration of the said period.

(3) As long as all the countries of the Union have not become Members of the Organization, the International Bureau of the Organization shall also function as the Bureau of the Union, and the Director-General as the Director of the said Bureau.

(4) Once all the countries of the Union have become Members of the Organization, the rights, obligations, and property, of the Bureau of the Union shall devolve on the International Bureau of the Organization.

IN WITNESS WHEREOF the undersigned, being authorised thereto, have signed this present Act.

DONE at Stockholm on 14 July, 1967.

# Appendix 5

# EC Directives and Regulations

COUNCIL DIRECTIVE (87/54/EEC) OF 16 DECEMBER 1986 ON THE
LEGAL PROTECTION OF TOPOGRAPHIES OF SEMICONDUCTOR
PRODUCTS

THE COUNCIL OF THE EUROPEAN COMMUNITIES

Having regard to the Treaty establishing the European Economic Community
and in particular Article 100 thereof,

Having regard to the proposal from the Commission,

Having regard to the opinion of the European Parliament,

Having regard to the opinion of the Economic and Social Committee,

Whereas semiconductor products are playing an increasingly important role in
a broad range of industries and semiconductor technology can accordingly be
considered as being of fundamental importance for the Community's industrial
development;

Whereas the functions of semiconductor products depend in large part on the
topographies of such products and whereas the development of such topographies
requires the investment of considerable resources, human, technical and financial,
while topographies of such products can be copied at a fraction of the cost needed
to develop them independently;

Whereas topographies of semiconductor products are at present not clearly
protected in all Member States by existing legislation and such protection, where
it exists, has different attributes;

Whereas certain existing differences in the legal protection of semiconductor
products offered by the laws of the Member States have direct and negative effects
on the functioning of the common market as regards semiconductor products and
such differences could well become greater as Member States introduce new
legislation on this subject;

Whereas existing differences having such effects need to be removed and new
ones having a negative effect on the common market prevented from arising;

Whereas, in relation to extension of protection to persons outside the
Community, Member States should be free to act on their own behalf in so far as
Community decisions have not been taken within a limited period of time;

Whereas the Community's legal framework on the protection of topographies
of semiconductor products can, in the first instance, be limited to certain basic
principles by provisions specifying whom and what should be protected, the
exclusive rights on which protected persons should be able to rely to authorise or

prohibit certain acts, exceptions to these rights and for how long the protection should last;

Whereas other matters can for the time being be decided in accordance with national law, in particular, whether registration or deposit is required as a condition for protection and, subject to an exclusion of licences granted for the sole reason that a certain period of time has elapsed, whether and on what conditions non-voluntary licences may be granted in respect of protected topographies;

Whereas protection of topographies of semiconductor products in accordance with this Directive should be without prejudice to the application of some other forms of protection;

Whereas further measures concerning the legal protection of topographies of semiconductor products in the Community can be considered at a later stage, if necessary, while the application of common basic principles by all Member States in accordance with the provisions of this Directive is an urgent necessity,

HAS ADOPTED THIS DIRECTIVE:

## CHAPTER 1

## Definitions

*Article 1*

**1.** For the purposes of this Directive:

    (a) a 'semiconductor product' shall mean the final or an intermediate form of any product:

        (i) consisting of a body of material which includes a layer of semi-conducting material; and

        (ii) having one or more other layers composed of conducting, insulating or semi-conducting material, the layers being arranged in accordance with a pre-determined three-dimensional pattern; and

        (iii) intended to perform, exclusively or together with other functions, an electronic function;

    (b) the 'topography' of a semiconductor product shall mean a series of related images, however fixed or encoded;

        (i) representing the three-dimensional pattern of the layers of which a semiconductor product is composed; and

        (ii) in which series, each image has the pattern or part of the pattern of a surface of the semiconductor product at any stage of its manufacture;

    (c) 'commercial exploitation' means the sale, rental, leasing or any other method of commercial distribution, or an offer for these purposes. However, for the purposes of Articles 3(4), 4(1), 7(1), (3) and (4) 'commercial exploitation' shall not include exploitation under conditions of confidentiality to the extent that no further distribution to third parties occurs, except where exploitation of a topography takes place under conditions of confidentiality required by a measure taken in conformity with Article 223 (1) (b) of the Treaty.

**2.** The Council acting by qualified majority on a proposal from the Commission, may amend paragraph 1(a) (i) and (ii) in order to adapt these provisions in the light of technical progress.

## CHAPTER 2

**Protection of topographies of semiconductor products**

*Article 2*

**1.** Member States shall protect the topographies of semiconductor products by adopting legislative provisions conferring exclusive rights in accordance with the provisions of the Directive.
**2.** The topography of a semiconductor product shall be protected in so far as it satisfies the conditions that it is the result of its creator's own intellectual effort and is not commonplace in the semiconductor industry. Where the topography of a semiconductor product consists of elements that are commonplace in the semiconductor industry, it shall be protected only to the extent that the combination of such elements, taken as a whole, fulfils the abovementioned conditions.

*Article 3*

**1.** Subject to paragraphs 2 to 5, the right to protection shall apply in favour of persons who are the creators of the topographies of semiconductor products.
**2.** Member States may provide that,

    (a) where a topography is created in the course of the creator's employment, the right to protection shall apply in favour of the creator's employer unless the terms of employment provide to the contrary;
    (b) where the topography is created under a contract other than a contract of employment, the right to protection shall apply in favour of a party to the contract by whom the topography has been commissioned, unless the contract provides to the contrary.

**3.**    (a) As regards the persons referred to in paragraph 1, the right to protection shall apply in favour of natural persons who are nationals of a Member State or who have their habitual residence on the territory of a Member State.
    (b) Where Member States make provision in accordance with paragraph 2, the right to protection shall apply in favour of:

        (i) natural persons who are nationals of a Member State or who have their habitual residence on the territory of a Member State;
        (ii) companies or other legal persons which have a real and effective industrial or commercial establishment on the territory of a Member State.

**4.** Where no right to protection exists in accordance with other provisions of this Article, the right to protection shall also apply in favour of the persons referred to in paragraph 3(b) (i) and (ii) who:

    (a) first commercially exploit within a Member State a topography which has not yet been exploited commercially anywhere in the world; and

(b) have been exclusively authorised to exploit commercially the topography throughout the Community by the person entitled to dispose of it.

**5.** The right to protection shall also apply in favour of the successors in title of the persons mentioned in paragraphs 1 to 4.

**6.** Subject to paragraph 7, Member States may negotiate and conclude agreements or understandings with third States and multilateral Conventions concerning the legal protection of topographies of semiconductor products whilst respecting Community law and in particular the rules laid down in this Directive.

**7.** Member States may enter into negotiations with third States with a view to extending the right to protection to persons who do not benefit from the right to protection according to the provisions of this Directive. Member States who enter into such negotiations shall inform the Commission thereof.

When a Member State wishes to extend protection to persons who otherwise do not benefit from the right to protection according to the provisions of this Directive or to conclude an agreement or understanding on the extension of protection with a non-Member State it shall notify the Commission. The Commission shall inform the other Member States thereof.

The Member State shall hold the extension of protection or the conclusion of the agreement or understanding in abeyance for one month from the date on which it notifies the Commission. However, if within that period the Commission notifies the Member State concerned of its intention to submit a proposal to the Council for all Member States to extend protection in respect of the persons or non-Member State concerned, the Member State shall hold the extension of protection or the conclusion of the agreement or understanding in abeyance for a period of two months from the date of the notification by the Member State.

Where, before the end of this two-month period, the Commission submits such a proposal to the Council, the Member State shall hold the extension of protection or the conclusion of the agreement or understanding in abeyance for a further period of four months from the date on which the proposal was submitted.

In the absence of a Commission notification or proposal or a Council decision within the time limits prescribed above, the Member State may extend protection or conclude the agreement or understanding.

A proposal by the Commission to extend protection, whether or not it is made following a notification by a Member State in accordance with the preceding paragraphs shall be adopted by the Council acting by qualified majority.

A Decision of the Council on the basis of a Commission proposal shall not prevent a Member State from extending protection to persons, in addition to those to benefit from protection in all Member States, who were included in the envisaged extension, agreement or understanding as notified, unless the Council acting by qualified majority has decided otherwise.

**8.** Commission proposals and Council decisions pursuant to paragraph 7 shall be published for information in the *Official Journal of the European Communities*.

*Article 4*

**1.** Member States may provide that the exclusive rights conferred in conformity with Article 2 shall not come into existence or shall no longer apply to the topography of a semiconductor product unless an application for registration in due form has been filed with a public authority within two years of its first commercial exploitation. Member States may require in addition to such registration that material identifying or exemplifying the topography or any combination thereof has been deposited with a public authority, as well as a statement as to the date of first commercial exploitation of the topography where it precedes the date of the application for registration.

**2.** Member States shall ensure that material deposited in conformity with paragraph 1 is not made available to the public where it is a trade secret. This provision shall be without prejudice to the disclosure of such material pursuant to an order of a court or other competent authority to persons involved in litigation concerning the validity or infringement of the exclusive rights referred to in Article 2.

**3.** Member States may require that transfers of rights in protected topographies be registered.

**4.** Member States may subject registration and deposit in accordance with paragraphs 1 and 3 to the payment of fees not exceeding their administrative costs.

**5.** Conditions prescribing the fulfilment of additional formalities for obtaining or maintaining protection shall not be admitted.

**6.** Member States which require registration shall provide for legal remedies in favour of a person having the right to protection in accordance with the provisions of this Directive who can prove that another person has applied for or obtained the registration of a topography without his authorisation.

*Article 5*

**1.** The exclusive rights referred to in Article 2 shall include the rights to authorise or prohibit any of the following acts:

    (a) reproduction of a topography in so far as it is protected under Article 2(2);

    (b) commercial exploitation or the importation for that purpose of a topography or of a semiconductor product manufactured by using the topography.

**2.** Notwithstanding paragraph 1, a Member State may permit the reproduction of a topography privately for non-commercial aims.

**3.** The exclusive rights referred to in paragraph 1(a) shall not apply to reproduction for the purpose of analysing, evaluating or teaching the concepts, processes, systems or techniques embodied in the topography or the topography itself.

**4.** The exclusive rights referred to in paragraph 1 shall not extend to any such act in relation to a topography meeting the requirements of Article 2(2) and created on the basis of an analysis and evaluation of another topography, carried out in conformity with paragraph 3.

**5.** The exclusive rights to authorise or prohibit the acts specified in paragraph 1 (b) shall not apply to any such act committed after the topography or the semiconductor product has been put on the market in a Member State by the person entitled to authorise its marketing or with his consent.

**6.** A person who, when he acquires a semiconductor product, does not know, or has no reasonable grounds to believe, that the product is protected by an exclusive right conferred by a Member State in conformity with this Directive shall not be prevented from commercially exploiting that product.

However, for acts committed after that person knows, or has reasonable grounds to believe, that the semiconductor product is so protected, Member States shall ensure that on the demand of the rightholder a tribunal may require, in accordance with the provisions of the national law applicable, the payment of adequate remuneration.

**7.** The provisions of paragraph 6 shall apply to the successors in title of the person referred to in the first sentence of that paragraph.

*Article 6*

Member States shall not subject the exclusive rights referred to in Article 2 to licences granted, for the sole reason that a certain period of time has elapsed, automatically, and by operation of law.

*Article 7*

**1.** Member States shall provide that the exclusive rights referred to in Article 2 shall come into existence:

    (a)  where registration is the condition for the coming into existence of the exclusive rights in accordance with Article 4, on the earlier of the following dates:

        (i)  the date when the topography is first commercially exploited anywhere in the world;

        (ii)  the date when an application or registration has been filed in due form; or

    (b)  when the topography is first commercially exploited anywhere in the world; or

    (c)  when the topography is first fixed or encoded.

**2.** Where the exclusive rights come into existence in accordance with paragraph 1(a) or (b), the Member States shall provide, for the period prior to those rights coming into existence, legal remedies in favour of a person having the right to protection in accordance with the provisions of this Directive who can prove that another person has fraudulently reproduced or commercially exploited or imported for that purpose a topography. This paragraph shall be without prejudice to legal remedies made available to enforce the exclusive rights conferred in conformity with Article 2.

**3.** The exclusive rights shall come to an end 10 years from the end of the calendar year in which the topography is first commercially exploited anywhere in the world or, where registration is a condition for the coming into existence or continuing application of the exclusive rights, 10 years from the earlier of the following dates:

    (a)  the end of the calendar year in which the topography is first commercially exploited anywhere in the world;

    (b)  the end of the calendar year in which the application for registration has been filed in due form.

**4.** Where a topography has not been commercially exploited anywhere in the world within a period of 15 years from its first fixation or encoding, any exclusive rights in existence pursuant to paragraph 1 shall come to an end and no new exclusive rights shall come into existence unless an application for registration in due form has been filed within that period in those Member States where registration is a condition for the coming into existence or continuing application of the exclusive rights.

*Article 8*

The protection granted to the topographies of semiconductor products in accordance with Article 2 shall not extend to any concept, process, system, technique or encoded information embodied in the topography other than the topography itself.

*Article 9*

Where the legislation of Member States provides that semiconductor products manufactured using protected topographies may carry an indication, the indication to be used shall be a capital T as follows: T, 'T', [T], T, T* or T.

## CHAPTER 3

### Continued application of other legal provisions

*Article 10*

**1.** The provisions of this Directive shall be without prejudice to legal provisions concerning patent and utility model rights.
**2.** The provisions of this Directive shall be without prejudice:

    (a) to rights conferred by the Member States in fulfilment of their obligations under international agreements, including provisions extending such rights to nationals of, or residents in, the territory of the Member State concerned;
    (b) to the law of copyright in Member States, restricting the reproduction of drawing or other artistic representations of topographies by copying them in two dimensions.

**3.** Protection granted by national law to topographies of semiconductor products fixed or encoded before the entry into force of the national provisions enacting the Directive, but no later than the date set out in Article 11(1), shall not be affected by the provisions of this Directive.

## CHAPTER 4

### Final provisions

*Article 11*

**1.** Member States shall bring into force the laws, regulations or administrative provisions necessary to comply with this Directive by 7 November 1987.
**2.** Member States shall ensure that they communicate to the Commission the texts of the main provisions of national law which they adopt in the field covered by this Directive.

*Article 12*

This Directive is addressed to the Member States.
    Done at Brussels, 16 December 1986.

COUNCIL DIRECTIVE (91/250/EEC) OF 14 MAY 1991 ON THE LEGAL
PROTECTION OF COMPUTER PROGRAMS

THE COUNCIL OF THE EUROPEAN COMMUNITIES,

Having regard to the Treaty establishing the European Economic Community
and in particular Article 100a thereof,

Having regard to the proposal from the Commission,

In cooperation with the European Parliament,

Having regard to the opinion of the Economic and Social Committee,

Whereas computer programs are at present not clearly protected in all Member
States by existing legislation and such protection, where it exists, has different
attributes;

Whereas the development of computer programs requires the investment of
considerable human, technical and financial resources while computer programs
can be copied at a fraction of the cost needed to develop them independently;

Whereas computer programs are playing an increasingly important role in a
broad range of industries and computer program technology can accordingly be
considered as being of fundamental importance for the Community's industrial
development;

Whereas certain differences in the legal protection of computer programs
offered by the laws of the Member States have direct and negative effects on the
functioning of the common market as regards computer programs and such
differences could well become greater as Member States introduce new legislation
on this subject;

Whereas existing differences having such effects need to be removed and new
ones prevented from arising, while differences not adversely affecting the
functioning of the common market to a substantial degree need not be removed
or prevented from arising;

Whereas the Community's legal framework on the protection of computer
programs can accordingly in the first instance be limited to establishing that
Member States should accord protection to computer programs under copyright
law as literary works and, further, to establishing who and what should be
protected, the exclusive rights on which protected persons should be able to rely
in order to authorize or prohibit certain acts and for how long the protection should
apply;

Whereas, for the purpose of this Directive, the term 'computer program' shall
include programs in any form, including those which are incorporated into
hardware; whereas this term also includes preparatory design work leading to the
development of a computer program provided that the nature of the preparatory
work is such that a computer program can result from it at a later stage;

Whereas, in respect of the criteria to be applied in determining whether or not
a computer program is an original work, no tests as to the qualitative or aesthetic
merits of the program should be applied;

Whereas the Community is fully committed to the promotion of international
standardization;

Whereas the function of a computer program is to communicate and work
together with other components of a computer system and with users and, for this
purpose, a logical and, where appropriate, physical interconnection and interaction
is required to permit all elements of software and hardware to work with other
software and hardware and with users in all the ways in which they are intended
to function;

Whereas the parts of the program which provide for such interconnection and interaction between elements of software and hardware are generally known as 'interfaces';

Whereas this functional interconnection and interaction is generally known as 'interoperability'; whereas such interoperability can be defined as the ability to exchange information and mutually to use the information which has been exchanged;

Whereas, for the avoidance of doubt, it has to be made clear that only the expression of a computer program is protected and that ideas and principles which underlie any element of a program, including those which underlie its interfaces, are not protected by copyright under this Directive;

Whereas, in accordance with this principle of copyright, to the extent that logic, algorithms and programming languages comprise ideas and principles, those ideas and principles are not protected under this Directive;

Whereas, in accordance with the legislation and jurisprudence of the Member States and the international copyright conventions, the expression of those ideas and principles is to be protected by copyright;

Whereas, for the purposes of this Directive, the term 'rental' means the making available for use, for a limited period of time and for profit-making purposes, of a computer program or a copy thereof; whereas this term does not include public lending, which, accordingly, remains outside the scope of this Directive;

Whereas the exclusive rights of the author to prevent the unauthorized reproduction of his work have to be subject to a limited exception in the case of a computer program to allow the reproduction technically necessary for the use of that program by the lawful acquirer;

Whereas this means that the acts of loading and running necessary for the use of a copy of a program which has been lawfully acquired, and the act of correction of its errors, may not be prohibited by contract; whereas, in the absence of specific contractual provisions, including when a copy of the program has been sold, any other act necessary for the use of the copy of a program may be performed in accordance with its intended purpose by a lawful acquirer of that copy;

Whereas a person having a right to use a computer program should not be prevented from performing acts necessary to observe, study or test the functioning of the program, provided that these acts do not infringe the copyright in the program;

Whereas the unauthorized reproduction, translation, adaptation or transformation of the form of the code in which a copy of a computer program has been made available constitutes an infringement of the exclusive rights of the author;

Whereas, nevertheless, circumstances may exist when such a reproduction of the code and translation of its form within the meaning of Article 4(a) and (b) are indispensable to obtain the necessary information to achieve the interoperability of an independently created program with other programs;

Whereas it has therefore to be considered that in these limited circumstances only, performance of the acts of reproduction and translation by or on behalf of a person having a right to use a copy of the program is legitimate and compatible with fair practice and must therefore be deemed not to require the authorization of the right-holder;

Whereas an objective of this exception is to make it possible to connect all components of a computer system, including those of different manufacturers, so that they can work together;

Whereas such an exception to the author's exclusive rights may not be used in a way which prejudices the legitimate interests of the rightholder or which conflicts with a normal exploitation of the program;

Whereas, in order to remain in accordance with the provisions of the Berne Convention for the Protection of Literary and Artistic Works, the term of protection should be the life of the author and fifty years from the first of January of the year following the year of his death or, in the case of an anonymous or pseudonymous work, 50 years from the first of January of the year following the year in which the work is first published;

Whereas protection of computer programs under copyright laws should be without prejudice to the application, in appropriate cases, of other forms of protection; whereas, however, any contractual provisions contrary to Article 6 or to the exceptions provided for in Article 5(2) and (3) should be null and void;

Whereas the provisions of this Directive are without prejudice to the application of the competition rules under Articles 85 and 86 of the Treaty if a dominant supplier refuses to make information available which is necessary for interoperability as defined in this Directive;

Whereas the provisions of this Directive should be without prejudice to specific requirements of Community law already enacted in respect of the publication of interfaces in the telecommunications sector or Council Decisions relating to standardization in the field of information technology and telecommunication;

Whereas this Directive does not affect derogations provided for under national legislation in accordance with the Berne Convention on points not covered by this Directive,

HAS ADOPTED THIS DIRECTIVE:

*Article 1*

**Object of protection**

**1.** In accordance with the provisions of this Directive, Member States shall protect computer programs, by copyright, as literary works within the meaning of the Berne Convention for the Protection of Literary and Artistic Works. For the purposes of this Directive, the term 'computer programs' shall include their preparatory design material.

**2.** Protection in accordance with this Directive shall apply to the expression in any form of a computer program. Ideas and principles which underlie any element of a computer program, including those which underlie its interfaces, are not protected by copyright under this Directive.

**3.** A computer program shall be protected if it is original in the sense that it is the author's own intellectual creation. No other criteria shall be applied to determine its eligibility for protection.

*Article 2*

**Authorship of computer programs**

**1.** The author of a computer program shall be the natural person or group of natural persons who has created the program or, where the legislation of the Member State permits, the legal person designated as the rightholder by that legislation. Where collective works are recognized by the legislation of a Member State, the person considered by the legislation of the Member State to have created the work shall be deemed to be its author.

**2.** In respect of a computer program created by a group of natural persons jointly, the exclusive rights shall be owned jointly.

**3.** Where a computer program is created by an employee in the execution of his duties or following the instructions given by his employer, the employer exclusively shall be entitled to exercise all economic rights in the program so created, unless otherwise provided by contract.

*Article 3*

**Beneficiaries of protection**

Protection shall be granted to all natural or legal persons eligible under national copyright legislation as applied to literary works.

*Article 4*

**Restricted acts**

Subject to the provisions of Articles 5 and 6, the exclusive rights of the rightholder within the meaning of Article 2, shall include the right to do or to authorize:

    (a) the permanent or temporary reproduction of a computer program by any means and in any form, in part or in whole. Insofar as loading, displaying, running, transmission or storage of the computer program necessitate such reproduction, such acts shall be subject to authorization by the rightholder;

    (b) the translation, adaptation, arrangement and any other alteration of a computer program and the reproduction of the results thereof, without prejudice to the rights of the person who alters the program;

    (c) any form of distribution to the public, including the rental, of the original computer program or of copies thereof. The first sale in the Community of a copy of a program by the rightholder or with his consent shall exhaust the distribution right within the Community of that copy, with the exception of the right to control further rental of the program or a copy thereof.

*Article 5*

**Exceptions to the restricted acts**

**1.** In the absence of specific contractual provisions, the acts referred to in Article 4 (a) and (b) shall not require authorization by the rightholder where they are necessary for the use of the computer program by the lawful acquirer in accordance with its intended purpose, including for error correction.

**2.** The making of a back-up copy by a person having a right to use the computer program may not be prevented by contract insofar as it is necessary for that use.

**3.** The person having a right to use a copy of a computer program shall be entitled, without the authorization of the rightholder, to observe, study or test the functioning of the program in order to determine the ideas and principles which underlie any element of the program if he does so while performing any of the acts of loading, displaying, running, transmitting or storing the program which he is entitled to do.

*Article 6*

**Decompilation**

**1.** The authorization of the rightholder shall not be required where reproduction of the code and translation of its form within the meaning of Article 4(a) and (b) are indispensable to obtain the information necessary to achieve the inter-operability of an independently created computer program with other programs, provided that the following conditions are met:

  (a) these acts are performed by the licensee or by another person having a right to use a copy of a program, or on their behalf by a person authorized to do so;

  (b) the information necessary to achieve interoperability has not previously been readily available to the persons referred to in subparagraph (a); and

  (c) these acts are confined to the parts of the original program which are necessary to achieve interoperability.

**2.** The provisions of paragraph 1 shall not permit the information obtained through its application:

  (a) to be used for goals other than to achieve the interoperability of the independently created computer program;

  (b) to be given to others, except when necessary for the interoperability of the independently created computer program; or

  (c) to be used for the development, production or marketing of a computer program substantially similar in its expression, or for any other act which infringes copyright.

**3.** In accordance with the provisions of the Berne Convention for the protection of Literary and Artistic Works, the provisions of this Article may not be interpreted in such a way as to allow its application to be used in a manner which unreasonably prejudices the right holder's legitimate interests or conflicts with a normal exploitation of the computer program.

*Article 7*

**Special measures of protection**

**1.** Without prejudice to the provisions of Articles 4, 5 and 6, Member States shall provide, in accordance with their national legislation, appropriate remedies against a person committing any of the acts listed in subparagraphs (a), (b) and (c) below:

  (a) any act of putting into circulation a copy of a computer program knowing, or having reason to believe, that it is an infringing copy;

  (b) the possession, for commercial purposes, of a copy of a computer program knowing, or having reason to believe, that it is an infringing copy;

  (c) any act of putting into circulation, or the possession for commercial purposes of, any means the sole intended purpose of which is to facilitate the unauthorized removal or circumvention of any technical device which may have been applied to protect a computer program.

**2.** Any infringing copy of a computer program shall be liable to seizure in accordance with the legislation of the Member State concerned.

**3.** Member States may provide for the seizure of any means referred to in paragraph 1(c).

*Article 8*

**Term of protection**

*1. Protection shall be granted for the life of the author and for fifty years after his death or after the death of the last surviving author; where the computer program is an anonymous or pseudonymous work, or where a legal person is designated as the author by national legislation in accordance with Article 2(1), the term of protection shall be fifty years from the time that the computer program is first lawfully made available to the public. The term of protection shall be deemed to begin on the first of January of the year following the abovementioned events.*

*2. Member States which already have a term of protection longer than that provided for in paragraph 1 are allowed to maintain their present term until such time as the term of protection for copyright works is harmonized by Community law in a more general way.*

*General note*

[Article 8 is repealed by 93/98/EEC.]

*Article 9*

**Continued application of other legal provisions**

**1.** The provisions of this Directive shall be without prejudice to any other legal provisions such as those concerning patent rights, trade-marks, unfair competition, trade secrets, protection of semi-conductor products or the law of contract. Any contractual provisions contrary to Article 6 or to the exceptions provided for in Article 5(2) and (3) shall be null and void.

**2.** The provisions of this Directive shall apply also to programs created before 1 January 1993 without prejudice to any acts concluded and rights acquired before that date.

*Article 10*

**Final provisions**

**1.** Member States shall bring into force the laws, regulations and administrative provisions necessary to comply with this Directive before 1 January 1993.

When Member States adopt these measures, the latter shall contain a reference to this Directive or shall be accompanied by such reference on the occasion of their official publication. The methods of making such a reference shall be laid down by the Member States.

**2.** Member States shall communicate to the Commission the provisions of national law which they adopt in the field governed by this Directive.

*Article 11*

This Directive is addressed to the Member States.

Done at Brussels, 14 May 1991.

**Information concerning the date of entry into force of the Cooperation Agreement between the European Economic Community and the Republic of Chile**

The exchange of instruments giving notice of completion of the procedures necessary for the entry into force of the aforementioned Agreement, signed in Rome on 20 December 1990, having been concluded on 30 April 1991, this Agreement entered into force, in accordance with Article 21 thereof, on 1 May 1991.

COUNCIL DIRECTIVE (92/100/EEC) OF 19 NOVEMBER 1992 ON RENTAL RIGHT AND LENDING RIGHT AND ON CERTAIN RIGHTS RELATED TO COPYRIGHT IN THE FIELD OF INTELLECTUAL PROPERTY

THE COUNCIL OF THE EUROPEAN COMMUNITIES,

Having regard to the Treaty establishing the European Economic Community, and in particular Articles 57(2), 66 and 100a thereof,

Having regard to the proposal from the Commission,

In cooperation with the European Parliament,

Having regard to the opinion of the Economic and Social Committee,

Whereas differences exist in the legal protection provided by the laws and practices of the Member States for copyright works and subject matter of related rights protection as regards rental and lending; whereas such differences are sources of barriers to trade and distortions of competition which impede the achievement and proper functioning of the internal market;

Whereas such differences in legal protection could well become greater as Member States adopt new and different legislation or as national case-law interpreting such legislation develops differently;

Whereas such differences should therefore be eliminated in accordance with the objective of introducing an area without internal frontiers as set out in Article 8a of the Treaty so as to institute, pursuant to Article 3(f) of the Treaty, a system ensuring that competition in the common market is not distorted;

Whereas rental and lending of copyright works and the subject matter of related rights protection is playing an increasingly important role in particular for authors, performers and producers of phonograms and films; whereas piracy is becoming an increasing threat;

Whereas the adequate protection of copyright works and subject matter of related rights protection by rental and lending rights as well as the protection of the subject matter of related rights protection by the fixation right, reproduction right, distribution right, right to broadcast and communication to the public can accordingly be considered as being of fundamental importance for the Community's economic and cultural development;

Whereas copyright and related rights protection must adapt to new economic developments such as new forms of exploitation;

Whereas the creative and artistic work of authors and performers necessitates an adequate income as a basis for further creative and artistic work, and the investments required particularly for the production of phonograms and films are especially high and risky; whereas the possibility for securing that income and recouping that investment can only effectively be guaranteed through adequate legal protection of the rightholders concerned;

Whereas these creative, artistic and entrepreneurial activities are, to a large extent, activities of self-employed persons; whereas the pursuit of such activities must be made easier by providing a harmonized legal protection within the Community;

Whereas, to the extent that these activities principally constitute services, their provision must equally be facilitated by the establishment in the Community of a harmonized legal framework;

Whereas the legislation of the Member States should be approximated in such a way so as not to conflict with the international conventions on which many Member States' copyright and related rights laws are based;

Whereas the Community's legal framework on the rental right and lending right and on certain rights related to copyright can be limited to establishing that Member States provide rights with respect to rental and lending for certain groups of rightholders and further to establishing the rights of fixation, reproduction, distribution, broadcasting and communication to the public for certain groups of rightholders in the field of related rights protection;

Whereas it is necessary to define the concepts of rental and lending for the purposes of this Directive;

Whereas it is desirable, with a view to clarity, to exclude from rental and lending within the meaning of this Directive certain forms of making available, as for instance making available phonograms or films (cinematographic or audiovisual works or moving images, whether or not accompanied by sound) for the purpose of public performance or broadcasting, making available for the purpose of exhibition, or making available for on-the-spot reference use; whereas lending within the meaning of this Directive does not include making available between establishments which are accessible to the public;

Whereas, where lending by an establishment accessible to the public gives rise to a payment the amount of which does not go beyond what is necessary to cover the operating costs of the establishment, there is no direct or indirect economic or commercial advantage within the meaning of this Directive;

Whereas it is necessary to introduce arrangements ensuring that an unwaivable equitable remuneration is obtained by authors and performers who must retain the possibility to entrust the administration of this right to collecting societies representing them;

Whereas the equitable remuneration may be paid on the basis of one or several payments at any time on or after the conclusion of the contract;

Whereas the equitable remuneration must take account of the importance of the contribution of the authors and performers concerned to the phonogram or film;

Whereas it is also necessary to protect the rights at least of authors as regards public lending by providing for specific arrangements; whereas, however, any measures based on Article 5 of this Directive have to comply with Community law, in particular with Article 7 of the Treaty;

Whereas the provisions of Chapter II do not prevent Member States from extending the presumption set out in Article 2(5) to the exclusive rights included in that chapter; whereas furthermore the provisions of Chapter II do not prevent Member States from providing for a rebuttable presumption of the authorization of exploitation in respect of the exclusive rights of performers provided for in those articles, in so far as such presumption is compatible with the International

Convention for the Protection of Performers, Producers of Phonograms and Broadcasting Organizations (hereinafter referred to as the Rome Convention);

Whereas Member States may provide for more far-reaching protection for owners of rights related to copyright than that required by Article 8 of this Directive;

Whereas the harmonized rental and lending rights and the harmonized protection in the field of rights related to copyright should not be exercised in a way which constitutes a disguised restriction on trade between Member States or in a way which is contrary to the rule of media exploitation chronology, as recognized in the Judgment handed down in *Société Cinéthèque v FNCF*,

HAS ADOPTED THIS DIRECTIVE:

## CHAPTER I
### RENTAL AND LENDING RIGHT

*Article 1*

### Object of harmonization

**1.** In accordance with the provisions of this Chapter, Member States shall provide, subject to Article 5, a right to authorize or prohibit the rental and lending of originals and copies of copyright works, and other subject matter as set out in Article 2(1).

**2.** For the purposes of this Directive, 'rental' means making available for use, for a limited period of time and for direct or indirect economic or commercial advantage.

**3.** For the purposes of this Directive, 'lending' means making available for use, for a limited period of time and not for direct or indirect economic or commercial advantage, when it is made through establishments which are accessible to the public.

**4.** The rights referred to in paragraph 1 shall not be exhausted by any sale or other act of distribution of originals and copies of copyright works and other subject matter as set out in Article 2(1).

*Article 2*

### Rightholders and subject matter of rental and lending right

**1.** The exclusive right to authorize or prohibit rental and lending shall belong:

— to the author in respect of the original and copies of his work,
— to the performer in respect of fixations of his performance,
— to the phonogram producer in respect of his phonograms, and
— to the producer of the first fixation of a film in respect of the original and copies of his film. For the purposes of this Directive, the term 'film' shall designate a cinematographic or audiovisual work or moving images, whether or not accompanied by sound.

**2.** For the purposes of this Directive the principal director of a cinematographic or audiovisual work shall be considered as its author or one of its authors. Member States may provide for others to be considered as its co-authors.

**3.** This Directive does not cover rental and lending rights in relation to buildings and to works of applied art.

**4.** The rights referred to in paragraph 1 may be transferred, assigned or subject to the granting of contractual licences.

**5.** Without prejudice to paragraph 7, when a contract concerning film production is concluded, individually or collectively, by performers with a film producer, the performer covered by this contract shall be presumed, subject to contractual clauses to the contrary, to have transferred his rental right, subject to Article 4.

**6.** Member States may provide for a similar presumption as set out in paragraph 5 with respect to authors.

**7.** Member States may provide that the signing of a contract concluded between a performer and a film producer concerning the production of a film has the effect of authorizing rental, provided that such contract provides for an equitable remuneration within the meaning of Article 4. Member States may also provide that this paragraph shall apply *mutatis mutandis* to the rights included in Chapter II.

*Article 3*

**Rental of computer programs**

This Directive shall be without prejudice to Article 4(c) of Council Directive 91/250/EEC of 14 May 1991 on the legal protection of computer programs.

*Article 4*

**Unwaivable right to equitable remuneration**

**1.** Where an author or performer has transferred or assigned his rental right concerning a phonogram or an original or copy of a film to a phonogram or film producer, that author or performer shall retain the right to obtain an equitable remuneration for the rental.

**2.** The right to obtain an equitable remuneration for rental cannot be waived by authors or performers.

**3.** The administration of this right to obtain an equitable remuneration may be entrusted to collecting societies representing authors or performers.

**4.** Member States may regulate whether and to what extent administration by collecting societies of the right to obtain an equitable remuneration may be imposed, as well as the question from whom this remuneration may be claimed or collected.

*Article 5*

**Derogation from the exclusive public lending right**

**1.** Member States may derogate from the exclusive right provided for in Article 1 in respect of public lending, provided that at least authors obtain a remuneration for such lending. Member States shall be free to determine this remuneration taking account of their cultural promotion objectives.

**2.** When Member States do not apply the exclusive lending right provided for in Article 1 as regards phonograms, films and computer programs, they shall introduce, at least for authors, a remuneration.

**3.** Member States may exempt certain categories of establishments from the payment of the remuneration referred to in paragraphs 1 and 2.

**4.** The Commission, in cooperation with the Member States, shall draw up before 1 July 1997 a report on public lending in the Community. It shall forward this report to the European Parliament and to the Council.

## CHAPTER II

**RIGHTS RELATED TO COPYRIGHT**

*Article 6*

**Fixation right**

**1.** Member States shall provide for performers the exclusive right to authorize or prohibit the fixation of their performances.

**2.** Member States shall provide for broadcasting organizations the exclusive right to authorize or prohibit the fixation of their broadcasts, whether these broadcasts are transmitted by wire or over the air, including by cable or satellite.

**3.** A cable distributor shall not have the right provided for in paragraph 2 where it merely retransmits by cable the broadcasts of broadcasting organizations.

*Article 7*

**Reproduction right**

**1.** Member States shall provide the exclusive right to authorize or prohibit the direct or indirect reproduction:

— for performers, of fixations of their performances,
— for phonogram producers, of their phonograms,
— for producers of the first fixations of films, in respect of the original and copies of their films, and
— for broadcasting organizations, of fixations of their broadcasts, as set out in Article 6(2).

**2.** The reproduction right referred to in paragraph 1 may be transferred, assigned or subject to the granting of contractual licences.

*Article 8*

**Broadcasting and communication to the public**

**1.** Member States shall provide for performers the exclusive right to authorize or prohibit the broadcasting by wireless means and the communication to the public of their performances, except where the performance is itself already a broadcast performance or is made from a fixation.

**2.** Member States shall provide a right in order to ensure that a single equitable remuneration is paid by the user, if a phonogram published for commercial purposes, or a reproduction of such phonogram, is used for broadcasting by wireless means or for any communication to the public, and to ensure that this remuneration is shared between the relevant performers and phonogram producers. Member States may, in the absence of agreement between the performers and phonogram producers, lay down the conditions as to the sharing of this remuneration between them.

**3.** Member States shall provide for broadcasting organizations the exclusive right to authorize or prohibit the rebroadcasting of their broadcasts by wireless means, as well as the communication to the public of their broadcasts if such communication is made in places accessible to the public against payment of an entrance fee.

*Article 9*

**Distribution right**

**1.** Member States shall provide:

— for performers, in respect of fixations of their performances,
— for phonogram producers, in respect of their phonograms,
— for producers of the first fixations of films, in respect of the original and copies of their films,
— for broadcasting organizations, in respect of fixations of their broadcast as set out in Article 6(2),

the exclusive right to make available these objects, including copies thereof, to the public by sale or otherwise, hereafter referred to as the 'distribution right'.
**2.** The distribution right shall not be exhausted within the Community in respect of an object as referred to in paragraph 1, except where the first sale in the Community of that object is made by the rightholder or with his consent.
**3.** The distribution right shall be without prejudice to the specific provisions of Chapter I, in particular Article 1(4).
**4.** The distribution right may be transferred, assigned or subject to the granting of contractual licences.

*Article 10*

**Limitations to rights**

**1.** Member States may provide for limitations to the rights referred to in Chapter II in respect of:

(a) private use;
(b) use of short excerpts in connection with the reporting of current events;
(c) ephemeral fixation by a broadcasting organization by means of its own facilities and for its own broadcasts;
(d) use solely for the purposes of teaching or scientific research.

**2.** Irrespective of paragraph 1, any Member State may provide for the same kinds of limitations with regard to the protection of performers, producers of phonograms, broadcasting organizations and of producers of the first fixations of films, as it provides for in connection with the protection of copyright in literary and artistic works. However, compulsory licences may be provided for only to the extent to which they are compatible with the Rome Convention.
**3.** Paragraph 1(a) shall be without prejudice to any existing or future legislation on remuneration for reproduction for private use.

CHAPTER III

**DURATION**

*Article 11*

*Duration of authors' rights*

*Without prejudice to further harmonization, the authors' rights referred to in this Directive shall not expire before the end of the term provided by the Berne Convention for the Protection of Literary and Artistic Works.*

*Article 12*

**Duration of related rights**

*Without prejudice to further harmonization, the rights referred to in this Directive of performers, phonogram producers and broadcasting organizations shall not expire before the end of the respective terms provided by the Rome Convention. The rights referred to in this Directive for producers of the first fixations of films shall not expire before the end of a period of 20 years computed from the end of the year in which the fixation was made.*

*General note*
Articles 11 and 12 are repealed by 93/98/EEC.

## CHAPTER IV

**COMMON PROVISIONS**

*Article 13*

**Application in time**

**1.** This Directive shall apply in respect of all copyright works, performances, phonograms, broadcasts and first fixations of films referred to in this Directive which are, on 1 July 1994, still protected by the legislation of the Member States in the field of copyright and related rights or meet the criteria for protection under the provisions of this Directive on that date.

**2.** This Directive shall apply without prejudice to any acts of exploitation performed before 1 July 1994.

**3.** Member States may provide that the rightholders are deemed to have given their authorization to the rental or lending of an object referred to in Article 2 (1) which is proven to have been made available to third parties for this purpose or to have been acquired before 1 July 1994. However, in particular where such an object is a digital recording, Member States may provide that rightholders shall have a right to obtain an adequate remuneration for the rental or lending of that object.

**4.** Member States need not apply the provisions of Article 2(2) to cinematographic or audiovisual works created before 1 July 1994.

**5.** Member States may determine the date as from which the Article 2(2) shall apply, provided that that date is no later than 1 July 1997.

**6.** This Directive shall, without prejudice to paragraph 3 and subject to paragraphs 8 and 9, not affect any contracts concluded before the date of its adoption.

**7.** Member States may provide, subject to the provisions of paragraphs 8 and 9, that when rightholders who acquire new rights under the national provisions adopted in implementation of this Directive have, before 1 July 1994, given their consent for exploitation, they shall be presumed to have transferred the new exclusive rights.

**8.** Member States may determine the date as from which the unwaivable right to an equitable remuneration referred to in Article 4 exists, provided that that date is no later than 1 July 1997.

**9.** For contracts concluded before 1 July 1994, the unwaivable right to an equitable remuneration provided for in Article 4 shall apply only where authors or performers or those representing them have submitted a request to that effect before 1 January 1997. In the absence of agreement between rightholders concerning the level of remuneration, Member States may fix the level of equitable remuneration.

## Article 14

**Relation between copyright and related rights**

Protection of copyright-related rights under this Directive shall leave intact and shall in no way affect the protection of copyright.

## Article 15

**Final provisions**

**1.** Member States shall bring into force the laws, regulations and administrative provisions necessary to comply with this Directive not later than 1 July 1994. They shall forthwith inform the Commission thereof.

When Member States adopt these measures, they shall contain a reference to this Directive or shall be accompanied by such reference at the time of their official publication. The methods of making such a reference shall be laid down by the Member States.

**2.** Member States shall communicate to the Commission the main provisions of domestic law which they adopt in the field covered by this Directive.

## Article 16

This Directive is addressed to the Member States.

Done at Brussels, 19 November 1992.

COUNCIL DIRECTIVE (93/83/EEC) OF 27 SEPTEMBER 1993 ON THE COORDINATION OF CERTAIN RULES CONCERNING COPYRIGHT AND RIGHTS RELATED TO COPYRIGHT APPLICABLE TO SATELLITE BROADCASTING AND CABLE RETRANSMISSION

THE COUNCIL OF THE EUROPEAN COMMUNITIES,

Having regard to the Treaty establishing the European Economic Community, and in particular Articles 57(2) and 66 thereof,

Having regard to the proposal from the Commission,

In cooperation with the European Parliament,

Having regard to the opinion of the Economic and Social Committee,

(1) Whereas the objectives of the Community as laid down in the Treaty include establishing an ever closer union among the peoples of Europe, fostering closer relations between the States belonging to the Community and ensuring the economic and social progress of the Community countries by common action to eliminate the barriers which divide Europe;

(2) Whereas, to that end, the Treaty provides for the establishment of a common market and an area without internal frontiers; whereas measures to achieve this include the abolition of obstacles to the free movement of services and the institution of a system ensuring that competition in the common market is not distorted; whereas, to that end, the Council may adopt directives for the coordination of the provisions laid down by law, regulation or administrative action in Member States concerning the taking up and pursuit of activities as self-employed persons;

(3) Whereas broadcasts transmitted across frontiers within the Community, in particular by satellite and cable, are one of the most important ways of pursuing these Community objectives, which are at the same time political, economic, social, cultural and legal;

(4) Whereas the Council has already adopted Directive 89/552/EEC of 3 October 1989 on the coordination of certain provisions laid down by law, regulation or administrative action in Member States concerning the pursuit of television broadcasting activities, which makes provision for the promotion of the distribution and production of European television programmes and for advertising and sponsorship, the protection of minors and the right of reply;

(5) Whereas, however, the achievement of these objectives in respect of cross-border satellite broadcasting and the cable retransmission of programmes from other Member States is currently still obstructed by a series of differences between national rules of copyright and some degree of legal uncertainty; whereas this means that holders of rights are exposed to the threat of seeing their works exploited without payment of remuneration or that the individual holders of exclusive rights in various Member States block the exploitation of their rights; whereas the legal uncertainty in particular constitutes a direct obstacle in the free circulation of programmes within the Community;

(6) Whereas a distinction is currently drawn for copyright purposes between communication to the public by direct satellite and communication to the public by communications satellite; whereas, since individual reception is possible and affordable nowadays with both types of satellite, there is no longer any justification for this differing legal treatment;

(7) Whereas the free broadcasting of programmes is further impeded by the current legal uncertainty over whether broadcastsing by a satellite whose signals can be received directly affects the rights in the country of transmission only or in all countries of reception together; whereas, since communications satellites and direct satellites are treated alike for copyright purposes, this legal uncertainty now affects almost all programmes broadcast in the Community by satellite;

(8) Whereas, furthermore, legal certainty, which is a prerequisite for the free movement of broadcasts within the Community, is missing where programmes transmitted across frontiers are fed into and retransmitted through cable networks;

(9) Whereas the development of the acquisition of rights on a contractual basis by authorization is already making a vigorous contribution to the creation of the desired European audiovisual area; whereas the continuation of such contractual agreements should be ensured and their smooth application in practice should be promoted wherever possible;

(10) Whereas at present cable operators in particular cannot be sure that they have actually acquired all the programme rights covered by such an agreement;

(11) Whereas, lastly, parties in different Member States are not all similarly bound by obligations which prevent them from refusing without valid reason to negotiate on the acquisition of the rights necessary for cable distribution or allowing such negotiations to fail;

(12) Whereas the legal framework for the creation of a single audiovisual area laid down in Directive 89/552/EEC must, therefore, be supplemented with reference to copyright;

(13) Whereas, therefore, an end should be put to the differences of treatment of the transmission of programmes by communications satellite which exist in the Member States, so that the vital distinction throughout the Community becomes whether works and other protected subject matter are communicated to the public;

whereas this will also ensure equal treatment of the suppliers of cross-border broadcasts, regardless of whether they use a direct broadcasting satellite or a communications satellite;

(14) Whereas the legal uncertainty regarding the rights to be acquired which impedes cross-border satellite broadcasting should be overcome by defining the notion of communication to the public by satellite at a Community level; whereas this definition should at the same time specify where the act of communication takes place; whereas such a definition is necessary to avoid the cumulative application of several national laws to one single act of broadcasting; whereas communication to the public by satellite occurs only when, and in the Member State where, the programme-carrying signals are introduced under the control and responsibility of the broadcasting organization into an uninterrupted chain of communication leading to the satellite and down towards the earth; whereas normal technical procedures relating to the programme-carrying signals should not be considered as interruptions to the chain of broadcasting;

(15) Whereas the acquisition on a contractual basis of exclusive broadcasting rights should comply with any legislation on copyright and rights related to copyright in the Member State in which communication to the public by satellite occurs;

(16) Whereas the principle of contractual freedom on which this Directive is based will make it possible to continue limiting the exploitation of these rights, especially as far as certain technical means of transmission or certain language versions are concerned;

(17) Whereas, in ariving at the amount of the payment to be made for the rights acquired, the parties should take account of all aspects of the broadcast, such as the actual audience, the potential audience and the language version;

(18) Whereas the application of the country-of-origin principle contained in this Directive could pose a problem with regard to existing contracts; whereas this Directive should provide for a period of five years for existing contracts to be adapted, where necessary, in the light of the Directive; whereas the said country-of-origin principle should not, therefore, apply to existing contracts which expire before 1 January 2000; whereas if by that date parties still have an interest in the contract, the same parties should be entitled to renegotiate the conditions of the contract;

(19) Whereas existing international co-production agreements must be interpreted in the light of the economic purpose and scope envisaged by the parties upon signature; whereas in the past international co-production agreements have often not expressly and specifically addressed communication to the public by satellite within the meaning of this Directive a particular form of exploitation; whereas the underlying philosophy of many existing international co-production agreements is that the rights in the co-production are exercised separately and independently by each co-producer, by dividing the exploitation rights between them along territorial lines; whereas, as a general rule, in the situation where a communication to the public by satellite authorized by one co-producer would prejudice the value of the exploitation rights of another co-producer, the interpretation of such an existing agreement would normally suggest that the latter co-producer would have to give his consent to the authorization, by the former co-producer, of the communication to the public by satellite; whereas the language exclusivity of the latter co-producer will be prejudiced where the language version or versions of the communication to the public, including where the version is dubbed or subtitled, coincide(s) with the language or the languages widely

understood in the territory allotted by the agreement to the latter co-producer; whereas the notion of exclusivity should be understood in a wider sense where the communication to the public by satellite concerns a work which consists merely of images and contains no dialogue or subtitles; whereas a clear rule is necessary in cases where the international co-production agreement does not expressly regulate the division of rights in the specific case of communication to the public by satellite within the meaning of this Directive;

(20) Whereas communications to the public by satellite from non-member countries will under certain conditions be deemed to occur within a Member State of the Community;

(21) Whereas it is necessary to ensure that protection for authors, performers, producers of phonograms and broadcasting organizations is accorded in all Member States and that this protection is not subject to a statutory licence system; whereas only in this way is it possible to ensure that any difference in the level of protection within the common market will not create distortions of competition;

(22) Whereas the advent of new technologies is likely to have an impact on both the quality and the quantity of the exploitation of works and other subject matter;

(23) Whereas in the light of these developments the level of protection granted pursuant to this Directive to all rightholders in the areas covered by this Directive should remain under consideration;

(24) Whereas the harmonization of legislation envisaged in this Directive entails the harmonization of the provisions ensuring a high level of protection of authors, performers, phonogram producers and broadcasting organizations; whereas this harmonization should not allow a broadcasting organization to take advantage of differences in levels of protection by relocating activities, to the detriment of audiovisual productions;

(25) Wheres the protection provided for rights related to copyright should be aligned on that contained in Council Directive 92/100/EEC of 19 November 1992 on rental right and lending right and on certain rights related to copyright in the field of intellectual property for the purposes of communication to the public by satellite; whereas, in particular, this will ensure that performers and phonogram producers are guaranteed an appropriate remuneration for the communication to the public by satellite of their performances or phonograms;

(26) Whereas the provisions of Article 4 do not prevent Member States from extending the presumption set out in Article 2(5) of Directive 92/100/EEC to the exclusive rights referred to in Article 4; whereas, furthermore, the provisions of Article 4 do not prevent Member States from providing for a rebuttable presumption of the authoriztion of exploitation in respect of the exclusive rights of performers referred to in that Article, in so far as such presumption is compatible with the International Convention for the Protection of Performers, Producers of Phonograms and Broadcasting Organizations;

(27) Whereas the cable retransmission of programmes from other Member States is an act subject to copyright and, as the case may be, rights related to copyright; whereas the cable operator must, therefore, obtain the authorization from every holder of rights in each part of the programme retransmitted; whereas, pursuant to this Directive, the authorizations should be granted contractually unless a temporary exception is provided for in the case of existing legal licence schemes;

(28) Whereas, in order to ensure that the smooth operation of contractual arrangements is not called into question by the intervention of outsiders holding

rights in individual parts of the programme, provision should be made, through the obligation to have recourse to a collecting society, for the exclusive collective exercise of the authorization right to the extent that this is required by the special features of cable retransmission; whereas the authorization right as such remains intact and only the exercise of this right is regulated to some extent, so that the right to authorize a cable retransmission can still be assigned; whereas this Directive does not affect the exercise of moral rights;

(29) Whereas the exemption provided for in Article 10 should not limit the choice of holders of rights to transfer their rights to a collecting society and thereby have a direct share in the remuneration paid by the cable distributor for cable retransmission;

(30) Whereas contractual arrangements regarding the authorization of cable retransmission should be promoted by additional measures; whereas a party seeking the conclusion of a general contract should, for its part, be obliged to submit collective proposals for an agreement; whereas, furthermore, any party shall be entitled, at any moment, to call upon the assistance of impartial mediators whose task is to assist negotiations and who may submit proposals; whereas any such proposals and any opposition thereto should be served on the parties concerned in accordance with the applicable rules concerning the service of legal documents, in particular as set out in existing international conventions; whereas, finally, it is necessary to ensure that the negotiations are not blocked without valid justification or that individual holders are not prevented without valid justification from taking part in the negotiations; whereas none of these measures for the promotion of the acquisition of rights calls into question the contractual nature of the acquisition of cable retransmission rights;

(31) Whereas for a transitional period Member States should be allowed to retain existing bodies with jurisdiction in their territory over cases where the right to retransmit a programme by cable to the public has been unreasonably refused or offered on unreasonable terms by a broadcasting organization; whereas it is understood that the right of parties concerned to be heard by the body should be guaranteed and that the existence of the body should not prevent the parties concerned from having normal access to the courts;

(32) Whereas, however, Community rules are not needed to deal with all of those matters, the effects of which perhaps with some commercially insignificant exceptions, are felt only inside the borders of a single Member State;

(33) Whereas minimum rules should be laid down in order to establish and guarantee free and uninterrupted cross-border broadcasting by satellite and simultaneous, unaltered cable retransmission of programmes broadcast from other Member States, on an essentially contractual basis;

(34) Whereas this Directive should not prejudice further harmonization in the field of copyright and rights related to copyright and the collective administration of such rights; whereas the possibility for Member States to regulate the activities of collecting societies should not prejudice the freedom of contractual negotiation of the rights provided for in this Directive, on the understanding that such negotiation takes place within the framework of general or specific national rules with regard to competition law or the prevention of abuse of monopolies;

(35) Whereas it should, therefore, be for the Member States to supplement the general provisions needed to achieve the objectives of this Directive by taking legislative and administrative measures in their domestic law, provided that these do not run counter to the objectives of this Directive and are compatible with Community law;

(36) Whereas this Directive does not affect the applicability of the competition rules in Articles 85 and 86 of the Treaty,

HAS ADOPTED THIS DIRECTIVE:

## CHAPTER I

## DEFINITIONS

*Article 1*

**Definitions**

**1.** For the purpose of this Directive, 'satellite' means any satellite operating on frequency bands which, under telecommunications law, are reserved for the broadcast of signals for reception by the public or which are reserved for closed, point-to-point communication. In the latter case, however, the circumstances in which individual reception of the signals takes place must be comparable to those which apply in the first case.

**2.**  (a)  For the purpose of this Directive, 'communication to the public by satellite' means the act of introducing, under the control and responsibility of the broadcasting organization, the programme-carrying signals intended for reception by the public into an uninterrupted chain of communication leading to the satellite and down towards the earth.

(b) The act of communication to the public by satellite occurs solely in the Member State where, under the control and responsibility of the broadcasting organization, the programme-carrying signals are introduced into an uninterrupted chain of communication leading to the satellite and down towards the earth.

(c) If the programme-carrying signals are encrypted, then there is communication to the public by satellite on condition that the means for decrypting the broadcast are provided to the public by the broadcasting organization or with its consent.

(d) Where an act of communication to the public by satellite occurs in a non-Community State which does not provide the level of protection provided for under Chapter II,

(i) if the programme-carrying signals are transmitted to the satellite from an uplink situation situated in a Member State, that act of communication to the public by satellite shall be deemed to have occurred in that Member State and the rights provided for under Chapter II shall be exercisable against the person operating the uplink station; or

(ii) if there is no use of an uplink station situated in a Member State but a broadcasting organization established in a Member State has commissioned the act of communication to the public by satellite, that act shall be deemed to have occured in the Member State in which the broadcasting organization has its principal establishment in the Community and the rights provided for under Chapter II shall be exercisable against the broadcasting organization.

**3.** For the purposes of this Directive, 'cable retransmission' means the simultaneous, unaltered and unabridged retransmission by a cable or microwave system for reception by the public of an initial transmission from another Member State, by wire or over the air, including that by satellite, of television or radio programmes intended for reception by the public.

**4.** For the purposes of this Directive 'collecting society' means any organization which manages or administers copyright or rights related to copyright as its sole purpose or as one of its main purposes.

**5.** For the purposes of this Directive, the principal director of a cinematographic or audiovisual work shall be considered as its author or one of its authors. Member States may provide for others to be considered as its co-authors.

## CHAPTER II

### BROADCASTING OF PROGRAMMES BY SATELLITE

*Article 2*

**Broadcasting right**

Member States shall provide an exclusive right for the author to authorize the communication to the public by satellite of copyright works, subject to the provisions set out in this chapter.

*Article 3*

**Acquisition of broadcasting rights**

**1.** Member States shall ensure that the authorization referred to in Article 2 may be acquired only by agreement.

**2.** A Member State may provide that a collective agreement between a collecting society and a broadcasting organization concerning a given category of works may be extended to rightholders of the same category who are not represented by the collecting society, provided that:

— the communication to the public by satellite simulcasts a terrestrial broadcast by the same broadcaster, and
— the unrepresented rightholder shall, at any time, have the possibility of excluding the extension of the collective agreement to his works and of exercising his rights either individually or collectively.

**3.** Paragraph 2 shall not apply to cinematographic works, including works created by a process analogous to cinematography.

**4.** Where the law of a Member State provides for the extension of a collective agreement in accordance with the provisions of paragraph 2, that Member States shall inform the Commission which broadcasting organizations are entitled to avail themselves of that law. The Commission shall publish this information in the *Official Journal of the European Communities* (C series).

*Article 4*

**Rights of performers, phonogram producers and broadcasting organizations**

**1.** For the purposes of communication to the public by satellite, the rights of performers, phonogram producers and broadcasting organizations shall be protected in accordance with the provisions of Articles 6, 7, 8 and 10 of Directive 92/100/EEC.

**2.** For the purposes of paragraph 1, 'broadcasting by wireless means' in Directive 92/100/EEC shall be understood as including communication to the public by satellite.

**3.** With regard to the exercise of the rights referred to in paragraph 1, Articles 2 (7) and 12 of Directive 92/100/EEC shall apply.

*Article 5*

**Relation between copyright and related rights**

Protection of copyright-related rights under this Directive shall leave intact and shall in no way affect the protection of copyright.

*Article 6*

**Minimum protection**

**1.** Member States may provide for more far-reaching protection for holders of rights related to copyright than that required by Article 8 of Directive 92/100/EEC.

**2.** In applying paragraph 1 Member States shall observe the definitions contained in Article 1(1) and (2).

*Article 7*

**Transitional provisions**

**1.** With regard to the application in time of the rights referred to in Article 4(1) of this Directive, Article 13(1), (2), (6) and (7) of Directive 92/100/EEC shall apply. Article 13(4) and (5) of Directive 92/100/EEC shall apply *mutatis mutandis*.

**2.** Agreements concerning the exploitation of works and other protected subject matter which are in force on the date mentioned in Article 14(1) shall be subject to the provisions of Articles 1(2), 2 and 3 as from 1 January 2000 if they expire after that date.

**3.** When an international co-production agreement concluded before the date mentioned in Article 14 (1) between a co-producer from a Member State and one or more co-producers from other Member States or third countries expressly provides for a system of division of exploitation rights between the co-producers by geographical areas for all means of communication to the public, without distinguishing the arrangement applicable to communication to the public by satellite from the provisions applicable to the other means of communication, and where communication to the public by satellite of the co-production would prejudice the exclusivity, in particular the language exclusivity, of one of the co-producers or his assignees in a given territory, the authorization by one of the co-producers or his assignees for a communication to the public by satellite shall require the prior consent of the holder of that exclusivity, whether co-producer or assignee.

## CHAPTER III

### CABLE RETRANSMISSION

*Article 8*

### Cable retransmission right

**1.** Member States shall ensure that when programmes from other Member States are retransmitted by cable in their territory the applicable copyright and related rights are observed and that such retransmission takes place on the basis of individual or collective contractual agreements between copyright owners, holders of related rights and cable operators.

**2.** Notwithstanding paragraph 1, Member States may retain until 31 December 1997 such statutory licence systems which are in operation or expressly provided for by national law on 31 July 1991.

*Article 9*

### Exercise of the cable retransmission right

**1.** Member States shall ensure that the right of copyright owners and holders or related rights to grant or refuse authorization to a cable operator for a cable retransmission may be exercised only through a collecting society.

**2.** Where a rightholder has not transferred the management of his rights to a collecting society, the collecting society which manages rights of the same category shall be deemed to be mandated to manage his rights. Where more than one collecting society manages rights of that category, the rightholder shall be free to choose which of those collecting societies is deemed to be mandated to manage his rights. A rightholder referred to in this paragraph shall have the same rights and obligations resulting from the agreement between the cable operator and the collecting society which is deemed to be mandated to manage his rights as the rightholders who have mandated that collecting society and he shall be able to claim those rights within a period, to be fixed by the Member State concerned, which shall not be shorter than three years from the date of the cable retransmission which includes his work or other protected subject matter.

**3.** A Member State may provide that, when a right-holder authorizes the initial transmission within its territory of a work or other protected subject matter, he shall be deemed to have agreed not to exercise his cable retransmission rights on an individual basis but to exercise them in accordance with the provisions of this Directive.

*Article 10*

### Exercise of the cable retransmission right by broadcasting organizations

Member States shall ensure that Article 9 does not apply to the rights exercised by a broadcasting organization in respect of its own transmission, irrespective of whether the rights concerned are its own or have been transferred to it by other copyright owners and/or holders of related rights.

*Article 11*

### Mediators

**1.** Where no agreement is concluded regarding authorization of the cable retransmission of a broadcast. Member States shall ensure that either party may call upon the assistance of one or more mediators.

**2.** The task of the mediators shall be to provide assistance with negotiation. They may also submit proposals to the parties.

**3.** It shall be assumed that all the parties accept a proposal as referred to in paragraph 2 if none of them expresses its opposition within a period of three months. Notice of the proposal and of any opposition thereto shall be served on the parties concerned in accordance with the applicable rules concerning the service of legal documents.

**4.** The mediators shall be so selected that their independence and impartiality and beyond reasonable doubt.

*Article 12*

**Prevention of the abuse of negotiating positions**

**1.** Member States shall ensure by means of civil or administrative law, as appropriate, that the parties enter and conduct negotiations regarding authorization for cable retransmission in good faith and do not prevent or hinder negotiation without valid justification.

**2.** A Member State which, on the date mentioned in Article 14(1), has a body with jurisdiction in its territory over cases where the right to retransmit a programme by cable to the public in that Member State has been unreasonably refused or offered on unreasonable terms by a broadcasting organization may retain that body.

**3.** Paragraph 2 shall apply for a transitional period of eight years from the date mentioned in Article 14(1).

CHAPTER IV

**GENERAL PROVISIONS**

*Article 13*

**Collective administration of rights**

This Directive shall be without prejudice to the regulation of the activities of collecting societies by the Member States.

*Article 14*

**Final provisions**

**1.** Member States shall bring into force the laws, regulations and administrative provisions necessary to comply with this Directive before 1 January 1995. They shall immediately inform the Commission thereof.

When Member States adopt these measures, the latter shall contain a reference to this Directive or shall be accompanied by such reference at the time of their official publication. The methods of making such a reference shall be laid down by the Member States.

**2.** Member States shall communicate to the Commission the provisions of national law which they adopt in the field covered by this Directive.

**3.** Not later than 1 January 2000, the Commission shall submit to the European Parliament, the Council and the Economic and Social Committee a report on the application of this Directive and, if necessary, make further proposals to adapt it to developments in the audio and audiovisual sector.

*Article 15*

This Directive is addressed to the Member States.
Done at Brussels, 27 September 1993.

COUNCIL DIRECTIVE (93/98/EEC) OF 29 OCTOBER 1993
HARMONIZING THE TERM OF PROTECTION OF COPYRIGHT AND
CERTAIN RELATED RIGHTS

THE COUNCIL OF THE EUROPEAN COMMUNITIES,
    Having regard to the Treaty establishing the European Economic Community, and in particular Articles 57(2), 66 and 100a thereof,
    Having regard to the proposal from the Commission,
    In cooperation with the European Parliament,
    Having regard to the opinion of the Economic and Social Committee,
(1) Whereas the Berne Convention for the Protection of Literary and Artistic Works and the International Convention for the protection of performers, producers of phonograms and broadcasting organizations (Rome Convention) lay down only minimum terms of protection of the rights they refer to, leaving the Contracting States free to grant longer terms; whereas certain Member States have exercised this entitlement; whereas in addition certain Member States have not become party to the Rome Convention;
    (2) Whereas there are consequently differences between the national laws governing the terms of protection of copyright and related rights, which are liable to impede the free movement of goods and freedom to provide services, and to distort competition in the common market; whereas therefore with a view to the smooth operation of the internal market, the laws of the Member States should be harmonized so as to make terms of protection identical throughout the Community;
    (3) Whereas harmonization must cover not only the terms of protection as such, but also certain implementing arrangements such as the date from which each term of protection is calculated;
    (4) Whereas the provisions of this Directive do not affect the application by the Member States of the provisions of Article 14a (2) (b), (c) and (d) and (3) of the Berne Convention;
    (5) Whereas the minimum term of protection laid down by the Berne Convention, namely the life of the author and 50 years after his death, was intended to provide protection for the author and the first two generations of his descendants; whereas the average lifespan in the Community has grown longer, to the point where this term is no longer sufficient to cover two generations;
    (6) Whereas certain Member States have granted a term longer than 50 years after the death of the author in order to offset the effects of the world wars on the exploitation of authors' works;
    (7) Whereas for the protection of related rights certain Member States have introduced a term of 50 years after lawful publication or lawful communication to the public;
    (8) Whereas under the Community position adopted for the Uruguay Round negotiations under the General Agreement on Tariffs and Trade (GATT) the term

of protection for producers of phonograms should be 50 years after first publication;

(9) Whereas due regard for established rights is one of the general principles of law protected by the Community legal order; whereas, therefore, a harmonization of the terms of protection of copyright and related rights cannot have the effect of reducing the protection currently enjoyed by rightholders in the Community; whereas in order to keep the effects of transitional measures to a minimum and to allow the internal market to operate in practice, the harmonization of the term of protection should take place on a long term basis;

(10) Whereas in its communication of 17 January 1991 'Follow-up to the Green Paper – Working programme of the Commission in the field of copyright and neighbouring rights' the Commission stresses the need to harmonize copyright and neighbouring rights at a high level of protection since these rights are fundamental to intellectual creation and stresses that their protection ensures the maintenance and development of creativity in the interest of authors, cultural industries, consumers and society as a whole;

(11) Whereas in order to establish a high level of protection which at the same time meets the requirements of the internal market and the need to establish a legal environment conducive to the harmonious development of literary and artistic creation in the Community, the term of protection for copyright should be harmonized at 70 years after the death of the author or 70 years after the work is lawfully made available to the public, and for related rights at 50 years after the event which sets the term running;

(12) Whereas collections are protected according to Article 2(5) of the Berne Convention when, by reason of the selection and arrangement of their content, they constitute intellectual creations; whereas those works are protected as such, without prejudice to the copyright in each of the works forming part of such collections, whereas in consequence specific terms of protection may apply to works included in collections;

(13) Whereas in all cases where one or more physical persons are identified as authors the term of protection should be calculated after their death; whereas the question of authorship in the whole or a part of a work is a question of fact which the national courts may have to decide;

(14) Whereas terms of protection should be calculated from the first day of January of the year following the relevant event, as they are in the Berne and Rome Conventions;

(15) Whereas Article 1 of Council Directive 91/250/EEC of 14 May 1991 on the legal protection of computer programs provides that Member States are to protect computer programs, by copyright, as literary works within the meaning of the Berne Convention; whereas this Directive harmonizes the term of protection of literary works in the Community; whereas Article 8 of Directive 91/250/EEC, which merely makes provisional arrangements governing the term of protection of computer programs, should accordingly be repealed;

(16) Whereas Articles 11 and 12 of Council Directive 92/100/EEC of 19 November 1992 on rental right and lending right and on certain rights related to copyright in the field of intellectual property make provision for minimum terms of protection only, subject to any further harmonization; whereas this Directive provides such further harmonization; whereas these Articles should accordingly be repealed;

(17) Whereas the protection of photographs in the Member States is the subject of varying regimes; whereas in order to achieve a sufficient harmonization of the

term of protection of photographic works, in particular of those which, due to their artistic or professional character, are of importance within the internal market, it is necessary to define the level of originality required in this Directive; whereas a photographic work within the meaning of the Berne Convention is to be considered original if it is the author's own intellectual creation reflecting his personality, no other criteria such as merit or purpose being taken into account; whereas the protection of other photographs should be left to national law;

(18) Whereas, in order to avoid differences in the term of protection as regards related rights it is necessary to provide the same starting point for the calculation of the term throughout the Community; whereas the performance, fixation, transmission, lawful publication, and lawful communication to the public, that is to say the means of making a subject of a related right perceptible in all appropriate ways to persons in general, should be taken into account for the calculation of the term of protection regardless of the country where this performance, fixation, transmission, lawful publication, or lawful communication to the public takes place;

(19) Whereas the rights of broadcasting organizations in their broadcasts, whether these broadcasts are transmitted by wire or over the air, including by cable or satellite, should not be perpetual; whereas it is therefore necessary to have the term of protection running from the first transmission of a particular broadcast only; whereas this provision is understood to avoid a new term running in cases where a broadcast is identical to a previous one;

(20) Whereas the Member States should remain free to maintain or introduce other rights related to copyright in particular in relation to the protection of critical and scientific publications; whereas, in order to ensure transparency at Community level, it is however necessary for Member States which introduce new related rights to notify the Commission;

(21) Whereas it is useful to make clear that the harmonization brought about by this Directive does not apply to moral rights;

(22) Whereas, for works whose country of origin within the meaning of the Berne Convention is a third country and whose author is not a Community national, comparison of terms of protection should be applied, provided that the term accorded in the Community does not exceed the term laid down in this Directive;

(23) Whereas where a rightholder who is not a Community national qualifies for protection under an international agreement the term of protection of related rights should be the same as that laid down in this Directive, except that it should not exceed that fixed in the country of which the rightholder is a national;

(24) Whereas comparison of terms should not result in Member States being brought into conflict with their international obligations;

(25) Whereas, for the smooth functioning of the internal market this Directive should be applied as from 1 July 1995;

(26) Whereas Member States should remain free to adopt provisions on the interpretation, adaptation and further execution of contracts on the exploitation of protected works and other subject matter which were concluded before the extension of the term of protection resulting from this Directive;

(27) Whereas respect of acquired rights and legitimate expectations is part of the Community legal order; whereas Member States may provide in particular that in certain circumstances the copyright and related rights which are revived pursuant to this Directive may not give rise to payments by persons who undertook

in good faith the exploitation of the works at the time when such works lay within the public domain,

HAS ADOPTED THIS DIRECTIVE:

*Article 1*

**Duration of authors' rights**

**1.** The rights of an author of a literary or artistic work within the meaning of Article 2 of the Berne Convention shall run for the life of the author and for 70 years after his death, irrespective of the date when the work is lawfully made available to the public.

**2.** In the case of a work of joint authorship the term referred to in paragraph 1 shall be calculated from the death of the last surviving author.

**3.** In the case of anonymous or pseudonymous works, the term of protection shall run for seventy years after the work is lawfully made available to the public. However, when the pseudonym adopted by the author leaves no doubt as to his identity, or if the author discloses his identity during the period referred to in the first sentence, the term of protection applicable shall be that laid down in paragraph 1.

**4.** Where a Member State provides for particular provisions on copyright in respect of collective works or for a legal person to be designated as the rightholder, the term of protection shall be calculated according to the provisions of paragraph 3, except if the natural persons who have created the work as such are identified as such in the versions of the work which are made available to the public. This paragraph is without prejudice to the rights of identified authors whose identifiable contributions are included in such works, to which contributions paragraph 1 or 2 shall apply.

**5.** Where a work is published in volumes, parts, instalments, issues or episodes and the term of protection runs from the time when the work was lawfully made available to the public, the term of protection shall run for each such item separately.

**6.** In the case of works for which the term of protection is not calculated from the death of the author or authors and which have not been lawfully made available to the public within seventy years from their creation, the protection shall terminate.

*Article 2*

**Cinematographic or audiovisual works**

**1.** The principal director of a cinematographic or audiovisual work shall be considered as its author or one of its authors. Member States shall be free to designate other co-authors.

**2.** The term of protection of cinematographic or audiovisual works shall expire 70 years after the death of the last of the following persons to survive, whether or not these persons are designated as co-authors: the principal director, the author of the screenplay, the author of the dialogue and the composer of music specifically created for use in the cinematographic or audiovisual work.

*Article 3*

## Duration of related rights

**1.** The rights of performers shall expire 50 years after the date of the performance. However, if a fixation of the performance is lawfully published or lawfully communicated to the public within this period, the rights shall expire 50 years from the date of the first such publication or the first such communication to the public, whichever is the earlier.

**2.** The rights of producers of phonograms shall expire 50 years after the fixation is made. However, if the phonogram is lawfully published or lawfully communicated to the public during this period, the rights shall expire 50 years from the date of the first such publication or the first such communication to the public, whichever is the earlier.

**3.** The rights of producers of the first fixation of a film shall expire 50 years after the fixation is made. However, if the film is lawfully published or lawfully communicated to the public during this period, the rights shall expire 50 years from the date of the first such publication or the first such communication to the public, whichever is the earlier. The term 'film' shall designate a cinematographic or audiovisual work or moving images, whether or not accompanied by sound.

**4.** The rights of broadcasting organizations shall expire 50 years after the first transmission of a broadcast, whether this broadcast is transmitted by wire or over the air, including by cable or satellite.

*Article 4*

## Protection of previously unpublished works

Any person who, after the expiry of copyright protection, for the first time lawfully publishes or lawfully communicates to the public a previously unpublished work, shall benefit from a protection equivalent to the economic rights of the author. The term of protection of such rights shall be 25 years from the time when the work was first lawfully published or lawfully communicated to the public.

*Article 5*

## Critical and scientific publications

Member States may protect critical and scientific publications of works which have come into the public domain. The maximum term of protection of such rights shall be 30 years from the time when the publication was first lawfully published.

*Article 6*

## Protection of photographs

Photographs which are original in the sense that they are the author's own intellectual creation shall be protected in accordance with Article 1. No other criteria shall be applied to determine their eligibility for protection. Member States may provide for the protection of other photographs.

*Article 7*

## Protection vis-à-vis third countries

**1.** Where the country of origin of a work, within the meaning of the Berne Convention, is a third country, and the author of the work is not a Community national, the term of protection granted by the Member States shall expire on the date of expiry of the protection granted in the country of origin of the work, but may not exceed the term laid down in Article 1.

**2.** The terms of protection laid down in Article 3 shall also apply in the case of rightholders who are not Community nationals, provided Member States grant them protection. However, without prejudice to the international obligations of the Member States, the term of protection granted by Member States shall expire no later than the date of expiry of the protection granted in the country of which the rightholder is a national and may not exceed the term laid down in Article 3.

**3.** Member States which, at the date of adoption of this Directive, in particular pursuant to their international obligations, granted a longer term of protection than that which would result from the provisions, referred to in paragraphs 1 and 2 may maintain this protection until the conclusion of international agreements on the term of protection by copyright or related rights.

*Article 8*

**Calculation of terms**

The terms laid down in this Directive are calculated from the first day of January of the year following the event which gives rise to them.

*Article 9*

**Moral rights**

This Directive shall be without prejudice to the provisions of the Member States regulating moral rights.

*Article 10*

**Application in time**

**1.** Where a term of protection, which is longer than the corresponding term provided for by this Directive, is already running in a Member State on the date referred to in Article 13(1), this Directive shall not have the effect of shortening that term of protection in that Member State.

**2.** The terms of protection provided for in this Directive shall apply to all works and subject matter which are protected in at least one Member State, on the date referred to in Article 13(1), pursuant to national provisions on copyright or related rights or which meet the criteria for protection under Directive 92/100/EEC.

**3.** This Directive shall be without prejudice to any acts of exploitation performed before the date referred to in Article 13(1). Member States shall adopt the necessary provisions to protect in particular acquired rights of third parties.

**4.** Member States need not apply the provisions of Article 2(1) to cinematographic or audiovisual works created before 1 July 1994.

**5.** Member States may determine the date as from which Article 2(1) shall apply, provided that date is no later than 1 July 1997.

*Article 11*

**Technical adaptation**

**1.** Article 8 of Directive 91/250/EEC is hereby repealed.

**2.** Articles 11 and 12 of Directive 92/100/EEC are hereby repealed.

*Article 12*

**Notification procedure**

Member States shall immediately notify the Commission of any governmental plan to grant new related rights, including the basic reasons for their introduction and the term of protection envisaged.

*Article 13*

**General provisions**

**1.** Member States shall bring into force the laws, regulations and administrative provisions necessary to comply with Articles 1 to 11 of this Directive before 1 July 1995.

When Member States adopt these provisions, they shall contain a reference to this Directive or shall be accompanied by such reference at the time of their official publication. The methods of making such a reference shall be laid down by the Member States.

Member States shall communicate to the Commission the texts of the provisions of national law which they adopt in the field governed by this Directive.

**2.** Member States shall apply Article 12 from the date of notification of this Directive.

*Article 14*

This Directive is addressed to the Member States.

Done at Brussels, 29 October 1993.

## PROPOSAL FOR A EUROPEAN PARLIAMENT AND COUNCIL DIRECTIVE ON THE LEGAL PROTECTION OF DESIGNS (93/C 345/09)

*COM(93) 344 final—COD 464*
*(Submitted by the Commission on 3 December 1993)*

THE EUROPEAN PARLIAMENT AND THE COUNCIL OF THE EUROPEAN UNION,

Having regard to the Treaty establishing the European Community and in particular Article 100a thereof,

Having regard to the proposal by the Commission,

Having regard to the opinion of the Economic and Social Committee,

**1.** Whereas the objectives of the Community as laid down in the Treaty include establishing an ever closer union among the peoples of Europe, fostering closer relations between the States belonging to the Community, and ensuring the economic and social progress of the Community countries by common action to eliminate the barriers which divide Europe, whereas to that end the Treaty provides for the establishment of an internal market and includes the abolition of obstacles to the free movement of goods and the institution of a system ensuring that competition in the common market is not distorted, whereas an approximation of the laws of the Member States on the legal protection of designs would further those objectives;

**2.** Whereas designs are not at present protected in all Member States by specific legislation and such protection, where it exists, has different attributes;

**3.** Whereas such differences in the legal protection of designs offered by the legislations of the Member States have direct and negative effects on the establishment and functioning of the internal market as regards goods embodying designs; whereas such differences will distort competition within the internal market;

**4.** Whereas it is therefore necessary for the proper functioning of the internal market to provide for specific design protection law in all Member States and to approximate the design protection laws of the Member States;

**5.** Whereas in doing so it is important to take into consideration the solutions and the advantages with which the Community design system will provide undertakings wishing to acquire design rights;

**6.** Whereas it is unnecessary to undertake a full-scale approximation of the design laws of the Member States, and it will be sufficient if approximation is limited to those national provisions of law which most directly affect the functioning of the internal market; whereas the objectives of this limited approximation cannot be sufficiently achieved by the Member States acting alone;

**7.** Whereas Member States should accordingly remain free to fix the procedural provisions concerning registration and invalidation of design rights and provisions concerning the effects of such invalidity;

**8.** Whereas this Directive does not exclude the application to designs of the legislation of the Member States other than that relating to the specific protection acquired by registration, such as the legislation relating to unregistered design rights, trademarks, patents and utility models, unfair competition or civil liability;

**9.** Whereas the attainment of the objectives of the internal market in the field of designs may only be fully realized following further harmonization of the relevant provisions of the copyright laws of Member States, in particular those relating to the criterion of originality; whereas, pending such further harmonization, it is important to establish the principle of cumulation of protection under specific registered design protection law and under copyright law, whilst leaving Member States free to establish the extent of copyright protection and the conditions under which such protection is conferred; whereas it is, however, necessary to abolish in the relationship between Member States the requirement that protection under copyright law shall be afforded only subject to reciprocity in the country of origin of the design, as such a requirement would run contrary to the principle of non-descrimination;

**10.** Whereas the attainment of the objectives of the internal market require that the conditions for obtaining a registered design right be not only identical in all the Member States but also identical to those required for obtaining a registered Community design; whereas to that end it is necessary to give a unitary definition of the notion of design and of the requirements as to novelty and individual character with which registered design rights must comply;

**11.** Whereas semiconductor products should not be excluded as products whose appearance could form the subject of a design right, since Member States may choose design legislation to implement the provisions of Council Directive 87/54/EEC of 16 December 1986 on the legal protection of topographies of semiconductor products.

**12.** Whereas it is essential, in order to facilitate the free movement of goods, to ensure that registered design rights confer upon the right holder the same protection in all Member States and that this protection is identical to the protection afforded by the registered Community design;

**13.** Whereas, in conformity with the applicable provisions on the Community

694

design, the interoperability of products of different makes should not be hindered by extending the protection to the design of mechanical fittings;

**14.** Whereas the mechanical fittings of modular products may nevertheless constitute an important element of the innovative characteristics of modular products and present a major marketing asset and therefore should be eligible for protection;

**15.** Whereas it is fundamental for the functioning of the internal market to unify the term of protection afforded by registered design rights in conformity with the solution adopted for the registered Community design;

**16.** Whereas the legal protection of design might in certain circumstances allow the creation of monopolies in generic products and captive markets by improperly binding consumers to a specific make of product, and thus the introduction of a provision is necessary in order to make the reproduction of designs applied to parts of complex products possible for repair purposes under very specific conditions;

**17.** Whereas the provisions of this Directive are without prejudice to the application of the competition rules under Articles 85 and 86 of the Treaty;

**18.** Whereas the grounds for refusal of registration in those Member States which provide for substantive examination of applications prior to registration, and the grounds for the invalidation of registered design rights in all the Member States, must be exhaustively enumerated,

HAVE ADOPTED THIS DIRECTIVE

*Article 1*

For the purpose of this Directive:

    (a)  'design' means the appearance of the whole or a part of a product resulting from the specific features of the lines, contours, colours, shape and/or materials of the product itself and/or its ornamentation;

    (b)  'product' means any industrial or handicraft item, including parts intended to be assembled into a complex item, sets or compositions of items, packaging, get-ups, graphic symbols and typographic typefaces, but excluding a computer program.

*Article 2*

This Directive shall apply to:

    (a)  design rights registered with the central industrial property offices of the Member States;

    (b)  design rights registered at the Benelux Design Office;

    (c)  design rights registered under international arrangements which have effect in a Member State;

    (d)  applications for design rights referred to under (a) to (c).

*Article 3*

**1.** Member States shall protect the designs upon registration, by conferring exclusive rights upon them in accordance with the provisions of the Directive.

**2.** A design shall be protected by a design right to the extent that it is new and has an individual character.

**3.** A design of a product which constitutes a part of a complex item shall only be considered to be new and to have an individual character in so far as the design applied to the part as such fulfils the requirement as to novelty and individual character.

## Article 4

**1.** A design shall be considered new if no identical design has been made available to the public before the date of filing the application for registration, or if a priority is claimed, the date of priority designs shall be deemed to be identical if their specific features differ only in immaterial details.
**2.** A design shall be deemed to have been made available to the public if it has been published following registration or otherwise, exhibited, used in trade or otherwise disclosed. It shall not, however, be deemed to have been made available to the public for the sole reason that it has been disclosed to a third person under explicit or implicit conditions of confidentiality.

## Article 5

**1.** A design shall be considered to have an individual character if the overall impression it produces on the informed user differs significantly from the overall impression produced on such a user by any design referred to in paragraph (2).
**2.** To be considered for the purpose of application of paragraph (1) a design must be:

   (a) commercialized in the market place, whether in the Community or elsewhere, at the date of the filing of the application for registration or, if a priority is claimed, at the date of priority; or
   (b) published following registration as a registered Community design or a design right of the Member State in question, the protection of which has not expired at the date of filing the application or registration or, if a priority is claimed, at the date of priority.

**3.** In order to assess individual character, common features shall as a matter of principle be given more weight than differences and the degree of freedom of the designer in developing the design shall be taken into consideration.

## Article 6

**1.** If a design for which protection is claimed under a registered design right of a Member State has been made available to the public by the designer or his successor in title or by a third person as a result of information provided or action taken by the designer or his successor in title or as a consequence of an abuse in relation to the designer or his successor in title during the 12-month period preceding the date of the filing of the application or, if a priority is claimed, the date of priority, such a disclosure shall not be taken into consideration for the purpose of applying Articles 4 and 5.
**2.** The provisions of paragraph (1) shall not apply if the subject of the abusive disclosure is a design which has resulted in a registered Community design or a registered design right of the Member State concerned.

## Article 7

**1.** A design right shall not subsist in a design to the extent that the realization of a technical function leaves no freedom as regards arbitrary features of appearance.

**2.** A design right shall not subsist in a design to the extent that it must necessarily be reproduced in its exact form and dimensions in order to permit the product in which the design is incorporated or to which it is applied to be mechanically assembled or connected with another product.

**3.** Notwithstanding paragraph (2), a design right shall under the conditions set out in Articles 4 and 5 subsist in a design serving the purpose of allowing simultaneous and infinite or multiple assembly or connection of identical or mutually interchangeable products within a modular system.

*Article 8*

A design right shall not subsist in a design the exploitation or publication of which is contrary to public policy or to the accepted principles of morality.

*Article 9*

**1.** The scope of the protection conferred by a design right shall include any design which produces on the informed user a significantly similar overall impression.

**2.** In order to assess the scope of protection, common features shall as a matter of principle be given more weight than differences and the degree of freedom of the designer in developing his design shall be taken into consideration.

*Article 10*

Upon registration a design which meets the requirements under Article 3 (2) shall be protected by a design right for a period of five years from the date of filing the application. The term of protection may be renewed for periods of five years each, up to a total term of 25 years from the date of filing.

*Article 11*

**1.** A design is excluded from registration, or if registered may be declared invalid, only in the following cases:

    (a) if the design does not fulfil the requirements under Article 3 (2), or
    (b) where its specific technical and/or interconnecting features are not eligible for protection under Article 7 (1) or (2), or
    (c) to the extent that its exploitation or publication is contrary to public policy or to accepted principles or morality, or
    (d) if the applicant for or the holder of the design right is not entitled to it under the law of the Member State concerned.

**2.** A design right may also be declared invalid if a conflicting design which has been made available to the public after the date of the filing of the application or, if a priority is claimed, the date of priority, is protected from a date prior to the said date by a registered Community design or a design right of the Member State concerned, or by an application for such a right.

**3.** Any Member State may provide that, by way of derogation from the preceding paragraphs, the grounds for refusal of registration or for invalidation in force in that State prior to the date on which the provisions necessary to comply with this Directive enter into force, shall apply to design rights for which application has been made prior to that date.

*Article 12*

**1.** Upon registration a design right shall confer on its holder the exclusive right to use the design and to prevent any third party not having his consent from using a design included within the scope of protection of the design right. The aforementioned use shall cover, in particular, the making, offering, putting on the market or using of a product in which such a design is incorporated or to which it is applied, or from importing, exporting or stocking such a product for those purposes.

**2.** Where, under the law of a Member State, acts referred to in paragraph (1) could not be prohibited before the date on which the provisions necessary to comply with this Directive entered into force, the rights conferred by the design right conferred by the design right may not be relied on to prevent continuation of such acts.

*Article 13*

**1.** The rights conferred by a design right upon registration shall not extend to:

    (a) acts done privately and for non-commercial purposes;

    (b) acts done for experimental purposes;

    (c) acts of reproduction for the purposes of making citations or of teaching, provided that such acts are compatible with fair trade practice and do not unduly prejudice the normal exploitation of the design, and that mention is made of the source.

**2.** In addition, the rights conferred by a design right upon registration shall not extend to:

    (a) the equipment on ships and aircraft registered in another country when these temporarily enter the territory of the Member State concerned;

    (b) the importation in the Member State concerned of spare parts and accessories for the purpose of repairing such craft;

    (c) the execution of repairs on such craft.

*Article 14*

The rights conferred by a design right shall not be exercised against third parties who, after three years from the first putting on the market of a product incorporating the design or to which the design is applied, use the design under Article 12, provided that:

    (a) the product incorporating the design or to which the design is applied is a part of a complex product upon whose appearance the protected design is dependent;

    (b) the purpose of such a use is to permit the repair of the complex product so as to restore its original appearance; and

    (c) the public is not misled as to the origin of the product used for the repair.

*Article 15*

The rights conferred by a design right upon registration shall not extend to acts relating to a product in which a design included within the scope of protection of the design right is incorporated or to which it is applied, when the product has been put on the market in the Community by the holder of the design right or with his consent.

*Article 16*

A design right may be declared invalid even after it has lapsed or has been surrendered.

*Article 17*

The provisions of this Directive shall be without prejudice to any legal provisions of the Community or of the Member State concerned relating to unregistered design rights, trademarks or other distinctive signs, patents and utility models, typefaces, civil liability, or unfair competition.

*Article 18*

**1.** Pending further harmonization of the laws of copyright of the Member States, a design protected by a design right registered in or for a Member State in accordance with this Directive shall also be eligible for protection under the law of copyright of that State as from the date on which the design was created or fixed in any form, irrespective of the number of products in which such design is intended to be incorporated or to which it is intended to be applied and irrespective of whether the design can be dissociated from the products in which it is intended to be incorporated or to which it is intended to be applied. The extent to which, and the conditions under which, such a protection is conferred, including the level of originality required, shall be determined by each Member State.
**2.** Pending further harmonization of the laws of copyright of the Member States, each Member State shall admit to the protection under its law of copyright a design protected by a design right registered in or for this State which fulfils the conditions required under such law, even if, in another Member State which is the country of origin of the design, the latter does not fulfil the conditions for protection under the law of copyright in that State.

*Article 19*

**1.** Member States shall bring into force the laws, regulations or administrative provisions necessary to comply with this Directive by 31 October 1996.

When Member States adopt these measures, these shall contain a reference to the Directive or shall be accompanied by such reference at the time of their official publication. The procedure for such reference shall be adopted by Member States.
**2.** Member States shall communicate to the Commission the provisions of national law which they adopt in the field governed by this Directive.

*Article 20*

This Directive is addressed to the Member States.

PROPOSAL FOR A EUROPEAN PARLIAMENT AND COUNCIL
REGULATION ON COMMUNITY DESIGN (94/C 29/02)

*COM(93) 342 final—COD 463*
*(Submitted by the Commission on 3 December 1993)*

THE EUROPEAN PARLIAMENT AND THE COUNCIL OF THE EUROPEAN UNION,
   Having regard to the Treaty establishing the European Community, and in
particular Article 100a thereof,
   Having regard to the proposal from the Commission,
   Having regard to the opinion of the Economic and Social Committee,
(1)  Whereas the objectives of the Community as laid down in the Treaty include
establishing an ever closer union among the peoples of Europe, fostering closer
relations between the States belonging to the Community, and ensuring the
economic and social progress of the Community countries by common action to
eliminate the barriers which divide Europe; whereas to that end the Treaty provides
for the establishment of an internal market and includes the abolition of obstacles
to the free movement of goods and the institution of a system ensuring that
competition in the common market is not distorted; whereas a unified system for
obtaining a Community design to which uniform protection is given with uniform
effect throughout the entire territory of the Community would further those
objectives;
   (2)  Whereas only the Benelux countries have introduced a uniform design
protection law; whereas the only other design protection that exists in the
Community is a matter for the relevant national law and is confined to the territory
of the Member State concerned; whereas there is no such relevant law in any one
Member State at the present time; whereas identical designs may be protected
differently in different Member States and for the benefit of different owners;
whereas this inevitably leads to conflicts in the course of trade between Member
States;
   (3)  Whereas the substantial differences between Member States' design laws
prevent and distort Community-wide competition between the producers of
protected goods, because in comparison with domestic trade in, and competition
between, products incorporating a design, trade and competition within the
Community are prevented and distorted by the large number of applications,
offices, procedures, laws, nationally circumscribed exclusive rights and the
combined administrative expense with correspondingly high costs and fees for the
applicant;
   (4)  Whereas the effect of design protection being limited to the territory of the
individual Member States whether or not their laws are approximated, leads to a
possible division of the internal market with respect to products incorporating a
particular design in areas with different right owners, and hence constitutes an
obstacle to the free movement of goods;
   (5)  Whereas this calls for the creation of a Community design right which is
directly applicable in each Member State, and of a Community design authority
with Community-wide powers, because only in this way will it be possible to
obtain, through one application made to one common design office in accordance
with a single procedure under one law, one design right for one area encompassing
all Member States;
   (6)  Whereas it is thus for the Community to adopt measures to achieve those
objectives, which cannot be achieved by the Member States acting individually

and which by reason of the scale and the effects of the creation of a Community design right and a Community design authority can only be achieved by the Community;

(7) Whereas superior design is an important attribute of Community industries in competition with industries from other countries, and is in many cases decisive in the commercial success of the associated product; whereas enhanced protection for industrial design not only promotes the contribution of individual designers to the sum of Community excellence in the field, but also encourages innovation and development of new products and investment in their production; whereas a more accessible design-protection system adapted to the needs of the internal market is therefore essential for Comunity industries;

(8) Whereas such a design-protection system would constitute the prerequisite for seeking corresponding design protection in the most important export markets of the Community;

(9) Whereas designs produced to meet a functional requirement and providing no opportunity for inclusion of further and arbitrary design features should, however, be excluded from such protection;

(10) Whereas interoperability of products of different makes should not be hindered by extending the protection to the design of mechanical fittings;

(11) Whereas mechanical fittings may nevertheless constitute an important element of the innovative characteristics of modular products especially designed to enable any number of such products, which may be identical or different but interchangeable, to be connected simultaneously in a modular system, and therefore should be eligible for protection; whereas this derogation should not prevent the replacement of one part of a non-modular system by a part of different make solely because the replacement part must possess a particular shape and configuration in order for the parts to work together in preforming the intended function of the system;

(12) Whereas the legal protection of design might in certain circumstances allow the creation of monopolies in generic products and captive markets by improperly binding consumers to a specific make of product and thus the introduction of a provision is necessary in order to make the reproduction of designs applied to parts of complex products possible for repair purposes under very specific conditions;

(13) Whereas the provisions of this Regulation are without prejudice to the application of the competition rules pursuant to Articles 85 and 86 of the Treaty;

(14) Whereas a Community design right should serve the needs of all sectors of industry in the Community; whereas those sectors are many and varied;

(15) Whereas some of the sectors produce large numbers of designs for products frequently having a short market life where protection without the burden of registration formalities is an advantage and the duration of protection is of lesser significance; whereas on the other hand, there are sectors of industry which value the advantages of registration for the greater legal certainty it provides and which require the possibility of a longer term of protection corresponding to the foreseeable market life of their products;

(16) Whereas this calls for two forms of protection, one being a short-term unregistered design right and the other being a longer term registered design right;

(17) Whereas a registered Community design right requires the creation and maintenance of a register in which will be registered all those applications which comply with formal conditions and which have been accorded a date of filing; whereas the performance of those functions requires a Community Design Office;

whereas the registration system should not be based upon substantive examination as to compliance with requirements for protection prior to registration, thereby keeping to a minimum the registration and other procedural burdens on applicants;

(18) Whereas a Community design right shall not be upheld unless the design is new in the sense that it is not identical to any other design previously made available to the public, and unless it also possesses an individual character in comparison with other designs which are currently exploited in the market, or which have previously been published following registration as being still valid Community designs or still valid design rights of a Member State;

(19) Whereas it is also necessary to allow the designer or his successor in title to test the products embodying the design in the market place before deciding whether the protection resulting from a registered Community design is desirable; whereas it is therefore necessary to provide that disclosures of the design by the designer or his successor in title, or abusive disclosures during a period of 12 months prior to the date of the filing of the application for a registered Community design should not be prejudicial in assessing the novelty or the individual character of the design in question;

(20) Whereas the exclusive nature of the right conferred by the registered Community design is consistent with its greater legal certainty; whereas it is appropriate that the unregistered Community design should, however, constitute a right only to prevent copying; whereas this right should also extend to trade in products embodying infringing designs;

(21) Whereas the enforcement of these rights is to be left to national laws and it is necessary therefore to provide for some basic uniform sanctions in all Member States; whereas these should make it possible, irrespective of the jurisdiction under which enforcement is sought, to stop the infringing acts, to obtain information about the infringer's source and distribution channels, and to seize infringing products;

(22) Whereas a procedure for hearing actions concerning validity of a registered Community design in a single place would bring savings in costs and time compared with procedures involving different national courts; whereas, if the single place were to be a court in the country where the design right holder is domiciled, undue costs and difficulties could still be encountered by a challenger to validity from another country; whereas it is appropriate in these cirumstances that the Community Design Office itself should hear direct actions raised by the Commission, Member States and third parties against validity;

(23) Whereas in particular the intervention of the Commission and Member States would contribute significantly to maintaining consistency of practice as regards the requirements for protection;

(24) Whereas it is necessary to provide safeguards including a right of appeal to a Board of Appeal, and ultimately to the Court of Justice of the European Communities; whereas such a procedure would assist the development of uniform interpretation of the requirements governing the validity of Community designs;

(25) Whereas it is a fundamental objective that the procedure for obtaining a registered Community design should present the minimum cost and difficulty to applicants, so as to make it readily available to small and medium-sized enterprises as well as to individual designers;

(26) Whereas sectors of industry producing large numbers of possibly short-lived designs over short periods of time of which only some may be eventually commercialized will find advantage in the unregistered Community design; whereas there is also a need for these sectors to have easier recourse to the

Registered Community design; whereas the option of combining a number of designs in one multiple application would satisfy that need;

(27) Whereas the normal publication following registration of a Community design could in some cases destroy or jeopardize the success of a commercial operation involving the design; whereas the facility of an adjournment of publication for a reasonable time affords a solution in such cases;

(28) Whereas it is essential that the rights conferred by the Community designs be enforced in an efficient manner throughout the territory of the Community; whereas specific rules concerning litigation based on Community designs must be provided in order to guarantee such a result; whereas for infringement actions and for actions for a declaration of invalidity a limitation in the number of national courts having jurisdiction may promote the specialization of the judges; whereas to that end Member States should designate Community Design Courts;

(29) Whereas the litigation system should avoid as far as possible 'forum shopping'; whereas it is therefore necessary to establish clear rules of international jurisdiction;

(30) Whereas this Regulation does not preclude the application to designs protected by Community designs or other relevant laws of the Member States, such as those relating to design protection acquired by registration or those relating to unregistered design rights, trade marks, patents and utility models, unfair competition or civil liability;

(31) Whereas, pending harmonization of copyright law, it is important to establish the principle of cumulation of protection under the Community design and under copyright law, whilst leaving Member States free to establish the extent of copyright protection and the conditions under which such protection is conferred; whereas in the relationship between Member States, Community law already prohibits Member States from requiring that protection under copyright law be afforded only subject to reciprocity; whereas it appears neccesary that national legal provisions and practice incompatible herewith be abolished,

HAVE ADOPTED THIS REGULATION:

TITLE I

**GENERAL PROVISIONS**

*Article 1*

**Community design**

**1.** Designs which comply with the conditions contained in this Regulation, hereinafter referred to as 'Community designs', shall be protected by a Community system of rights.

**2.** A design shall be protected under the terms of this Regulation:

    (a) by an 'unregistered Community design', without any formalities;

    (b) by a 'registered Community design', if registered in the manner provided for in this Regulation.

**3.** A Community design shall have a unitary character. It shall have equal effect throughout the Community; it shall not be registered, transferred or surrendered or be the subject of a decision declaring it invalid, save in respect of the whole Community. This principle and its implications shall apply unless otherwise provided in this Regulation.

*Article 2*

**Community Design Office**

A Community Design Office, hereinafter referred to as 'the Office', is hereby established.

TITLE II

**THE LAW RELATING TO DESIGNS**

Section 1
Requirements for protection

*Article 3*

**Definitions**

For the purposes of this Regulation:

    (a) 'design' means the appearance of the whole or a part of a product resulting from the specific features of the lines, contours, colours, shape and/or materials of the product itself and/or its ornamentation;

    (b) 'product' means any industrial or handicraft item, including parts intended to be assembled into a complex item, sets or compositions of items, packaging, get-ups, graphic symbols and typographic typefaces, but excluding a computer program or a semi-conductor product.

*Article 4*

**General requirements**

**1.** A design shall be protected by a Community design to the extent that it is new and has an individual character.

**2.** A design of a product which constitutes a part of a complex item shall only be considered to be new and to have an individual character in so far as the design applied to the part as such fulfils the requirements as to novelty and individual character.

*Article 5*

**Novelty**

**1.** A design shall be considered to be new if no identical design has been made available to the public before the date of reference. Designs shall be deemed to be identical if their specific features differ only in immaterial details.

**2.** A design shall be deemed to have been made available to the public if it has been published following registration or otherwise, exhibited, used in trade or otherwise disclosed. It shall not, however, be deemed to have been made available to the public for the sole reason that it has been disclosed to a third person under explicit or implicit conditions of confidentiality.

*Article 6*

**Individual character**

**1.** A design shall be considered to have an individual character if the overall impression it produces on the informed user differs significantly from the overall impression produced on such a user by any design referred to in paragraph 2.

**2.** To be considered for the purpose of application of paragraph 1, a design must be:

    (a)  commercialized in the market place at the date of reference whether in the Community or elsewhere; or

    (b)  published following registration as a registered Community design or as a design right of a Member State, provided that protection has not expired at the date of reference.

**3.** In order to assess individual character, common features shall as a matter of principle be given more weight than differences and the degree of freedom of the designer in developing design shall be taken into consideration.

*Article 7*

**Date of reference**

The date of reference within the meaning of the first sentence of Articles 5(1) and Article 6 (2) shall be:

    (a)  in the case of an unregistered Community design, the date on which the design for which protection is claimed was first made available to the public by the designer or his successor in title or by a third person as a result of information provided or action taken by the designer or his successor in title;

    (b)  in the case of registered Community design, the date of filing the application for registration or, if a priority is claimed, the date of priority.

*Article 8*

**Non-prejudicial disclosures**

**1.** If a design for which protection is claimed under a registration Community design has been made available to the public by the designer or his successor in title or by a third person as a result of information provided or action taken by the designer or his successor in title or as a consequence of an abuse in relation to the designer or his successor in title during the twelve-month period preceding the date of the filing of the application or, if a priority is claimed, the date of priority, such disclosure shall not be taken into consideration for the purpose of applying Articles 5 and 6.

**2.** The provisions of paragraph 1 shall not apply if the subject of the abusive disclosure is a design which has resulted in a registration Community design or a design right of a Member State.

*Article 9*

**Non-arbitrary technical designs, and designs of interconnections**

**1.** A Community design right shall not subsist in a design to the extent that the realization of a technical function leaves no freedom as regards arbitrary features of appearance.

**2.** A Community design right shall not subsist in a design to the extent that it must necessarily be reproduced in its exact form and dimensions in order to permit the product in which the design is incorporated or to which it is applied to be mechanically assembled or connected with another product.

**3.** Notwithstanding paragraph 2 a Community design right shall under the conditions set out in Articles 5 and 6 subsist in a design serving the purpose of allowing simultaneous and infinite or multiple assembly or connection of identical or mutually interchangeable products within a modular system.

*Article 10*

**Designs contrary to public policy**

A Community design right shall not subsist in a design the exploitation or publication of which is contrary to public policy or to accepted principles of mortality.

Section 2
Scope and term of protection

*Article 11*

**Scope of protection**

**1.** The scope of the protection conferred by a Community design shall include any design which produces on the informed user a significantly similar overall impression.

**2.** In order to assess the scope of protection, common features shall as a matter of principle be given more weight than differences and the degree of freedom of the designer in developing his design shall be taken into consideration.

*Article 12*

**Commencement and term of protection of the unregistered Community design**

A design which meets the requirements under Section 1 shall be protected without any formalities by an unregistered Community design for a period of three years as from the date referred to in Article 7(a).

*Article 13*

**Commencement and term of protection of the registered Community design**

Upon registration by the Office, a design which meets the requirements under Section 1 shall be protected by a registered design for a period of five years as from the date of the filing of the application. The term of protection may be extended in accordance with Article 53.

Section 3
Entitlement to the Community design

*Article 14*

**Right to the Community design**

**1.** The right to the Community design shall vest in the designer or his successor in title.

**2.** Where a design is developed by an employee in the execution of his duties or following the instructions given by his employer, the right to the Community design shall vest in the employer, unless otherwise provided by contract.

*Article 15*

**Plurality of designers**

If two or more persons have jointly developed a design, the right to the Community design shall vest in them jointly.

*Article 16*

**Claims relating to the entitlement to a Community design**

**1.** If the right to an unregistered Community design is claimed by, or a registered Community design has been registered in the name of, a person who is not entitled to it under Article 14, the person entitled to it under that provision may, without prejudice to any other remedy which may be open to him, claim to have the Community design transferred to him.

**2.** Where a person is jointly entitled to a Community design, that person may, in accordance with paragraph 1, claim to be made a joint holder.

**3.** In the case of a registered Community design, legal proceedings to seek the transfer under paragraph 1 may be instituted only within a period of not more than two years after the date of publication of the registered Community design. This provision shall not apply if the holder of the registered Community design knew that he was not entitled to it at the time when such design was registered or transferred to him.

**4.** In case of a registered Community design, the fact that legal proceedings under paragraph 1 have been instituted shall be entered in the register. Entry shall also be made of the final decision in, or of any other termination of, the proceedings.

*Article 17*

**Effects of a judgment on entitlement to a registered Community design**

**1.** Where there is a complete change of ownership of a registered Community design as a result of legal proceedings under Article 16(1), licences and other rights shall lapse upon the entering in the register of the person entitled.

**2.** If, before the institution of the legal proceedings under Article 16(1) has been registered, the holder of the registered Community design or a licensee has exploited the design within the Community or made serious and effective preparations to do so, he may continue such exploitation provided that he requests within the period prescribed by the implementing Regulation a non-exclusive licence from the new holder whose name is entered in the register. The licence shall be granted for a reasonable period and upon reasonable terms.

**3.** Paragraph 2 shall not apply if the right holder or the licensee was acting in bad faith at the time when he began to exploit the design or to make preparations to do so.

*Article 18*

**Presumption in favour of the registered person**

The person in whose name the application for a registered Community design was filed shall be deemed to be the person entitled in any proceedings before the Office.

*Article 19*

**Specific rights of the designer**

The designer shall have the right, as against the applicant for or the holder of a registered Community design, to be cited as such before the Office or in the register. If the design is the result of team-work, the indication of the team may replace the citation of the individual designers.

Section 4
Effects of the Community design

*Article 20*

**Rights conferred by the unregistered Community design**

An unregistered Community design shall confer on its holder the right to prevent any third party not having his consent from copying the design or from using a design included within the scope of protection of the unregistered Community design and resulting from such copying. The aforementioned use shall, in particular, cover the making, offering, putting on the market or using of a product in which such a design is incorporated or to which it is applied, and the importing, exporting or stocking of such a product for those purposes.

*Article 21*

**Rights conferred by the registered Community design**

**1.** A registered Community design shall confer on its holder the exclusive right to use the design and to prevent any third party not having his consent from using a design included within the scope of protection of the registered Community design. The aforementioned use shall, in particular, cover the making, offering, putting on the market or using of a product in which such a design is incorporated or to which it is applied, and the importing, exporting or stocking of such a product for those purposes.

**2.** Notwithstanding paragraph 1a registered Community design whose publication is deferred in accordance with Article 52 shall confer on its holder the rights referred to in Article 20.

*Article 22*

**Limitation of the rights conferred by a Community design**

**1.** The rights conferred by a Community design shall not extend to:

    (a)  acts done privately and for non-commercial purposes;
    (b)  acts done for experimental purposes;
    (c)  acts of reproduction for the purpose of making citations or of teaching, provided that such acts are compatible with fair trade practice and do

not unduly prejudice the normal exploitation of the design, and that mention is made of the source.

**2.** In addition, the rights conferred by a Community design shall not extend to:

(a) the equipment on ships and aircraft registered in a third country, when these temporarily enter the territory of the Community;

(b) the importation in the Community of spare parts and accessories for the purpose of repairing such craft;

(c) the execution of repairs on such craft.

*Article 23*

**Use of a registered Community design for repair purposes**

The rights conferred by a registered Community design shall not be exercised against third parties who, after three years from the first putting on the market of a product incorporating the design or to which the design is applied, use the design under Article 21, provided that:

(a) the product incorporating the design or to which the design is applied is a part of a complex product upon whose appearance the protected design is dependent;

(b) the purpose of such a use is to permit the repair of the complex product so as to restore its original appearance; and

(c) the public is not misled as to the origin of the product used for the repair.

*Article 24*

**Exhaustion**

The rights conferred by a Community design shall not extend to acts relating to a product in which a design included within the scope of protection of the Community design is incorporated or to which it is applied, when the product has been put on the market in the Community by the holder of the Community design or with his consent.

*Article 25*

**Rights of prior use in respect of a registered Community design**

The rights conferred by a registered Community design shall not become effective against any third person who can establish that:

(a) before the date of filing the application; or

(b) if a priority is claimed, before the date of priority,

he has, in good faith, commenced use within the Community—or has made serious preparations to that end—of a design included within the scope of protection of the registered Community design, which has been developed independently of the latter and which at such a date had not yet been made available to the public. Such a person shall be entitled to exploit the design for the needs of the undertaking in which the use was effected or anticipated. That right cannot be transferred separately from the undertaking.

Section 5
Invalidity

*Article 26*

**Declaration of invalidity**

**1.** A Community design may only be declared invalid by a Community Design Court. A registered Community design may also be declared invalid by the Office in accordance with the procedure in Title VII.
**2.** An application for a declaration of invalidity may be submitted even after the Community design has lapsed or has been surrendered.

*Article 27*

**Grounds for invalidity**

**1.** A Community design may be declared invalid only in the following cases:

    (a) if the design protected does not fulfil the requirements pursuant to Article 4; or
    (b) to the extent that its specific technical and/or interconnecting features are not eligible for protection under Article 9(1) or (2); or
    (c) to the extent that its exploitation or publication is contrary to public policy or to accepted principles of morality; or
    (d) if the right holder in the Community design is, by virtue of a court decision, not entitled under Articles 14 and 15.

**2.** A Community design may also be declared invalid if a conflicting design which has been made available to the public after the date of reference within the meaning of Article 7(a) or (b), as the case may be, is protected from a date prior to the said date of reference by a registered Community design or a registered design right of one or more Member States, or an application for such a right.
**3.** By derogation from Article 1(3):

    (a) in the case specified in paragraph 1(c), invalidity shall be declared only ·in respect of the Member State or States where the ground for invalidation obtains;
    (b) in the case specified in paragraph 2, to the extent that the rights in question, or applications for such rights, have effect only in respect of a Member State or States, invalidity shall be declared only in respect of such a Member State or States.

*Article 28*

**Effects of invalidity**

**1.** A Community design which has been declared invalid shall be deemed not to have had, from the outset, the effects specified in this Regulation.
**2.** Subject to the national provisions relating either to claims for compensation for damage caused by negligence or lack of good faith on the part of the holder of the Community design, or to unjust enrichment, the retroactive effect of invalidity of the Community design shall not affect:

    (a) any decision on infringement which has acquired the authority of a final decision and been enforced prior to the invalidity decision;

(b) any contract concluded prior to the invalidity decision, in so far as it has been performed before the decision; however, repayment, to an extent justified by the circumstances, of sums paid under the relevant contract, may be claimed on grounds of equity.

TITLE III

**COMMUNITY DESIGNS AS OBJECTS OF PROPERTY**

*Article 29*

**Dealing with Community designs as national design rights**

**1.** Save where Articles 30 to 34 provide otherwise, a Community design as an object of property shall be dealt with in its entirety, and for the whole area of the Community, as a national design right of the Member State in which:

(a) the holder has his seat or his domicile on the relevant date; or
(b) where subparagraph (a) does not apply, the holder has an establishment on the relevant date.

**2.** In the case of registered Community design, paragraph 1 shall apply according to the entries in the register.

**3.** In the case of joint holders, if two or more of them fulfil the condition under paragraph 1(a) or, where that provision does not apply, the condition under paragraph 1(b), the Member State referred to in paragraph 1 shall be determined:

(a) in the case of an unregistered Community design, by reference to the relevant joint holder designated by them by common agreement;
(b) in the case of a registered Community design, by reference to the first of the relevant joint holders in the order in which they are mentioned in the register.

**4.** Where paragraphs 1, 2 and 3 do not apply, the Member State referred to in paragraph 1 shall be the Member State in which the Office is situated.

*Article 30*

**Transfer**

**1.** A Community design may be transferred.

**2.** The transfer of a registered Community design shall be subject to the following provisions:

(a) at the request of one of the parties, a transfer shall be entered in the register and published;
(b) until such time as the transfer has been entered in the register, the successor in title may not invoke the rights arising from the registered Community design;
(c) where there are time limits to be observed in dealings with the Office, the successor in title may make the corresponding statements to the Office once the request for registration of the transfer has been received by the Office;
(d) all documents which require notification to the holder of the registered Community design shall be addressed to the person registered as holder or his representative, if one has been appointed.

*Article 31*

### Rights *in rem* on a registered Community design

**1.** A registered Community design may be given as security or be the subject of rights *in rem*.
**2.** At the request of one of the parties, rights mentioned in paragraph 1 shall be entered in the register and published.

*Article 32*

### Levy of execution on a registered Community design

**1.** A registered Community design may be levied in execution.
**2.** As regards the procedure for levy of execution in respect of a registered Community design, the courts and authorities of the Member State determined in accordance with Article 29 shall have exclusive jurisdiction.
**3.** On request of one of the parties, levy of execution shall be entered in the register and published.

*Article 33*

### Bankruptcy or like proceedings

**1.** Until such time as common rules for the Member States in this field enter into force, the only Member State in which a Community design may be involved in bankruptcy or like proceedings shall be that in which such proceedings are first brought under national law or conventions applicable in this field.
**2.** Where a registered Community design is involved in bankruptcy or like proceedings, an entry to that effect shall be made in the register at the request of the competent national authority and shall be published.

*Article 34*

### Licensing

**1.** A Community design may be licensed for the whole or part of the Community. A licence may be exclusive or non-exclusive.
**2.** Without prejudice to the provisions of the licensing contract, the licensee may bring proceedings for infringement of a Community design only if the right holder consents thereto. However, the holder of an exclusive licence may bring such proceedings if the right holder in the Community design, having been given notice to do so, does not himself bring infringement proceedings within an appropriate period.
**3.** A licensee shall, for the purpose of obtaining compensation for damage suffered by him, be entitled to intervene in an infringement action brought by the right holder in a Community design.
**4.** In the case of a registered Community design, the grant or transfer of a licence in respect of such right shall, at the request of one of the parties, be entered in the register and published.

*Article 35*

### Effects *vis-à-vis* third parties

**1.** The effects *vis-à-vis* third parties of the legal acts referred to in Articles 30, 31,

32 and 34 shall be governed by the law of the Member State determined in accordance with Article 29.

**2.** However, as regards registered Community designs, legal acts referred to in Article 30, 31 and 34 shall have effect only *vis-à-vis* third parties in all the Member States after entry in the register. Nevertheless, such an act, before it is so entered, shall have effect *vis-à-vis* third parties who have acquired rights in the registered Community design after the date of that act but who knew of the act at the date on which the rights were acquired.

**3.** Paragraph 2 shall not apply to a person who acquires the registered Community design or a right relating to it by way of transfer of the whole of the undertaking or by any other universal succession.

**4.** Until such time as common rules for the Member States in the field of bankruptcy enter into force, the effects *vis-à-vis* third parties of bankruptcy or like proceedings shall be governed by the law of the Member State in which such proceedings are first brought under national law or the conventions applicable in this field.

*Article 36*

**The application for a registered Community design as an object of property**

**1.** An application for a registered Community design as an object of property shall be dealt with in its entirety, and for the whole area of the Community, as a national design right of the Member State determined in accordance with Article 29.

**2.** Articles 30 to 35 shall apply *mutatis mutandis* to applications for registered Community designs. Where the effect of one of these provisions is conditional upon an entry in the register, that formality shall have to be performed upon registration of the resulting registered Community design.

TITLE IV

**APPLICATION FOR A REGISTERED COMMUNITY DESIGN**

Section 1
Filing of applications and the conditions which govern them

*Article 37*

**Filing of applications**

**1.** An application for a registered Community design shall be filed, at the option of the applicant:

  (a)  at the Office; or
  (b)  if the law of the Member State so permits, at the central industrial property office of a Member State or at the Benelux Design Office.

**2.** An application filed at the central industrial property office of a Member State or at the Benelux Design Office shall have the same effect as if it had filed on the same date at the Community Design Office.

*Article 38*

**Forwarding of the application**

**1.** Where the application is filed at the central industrial property office of a

Member State or at the Benelux Design Office, that office shall take all steps to forward the application to the Office within two weeks after filing. It may charge the applicant a fee which shall not exceed the administrative costs of receiving and forwarding the application.

**2.** As soon as the Office has received an application which has been forwarded by a central industrial property office or by the Benelux Design Office, it shall inform the applicant accordingly, indicating the date of its receipt at the Office.

**3.** No less than ten years after the entry into force of this Regulation, the Commission shall draw up a report on the operation of the system of filing applications for registered Community designs, accompanied by any proposals for revision that it may deem appropriate.

*Article 39*

**Conditions with which applications must comply**

**1.** An application for a registered Community design shall contain:

    (a) a request for registration;
    (b) information identifying the applicant;
    (c) a representation of the design suitable for reproduction.

**2.** If the object of the application is a two-dimensional design and the application contains a request for deferment of publication in accordance with Article 52, the representation of the design may be replaced by a specimen or a sample of the product in which the design is incorporated or to which it is applied.

**3.** In addition, the application may contain:

    (a) a description explaining the representation;
    (b) an indication of the products in which the design is intended to be incorporated or to which it is intended to be applied;
    (c) the classification of the products in which the design is intended to be incorporated or to which it is intended to be applied according to class and sub-class;
    (d) a specimen or a sample of the product in which the design reproduced in the representation is incorporated or to which it is applied;
    (e) a request for deferment of publication of the application in accordance with Article 52.

**4.** The application shall cite the designer or indicate the team of designers. If the applicant is not the designer, or not the sole designer, the entry shall contain a statement indicating the origin of the right of the Community design.

**5.** The application shall be subject to the payment of the registration fee and the publication fee. Where a request for deferment under paragraph 3(e) is filed, the publication fee shall be replaced by the fee for deferment of publication.

**6.** The application shall comply with the conditions laid down in the implementing Regulation.

*Article 40*

**Multiple applications**

**1.** Several designs may be combined in one multiple application for registered Community designs. Except in cases of ornamentation, this possibility is subject to the condition that the products in which the designs are intended to be incorporated or to which they are intended to be applied all belong to the same sub-class, or to the same set or composition of items.

**2.** Besides the fees referred to in Article 39(5), the multiple application shall be subject to payment of an additional registration fee and an additional publication fee. Where the multiple application contains a request for deferment of publication, the additional publication fee shall be replaced by the additional fee for deferment of publication. The additional fees shall correspond to a percentage of the basic fees for each additional design.

**3.** The multiple application shall comply with the conditions of presentation laid down in the implementing Regulations.

*Article 41*

**Date of filing**

The date of filing of an application for a registered Community design shall be the date on which documents containing the information specified in Article 39 (1) or (2) are filed with the Office by the applicant, or, if the application has been filed with the central industrial property office of a Member State or with the Benelux Design Office, with that office subject to payment of the fees referred to in Article 39(5) and, where appropriate, Article 40(2) within a period of two months of the filing of the abovementioned documents.

*Article 42*

**Classification**

For the purpose of this Regulation, use shall be made of the classification for designs provided for in the Annex to the Agreement Establishing an International Classification for Industrial Designs, signed at Locarno on 8 October 1968.

Section 2
Priority

*Article 43*

**Right of priority**

**1.** A person who has duly filed an application for a design in or for any State party to the Paris Convention for the Protection of Industrial Property, hereinafter referred to as 'the Paris Convention', or his successors in title, shall enjoy, for the purpose of filing an application for a registered Community design in respect of the same design, a right of priority of six months from the date of filing of the first application.

**2.** Every filing that is equivalent to a lawful national filing under the national law of the State where it took place or under bilateral or multilateral agreements shall be recognized as giving rise to a right of priority.

**3.** Lawful national filing means any filing that is sufficient to establish the date on which the application was filed, whatever may be the outcome of the application.

**4.** A subsequent application for a design which was the subject of a previous first application, and which is filed in or in respect of the same State, shall be considered as the first application for the purpose of determining priority, provided that, at the date of the filing of the subsequent application, the previous application has been withdrawn, abandoned or refused without being open to public inspection and without leaving any right outstanding, and has not served as a basis for claiming priority. The previous application may not thereafter serve as a basis for claiming a right of priority.

**5.** If the first filing has been made in a State which is not a party to the Paris Convention, paragraphs 1 to 4 shall apply only in so far as that State, according to published findings, grants, on the basis of a filing made at the Office and subject to conditions equivalent to those laid down in this Regulation, a right of priority having equivalent effect.

*Article 44*

**Claiming priority**

An applicant for a registered Community design desiring to take advantage of the priority of a previous application shall file a declaration of priority and a copy of the previous application. If the language of the latter is not one of the languages of procedure of the Office, the latter may require a translation of the previous application in one of the languages of procedure of the Office. The procedure to be followed in carrying out this provision is laid down in the implementing Regulation.

*Article 45*

**Effect of priority right**

The effect of the right of priority shall be that the date of priority shall count as the date of the filing of the application for a registered Community design for the purpose of Articles 5, 6, 8, 25 and 27(2).

*Article 46*

**Equivalence of Community filing with national filing**

An application for a registered Community design which has been accorded a date of filing shall, in the Member States, be equivalent to a lawful national filing, including where appropriate the priority claimed for the said application.

*Article 47*

**Exhibition priority**

**1.** If an applicant for a registered Community design has displayed products in which the design is incorporated, or to which it is applied, at an official or officially recognized international exhibition falling within the terms of the Convention on International Exhibitions signed in Paris on 22 November 1928 and last revised on 30 November 1972, he may, if he files the application within a period of six months from the date of the first display of such products, claim a right of priority from that date within the meaning of Article 45.

**2.** An applicant who wishes to claim priority pursuant to paragraph 1 must file evidence of the display of the products in which the design is incorporated or to which it is applied under the conditions laid down in the implementing Regulation.

**3.** An exhibition priority granted in a Member State or in a third country does not extend the period of priority laid down in Article 43.

TITLE V

**REGISTRATION PROCEDURE**

*Article 48*

**Examination as to formal requirements**

**1.** The Office shall refuse any application for a registered Community design the subject of which is obviously not covered by the definition in Article 3.
**2.** The office shall examine whether:

    (a)  the application complies with the conditions laid down in Article 39(1) and (2) for the accordance of a date of filing;
    (b)  the application complies with the other conditions laid down in Article 39 and, in the case of a multiple application, Article 40;
    (c)  the requirements concerning the claim to priority are satisfied, if a priority is claimed.

*Article 49*

**Remediable deficiencies**

**1.** Where the application does not satisfy the requirements referred to in Article 48(2) (a) and (b), the Office shall request the applicant to remedy the deficiencies or the default on payment of the fees within the prescribed period.
**2.** If the applicant complies with the Office's request in due time, the Office shall allow as the date of filing the date on which the deficient application was originally filed. If, however, compliance with the Office's request concerns deficiencies relating to the conditions referred to in Article 39(1) or (2), the Office shall allow as date of filing the date on which the deficiencies are remedied.
**3.** If the deficiencies or the default in payment established pursuant to paragraph 1 are not remedied within the prescribed period, the Office shall refuse the application.
**4.** Failure to satisfy the requirements concerning the claim to priority shall result in the loss of the right of priority for the application.

*Article 50*

**Registration**

An application which has been accorded a date of filing shall forthwith be registered as a registered Community design. The registration shall bear the date on which the date of filing was accorded.

*Article 51*

**Publication**

Upon registration, the Office shall publish the registered Community design in the *Community Design Bulletin* as mentioned in Article 77(a). The publication shall contain:

    (a)  information identifying the right holder in the registered Community design;

    (b)  the number and the date of filing and, if a priority has been claimed, the priority date;

    (c)  the citation of the designer or the indication of the team;

    (d)  the reproduction of the representation of the design;

    (e)  where a specimen or a sample has been filed, a reference to such filing;

    (f)  any other particulars prescribed by the implementing Regulation.

*Article 52*

**Deferment of publication**

**1.** The application for a registered Community design may request, when filing the application, that the publication of the registered Community design be deferred for a period not exceeding 30 months from the date of filing the application or, if a priority is claimed, from the date of priority.

**2.** Upon such request, where the application has been accorded a date of filing, the registered Community design shall be registered, but neither the representation of the design nor any file relating to the application shall, subject to Article 78(2), be open to public inspection.

**3.** The Office shall publish in the *Community Design Bulletin* a mention of the deferment of the publication of the registered Community design. The mention shall be accompanied by information identifying at least the right holder in the registered Community design, the date of filing the application, the length of the period for which deferment has been requested and any other particulars perscribed by the implementing Regulation.

**4.** At the expiry of the period of deferment, or at any earlier date on request by the right holder, the Office shall open to public inspection all the entries in the register and the file relating to the application and shall publish the registered Community design in the *Community Design Bulletin*, provided that, within the time limit laid down in the implementing Regulation:

    (a)  the publication fee and, in the event of a multiple application, the additional publication fee are paid;

    (b)  where use has been made of the option pursuant to Article 39(2), the right holder has filed with the Office a representation of the design suitable for reproduction.

If the right holder fails to comply with these requirements, the registered Community design shall, unless surrendered in accordance with the provisions of Article 55, be deemed from the outset not to have had the effects specified in this Regulation.

**5.** In the case of a multiple application, the provisions of this Article may be applied to only some of the designs included therein.

**6.** The institution of legal proceedings on the basis of a registered Community design during the period of deferment of publication shall be subject to the condition that the information contained in the register and in the file relating to the application has been communicated to the person against whom the action is brought.

**7.** References in this Regulation to the date of publication of the registered Community design shall be understood, in the case of a registered Community design subject to deferment of publication, to mean the date on which the Office performs the act referred to in paragraph 4.

TITLE VI

## TERM OF PROTECTION OF THE REGISTERED COMMUNITY DESIGN

*Article 53*

### Term of protection

The term of protection of the registered Community design shall be five years as from the date of filing of the application. It may be renewed pursuant to Article 54 for periods of five years each up to a total term of 25 years as from the date of filing of the application.

*Article 54*

### Renewal

**1.** Registration of the registered Community design shall be renewed at the request of the right holder or of any person expressly authorized by him, provided that the renewal fee has been paid.

**2.** The Office shall inform the right holder in the registered Community design and any person having a registered right in respect of the registered Community design, of the expiry of the registration in good time before the said expiry. Failure to give such information shall not involve the responsibility of the Office.

**3.** The request for renewal shall be submitted and the renewal fee paid within a period of six months before the last day of the month in which protection ends. Failing this, the request may be submitted and the fee paid within a further period of six months from the day referred to in the first sentence, provided that an additional fee is paid within this further period.

**4.** Renewal shall take effect from the day following the date on which the existing registration expires. The renewal shall be registered.

TITLE VII

### SURRENDER AND INVALIDITY OF THE REGISTERED COMMUNITY DESIGN

*Article 55*

### Surrender

**1.** The surrender of a registered Community design shall be declared to the Office in writing by the right holder. It shall not have effect until it has been registered.

**2.** Surrender shall be registered only with the agreement of the holder of a right entered in the register. If a licence has been registered, surrender shall be entered in the register only if the right holder in the registered Community design proves that he has informed the licensee of his intention to surrender; this entry shall be made on expiry of the period prescribed by the implementing Regulation.

*Article 56*

### Application for a declaration of invalidity

**1.** The Commission, Member States and any other natural or legal person may submit to the Office an application for a declaration of invalidity of a registered Community design; however, in the case envisaged in Article 27(1)(d), the application may be filed only by the person or persons entitled and, in the case envisaged in Article 27(2), only by the right holder of the earlier right.

**2.** The application shall be filed in a written reasoned statement. It shall not deem to have been filed until the fee has been paid.

**3.** The application for a declaration of invalidity shall not be admissible if an application relating to the same subject matter and cause of action, and involving the same parties, has been adjudicated on by a Community Design Court and has acquired the authority of a final decision.

*Article 57*

**Examination of the application**

**1.** If the application for a declaration of invalidity is admissible, the Office shall examine whether the grounds for invalidity referred to in Article 27 prejudice the maintenance of the registered Community design

**2.** In the examination of the application, which shall be conducted in accordance with the implementing Regulation, the Office shall invite the parties, as often as necessary, to file observations, within a period to be fixed by the Office, on communications by the other parties or those issued by itself.

**3.** The decision declaring the registered Community design invalid shall be entered in the register upon becoming final.

*Article 58*

**Participation in the proceedings of the alleged infringer, the Commission and the Member States**

**1.** If an application for a declaration of invalidity of a registered Community design is filed, and as long as no final decision has been taken by an Invalidity Division, any third party who proves that proceedings for infringement of the same design have been instituted against him may intervene in the invalidity proceedings, if he gives notice of intervention within three months of the date on which the infringement proceedings were instituted. The same shall apply in respect of any third party who proves both that the right holder of the design has requested that he cease an alleged infringement of the design and that he has instituted proceedings for a court ruling that he is not infringing the design.

**2.** The Commission and Member States shall have the right to be joined as parties to the proceedings in accordance with the provisions hereon set out in the implementing Regulation.

**3.** Notice of intervention or the request to be joined as a party shall be filed in a written reasoned statement. It shall not be deemed to have been filed until the fee referred to in Article 56(2) has been paid. Thereafter the intervention or the request shall, subject to any exceptions laid down in the implementing Regulation, be treated as an application for a declaration of invalidity.

TITLE VIII

**APPEALS FROM DECISIONS OF THE OFFICE**

*Article 59*

**Decisions subject to appeal**

**1.** An appeal shall lie from decisions of the Formalities Examination Divisions, Design Administration and Legal Division and Invalidity Divisions. It shall have suspensive effect.

**2.** A decision which does not terminate proceedings as regards one of the parties can only be appealed against if joined with the final decision, unless the decision allows separate appeal.

*Article 60*

### Persons entitled to appeal and to be parties to appeal proceedings

Any party to proceedings adversely affected by a decision may appeal. Any other parties to the proceedings shall be parties to the appeal proceedings as of right.

*Article 61*

### Time limit and form of appeal

Notice of appeal must be filed in writing at the Office within two months after the date of notification of the decision appealed against. The notice shall not be deemed to have been filed until after the appeal fee has been paid. Within four months after the date of notification of the decision, a written statement setting out the grounds of appeal must be filed.

*Article 62*

### Interlocutory revision

**1.** If the department whose decision is contested considers the appeal to be admissible and well founded, it shall amend its decision. This shall not apply where the appellant is opposed by another party to the proceedings.
**2.** If the decision is not amended within one month after receipt of the statement of grounds, the appeal shall be remitted to the Board of Appeal without delay and without comment as to its merits.

*Article 63*

### Examination of appeals

**1.** If the appeal is admissible, the Board of Appeal shall examine whether the appeal is to be allowed.
**2.** In the examination of the appeal, the Board of Appeal shall invite the parties, as often as necessary, to file observations, within a period to be fixed by the Board of Appeal, on communications from the other parties or those issued by itself.

*Article 64*

### Decisions in respect of appeals

**1.** Following the examination as to the merits of the appeal, the Board of Appeal shall decide on the appeal. The Board of Appeal may either exercise any power within the competence of the department which was responsible for the decision appealed against or remit the case to that department for further action.
**2.** If the Board of Appeal remits the case for further action to the department whose decision was appealed against, that department shall be bound by the *ratio decidendi* of the Board of Appeal, in so far as the facts are the same.
**3.** The decisions of the Boards of Appeal shall take effect only as from the date of expiration of the period referred to in Article 65(5) or, if an action has been

brought before the Court of Justice within that period, as from the date of dismissal of such action.

*Article 65*

## Actions before the Court of Justice

**1.** Actions may be brought before the Court of Justice against decisions of the Office taken by the Boards of Appeal on appeals.
**2.** The action may be brought on grounds of lack of competence, infringement of an essential procedural requirement, infringement of the Treaty, of this Regulation or of any rule of law relating to their application or misuse of power.
**3.** The Court of Justice has jurisdiction to annul or alter the contested decision.
**4.** The action shall be open to any party to proceedings before the Board of Appeal adversely affected by its decision.
**5.** The action shall be brought before the Court of Justice within two months of the date of notification of the decision of the Board of Appeal.
**6.** The Office shall be required to take the necessary measures to comply with the judgment of the Court of Justice.

TITLE IX

**PROCEDURE BEFORE THE OFFICE**

Section 1
General provisions

*Article 66*

## Statement of reasons on which decisions are based

Decisions of the Office shall state the reasons on which they are based. They shall be based only on reasons or evidence on which the parties concerned have had an opportunity to present their comments.

*Article 67*

## Examination of the facts by the Office of its own motion

**1.** In proceedings before it the Office shall examine the facts of its own motion; however, in proceedings relating to a declaration of invalidity, the Office shall be restricted in this examination to the facts, evidence and arguments provided by the parties and the relief sought.
**2.** The Office may disregard facts or evidence which are not submitted in due time by the parties concerned.

*Article 68*

## Oral proceedings

**1.** If the Office considers that oral proceedings would be expedient, they shall be held either at the instance of the Office or at the request of any party to the proceedings.
**2.** Oral proceedings, including delivery of the decision, shall be public, unless the Office decides otherwise in cases where admission of the public could have serious and unjustified disadvantages, in particular for a party to the proceedings.

*Article 69*

**Taking of evidence**

**1.** In any proceedings before the Office the means of giving or obtaining evidence shall include the following:

    (a)  hearing the parties;
    (b)  requests for information;
    (c)  the production of documents and items of information;
    (d)  hearing the witnesses;
    (e)  opinions by experts;
    (f)  statements in writing, sworn or affirmed or having a similar effect under the law of the State in which the statement is drawn up.

**2.** The relevant department of the Office may commission one of its members to examine the evidence adduced.
**3.** If the Office considers it necessary for a party, witness or expert to give evidence orally, it shall issue a summons to the person concerned to appear before it.
**4.** The parties shall be informed of the hearing of a witness or expert before the Office. They shall have the right to be present and to put questions to the witness or expert.

*Article 70*

**Notification**

The Office shall, as a matter of course, notify those concerned of decisions and summonses and of any notice or other communication from which a time limit is reckoned, or of which those concerned must be notified under other provisions of this Regulation or of the Implementing Regulation, or of which notification has been ordered by the President.

*Article 71*

*Restitutio in integrum*

**1.** The applicant for or right holder of a registered Community design or any other party to proceedings before the Office who, in spite of all due care required by the circumstances having been taken, was unable to observe a time limit in dealings with the Office shall, upon application, have his rights re-established if the non-observance in question has the direct consequence, by virtue of the provisions of this Regulation, of causing the loss of any rights or means of redress.
**2.** The application must be filed in writing within two months of the removal of the cause of non-compliance with the time limit. The omitted act must be completed within this period. The application shall only be admissible within the year immediately following the expiry of the infringed time limit. In the case of non-submission of the request for renewal of registration or of non-payment of a renewal fee, the further period of six months provided for in the second sentence of Article 54(3) shall be deducted from the period of one year.
**3.** The application must state the grounds on which it is based and must set out the facts on which it relies. It shall not be deemed to be filed until the fee for the re-establishment of rights has been paid.
**4.** The department of the Office empowered to decide on the omitted act shall decide upon the application.

**5.** The provisions of this Article shall not be applicable to the time limits referred to in paragraph 2 and in Article 43(1).

**6.** Where the applicant for or right holder in a registered Community design has his rights re-established, he may not invoke his rights *vis-à-vis* a third party who, in good faith, during the period between the loss of rights in the application or in the registered Community design and publication of the mention of re-establishment of those rights, has put products on the market in which a design is incorporated or to which it is applied, which is comprised within the scope of protection of the registered Community design.

**7.** A third party who may avail himself of the provisions of paragraph 6 may bring third party proceedings against the decision re-establishing the rights of the applicant for or right holder in the registered Community design within a period of two months as from the date of publication of the mention of re-establishment of those rights.

**8.** Nothing in this Article shall limit the right of a Member State to grant *restitutio integrum* in respect of time limits provided for in this Regulation and to be complied with *vis-à-vis* the authorities of such State.

*Article 72*

**Reference to general principles**

In the absence of procedural provisions in this Regulation, the implementing Regulation, the fees Regulations or the rules of procedure of the Boards of Appeal, the Office shall take into account the principles of procedural law generally recognized in the Member States.

*Article 73*

**Termination of financial obligations**

**1.** Rights of the Office to payment of a fee shall be extinguished after four years from the end of the calendar year in which the fee fell due.

**2.** Rights against the Office for the refunding of fees or sums of money paid in excess of a fee shall be extinguished after four years from the end of the calendar year in which the right arose.

**3.** The periods laid down in paragraphs 1 and 2 shall be interrupted, in the case covered by paragraph 1, by a request for payment of the fee and, in the case covered by paragraph 2, by a reasoned claim in writing. On interruption it shall begin again immediately and shall end at the latest six years after the end of the year in which it originally began, unless in the meantime judicial proceedings to enforce the right have begun; in such case the period shall end no earlier than one year after the judgment has acquired the authority of a final decision.

Section 2
Costs

*Article 74*

**Allocation of costs**

**1.** The losing party in proceedings for a declaration of invalidity of a registered Community design or appeal proceedings shall bear the fees incurred by the other party as well as all costs incurred by him essential to the proceedings, including travel and subsistence and the remuneration of an agent, adviser or advocate, within the limits of scales set for each category of costs under the conditions laid down in the implementing Regulation.
**2.** However, where each party succeeds on some and fails on other heads, or if reasons of equity so dictate, the Invalidity Division or Board of Appeal shall decide a different apportionment of costs.
**3.** The party who terminates the proceedings by surrendering the registered Community design or by not renewing its registration or by withdrawing the application for a declaration of invalidity or the appeal, shall bear the fees and the costs incurred by the other party as stipulated in paragraph 1 and 2.
**4.** Where a case does not proceed to judgment, the costs shall be in the discretion of the Invalidity Division or Board of Appeal.
**5.** Where the parties conclude before the Invalidity Division or Board of Appeal a settlement of costs differing from that provided for in paragraphs 1 to 4, the body concerned shall take note of that agreement.
**6.** On request, the registry of the Invalidity Division or, Board of Appeal shall fix the amount of the costs to be paid pursuant to the preceding paragraphs. The amount so determined may be reviewed by a decision of the Invalidity Division or Board of Appeal on a request filed within the period prescribed by the implementing Regulation.

*Article 75*

**Enforcement of decisions fixing the amount of costs**

**1.** Any final decision of the Office fixing the amount of costs shall be enforceable.
**2.** Enforcement shall be governed by the rules of civil procedure in force in the State in the territory of which it is carried out. The order for its enforcement shall be appended to the decision, without any other formality than verification of the authenticity of the decision, by the national authority which the government of each Member State shall designate for this purpose and shall make known to the Office and to the Court of Justice.
**3.** When these formalities have been completed on application by the party concerned, the latter may proceed to enforcement in accordance with the national law, by bringing the matter directly before the competent authority.
**4.** Enforcement may be suspended only by a decision of the Court of Justice. However, the courts of the Member State concerned shall have jurisdiction over complaints that enforcement is being carried out improperly.

Section 3
Information of the public and of the official authorities of the Member States

*Article 76*

**Register**

The Office shall keep a register to be known as the Community design register, which shall contain those particulars of which the registration is provided for by this Regulation or by the implementing Regulation. The register shall be open to public inspection, except to the extent that Article 52(2) provides otherwise in relation to entries relating to registered Community designs subject to deferment of publication.

*Article 77*

**Periodical publications**

This Office shall periodically publish:

  (a) a *Community Design Bulletin* containing entries open to public inspection in the register as well as other particulars the publication of which is prescribed by this Regulation or by the implementing Regulation;
  (b) an *Official Journal of the Community Design Office*, containing notices and information of a general character issued by the President of the Office, as well as any other information relevant to this Regulation or its implementation.

*Article 78*

**Inspection of files**

**1.** The files relating to applications for registered Community designs which have not yet been published or the files relating to registered Community designs which are subject to deferment of publication in accordance with Article 52 or which, being subject to such deferment, have been surrendered before or on the expiry of that period, shall not be made available for inspection without the consent of the applicant for or the right holder in the registered Community design.
**2.** Any person who can establish a legitimate interest may inspect a file without the consent of the applicant for or right holder in the registered Community design prior to the publication or after the surrender of the latter in the case provided for pursuant to paragraph 1. This shall in particular apply if the interested person proves that the applicant for, or the right holder in, a registered Community design has taken steps with a view to invoking against him the right under the registered Community design.
**3.** Subsequent to the publication of the registered Community design, the file may be inspected on request.
**4.** However, where a file is inspected pursuant to paragraph 2 or 3, certain documents in the file may be withheld from inspection in accordance with the provisions of the implementing Regulation.

*Article 79*

**Administrative and legal cooperation**

Unless otherwise provided in this Regulation or in national laws, the Office and the courts or authorities of the Member States shall on request give assistance to each other by communicating information or opening files for inspection. Where the Office opens files to inspection by courts, Public Prosecutors' Offices or central industrial property offices, the inspection shall not be subject to the restrictions laid down in Article 78.

*Article 80*

**Exchange of publications**

**1.** The Office and the central industrial offices of the Member States shall despatch to each other on request and for their own use one or more copies of their respective publications free of charge.
**2.** The Office may conclude agreements relating to the exchange or supply of publications.

Section 4
Representation

*Article 81*

**General principles of representation**

**1.** Subject to the provisions of paragraph 2, no person shall be compelled to be represented before the Office.
**2.** Without prejudice to the second sentence of paragraph 3, natural or legal persons not having either their domicile or their principal place of business or a real and effective industrial or commercial establishment in the Community must be represented before the Office in accordance with Article 82(1) in all proceedings before the Office established by this Regulation, other than in filing an application for a registered Community design.
**3.** Natural or legal persons having their domicile or principal place of business or a real and effective industrial or commercial establishment in the Community may be represented before the Office by one of their employees, who must file with it a signed authorization for inclusion in the files, the details of which are set out in the implementing Regulation. An employee of a legal person to which this paragraph applies may also represent other legal persons which have economic connections with the first legal person, even if those other legal persons have neither their domicile nor their principal place of business nor a real and effective industrial or commerical establishment within the Community.

*Article 82*

**Professional representatives**

**1.** Representation of natural or legal persons before the Office may only be undertaken by:

    (a)  any legal practitioner qualified in one of the Member States and having his place of business within the Community, to the extent that he is entitled, within the said State, to act as a representative in industrial property matters; or

(b) professional representatives whose names appear on the list maintained for this purpose by the Office.

Representatives acting before the Office must file with it a signed authorization for inclusion on the files, the details of which are set out in the implementing Regulation.

**2.** Any natural person who fulfils the following conditions may be entered on the list of professional representatives:

(a) he must have his place of business or employment in the Community;

(b) he must be entitled to represent natural or legal persons:

— in patent matters before the European Patent Office, or

— in trade mark matters before the Community Trade Mark Office, or

— in industrial property matters, including design matters, before the central industrial property office of the Member State in which he has his place of business or employment. Where, in that State, the entitlement is not conditional upon the requirement of special professional qualifications, persons applying to be entered on the list who act in industrial property matters, including design matters, before the central industrial property office of the said State must have habitually so acted for at least five years. However, persons whose professional qualification to represent natural or legal persons in industrial property matters, including design matters, before the central industrial property office of one of the Member States is officially recognized in accordance with the regulations laid by such State, shall not be subject to the condition of having exercised the profession.

**3.** Entry shall be effected upon request, accompanied by a certificate furnished by the central industrial property office of the Member State concerned, or by the European Patent Office or by the Community Trade Mark Office, which must indicate that the conditions laid down in paragraph 2 are fulfilled.

**4.** The President of the Office may grant exemption from the requirement of the second sentence of paragraph 2(b), third indent, if the applicant furnishes proof that he has acquired the requisite qualification in some other way.

**5.** The conditions under which a person may be removed from the list of professional representatives shall be laid down in the implementing Regulation.

TITLE X

**JURISDICTION AND PROCEDURE IN LEGAL ACTIONS RELATING TO COMMUNITY DESIGNS**

Section 1
Jurisdiction and Enforcement

*Article 83*

**Application of the Convention on Jurisdiction and Enforcement**

**1.** Unless otherwise specified in this Regulation, the Convention on Jurisdiction and the Enforcement of Judgments in Civil and Commercial Matters, signed in

Brussels on 27 September 1968, as amended by the Conventions on the Accession to that Convention of the States acceding to the European Communities, the whole of which Convention and of which Conventions of Accession are hereinafter referred to as the 'Convention on Jurisdiction and Enforcement', shall apply to proceedings relating to Community designs and applications for registered Community designs, as well as to proceedings relating to actions on the basis of Community designs and national design rights enjoying simultaneous protection.
**2.** In the event of proceedings in respect of the actions and claims referred to in Article 85:

    (a) Articles 2, 4, 5 (1), (3), (4) and (5) and 24 of the Convention on Jurisdiction and Enforcement shall not apply;

    (b) Articles 17 and 18 of that Convention shall apply subject to the limitations in Article 86(4) of this Regulation;

    (c) the provisions of Title II of that Convention which are applicable to persons domiciled in a Member State shall also be applicable to persons who do not have a domicile in any Member State but have an establishment therein.

**3.** Article 16(3) of the Convention on Jurisdiction and Enforcement shall be complied with by bringing proceedings in respect of an action or claim referred to in Article 85(c) and (d) before any Community Design Court having jurisdiction pursuant to Article 86.

Section 2

Disputes concerning the infringement and validity of Community designs

*Article 84*

**Community Design Courts**

**1.** The Member States shall designate in their territories as limited a number as possible of national courts and tribunals of first and second instance (Community Design Courts), which shall perform the functions assigned to them by this Regulation.
**2.** Each Member State shall communicate to the Commission within three years of the entry into force of this Regulation a list of Community Design Courts, indicating their names and their territorial jurisdiction.
**3.** Any change made after communication of the list referred to in paragraph 2 in the number, the names or territorial jurisdiction of the Community Design Courts shall be notified without delay by the Member State concerned to the Commission.
**4.** The information referred to in paragraphs 2 and 3 shall be notified by the Commission to the Member States and published in the *Official Journal of the European Communities*.
**5.** As long as a Member State has not communicated the list as stipulated in paragraph 2, jurisdiction for any proceedings resulting from an action covered by Article 85 for which the courts of that State have jurisdiction pursuant to Article 86, shall lie with that court of the State in question which would have jurisdiction *ratione loci* and *ratione materiae* in the case of proceedings relating to a national design right of that State.

*Article 85*

**Jurisdiction over infringement and validity**

The Community Design Courts shall have exclusive jurisdiction:

  (a) for infringement actions and — if they are permitted under national law — actions in respect of threatened infringement of Community designs;
  (b) for actions for declaration of non-infringement of Community designs, if they are permitted under national law;
  (c) for actions for a declaration of invalidity of an unregistered Community design;
  (d) for counter-claims for a declaration of invalidity of a Community design raised in connection with actions under (a).

*Article 86*

**International jurisdiction**

**1.** Subject to the provisions of this Regulation and to any provisions of the Convention on Jurisdiction and Enforcement applicable by virtue of Article 83, proceedings in respect of the actions and claims referred to in Article 85 shall be brought in the courts of the Member State in which the defendant is domiciled or, if he is not domiciled in any of the Member States, in which he has an establishment.
**2.** If the defendant is neither domiciled nor has an establishment in any of the Member States, such proceedings shall be brought in the courts of the Member State in which the plaintiff is domiciled or, if he is not domiciled in any of the Member States, in which he has an establishment.
**3.** If neither the defendant nor the plaintiff is so domiciled or has such an establishment, such proceedings shall be brought in the courts of the Member States where the Office is situated.
**4.** Notwithstanding the provisions of paragraphs 1, 2 and 3:

  (a) Article 17 of the Convention on Jurisdiction and Enforcement shall apply if the parties agree that a different Community Design Court shall have jurisdiction;
  (b) Article 18 of that Convention shall apply if the defendant enters an appearance before a different Community Design Court.

**5.** Proceedings in respect of the actions and claims referred to in Article 85(a) and (d) may also be brought in the courts of the Member State in which the act of infringement has been committed or threatened.

*Article 87*

**Extent of jurisdiction on infringement**

**1.** A Community Design Court whose jurisdiction is based on Article 86(1), (2) (3) or (4) shall have jurisdiction in respect of acts of infringement committed or threatened within the territory of any of the Member States.
**2.** A Community Design Court whose jurisdiction is based on Article 86(5) shall have jurisdiction only in respect of acts of infringement committed or threatened within the territory of the Member State in which that court is situated.

*Article 88*

**Action or counter-claim for a declaration of invalidity of a Community design**

**1.** An action or a counter-claim for a declaration of invalidity of a Community design may only be based on the grounds for invalidity mentioned in Article 27.

**2.** In the case specified in Article 27(1) (d), the action or the counter-claim may be brought only by the person or persons entitled to the Community design and, in the case specified in Article 27(2), only by the right holder of the earlier right.

**3.** If the counter-claim is brought in a legal action to which the right holder in the Community design is not already a party, he shall be informed thereof and may be joined as a party to the action in accordance with the conditions set out in the law of the Member State where the court is situated.

**4.** The validity of a Community design may not be put in issue in an action for a declaration of non-infringement.

*Article 89*

**Presumption of validity — defence as to the merits**

**1.** In proceedings in respect of an infringement action or an action for threatened infringement, the Community Design Court shall treat the Community design as valid unless its validity is put in issue by the defendant with a counter-claim for a declaration of invalidity.

**2.** In proceedings in respect of an infringement action or an action for threatened infringement, the Community Design Court shall, when the right holder presents evidence to sustain his claim that the design has an individual character, treat the design as new within the meaning of Article 5 unless in any counter-claim for a declaration of invalidity proof is presented to the contrary by the defendant in the main action.

**3.** In proceedings referred to in paragraph 1, a plea relating to the invalidity of a Community design submitted otherwise than by way of counter-claim shall be admissible in so far as the defendant claims that the Community design should be declared invalid on account of a national design right within the meaning of Article 27(2) belonging to him.

*Article 90*

**Judgments of validity**

**1.** Where in a proceeding before a Community Design Court the Community design has been put in issue by way of a counter-claim for a declaration of invalidity:

    (a) if any of the grounds mentioned in Article 27 are found to prejudice the maintenance of the Community design, the Court shall declare the Community design invalid;

    (b) if none of the grounds mentioned in Article 27 is found to prejudice the maintenance of the Community design, the Court shall reject the counter-claim.

**2.** The Community Design Court with which a counter-claim for a declaration of invalidity of a registered Community design has been filed shall inform the Office of the date on which the counter-claim was filed. The latter shall record this fact in the register.

**3.** The Community Design Court hearing a counter-claim for a declaration of invalidity of a registered Community design may, on application by the right holder in the registered Community design and after hearing the other parties, stay the proceedings and request the defendant to submit an application for a declaration of invalidity to the Office within a time limit which it shall determine. If the application is not made within the time limit, the proceedings shall continue; the counter-claim shall be deemed withdrawn. Article 95(3) shall apply.

**4.** Where a Community Design Court has given a judgment which has become final on a counter-claim for a declaration of invalidity of a registered Community design, a copy of the judgment shall be sent to the Office. Any party may request information about such transmission. The Office shall mention the judgment in the register in accordance with the provisions of the implementing Regulation.

**5.** No counter-claim for a declaration of invalidity of a registered Community design may be made if an application relating to the same subject-matter and cause of action, and involving the same parties, has already been determined by the Office in a decision which has become final.

*Article 91*

**Effects of the judgment on validity**

When it has become final, a judgment of a Community Design Court declaring a Community design invalid shall have, subject to Article 27(3), in all the Member States the effects specified in Article 28.

*Article 92*

**Applicable law**

**1.** The Community Design Courts shall apply the provisions of this Regulation.

**2.** On all matters not covered by this Regulation, a Community Design Court shall apply its national law, including its private international law.

**3.** Unless otherwise provided in this Regulation, a Community Design Court shall apply the rules of procedure governing the same type of action relating to a national design right in the Member State where it is situated.

*Article 93*

**Sanctions in actions for infringement**

**1.** Where in an action for infringement or for threatened infringement a Community Design Court finds that the defendant has infringed or threatened to infringe a Community design, it shall, unless there are special reasons for not doing so, issue an order prohibiting the defendant from proceeding with the acts which have infringed or would infringe the Community design.

**2.** Where in an action for infringement a Community Design Court finds that the defendant has infringed a Community design, the Court shall, unless there are special reasons for not doing so:

    (a) enjoin the infringer to provide forthwith information concerning the origin of the infringing products and the channels through which they are commercialized;

    (b) issue an order to seize the infringing products.

**3.** The Community Design Court shall take such measures in accordance with its national law as are aimed at ensuring the orders referred to in paragraphs 1 and 2 are complied with.

**4.** In all other respects the Community Design Court shall apply the law of the Member State in which the acts of infringement or threatened infringement were committed, including its private international law.

*Article 94*

**Provisional measures, including protective measures**

**1.** Application may be made to the courts of a Member State, including Community Design Courts, for such provisional measures, including protective measures, in respect of a Community design as may be available under the law of that State on national design rights, or those which follow from the application of the provision in Article 93(2) (a), even if, under this Regulation, a Community Design Court of another Member State has jurisdiction as to the substance of the matter.

**2.** In proceedings relating to provisional measures, including protective measures, a plea otherwise than by way of counter-claim relating to the invalidity of a Community design submitted by the defendant shall be admissible. Article 88(2) shall, however, apply *mutatis mutandis.*

**3.** A Community Design Court whose jurisdiction is based on Article 86(1), (2), (3) or (4) shall have jurisdiction to grant provisional measures, including protective measures, which, subject to any necessary procedure for recognition and enforcement pursuant to Title III of the Convention on Jurisdiction and Enforcement, are applicable in the territory of any Member State. No other court shall have such jurisdiction.

*Article 95*

**Specific rules on related actions**

**1.** A Community Design Court hearing an action referred to in Article 85, other than an action for a declaration of non-infringement, shall, unless there are special grounds for continuing the hearing, of its own motion after hearing the parties, or at the request of one of the parties and after hearing the other parties, stay the proceedings where the validity of the Community design is already in issue before another Community Design Court on account of a counter-claim or, in the case of a registered Community design, where an application for a declaration of invalidity has already been filed at the Office.

**2.** The Office, when hearing an application for a declaration of invalidity of a registered Community design, shall, unless there are special grounds for continuing the hearing, of its own motion after hearing the parties, or at the request of one of the parties and after hearing the other parties, stay the proceedings where the validity of the registered Community design is already in issue on account of a counter-claim before a Community Design Court. However, if one of the parties to the proceedings before the Community Design Court so requests, the court may, after hearing the other parties to these proceedings, stay the proceedings. The Office shall in this instance continue the proceedings pending before it.

**3.** Where the Community Design Court stays the proceedings it may order provisional measures, including protective measures, for the duration of the stay.

*Article 96*

## Jurisdiction of Community Design Courts of second instance — further appeal

**1.** An appeal to the Community Design Courts of second instance shall lie from judgments of the Community Design Courts of first instance in respect of proceedings arising from the actions and claims referred to in Article 85.

**2.** The conditions under which an appeal may be lodged with a Community Design Court of second instance shall be determined by the national law of the Member State in which that court is located.

**3.** The national rules concerning further appeal shall be applicable in respect of judgments of Community Design Courts of second instance.

Section 3
Other disputes concerning Community designs

*Article 97*

## Supplementary provisions on the jurisdiction of national courts other than Community Design Courts

**1.** Within the Member State whose courts have jurisdiction pursuant to Article 83(1), the courts having jurisdiction for actions relating to Community designs other than those referred to in Article 85 shall be those which would have jurisdiction *ratione loci* and *ratione materiae* in actions relating to a national design right in that State.

**2.** Actions relating to Community designs other than those referred to in Article 85, for which no court has jurisdiction pursuant to Article 83(1) and paragraph 1 of this Article may be heard before the courts of the Member State in which the Office is situated.

*Article 98*

## Obligation of the national court

A national court which is dealing with an action relating to a Community design other than the actions referred to in Article 85 shall treat the design as valid. Articles 89(2) and 94(2) shall, however, apply *mutatis mutandis*.

TITLE XI

## EFFECTS ON THE LAWS OF THE MEMBER STATES

*Article 99*

## Parallel actions on the basis of Community designs and national design rights

**1.** Where actions for infringement or for threatened infringement involving the same cause of action and between the same parties are brought before the courts of different Member States, one being seized on the basis of a Community design and the other seized on the basis of a design right providing simultaneous protection, the court other than the court first seized shall of its own motion decline jurisdiction in favour of that court. The court which would be required to decline jurisdiction may stay its proceedings if the jurisdiction of the other court is contested.

**2.** The Community Design Court hearing an action for infringement or threatened infringement on the basis of a Community design shall reject the action if a final judgment on the merits has been given on the same cause of action and between the same parties on the basis of a design right providing simultaneous protection.
**3.** The court hearing an action for infringement or for threatened infringement on the basis of a national design right shall reject the action if a final judgment on the merits has been given on the same cause of action and between the same parties on the basis of a Community design providing simultaneous protection.
**4.** The preceding paragraphs shall not apply in respect of provisional measures, including protective measures.

*Article 100*

**Relationship to other forms of protection under national law**

**1.** Nothing in this Regulation shall prevent actions concerning designs protected by Community designs from being brought under any legal provisions of the Community or of a Member State relating to trade marks or other distinctive signs, patents and utility, models, typefaces, civil liability and unfair competition.
**2.** Pending further harmonization of the laws of copyright of the Member States, a design protected by a Community design shall also be eligible for protection under such laws as from the date the design was created or fixed in any form, irrespective of the number of products to which such design is intended to be incorporated or to be applied and irrespective of whether the design can be dissociated from the products to which it is intended to be incorporated or applied. The extent and the conditions under which such a protection is conferred, including the level of originality required, shall be determined by each Member State.
**3.** Each Member State shall admit to the protection under its law of copyright a design protected by a Community design which fulfils the conditions required by such law, even if in another Member State which is the country of origin of the design, the latter does not fulfil the conditions for protection under the law of copyright of that State.

TITLE XII

**THE COMMUNITY DESIGN OFFICE**

Section 1
General provisions

*Article 101*

**Legal status**

**1.** The Office shall be a body of the Community. It shall have legal personality.
**2.** The Office shall be located at the seat of the Community Trade Mark Office.
**3.** In each of the Member States, the Office shall enjoy the most extensive legal capacity accorded to legal persons under their laws; it may, in particular, acquire or dispose of movable and immovable property and may be a party to legal proceedings. For these purposes, the Office shall be represented by its President.

*Article 102*

**Administrative services**

The Community Design Office may have recourse to the administrative services of the Community Trade Mark Office under conditions defined in the implementing regulations established pursuant to Council Regulation (EEC) No. .../... on the Community trade mark and those established pursuant to the present Regulation.

*Article 103*

**Staff**

**1.** The Staff Regulations of officials of the European Communities, the Conditions of Employment of other servants of the European Communities and the rules adopted by agreement between the institutions of the European Communities for giving effect to those Staff Regulations and Conditions of Employment shall apply to the staff of the Office, without prejudice to the application of Article 118 to the members of the Boards of Appeal.
**2.** Without prejudice to Article 108, the powers conferred on each institution by the Staff Regulations and by the Conditions of Employment of other servants shall be exercised by the Office in respect of its staff.

*Article 104*

**Privileges and immunities**

The Protocol on the Privileges and Immunities of the European Communities shall apply to the Office.

*Article 105*

**Liability**

**1.** The contractual liability of the Office shall be governed by the law applicable to the contract in question.
**2.** The Court of Justice of the European Communities shall be competent to give judgment pursuant to any arbitration clause contained in a contract concluded by the Office.
**3.** In the case of non-contractual liability, the Office shall, in accordance with the general principles common to the laws of the Member States, make good any damage caused by its departments or by its servants in the performance of their duties.
**4.** The Court of Justice shall have jurisdiction in disputes relating to compensation for the damage referred to in paragraph 3.
**5.** The personal liability of its servants towards the Office shall be governed by the provisons laid down in their Staff Regulations or in the Conditions of Employment applicable to them.

*Article 106*

**Jurisdiction of the Court of Justice**

The Court of Justice shall have jurisdiction in actions brought against the Office under the conditions provided for in Articles 173 and 175 of the Treaty unless the decision in question is subject to appeal to the Board of Appeal pursuant to the provisions of this Regulation.

Section 2
Management of the Office

*Article 107*

**Powers of the President**

**1.** The Office shall be managed by the President.
**2.** In addition to the powers conferred on the President by the present Regulation:

(a) he shall take all necessary steps, including the adoption of internal administrative instructions and the publication of notices, to ensure the functioning of the Office;

(b) he may place before the Commission any proposal to amend this Regulation, to the extent that it applies to registered Community designs, the implementing Regulation, the rules of procedure of the Boards of Appeal, the fees Regulation and any other rule applying to registered Community designs after consulting the Administrative Board;

(c) he shall submit a management report to the Commission, the European Parliament and the Administrative Board each year;

(d) he shall exercise in respect of the staff the powers referred to in Article 103(1);

(e) he may delegate his powers.

**3.** The President shall be assisted by one or more Vice-presidents. If the President is unable to act, the Vice-President or one of the Vice-presidents shall take his place in accordance with the procedure laid down by the Administrative Board.

*Article 108*

**Appointment of senior officials**

**1.** The President of the Office shall be appointed by the Commission from a list of at most three candidates, which shall be prepared by the Administrative Board. Power to dismiss the President shall lie with the Commission, acting on a proposal from the Administrative Board.
**2.** The term of office of the President shall not exceed five years. This term of office shall be renewable.
**3.** The Vice-President or Vice-Presidents of the Office shall be appointed or dismissed as in paragraph 1, after consultation of the President.
**4.** The Commission shall exercise disciplinary authority over the officials referred to in paragraphs 1 and 3 of this Article.

Section 3
Administrative Board

*Article 109*

**Creation and powers**

**1.** An Administrative Board is hereby set up, attached to the Office.

**2.** In addition to any powers conferred on it by other provisions of the present Regulation:

    (a) it shall set the date for the first filing of applications for registered Community designs pursuant to Article 128(2);

    (b) it shall advise the President on matters for which the Office is responsible;

    (c) it shall be consulted before adoption of the guidelines for examination as to formal requirements and invalidity proceedings in the Office and in the other cases provided for in this Regulation;

    (d) it shall, at regular intervals, hold an exchange of views on the development of the case-law communicated under the system of exchange of information established by Article 125;

    (e) it may deliver opinions and requests for information to the President and to the Commission where it considers that this is necessary.

*Article 110*

**Composition**

**1.** The Administrative Board shall be composed of one representative of each Member State and one representative of the Commission and their alternates.

**2.** The members of the Administrative Board may, subject to the provisions of its rules of procedure, be assisted by advisers or experts.

*Article 111*

**Chairmanship**

**1.** The Administrative Board shall elect a chairman and a deputy chairman from among its members. The deputy chairman shall *ex officio* replace the chairman in the event of his being prevented from attending to his duties.

**2.** The duration of the terms of the chairman and the deputy chairman shall be three years. The terms of office shall be renewable.

*Article 112*

**Meetings**

**1.** Meetings of the Administrative Board shall be convened by its chairman.

**2.** The President of the Office shall take part in the deliberations, unless the Administrative Board decides otherwise. He shall not have the right to vote.

**3.** The Administrative Board shall hold an ordinary meeting once a year; in addition, it shall meet on the initiative of its chairman or at the request of the Commission or of one-third of the Member States.

**4.** It shall adopt rules of procedure.

**5.** The Administrative Board shall take its decisions by a simple majority of the representatives of the Member States. However, a majority of three-quarters of the representatives of the Member States shall be required for the decisions which the Administrative Board is empowered to take pursuant to Article 108(1) and (3). In both cases each Member State shall have one vote.

**6.** The Administrative Board may invite observers to attend its meetings.

**7.** The secretariat for the Administrative Board shall be provided by the Office.

Section 4
Implementation of procedures

*Article 113*

**Competence**

The following departments of the Office shall be competent for taking decisions in connection with the procedures laid down in this Regulation:

    (a)  Formalities Examining Divisions;
    (b)  a Design Administration and Legal Division;
    (c)  Invalidity Divisions;
    (d)  Boards of Appeal.

*Article 114*

**Formalities Examining Division**

A Formalities Examining Division shall be responsible for taking decisions in relation to an application for a registered Community design.

*Article 115*

**Design Administration and Legal Division**

**1.** The Design Administration and Legal Division shall be responsible for those decisions required by this Regulation which do not fall within the competence of a Formalities Examining Division or an Invalidity Division. It shall in particular be responsible for decisions in respect of entries in the register.

**2.** It shall also be responsible for keeping the list of professional representatives which is referred to in Article 82.

**3.** A decision of the Division shall be taken by one member.

*Article 116*

**Invalidity Divisions**

**1.** An Invalidity Division shall be responsible for taking decisions in relation to an application for a declaration of invalidity of a registered Community design.

**2.** An Invalidity Division shall consist of three members. At least two of these members must be legally qualified.

*Article 117*

**Boards of Appeal**

**1.** A Board of Appeal shall be responsible for deciding on appeals from decisions of the Formalities Examining Divisions, Design Administration and Legal Division and Invalidity Divisions.

**2.** A Board of Appeal shall consist of three members. At least two of these members must be legally qualified.

*Article 118*

**Independence of the members of the Boards of Appeal**

**1.** The members, including the chairmen, of the Boards of Appeal shall be appointed for a term of five years in accordance with the procedure laid down in Article 108 for the appointment of the President. They may not be removed from office during this term, unless there are serious grounds for such removal and the Court of Justice, on application by the body which appointed them, takes a decision to this effect. Their term of office shall be renewable.
**2.** The members of the Boards of Appeal shall be independent. In their decisions they shall not be bound by any instructions.
**3.** The members of the Boards of Appeal may neither be members of any other department of the Office, nor be members of any department of the Community Trade Mark Office, except its Boards of Appeal.

*Article 119*

**Exclusion and objection**

**1.** Members of the Invalidity Divisions and Boards of Appeal may not take part in any proceedings if they have any personal interest therein, or if they have previously been involved as representatives of one of the parties. Members of the Boards of Appeal may not take part in appeal proceedings if they participated in the decision under appeal.
**2.** If, for one of the reasons mentioned in paragraph 1 of for any other reason, a member of an Invalidity Division or Board of Appeal considers that he should not take part in any proceedings, he shall inform the Division or Board accordingly.
**3.** Members of an Invalidity Division or Board of Appeal may be objected to by any party for one of the reasons mentioned in paragraph 1, or if suspected of partiality. An objection shall not be admissible if, while being aware of a reason for objection, the party has taken a procedural step. No objection may be based upon the nationality of members.
**4.** The Invalidity Division or Board of Appeal shall decide as to the action to be taken in the cases specified in paragraphs 2 and 3 without the participation of the member concerned. For the purposes of taking this decision, the member who withdraws or has been objected to shall be replaced by alternate.

*Article 120*

**Appointment of members of Invalidity Divisions and Boards of Appeal during a transitional period**

**1.** During a transitional period, the expiry of which shall be determined by the Commission on a proposal by the President of the Office, the President may appoint on a short-term contract basis as members of the Invalidity Divisions persons employed in the central industrial property Offices of the Member States or in the Benelux Design Office or in courts or other authorities of the Member States and having an experience in issues relating to the validity of design rights or applications for such rights in the Member States. These persons may continue their existing employment. They may be reappointed.
**2.** During a transitional period, the expiry of which shall be determined by the Commission on a proposal by the President of the Office, the Commission may appoint as members of the Boards of Appeal members of courts or other authorities

of the Community of the Member States who may continue their activities in the court or the authority of origin. These persons may be appointed for a term of less than five years, though this shall not be less than one year, and may be reappointed.

Section 5
Financial provisions

*Article 121*

**Budget**

**1.** The revenues of the Office shall consist of the fees paid in accordance with the provisions of this Regulation and, to the extent necessary, of a contribution from the Community.

**2.** The expenditure of the Office shall include the costs of staff, administrative, infrastructure and operational expenses.

**3.** By 15 February each year at the latest, the President shall draw up a preliminary draft budget covering expenditure and the program of work anticipated for the following financial year, and shall forward this preliminary draft to the Administrative Board together with an establishment plan.

**4.** Revenue and expenditure shall be in balance.

**5.** By 31 March each year at the latest, the Administrative Board shall establish the draft budget and forward it together with the establishment plan to the Commission which on that basis shall establish the relevant estimates in the preliminary draft general budget of the European Communities.

**6.** The Administrative Board shall adopt the Office's budget before the beginning of the financial year, adjusting it where necessary to the Community contribution and the Office's other resources.

**7.** The President shall implement the Office's budget.

**8.** Control of the commitment and payment of all the Office's expenditure and control of the existence and recovery of all the Office's revenue shall be exercised by the Commission's financial controller.

**9.** By 31 March each year at the latest, the President shall forward to the Commission, the Administrative Board and the Court of Auditors the accounts for all the Office's revenue and expenditure in respect of the preceding financial year.

The Court of Auditors shall examine them in accordance with Article 206a of the Treaty.

**10.** The Administrative Board shall give a discharge to the President in respect of the implementation of the budget.

**11.** The Administrative Board shall adopt the internal financial provisions of the Office after consultation with the Commission and the Court of Auditors.

*Article 122*

**Fees**

The amount of the fees referred to in this Regulation shall be established by the Commission following consultation of the committee referred to in Article 126.

TITLE XIII

**FINAL PROVISIONS**

*Article 123*

**Official languages**

The official languages and the languages of proceedings of the Office shall be the same as those for the Community Trade Mark Office.

*Article 124*

**Community implementing provisions**

The rules implementing this Regulation, in particular the rules concerning the filing of applications, multiple applications, examinations as to formal requirements, registration, publication, and the deferment of the publication, and the rules of procedure of the Boards of Appeal shall be adopted in an implementing Regulation in accordance with the procedure laid down in Article 126.

*Article 125*

**System of exchange of information**

A system of exchange of information is hereby established concerning decisions relating to the compliance with the requirements for protection both as regards Community designs and design rights of Member States. The implementing Regulation shall set out how and by which authority such a system will be operated.

*Article 126*

**Establishment of a committee and procedure for the adoption of implementing regulations**

The Commission shall be assisted by a committee of an advisory nature on fees, implementation rules, and the procedure of the Boards of Appeal, which shall be composed of the representatives of the Member States and chaired by the representative of the Commission.

The representative of the Commission shall submit to the committee a draft of the measures to be taken. The committee shall deliver its opinion on the draft, within a time limit which the chairman may lay down according to the urgency of the matter, if necessary by taking a vote.

The opinion shall be recorded in the minutes; in addition, each Member State shall have the right to ask to have its position recorded in the minutes.

The Commission shall take the utmost account of the opinion delivered by the committee. It shall inform the committee of the manner in which its opinion has been taken into account.

*Article 127*

**Fees Regulation**

**1.** The fees Regulation shall determine in particular the amounts of the fees and the ways in which they are to be paid.

**2.** In addition to the fees already provided for in this Regulation, fees shall be charged, in accordance with the detailed rules of application laid down in the implementing Regulation, in the cases listed below:

  (a)  late payment of the registration fee;
  (b)  late payment of the publication fee;
  (c)  late payment of the fee for deferment of publication;
  (d)  late payment of additional fees for multiple applications;
  (e)  issue of a copy of the certificate of registration;
  (f)  registration of the transfer of a registered Community design;
  (g)  registration of a licence or another right in respect of a registered Community design;
  (h)  cancellation of the registration of a licence or another right;
  (i)  issue of an extract from the register:
  (j)  inspection of the files;
  (k)  issue of copies of file documents;
  (l)  communication of information of a file;
  (m) review of the determination of the procedural costs to be refunded;
  (n)  issue of certified of the application.

**3.** The amounts of the fees shall be fixed at such a level as to ensure that the revenue in respect thereof is in principle sufficient for the Office's revenue and expenditure to be balanced.

*Article 128*

**Entry into force**

**1.** This Regulation shall enter into force on the 60th day following its publication in the *Official Journal of the European Communities.*
**2.** Applications for registered Community designs may be filed at the Office from the date fixed by the Administrative Board on the recommendation by the President.
**3.** Applications for registered Community designs filed within three months before the date referred to in paragraph 2, shall be deemed to have filed on that date.

    This Regulation shall be binding in its entirety and directly applicable in all Member States.

PROPOSAL FOR A COUNCIL REGULATION (EEC) LAYING DOWN
MEASURES TO PROHIBIT THE RELEASE FOR FREE CIRCULATION,
EXPORT OR TRANSIT OF COUNTERFEIT AND PIRATED GOODS
(93/C 238/15)

*COM(93) 329 final*
*(Submitted by the Commission on 16 August 1993)*

*General note*

Amended by the Proposal for a Council Regulation (EC) on Laying Down
Measures to Prohibit the Release for Free Circulation, Export, Re-Export or
Placing under a Suspensive Procedure of Counterfeit and Pirated Goods (94/C
86/06)

THE COUNCIL OF THE EUROPEAN COMMUNITIES,

Having regard to the Treaty establishing the European Economic Community
and in particular Article 113 thereof,

Having regard to the proposal from the Commission,

Having regard to the opinion of the European Parliament,

Having regard to the opinion of the European Economic and Social Committee,

Whereas Council Regulation (EEC) No 3842/86 of 1 December 1986 laying
down measures to prohibit the release for free circulation of counterfeit goods has
been in force since 1 January 1988; whereas conclusions should be drawn from
experience gained during the early years of its implementation with a view to
improving the operation of the system instituted thereunder;

Whereas the marketing of counterfeit goods and pirated goods causes
considerable injury to law-abiding manufacturers and traders and misleads
consumers, whereas such goods should as far as possible be prevented from being
placed on the market and measures should be adopted to that end to deal effectively
with this unlawful activity without impeding the freedom of legitimate trade,
whereas this objective is also being pursued through efforts being made along the
same lines at international level;

Whereas in so far as counterfeit or pirated goods are imported from third
countries it is important to prohibit their release for free circulation in the
Community and to introduce an appropriate procedure enabling the customs
authorities to act to ensure that such a prohibition can be properly enforced;

Whereas action by the customs authorities to prohibit the release for free
circulation of counterfeit or pirated goods should also apply to the export of such
goods from the Community and to those which are carried under a transit
procedure;

Whereas the Community should take into account the terms of the draft GATT
agreement on trade-related intellectual property issues, including trade in
counterfeit goods, in particular the measures to be taken at the frontier;

Whereas it must be stipulated that the customs authorities are empowered to
take decisions on applications for action to be taken that are submitted to them;

Whereas action by the customs authorities must consist either in suspending the
release for free circulation or the export of goods suspected of being counterfeit
or pirated or in seizing such goods when they are carried to the Community under
transit procedure, for as long as is necessary to enable it to be determined whether
the goods are actually counterfeit;

Whereas the objective to be achieved by the introduction of such a procedure does not require the drawing up of Community provisions either as regards the designation of the judicial authority competent to determine whether the goods entered for free circulation or for export or seized during a transit procedure are counterfeit or pirated, or as regards the procedures to be followed for referral to that authority; whereas in the absence of Community rules on the subject the said competent authority should furthermore decide cases submitted to it by reference to the criteria which are used to determine whether goods produced in the Member State concerned infringe intellectual property rights;

Whereas it is necessary to determine the measures to be applied to goods entered for free circulation or for export or carried under a transit procedure where it is established that they are counterfeit or pirated; whereas those measures must not only deprive those responsible for trading in such goods of the economic benefits of the transaction but also constitute an effective deterrent to further transactions of the same kind;

Whereas in order to avoid serious disruption to the clearing of goods contained in travellers' personal luggage, it is necessary to exclude from the scope of this Regulation goods which may be counterfeit or pirated which are imported from third countries within the limits laid down by Community rules in respect of relief from customs duty;

Whereas uniform application of the common rules laid down by this Regulation must be ensured and to that end a Community procedure must be established enabling measures implementing these rules to be adopted within appropriate periods;

Whereas it will be appropriate to consider the possibility of increasing the number of intellectual property rights covered by this Regulation in the light, *inter alia*, of the experience gained in its implementation;

Whereas Regulation (EEC) No 3842/86 should therefore be repealed,

HAS ADOPTED THIS REGULATION:

CHAPTER I

**General**

*Article 1*

1. This Regulation lays down:

   (a) the conditions under which the customs authorities shall take action where goods entered for free circulation or for export are suspected of being counterfeit or pirated or where such goods are carried under a transit procedure; and

   (b) the measures which shall be taken by the competent authorities with regard to those goods where it has been established that they are indeed counterfeit or pirated.

2. For the purposes of this Regulation:

   (a) 'counterfeit goods' means:

   — goods, including the packaging, thereof, bearing without authorization a trademark which is identical to the trademark validly registered in respect of the same type of goods, or which cannot be distinguished in its essential aspects from such trademark, and which thereby infringes the rights of the owner of the trademark in question under Community law or the law of the Member State where the application for action by the customs authorities is made,

— any trademark symbol (logo), whether or not presented separately, in the same circumstances as the goods referred to in the first indent;

— any tool, mould or similar material specifically intended for the manufacture of a counterfeit trademark or of a product bearing such a trademark, provided such tools, moulds or materials infringe Community law or the law of the Member State where the application for action by the customs authorities is made;

— packaging materials bearing the trademarks of counterfeit products, presented separately, in the same circumstances as the goods referred to in the first indent;

(b) 'pirated goods' means goods made without the consent of the holder of the copyright or neighbouring rights, or of the holder of a design right, whether or not registered under national law, or of a person duly authorized by him in the country of production and which are made directly or indirectly from an article, where the making of those goods would have constituted an infringement of the right in question under Community law or the law of the Member State where the application for action by the customs authorities is made;

(c) 'owner or holder of a right' means the owner of a trademark, as referred to in (a), and/or one of the rights referred to in (b), or any other person authorized to use the trademark and/or rights, or their representative;

(d) 'transit' means the external transit procedure referred to in Article 91 of Council Regulation (EEC) No 2913/92 of 12 October 1992 establishing the Community Customs Code.

**3.** This Regulation shall not apply to goods which bear a trademark with the consent of the owner of that trademark or which are protected by a copyright or neighbouring right or a design right and which have been made with the consent of the holder of the right but which are entered for free circulation or for export without the owner's or the holder's consent.

Nor shall it apply to goods referred to in the first subparagraph entered for free circulation or for export which bear a trademark under conditions other than those agreed with the owner of the rights in question.

CHAPTER II

**Prohibition of the release for free circulation, export or transit of counterfeit goods and pirated goods**

*Article 2*

The release for free circulation, export or carriage under a transit procedure of goods found to be counterfeit or pirated on completion of the procedure provided for in Article 5 shall be prohibited.

CHAPTER III

## Application for action by the custom authorities

*Article 3*

**1.** In each Member State, an owner or holder of a right may lodge an application in writing with the competent authority for the release of counterfeit or pirated goods entered for free circulation or for export in that Member State to be refused by the customs authorities or for the seizure of such goods where they are carried to that Member State under a transit procedure, where he has valid grounds for suspecting that the importation, exportation or carriage under a transit procedure of such counterfeit or pirated goods is contemplated in that Member State.

For the purposes of this Article, 'entered for free circulation' and and 'for export' mean entered on the basis of declarations made in writing or orally or by any other means.

**2.** The application referred to in paragraph 1 shall contain:

— a sufficiently detailed description of the goods to enable them to be recognized by the customs authorities, and
— proof that the applicant is the owner or holder of the right for the goods in question.

The owner or holder of the right must also provide all other pertinent information available to him to enable the competent authority to act on the application in full knowledge of the facts, without, however, this information being a condition of admissibility of the application.

As regards pirated goods, this information shall, wherever possible, contain the following:

— the place where the goods are situated or the intended destination,
— particulars identifying the consignment or packages,
— scheduled date of arrival or departure of the goods,
— the means of transport used,
— the identity of the importer or exporter.

**3.** The application must specify the length of the period during which the customs authorities are requested to take action.

**4.** The applicant may be charged a fee to cover the administrative costs incurred in dealing with the application. The fee must be commensurate with the costs incurred and must not have the effect of deterring the applicant.

**5.** The authority with which an application drawn up pursuant to paragraph 2 has been lodged shall take a decision on the application and shall immediately notify the applicant in writing of that decision.

Where the application is granted, it shall specify the period during which the customs authorities shall take action. That period may, upon application by the owner or holder of the right, be extended by the authority which took the initial decision.

Refusals to grant an application must contain the reasons for the refusal and shall be open to appeal.

**6.** Member States may require the owner or holder of a right, where his application has been granted, or where the release of a consignment of goods is suspended or the goods are seized whilst under a transit procedure pursuant to Article 5(1), to provide a security:

— to cover any liability on his part *vis-a-vis* the importer, exporter or the persons involved in the transit procedure where the procedure initiated pursuant to Article 5 (1) is discontinued owing to an act or omission by the owner or holder of the right or where the goods in question are subsequently found not to be counterfeit or pirated,

— to ensure payment of the costs incurred in accordance with the provisions of this Regulation in keeping the goods under customs control pursuant to Article 5.

The security must not be such as to constitute an undue deterrent to initiating or implementing this procedure.

**7.** The owner or holder of the right shall be obliged to inform the authority referred to in paragraph 1 should the right cease to be validly registered or should it expire.

**8.** Member States shall designate the customs department competent to decide on the application referred to in this Article.

Member States may, in addition to the department referred to in the first subparagraph, designate another authority as the authority competent to decide on the application.

*Article 4*

The decision granting the application by the owner or holder of the right shall be forwarded immediately to the customs offices of the Member State which are liable to be concerned with imports, exports or transit operations involving the counterfeit or pirated goods referred to in the application.

CHAPTER IV

**Conditions governing action by the customs authorities and by the authority competent to take a substantive decision**

*Article 5*

**1.** Where a customs office to which the decision granting an application by the owner or holder of a right has been forwarded pursuant to Article 4 is satisfied, after consulting the applicant where necessary, that goods entered for free circulation or for export or which are under a transit procedure correspond to the description of the counterfeit or pirated goods contained in that decision, it shall suspend release of the goods or seize them.

The customs office shall immediately inform the authority which decided on the application in accordance with Article 4. The customs office, or the competent authority which decided on the application, shall immediately inform the person making the entry and the person who applied for action to be taken. Without prejudice to the protection of confidential information, they shall afford the applicant and the importer, the exporter or the persons involved in the transit procedure the opportunity to inspect the goods the release of which has been suspended or which have been seized.

When examining the goods the customs office may take samples in order to expedite the procedure.

**2.** The law in force in the Member State in whose territory the goods were entered for free circulation or for export or where they were seized during a transit operation shall apply as regards:

(a) the referral to the authority competent to take a substantive decision and inform without delay the customs office specified in paragraph 1 of such referral, unless referral is undertaken by that customs office;

(b) reaching the decision to be taken by that authority. In the absence of Community rules in this regard, the criteria to be used in reaching that decision shall be the same as those used to determine whether goods produced in the Member State concerned infringe the rights of the owner or holder. Reasons shall be given for decisions adopted by the competent authority.

*Article 6*

**1.** If, within ten working days of notification of suspension of release or of seizure, the customs office referred to in Article 5(1) has not been informed that the matter has been referred to the authority competent to take a substantive decision on the case in accordance with Article 5(2) or that the duly empowered authority has adopted interim measures, the goods shall be released, provided all the import or export formalities have been complied with and the seizure has been lifted.

**2.** In the case of goods suspected of infringing design rights, the owner, the importer or the consignee of the goods shall be able to have the goods in question released or their seizure lifted, against provision of a security, provided that:

— the customs office referred to in Article 5(1) has been informed, within the time limit referred to in paragraph 1 of this Article, that the matter has been referred to the authority competent to take a substantive decision referred to in paragraph 1 of this Article,

— on expiry of the time limit, the authority empowered for this purpose has not imposed interim measures, and

— all the import or export formalities have been completed.

The security must be sufficient to protect the interests of the owner or holder of the right. Payment of the security shall be without prejudice to the other actions open to the owner or holder of the right. The security shall be released if that person does not exercise his right to institute legal proceedings within 20 working days of the date when he is notified of the suspension of release or the seizure.

**3.** The conditions governing storage of the goods during the period of suspension of release or seizure shall be determined by each Member State.

CHAPTER V

**Provisions applicable to goods found to be counterfeit or pirated goods**

*Article 7*

**1.** Without prejudice to the other rights of action open to the owner of a trademark which has been found to be counterfeit or the holder of a copyright or neighbouring right or a design right which has been found to be pirated, Member States shall adopt the measures necessary to allow the competent authorities:

(a) as a general rule, and in accordance with the relevant provisions of national law, to destroy goods found to be counterfeit or pirated, or dispose of them outside the channels of commerce in such a way as to preclude injury to the owner or holder of the right, without compensation of any sort;

(b) to take, in respect of such goods, any other measures having the effect of effectively depriving those responsible for importation, exportation or transit of the economic benefits of the transaction.

The following, *inter alia*, shall not be regarded as having such effect:

— re-exporting the counterfeit or pirated goods in the unaltered state,
— other than in exceptional cases, simply removing the trademarks which have been affixed to the counterfeit goods without authorization,
— entering the goods for a different customs procedure.

Moreover, each Member State shall impose penalties to discourage further transactions of the same kind. Such penalties must be effective, commensurate with their purpose and have adequate deterrent effect.

**2.** The counterfeit or pirated goods may be handed over to the public exchequer. In that case, the provisions of point (a) of paragraph 1 shall apply.

**3.** Without prejudice to the protection of confidential information, the customs office concerned or the competent authority shall inform the owner or holder of the right, upon request, of the names and addresses of the consignor, of the importer or exporter, of the manufacturer and of the consignee of the goods found to be counterfeit or pirated and of the quantity of the goods in question.

## CHAPTER VI

**Final provisions**

*Article 8*

**1.** Save as otherwise provided by the law of the Member State concerned, the acceptance of an application drawn up in accordance with Article 3(2) shall not entitle the owner or holder of a right to compensation where counterfeit or pirated goods are not detected by a customs office and their release is not therefore suspended or no measure is taken interrupting the transit operation as provided for Article 5(1).

**2.** Save as otherwise provided by the law of the Member State concerned, exercise by a customs office or by another duly empowered authority of the powers conferred on them in regard to combating counterfeit or pirated goods shall not render them liable to the importer or exporter or any other person holding rights with respect to the goods entered for free circulation or for export or carried under a transit procedure, in the event of his suffering loss or damage as a result of their action.

**3.** The civil liability of the owner or holder of a right shall be governed by the law of the Member State in which the goods in question were entered for free circulation or for export or seized during a transit procedure.

*Article 9*

This Regulation shall not apply to goods of a non-commercial nature contained in travellers' personal luggage within the limits laid down in respect of relief from customs duty.

*Article 10*

The provisions required for applying this Regulation shall be adopted in accordance with the procedure laid down in Article 11.

*Article 11*

**1.** The Commission shall be assisted by the committee set up by Article 247 of Regulation (EEC) No 2913/92.

**2.** The representative of the Commission shall submit to the committee a draft of the measures to be taken. The committee shall deliver its opinion on the draft within a time limit which the chairman may lay down according to the urgency of the matter, if necessary by taking a vote.

The opinion shall be recorded in the minutes; in addition, each Member State shall have the right to ask to have its position recorded in the minutes.

The Commission shall take the utmost account of the opinion delivered by the committee. It shall inform the committee of the manner in which its opinion has been taken into account.

**3.** The Committee may examine any matter concerning the prohibition of release for free circulation, export or transit of counterfeit or pirated goods raised by the chairman, on his own initiative or at the request of a Member State.

*Article 12*

Member States shall communicate all relevant information on the application of this Regulation to the Commission.

The Commission shall communicate this information to the other Member States.

The details of the information procedure shall be drawn up in the framework of the implementing provisions in accordance with Article 11(2) and (3).

*Article 13*

Within two years following the entry into force of this Regulation, the Commission shall, on the basis of the information referred to in Article 12, report to the European Parliament and the Council on the operation of the system instituted thereunder and shall propose such amendments and additions as need to be made thereto. An initial evaluation shall be carried out at the end of the first year.

*Article 14*

Council Regulation (EEC) No 3842/86 of 1 December 1986 is repealed.

*Article 15*

This Regulation shall enter into force on 1 July 1994.

This Regulation shall be binding in its entirety and directly applicable in all Member States.

AMENDED PROPOSAL FOR A COUNCIL REGULATION (EC) LAYING
DOWN MEASURES TO PROHIBIT THE RELEASE FOR FREE
CIRCULATION, EXPORT, RE-EXPORT OR PLACING UNDER A
SUSPENSIVE PROCEDURE OF COUNTERFEIT AND PIRATED GOODS
(94/C 86/06)

(Amendment to the Proposal for a Council Regulation (EEC) laying down
measures to Prohibit the Release for Free Circulation, Export or Transit of
Counterfeit and Pirated Goods)

*COM(94) 43 final*

*(Submitted by the Commission pursuant to Article 189a (2) of the EC Treaty on
18 February 1994)*

The Commission hereby amends its proposal as follows:
**1.** The title of the Regulation is replaced by the following:

'Amended proposal for a Council Regulation (EC) laying down measures to
prohibit the release for free circulation, export, re-export or placing under a
suspensive procedure of counterfeit and pirated goods';

**2.** The second recital is replaced by the following:

'Whereas the marketing of counterfeit goods and pirated goods causes
considerable injury to law-abiding manufacturers and traders and to owners or
holders of copyright or related rights, and misleads consumers; whereas such
goods should as far as possible be prevented from being placed on the Community
market and measures should be adopted to that end to deal effectively with this
unlawful activity without impeding the freedom of legitimate trade; whereas this
objective is also being pursued through efforts being made along the same lines
at international level;'

**3.** The fourth recital is replaced by the following:

'Whereas action by the customs authorities to prohibit the release for free
circulation or placing under a suspensive procedure of counterfeit or pirated goods
should also apply to the export or re-export of such goods from the Community;'

**4.** The seventh recital is replaced by the following:

'Whereas action by the customs authorities must consist in suspension of the
release for free circulation, export or re-export of goods suspected of being
counterfeit or pirated or in detention of such goods if they are placed under a
suspensive procedure or re-exported with notification for as long as is necessary
to enable it to be determined whether the goods are actually counterfeit;'

**5.** The eighth recital is replaced by the following:

'Whereas the objective to be achieved by the introduction of such a procedure
does not require the drawing up of Community provisions either as regards the
designation of the judicial authority competent to determine whether the goods
entered for free circulation, export or re-export, or detained when placed under a
suspensive procedure or re-exported subject to notification, are counterfeit or
pirated, or as regards the procedures to be followed for referral to that authority;
whereas in the absence of Community rules on the subject the said competent

authority should furthermore decide cases submitted to it by reference to the criteria which are used to determine whether goods produced in the Member State concerned infringe intellectual property rights;'

**6.** The ninth recital is replaced by the following:

'Whereas it is necessary to determine the measures to be applied to the goods in question where it is established that they are counterfeit or pirated; whereas those measures must not only deprive those responsible for trading in such goods of the economic benefits of the transaction and penalize them, but also constitute an effective deterrent to further transactions of the same kind;'

**7.** The eleventh recital is replaced by the following:

'Whereas the common rules laid down by this Regulation should be uniformly applied and to that end provision made for a Community procedure to ensure that measures to implement these rules are adopted in good time and their implementation coordinated in the interests of greater effectiveness;'

**8.** Article 1(1)(a) is replaced by the following:

'1. This Regulation lays down:

(a) the conditions under which the customs authorities shall take action where goods suspected of being counterfeit or pirated, are:

— entered for free circulation, export or re-export,
— found when checks are made on goods placed under a suspensive procedure within the meaning of Article 84(1) (a) of Council Regulation (EEC) No 2913/92 establishing the Community Customs Code, or re-exported subject to notification;'

**9.** The third indent of Article 1(2)(a) is deleted;
**10.** Article 1(2)(b) is replaced by the following:

'(b) "pirated goods" means goods which are or contain copies of protected works, performances or designs made without the consent of the holder of the copyright or related rights, or of the owner or holder of a design right, whether registered under national law or not, or of a person duly authorized by him in the country of production in cases where the making of those copies would have constituted an infringement of the right in question under Community law or the law of the Member State in which the application for action by the customs authorities is made';

**11.** The following new paragraph 3 is inserted after Article 1(2):

'3. Any tool, mould or matrix or similar equipment (including printing equipment and films likely to be used to apply the trademark to goods) which is specifically designed or adapted for the manufacture of a counterfeit trademark, products bearing such a trademark or pirated goods shall be treated as a counterfeit or pirated good, as appropriate, provided that the use of such tools, moulds, matrices or equipment infringes the rights of the owner or holder of the right under Community law or the law of the Member State where the application for action by the customs authorities is made.';

**12.** Article 1(3) is replaced by the following, which becomes paragraph 4:

'4. This Regulation shall not apply to goods which bear a trademark with the consent of the owner or holder of that trademark or which are protected by a copyright or related right or a design right, and which have been manufactured with the consent of the owner or holder of the right but are placed in one of the situations referred to in paragraph 1(a) without his consent.

Nor shall it apply to goods referred to in the first subparagraph which have been manufactured, or bear a trademark, under conditions other than those agreed with the owners or holders of the rights in question.';

**13.** Article 2 is replaced by the following:

*'Article 2*
The release for free circulation, export, re-export or placing under a suspensive procedure of goods found to be counterfeit on completion of the procedure provided for in Article 5 shall be prohibited.';

**14.** Article 3(1) is replaced by the following:

'1. In each Member State, the owner or holder of a right may lodge an application in writing with the competent authority for action by the customs authorities if the goods are in one of the situations referred to in Article 1(2)(a).';

**15.** The first indent of Article 3(2) is amended as follows:

'— a sufficiently detailed description of the goods to enable the customs authorities to recognize them or a reference to the work or performance and';

**16.** The third subparagraph of Article 3(2) is amended as follows:

'By way of indication in the case of pirated goods, this information shall, wherever possible, include:';

**17.** Article 3(5) is amended as follows:

'5. The authority with which an application drawn up pursuant to paragraph 2 has been lodged shall take a decision on the application and notify the applicant in writing of that decision within five working days.';

**18.** Article 3(6) is amended as follows:

'6. Member States may require the owner or holder of a right, where his application has been granted, or where action referred to in Article 1(1)(a) has been taken pursuant to Article 5(1), to provide security to:

— cover any liability on his part *vis-a-vis* the persons involved in one of the operations referred to in Article 1(1)(a) where the procedure initiated pursuant to Article 5(1) is discontinued owing to an act or omission by the owner or holder of the right or where the goods in question are subsequently found not to be counterfeit or pirated.';

**19.** Article 3a is inserted:

*'Article 3a*
Where, in the course of checks made under one of the customs procedures referred to in Article 1(1)(a) and before an application by the owner or holder of the right has been lodged or approved, it is clear to the customs service that goods are

counterfeit or pirated, the customs authority may, in accordance with the rules in force in the Member State concerned, notify the owner or holder of the right, where known, of a possible infringement thereof. In that case the customs authority shall be allowed to suspend release of the goods or detain them for a period of three working days to enable the owner or holder of the right to lodge an application for action in accordance with Article 3.';

**20.** Article 4 is replaced with the following:

*'Article 4*
The decision granting the application by the owner or holder of the right shall be notified immediately to the relevant customs offices of the Member State.';

**21.** Article 5(1) is amended as follows:

'1. Where a customs service to which a decision granting an application by the owner of a trademark has been forwarded pursuant to Article 4 is satisfied, after consulting the applicant where necessary, that goods in one of the situations referred to in Article 1(1)(a) correspond to the description of the counterfeit or pirated goods contained in that decision, it shall suspend release of the goods or detain them.

The said service shall immediately inform the authority which dealt with the application in accordance with Article 4. The service, or the competent authority which dealt with the application, shall immediately inform the declarant and the person who applied for action to be taken. In accordance with national provisions on the protection of personal data and commercial, industrial, professional and official secrets, the customs office or competent authority shall notify the owner or holder of the right, at his request, of the name and address of the declarant and, where known, of the consignee so as to enable the owner or holder of the right to ask the competent authorities to take a substantive decision. They shall afford the applicant and the persons involved in the operations referred to in Article 1(1)(a) the opportunity to inspect the goods whose release has been suspended or which have been detained.';

**22.** The introductory sentence of Article 5(2) is amended as follows:

'2. The law in force in the Member State on whose territory goods are found in one of the situations referred to in Article 1(1)(a) shall apply as regards:';

**23.** Article 6(1) is replaced by the following:

'1. If, within 10 working days of notification of suspension of release or of detention, the customs service referred to in Article 5(1) has not been informed that the matter has been referred to the authority competent to take a substantive decision on the case in accordance with Article 5(2) or that interim measures have been adopted by the duly empowered authority, the goods shall be released, provided all the import formalities have been complied with, and the detention order revoked.

Where appropriate, this period may by extended by not more than 10 working days.';

**24.** Article 7(1)(a) and (b) are replaced by the following:

'(a) as a general rule, and in accordance with the relevant provisions of national law, to destroy goods found to be counterfeit or pirated, without compensation of any sort and at no cost to the exchequer. The goods in question may be disposed of outside commercial channels, subject to

the explicit authorization of the owner or holder of the right, for socially useful purposes;
(b) to take in respect of such goods any other measures having the effect of effectively depriving the persons concerned of the economic benefits of the transaction.
The following in particular shall not be regarded as having such effect:

— re-exporting the counterfeit or pirated goods in the unaltered state,
— other than in exceptional cases, and subject to the explicit authorization of the owner or holder of the right, simply removing the trademarks which have been affixed to the counterfeit goods without authorization,
— entering the goods for a different customs procedure.';

**25.** Article 7(2) is replaced by the following:

'2. The counterfeit or pirated goods may be handed over to the exchequer, which may dispose of them subject to paragraph 1(a).';

**26.** Article 9a is inserted:

*'Article 9a*
Moreover, each Member State shall introduce penalties to apply in the event of infringements of Article 2. Such penalties must be sufficiently severe to encourage compliance with the rules.';
**27.** The following subparagraph is inserted before the last subparagraph of Article 12:

'The Commission shall coordinate the fight against trade in counterfeit and pirated goods.';

**28.** Article 13 is replaced by the following:

*'Article 13*

The Commission shall, on the basis of the information referred to in Article 12, report on a regular basis to the European Parliament and the Council on the operation of the system and within one year dating from the first application of this Regulation, shall propose such amendments and additions as need to be made thereto.
The Commission in its assessment shall seek to analyse both the macro-economic and sectoral impact of counterfeiting and shall propose indicators suitable for the purposes of tracking the evolution of such changes.'